# The Minister's Library™
## Volume 2

# The Minister's Library™

Volume 2
1971-1985

by

## Cyril J. Barber

**MOODY PRESS**
CHICAGO

**Library of Congress Cataloging in Publication Data**
(Revised for vol. 2)

Barber, Cyril J.
   The minister's library.

   On t.p. the registered trademark symbol "TM" is
superscript following "library" in the title.
   Includes indexes.
   Contents: v. 1. [without special title]—
v. 2. 1971-1985.
   1. Theology—Bibliography.   2. Christianity—
Bibliography.   3. Religion—Bibliography.
4. Theological libraries.   I. Title.
Z7751.B277   1985        027.6'7        84-25500
ISBN 0-8024-5296-5 (v. 1)
ISBN 0-8024-5299-X (v. 2)


1 2 3 4 5 6 7 Printing/ AF /Year 92 91 90 89 88 87

To the faculty of the
**Dallas Theological Seminary**
in appreciation

# Contents

# Foreword

The somewhat frustrated assessment of King Solomon in Ecclesiastes 12:12 was that "the writing of many books is endless" (NASB). If he had known the explosion of books facing the minister today, perhaps he would have included a few more descriptives. The proliferation of books that characterizes our age, together with the time and professional commitments of the pastor, create the need for assistance in discerning the wheat from the chaff.

In an effort to do just that, Cyril Barber, in *The Minister's Library*, has purposed "to assist the busy pastor to select . . . those works that will be of lasting benefit to him in the discharge of his duties" (p. xii). It is my opinion that this volume has successfully accomplished its goal.

Taking seriously the time constraints of a pastor's schedule, *The Minister's Library* not only provides succinct and factual book reviews, but the format also affords the pastor quick retrieval of the information. Because information is only as valuable as the ease of its accessibility, Dr. Barber has diligently arranged each work alphabetically, indexing each author under a topical heading.

Says Dr. Barber: "The emphasis of this volume remains the same as for Volume 1. The focus is on expository preaching, which enables the pastor to declare the whole counsel of God to his congregation (cf. Acts 20:27)." And, because a broad base of works is needed by the capable expositor, *The Minister's Library* is not limited exclusively to a review of biblical works. Noting that the pastor cannot afford to be ignorant of other issues, the author explains that "works regarded as secular may be used profitably to illustrate or apply the teaching of the biblical text."

The reviews are not limited to books by contemporary authors. Citing and embracing the philosophy espoused by C. S. Lewis, that every new book is still on trial and has to be tested against the great body of Christian thought down through the ages, Dr. Barber has afforded the reader an excellent sprinkling of noteworthy reprints, books that have stood the test of time.

Another significant inclusion is his sizeable section on comparative religions. He cites works from a broad spectrum, including many religions and cults from ancient to modern, and provides substantive and insightful reviews on most.

On the whole, however, the books he reviews are along the pastoral theme, including everything from the arrangement of the worship service to the maintenance of buildings. That makes a substantial contribution to the broad area of pastoral ministry. He seeks to differentiate between the superficial books that sprinkle a few principles "with personal anecdotes and Bible verses" and those that make significant contribution through allowing the accurate exposition of the Scriptures to speak with practical wisdom to our uncertain times.

In addition to the reviews themselves, many pastors will find the Dewey Decimal System that is included with each entry quite valuable, making the very tedious task of cataloging one's library efficient and accurate. The inclusion of various other devices, such as the asterisk to designate those works that are highly recommended, provide quick visual assistance in understanding the author's evangelical, theologically conservative recommendations.

A wealth of information is contained in this book. The comments are succinct, yet descriptive, analytical, and generally helpful. It is my opinion that *The Minister's Library* is a tool that will provide valuable and informative assistance to the busy pastor.

JOHN F. MACARTHUR, JR.

# Introduction

T. R. Glover wrote:

> The minds of most of us are like palimpsests, written over and over again; here the latest notion stands out in the newest script, but between the letters are to be found traces of ideas much older, obliterated but legible; there the old is almost untouched, but the closer observer finds hints of a "later hand." Every great thinker sets men writing these palimpsests.[1]

As we reflect on the books published over the last fifteen years (1971-1985), the same pattern is discernible. Here and there creative men and women, building on their training and research and indebted to those whose writings have enriched their lives, have made a new, fresh contribution. In some instances, however, reprints of older books, like the still legible but partly obscured writing on the palimpsests, are worthy of serious consideration.

In some circles a certain degree of disdain is manifest whenever older works are mentioned. The impression conveyed is that only those books published in the last five to ten years are of value. Any mention of reissued works immediately arouses the ire of those who hold that point of view. C. S. Lewis, however, forever exposed the fallacy of such shallow thinking.

> A new book is still on its trial, and an amateur is not in a position to judge it. It has to be tested against the great body of Christian thought down the ages, and all its hidden implications (often unsuspected by the author himself) have to be brought to light. Often it cannot be fully understood without the knowledge of a good many other modern books. . . . It is a good rule, after reading a new book, never to allow yourself another new one till you have read an old one in between.[2]

1. T. R. Glover, *Jesus in the History of Men* (Folcroft, Pa.: Folcroft, 1921), p. xiii.
2. C. S. Lewis, *Screwtape Letters* (New York: Macmillan, 1961), pp. 128-29; cf. also *God in the Dock,* ed. Walter Hooper (Grand Rapids: Eerdmans, 1970), pp. 200ff.

That is sound advice, and those who peruse these pages will find that *notable* reprints have been included. By checking the imprint data, users will be able to locate the most recent publisher, thus saving themselves much time scouring for books in secondhand bookstores or in a variety of trade catalogs.

In reviewing the entries since the completion of Volume 1, it will be noted that the statement made by King Solomon in Ecclesiastes 12:12 regarding his age is also true of our own. All of us who are in any way associated with the publishing industry know that of the making of many books there seems to be no end. Furthermore, those of us who are also involved in education can understand the perennial complaint of students that much study is a weariness of the flesh (KJV).

Some indication of the proliferation of published works may be gleaned from the pages of the *American Book Publishers Record* (also known as *BPR*). That unique resource lists about 45,000 *new* books each year—all cataloged by the Library of Congress—indicating all too clearly that *mania scribendi* is a well-established characteristic of our age.

No doubt future historians will discern trends in our publishing fads and fancies. They will probably point with unerring finger to many of the sensational works that were regarded as in vogue for a time, but that went out of print within a decade. Such ephemeral books will undoubtedly glut the shelves of secondhand bookstores several years from now. But in the light of eternity they will be shown to have made little lasting impact on people's lives.

Pastors have neither the time nor the money to spend on these peripheral publications. Their system of values and professional needs requires them to be wise discerners of the wheat among new books, with a corresponding awareness of the chaff. The task of selecting books of lasting significance is difficult, however. And publishing houses often promote their respective titles with a fervor that may deceive us into buying books that are of little intrinsic worth.

*The Minister's Library* seeks to evaluate the strengths and weaknesses of books being offered for professional consumption. It is an attempt to assist the busy pastor to select wisely those works that will be of lasting benefit to him in the discharge of his duties. Having said that, I also need to point out that I make no claim to omniscience. In addition, many good books have unfortunately escaped my attention. Such omissions are regretted, and where they exist I offer my apologies to the writer and the consumer.

I am most grateful to Moody Press for publishing *The Minister's Library* and wish to thank them for the many courtesies they have extended to me. I also thank those publishers who graciously have made available to me copies of their new titles. Their courtesy has been truly helpful, and their kindness is deeply appreciated. I am thankful, too, for the gracious reviews given Volume 1.

The emphasis of this volume remains the same as for Volume 1. The focus is on expository preaching, which enables the pastor to declare the whole counsel of God to his congregation (cf. Acts 20:27). That does not mean the pastor can afford to be ignorant of other issues. Sometimes works regarded as secular may be used profitably to illustrate or apply the teaching of the biblical text. Certain sections of this volume are quite extensive and contain references to such books when that has been considered useful for pastors.

As I mentioned in the Introduction to Volume 1, *this book is not intended for the seminary professor.* Its aim is to be practical and helpful, and it is geared to the needs of those in the ministry (or those who are preparing for it) whose task is to be a pastor-teacher. Others, however, have not been ignored or forgotten. Where appropriate, space has been given to the needs of church administrators and pastoral counselors. And because I believe the home to be of vital importance in our society, considerable space has been given to books on that subject.

Books that are of particular significance and represent a worthwhile investment of a pastor's funds have been marked with an asterisk (*). The annotations are designed to provide a brief evaluation of the nature, scope, and value of the book from a conservative, evangelical point of view. Those books that have been written from a theologically liberal perspective have been identified with a dagger (†).

In concluding this brief statement of the purpose and scope of this volume, it would be remiss of me not to thank my wife, Aldyth. I am deeply grateful to her for her support.

In addition, I wish to thank my son Stephen for the many hours he spent writing the software that made it possible for this material to be typed on a word processor and for the entries to be sorted by computer. Without his timely assistance, I would have been compelled to spend untold hours of tedious work sorting and arranging the material by hand.

Special thanks is also due to Moody Press, and in particular to Garry Knussman, Senior Editor/Academic Books, and Jim Fann, Manuscript Editor/Academic Books, for their diligent efforts in preparing this volume for publication.

And I also wish to express my deep appreciation to my good friend, Dr. John F. MacArthur, Jr., pastor-teacher of the Grace Community Church, Sun Valley, California, for his willingness to read the manuscript and write the Foreword.

May the work now before the reader fulfill Ephesians 4:15 so that together we may *"grow up in all aspects into Him,* who is the head, even Christ" (NASB; italics added).

# Abbreviations

| | |
|---|---|
| *ANEP* | *Ancient Near East in Pictures* |
| *ANET* | *Ancient Near Eastern Texts* |
| ASV | *American Standard Version*, 1901 |
| BDB | Gesenius's *Hebrew-English Lexicon of the Old Testament*, ed. Brown, Driver, and Briggs. |
| *BIP* | *Books in Print* |
| *BPR* | *Book Publishers' Record* |
| *DAC* | Hastings, *Dictionary of the Apostolic Church* |
| *DCG* | Hastings, *Dictionary of Christ and the Gospels* |
| DDC | Dewey Decimal Classification |
| DDS | Dead Sea Scrolls |
| *HDB* | Hastings, *Dictionary of the Bible* |
| *HERE* | Hastings, *Encyclopedia of Religion and Ethics* |
| *IB* | *Interpreter's Bible* |
| *IDB* | *Interpreter's Dictionary of the Bible* |
| ICC | International Critical Commentary |
| *IRPL* | *Index to Religious Periodical Literature* |
| *ISBE* | *International Standard Bible Encyclopedia* |
| KD | Keil and Delitzsch, *Commentary on the Old Testament* |
| KJV | King James Version |
| LC | Library of Congress |
| LS | Liddell and Scott, *Greek-English Lexicon* |
| LXX | Septuagint |
| MM | Moulton and Milligan, *The Vocabulary of the Greek Testament* |
| MS(S) | Manuscript(s) |
| MT | Masoretic Text |
| NAB | *New American Bible* |
| NASB | *New American Standard Bible* |

| | |
|---|---|
| *NBD* | *New Bible Dictionary* |
| NEB | *New English Bible* |
| NICNT | New International Commentary on the New Testament |
| NICOT | New International Commentary on the Old Testament |
| NIV | *New International Version* |
| *NIDCC* | *New International Dictionary of the Christian Church* |
| *NIDNTT* | *New International Dictionary of New Testament Theology* |
| NT | New Testament |
| OT | Old Testament |
| *POTT* | *People of Old Testament Times,* ed. D. J. Wiseman |
| *RIO* | *Religious Index One: Periodicals* |
| RSV | *Revised Standard Version* |
| *SHERK* | *New Schaff-Herzog Encyclopedia of Religious Knowledge* |
| *TDNT* | *Theological Dictionary of the New Testament* |
| *TDOT* | *Theological Dictionary of the Old Testament* |
| TEV | *Today's English Version* |
| TNTC | Tyndale New Testament Commentaries |
| TOTC | Tyndale Old Testament Commentaries |
| TWOT | *Theological Wordbook of the Old Testament,* ed. Harris, Archer, and Waltke. |

# 1

# General Reference Works and Bible Commentaries

Speaking at a luncheon during the 1982 International Congress on Biblical Inerrancy, San Diego, Walter C. Kaiser, Jr., of the Trinity Evangelical Divinity School outlined an agenda for evangelicals. He assessed the contemporary scene and stressed several areas that he believed need to receive attention during the closing decades of this century. These include:

1. The danger of having a canon within a canon, that is, of paying deference to the whole biblical canon of sixty-six books, yet maintaining favorites within the Old and New Testament
2. The correction of confusion that exists between the interpretation of the biblical text and its application
3. The probing of the role of the biblical writer, keeping in mind the needs of the modern reader, so as to bridge the gap between the biblical narrative and the present

Dr. Kaiser's points are well taken. Unconsciously, perhaps, yet nonetheless persistently, we have all favored certain books of the Bible (e.g., John's gospel, Romans, Hebrews) to the exclusion of certain others (Judges, Nehemiah, Ecclesiastes, Lamentations, the Minor Prophets, the General Epistles). But the need for evangelicals is to master all that God so graciously chose to reveal. As John R. W. Stott pointed out in his excellent treatise *The Preacher's Portrait*:

> The household of God urgently needs faithful stewards who will dispense to it systematically the whole Word of God, not the New Testament only but the Old as well, not the best known texts only, but also the less known, not just passages that favor the preacher's particular prejudices, but those which do not. . . . The wise

steward [of the mysteries of God] varies the diet which he gives to the household. He studies their needs and uses his discretion in supplying them with suitable food.[1]

As expositors, we have incurred a double burden. We are responsible to open up the inspired text of Scripture with faithfulness and relevancy. The Bible is God's disclosure of His will for His people. That means we have an obligation to be loyal to its teaching and wise in applying its message to the needs of those to whom we minister. It is the combination of faithfulness and relevancy that makes exposition effective.

It is this double burden that causes so much confusion to evangelicals. In fact, it is this that often distinguishes theological conservatives from liberals. The conservative finds it easy to be loyal to the Word, but his training has often not prepared him to be contemporary. The liberal, by contrast, has been trained to be contemporary but is seldom biblical. Few can maintain a balance and be both biblical and contemporary at the same time.

We are quick to point out in our books on Bible study methodology that we progress through four distinct stages: observation, interpretation, application, and correlation, corresponding to exegesis, exposition, devotional application, and the development of a biblical philosophy of life. Few commentators, however, follow that procedure, and that makes the task of the expository preacher more difficult.

Obviously, in dealing with any portion of Scripture we need to have a clear understanding of history and of progressive revelation. We also need to ground our communication of God's truth in a clear, well-identified, systematic, and consistent hermeneutic. And then we should seek to enrich our understanding of the biblical text by consulting a variety of general and specific resource tools. Those will provide us with helpful information on the culture and customs of the times.

To help us succeed in that undertaking, a vast resource is available. This includes reference works and Bible commentaries that bring within easy reach a vast storehouse of usable information. Among them are John A. Bollier's *The Literature of Theology* (1979), Joseph A. Fitzmyer's *An Introductory Bibliography to the Study of Scripture* (rev. ed., 1981), Robert J. Kepple's *Reference Works for Theological Research* (2d ed., 1981), and my own *Introduction to Theological Research* (1982). Individually or collectively, these works serve to enhance the scope of our research. They provide a wealth of helpful information, and by enriching our own experience, they also make it possible for us to minister to others out of the overflow of what we have learned.

1. John R. W. Stott, *The Preacher's Portrait* (Grand Rapids: Eerdmans, 1964), pp. 25, 27.

# INTRODUCTORY STUDIES
## ON RELIGION

**Adler, Mortimer J.** *Six Great Ideals.* New York: Macmillan Publishing Co., 1981.

A cogent discussion of truth, goodness, and beauty (ideas we judge by), and liberty, equality, and justice (the ideas we act on) that readily brings to the surface the author's dedication to the central tenets of Western thought. Highly recommended. 111.8.AD5

**Altizer, Thomas J. J.** *The Self Embodiment of God.* New York: Harper & Row, 1977.

†Having spawned the Death of God movement in the 1960s, Altizer now seeks to probe the psychology of self-actualization and, by focusing on speech as a means of growth, demonstrates how God can become the center and foundation of our self-actualization. 201.4.AL7

**Argyle, Michael,** and **Benjamin Beit-Hallahmi.** *The Social Psychology of Religion.* Boston: Routledge and Kegan Paul, 1975.

Based on the work entitled *Religious Behaviour* (1958), this book presents the main empirical findings from social surveys, field studies, and experiments about religious behavior, beliefs, and experience. It is of value to all those who wish to know what the masses think and believe, and why. 301.5′8.AR3

**Aune, David E.** *Prophecy in Early Christianity and the Ancient Mediterranean World.* Grand Rapids: Wm. B. Eerdmans Publishing Co., 1983.

"[The author] has written the most comprehensive and detailed study of early Christian prophecy yet to appear. He puts his encyclopedic knowledge of ancient Judaism and the Greco-Roman world to excellent [use by] placing Christian prophecy within its context. . . . This book is a major contribution to NT scholarship and will become the standard textbook on [this] subject" (I. Howard Marshall). 200.1′5.AU5

**\*Barber, Cyril John.** *Introduction to Theological Research.* Chicago: Moody Press, 1982.

Helps students and pastors "gain bibliographical control over the whole range of theological literature. . . . Any student of the Bible who loves to explore its text and the various theological disciplines, will bristle with delight as he or she is led [to use the] general and specific reference tools" introduced via this book (Walter C. Kaiser, Jr.). 016.23.B23I

**Barclay, William.** *By What Authority?* Valley Forge, Pa.: Judson Press, 1975.

Examines the meaning of authority in both Testaments and assesses the reasons for the tension between authority and freedom. 201.1.B23

**Barrett, David B.,** ed. *World Christian Encyclopedia.* New York: Oxford University Press, 1982.

This impressive reference work brings together a wealth of information, much of it never published before. It is slanted in favor of liberal Christianity and ecumenism. It surveys more than 150 major ecclesiastical traditions, 20,800 distinct denominations, and the status of Christianity and other religions in 223 countries. Well illustrated. 203.W89B

**\*Bollier, John Albert.** *The Literature of Theology: A Guide for Students and Pastors.* Philadelphia: Westminster Press, 1979.

Lists 542 reference works covering all aspects of theology, church history, and the pastoral ministry. Each entry is annotated. Meets a need. Highly recommended. 016.23.B63

**Brenneman, Walter L., Jr., Stanley O. Yarian,** and **Alan M. Olson.** *The Seeing Eye: Hermeneutical Phenomenology in the Study of Religion.* University Park, Pa.: Pennsylvania State University Press, 1982.

Part of the continuing debate in which the hermeneutics of Heidegger and Hesserl is applied to modern religious movements. Discusses the contribution of Eliade and van der Leeuw in developing a new "creative hermeneutics." Concludes with an analysis of folklore and the development of beliefs and values. 200.1.B75

**Brown, Colin, ed.** *History, Criticism and Faith.* Downers Grove, Ill.: InterVarsity Press, 1976.

An important contribution that focuses attention on the interplay between history and faith in the OT and NT and in the development of a philosophy of life. 201. B81

_____. *Philosophy and Christian Faith.* Downers Grove, Ill.: InterVarsity Press, 1969.

Introduces the main thinkers and schools of thought from the Middle Ages to the present day. The material is succinct and admirably serves the purpose for which the book was written. 201.B78

**Clark, Stephen R. L.** *From Athens to Jerusalem: The Love of Wisdom and the Love of God.* Oxford: Clarendon Press, 1984.

†Contains the Gifford Lectures, University of Glasgow, 1982. Advocates a return to the Neo-Platonism that served the purposes of the different religious systems of antiquity. Ironically, makes little use of the Bible in trying to establish a doctrine of theism. 211'.3.C54

**Collins, Gary R.** *The Christian Psychology of Paul Tournier.* Grand Rapids: Baker Book House, 1973.

Provides a helpful summary of Tournier's ideas. Of particular value is Collins's delineation of Tournier's theological commitments. 201.T64.C69

**Custance, Arthur C.** *The Mysterious Matter of Mind.* With a Response by Lee Edward Travis. Grand Rapids: Zondervan Publishing House, 1980.

Another important monograph on the origin and nature of the mind. Underscores the psychology of human worth, the philosophy of human life, and the practicability of each person's potential. 128.2.C96

**Diamond, Malcolm Luria.** *Contemporary Philosophy and Religious Thought.* New York: McGraw-Hill Book Co., 1974.

†A contemporary approach to the philosophy of religion with extensive discussions of Rudolph Otto, Martin Buber, Søren Kierkegaard, Rudolf Bultmann, and others. 200.1.D54

**Donovan, Peter.** *Interpreting Religious Experience.* New York: Seabury Press, 1979.

†Follows in the wake of the relational revolution and, by setting aside the teaching of Scripture, seeks to find validity in religious experiences. Then, after formulating philosophic principles based on these experiences, seeks to validate the conclusions reached either by an appeal to Scripture or quotations from a variety of theologians. 200'.1.D71

**Ellul, Jacques.** *The New Demons.* New York: Seabury Press, 1975.

A careful critique of the resurgence of interest in religion within secular Occidental cultures. The new "gods," however, are national, racial, or social, not biblical, and in the rejection of revealed religion as found in the Bible, Ellul sees a very grave danger. He rightly warns against using God to further secular aims and clearly delineates between true faith and religious belief. This is a powerful book, and it deserves careful reading by everyone who wishes to remain informed on the pressures facing evangelicalism in the closing years of this century. 211'.6.EL5

**Evans, C. Stephen.** *Philosophy of Religion: Thinking About Faith.* Downers Grove, Ill.: InterVarsity Press, 1985.

Although philosophy came to the fore only as religion declined—and that was true in the case of Christianity as well as in pagan cultures—this work succeeds in providing believers with a concise introduction to the crosscurrents of thought. Usable as an introductory text. 200'.1.EV1

————. *Subjectivity and Religious Belief: An Historical, Critical Study.* Grand Rapids: Wm. B. Eerdmans Publishing Co., 1978.

A critique of the nontheoretical justification of belief in the philosophical systems of Kant, Kierkegaard, and William James. A handy text for college students. 200.1.EV1 1978

**Ewing, A. C.** *The Fundamental Questions of Philosophy.* London: Routledge and Kegan Paul, 1985.

First published in 1951, this is "a clear and reliable account of the main problems of philosophy without departing at any point from serious philosophical argument. . . . [It] properly warns the reader that mental effort is needed. . . . Ewing's style makes the mastery of the material easy to understand" *(Philosophy).* 190.9.EW5 1985

**Faber, Heije.** *Psychology of Religion.* Translated by M. Kohl. Philadelphia: Westminster Press, 1976.

An interesting attempt to arrange a marriage between two proud disciplines: psychotherapy and theology. Blends the theories of Freud and Jung with traditional liberal theology. Of value for its honest attempt to treat the problems of integration. 200'.1'9.F11

**\*Fitzmyer, Joseph Augustine.** *An In-*troductory Bibliography for the Study of Scripture.* Subsidia Biblica, 3. Rev. ed. Rome: Biblical Institute Press, 1981.

A valuable guide to the best reference works in all areas of biblical research. Worthy of repeated consultation. 016.2.F58 1981

**Flew, Anthony.** *God: A Critical Enquiry.* LaSalle, Ill.: Open Court Publishing Co., 1984.

This lucid introduction to theology probes the existence of God from Aquinas to C. S. Lewis. Flew approaches his theme with the intent of providing the strongest case possible, though continuing to work within the monotheistic framework provided by Judaism, Christianity, and Islam. As a work of philosophy, this treatise has much to commend it. As a work making use of natural and special revelation, it is sadly lacking. 212.F62

**Frankl, Victor Emil.** *The Unconscious God: Psychotherapy and Theology.* New York: Simon and Schuster, 1975.

Frankl explains his logotherapy and applies its principles to counseling. The material in this book is based on lectures delivered after the close of World War II. 616.89'14.F85

**Funk, Robert Walter.** *Jesus as Precursor.* Philadelphia: Fortress Press, 1976.

Traces the influence of Christ in the writings of Kafka, Borges, Thoreau, John Fowles, Carlos Castaneda, Nietzsche, Camus, Henry Miller, Ludwig Wittgenstein, and Samuel Beckett. 809'.933'51.F96

**Geisler, Norman L.** *Philosophy of Religion.* Grand Rapids: Zondervan Publishing House, 1974.

A Thomistic philosopher discusses God and experience, reason, language, and evil and argues that though it is not logically necessary to believe in God, it is ontologically necessary to do so. 201.G27

————, and **Paul David Feinberg.** *In-*

troduction to Philosophy: A Christian Perspective. Grand Rapids: Baker Book House, 1980.

A fine text that ably sifts through the maze of human theories and systems and provides a clear, concise, and convincing approach to philosophy. 101.G27

————. The Roots of Evil. Grand Rapids: Zondervan Publishing House, 1978.

Brief, but of sufficient depth to adequately probe the source of evil. Contains a response by John W. Wenham of Oxford. No reader will put down this book without an awareness of the issues and a realization of the plan and purpose of God. Recommended. 216.G27

*Gorman, G. E., and Lyn Gorman. Theological and Religious Reference Materials. Vol. 1: General Resources and Biblical Studies. Westport, Conn.: Greenwood Press, 1984.

Scheduled for four volumes. This volume is about as complete as one could desire. Although the sources cited are not evangelical, that is to be expected in a work of this nature. The suggested references are all worthy of consultation, however, and the brief annotation that accompanies each entry will guide the researcher in his/her investigation. The biblical and historical books mentioned within these pages show few significant omissions, and the compilers and publisher are to be commended for having undertaken such a noteworthy project. 016.2.G68 v. 1

————, and Lyn Gorman. Theological and Religious Reference Materials. Vol. 2: Systematic Theology and Church History. Westport, Conn.: Greenwood Press, 1985.

The authors provide a comprehensive, basic guide to a full range of theological and religious reference materials. Ranging from the concerns of philosophical theory to the more concrete areas of history and literature to the practical fields of social ethics, psychology, education, and politics, their coverage is about as comprehensive as one could wish for. 016.2.G68 v.2

**Grounds, Vernon Carl.** Emotional Problems and the Gospel. Grand Rapids: Zondervan Publishing House, 1976.

In his own inimitable way, the author combines theological insights with the teaching of psychoanalysis and applies the results to mental health and the problems of anxiety, anger, pride, and guilt. Worthy of serious consideration. 201'.9.G91

**Guest, John.** In Search of Certainty. Ventura, Calif.: Regal Books, 1983.

Designed for the intelligent layperson, this work on agnosticism deals empathetically with the struggles of those whose early academic training has ill-equipped them to interact with the truth of Christianity. Described as "answers to doubt when values are eroding and unbelief is fashionable." 149.72.G93

**Hefner, R.,** and **W. W. Schroeder, eds.** Belonging and Alienation: Religious Foundations for the Human Future. Chicago: Center for the Scientific Study of Religion, 1976.

Composed of papers presented at the Center over a three-year period. Main theme ably fulfills the subtitle. 201.B41

**Heisig, James V.** Imago Dei: A Study of C. G. Jung's Psychology of Religion. Lewisburg, Pa.: Bucknell University Press, 1979.

A historical inquiry into Jungian psychology with a penetrating critique of his methodology. This is a scholarly assessment of the nature of human personality. 200.1'9.J95.H36

**Hesselgrave, David John, ed.** Dynamic Religious Movements: Case Studies of Rapidly Growing Religious Movements Around the World. Grand Rapids: Baker Book House, 1978.

A series of essays on various contemporary religious movements that have experienced unusual growth. A concluding chapter considers what these movements can teach evangelicals about church growth. 200.9.H46D

**Higham, John, Leonard Krieger, and Felix Gilbert.** *History.* New York: Garland Publishing, 1985.

Contains scholarly essays first published by the trustees of Princeton University, 1965. Explores the theory of historiography and how history is communicated. 907.2.H53 1985

**Holm, Jean.** *The Study of Religions.* New York: Seabury Press, 1977.

This appraisal of religious phenomena draws attention to the nature of religious belief, the authority of religion over its adherents, changes taking place as dogma is influenced by culture, and interfaith dialogue. 200.7.H73

**\*Holmes, Arthur F.** *All Truth Is God's Truth.* Grand Rapids: Wm. B. Eerdmans Publishing Co., 1977.

Carefully distinguishes between faith and knowledge, and exposes the limitations of human wisdom. Emphasizes the Christological perspective that is vital if the integration of one's beliefs and learning is to be effective. 201.1.H73

**Hooker, Douglas.** *The Healthy Personality and the Christian Life.* North Quincy, Mass.: Christopher Publishing House, 1977.

Presents Karl Barth's understanding of the Christian life in a way that is helpful to Christians and students of psychology. 201.9.H76

**Hudson, W. Donald.** *A Philosophical Approach to Religion.* New York: Barnes and Noble, 1974.

This objective examination of the structure of religious belief treats, among others, the theories of Dietrich Bonhoeffer, Henry P. Van Dusen, Paul Van Buren, Paul Tillich, and Harvey Cox

and finds them deficient. 201.H86

**\*Hughes, Philip Edgcumbe.** *Hope for a Despairing World: The Christian Answer to the Problem of Evil.* Grand Rapids: Baker Book House, 1977.

A well-reasoned treatise that demonstrates the author's awareness of contemporary issues and of modern man's dilemma. Provides theologically sound, workable solutions to many of the tensions of modern life. Practical; not idealistic. 216.H87

**James, William.** *The Varieties of Religious Experience.* The Works of William James. Cambridge, Mass.: Harvard University Press, 1985.

Still eagerly sought after, these lectures, delivered at Edinburgh University in 1901-1902, have been carefully compiled from James's notes. Few works have exerted such influence on Christians and non-Christians alike. Though insightful, they lack an awareness of the spiritual dynamics of conversion. 201.6.J23 1985

**Kalsbeek, L.** *Contours of a Christian Philosophy: An Introduction to Herman Dooyeweerd's Thought.* Toronto: Wedge Publishing Co., 1975.

A clear, concise introduction to Dooyeweerd's *New Critique of Theoretical Thought.* 201.D72.K12

**Kepple, Robert J.** *Reference Works for Theological Research: An Annotated Selective Guide.* 2d ed. Washington, D.C.: University Press of America, 1981.

An informative guide listing all the reference works a researcher could possibly wish to consult. Duplicates much of Bollier's *The Literature of Theology* (1979). Well indexed. Worthy of repeated consultation. 016.2.K44 1981

**Kinsler, F. Ross.** *The Extension Movement in Theological Education: A Call to the Renewal of Ministry.* South Pasadena, Calif.: William Carey Library, 1978.

Recounts the events of theological education by extension and deals specifically with the self-study materials, the practical work with congregations, and encounter seminars. An important work for missiologists and all engaged in the educational task of the church. 207.11.K62

**Kirkemo, Ronald.** *Between the Eagle and the Dove: The Christian and American Foreign Policy.* Downers Grove, Ill.: Inter-Varsity Press, 1976.

Deals with the tension Christians in America experience as citizens of two kingdoms: the country (symbolized by the eagle) and the Spirit (symbolized by the dove). Although not definitive, this work is provocative. 200.AM3.K63

**Levinson, Henry Samuel.** *The Religious Investigations of William James.* Chapel Hill, N.C.: University of North Carolina Press, 1981.

A scholarly critique of James's lifelong absorption with religious experience and parapsychology. Illumines much of the data found in *Varieties of Religious Experience*. Also evaluates James's psychology and pantheistic ideas. 201.J23.L57

**Macquarrie, John.** *Twentieth Century Religious Thought: The Frontiers of Philosophy and Theology, 1900-1980.* New York: Charles Scribner's Sons, 1981.

An assessment of the influence of neo-Hegelianism, neo-Marxism, and neo-orthodoxy on the contemporary theological scene. 200.9'04.M24 1981

**Malony, H. Newton,** ed. *Current Perspectives in the Psychology of Religion.* Grand Rapids: Wm. B. Eerdmans Publishing Co., 1977.

Contains readings on the history and trends, methodology, and orientation of psychology of religion. Explores such areas as psychodynamics, religious experience, religious development, and measurement. Of particular value to DCEs and students doing research in these areas. 201.6.M29

**Marty, Martin Emil.** *A Nation of Behavers.* Chicago: University of Chicago Press, 1976.

Marty, a church historian frequently regarded as an evangelical (see *The Young Evangelicals* by Quebedeaux and *The Evangelicals* by Wells and Woodbridge), examines social behavior and group identity in an endeavor to ascertain the climate of American religious consciousness. What he has to say is of value for its breadth of vision and sociological understanding. 200'.AM3.M36

**Melton, J. Gordon.** *The Encyclopedia of American Religions.* 2 vols. Wilmington, N.C.: Consortium Books, 1982.

A comprehensive survey of religious sects and denominations in the U. S. today. This is the first reference work of its kind to bring together detailed information on all American religions, from major institutional churches to lesser known cults. Examines nearly 1,200 distinct groups and describes the unique history, practices, and beliefs of each. These volumes are the culmination of sixteen years of research and writing. Destined to become a standard reference work on American denominations and sects. 200.2.AM3.M49

**Oates, Wayne Edward.** *The Psychology of Religion.* Waco, Tex.: Word Books, 1973.

Realizing that the disciplines of theology and psychology have long been at enmity with one another, Oates attempts to define their approach to human life and provide a common meeting ground for both. He is correct in assuming that psychology can serve as the handmaid of the theologian, but manifests a distinct weakness in his understanding of the nature of man. Discusses such issues as mysticism, LSD, operant conditioning, the counterculture, and demon possession. 200'.1.0A8

**Oden, Thomas C.** *Game Free.* New York: Harper & Row, 1974.

†An attempt to apply the Scriptures in terms of Transactional Analysis. Oden makes important observations and correlations but fails to emphasize the need for any redemptive act. 158.2.OD2

**Pannenberg, Wolfhart.** *The Idea of God and Human Freedom.* Translated by R. A. Wilson. Philadelphia: Westminster Press, 1973.

†Continuing the train of thought begun in *Basic Issues in Theology,* Pannenberg opposes Bultmann's approach to the NT. He draws heavily on form-criticism and painstakingly probes into texts referring to the Spirit of God. The material presented in this volume lacks cohesion, but it does have value for those scholars who are interested in keeping abreast of the latest European thought. 201'.1.P19

**Pruyser, Paul W.** *Between Belief and Unbelief.* New York: Harper & Row, 1974.

Evaluates modern man's preoccupation with religious quests, examines belief and unbelief from the perspective of a clinical psychologist, and concludes with an analysis of love and hate objects. Of value for its insights into man's innate religiosity. Fails to demonstrate an awareness of the uniqueness of Christ or of the value of His redemption. 121.P95

*The Religious Life of Man: Guide to Basic Literature.* Compiled by Lesek M. Karpinski. Metuchen, N.J.: Scarecrow Press, 1978.

This bibliography of more than 2,000 entries acquaints researchers with sources of information about the rise and development of all the major religions of the world and the countries in which they are found today. Well indexed. 016.2.R27K 1978

*Religious Books and Serials in Print.* New York: R. R. Bowker, 1978.

This first edition extends to 1,259 pages and lists 47,400 books and 3,140 serials in print at the present time. It includes a "Subject Area Directory," giving Library of Congress subject headings, a "Sacred Word Index," and a listing of various editions of the Bible. It is valuable as a resource tool and serves as a useful supplement to *Books in Print* and *A Subject Guide to Books in Print.* Should be in every Christian college and seminary library. 016.22.R27

**Rust, Eric Charles.** *Religion, Revelation and Reason.* Macon, Ga.: Mercer University Press, 1981.

Discusses the essence of reality, how we come to know, the philosophical rationale for belief in the existence of God, the place of man, and theodicy. Wide-ranging. Needs to be read with discernment. 200'.1.R92

**Sall, Millard J.** *Faith, Psychology and Christian Maturity.* Grand Rapids: Zondervan Publishing House, 1975.

A provocative, well-written, well-intentioned but somewhat naive approach to integrating psychological and theological concepts of the nature of man. 201.SA3

**Scobie, Geoffrey E. W.** *Psychology of Religion.* New York: Halsted Press, 1975.

In keeping with the pace of new developments in this area of integrative study, this work provides a guide to the problem of a definition of religion, the method of research, religious variables, dimensions of religion, psychological and sociological factors affecting behavior, and the role of religious beliefs in attitude change. 200.1'9.SC1

**Sims, James H.,** and **Leland Ryken, eds.** *Milton and Scriptural Tradition: The Bible into Poetry.* Columbia, Mo.: University of Missouri Press, 1984.

Focuses on Milton as an artist and interpreter of Scripture. What is ambiguous in this work are the terms used by the contributors to describe Milton's theological ideas. In spite of this weakness, the essays reveal the genius of Milton as an epic poet. 821.4.SI5

**Sire, James W.** *The Universe Next Door: A Basic World View Catalog.* Downers Grove, Ill.: InterVarsity Press, 1976.

A concise survey of seven world views: Christian theism, deism, naturalism, nihilism, existentialism, Eastern pantheism, monism, and the new consciousness. Well researched and well written. Recommended. 110.SI7

**Smart, Ninian.** *Beyond Ideology: Religion and the Future of Western Civilization.* San Francisco: Harper & Row, 1981.

†Sifts through all major religious and philosophical systems to discern the elements of an optimistic, positive synthesis of spiritual and secular, Eastern and Western, Christian and Buddhist thought, with a view to creating a new role for religion, namely, criticism, not authority. Lays the theoretical and creative groundwork on which to build the global community that Smart believes is the challenge and hope of the future. 201.SM2

**Smith, John E.** *The Analog of Experience: An Approach to Understanding Religious Truth.* New York: Harper & Row, 1973.

Constituting the Warfield Lectures, Princeton Theological Seminary, 1970, these philosophically oriented studies probe the centrality of experience in the Christian faith. 201.SM6

**Stater, Peter.** *The Dynamics of Religion: Meaning and Change in Religious Traditions.* San Francisco: Harper & Row, 1978.

Much of the book is devoted to questions of meaning regarding symbols, stories, and patterns of change in different religions. 201.ST2

**Tart, C. T., ed.** *Transpersonal Psychologies.* New York: Harper & Row, 1975.

This attempt to bridge the gap between "orthodox Western psychology" and "transpersonal psychologies that are an integral part of spiritual disciplines" succeeds in focusing attention on parapsychology and cultic groups devoted to different forms of Oriental mysticism. The contributors fail to fulfill their stated purpose. 200.1'9.T68

**\*Towns, Elmer L., ed.** *A History of Religious Educators.* Grand Rapids: Baker Book House, 1975.

Includes a treatment of leading educators from Christ and Paul to William James and John Dewey. The chapters assess each person's philosophy of education and the way in which the strengths of his views may be implemented. Not all chapters are of equal value. 209'.2'2.T66

**Webb, Eugene.** *The Dark Dove: The Sacred and the Secular in Modern Literature.* Seattle, Wash.: University of Washington Press, 1975.

Evaluates the tensions between sacred and profane themes in twentieth-century literature, and demonstrates the vital link between modern literature and religious tradition. Concludes that the spiritual has been influenced by the temporal, not vice versa. 809'.933.W38

**Welch, Claude.** *Protestant Thought in the Nineteenth Century: Volume 2, 1870-1914.* New Haven, Conn.: Yale University Press, 1985.

This volume discusses both major and minor thinkers of the late nineteenth century and the ideas that concerned them most: the nature of faith, the questions posed by historical studies of the Bible and the history of Christianity, and the relation of church and society. Together with volume 1 (now revised by Yale University Press to coincide with publication of volume 2), this book presents an inclusive account of the principal Protestant theological concerns and writers of the nineteenth century in continental Europe, Great Britain, and the United States. 209'.034.W46 v. 2

**\*White, Jerry E.** *Honesty, Morality and Conscience.* Colorado Springs, Colo.: Navpress, 1981.

Reissue of the 1979 edition, which Vernon C. Grounds appropriately described as "helpful, down-to-earth. . . . This book will be used of God to remind Christians that their lifestyle ought to be qualitatively different from that of our relativistic society." 241.W58 1981

**Whittaker, John H.** *Matters of Faith and Matters of Principle: Religious Truth Claims and Their Logic.* San Antonio, Tex.: Trinity University Press, 1981.

Seeks to establish a basis for understanding religious assertions to distinguish between fact and faith, taste and temperament, to provide a valid experience, and to establish the need for experimental research in matters of dogma and man's quest for meaning. 201.W58

**\*Wilberforce, William.** *Real Christianity Contrasted with the Prevailing Religious System.* Abridged and edited by J. M.

Houston. Portland, Oreg.: Multnomah Press, 1982.

This outstanding classic first appeared in 1829. It is a brilliant and sorely needed presentation of authentic Christianity—a Christianity marked by power, not pragmatism. Recommended. 209'.033.W65H 1982

**Wilson, John Francis.** *Religion: A Preface.* Englewood Cliffs, N.J.: Prentice-Hall, 1982.

A comprehensive, philosophical introduction to mankind's well-attested religiosity. Considers some of the major movements and the tensions they face in the world today. 200.W69

**Yankelovich, David.** *The New Morality: A Profile of American Youth in the 70's.* New York: McGraw-Hill Book Co., 1974.

Brief and to the point. This work by a social scientist is based on more than 3,500 personal interviews of people aged sixteen to twenty-five. His analysis tolls out a warning and tells us what we may expect in "Christian" America in the next ten to twenty years. 201.43'15.AM3.Y1

## CREATION, SCIENCE, AND THE BIBLE

**Blacker, Carmen,** and **Michael Loewe.** *Ancient Cosmologies.* London: Allen and Unwin, 1975.

With contributions by leading authorities, this work adequately surveys the theory of origins of ancient civilizations. 113.B56

**Brooks, James.** *Origins of Life.* Belleville, Mich.: Lion Publishing Corporation, 1985.

The author, a geologist, draws on the disciplines of chemistry, physics, biology, cosmology, and the like as he discusses the issues surrounding creation. Beautifully illustrated. This work provides some interesting sidelights on the origin

of life, but it also leaves some important questions unanswered. 213.B79

**Davidheiser, Bolton.** *Science and the Bible.* Grand Rapids: Baker Book House, 1971.

A biologist's critical evaluation of the methods used and the conclusions reached by scientists in their attempt to prove the evolutionary hypothesis. A valuable apologetic. 215.D28

**Gale, Barry George.** *Evolution Without Evidence: Charles Darwin and The Origin of Species.* Albuquerque: University of New Mexico Press, 1982.

This extensively documented work exposes the superficiality of the evolutionary hypothesis. Though not supporting creationism, Gale does demonstrate the biological and scientific inadequacies of Darwinism. 575.D25.G13

**\*Geisler, Norman Leo, A. F. Brooke II,** and **M. J. Keough.** *The Creator in the Courtroom: Scopes II, The 1981 Arkansas Creation-Evolution Trial.* Milford, Mich.: Mott Media, 1982.

This eye-opening study of the historical trial provides readers with a detailed eyewitness account of several aspects of the proceedings. The way the secular media blatantly slanted their coverage, the discussion of the strategy used by creationism's defense team, and the misconceptions about the law in question are all included in documentary fashion, as are the related briefs and testimonies and the judge's final ruling. Geisler's analysis of the event is something every thinking Christian will welcome. 370.11.G27

**\*Gish, Duane T.** *Evolution: The Challenge of the Fossil Record.* El Cajon, Calif.: Creation-Life Publishers, 1985.

"This book constitutes one of the most devastating critiques of the evolutionary philosophy one could find. It goes right to the stronghold of the supposed scientific evidence for evolution and demolishes its central bastion" (Henry M. Morris). 575.G4

**Howe, George F., ed.** *Speak to the Earth.* San Diego: Creation-Life Publishers, 1976.

Learned essays (published between June 1969 and March 1974) offering convincing evidence for the scientific viability of creationism. 213.H83 1976

**Jaki, Stanley L.** *Brain, Mind and Computers.* South Bend, Ind.: Gateway Editions, 1969.

The author, Hungarian-born Distinguished Professor of Seton Hall Univer-

sity, holds unquestioned credentials in both physics and theology. In this valuable volume he presents sustained, well-informed, and persuasive arguments for mind-body dualism. Sir John C. Eccles, Nobel Laureat in 1963, wrote of his work: "Certainly, it is rewarding and refreshing to read such penetrating criticism of a field in which gratuitous theorizing and dogmatism are able to flourish because our science of understanding is so small." This is a welcome, provocative apologetic, and it is deserving of careful reading. 510.78.J21

**\*Lammerts, Walter Edward, ed.** *Scientific Studies in Special Creation.* Grand Rapids: Baker Book House, 1971.

A fascinating, scholarly volume that deals with the basic questions in the areas of special creation and presents strong arguments for its support. 215.L18

**Lester, Lane P.,** and **Raymond G. Bohlin.** *The Natural Limits to Biological Change.* Grand Rapids: Zondervan Publishing House, 1984.

Tackles the theory of evolution head-on and demonstrates the functional inadequacy of Neo-Darwinianism. Also shows how theories of evolution rest on very shaky, tottering pillars that any rational scientist would be compelled to discard. 575.L56

**MacBeth, Norman.** *Darwin Retried.* Boston: Gambit Publishing Co., 1971.

Building on the laws of evidence, the writer evaluates Darwinism and concludes that the basis on which it rests cannot be closely scrutinized without leading to the collapse of the system. 575.M12

**Montenat, Christian, Luc Platenux,** and **Pascal Toux.** *How to Read the World: Creation in Evolution.* Translated by J. Bowden. New York: Crossroad Publishing, 1985.

The writers—a geologist, a biologist, and a priest, who were later joined by J.-P. Signoret, an ethnologist, and M. Godinot, a paleontologist—seek to provide a new, scholarly rationale for creation-evolution that will be acceptable to Christians and scientists. In presenting their material, they have used the "language of faith," as they try to show how creationism can be understood within an evolutionary framework. Unconvincing. 213.M74

**\*Morris, Henry Madison.** *The Biblical Basis for Modern Science.* Grand Rapids: Baker Book House, 1984.

The scientifically accurate, highly responsible, and articulate study provides comprehensive coverage of those salient and revelant issues supporting biblical creationism. Recommended. 215.M83M 1984

\*_____. *Evolution in Turmoil.* San Diego: Creation-Life Publishers, 1982.

Formerly published under the title *The Troubled Waters of Evolution,* this work champions creationism and furnishes readers with a concise, reliable refutation of the major tenets of evolution. This is a good book. Buy it, read it, and see that a copy is placed in your church library as well. 575.M83E 1982.

\*_____. *A History of Modern Creationism.* San Diego: Master Book Publishers, 1984.

The fascinating story of the modern revival of scientific interest in biblical creationism. Describes the roots of the ancient conflict in polytheism and animinism, through the Darwinian era to the Scopes trial and the fundamentalist/modernist controversy of the 1920s, up to the present day. Scientific creationism has been both ridiculed and ignored by the intelligentsia. This attitude is changing. Anger is now evident, and there is also the marshaling of the media as well as educational/political forces against creationism. This involves a violation of constitutional rights as well as an unwillingness to abide by the scientific process in searching out the truth. All of this and more is documented in this book. 213.M83

_____. *Men of Science/Men of God.* San Diego: Creation-Life Publishers, 1982.

The author gives a brief biography and Christian testimony of a number of scientists who believed they were "thinking God's thoughts after Him." Appendixes include "Scientific Disciplines Established by Bible-Believing Scientists" and "Notable Inventions, Discoveries, or Developments by Bible-Believing Scientists." Emphasizes truths noncreationists would rather forget. 509.2.M83

_____. *The Troubled Waters of Evolution.* San Diego: Creation-Life Publishers, 1974.

Another of the author's exposés of the evolutionary hypothesis. This one demonstrates the logical inconsistencies of evolution when compared with factual evidence from other related sciences. 213.M83T 1974

_____, and **Gary E. Parker.** *What Is Creation Science?* San Diego: Creation-Life Publishers, 1982.

The authors answer the question of the title and many others with fairness and straightforward honesty. Best of all, these scientists explain the scientific theories and evidences that make up creation science in language we can understand. Nearly sixty illustrations help to explain some of the more technical aspects. Recommended. 213.M83W

**Wilder-Smith, A. E.** *The Natural Sci-*

*ences Know Nothing of Evolution.* San Diego: Master Books, 1981.

A valuable contribution to the whole issue of natural history, evolution, and the origin of life on this planet. Highly recommended. 500.W64

## BIBLICAL STUDIES

**Blair, Edward Payson.** *Abingdon Bible Handbook.* Nashville: Abingdon Press, 1975.

This lavishly illustrated work serves also as an introduction to the books of the Bible. The author adheres to the standard critical conclusions of OT scholarship but is more conservative in treating the NT. 220'.02.B57

**Gibson, Arthur.** *Biblical Semantic Logic: A Preliminary Analysis.* Oxford: Basil Blackwell, 1981.

†The author, a pupil of James Barr, has written an incisive, stimulating, but generally destructive work. As a philosopher, his statements are made with telling logic. When logic is applied to the theory of meaning in biblical studies, the results challenge the scholar but may also lead the unwary astray. 220'.01'4.G35

**\*Jensen, Irving Lester.** *Jensen's Bible Study Charts.* Chicago: Moody Press, 1981.

Now complete in one volume, this indispensable work should be in the hands of every Sunday school teacher. 220'.02'.02.J45 1981

**\*MacArthur, John F., Jr.** *Why Believe the Bible?* Ventura, Calif.: Regal Books, 1980.

Twelve chapters that provide a rationale for confidence in the Bible and an explanation of the importance of the Word of God in the life of the believer. 220'.01.M11

**McDonald, Hugh Dermot.** *What the Bible Teaches About the Bible.* Wheaton, Ill.: Tyndale House Publishers, 1979.

An able discussion of the theological issues surrounding the doctrines of revelation and inspiration. Well-reasoned; communicates the teaching of Scripture in terms laypeople can understand. 220'.01.M14

## BIBLE STUDY

**\*Allison, Joseph D.** *The Bible Study Resource Guide.* Nashville: Thomas Nelson Publishers, 1982.

Covers study Bibles, concordances, commentaries, dictionaries, encyclopedias, atlases, and language helps. A very handy bibliography that users will find most helpful. 016.22.AL15

**\*Barber, Cyril John.** *Dynamic Personal Bible Study: Principles of Inductive Bible Study Based on the Life of Abraham.* Neptune, N.J.: Loizeaux Brothers, 1981.

Designed for use in Bible colleges or as an introductory course in churches, these chapters seek to make Bible study an exciting experience. "The treatment of the [principles of inductive Bible study] is refreshing and stimulating. Seasoned with appropriate illustrations, [the author] serves up the material in an attractive way" (Charles C. Ryrie). 220'.07.B23

**Braga, James.** *How to Study the Bible.* Portland, Oreg.: Multnomah Press, 1982.

An excellent resume of the basic principles of Bible study. Recommended. 220'.07.B73

**Coleman, Lucien E., Jr.** *How to Teach the Bible.* Nashville: Broadman Press, 1979.

A helpful work for use by DCEs and

those involved in the training of teachers. 220.07.C67 1979

**DeLoe, Jesse B.** *Sweeter Than Honey: A Guide to Effective Bible Study.* Winona Lake, Ind.: Brethren Missionary Herald Press, 1979.

A basic introduction to Bible study. Intended for laypeople. Recommended. 220'.07.D37

**Hromas, R. P.** *Passport to the Bible.* Wheaton, Ill.: Tyndale House Publishers, 1980.

The author teaches Bible study groups in her home and church. In this handy book she shares with her readers the principles of personal study that she has found successful. 220.07.H85

***Jensen, Irving Lester.** Jensen's Survey of the Old Testament.* Chicago: Moody Press, 1978.

A helpful introduction that avoids the traditional matters of authorship, date, and the like, and instead assists readers to come to grips with and understand the text of each canonical book of the OT. Can be recommended to laypeople who wish to study the Bible for themselves. 221'.07.J45

**LaHaye, Tim.** *How to Study the Bible for Yourself.* Irvine, Calif.: Harvest House Publishers, 1976.

A simply written, practical how-to book for laymen. Recommended. 220.07.L13

**Laymon, Charles M., ed.** *Interpreter's One Volume Commentary on the Bible.* Nashville: Abingdon Press, 1971.

†This abridgment of the twelve-volume commentary includes the Apocrypha and contains some helpful general articles. 220.7.IN8L

**Lockerbie, D. Bruce.** *Asking Questions: A Classroom Model for Teaching the Bible.* Milford, Mich.: Mott Media, 1970.

A commendable book on Bible study methodology. Analyzes the technique of asking questions used by the Lord Jesus

and then applies the principles to select passages of the OT. Recommended. 220.07.L79

***Martin, John Richard.** Keys to Successful Bible Study.* Kitchener, Ontario: Herald Press, 1981.

A wise, discerning, and in some repects unusual approach to inductive Bible study. Provides clear guidance on how to find God's will in His Word. 220'.07.M36

**McDowell, Josh.** *Guide to Understanding Your Bible.* San Bernardino, Calif.: Here's Life Publishers, 1982.

Shows his readers how to become more consistent in Bible study, how to uncover the meaning of a passage, the importance of making charts as a means of review, the benefit of studying in a group, and how to relate the teaching of Scripture to the crises of life. 220.07.M14G

**Olsson, Karl A.** *Find Yourself in the Bible: A Guide to Relational Bible Study for Small Groups.* Minneapolis: Augsburg Publishing House, 1974.

The evangelical renaissance that began in the 1950s has merged with the relational emphasis of the 1960s, resulting in a demand for books that vitally relate the Bible to life. This treatise goes a long way toward meeting that need. 220.07.OL8

***Richards, Lawrence O.** Creative Bible Study.* Grand Rapids: Zondervan Publishing House, 1971.

A new approach to Bible study designed to encourage individuals to discover God's Word for themselves. The treatment is objective and revitalizing. This is an ideal book for group or personal use. 220.07.R39

**Scroggie, William Graham.** *Unfolding Drama of Redemption.* 3 vols. London: Pickering and Inglis, 1953-1971.

A valuable set for the expositor. Each book of the Bible is outlined and receives careful comment. Numerous charts highlight God's redemptive program. 220.07.SCR5U

**Sproule, Robert Charles.** *Knowing Scripture.* Downers Grove, Ill.: InterVarsity Press, 1977.

A complete discussion of the dynamics of Bible study from a basic rationale to hermeneutics and from cultural considerations to a discussion of appropriate tools and translations. 220'.07.SP8

**Stibbs, Alan Marshall.** *How to Understand Your Bible.* Revised by D. Wenham and G. Wenham. Wheaton, Ill.: Harold Shaw Publishers, 1977.

Formerly published under the title *Understanding God's Word* (1950), this practical guide is relevant to the needs of laypeople. Excellent. 220'.07.ST5H

**Stott, John Robert Walmsey.** *Understanding the Bible.* Grand Rapids: Zondervan Publishing House, 1979.

First published in England in 1972, this study guide by one of the great expository preachers of our generation answers questions new Christians are asking and shows how they may benefit from, and be nurtured by, the Word of God. 220.07.S7

**\*Traina, Robert A.** *Methodical Bible Study: A New Approach to Hermeneutics.* Grand Rapids: Francis Asbury Press, 1985.

The reissuing of a work that has been a standard text on Bible study methodology for more than three decades. A welcome reprint. 220.07.T68 1985

**Wald, Oletta.** *The Joy of Discovery in Bible Study.* Rev. ed. Minneapolis: Augsburg Publishing House, 1977.

A revision and expansion of the author's ever-popular study guide. Uses the text of TEV. 220'.07.W14 1977

**\*_____.** *The Joy of Teaching Discovery in Bible Study.* Minneapolis: Augsburg Publishing House, 1976.

A companion volume to *Joy of Discovery in Bible Study.* Helpful. 220.07.W14T

**Warren, Richard,** and **William A. Shell.** *Twelve Dynamic Bible Study Methods.* Wheaton, Ill.: Victor Books, 1981.

Combines methodology with a devotional approach to the text. Elementary. 220'.07.W25

**\*Willmington, Harold L.** *Willmington's Guide to the Bible.* Wheaton, Ill.: Tyndale House Publishers, 1981.

A massive work in which each book of the Bible receives careful analysis and comment. The main theological doctrines are outlined with appropriate quotations and proof texts, and the concluding sections treat issues of interest to Bible students. An essential reference work. 220'.07.W68

## ORIGIN AND AUTHENTICITY OF THE BIBLE

**Achtemeier, Paul J.** *The Inspiration of Scripture: Problems and Proposals.* Philadelphia: Westminster Press, 1980.

The author adopts a mediating stance. He refers to the works of A. A. Hodge and B. B. Warfield but fails to interact with other evangelical writers. He does discuss the use of the Bible in the church and advocates its authority, but not in the sense of "Thus saith the Lord." 220.13.AC4

**Anderson, Bernhard W.** *The Living Word of the Bible.* Philadelphia: Westminster Press, 1979.

†This collection of sermons reveals the author's unwillingness to separate the biblical narrative from history of higher critical theories, yet treats the Bible as authoritative. 220.1.AN2

**Bavinck, Herman.** *The Philosophy of Revelation.* Grand Rapids: Baker Book House, 1979.

Contains the L. P. Stone Lectures, Princeton Seminary, 1908-1909. Traces the idea of revelation in its biblical form and content and develops a view of man in relation to the creation that paves the way for an understanding of the plan and purpose of God in revelation. Reformed. 220.1.B32

**Beckwith, Roger.** *The Old Testament Canon of the New Testament Church and Its Background in Early Judaism.* Grand Rapids: Wm. B. Eerdmans Publishing Co., 1985.

"It is a pleasure to commend a work of high scholarship on an important subject which cries out for fresh and up-to-date treatment" (F. F. Bruce). 221.1'2.B38

**Blenkinsopp, Joseph.** *Prophecy and Canon: A Contribution to the Study of Jewish Origins.* Notre Dame, Ind.: University of Notre Dame Press, 1977.

Suggests ways in which a fresh understanding of the Hebrew canon can enhance the study of biblical theology and bring into clearer focus the main tenets of Judaism. 221.12.B61

**\*Boice, James Montgomery.** *Standing on the Rock.* Wheaton, Ill.: Tyndale House Publishers, 1984.

Strong in his advocacy of biblical inerrancy, Boice challenges those who may be wavering in their allegiance to God's Word and also provides a powerful apologetic, which those who have abandoned the church's historic position will do well to consider. And to those who need convincing, he offers a stimulating, rational basis for belief in the inspiration of Scripture. 220.13.B63

**Bush, L. Russ,** and **Tom J. Nettles.** *Baptists and the Bible: The Baptist Doctrine of Biblical Inspiration and Religious Authority in Historical Perspective.* Chicago: Moody Press, 1980.

A singularly thorough blending of the history of the inerrancy controversy with a fine refutation of the theories that have been advanced against the orthodox, conservative position. 220.13.B96

**\*Carroll, Benajah Harvey.** *Inspiration of the Bible.* Nashville: Thomas Nelson Publishers, 1980.

Originally published in 1930 (at the height of the Fundamentalist-Modernist controversy), this trenchant statement of the historic Baptist position on the inspiration of the Scriptures is a classic in the field that can be read with profit by pastors and laypeople today. 220.13.C23 1980

**\*Clark, Gordon Haddon.** *God's Hammer: The Bible and Its Critics.* Jefferson, N.Y.: Trinity Foundation, 1982.

Another important work in the growing corpus of literature on the inspiration and inerrancy of the Bible. Worthy of serious consideration. 220.13.C54

**Coats, George W.,** and **Burke O. Long, eds.** *Canon and Authority.* Philadelphia: Fortress Press, 1977.

Studies the relationship between the biblical canon and biblical authority. Marred by higher critical theories but does elucidate the problem surrounding these important themes. Individual essays dealing with such topics as superscriptions are worth consulting. 221.12.C63

**Countryman, William.** *Biblical Authority or Biblical Tyranny?* Scripture and the Christian Pilgrimage. Philadelphia: Fortress Press, 1981.

†An innocent work that readily employs evangelical terminology. Accepts the Bible's authority, but advocates biblical errancy. Also of interest is the writer's critique of modern fundamentalism. Unreliable. 220.13.C83

**Davis, Stephen T.** *The Debate About the Bible: Inerrancy Versus Infallibility.* Philadelphia: Westminster Press, 1977.

Evades the real issues surrounding the inscripturation of God's revelation. Beclouds the issues by affirming infallibility and yet allowing for errors in the Bible. 220.1.D29

**\*Feinberg, Charles Lee.** *Israel at the Center of History and Revelation.* Portland, Oreg.: Multnomah Press, 1980.

This revised edition of *Israel in the Spotlight* brings up to date the author's earlier treatise dealing with God's plan and purpose for His chosen people—past, present, and future. Recommended. 220.15.F32 1980.

———, **ed.** *Prophecy and the Seventies.* Chicago: Moody Press, 1971.

A symposium on biblical prophecy by nine outstanding Bible teachers. Lucid, informative, and generally reliable. 220.15.F32

**\*Geisler, Norman Leo, ed.** *Inerrancy.* Grand Rapids: Zondervan Publishing House, 1979.

One part of a series of monographs stemming from the International Conference on Biblical Inerrancy, 1978. Chapters treat crucial aspects of the debate from an evangelical perspective. 220.13.IN3G 1979

**Greenspahn, Frederick E., ed.** *Scripture in Jewish and Christian Traditions: Authority, Interpretation, Relevance.* Nashville: Abingdon Press, 1982.

This book is a part of the University of Denver's Judaic studies. The essays cover the three areas of the subtitle. John Gerstner is the only evangelical to contribute to this symposium. As a whole, the choice of topics and the variety of views presented makes this a valuable contribution. 220.1.G85

**\*Haldane, Robert.** *The Authenticity and Inspiration of the Holy Scriptures.* Minneapolis: Klock & Klock Christian Publishers, 1985.

First published in 1845. This work is of contemporary relevance because history has repeated itself and the same issues Haldane confronted are facing the church again. Haldane's material is clear

and cogent; his presentation is biblical; his defense of this cardinal doctrine of the faith is one of the best ever penned. What is to be found between the covers of this book is worthy of serious consideration. 220.13.H12 1985

**Hannah, John D., ed.** *Inerrancy and the Church.* Chicago: Moody Press, 1984.

Believing that evangelicals need to respond to *Authority and Interpretation of the Bible,* by Rogers and McKim, Hannah has gathered together a team of competent evangelical scholars who probe the origins of inerrancy in the writings of leaders of the church. The result is a positive apologetic and a clear, concise rebuttal that detractors of the doctrine as well as those who are unsure of the issues would do well to read. 220.13.H19

**Hodge, Archibald A.,** and **Benjamin B. Warfield.** *Inspiration.* Grand Rapids: Baker Book House, 1979.

These brief essays, reprinted from the 1881 edition, lay bare and defend the evangelical doctrine of the self-disclosure of God to man. 220.12.H66 1979

**Inch, Morris Alton.** *Understanding Bible Prophecy.* New York: Harper & Row, 1977.

Intended for adult discussion groups. Explains biblical prophecy as a living encounter between God and man. 220.15.IN2

**\*Johnson, Samuel Lewis, Jr.** *The Old Testament in the New: An Argument for Biblical Inspiration.* Grand Rapids: Zondervan Publishing House, 1980.

Delightful studies that ably correlate the OT Scripture with the New. Demonstrates convincingly the accuracy of the Word and the viability of the doctrine of inspiration. 220.13.J63

**\*Lewis, Gordon Russell,** and **Bruce Demarest, eds.** *Challenges to Inerrancy: A Theological Response.* Chicago: Moody Press, 1984.

Part of the growing corpus of literature produced by those who participated in the various congresses sponsored by the International Council on Biblical Inerrancy. This volume focuses on theological and historical issues and contains insightful chapters covering a variety of themes. 220.13.L58

**Lightner, Robert Paul.** *The Saviour and the Scriptures.* Grand Rapids: Baker Book House, 1978.

First published in 1966, and with the original foreword by Edward J. Young, this volume ably sets forth the case for biblical inerrancy. Its reappearance is welcomed. 220.12.L64 1978

**\*Lindsell, Harold.** *The Battle for the Bible.* Grand Rapids: Zondervan Publishing House, 1976.

A highly controversial work that boldly champions the inspiration of Scripture and calls on believers to recognize its authority. 220.13.L64

————. *The Bible in the Balance.* Grand Rapids: Zondervan Publishing House, 1979.

This sequel to the *Battle for the Bible* deals with the criticisms and objections leveled against the former work. It continues the history of certain church and education groups facing the current inroads of those who do not espouse inerrancy and concludes with an assessment of what the future holds with regard to the position of biblical inerrancy. Popular. 220.13.L64B 1979

**\*M'Intosh, Hugh.** *Is Christ Infallible and the Bible True?* Minneapolis: Klock & Klock Christian Publishers, 1981.

A refreshing, thoroughly biblical defense of the inspiration and authority of the Scriptures. Draws attention to the consequences of negative biblical criticism and describes the results to individuals and nations when divine revelation is first deprecated and then ignored. Recommended. 220.1.M66 1981

**McCall, Thomas S.,** and **Zola Levitt.**

*Satan in the Sanctuary.* Chicago: Moody Press, 1973.

A popular book dealing with the events that the authors believe are leading up to the Tribulation. 220.15.M12

**McDowell, Josh,** and **Dale E. Belles.** *The Uniqueness of the Bible.* San Bernardino, Calif.: Here's Life Publishers, 1982.

Leads the reader through the steps that eventuate in an understanding of bibliology. Excellent. 220.12.M14U

————. *The Trustworthiness of the Bible.* San Bernardino, Calif.: Here's Life Publishers, 1981.

Part of a growing series of self-help workbooks designed to guide users in their pursuit of a grasp of the basic concepts of Christianity. 220.1.M14T

**Neil, William.** *Can We Trust the Old Testament?* New York: Seabury Press, 1979.

†Intended as a companion volume to J. Robinson's *Can We Trust the New Testament?* Adheres to the major tenets of modern critical scholarship. Though well written, this work fails to treat seriously the traditional beliefs of evangelicals and ignores the contribution of conservative scholars. The result is a treatment that, for all its scholarship, does not honor the Word of God as His progressive revelation to man and will mislead the uninformed. 221.12.N31

**Packer, James Innell.** *God Has Spoken.* Downers Grove, Ill.: InterVarsity Press, 1979.

Published in England in 1965, these messages reveal what has taken place in the Christian church following the neglect of the Bible as the revelation of God to man. Concludes with "The Chicago Statement on Biblical Inerrancy." 220.12.P12

**Pentecost, John Dwight.** *Will Man Survive? Prophecy You Can Understand.* Chicago: Moody Press, 1971.

An easy-to-understand survey of God's

future program. Rich in insights and valuable as a synthesis of coming events. 220.15.P38W

**Pinnock, Clark H.** *Biblical Revelation, the Foundation of Christian Theology.* Chicago: Moody Press, 1971.

An evaluation of present-day religious philosophies with an analysis of modern concepts of inspiration. Pinnock's position seems to have undergone change since writing this book. 220.13.P56B

**\*Radmacher, Earl D., ed.** *Can We Trust the Bible?* Wheaton, Ill.: Tyndale House Publishers, 1979.

Continues the authoritative works growing out of the International Council on Biblical Inerrancy, 1977. Stimulating. 220.1.C16 1979

**Robinson, John Arthur Thomas.** *Redating the New Testament.* Philadelphia: Westminster Press, 1976.

No one has ever doubted Bishop Robinson's scholastic ability or his identification with those on the far left fringe of theological thought. In this treatise he abandons the liberal dating of NT books by assigning very early dates for their composition, outdoing even the most conservative of evangelicals. 225.1'4.R56

**\*Rushdoony, Rousas John.** *Infallibility: An Inescapable Concept.* Vallecito, Calif.: Ross House Books, 1978.

Amid the furor over inerrancy, certain writers have grasped the truth of the matter and have written about it with clarity and insight. This is one such book. The chapters are brief but cover the bases adequately. 220.13.R89

**Ryrie, Charles Caldwell.** *The Best Is Yet to Come.* Chicago: Moody Press, 1980.

In thirteen moving chapters Ryrie covers prophetic themes relating to the future. In each chapter he treats a new facet of eschatology and offers hope in the midst of doubt and uncertainty. 220.15.R99B

**\*Saphir, Adolph.** *Divine Unity of Scripture.* Grand Rapids: Kregel Publications, 1984.

This helpful study, first published in 1885, is still of the utmost importance. Devout readers of Scripture will benefit greatly from this discussion. 220.1.SA6 1984.

**\*Turretin, Francis.** *The Doctrine of Scripture: Locus 2 of "Institutio Theologiae Elencticae."* Translated and edited by J. W. Beardslee III. Grand Rapids: Baker Book House, 1981.

The writer, professor of theology, University of Geneva (1648-1687), exercised considerable influence on the American Princeton theologians. In this work he presents his doctrine of Scripture and discourses at length on its inspiration and authority. 220.1.T86

**\*Woodbridge, John D.** *Biblical Authority: A Critique of the Rogers/McKim Proposal.* Grand Rapids: Zondervan Publishing House, 1982.

A careful refutation of the erroneous interpretations of history of Rogers and McKim, showing the logical fallacies inherent in their thinking. A valuable treatise. 220.13.W85

**Youngblood, Ronald, ed.** *Evangelicals and Inerrancy.* Nashville: Thomas Nelson Publishers, 1984.

Containing essays from the *Journal of the Evangelical Theological Society* (published 1954-1979), this volume provides readers with some excellent information on the growing debate over inerrancy. This is a most helpful contribution. 220.13.Y8

## Bible Concordances

*The Complete Concordance to the Bible; New King James Version.* Nashville: Thomas Nelson Publishers, 1983.

With the publication of the *New King*

*James Version* (NKJV) of the Bible, a need was felt for a concordance similar to the magisterial work of Strong. There are more than 265,000 entries in this volume to 13,331 words. A list of nonindexed words is provided at the beginning. 220.2.AU8 1983

**Einspahr, Bruce, et al., comps.** *Index to Brown, Driver and Briggs Hebrew Lexicon.* Chicago: Moody Press, 1976.

This is a work of merit. It is also worthy of acquisition. It builds on BDB. Because BDB lists words by their root, students with little grasp of Hebrew have experienced difficulty in using it. This index removes the problem by following the canonical arrangement of the books of the Bible (Genesis, Exodus, etc.) and dealing with each word as it appears in the text. It also provides the meaning, page, and section in BDB where the word is discussed. Recommended. 221.2.B81.EI6

**Graham, William Franklin.** *The Secret of Happiness.* Revised and expanded edition. Waco, Tex.: Word Books, 1985.

The timeless message of true happiness, based on the Beatitudes, is even more urgently needed now than it was thirty years ago when this book was first published. The messages here turn human values upside down. Christ's words are shown to provide a new way of looking at life. Richly illustrated from Graham's own experiences, this book is a welcome addition to other works covering the introductory verses to the Sermon on the Mount. 225.2.5.G76 1985

**Hartdegen, Stephen J., ed.** *Nelson's Complete Concordance to the New American Bible.* Nashville: Thomas Nelson Publishers, 1977.

This beautifully produced concordance to the NAB (1970) version of the Bible and Apocrypha should not be confused with the concordance to the NASB. Nelson's concordance is to the highly acclaimed Roman Catholic version and is a work to which researchers

will turn again and again. 220.2.N33

**Morrison, Clinton.** *An Analytical Concordance to the Revised Standard Version of the New Testament.* Philadelphia: Westminster Press, 1979.

A skillfully prepared work that will be welcomed by users of the RSV. Also of value to those who wish to obtain insights into the meaning of specific Greek words and terms. Exceptionally well produced. 225.2.M83A 1979

**Moulton, Harold K.** *The Challenge of the Concordance: New Testament Words Studied in Depth.* London: Samuel Bagster and Sons, 1977.

True to its subtitle, this work treats 163 words and their meaning, interpreting them historically as they apply to the life of Christ, the development of doctrine, the ministry of the church, and the like. A welcome volume. 225.2.M86C

**Robinson, David, ed.** *Concordance to the Good News Bible.* Nashville: Thomas Nelson Publishers, 1983.

This computer-produced concordance to TEV contains 250,000 entries. Theological words from the KJV are cross-referenced to TEV. Although this work has been beautifully produced, one questions its usefulness (except for Bible translators using TEV) because the text of the *Good News Bible* is such as to disqualify it for use in serious Bible study. 220.2.G62R

**Walker, James Bradford Richmond.** *Walker's Comprehensive Bible Concordance.* Grand Rapids: Kregel Publications, 1976.

Based on the KJV, this alphabetically arranged concordance contains more than 50,000 entries. It ranks with Strong's *Exhaustive Concordance* (1890) for usefulness and versatility. Reprinted from the 1894 edition. 220.2.W15 1976

**Wigram, George V.,** and **Ralph D. Winter.** *The Word Study Concordance.* Pasadena, Calif.: William Carey Library, 1978.

This unique work contains Wigram's popular *Englishman's Greek Concordance of the New Testament* coded to Strong's *Exhaustive Concordance of the Bible*, the 4th edition of Arndt and Gingrich's *Greek Lexicon of the New Testament*, and Kittel's *TDNT* (using the text of the KJV). Each word is located in Strong's *Concordance*, thus providing via Strong's work access to the original. Of value to lay Bible students. 225.2W63W 1978

## BIBLE ENCYCLOPEDIAS AND DICTIONARIES

**Bauer, Walter.** *A Greek-English Lexicon of the New Testament and Other Early Christian Literature.* Translated and adapted from the 5th German ed. by W. F. Arndt and F. W. Ginrich. Revised by F. W. Ginrich and F. W. Danker. Chicago: University of Chicago Press, 1979.

A new edition of a standard work. Besides adding Bauer's new material, the editors have corrected errors in the first edition, increased the references to include textual variants and parallel usage, added new words, made references to Qumran and the Bodmer Papyri, and enhanced the bibliographies by inserting literally thousands of entries. This is a most important resource, and pastors should make extensive use of it. 487.4.B32 1979

**Bromiley, Geoffrey William, et al.** *The International Standard Bible Encyclopedia.* In process. Grand Rapids: Wm. B. Eerdmans Publishing Co., 1979-.

Originally published in 1915 and revised in 1929, this work is now in the process of a fresh revision. The new edition is based on the text of the RSV and includes articles on every person and place mentioned in Scripture. Some articles have been retained from the earlier edition. The contributors, however, are not all conservative theologians, and the different viewpoints adhered to is evident in many of the leading articles. This work has been well illustrated and beautifully produced. It is deserving of consultation, and the appearance of the other volumes is anxiously awaited. Only two volumes are in print at this time. 220.3.IN8B

**\*Brown, Colin, ed.** *The New International Dictionary of New Testament Theology.* 3 vols. Grand Rapids: Zondervan Publishing House, 1975-1978.

This is a work of great merit. It consists of a translation and revision of the famous *Theologisches Begriffslexikon zum Neuen Testament* and makes available in English the valuable material heretofore accessible only to those with a command of theological German. More conservative than *TDNT*, these volumes deserve a place in every preacher's library. 225.3.N42.B39

**\****Computer-Konkordanz zum Novum Testamentum Graece.* Edited by the Institut für Neutestamentliche Textforschung. Berlin: Walter de Gruyter, 1980.

Based on the 26th edition of the Nestle-Aland *Novum Testamentum Graece* and the 3d edition of the United Bible Societies' *Greek New Testament*, this computer concordance is more compete than any of its predecessors and includes occurrences of conjunctions, participles, pericope, and the like. It gives promise of becoming one of the most widely consulted Greek concordances ever produced. Highly recommended. 283.C73

**Douglas, James D., ed.** *The Illustrated Bible Dictionary.* 3 vols. Wheaton, Ill.: Tyndale House Publishers, 1980.

Formerly published as the *New Bible Dictionary*, this new, revised, updated, and lavishly illustrated edition retains many of the excellencies of the older work. Some articles in the former edition have been omitted, whereas others have been merged with similar topics for easier reference. Coverage is excellent; the dates of certain OT events tend to reflect the opinion of liberal scholarship. The index in vol. 3 is most valuable and complete. All things considered, this is a timely and helpful work that has been exceptionally well produced. 220.3.IL6 1980

————. *New Bible Dictionary.* 2d ed. Wheaton, Ill.: Tyndale House Publishers, 1982.

Beautifully reproduced, with up-to-date bibliographies, this resource tool will long be a standard work throughout the English-speaking world. "I doubt if there is any better value for money today. As a basic book for every thinking Christian's library, it is indispensable" (John R. W. Stott). 220.3.N42 1982

**\*Harris, Robert Laird, Gleason Leonard Archer, Jr.,** and **Bruce Kenneth Waltke,** eds. *Theological Wordbook of the Old Testament.* 2 vols. Chicago: Moody Press, 1980.

Less comprehensive than the *Theologisches Worterbuch zum Alten Testament,* *TWOT* will nevertheless prove to be an invaluable resource tool for those engaged in, or preparing for, the ministry. Each word is arranged according to its root form, cognate terms are dealt with adequately, definitions are concise, and the usage of the word is employed to establish its meaning. Every word in BDB is included, and each word is keyed to Strong's *Exhaustive Concordance. TWOT* must stand as one of the most valuable OT resource tools produced to date. Highly recommended. 221.4′4.H24

**Kittel, Gerhard,** and **Gerhard Frederich,** eds. *Theological Dictionary of the New Testament.* Translated and abridged by G. W. Bromiley. Grand Rapids: Wm.

B. Eerdmans Publishing Co., 1985.

Considered by many biblical scholars to be the best NT dictionary ever compiled, *TDNT* has established itself as an indispensable resource tool. Exemplifying the best of German liberal scholarship, it was too extensive and too technical for lay use. Now Bromiley has abridged the monumental work into a convenient one-volume "Little Kittel." In doing so, he has eliminated a great deal of scholarly detail and given to those with little knowledge of Greek a useful, easy-to-use reference work. 225.3.T34B 1985

**Leon-DuFour, Xavier,** ed. *Dictionary of the New Testament.* Translated by T. Prendergast. 3d ed. San Francisco: Harper & Row, 1980.

†This up-dated edition continues the many excellencies of its predecessors. Tables of money equivalencies, linear measures, a chronology of the life of the apostle Paul, and the like further enhance the usefulness of this fine work. Roman Catholic. 225.3.L55 1980

**Miller, Madeline Sweeny,** and **J. Lane Miller.** *Harper's Bible Dictionary.* Rev. ed. New York: Harper & Row, 1975.

†Lacks consistent bibliographical improvement, is uneven in revision, and is more liberal than the previous edition in its orientation. Disappointing. 220.3.M61 1975

**\*Pitkin, Ronald E.,** comp. *Theological Dictionary to the New Testament.* Vol. X, *Index.* Grand Rapids: Wm. B. Eerdmans Publishing Co., 1976.

Compiled by a busy pastor, this index volume provides an indispensable key to unlocking the full treasures of *TDNT.* The respective indexes fall into four primary areas: English keywords, Greek keywords, Hebrew and Aramaic words, and biblical references. The arrangement is such that the lecturer, minister, or student can tell at a glance if relevant material has been treated anywhere in the previous nine volumes, and exactly where it may be found. This is a priceless addition to an excellent resource tool, and we are most grateful that it has been made available to facilitate research. The publisher and the compiler are deserving of our hearty thanks. 487.2.K65 v.10

*Richards, Lawrence O.* Expository Dictionary of Bible Words. Grand Rapids: Zondervan Publishing House, Regency Reference Library, 1985.

"Richards shows a fine sense of discrimination in the handling of the technical material of biblical lexicography, and he clarifies the distinctives of the many near-synonyms that serve as key terms in Biblical theology. . . . For the sincere Bible student who has had to rely on brief and sometimes oversimplifed comments in [study] Bibles, this new volume will furnish much more detailed and satisfying input" (Gleason L. Archer, Jr.). 220.3.R39

**Smith, William.** *Dr. William Smith's Dictionary of the Bible.* Revised and edited by H. B. Hackett. 4 vols. Grand Rapids: Baker Book House, 1981.

Though old, this work has retained much of its value. It is obviously dated in historical and archaeological matters, yet the writings of many of the great theologians are to be found in these volumes, and what they wrote has stood the test of time. 220.3.SM6 1981

*Townsley, David, and Russell Bjork.* Scripture Index to the New International Dictionary of New Testament Theology. Grand Rapids: Zondervan Publishing House, Regency Reference Library, 1985.

Opens the way for the serious user to benefit from the wealth of background material, philological information, and helpful data that can add depth as well as interest to one's study of the NT. Cross-

referenced and arranged in biblical sequence (Genesis through Revelation), followed by references to the Apocrypha, the Pseudepigrapha, the DDS, and the like, this computer-produced index is easy for preachers to use in the preparation of their messages. Invaluable. 225.3.N42 v.4

**Unger, Merrill Frederick,** and **William White, Jr.** *Nelson's Expository Dictionary of the Old Testament.* Nashville: Thomas Nelson Publishers, 1980.

A handy dictionary arranged alphabetically by English word, with the Hebrew equivalent(s) listed according to their verbal, nounal, adverbial, and adjectival forms. Theological issues are blended with etymological distinctions and word usage to make this a handy resource tool for laypeople. Should be in every church library. 221.4'4.N33

———, and **William Edwy Vine.** *An Expositional Dictionary of Biblical Words.* Nashville: Thomas Nelson Publishers, 1984.

Combines Vine's famous *Expository Dictionary of New Testament Words* (1939) with Unger and White's *Nelson's Expository Dictionary of Old Testament Words* (1982). Users of these works can study the meanings of biblical words in the original languages with little or no formal training in either Hebrew or Greek. 220.3.UN3 1984

**Vine, William Edwy.** *An Expository Dictionary of Old Testament Words.* Old Tappan, N.J.: Fleming H. Revell Co., 1978.

This posthumous work is much briefer than the author's fine work on the NT. Though highly commended by F. F. Bruce, it is doubtful it will ever share the popularity its NT counterpart enjoys. This edition includes essays by other writers. 221.3.V73

**Young, G. Douglas,** ed. *Young's Bible*

*Dictionary.* Wheaton, Ill.: Tyndale House Publishers, 1984.

Deceptively simple in its arrangement, and with an emphasis on pithy comments, this work is a masterpiece of succinct condensation. Accurate, reliable. 220.3.Y8

## BIBLE VERSIONS

**\*Beekman, John,** and **John Callow.** *Translating the Word of God.* Grand Rapids: Zondervan Publishing House, 1974.

This book, written by experienced linguists, sets forth the principles of biblical translation with examples of problems and suggested solutions. This is an excellent book and a must for missionary translators. It also has value for pastors and seminarians as well. Well indexed. 220.4.B39

**Bratcher, Robert G., trans.** *Good News Bible: The Bible in Today's English Version.* New York: American Bible Society, 1975.

*Good News for Modern Man,* Bratcher's translation of the NT, has now been expanded to include the OT. Although the style is lucid, the same theological shortcomings that characterized the NT are apparent in the edition of the entire Bible. Although lauded by scholars on both sides of the Atlantic and used extensively in the materials of the American and United Bible Societies, we find the deficiencies too great to merit praise. 220.52.G62

**Bruce, Frederick Fyvie.** *The History of the Bible in English.* 3d ed. New York: Oxford University Press, 1978.

This new edition includes a discussion of the NEB, NASB, *Living Bible,* and *Good News Bible.* Bruce is critical of the NASB and speaks approvingly of the *Good News Bible.* See *The Minister's Library* (1984), p. 65, for comments on the earlier edition. 220.52'09.B83 1978

**\*Callow, Kathleen.** *Discourse Considerations in Translating the Word of God.* Grand Rapids: Zondervan Publishing House, 1974.

A brilliant and informative work that ably handles the problems of direct and indirect discourse and other matters of importance to translators. Recommended. 220.4.C13

*The Christian Life Bible: The New King James Version.* Nashville: Thomas Nelson Publishers, 1985.

This translation retains the beauty and poetry of the KJV, includes all the verses found in the Traditional Text, and is widely accepted for preaching and teaching because of its accuracy, authority, and clarity. Included is a subject index, a résumé of the history of the intertestamental period, a summary of people and places mentioned in the Bible, and a concordance. 220.52.C46 1985

**\*deVaux, Roland.** *Archaeology and the Dead Sea Scrolls.* London: The British Academy, 1973.

A detailed discussion of the site of ancient Qumran, the authenticity of the Dead Sea material, and the relevance of these studies to biblical scholarship. 221.44.D49

**Foster, Lewis.** *Selecting a Translation of the Bible.* Cincinnati: Standard Publishing, 1983.

Written in a popular vein, this well-outlined, capable assessment of modern versions evaluates the AV, NASB, NEB, RSV, GNB, LB, JB, and New KJV. Helpful. 220.52.F78

**Glassman, Eugene H.** *The Translation Debate: What Makes a Bible Translation*

*Good?* Downers Grove, Ill.: InterVarsity Press, 1981.

Weighs carefully the merits of paraphrases and translations, traces the history of each, and provides guidelines for translators and readers. Stresses the importance of communication for meaning but minimizes the importance of accuracy for Bible study. Interesting to read but unreliable as a guide for a study Bible. 220.5.G46

**Goodrick, Edward W.,** and **John R. Kohlenberger, III, eds.** *The NIV Complete Concordance: The Complete English Concordance to the New International Version.* Grand Rapids: Zondervan Publishing House, 1981.

Includes biblical references to a particular word included under the key word. In all, 12,800 words are indexed, with the entire work comprising about 250,000 entries. Ideal for users of the NIV. 220.52.G62

**\*Larson, Mildred.** *A Manual on Problem Solving in Bible Translation.* Grand Rapids: Zondervan Publishing House, 1975.

Reflects the obvious desire of the author to faithfully communicate the Word of God. The value of this work increases with its use. Will become indispensable to Bible translators. Highly recommended. 220.4.L32

**Lewis, Jack Pearl.** *The English Bible from KJV to NIV: A History and Evaluation.* Grand Rapids: Baker Book House, 1981.

A penetrating evaluation of the history of the English Bible from the KJV to the present. Evaluates the strengths and weaknesses of each version with rare evangelical skill and theological acumen. Recommended. 220.52'09.L58

**May, H. G.,** and **B. M. Metzger, eds.** *The Oxford Annotated Bible with the Apocrypha: An Ecumenical Study Bible.* New York: Oxford University Press, 1977.

†Using the text of the RSV, this edition has notes supporting an unorthodox approach to Scripture and includes 3 and 4 Maccabees and Psalm 151 (a supposed psalm of David). 220.52'04.OX2E 1977

*\*The New American Standard Bible.* Carol Stream, Ill.: Creation House, 1971.

This work by an outstanding team of biblical scholars is perhaps the most accurate and reliable translation available. 220.52'06.AM3 1971

*New English Bible with the Apocrypha.* New York: Oxford and Cambridge University Presses, 1971.

†Includes the second edition of the NT together with the translation of the OT Apocrypha. The translators failed to avail themselves of the Ugaritic materials, which could have been used to good advantage in translating numerous OT passages. In spite of its excellent literary qualities, this translation is disappointing in that it too often reflects the theological biases of the translators. 220.52'06.N42

*New International Version Study Bible.* Grand Rapids: Zondervan Publishing House, 1985.

"Represents a notable advance on earlier study Bibles. It will enable both ministers and laypeople to have a better understanding of the Bible" (Colin Brown). 220.52.N42

**Nida, Eugene Albert.** *Language Structure and Translation.* Stanford, Calif.: Stanford University Press, 1975.

Concerned primarily with semantic structure, this volume offers timely counsel on the bridging of cultural gaps in translation and how that affects the work of the translator. 410.N54

————, and **William David Reyburn.** *Meaning Across Cultures.* American Society of Missiology. Maryknoll, N.Y.: Orbis Books, 1981.

Part of the continuing quest to make Bible translation and the communication of the gospel relevant to all cultures around the world. Informative. 220.5.N54

**Taylor, Kenneth N.** *The Living Bible.* Wheaton, Ill.: Tyndale House Publishers, 1971.

This is not and should not be regarded as an accurate version of the Holy Scriptures. As a paraphrase, it is a deservedly famous work. It appeals to young Christians and young people. 220.52'06.T21

**\*Westcott, Brooke Foss.** *The Bible in the Church: A Popular Account of the Collection and Reception of the Holy Scriptures in the Christian Churches.* Grand Rapids: Baker Book House, 1979.

Growing out of Westcott's excellent *History of the Canon of the New Testament,* these chapters treat relevantly and practically the reception of the biblical writings by the church. Historically reliable. Evangelical. Deserves careful reading, particularly by those who are troubled by denials of inspiration, authority, and canonicity. Recommended. 220.52'09.W52

OLD TESTAMENT

**Allen, Leslie C.** *The Greek Chronicles.* 2 vols. Leiden, The Netherlands: E. J. Brill, 1975.

Explains the methodology used in, and the results of, a comparison of the LXX and the MT. A definitive work. 221.4.AL5

**Alter, Robert.** *The Art of Biblical Narrative.* New York: Basic Books, 1981.

Advocates a return to the basic interpretation of the biblical narrative unencumbered by higher critical theories. Supports his theories with data on archaeological, sociological, and historical grounds. 221.4'4.AL7

**Brockington, L. H.** *The Hebrew Text of the Old Testament.* Malta: St. Paul's Press, 1973.

A discussion of the text used to support the NEB translation of the OT. One important feature of this work is the record of all variants (whether in pointing, word division, or text) from the third edition of Kittel's *Biblia Hebraica.* 221.4.B78

**Cross, Frank Moore, and S. Talmon, eds.** *Qumran and the History of the Biblical Text.* Cambridge, Mass.: Harvard University Press, 1975.

Essays on textual criticism and an attempt to assess the advances made in the area of scholarly pursuit since the discovery of the DDS. 221.4'4.C87

**Finley, Harvey E., and Charles D. Isbell.** *Biblical Hebrew.* Grand Rapids: Baker Book House, 1975.

An introductory grammar that is valuable for its methodology. It has been tested in the classroom. 492.45.F49

**Fitzmyer, Joseph A.** *The Dead Sea Scrolls: Major Publications and Tools for Study.* Missoula, Mont.: Scholars Press, 1975.

A reference volume providing access to an abundance of essential material. Recommended. 016.2214'4.F57

**Gaster, Theodor H., trans.** *The Dead Sea Scrolls.* 3d ed. revised. Garden City, N.Y.: Doubleday and Company, 1976.

A lucid translation that makes available to English readers a vast wealth of information, thus permitting them to ascertain first-hand the beliefs and practices of the Essenes of Qumran. This edition has been expanded to include twenty-four additional texts. 221.4.D34.G21 1976

**\*Gesenius, Wilhelm.** *Hebrew and Chaldee Lexicon to the Old Testament.* Translated by S. P. Tregelles. Milford, Mich.: Mott Media, 1982.

Coded to Strong's *Exhaustive Concordance,* this work makes available in a handy format the essence of Gesenius's famous *Lexicon Manuale Hebraicum et Chaldaicum in Veteris Testamenti Libros.* Contains entries to more than 12,000 words. 492.43.G33T 1982

**Greenspahn, Frederick E.** *Hapax Legomena in Biblical Hebrew: A Study of the Phenomenon and Its Treatment Since Antiquity with Special Reference to Verbal Forms.* Chico, Calif.: Scholars Press, 1984.

Although scholars have for centuries referred to the fact that certain words occur only once in the Hebrew Bible, no comprehensive effort has been made to determine the significance of their isolation. This book reviews the history of interest in this phenomenon and evaluates the relevance of these words and their form. Included is a detailed description of the methods applied to such words from antiquity to the present as well as a historical survey of how the 140 verbs have been understood. 492.4′028.G85

***Holladay, William L.** A Concise Hebrew and Aramaic Lexicon of the Old Testament.* Grand Rapids: Wm. B. Eerdmans Publishing Co., 1971.

A recent, up-to-date working tool. Not as extensive as BDB, but easy to use. It will greatly facilitate the rapid reading of Hebrew. 492.43.H71

**Klein, Ralph W.** *Textual Criticism of the Old Testament: The Septuagint After Qumran.* Philadelphia: Fortress Press, 1974.

Explains the importance of the LXX in the study of the OT, the relationship to the Greek text to the MT, and the way in which the discoveries of Qumran have influenced modern OT textual criticism. 221.4′8.K67

**Kugel, James L.** *The Idea of Biblical Poetry: Parallelism and Its History.* New Haven, Conn.: Yale University Press, 1981.

Traces the history of the interpretation of hymnic literature and provides an extensive analysis of the different forms as they appear in the milieu of the ancient Near East. An excellent discussion. 221.4′4.K95

**Kutscher, E. Y.** *The Language and Linguistic Background of the Isaiah Scroll.* Leiden, The Netherlands: E. J. Brill, 1974.

This study of 1QIsa(a) was first published in Hebrew in 1959. It contains a veritable trove of valuable data on linguistic and textual matters. 221.4.K96

**Mitchel, Larry A.** *A Student's Vocabulary for Biblical Hebrew and Aramaic.* Grand Rapids: Zondervan Publishing House, Academie Books, 1984.

Concentrates on the most frequently used words, and after explaining how that list may be used to maximum advantage, lists the words in accordance with their frequency of occurrence and also provides a key to their pronunciation. Recommended. 221.4′4.M69

**Walters, Peter.** *The Text of the Septuagint: Its Corruptions and Their Emendations.* Edited by D. W. Gooding. Cambridge: At the University Press, 1973.

An excellent prolegomena to the critical text of the LXX. Brings up to date Thackery's *Grammar of the Old Testament in Greek.* 221.48.W17

**Weingreen, Jacob.** *Introduction to the Critical Text of the Hebrew Bible.* Oxford: Clarendon Press, 1982.

A brief, clearly written, accurate work. Ideal for use as an introduction. 221.4′4.W43

**Wurthwein, Ernest.** *The Text of the Old Testament: An Introduction to the "Biblia Hebraica."* Translated by E. F. Rhodes. Grand Rapids: Wm. B. Eerdmans Publishing House, 1979.

Based on the 4th German edition (1973), this work is of the utmost value to the student of the OT. It surveys the transmission of the text and includes pertinent historical and philological comments on the MT, Samaritan Pentateuch, the different Targums, the Syriac Version, and the like. A valuable introduction. 221.4.W95 1979

NEW TESTAMENT

**Aland, Kurt, et al.** *The Greek New Testament.* 3d ed. New York: United Bible Societies, 1977.

With a new preface and a completely revised textual apparatus, this latest edition should be a constant source of delight to users. 225.4.G81 1977

**Alsop, John R., ed.** *An Index to the Revised Bauer-Arndt-Gingrich Greek Lexicon.* 2d ed. Grand Rapids: Zondervan Publishing House, 1981.

First published by the Wycliffe Bible Translators, this work is designed to facilitate the reading and study of the NT. Each entry carries a reference to the *Lexicon,* where a fuller explanation of the etymology of the word may be found. 487.4.AL7B 1981

**Berry, Harold J.** *Treasures from the Original.* Chicago: Moody Press, 1985.

These brief studies, first published in 1972, focus attention on some of the obscure, problematic words or phrases of the NT and explain their meaning in light of the semantics of language. 225.4'8.B45 1985

**\*Bruce, Frederick Fyvie.** *The Books and the Parchments: How We Got Our English Bible.* Revised and updated ed. Old Tappan, N.J.: Fleming H. Revell Co., 1984.

A thorough review of the translations of the Bible from the earliest versions to the NIV, *New KJV,* and *Reader's Bible.* Becomes less reliable in assessing the worth of those translations from the NEB onwards. Includes appendixes on the lost books mentioned in the Bible, and the NT Apocrypha. 225.4.B83 1984

**Burgon, John William.** *The Revision Revised.* Paradise, Pa.: Conservative Classics, 1979.

Long out-of-print, this classic by the renowned dean of Chichester, England, was first published in 1883. In this work Burgon takes issue with Westcott and Hort and advocates the acceptance of the Textus Receptus. 225.4.B91 1979

**Burton, Ernest DeWitt.** *Syntax of the Moods and Tenses in New Testament Greek.* Grand Rapids: Kregel Publications, 1976.

Though dated, this work still is of inestimable value to students of NT Greek, for it contains one of the best treatments available on the translation of direct and indirect discourse. Reprinted from the 1900 edition. 487.5.B95 1976

**Carson, Donald A.** *The King James Version Debate: A Plea for Realism.* Grand Rapids: Baker Book House, 1979.

A powerful polemic in favor of modern translations of the Bible coupled with an equally powerful repudiation of Pickering's *The Identity of the New Testament Text.* The work should be read by all who are interested in the facts. 225.4.C23

**Chamberlain, William Douglas.** *An Exegetical Grammar of the Greek New Testament.* Grand Rapids: Baker Book House, 1979.

First published in 1941, this introductory text has been widely used in Bible colleges and seminaries. It is comprehensive and helpful. 485.C35 1979

**Estrada, David,** and **William White.** *The First New Testament.* Nashville: Thomas Nelson Publishers, 1978.

Elaborates on the proposal made by Fr. Jose O'Callahan of Barcelona, that Fragment 5 from Qumran and other fragments from the same period came from Mark's gospel and other NT books. Contains photographs, drawings, and inscriptions of fragments. 225.48.ES8

**\*Friberg, Barbara,** and **Timothy Fri-**

berg, eds. *Analytical Greek New Testament: Greek-Text Analysis.* Grand Rapids: Baker Book House, 1981.

A prodigious work that analyzes by means of symbols every verbal and noun form of the Greek NT. Will be used extensively by pastors and Bible translators. 225.48.F91

**Greenlee, Jacob Harold.** *Scribes, Scrolls, and Scripture: A Student's Guide to New Testament Textual Criticism.* Grand Rapids: Wm. B. Eerdmans Publishing Co., 1985.

"[This book] is the finest primer on NT textual criticism for both the student and the general reader on several counts. Besides being up-to-date and well researched, it is clearly written, with no untranslated Greek or technical jargon. It is judicious and fair in its treatment of the innovators and modern schools of textual criticism. But above all, it is extremely sensitive throughout to those who fear textual criticism is destructive of the biblical text and should help greatly to assure its readers that this discipline seeks only to restore the text of the autographs and jeopardize no doctrine of orthodox Christianity" (John R. Kohlenberger III). 225.4.G84S

**Hodges, Zane C.,** and **Arthur L. Farstad, eds.** *The Greek New Testament According to the Majority Text.* Nashville: Thomas Nelson Publishers, 1982.

This theologically conservative edition of the Greek NT rejects the theory that the oldest MSS represent the most accurate text of the NT and, instead, seeks to establish the viability of a text based upon a consensus of the bulk of extant MSS. The result is a recension that approximates the Greek text of the KJV. Footnotes contain two sets of data for easy comparison. 225.48.H66

***Kaiser, Walter Christian, Jr.** The Uses of the Old Testament in the New.* Chicago: Moody Press, 1985.

Investigates the use of the OT in the NT. Finds it impossible to justify modern redaction or canonical criticism. Exposes the dubious assumptions of those who seek to preserve the Bible's authority yet deny the inerrancy of the autographs. Lays before each reader clear and irrefutable proof for the accuracy and reliability of the biblical text. Recommended. 225.4'8.K12

**Kenyon, Frederick George.** *The Text of the Greek Bible.* 3d ed. revised and augmented by W. Adams. London: G. Duckworth, 1975.

This well-researched, balanced treatment is now fully abreast of the manuscript evidence that has come to light since Sir Frederick's death. It remains an invaluable aid to students of textual criticism. 225.4.K42Ad 1975

**La Sor, William Sanford.** *The Dead Sea Scrolls and the New Testament.* Grand Rapids: Wm. B. Eerdmans Publishing Co., 1973.

Marshals a vast amount of material and presents it with fairness and skill. Of particular interest is the comparison between the early church and the Qumran community. 225.4.L33

**Lattimore, Richmond, trans.** *The Four Gospels and the Revelation.* London: Hutchinson and Co., 1980.

Lattimore's aim was to make a translation that was as faithful as possible to the original, in which the syntax and order of words permitted a delicate use of English and where the style truly conveyed the thought of the biblical writer. The result is a version in which the words of the evangelists are allowed to speak for themselves, and which, though thoroughly modern, will nevertheless astonish and delight the reader. 225.4.L35

***Longenecker, Richard Norman.** Biblical Exegesis in the Apostolic Period.* Grand Rapids: Wm. B. Eerdmans Publishing Co., 1975.

An assessment of first-century hermeneutics against the background of intertestamental Judaism, the DDS, the Gnostic texts from Nag Hammadi, and Talmudic material. A judicious study by a competent scholar. 225.5′6.L85

**Mare, W. Harold.** *Mastering New Testament Greek.* Grand Rapids: Baker Book House, 1979.

Designed for the beginner, with "lesson plans for intermediate and advanced students," this able manual succeeds in helping users gain a mastery of the NT. May well become a standard in Bible colleges and seminaries. 487.5.M33

**Metzger, Bruce Manning.** *The Text of the New Testament.* 2d ed. New York: Oxford University Press, 1970.

An extensive treatment of the transmission, corruption, and restoration of the text of the NT. 225.4.M56T 1970

**Moulton, James Hope.** *Grammar of New Testament Greek.* Vol. IV: *Style,* by Nigel Turner. Edinburgh: T. & T. Clark, 1976.

Contains a careful analysis of the writing style of each NT author. Will help sharpen the focus of every expository preacher. Of great value for its insights. Deserves to be studied until the contents are well-known and capable of being reproduced in one's spoken messages. 487.5.M86 v.4

**Mueller, Walter.** *Grammatical Aids for Students of New Testament Greek.* Grand Rapids: Wm. B. Eerdmans Publishing Co., 1972.

Designed to supplement a regular grammar. Its chief value is for those who either have no prior knowledge of the language or stand in need of a refresher course. 487.4.M88

**Nestle, E., and E. Nestle.** *Novum Testament Graece.* Edited by K. Aland, et al. 26th ed. Stuttgart, Germany: Deutsche Bibelstiftung, 1979.

Containing a completely revised text, with the latest manuscript evidence in the footnotes, this work represents the latest consensus of modern NT scholars.

Also of considerable interest are the new introduction and the editors' comments relating to the discarding of symbols for the Hesychian and Koine texts, and the inclusion of *M*, signifying the "Majority text." 225.48.N85 1979

**Nestle, Eberhard.** *The NASB Interlinear Greek-English New Testament.* The Nestle Text with a literal English translation by A. Marshall. Grand Rapids: Regency Reference Library, 1984.

With a foreword by the late J. B. Phillips and an introduction to the problems of translating the NT by Alfred Marshall, this interlinear has already proved its worth to pastors who wish to prepare their sermons based on the Greek text. 225.4′8.NE36.M35

***Owings, Timothy.** *A Cumulative Index to New Testament Greek Grammars.* Grand Rapids: Baker Book House, 1983.

By following the order of the NT writings, Owings lists against each chapter and verse the location in leading grammars where important discussions of syntax and the nuances of the original text may be found. A most useful volume. 487.5.OW3

**Pickering, Wilbur N.** *The Identity of the New Testament Text.* Nashville: Thomas Nelson Publishers, 1977.

This detailed examination of the principles and practices of NT textual criticism has created considerable furor (1) for its attack on the theories of Westcott and Hort and (2) for its advocacy of the Byzantine text. Not accepting the Textus Receptus, Pickering makes a case for going with the majority of MSS, not the oldest. 225.4.P58

***Powers, Ward.** *Learn to Read the Greek New Testament: An Approach to New Testament Greek Based on Linguistic Principles.* Grand Rapids: Wm. B. Eerdmans Publishing Co., 1982.

The "Powers Method" was developed in the classroom and has been proved highly successful. It applies the principles of linguistic science to the analysis of NT Greek and to its teaching and learning. The method is based on these six principles: framework learning, natural language acquisition, immediate introduction to the target material, low threshold of utility, morphological analysis and pattern recognition (with rote learning of basic paradigms kept to a minimum), and progressive presentation followed by systematic revision. This volume includes the beginner's course, the intermediate course, and several appendixes, including a student's guide, a teacher's guide, and a Greek vocabulary and index. 487.4.P87

**\*Rienecker, Fritz.** *A Linguistic Key to the Greek New Testament.* 2 vols. Translated, with additions and revisions, and edited by Cleon L. Rogers, Jr. Grand Rapids: Zondervan Publishing House, 1977-1980.

This translation of *Sprachlicher Schluessel zum Griechischen Neuen Testament* makes available to English readers a vast amount of material pertaining to the grammar of the NT. Words are parsed and translated, and brief notes highlight important facts. This is an ideal work for the pastor and should help to provide greater accuracy in the exposition of the text. Recommended. 225.48.R44R

**\*Ryrie, Charles Caldwell.** *The Ryrie Study Bible. New American Standard* version, with Introductions, etc. Chicago: Moody Press, 1978.

As a study Bible, this one ranks among the most useful ever produced. The text is clear, the outlines follow the theme of the book, and the notes are enlightening. This is a work that can be highly recommended, and it is hoped that laypeople everywhere will acquire it and use it to their own great profit. 220.52.N42.R99 1976

**Simcox, William Henry.** *The Language of the New Testament.* Winona Lake, Ind.: Alpha Publications, 1980.

A clear, concise introduction to the grammar of the NT. Recommended for beginners. 487.SI4 1980

**\*Sturz, Harry A.** *The Byzantine Text-type and New Testament Textual Criticism.* Nashville: Thomas Nelson Publishers, 1984.

"[Sturz's] conclusions can have revolutionary consequences for the text of the Greek Testament. The Byzantine text is not just a later recension, but contains distinctive readings, going back to the second century, which may sometimes prove original. We now need editions of the Greek Testament which will reflect [his] views" (George D. Kilpatrick, Oxford University). A valuable precursor to the development of a new text of the NT. 225.4'8.ST9

**Thayer, Joseph Henry.** *A Greek-English Lexicon of the New Testament.* Milford, Mich.: Mott Media, 1982.

Numerically coded to Strong's *Exhaustive Concordance,* this old and now dated lexicon may nevertheless be used with profit when doing word studies limited to the NT text. 487.3.T33

## INTERPRETATION AND CRITICISM OF THE BIBLE

**Anderson, Bernhard W.** *Understanding the Old Testament.* 3d ed. Englewood Cliffs, N.J.: Prentice-Hall, 1975.

†This revision of the text that appeared in 1957 and 1966 maintains the author's adherence to source criticism. The pre-Davidic material has been enlarged and the bibliographies brought up to date. 220.6'6.AN2 1975

**\*Archer, Gleason Leonard, Jr.** *Encyclopedia of Bible Difficulties.* 2d ed. Grand Rapids: Zondervan Publishing House, 1982.

Vigorously defends the integrity of

Scripture by tackling the supposed contradictions and many of the interpretative problems and shows how the Bible is both internally consistent and authoritative. Some articles appeared in *Decision* magazine. A valuable reference tool. 220.6.AR2

**Baker, D. L.** *Two Testaments: One Bible. A Study of Some Modern Solutions to the Theological Problem of the Relationship Between the Old and New Testaments.* Downers Grove, Ill.: InterVarsity Press, 1977.

Contains an insightful biblical, historical, and methodological introduction to the problem of the relationship between the Testaments. This is followed by an assessment of the value and viability of eight modern theories. 220.6.B17

**Barton, John.** *Reading the Old Testament: Method in Biblical Study.* Philadelphia: Westminster Press, 1984.

†"By integrating the ideas of biblical scholars with recent developments in literary appreciation [this book] makes readily intelligible the role of traditional historical methods on the one hand and that of newer trends like structuralism on the other. The work is well-informed, its expression clear and attractive; it can be read without previous technical knowledge, and its total point of view carries conviction" (James Barr). 220.6′01.B28

**Caird, George Bradford.** *The Language and Imagery of the Bible.* Philadelphia: Westminster Press, 1981.

A systematic approach to the linguistic treasures of the Bible. Covers hermeneutics, anthropomorphisms and other figures of speech, and the literary framework in which different forms of revelation are to be found. A scholarly study. Recommended. 220.6.C12

**Carson, Donald A., ed.** *Biblical Interpretation and the Church: The Problem of Contextualization.* Nashville: Thomas Nelson Publishers, 1984.

Whereas most texts on hermeneutics are purely theoretical, this one is concerned with practical missiological applications. The eight sharply focused essays are the result of the World Evangelical Fellowship's *Faith and Life* study. 220.6.C23

**Dunnett, Walter M.** *The Interpretation of Holy Scripture.* Nashville: Thomas Nelson Publishers, 1984.

A number of issues are involved in the task of interpreting the Bible: methodology, ideology, history, and application. These issues are diverse, yet all contribute to a more complete understanding of the Bible, and their mastery facilitates the expression and communication of the truth. In these pages Dunnett has made available an excellent introduction to the science of hermeneutics. His book deserves wide circulation. 220.6.D92

**Efird, James M.** *How to Interpret the Bible.* Atlanta: John Knox Press, 1984.

†Declaring that, contrary to popular misconception, the Bible is not easy to understand, Efird suggests an approach that leads the reader to discover what the biblical writers meant when they wrote the books that are now a part of the OT canon. He provides an introduction to who wrote these books, when, where, and for whom. This approach is basic and truly commendable. Unfortunately, liberal presuppositions are introduced into the book, and these can only mislead users whose lack of knowledge have ill-prepared them for such a treatment. 220.61.EF3

**\*Fairbairn, Patrick.** *The Typology of Scripture.* Grand Rapids: Zondervan Publishing House, 1975.

Reprinted from the 1900 edition, this masterful study continues to rank among the foremost works on the hermeneutics of biblical typology. 220.64.F15 1975

**Fee, Gordon D.,** and **Douglas Stuart.** *How to Read the Bible for All It's Worth: A*

*Guide to Understanding the Bible.* Grand Rapids: Zondervan Publishing House, 1982.

A most capable work that serves to introduce the reader to different kinds of biblical literature and assists him/her to obtain a fuller understanding of God's plan and purpose. 220.6'1.F32

**Gasque, W. W.,** and **W. S. LaSor, eds.** *Scripture, Tradition, and Interpretation: Essays Presented to Everett F. Harrison by His Students.* Grand Rapids: Wm. B. Eerdmans Publishing Co., 1978.

This festschrift is a fitting tribute to one whose interest in and contribution to biblical scholarship has spanned more than half a century. 220.6.H24, SC3 1978

**\*Geisler, Norman Leo.** *Decide For Yourself: How History Views the Bible.* Grand Rapids: Zondervan Publishing House, 1982.

Treats clearly and concisely the view of Scripture held by people throughout church history. Provides a valuable survey and serves as a reliable apologetic. Insightful. 220.6'01.G27

**Goppelt, Leonhard.** *Typos: The Typological Interpretation of the Old Testament in the New.* Translated by D. H. Madvig. Grand Rapids: Wm. B. Eerdmans Publishing Co., 1982.

In his search for a normative hermeneutic, Goppelt offers "a study of the interpretation of Scripture that is characteristic of the NT" in order to provide a standard guide for interpreting the Bible today. The focal question for Goppelt is how the OT and Jesus Christ are related. Goppelt's answer to that question is found in how the NT interprets the OT typologically. He begins with a brief survey of the various definitions of typology to determine how it is distinguished from allegory (with which it is often confused). After the introductory chapter, Goppelt divides his work into three parts: typology in late Judaism, typology

in the NT, and apocalypticism and typology in Paul. Well-researched and informative. 220.6'4.G64

**Hagen, Kenneth, et al.** *The Bible in the Churches: How Different Christians Interpret the Scriptures.* New York: Paulist Press, 1985.

†Contains four major essays and a conclusion. Deals with the views of Augustine, Aquinas, Erasmus, and Luther. Leaves much to be desired. 220.6'1.H12

**Harrison, Roland Kenneth, et al.** *Biblical Criticism: Historical, Literary and Textual.* Grand Rapids: Zondervan Publishing House, 1978.

Essays by competent Bible scholars. Taken from vol. 1 of the *Expositor's Bible Commentary.* 220.6H24 1978

**\*Huey, F. B., Jr.,** and **Bruce Corley.** *A Student's Dictionary for Biblical and Theological Studies.* Grand Rapids: Zondervan Publishing House, Academie Books, 1983.

Another handy and important work, providing easy access to nearly 1,300 terms in common use in biblical and theological circles. A most helpful volume. 220.6'03.H87

**\*Jensen, Irving Lester.** *How to Profit from Bible Reading.* Chicago: Moody Press, 1985.

A handy book to use with new converts. Outlines a proved methodology for deriving more profit from Bible reading. 220.6.J45

**\*Kaiser, Walter Christian, Jr.** *Toward an Exegetical Theology: Biblical Exegesis for Preaching and Teaching.* Grand Rapids: Baker Book House, 1981.

One of the most capable explanations of the place and importance of biblical exegesis ever written. Should be must reading in every homiletics course in seminary. 220.6'01.K12

**Larue, Gerald A.** *Ancient Myth and Modern Man.* Englewood Cliffs, N.J.: Prentice-Hall, 1975.

An examination of the way in which hero stories of the past are projected into the future and find their expression in personal attitudes and social values. Unreliable. 220.6.L32

**Lundin, Roger, Anthony C. Thiselton,** and **Clarence Walhout.** *The Responsibility of Hermeneutics.* Grand Rapids: Wm. B. Eerdmans Publishing Co., 1985.

"The authors' proposal for a hermeneutics of action and responsibility is compelling. In the end, the thing that makes this book so satisfying is the self-conscious effort to interact faithfully with modern hermeneutical theory from a firm grounding in historic Christian faith" (Mark A. Noll). 121.68.L96

**Morris, Henry Madison.** *The Bible Has the Answer.* Grand Rapids: Baker Book House, 1973.

Basing his approach on a question-and-answer method, the author covers a wide variety of themes ranging from the Word of God to things to come. Includes sections on misunderstood Bible characters and Christian holidays. 220.6′6.M83

**Nineham, Dennis Eric.** *The Use and Abuse of the Bible: A Study of the Bible in an Age of Rapid Cultural Change.* New York: Barnes and Noble, 1977.

†Grapples realistically with contemporary views relating to the Bible, but fails to assert the Bible's authority or to demonstrate how it may be used in meeting the needs of people in an era of change. Scholarly. 220.6.N62

**Orlinsky, Harry Mayer.** *Essays in Biblical Culture and Bible Translation.* New York: Ktav Publishing House, 1974.

This book by a renowned Hebraist contains a wide variety of essays that have been collected and published by his students. 220.6.OR5

**Pink, Arthur Walkington.** *The Doctrine of Revelation.* Grand Rapids: Baker Book House, 1975.

Based on articles from *Studies in Scripture,* these chapters draw attention to God's revelation of Himself in creation, the moral nature of man, history, the incarnation, and the Scriptures. The material probes many of modern man's dilemmas and shows that only in the revelation of God can man understand His all-wise providence. 220.6.P65

**Pinnock, Clark H.** *The Scripture Principle.* San Francisco: Harper & Row. 1984.

A mediating work that satisfies neither the theological liberal nor the evangelical conservative. Champions the Bible's authority but not its nature as "God-breathed." Leaves many questions unanswered. 220.6.P65

**Prince, Derek.** *The Last Word on the Middle East.* Lincoln, Va.: Chosen Books, 1982.

A well-written, carefully documented account of the events that have taken place in the Middle East since 1948. Surveys Israel's recent past as well as the nation's prophetic future. 220.6′8.J55.P93

**Radmacher, Earl D.,** and **Robert D. Preus, eds.** *Hermeneutics, Inerrancy, and the Bible.* Grand Rapids: Zondervan Publishing House, Academie Books, 1984.

Contains papers read at the second International Congress on Biblical Inerrancy. Focuses primarily on the interpretation of Scripture and how believers may know what God has said and what is meant by terms such as *authority, infallibility,* the *science of interpretation,* and the *Spirit's illumination.* 220.6′01.R11

**Ricoeur, Paul.** *Essays on Biblical Interpretation.* Edited by L. S. Mudge. Philadelphia: Fortress Press, 1980.

†These extensively documented essays advance and refine the idea of the testimonia of the NT and the methodology whereby they may be uncovered and understood. 220.6′01.R42

**Rogers, Jack B.,** and **Donald K. McKim.** *The Authority and Interpretation of* *the Bible.* San Francisco: Harper & Row, 1979.

Rogers and McKim provide an assessment of the views of leading theologians from Clement to the present in an endeavor to prove that the view of Scripture held by conservative evangelicals today is not the traditional viewpoint of the church through the ages. They do not consider the evidence of Scripture. Scholarly, but with a selective use of information that distorts the truth. 220.6'09.R63

**Sabourin, Leopold.** *The Bible and Christ: The Unity of the Two Testaments.* Staten Island, N.Y.: Alba House, 1980.

Known for his scholarship, Sabourin here turns from exegesis and exposition to bibliography and the nature of revelation. He delineates the scope of the OT covenants and the use of typology as the bridge by which to unite the teaching of the Testaments. 220.6.S1

**Schultz, Samuel J.,** and **Morris A. Inch.** *Interpreting the Word of God: Festschrift in Honor of Steven Barabas.* Chicago: Moody Press, 1976.

Essays on a wide range of topics showing the way in which proper research enhances our understanding of the Bible and its interpretation. 220.63.IN8.SCH8

**Soulen, Richard N.** *Handbook of Biblical Criticism.* 2d ed. Atlanta: John Knox Press, 1981.

†Believing that NT scholarship has undergone a second revolution, analogous to the introduction of historico-criticism two centuries ago, Soulen here tries to bring the student up to date with these new developments. In doing so, he concentrates on fields of study rather than on a plethora of technical terms within these larger areas. More than forty new articles have been added to this revision, including "Canonical Criticism," "Semiology," "Structure," "Sociological Interpretation," "Reception Theory," "Rhetorical Analysis," "Biblical Theology (Movement)," "Linguistics," and "Topos." An equal number have been expanded and revised. 220.6.SO8 1981

**Stendahl, Krister.** *Meanings: The Bible as Document and as Guide.* Philadelphia: Fortress Press, 1984.

†A scholarly attempt to show how certain biblical themes or passages of Scripture speak about different situations or issues facing the church today. Provocative. 220.6.ST4

**Tollers, Vincent L.,** and **John R. Maier, eds.** *The Bible in Its Literary Milieu: Contemporary Essays.* Grand Rapids: Wm. B. Eerdmans Publishing Co., 1979.

A stimulating collection of essays by both conservative and liberal scholars, each discussing a form of literature or the contribution of some other discipline to our awareness of the meaning and message of different portions of Scripture. For the informed reader. 220.6.T57

**\*Turner, Nicholas.** *Handbook for Biblical Studies.* Oxford: Basil Blackwell, 1982.

Though he presents a faulty chronology of the main biblical events, Turner nevertheless provides seminarians with a highly usable handbook to various scholars and their schools of thought. There is also a glossary of terms. That division of the book (which is by far the largest) will serve to acquaint readers with concise definitions for the different terms they are likely to encounter in the writings of contemporary scholars. All things considered, this is a most helpful handbook. 016.2.T85

**Tuttle, G. A., ed.** *Biblical and Near Eastern Studies: Essays in Honor of William Sanford LaSor.* Grand Rapids: Wm. B. Eerdmans Publishing Co., 1978.

This festschrift by OT and NT scholars—over half of whom are former students of LaSor—covers a variety of themes and gives evidence of the respect in which LaSor is held by conservatives and liberals alike. 220.6.L33.B47

**Virkler, Henry A.** *Hermeneutics: Principles and Processes of Biblical Interpretation.* Grand Rapids: Baker Book House, 1981.

A welcome addition to the fast-growing corpus of literature on the science of biblical interpretation. Historically and biblically viable, this work discusses a variety of literary forms and their principles of interpretation. 220.63.V81

**Walsh, K. J., et al., comps.** *Religious Bibliographies in Serial Literature: A Guide.* Westport, Conn.: Greenwood Press, 1981.

This volume was sponsored by the Association of British Theological and Philosophical Libraries. It is limited to 175 current sources: journals containing occasional bibliographic essays, indexes, abstracts, and bibliographies. The annotations are longer than Bollier's *Literature of Theology* and Kepple's *Reference Works for Theological Research.* The arrangement, however, makes it difficult to use unless one knows what to look for. 016.2.AS7

**Wenham, John William.** *Christ and the Bible.* Downers Grove, Ill.: InterVarsity Press, 1972.

The first of four volumes on the nature, interpretation, and application of Scripture. This one is designed to update and supplement the work of B. B. Warfield. Attempts to show that belief in the Bible comes from faith in Christ, not vice versa. 220.6.W48

OLD TESTAMENT

**Anderson, G. W., ed.** *Tradition and Interpretation: Essays by Members of the Society for Old Testament Study.* Oxford: Clarendon Press, 1979.

Continues the series begun by A. S. Peake in *The People and the Book* (1925).

Contains thirteen essays on different problem areas of the OT, from Pentateuchal criticism to apocalyptic literature. 221.6.T67

**\*Archer, Gleason Leonard, Jr.** *A Survey of Old Testament Introduction.* Rev. ed. Chicago: Moody Press, 1974.

A definitive study that in this revision perpetuates the finest conservative scholarship. A must for evangelicals who wish to have an intelligent grasp of the OT. 221.61.AR2 1974

**\*Baron, David.** *Types, Psalms, and Prophecies.* Minneapolis: Klock & Klock Christian Publishers, 1981.

Provides a pleasant blending of sound interpretation with true spiritual instruction. Succeeds in highlighting much of the NT's teaching on Christ and God's plan for His people. Preachers, especially, will welcome the reprinting of this fine work. 221.6.B26 1981

**Berlin, Adele.** *The Dynamics of Biblical Parallelism.* Bloomington, Ind.: Indiana University Press, 1985.

This book offers a new way of analyzing biblical parallelism and presents a more comprehensive understanding of that phenomenon than has been available to date. Though many biblicists have equated parallelism with poetic literature, Berlin takes the position that parallelism is a linguistic device that occurs in other kinds of literature as well. Her book illustrates her point. 221.6.B46 (Alt. DDC 809'.93522)

**Boadt, Lawrence.** *Reading the Old Testament: An Introduction.* New York: Paulist Press, 1984.

†Designed as an introductory work for beginning theologues, this study succeeds in alerting readers to the history of OT times as well as the literature of God's ancient people. 221.6.B63

**Childs, Brevard S.** *Introduction to the Old Testament as Scripture.* Philadelphia: Fortress Press, 1979.

†Not since Harrison's *Introduction to the Old Testament* has anything as comprehensive as this been attempted. Based on the latest critical theories, this scholarly study exhibits the best that liberal theological scholarship has to offer. Childs makes a case for canonical criticism and uses this criterion as the basis for the Bible's authority. 221.6.C43

**Clements, Ronald Ernest.** *One Hundred Years of Old Testament Interpretation.* Philadelphia: Westminster Press, 1976.

Demonstrates how each part of the OT canon has been treated and what contributions have been made since the time of Wellhausen. 221.6'6.C59

**Efird, James M.** *The Old Testament Writings: History, Literature, and Interpretation.* Atlanta: John Knox Press, 1982.

†This book was written for the beginning student of the OT. It serves to introduce him/her to the complex world of the OT, its history, literature, and the scope of the religious writings. The procedure follows the title, and the discussion is divided into three major parts corresponding to the three divisions of the subtitle. The author adheres to virtually all of the subjective views commonly associated with negative higher criticism, and it is disappointing to note that this book was written with the beginning student in mind. For those well-versed in OT history and criticism, and who can read with discernment, the work has much to commend it. 221.61.EF3

***Ellisen, Stanley A.** *Knowing God's Word.* Nashville: Thomas Nelson Publishers, 1984.

The main purpose of this book is to provide a simple guide to reading the OT. By using charts and outlines, coupled with a clear and concise explanation of the theme of each book, Ellisen leads the reader into an understanding of the contribution of each book to the OT and how they all fit together. This is an inval-uable resource for students, pastors, and especially laypeople. 221.61.EL5

**Ellison, Henry Leopold.** *The Message of the Old Testament.* Palm Springs, Calif.: Ronald N. Haynes Publishers, 1981.

A brief introduction to the central teaching of the books of the OT canon. 221.6.EL5 1981

**Feinberg, John S.,** and **Paul D. Feinberg, eds.** *Tradition and Testament: Essays in Honor of Charles Lee Feinberg.* Chicago: Moody Press, 1981.

This festschrift, prepared by Feinberg's sons, commemorates their father's unique Hebrew-Christian ministry. The essays fall into four areas: hermeneutics; exegetical; textual and linguistic; and integrative. 221.6.F32F 1981

**Fishbane, Michael.** *Biblical Interpretation in Ancient Israel.* Oxford: Clarendon Press, 1985.

†The author grounds his approach in the mental/cultural milieu that formed the backdrop of revelatory history. Uses that to highlight the exegetical practices and traditions that lie latent in the text. Fishbane divides his work into four parts: scribal comments and corrections, legal issues, Aggadic influence, and mantological matters. A work of rare scholarship. 221.6.F52

**Godet, Frederic Louis.** *Studies in the Old Testament.* Grand Rapids: Kregel Publications, 1984.

Reprinted from the 1884 edition. These six essays cover a wide range of subjects including angels, the plan of the development of life on earth, the six days of creation, and the interpretation of the Song of Solomon. Though one may not always agree with Godet, he is always worth consulting. 221.6.G54 1984

**Gordis, Robert.** *The Word and the Book.* New York: Ktav Publishing House, 1976.

This collection of essays should be of interest to all engaged in a study of OT wisdom literature, particularly the

Qoheleth. The word studies are of major significance. 221.6.G65

**Gottwald, Norman K.** *The Hebrew Bible: A Socio-Literary Introduction.* Philadelphia: Fortress Press, 1985.

†This book offers a different approach to the text of the OT and the influence of the people's culture on the formation of the canon. An important contribution. 221.6.G71

**Gunneweg, Antonius H. J.** *Understanding the Old Testament.* Translated by J. Bowden. Philadelphia: Westminster Press, 1978.

†Aims to "describe and give a critical evaluation of the different and often contradictory possibilities of understanding the OT." Does so by treating the text in the light of historical criticism. 221.6.G92

**Habersohn, Ada Ruth.** *Hidden Pictures in the Old Testament; or How the New Testament is Concealed in the Old Testament.* Grand Rapids: Kregel Publications, 1982.

This 1916 publication discusses the relevance of twenty-seven OT incidents in light of the teaching of the NT. The result is a work illustrating the principles of typological interpretation, a devotional treatise of real merit, and an enriched understanding of God's revelation. 221.6'4.H11 1982

**Kaiser, Otto.** *Introduction to the Old Testament: A Presentation of Its Results and Problems.* Translated by John Sturdy. Minneapolis: Augsburg Publishing House, 1975.

†A thorough work identifying and dealing with the problems of OT introduction. Helpful bibliographies. 221.61.K12

**Kaiser, Walter Christian, Jr.** *The Old Testament and Contemporary Preaching.* Grand Rapids: Baker Book House, 1973.

A popular presentation of the relevance of the OT in developing a meaningful philosophy of life. 221.6'6.K12

**McCurley, Foster R., Jr.** *Proclaiming the Promise: Christian Preaching from the Old Testament.* Philadelphia: Fortress Press, 1974.

†This work, designed to be practical, emphasizes the need for using the results of modern higher criticism (documentary, form, and redaction) in proclaiming the OT to Christians today. The discussion of the use of exegesis in sermon preparation is helpful. 221.6'6.M13

**Morgan, Donn F.** *Wisdom in the Old Testament Traditions.* Atlanta: John Knox Press, 1981.

†Morgan evaluates the contribution of nonwisdom literature and shows that wisdom literature is an integral part of the message of the Bible. He offers some significant clues to understanding and interpreting this form of literature and explains some of the short-comings of recent attempts to analyze its contents and contribution. 221.6.M82

**Patte, Daniel.** *Early Jewish Hermeneutic in Palestine.* Missoula, Mont.: Scholar's Press, 1975.

Deals with the attitude of early Palestinian Jews toward their sacred writings. Outlines and compares the hermeneutics of rabbinic Judaism with sectarian Judaism (particularly as found among the apocalyptists and the Qumran community). 221.6'3.P27

**Rogerson, John William.** *Old Testament Criticism in the Nineteenth Century: England and Germany.* Philadelphia: Fortress Press, 1985.

†"There is no comparable work in any language and [Rogerson's] discussion of German scholarship provides many new insights on developments in Germany not previously noted in what is a well-explored area" (John H. Hayes). 221.6'09.R63

**Sandmel, Samuel.** *The Hebrew Scriptures: An Introduction to Their Literature and*

*Religious Ideas.* New York: Oxford University Press, 1978.

†Written from a Jewish point of view, this work probes the techniques and findings of modern biblical scholarship. Disappointing as a survey of the OT. 221.6.SA5

**Schmidt, Werner H.** *Old Testament Introduction.* Translated by M. J. O'Connell. New York: Crossroad, 1984.

†This *Einfuhrung* differs from the usual introductions in certain of its limitations and in the inclusion of a history of Israel, literature criticism, and OT theology. Interacts with the schools of thought that have grown up around G. von Rad, M. Noth, and A. Alt. 221.6'1.SCH5

————. *The Faith of the Old Testament: A History.* Translated by J. Sturdy. Philadelphia: Westminster Press, 1983.

†Correlates information from Israelite history and theology and attempts to mediate between these schools of thought. The result is an OT theology that correlates social, political, and religious features of Israelite culture. 221.6'7.SCH5

**\*Schultz, Samuel J.** *The Bible Speaks Today.* 3d ed. San Francisco: Harper & Row, 1980.

Having served the needs of collegians for twenty years, this work in its revised form continues to be one of the ablest historical introductions to the OT. 221.61.SCH8 1980

**Soggin, J. Alberto.** *Introduction to the Old Testament from Its Origin to the Closing of the Alexandrian Canon.* Old Testament Library. Rev. ed. Philadelphia: Westminster Press, 1982.

†A most capable treatment that ranks among the finest of its kind. 221.6'1.S02 1982

**Stuart, Douglas K.** *Old Testament Exegesis: A Primer for Students and Pastors.* 2d ed. Revised and enlarged. Philadelphia: Westminster Press, 1984.

†"Helpful without being overly techni-cal, its goal is to bring serious Old Testament exegesis back into the life of the average seminary student and working pastor. It explains the procedures and aims of exegesis, tells how to use the tools of exegesis, and emphasizes preaching and teaching values. . . . Excellent bibliographies" *(Christianity Today).* 221.6'01.ST9 1984

**Tullock, John** *The Old Testament Story.* Englewood Cliffs, N.J.: Prentice-Hall, 1981.

†This historical introduction to the events of the OT is well-outlined, illustrated, and deals with the crucial issues raised by biblical scholars from Wellhausen to the present. 221.6'1.T82

**Van Ruler, Arnold Albert.** *The Christian Church and the Old Testament.* Translated by W. Bromley. Grand Rapids: Wm. B. Eerdmans Publishing Co., 1971.

An examination of the manner in which the church through the ages has considered the OT. 221.63.V35

**Zimmerli, W.** *The Old Testament and the World.* London: S.P.C.K., 1976.

†First published in German in 1971, this work vigorously rebuts Bultmann's views of the OT. In vindicating his beliefs, Zimmerli explores the OT world and man's relation to it. 221.6'6.Z6

NEW TESTAMENT

**Barclay, William.** *Many Witnesses, One Lord.* Grand Rapids: Baker Book House, 1973.

Though designed to show the diversity of viewpoints existing in the NT, the writer exhibits something of his own ambivalence to crucial areas of theology by alternately defending and then detracting from the Person of Christ. 225.6.B23

**Barrett, L. Bammel,** and **W. D. Davies, eds.** *Donum Gentilicium.* New York: Oxford University Press, 1977.

†This festschrift contains essays in

honor of David Daube. The focal point around which these studies revolve is the intertestamental period and the Jewish background to the NT. Informative and enlightening. 225.6.D26.D61

**Brown, Schuyler.** *The Origins of Christianity: A Historical Introduction to the New Testament.* Oxford: Oxford University Press, 1984.

†Brown deals concisely with the history of the NT, the transmission of the text, dating of various documents, and the sources supposedly used by different writers. He then launches into a theological consideration of Jesus of Nazareth, His resurrection, the dissemination of the gospel, and the historical/theological development of the church. Though written for laypeople, this is unquestionably the work of a scholar, and those who read this book will need to exercise discernment. 225.6'7.B81

**Bruce, Frederick Fyvie.** *The Time Is Fulfilled: Five Aspects of the Fulfillment of the Old Testament in the New.* Grand Rapids: Wm. B. Eerdmans Publishing Co., 1978.

Contains the Moore Theological College (Sydney, Australia) Lectures, 1977. Ably fulfills the subtitle and succeeds in opening up the use of the OT in the NT. 225.6.B83T

**Childs, Brevard S.** *The New Testament as Canon: An Introduction.* Philadelphia: Fortress Press, 1985.

†This important, scholarly work furthers the author's earlier studies of canonical criticism on which he based his introduction to the OT. Though the underlying presuppositions place Childs at odds with evangelical and conservative theologians, this is a work that must be reckoned with, and researchers of all persuasions will turn to it repeatedly in years to come. 225.61.C43

**Efird, James M.** *The New Testament Writings: History, Literature, and Interpretation.* Atlanta: John Knox Press, 1980.

†This book is written with the uniniti-ated student in mind. The approach adopted by the author attempts to involve the student with the NT text as much as possible. The basic approach to the investigation of the NT literature is historical and critical. The tenets long associated with the negative aspects of biblical criticism are to be found in this work. Though it has much that is commendable, it is lamentable that this introductory text was designed for those who lack the discernment necessary to be able to use it effectively. 225.61.EF3

**Ellis, Edward Earle.** *Prophecy and Hermeneutic in Early Christianity.* Grand Rapids: Wm. B. Erdmans Publishing Co., 1978.

Contains vol. 18 of *Wissenschaftliche Untersuchungen zum Neuen Testament.* Treats the pneumatics in the missionary enterprise of the early church and the formation of Christian theology. The final chapter discusses new directions in form-criticism. 225.63.EL5

**Finegan, Jack.** *Encountering New Testament Manuscripts.* Grand Rapids: Wm. B. Eerdmans Publishing Co., 1974.

A well-written, exciting excursus into the realm of NT textual criticism. Combines the fascinating saga of manuscript discoveries with the techniques of translation. 225.61.F49

**Godet, Frederic Louis.** *Studies in the New Testament.* Grand Rapids: Kregel Publications, 1984.

First published in England in 1876, these studies cover differences in the four gospels, the Person and work of Christ, the leading apostles, and the structure of the book of Revelation. Reaffirms some long-held truths that are in danger of being overlooked today due to modern (and in some respects), misguided aspects of NT criticism. 225.6.G54 1984

**\*Gromacki, Robert Glenn.** *New Testament Survey.* Grand Rapids: Baker Book House, 1974.

Of primary value as a college text, this book nevertheless deserves a place in the pastor's library. Portrays not only what happened in NT times, but also explains why, and describes the way in which it became a part of the biblical writer's inspired record. 225.6.G89

**Guelich, R. A., ed.** *Unity and Diversity in New Testament Theology: Essays in Honor of George E. Ladd.* Grand Rapids: Wm. B. Eerdmans Publishing Co., 1978.

The scholarly essays that make up this festschrift commemorate Ladd's many years as a teacher and bear eloquent witness to the esteem in which he was held by his peers. 225.6.L12U 1979

**\*Guthrie, Donald.** *New Testament Introduction.* Downers Grove, Ill.: InterVarsity Press, 1971.

Formerly published in three volumes, but now issued in one. Quite abreast of the latest developments in the field of NT studies, favors a more mediating view of the synoptic problem than is necessary and provides detailed, up-to-date discussions on the many and varied historical problems. Generally conservative. 225.61.G98

**Hahn, Ferdinand.** *Historical Investigation and New Testament Faith: Two Essays.* Translated by R. Maddox. Edited by E. Krentz. Philadelphia: Fortress Press, 1983.

†Seeks to relate historical-critical methods of interpretation to the spirit of the times that gave rise to the NT writings. As commendable as Hahn's investigation is, it is marred by his theological presuppositions. 225.6′7.H12

**\*Harrison, Everett Falconer.** *Introduction to the New Testament.* 2d ed. Grand Rapids: Wm. B. Eerdmans Publishing Co., 1971.

Vies with Guthrie's book for preeminence among modern conservative introductions. Recommended. 225.61.H24 1971.

**Hawthorne, Gerald F., ed.** *Current Issues in Biblical and Patristic Interpretation. Studies in Honor of Merrill C. Tenney.* Grand Rapids: Wm. B. Eerdmans Publishing Co., 1975.

A festschrift honoring one whose lifetime of dedication to NT scholarship has resulted in a harvest of achievements. Covers a wide range of subjects, historical, biblical, patristic, and theological. 225.6′6.T25.H31

**\*Hiebert, David Edmond.** *An Introduction to the New Testament.* 3 vols. Chicago: Moody Press, 1975-1977.

In keeping with what we have come to expect of this capable author. Each book is carefully introduced and outlined, and critical problems are faced. These volumes are of the utmost value, and inasmuch as Hiebert's outlines are based on a painstaking analysis of the Greek text, preachers should consult them whenever preaching on the NT. 225.61.H53

**Hunter, Archibald Macbride.** *Probing the New Testament.* Atlanta: John Knox Press, 1972.

Published in the United Kingdom under the title *Exploring the New Testament* (1971), this work concentrates attention on words, phrases, or meanings in the NT and discusses their relevance to people today. 225.61.H91

**\*Jensen, Irving Lester.** *Jensen's Survey of the New Testament.* Chicago: Moody Press, 1981.

A welcome introduction to the contents of the NT. Of inestimable help to those studying a book of the NT for the first time, seeking to obtain an accurate overview of its contents. 225.6′1.J45

**Johnson, Roger A.** *The Origins of Demythologizing.* Leiden: E. J. Brill, 1974.

A highly intelligent examination of the philosophy and historiography underlying Bultmann's theology. 225.6.J63

**Keck, Leander E.** *The New Testament Experience of Faith.* St. Louis: CBP Press, 1984.

†First published in 1976, this book

focuses on the development of Christianity in the major centers of the NT: Jerusalem, Ephesus, Corinth, and Rome. Insightful. 225.6.K23 1984

**Kennedy, George Alexander.** *New Testament Interpretation Through Rhetorical Criticism.* Studies in Religion. Chapel Hill, N.C.: University of North Carolina Press, 1984.

"In the past few years we have seen growing interest in ancient rhetoric as one context for the comparative study of the NT, but up until now there has been no general introduction to this kind of analysis. [This] book is therefore sure to find an eager audience, especially because of [Kennedy's] acknowledged stature as one of the leading scholars of classical rhetoric" (Wayne A. Meeks). 225.6'6.K38

**Kummel, Werner George.** *The New Testament: The History of the Investigation of Its Problems.* Translated by S. McLean Gilmour and Howard C. Kee. Nashville: Abingdon Press, 1972.

This historic survey into the problems of NT study from ancient times to 1930 is of value for its general discussion and the lengthy quotations from leading scholars. It is not evaluative and manifests a tendency to accept the theories of others without adequate investigation. 225.6.K96

**Leitch, Addison H.** *The Reader's Introduction to the New Testament.* Garden City, N.Y.: Doubleday and Co., 1971.

Designed to get people to read the NT with enlightenment and understanding. Amillennial. 225.61.L53

**Longenecker, Richard N.,** and **Merrill C. Tenney, eds.** *Directions in New Testament Study.* Grand Rapids: Zondervan Publishing House, 1974.

Contains papers of exceptional quality presented at the 1973 meeting of the Evangelical Theological Society. 225.6.L 1974

**Machen, John Gresham.** *The New Testament: An Introduction to Its Literature and History.* Carlisle, Pa.: Banner of Truth Trust, 1977.

Contains brief chapters covering six major sections: "The Historical Background of Christianity," "The Early History of Christianity," "Christianity Established Among the Gentiles," "The Principles and Practice of the Gospel," "The Presentation and Defense of Christianity," and "The Apostolic Church and the Church Today." 225.61.M18 1977

**Marshall, I. Howard, ed.** *New Testament Interpretation: Essays on Principles and Methods.* Grand Rapids: Wm. B. Eerdmans Publishing Co., 1977.

Aims at presenting evangelical views on the history, presuppositions, and types of critical study and research methodology presently in vogue. 225.6.M35

**Mays, James Luther, ed.** *Interpreting the Gospels.* Philadelphia: Fortress Press, 1981.

†In twenty scholarly chapters taken from the pages of *Interpretation*, contributors deal with thorny problems in hermeneutics, ranging from Paul's view of the gospels to Johannine eschatology. This book is of value to seminarians for its helpful discussion of the issues. The conclusions, however, are often misleading or faulty. 225.6.IN8M

**McKay, J. R.,** and **J. F. Miller, eds.** *Biblical Studies: Essays in Honour of William Barclay.* Philadelphia: Westminster Press, 1976.

Following two tributes to Professor Barclay are essays that cover a variety of biblical themes. These essays are not all of equal value. 225.6.B23.M19

**\*Moule, Charles Francis Digby.** *The Birth of the New Testament.* 3d ed. rev. San Francisco: Harper & Row, 1981.

This form-critical revision of the author's epoch-making earlier work will be welcomed by all students of the NT. Though it needs to be read with discernment it offers a great deal of instruction on the history of the canon and the development of the early church. 225.6′7.M86 1981

**Petersen, Norman R.** *Literary Criticism for New Testament Critics.* Philadelphia: Fortress Press, 1978.

†By utilizing case studies based on Mark and Luke-Acts, Petersen draws attention to the process of redaction. 225.61.P44

**Simcox, William Henry.** *The Writers of the New Testament, Their Style and Characteristics.* Winona Lake, Ind.: Alpha Publications, 1980.

A remarkably perceptive introduction to the literary style of the writers of the NT. Though brief, the comments are accurate and succinct. The work abounds with important insights, and users will find it a valuable guide. 225.6.SI3 1980

**\*Tenney, Merrill Chapin.** *New Testament Survey, Revised.* Revised by W. M. Dunnett. Grand Rapids: Wm. B. Eerdmans Publishing Co., 1985.

This work has been a favorite of college professors since its first appearance a quarter of a century ago. Now completely revised and updated, this able text should serve another generation. 225.61.T25D 1985

**Thistleton, Anthony C.** *The Two Horizons: New Testament Hermeneutics and Philosophical Description with Special Reference to Heidegger, Bultmann, Gadamer, and Wittgenstein.* Grand Rapids: Wm. B. Eerdmans Publishing Co., 1980.

†This scholarly study admirably fulfills the subtitle of the book. It provides a masterly introduction to the science of hermeneutics and, were it not for the author's presuppositions, would be highly commended. In spite of that, Thistleton seeks to bridge the gap between the era of the NT and our own. Much of what he says is most apropos. 225.6′01.T34

**Vos, Howard Frederick.** *Beginnings in the New Testament.* Chicago: Moody Press, 1973.

A useful work for laypeople in Bible discussion groups. 225.6.V92

**Zahn, Theodor.** *Introduction to the New Testament.* 3 vols. Minneapolis: Klock & Klock Christian Publishers, 1977.

Reprinted from the 1909 translation of the 3d German edition, this work treats the epistles in chronological order before focusing on the synoptic problem and the gospels. Though obviously dated, Zahn's work is nevertheless extensive and contains a mine of valuable material. It should be consulted by all students of the NT. 225.61.Z2 1977

## BIBLE COMMENTARIES

**\*Bengel, John Albert.** *Bengel's New Testament Commentary.* 2 vols. Translated by C. T. Lewis and M. R. Vincent. Grand Rapids: Kregel Publications, 1982.

This edition of Bengel's famous *Gnomon of the New Testament* was published in 1860-1861. The comments are judicious, and this set is worthy of repeated consultation. 225.7′07.B43 1982

**Calvin, John.** *Commentaries.* Translated and edited by J. Haroutunian. Library of Christian Classics. Philadelphia: Westminster Press, 1979.

Selections from Calvin's commentaries on topics like the Bible, the knowledge of God, Jesus Christ, the Christian life, faith, providence, election and predestination, ethics and the common life, and the church. 220.08.C11 1979

**Cook, F. C., ed.** *The Bible Commentary.* 10 vols. Grand Rapids: Baker Book House, 1981.

This Anglican work was first published between 1871 and 1881 and has been variously known as *The Speaker's Bible* or *The Holy Bible with an Explanatory and*

*Critical Commentary.* Westcott wrote on John's gospel and Gifford on Romans. Those works were deemed to be of such superlative merit that they were published separately. The other works in this series were not of comparable worth. Some of the expositions began well, but ended with sparse comments and every evidence of haste. All things considered, this is not worthy of one's investment and ranks low on the list of available and usable Bible commentaries. 220.7.C77 1981

**Gaebelein, Arno Clemens.** *Gaebelein's Concise Commentary on the Whole Bible.* Rev. ed. Neptune, N.J.: Loizeaux Brothers, 1985.

The earlier four-volume set is here presented unabridged and in a handy format to serve the needs of a new generation. This work has been beautifully produced, is easy-to-use, and presents an overview of the theme and scope of each book in the Bible. Recommended for use by laypeople. 220.7'07.G11 1985

**\*Gaebelein, Frank Ely, ed.** *The Expositor's Bible Commentary.* In process. Grand Rapids: Zondervan Publishing House, 1976-.

Based on the text of the *New International Version* of the Bible (NIV) and scheduled for twelve volumes, this work gives promise of replacing other sets for general reliability and practicality. The contributors are all competent scholars of international repute. Their work transcends denominational boundaries. Critical notes are kept separate, thereby ensuring the value of this series to a wider readership. 220.7.EX7.G11

**Gray, James Martin.** *Home Bible Study Commentary.* Grand Rapids: Kregel Publications, 1985.

Formally published as the *Christian Worker's Commentary*, this book has served the needs of three generations. The thoroughness and soundness of Gray's teaching continue to make this an important

work for the lay church-worker. 220.7'07.G79 1985

**Jensen, Irving Lester.** *Do-It-Yourself Bible Studies.* San Bernardino, Calif.: Here's Life Publishers, 1983-.

Leads users in the discovery of the books of the Bible. Shows how Bible study can be personal, independent, practical, and rewarding. Pastors will do well to recommend these guides to laypeople in their churches. Each volume is complete in itself and makes inductive study an exciting experience. Most of the NT is presently available, and other volumes are to follow. 220.7'07.J45D

**\*Kitto, John.** *Kitto's Daily Bible Illustrations.* 2 vols. Grand Rapids: Kregel Publications, 1981.

First published between 1851 and 1854. This reprint of the 1901 edition contains an excellent biographical essay explaining to twentieth-century Christians something of the life and labors, hardships and triumphs of this great man of God. Few readers can remain unmoved by Kitto's wealth of insight into the biblical text and his skill in explaining it. These volumes are heartily commended to all who wish for a deeper understanding of God's inspired Word. 220.7'06.K65 1981

**Lightfoot, John.** *A Commentary on the New Testament from the Talmud and Hebraica.* 4 vols. Grand Rapids: Baker Book House, 1979.

Preceded Strack and Billerbeck's *Kommentar zum Neuen Testament* by nearly 300 years, yet remains the only work of its kind in English. Covers Matthew through 1 Corinthians only. Relates the teaching of the rabbis to the writings of the NT. 225.7.L62 1979

**McNicol, John.** *Thinking Through the Bible.* Grand Rapids: Kregel Publications, 1976.

An impressive synopsis of the books of the Bible. Helpful in survey courses in Bible institutes. Reprinted from the 1944 edition. 220.7.M23 1976

**Meyer, Heinrich August Wilhelm.** *Commentary on the New Testament.* 11 vols. Winona Lake, Ind.: Alpha Publications, 1979-1980.

Beautifully produced from the 1906 edition. The translation was carefully checked by some of the most capable scholars of the day. These volumes make available again the rich treasures that made this work one of the most eagerly sought after at the turn of the century. In areas where this work is now dated, reference will need to be made to more recent treatments. Readers, however, should not neglect the solid evangelical scholarship that made this set justifiably famous. 225.7.M57

**\*Morgan, George Campbell.** *Living Messages of the Books of the Bible.* Grand Rapids: Baker Book House, 1982.

Seventy years after its first appearance, this unique and handy work has been reissued in one volume. Morgan was never conventional in his approach to the study of the Bible. In him the stereotypical mold was broken. What is to be found between these covers is a refreshing analysis together with new insights into the teaching of Scripture. 220.7'06.M82 1982

**North, Gary.** *The Dominion Covenant: Genesis.* Vol. 1 of An Economic Commentary on the Bible. Tyler, Tex.: Institute for Christian Economics, 1982.

North, who has already provided devastating critiques of the economic theories of Marx, Sider, and others, here turns to the book of beginnings and the only time when the world's resources exceeded mankind's demands. In this volume—the first of a series—he undertakes a bold project: the development of an economic system based on a theocratic understanding of God's Word. North's approach is Van Tillian and postmillennial. His handling of Genesis—within the boundaries he established for the series—meets a felt need. Three concluding essays deal with cosmology, evolution, and creationism. Seen as a whole, this work is to be commended. The remaining volumes in this series are eagerly awaited. Reformed. 220.7.N81 v.1

**Ogilvie, Lloyd John, ed.** *The Communicator's Commentary.* In process. Waco, Tex.: Word Books, 1982-.

Scheduled for twelve volumes, this series of commentaries is largely the product of pastors. Each book of the NT is introduced before a section-by-section commentary is given. The style is not homiletical, even though the reader can easily discern that each writer is comfortable in the pulpit. Those selected to supply expository studies are evangelicals, but one wonders why some of the finest expositors of our day—J. M. Boice, J. Borror, M. Cronk, S. L. Johnson, J. D. Pentecost, R. Stedman, C. R. Swindoll—were omitted. Publisher's and editor's rhetoric will not be able to make up for what individual volumes lack in quality. 225.7'07.C73

**Parker, Thomas Henry Louis.** *Calvin's New Testament Commentaries.* Grand Rapids: Wm. B. Eerdmans Publishing Co., 1971.

Written by a man who has contributed to the presently in-progress translation of Calvin's commentaries. This work about their production is of great interest and is highly informative. 225.7'09.P22

**Ryrie, Charles Caldwell.** *Ryrie's Concise Guide to the Bible.* San Bernardino, Calif.: Here's Life Publishers, 1984.

Contains excellent introductory material on the Bible's origin, inspiration, authenticity, and reliability. These are followed by brief resumés of the contents of each canonical book. 220.7.R99C

**\*Spurgeon, Charles Haddon.** *Commenting and Commentaries: A Reference*

*Guide to Book Buying for Pastors, Students, and Christian Workers.* Grand Rapids: Baker Book House, 1981.

An indispensable catalog of the best expository studies from the Reformation to 1876. Emphasis is placed on those works making relevant application of truth to life. Substantive works (where exposition is based on thorough exegesis) do not receive the same praise. 016.2.SP9 1981

**Tasker, R. V. G., ed.** *Tyndale New Testament Commentaries.* 20 vols. Grand Rapids: Wm. B. Eerdmans Publishing Co., 1957-1971.

An up-to-date, moderately priced, evangelical series of commentaries written by British and Australian theologians. Though these works vary in value, each writer bases his exposition on an exegesis of the Greek text. Reformed. 225.7.T97

**\*Unger, Merrill Frederick.** *The New Unger's Bible Handbook.* Revised by G. N. Larson. Chicago: Moody Press, 1984.

Almost two decades after the appearance of *Unger's Bible Handbook,* the publishers have seen fit to issue this lavishly illustrated revision, replete with charts and abreast of the latest archaeological and historical data. Though an attempt has been made to retain the distinctives of the original work, the revising editor has taken it on himself to broaden the scope of some of the interpretative positions held by the writer. Not having studied under Unger, this is a bold and perhaps presumptuous task. This new work also includes the text of the NIV, which makes for good reading, but lacks accuracy. 220.7.UN3L 1984

\*————. *Unger's Commentary on the Old Testament.* 2 vols. Chicago: Moody Press, 1981.

These volumes represent the fruit of a lifetime dedicated to the sacred text. Unger, however, chose not to write for the scholar. He directed his thoughts instead to laypeople and sought at all times to place in their hands the kind of books that would edify them and build them up in the faith. These volumes are an example of that dedication. Though manifesting a tendency toward a typological hermeneutic, Unger's rich thoughts are readily made available. We are happy to be able to commend these volumes to laypeople everywhere. 221.7'07.UN3

**\*Walvoord, John Flipse,** and **Roy B. Zuck, eds.** *The Bible Knowledge Commentary.* 2 vols. Wheaton, Ill.: Victor Books, 1983-1985.

Based on the text of the NIV, these up-to-date volumes faithfully expound each book of the Bible. Accompanying each study is an introduction and bibliography. The former is nontechnical and yet covers all of the major issues of importance to Bible students. The latter is not extensive, but does direct readers to some of the more important full-length commentaries. Together these volumes provide an indispensable resource for Sunday school teachers and laypeople generally. The faculty of Dallas Seminary is to be commended for such a fine condensation of biblical information. 220.7.W17B

## SPECIAL SUBJECTS

**Adams, Jay Edward.** *Marriage, Divorce and Remarriage in the Bible.* Grand Rapids: Baker Book House, 1980.

Treats fairly the problems leading to divorce and, after discussing the biblical teaching for the resolution of these difficulties, makes a plea for forgiveness, particularly on the part of the Christian community. 220.8.M35.AD1

**Anderson, David A.** *All the Trees and Woody Plants of the Bible.* Waco, Tex.: Word Books, 1979.

After years of service in the U.S. Forestry Service and five trips to the Middle East, Anderson has brought his expertise to bear on the trees and shrubs mentioned in the Bible. The result is a handy, well-indexed volume that should be of value to preachers and teachers. 220.8′58.AN2

**Anderson, J. Kerby,** and **Harold G. Coffin.** *Fossils in Focus.* Grand Rapids: Zondervan Publishing House, 1977.

A brief, informative book relating recent geological discoveries (specifically in paleontology) to the biblical account of creation and the theory of evolution. Recommended. 560.AN2

**Armerding, George D.** *The Fragrance of the Lord: Toward a Deeper Appreciation of the Bible.* New York: Harper & Row, 1979.

Gleans devotional lessons from passages in which odors (sweet fragrances) of the Bible are mentioned. 220.8.0D5.AR5

***Baron, David.** *Rays of Messiah's Glory: Christ in the Old Testament.* Winona Lake, Ind.: Alpha Publications, n.d.

This reprint makes available again the delightful exposition of select OT passages relating to Christ and His ministry. 220.8.B26

**Baxter, James Sidlow.** *Divine Healing of the Body.* Grand Rapids: Zondervan Publishing House, 1979.

A valiant attempt to arbitrate between those who disagree as to whether or not special, divine healing occurs today. Gives the author's perception of what the Bible really teaches on the subject. Contains some startling conclusions for readers of all persuasions. 615′.852.B33

**Bennett, Georgann.** *What the Bible Says About Goodness.* Joplin, Mo.: College Press Publishing Co., 1981.

A valuable contribution that rightly centers goodness in the nature of God. Following this, there is an assessment of the virtue of goodness in both Testaments. Concludes with pointers for practical application. 220.8.G62.B43

**Bruce, Frederick Fyvie.** *Answers to Questions.* Grand Rapids: Zondervan Publishing House, 1973.

Contains candid replies to frequently asked questions. Insightful. 220.8.B83

***Clark, Gordon Haddon.** *Logic.* Jefferson City, Md.: Trinity Foundation, 1985.

This introductory work explains in clear, concise terms how a person may think correctly and reason effectively. For those desiring a reliable guide to sharpening the focus of their thoughts, this will meet that need. 160.C54

**Clements, Ronald Ernest.** *In Spirit and in Truth: Insights from Biblical Prayers.* Atlanta: John Knox Press, 1985.

A valuable compendium of prayers in the Bible. Well illustrated from incidents from life and happily free from higher critical theories, this work brings true scholarship to the fore and shows how a thorough analysis of the biblical text may aid the expository preacher. Excellent. 220.8.P89.C59

**Cottrell, Jack.** *What the Bible Says About God the Ruler.* Joplin, Mo.: College Press Publishing Co., 1984.

Continues this valuable series and provides a scholarly and accurate theological analysis of God's providence, purpose, sovereignty, and related topics. Weak in handling eschatological matters, but nonetheless stimulating and well-deserving of a place in the preacher's library. Provides a powerful stimulus for further study in this area. 220.8.G54.C82

***Culver, Robert Duncan.** *Toward a Biblical View of Civil Government.* Chicago: Moody Press, 1974.

A landmark work that deserves a place

in every church library. 220.8.G74.C89

**\*Custance, Arthur C.** *The Doorway Papers.* 10 vols. Grand Rapids: Zondervan Publishing House, 1975-1980.

These previously published essays ably integrate modern anthropology with the teaching of the Bible. The author, who has a Ph.D. in anthropology, boldly faces problems such as the preparation of the earth (creation), evolution, the uniqueness of man, the origin of evil, and the development of personality. His treatment, though dealing preeminently with OT themes, includes a consideration of the progress of revelation and concludes with a presentation of the teaching of the NT. Throughout his work, Custance is judicious and, allowing for minor differences in interpretation, provides an abundance of information for the zealous Bible student. Highly recommended. 220.8.M31.C96

————. *Indexes of the Doorway Papers.* Grand Rapids: Zondervan Publishing House, 1980.

This index to the author's famous essays is complete with a listing of all papers; diagrams, figures, maps, and tables; subject, name, and Scripture indexes; and a listing of the discussion of Hebrew and Greek words. This volume should not be neglected, as it provides easy access to a lifetime of research. Of apologetic value. 220.8.M31.C96 v.10

\*————. *The Seed of the Woman.* Brockville, Ontario, Canada: Doorway Publications, 1980.

The author who gave the Christian world the inestimably rich *Doorway Papers* here makes available another massive treatise in which he discusses such topics as the longevity of those living before the Flood, the nature of the forbidden fruit, the promise of God to Eve, and how the Word became flesh. Well researched, this volume is an able synthesis of the Bible with anthropology, physiology, and theology. 220.8.W84.C96

**Daniel, Eleanor.** *What the Bible Says About Sexual Identity.* Joplin, Mo.: College Press Publishing Co., 1981.

Considers the biblical teaching on sexuality, the misuses of sex, the NT teaching, and the way believers may control their own drives and emotions. 220.8.SE9.D22

**Epstein, Louis M.** *The Jewish Marriage Contract: A Study in the Status of the Woman in Jewish Law.* New York: Arno Press, 1973.

First published in 1927, this volume contributes immensely to our knowledge of marriage in OT times. 346.01.EP8 1973

**\*Fairbairn, Patrick.** *The Revelation of Law in Scripture.* Winona Lake, Ind.: Alpha Publications, 1979.

These lectures, first published in 1869, treat the moral law implanted in the heart of man and trace its use throughout the Bible. Complete with supplementary dissertations. Excellent. Reformed. 220.8.L41.F15 1979

**Ferguson, Walter W.** *Living Animals of the Bible.* New York: Charles Scribner's Sons, 1974.

A magnificently illustrated volume containing paintings of animals (including mammals, birds, etc.) mentioned in the Bible and still living today. The Hebrew names are given with the English equivalents, followed by their Latin phyla and selected passages of Scripture in which they are mentioned. 220.859.F38

**Foh, Susan T.** *Women and the Word of God: A Response to Biblical Feminism.* Phillipsburg, N.J.: Presbyterian and Reformed Publishing Co., 1980.

This discussion of feminism treats fairly the difficult issues and grapples realistically with the hard problems. The teaching of Scripture is referred to frequently and the nitty-gritty issues of submission are discussed in light of the evident androgeny within the Godhead and the willing subordination of members of the Godhead to one another. 220.8.W84.F69

**Gerhardsson, Birger.** *The Ethos of the Bible.* Translated by S. Westerholm. Philadelphia: Fortress Press, 1981.

An historical and biblical study of ethics and the contribution of the historic development of social norms to the formation of the Christian faith. 220.8.ET13.G31

**\*Govett, Robert.** *The Three Eatings.* Miami Springs, Fla.: Conley and Schoettle Publishing Co., 1985.

This is the kind of volume that can easily escape a person's notice. Its significance, however, is exactly opposite of its notoriety. Govett, whose thought was always fresh, describes the theological significance of Adam's eating the forbidden fruit; the Passover, with discourses on the bread of the Presence and Christ's invitation in John 6; and the Lord's Supper. In these "three eatings" Govett discerns an outline of the Fall, redemption through personal appropriation, and fellowship. 220.8.G74 1985

**Gunn, Giles, ed.** *The Bible and American Arts and Letters.* Philadelphia: Fortress Press, 1983.

Contains articles contributed by some of the leading authorities in the U.S. Highlights the presence (or absence, depending on one's point of view) of biblical motifs in American traditions. 220.8.AR7.G95

**Hals, Ronald M.** *Grace and Faith in the Old Testament.* Minneapolis: Augsburg Publishing House, 1980.

A judicious discussion that leads the author to conclude that "the basic shape in which we encounter grace and faith in both testaments is the same." 221.8.G75.H16

**Hieronymus, Lynn.** *What the Bible Says*

*About Worship.* Joplin, Mo.: College Press Publishing Co., 1984.

Part of the growing corpus of literature on church worship. A pastor of the Christian Churches/Churches of Christ here shares his philosophy of worship and guides his fellow-pastors in the form and function of praise. 220.8.W89.H53

**Ide, Arthur Frederick.** *Women in the Ancient Near East.* Mesquite, Tex.: Ide House, 1982.

Part of the series *Women in History,* this sequel to *Women in Ancient Israel* surveys the role and community relationships of women in the nations surrounding Palestine. A very brief, cursory survey. 305.4.ID2

**Jewett, Paul King.** *Man as Male and Female: A Study of Sexual Relationships from a Theological Point of View.* Grand Rapids: Wm. B. Eerdmans Publishing Co., 1975.

†Stresses the equality of the sexes from a pro-Barthian perspective. Blames rabbinic traditions for the social roles that have become part of our Western heritage. Scriptures that teach a position contrary to Jewett's are dismissed as culturally conditioned. Galatians 3:28 is wrongly construed as abolishing subordination instead of referring to the privileges of all believers. This book does more harm than good, and its publication has served only to becloud the issues further. 220.8′301.J54

**Kaye, B.,** and **G. Wenham, eds.** *Law, Morality and the Bible: A Symposium.* Downers Grove, Ill.: InterVarsity Press, 1978.

These essays by evangelical Anglicans probe the theological, philosophical, and legal aspects of ethical theory and practice. 220.8′17.L41

**Larue, Gerald.** *Sex and the Bible.* Buffalo, N.Y.: Prometheus Books, 1983.

†Draws together a variety of information, but fails to offer much that is new or of lasting significance. 220.8.SE9.L32

**Little, Robert J.** *Insight.* Chicago: Moody Press, 1971.

Provides answers to some of the questions featured on the radio programs "Moody Presents" and "The Question Box." Covers topics such as "Was Jesus a Revolutionary?" "The If's and Ought's of Prayer," and "Christian Ethics." 220.8.L72

**Long, A. A.** *Hellenistic Philosophy: Stoics, Epicureans, Sceptics.* New York: Charles Scribner's Sons, 1974.

Provides a vivid portrayal of the intellectual climate in Greek cities visited by the apostle Paul. Forms a valuable backdrop to the study of many of his letters. 180.L25

**\*Morris, Leon Lamb.** *Testaments of Love: A Study of Love in the Bible.* Grand Rapids: Wm. B. Eerdmans Publishing Company, 1981.

A thorough and instructive analysis of "love" in both the OT and NT. The importance of this study is explained by Morris: "Love is at the core of almost all biblical events. Throughout the Bible love is at the heart of God's dealings with men, little of which can be understood if this basic fact is not recognized. And little of what is expected of men can be appreciated until we realize that the commands to love God and our neighbor are basic." 220.8.L94.M83

**Noble, Lowell.** *Naked and Not Ashamed: An Anthropological, Biblical, and Psychological Study of Shame.* Jackson, Mich.: Lowell Noble, 1975.

Makes up for the lack of a thorough study of conscience, sin, and guilt in anthropological literature. An excellent treatise. 220.8.N66

**Norris, Bill,** and **Judy Norris.** *What the Bible Says About Families.* Joplin, Mo.: College Press Publishing Co., 1985.

This book covers the entire history of biblical revelation. Beginning with Adam and Eve and concluding with the apostolic era, the Norrises seek to unfold God's progressive revelation. The book manifests an unfortunate shallowness, and however much the efforts of the authors may be applauded, what is presented manifests little awareness of the changing social milieu of the OT, or of the NT, for that matter. Though the undertaking is prodigious, the comments made by the authors on different passages of Scripture fail to elicit any abiding principles, and a careful perusal of this book leaves one with the impression that the information could have been gained simply by a careful reading of the Bible itself. 220.8.M34.N79

**Parmelee, Alice.** *All the Birds of the Bible.* New Canaan, Conn.: Keats Publishing, 1977.

Bible students and ornithologists will welcome this handy, well-illustrated volume. Recommended. 220.859.P24A 1977

**Robinson, Henry Wheeler.** *Corporate Personality in Ancient Israel.* Rev. ed. Philadelphia: Fortress Press, 1980.

†First published in 1937 under the title *The Group and the Individual in Israel,* this book constructs a theological foundation for understanding personality in the OT and considers how each Israelite contributed to the complexion of the family, tribe, and nation. 301.29′33.R56 1980

**\*Ryken, Leland.** *The Literature of the Bible.* Grand Rapids: Zondervan Publishing House, 1974.

Deals admirably with all the categories of modern literary criticism and thus adds new meaning to the study of the Bible. 220.88.R98 (Alt. DDC 809.93522)

**\*Ryrie, Charles Caldwell.** *You Mean the Bible Teaches That?* Chicago: Moody Press, 1974.

Clear, concise chapters on subjects such as civil obedience, women's lib, divorce, situation ethics, and abortion. Valuable to those who are disturbed over today's ethical dilemmas. 220.817.R99

**Schochet, Elijah Judah.** *Animal Life in Jewish Tradition: Attitudes and Relations.* New York: Ktav Publishing House, 1984.

This encyclopedic work deals with animal lore and legend. It is divided into three sections: biblical, rabbinic, and medieval and modern. Preachers will find an abundance of information either to elucidate the biblical text or to illustrate their messages. 220.8.AN5.SCH6

**Smart, James D.** *The Past, Present, and Future of Biblical Theology.* Philadelphia: Westminster Press, 1979.

†Continues the discussion begun by Childs in *Biblical Theology in Crisis.* Points to the continued resurgence of interest in biblical theology and charts a course for the future. 220.8'23.SM2

**Smith, Willard S.** *Animals, Birds and Plants of the Bible.* Needham Heights, Mass.: Church Art, 1971.

A recent, colorful, reliable work. Exceptionally well produced. Will enhance one's library and serve the pastor well as a resource tool. 220.859.SM6

**Smith, James E.** *What the Bible Says About the Promised Messiah.* Joplin, Mo.: College Press Publishing Co., 1984.

Treats specific OT passages of Scripture dealing with Christ's messiahship. Preachers will find enough ideas in this volume to provide them with more than a year's sermonic material. 220.8.M56.SM6

**\*Unger, Merrill Frederick.** *Biblical Demonology: A Study of the Spiritual Forces Behind the Present World Unrest.* Wheaton, Ill.: Scripture Press, 1974.

First published in 1952. Exposes the fallacies inherent in Satanism and explains the resurgence of interest in the occult. 220.813.UN3

**Veith, Gene Edward, Jr.** *The Gift of Art: The Place of the Arts in Scripture.* Downers Grove, Ill.: InterVarsity Press, 1983.

Examines the biblical teaching on art, and, by drawing on information surrounding the person of Bezalel, establishes guidelines for the cultivation of the arts today. 220.8.AR7.V53

**White, Reginald Ernest Oscar.** *Biblical Ethics.* Grand Rapids: Wm. B. Eerdmans Publishing Co., 1979.

A learned, but disappointing work. The author grounds his teaching on the Scriptures, but only after he has interpreted them in the light of the latest *Formgeschichte* and *Redactiongeschichte.* 220.8'17.W58

**White, Willie W.** *What the Bible Says About Suffering.* Joplin, Mo.: College Press Publishing Co., 1984.

A compassionate work growing out of the loss of his sons. Takes the reader from the early stages of bereavement—and growing perfect through suffering—to the glad assurance of an eternal home. 220.8.SU2.W58

**\*Zohary, Michael.** *Plants of the Bible.* Cambridge: Cambridge University Press, 1982.

This lavishly illustrated handbook introduces readers to the plants of the Bible: fruit trees, field crops, and garden plants; wild herbs, forest trees, and shrubs; plants by rivers and marshes; plants of the wilderness; thorns and thistles; flowers of the field; drugs and spices; incense and perfume. Provides a brief informative description of each. Excellent. 220.858.Z7

OLD TESTAMENT

**Becker, Joachim.** *Messianic Expectation in the Old Testament.* Translated by David E. Green. Edinburgh: T. & T. Clark, 1980.

Based on the historical-critical interpretation of the OT, these chapters scrutinize some key passages and then succinctly relate the essence of their teaching to the NT. 221.8.M56.B38

**Bergren, Richard Victor.** *The Prophets and the Law.* Jerusalem: Hebrew Union College Press, 1974.

Following an extensive introduction on the relationship between the prophets and the law, Bergren focuses attention on the judgment speeches of Amos, Micah, Isaiah, and Jeremiah. Also of value for its critique of OT scholars from Alt to Westermann. 221.8.B45

**Blanch, Stuart.** *The Trumpet in the Morning: Law and Freedom Today in the Light of the Hebraeo-Christian Tradition.* New York: Oxford University Press, 1979.

†Contains the Chavasse Lectures for 1977. Each chapter treats with theological acumen and practical relevance some aspect of the OT law and its application to the present. Stimulating. 221.8.L41.B59

**Childs, Brevard S.** *Old Testament Books for Pastor and Teacher.* Philadelphia: Westminster Press, 1977.

†Concentrates on form-critical and redaction-critical works that the writer believes can be of value to pastors and those preparing for the ministry. These bibliographic essays can be read with profit by the discerning reader. 016.22′16.C43

**Cohen, H. Hirsch.** *The Drunkenness of Noah.* University, Ala.: University of Alabama Press, 1974.

†A scholarly study by a rabbi whose extensive research into the social conditions prevailing at the time of the Deluge makes a distinct contribution to our knowledge of that era. Includes a chapter on man as God's representative and the sin and affliction of Cain. 221.8.C66

**Craigie, Peter Campbell.** *The Problem of War in the Old Testament.* Grand Rapids: Wm. B. Eerdmans Publishing Co., 1978.

A bold approach to the topic of war in Scripture with a careful discussion of the ethical ramifications of the Bible's teaching for contemporary Christians. Omits a discussion of the theocracy. Does provide helpful insights when treating problematical passages. 221.8.W19.C84 (Alt DDC 261.8)

***Delitzsch, Franz Julius.** *Old Testament History of Redemption.* Translated by S. I. Curtis. Winona Lake, Ind.: Alpha Publications, 1980.

Contains lectures delivered in Leipzig in 1880. This companion volume to the author's *Messianic Prophecies* follows the history of God's progressive revelation and explains the development of the doctrine of salvation in the OT. 221.8.SA3.D37

**DeVries, Simon J.** *The Achievement of Biblical Religion: A Prolegomenon to Old Testament Theology.* New York: University Press of America, 1983.

A thought-provoking text that suggests abandoning current habits of judging the Judaeo-Christian Scriptures by contemporary standards. Instead, the author sets out to measure the OT by standards held at the time of the Scriptures' writing. 221.823.D49

**Dyrness, William.** *Themes in Old Testament Theology.* Downers Grove, Ill.: Inter-Varsity Press, 1979.

Provocative studies of the revelation and nature of God, creation and providence, man and woman, sin, the covenant and the law, and other themes. Missing is a development of the theocracy and the grounding of ethics in the "fear of the Lord." Enlightening and rewarding. 221.8′23.D84

**Frick, Frank S.** *The City in Ancient Israel.* Missoula, Mont.: Scholars Press, 1977.

Assesses the place and importance of the city in Israelite society from the thirteenth century B.C. to the destruction of Jerusalem in 587 B.C. 221.8.C49.F91

**Geodicke, H.,** and **J. J. M. Roberts, eds.** *Unity and Diversity: Essays in the History, Literature, and Religion of the Ancient*

*Near East.* Baltimore: Johns Hopkins University Press, 1975.

Essays presented in memory of noted archaeologist William Foxwell Albright reveal the multifaceted social life and religious beliefs of those living in the Near East in biblical times. 956.G55

**Hassel, Gerhard F.** *Old Testament Theology: Basic Issues in the Current Debate.* Grand Rapids: Wm. B. Eerdmans Publishing Co., 1972.

A critical appraisal of the history and methodology of contemporary OT study. Hassel rejects the *Religionsgeschichtliche Schule* and the *Weltanschauung* of modern rationalism. Also repudiates the confession approach of some European writers, and corrects many ideas inherent in *Heilsgeschichte.* Exposes the inadequacies of these theories to OT theology, and then lays a foundation for a constructive approach to the teaching of the OT. 221.823.H27

**Hayes, John H.,** and **Frederick Prussner.** *Old Testament Theology: Its History and Development.* Atlanta: John Knox Press, 1985.

†A valuable revision of Prussner's doctoral dissertation, University of Chicago, 1952. 221.823.H32P 1985

**Herzog, Chaim,** and **Mordechai Gichon.** *Battles of the Bible.* New York: Random House, 1978.

Well illustrated with pictures, maps, and charts, this book provides a modern military evaluation of the wars and border skirmishes that took place in Palestine from the time of Joshua to the close of the intertestamental period. 221.8.W19.H44

**Ide, Arthur Frederick.** *Women in Ancient Israel Under the Torah and Talmud, with a Translation and Critical Commentary on Genesis 1-3.* Mesquite, Tex.: Ide House, 1982.

Uses Israel's ancient traditions to provide an account of the place of women within Judaism. Readers are left with the impression that the Bible accords women more respect and honor. 305.4'2.IS7.ID2

**Ishida, Tomoo.** *The Royal Dynasties in Ancient Israel: At Study on the Formation and Development of Royal-Dynastic Ideology.* Berlin: Walter de Gruyter, 1977.

†A scholarly discussion of the monarchies of the ancient Near East, and in particular the Davidic dynasty. Stops short of carrying the OT teaching into the New and showing how Christ will fulfill all that the OT foreshadowed in type and prophecy. 221.8.K61.IS3

**Joines, Karen Randolph.** *Serpent Symbolism in the Old Testament: A Linguistic, Archaeological and Literary Study.* Haddonfield, N.J.: Haddonfield House, 1974.

†A comprehensive study of the serpent motif in the OT. Links OT references to ethnic and cultural movements in the ancient Near East. 221.8.J66

**\*Kaiser, Walter Christian, Jr.** *Toward an Old Testament Theology.* Grand Rapids: Zondervan Publishing House, 1978.

Of surpassing excellence. This treatment lays a foundation for a return to biblical theology as a respected discipline. In it Kaiser also advances his views in support of promise theology. All things considered, this is a most valuable contribution. 221.823.C59

**\*_____.** *Toward Old Testament Ethics.* Grand Rapids: Zondervan Publishing House, Academie Books, 1983.

A magisterial work that now takes its place in the forefront of works on this subject. Kaiser is always gracious and leaves room for dissenting opinion. He is cognizant of the issues, and his discussion is both timely and helpful. Recommended. 221.8.EI9.K12

**Keel, Othmar.** *The Symbolism of the Biblical World: Ancient Near Eastern Iconography and the Book of Psalms.* Translated by

T. J. Hallett. New York: Seabury Press, 1978.

A fascinating and insightful volume that sets the OT, and particularly the Psalms, in the *Sitz im Leben* of the times. Well illustrated. 221.8.SY6.K24

**\*Kurtz, Johann Heinrich.** *Sacrificial Worship in the Old Testament.* Translated by J. Martin. Minneapolis: Klock & Klock Christian Publishers, 1980.

A work of genius that grasps the significance of the Levitical system of sacrifices and explains their symbolism in relation to the forgiveness of sins. Kurtz, however, fails to treat Israel's worship in light of the theocracy and does not lay a foundation for the development of the priesthood of all believers in the NT. In spite of these weaknesses, this is a commendable volume. 221.8.SA11.K96

**LaSor, William Sanford.** *Israel: A Biblical View.* Grand Rapids: Wm. B. Eerdmans Publishing Co., 1976.

Treats specific themes such as the "Servant of the Lord," "Israel in History," "Israel in Prophecy," and the "Church as Israel." Amillennial. 221.8'.IS7.133

**Leggett, Donald A.** *The Levirate and Goel Institutions in the Old Testament with Special Attention to the Book of Ruth.* Cherry Hill, N.J.: Mack Publishing, 1974.

A readable account of the OT levirate and *goel* institutions. Illustrates the legal formalities and shows how they were met by Boaz. 221.8.L52

**Littauer, M. A.,** and **J. H. Crouwel.** *Wheeled Vehicles and Ridden Animals in the Ancient Near East.* Leiden: E. J. Brill, 1979.

A historical survey of vehicles for conveyance—domestic, economic, and military—from the first to the third millennia B.C. This well-researched volume highlights the use of animals in the OT, particularly in warfare. 221.8.T68.L71

**Martens, Elmer Arthur.** *God's Design: A Focus on Old Testament Theology.* Grand Rapids: Baker Book House, 1981.

Avoids the basic approaches to OT theology and stresses instead the kingdom concept, but falls short of developing a truly theocratic approach through the main leaders of the pre-Diluvian period to Abraham and God's chosen people, Israel. 221.8'23.M36

**McKenzie, John L.** *A Theology of the Old Testament.* Garden City, N.Y.: Doubleday and Co., 1974.

†This scholarly work by a Roman Catholic theologian approaches the OT on the basis of its cultus, revelation, history, nature, wisdom, institutions, and eschatology. The author sees no vital connection between OT theology and the development of NT doctrine. 221.823.M19

**Oehler, Gustav Friedrich.** *Theology of the Old Testament.* Minneapolis: Klock & Klock Christian Publishers, 1978.

First published in 1873, this work admirably treats Mosaism, prophetism, and the wisdom literature. It is valuable for its nuggets of thought on topics such as man, OT history, the theocracy (limited to the period of the Exodus and Joshua/Judges). Amillennial. 221.823.OE5 1978

**Patrick, Dale.** *Old Testament Law.* Atlanta: John Knox Press, 1985.

†Though adhering to those tenets commonly identified with liberal higher criticism, this work nonetheless provides a careful analysis of the Decalogue, the Book of the Covenant, the Deuteronomic law, the Holiness Code, and the Priestly law. The result is a concise handling of an important theme. 221.8.L41.P27

**\*Raven, John Howard.** *The History of the Religion of Israel: An Old Testament Theology.* Grand Rapids: Baker Book House, 1979.

Written by one of the great conservative theologians of the past, this work was first published privately in 1933. It contains a fine delineation of OT theology from the time of Moses to Manasseh. All things considered, this is an outstanding contribution. Reformed. 221.823.R19 1979

**Rogerson, J. W.** *Anthropology and the Old Testament.* Atlanta: John Knox Press, 1979.

A careful discussion of the OT teaching on the nature of man. Well executed in research and design and only impaired by the author's adherence to theologically liberal tenets. 221.8.M31.R63

**\*Skilton, John H. ed.** *The Law and the Prophets: Old Testament Studies Prepared in Honor of Oswald Thompson Allis.* Philadelphia: Presbyterian and Reformed Publishing Co., 1974.

These essays, in honor of one of the great OT scholars of all time, cover a wide variety of themes. 221.8.AL5.SK3

**Thompson, Reginald Campbell.** *Semitic Magic, Its Origins and Development.* New York: AMS Press, 1976.

Of importance in understanding the cultural milieu of the OT and God's warnings against idolatry. Reprinted from the 1908 edition. 133.4.T37 1976

**Vermes, Gaza.** *Scripture and Tradition in Judaism. Studia Post-Biblica.* 2d rev. ed. Leiden: E. J. Brill, 1973.

A detailed study of *haggadic* exegesis highlighting eight incidents in the Bible. 221.8.V59

**Von Rad, Gerhard.** *God at Work in Israel.* Translated by J. H. Marks. Nashville: Abingdon Press, 1980.

†First published in German in 1974, this series of lectures/essays covers a variety of OT themes from "How to Read the OT" to concepts of life and death. It includes character studies and a few critical chapters on Mosaic monotheism, creation, and the like. 221.8.V89

**Westermann, Claus.** *Elements of Old Testament Theology.* Translated by D. W. Stott. Atlanta: John Knox Press, 1982.

The writer suggests that the rediscovery of the theme of blessing is a necessary supplement to a one-sided emphasis on the mighty acts of God. The book includes an exposition of Exodus and points to the importance of creation throughout the OT. 221.823.W52

**Wright, Christopher J. H.** *An Eye for an Eye, The Place of Old Testament Ethics Today.* Downers Grove, Ill.: InterVarsity Press, 1983.

With renewed interest in biblical ethics, Christians of all persuasions will find this work helpful. The assessment of the theological, social, and economic aspects of ethics is particularly enlightening. 221.8.EI3.W93

NEW TESTAMENT

**Banks, Robert J.** *Jesus and the Law in Synoptic Tradition.* New York: Cambridge University Press, 1975.

After surveying the concept of law in the OT, intertestamental period, and later Jewish literature, the author studies in detail the attitude of Christ toward Mosaic legislation. 225.8.B22

**Barrett, Charles Kingsley.** *The Signs of an Apostle.* Philadelphia: Fortress Press, 1972.

An in-depth treatment of what was involved in apostleship in the first century A.D. 225.8.AP4.B27

_____. *New Testament Essays.* London: SPCK, 1972.

Studies giving evidence of deep scholarship and awareness of the contemporary NT debate. 225.8.B27

**\*Bernard, Thomas D.** *The Progress of Doctrine in the New Testament.* Minneapolis: Klock & Klock Christian Publishers, 1979.

The reissuing of this highly acclaimed treatment is well worth the pastor's investment of both time and money. Bernard provides something good on every aspect of NT theology, and no evangelical worthy of the name should be without this fine study. 225.823.B45 1979

**Berry, Harold J.** *Treasures from the Original.* Chicago: Moody Press, 1985.

Originally entitled *Gems from the Original, Vol. 1.* Brief, devotional studies on such topics as "The Believer's Old Nature" and "The Great Commission." Helpful to laypeople. Of value for ideas when called on occasionally to give a talk. 255.84.B45

**Blaiklock, Edward Musgrave.** *Word Pictures from the Bible.* Grand Rapids: Zondervan Publishing House, 1971.

This work by a gifted writer and classical scholar lacks depth but is an ideal reference work in the pastor's library. 225.84.B57

**Catchpole, David R.** *The Synoptic Divorce Material as a Traditio-Historical Problem.* Manchester, England: John Rylands Library, 1974.

An exemplary study of Matthew 5:31-32; 19:1-9; Mark 10:1-12; Luke 17:18; and 1 Corinthians 7:10-16. 301.428.C28

**Couasnon, Charles.** *The Church of the Holy Sepulchre in Jerusalem.* New York: Oxford University Press, 1974.

A beautifully illustrated, detailed history. 726.5.C83

**Cullmann, Oscar.** *The Christology of the New Testament.* Rev ed. Translated by S. C. Guthrie and C. A. M. Hall. Philadelphia: Westminster Press, 1981.

†The reissue in paperback of the writer's famous 1957 work (translated into English in 1963). A most important study. 225.82.C89

**Deissmann, Gustav Adolf.** *Bible Studies.* Translated by A. Grieve. Winona Lake, Ind.: Alpha Publications, 1979.

First published in English in 1901, this companion to *Light from the Ancient East* relates the usage of specific words found in papyri fragments and on inscriptions to the text of the NT. The result is an illuminating series of studies that enriches the user's understanding of NT times. 225.848.D36B 1979

**Derrett, John Duncan Martin.** *Law in the New Testament.* London: Darton, Longman and Todd, 1971.

A collection of essays that is remarkable for its concise reconstruction of events. A model of historical scholarship drawing on a wide knowledge of rabbinic and Oriental legal codes. 225.834.D44

———. *Studies in the New Testament.* 3 vols. Leiden: E. J. Brill, 1977-1982.

A brilliant series of studies relating the law to the discourses of the Lord Jesus and/or incidents in His life. Each chapter is a model of historical scholarship exhibiting a wide range of knowledge of rabbinic and Oriental laws. Indispensable. 225.834.D44S

**France, R. T.** *Jesus and the Old Testament.* London: Tyndale Press, 1971.

A valuable study that provides a generally conservative, thorough, and scholarly examination of the OT passages in the gospels that apply to Christ and His mission. Stops short of adherence to the doctrine of inspiration. Valuable. 225.848.F84

**Goppelt, Leonhard.** *Theology of the New Testament.* 2 vols. Edited by J. Roloff. Translated by J. E. Alsup. Grand Rapids: Wm. B. Eerdmans Publishing Co., 1981-1983.

This study of the life and ministry of Jesus and the apostolic witness makes a thorough application of contemporary NT scholarship to the gospel records and epistles. Although Goppelt sees his study as a "qualified conversation between exegetical and systematic theology," his goal is always to come to terms with the intent of the NT authors without losing sight of the meaning of the message of the NT today. 225.823.G64 v.1

*Gundry, Robert Horton.** *"Soma" in Biblical Theology, With Emphasis on Pauline Anthropology.* New York: Cambridge University Press, 1976.

A scholarly treatise demonstrating that *soma* frequently refers to the whole person rather than simply the physical body. 225.8.M21.G95

*Guthrie, Donald.** *New Testament Theology.* Downers Grove, Ill.: InterVarsity Press, 1981.

The climax of a lifetime of research, this magisterial study combines thorough scholarship with a sound Christocentric approach to theology. Of particular significance is Guthrie's handling of the NT teaching on the kingdom. 225.823.G98

**Hasel, Gerhard F.** *New Testament Theology: Basic Issues in the Current Debate.* Grand Rapids: Wm. B. Eerdmans Publishing Co., 1978.

†A companion volume to the writer's earlier work on the OT, this study surveys the rise, progress, and contribution of NT theology in light of current critical scholarship. 225.823.H27

**Jeremias, Joachim.** *The Central Message of the New Testament.* Philadelphia: Fortress Press, 1981.

First published in 1965, these essays are at once perceptive and complete and zero in on the heart of NT theology. 225.823.J47 1981

*Knight, George William, III.** *The Role Relationship of Men and Women.* Chicago: Moody Press, 1985.

Originally issued by Baker Book House in 1977 under the title *The New Testament Teaching on the Role Relationship of Men and Women.* Based on three previously published essays, this revision of the Baker book provides a powerful, biblically based rebuttal to Scanzoni and Hardesty's *All We're Meant to Be* and Jewett's *Man as Male and Female.* This is a work of thorough scholarship that deals

practically with the issue of husband-wife equality and treats the topic of headship-subordination in a truly praiseworthy manner. Contains a valuable new appendix on the meaning of *kephalē* ("head") in the New Testament. 225.8.W84.K74

**Ladd, George Eldon.** *A Theology of the New Testament.* Grand Rapids: Wm. B. Eerdmans Publishing Co., 1974.

An important contribution covering the synoptics, Johannine and Pauline writings, and including material from the Acts and catholic epistles. 225.823.L12

**Lehman, Chester K.** *Biblical Theology: New Testament.* Scottdale, Pa.: Herald Press, 1974.

Not since G. Vos's treatment has anything quite like this been attempted. Lehman's approach differs from G. E. Ladd's *Theology of the New Testament.* This is not an in-depth study and will probably be most widely used in Bible colleges. 225.823.L52

**Lightfoot, Joseph Barber.** *Biblical Essays.* Grand Rapids: Baker Book House, 1979.

A series of brilliant, devout essays on John's gospel, the preparation of Paul for the ministry, the churches of Macedonia, the structure of Paul's letter to the Romans, and other topics. A valuable acquistion. 225.8.L62

**Longenecker, Richard Norman.** *New Testament Social Ethics for Today.* Grand Rapids: Wm. B. Eerdmans Publishing Co., 1984.

Answers the question of what role the NT should play in the formation and expression of Christian social morality today. Longenecker proposes a developmental hermeneutic that distinguishes between "declared principles" and "described practices" in the NT writings. 225.8.EI9.L85

**Mealand, David L.** *Poverty and Expectation in the Gospels.* London: Society for

Promoting Christian Knowledge, 1981.

An assessment of the teaching of the gospels on the subjects of poverty and deprivation. Combines textual criticism with an assessment of the socio-economic conditions of the times. 225.8.P86.M46

**Morrice, William G.** *Joy in the New Testament.* Grand Rapids: Wm. B. Eerdmans Publishing Co., 1984.

This book focuses on the various words used in the NT to express the joy that comes from belief in the gospel of Jesus Christ. The first half of the book consists of an examination of various groups of Greek words for joy, including their use in classical Greek, the LXX, the Apocrypha, Pseudepigrapha, and elsewhere. In Part 2 Morrice looks at our heritage of joy, particularly as evidenced in the life and teachings of Christ. He then examines the place of joy in the writings of the rest of the NT. 225.8.K84.M83

**Pearson, Birger Albert.** *The Pneumatikos-Psychikos Terminology in I Corinthians: A Study in the Theology of the Corinthian Opponents of Paul and Its Relation to Gnosticism.* Missoula, Mont.: Scholars Press, 1973.

Traces Paul's usage of allegedly Gnostic terms and shows that *pneumatikos* and *psychikos* occur in non-Gnostic writings prior to the time of the apostle. Demonstrates how the Gnostic writers used tenets of Judaism and Jewish exegesis to suit their own purpose. 225.8.M31.P31

**Perkins, Pheme.** *Love Commands in the New Testament.* New York: Paulist Press, 1982.

In endeavoring to establish a NT ethic for the people of God, Perkins deals with Christ's command and illustrates this principle from different incidents in the NT. Stimulating. 225.8.L94.P41

**Perrin, Norman.** *A Modern Pilgrimage in New Testament Christology.* Phila-

delphia: Fortress Press, 1974.

†These essays apply the author's process theology to the synoptic gospels in the vain hope of drawing from them a NT Christology. 225.823.P41

**Sanders, Jack T.** *Ethics in the New Testament: Change and Development.* Philadelphia: Fortress Press, 1975.

Considers whether an Occidental may gain valid insights for present behavior from the NT. Concludes that NT precepts are so intimately connected with eschatology that their ethical teaching is no longer relevant. 225.8'17.SA5

**Shires, Henry M.** *Finding the Old Testament in the New.* Philadelphia: Westminster Press, 1974.

†Builds on previous works and enhances our knowledge of the way the NT uses the OT. Written in a style that is easily comprehended. Its approach to and handling of problem areas is forthright and helpful. 225.84.SH6

**Stephens, Shirley.** *A New Testament View of Women.* Nashville: Broadman Press, 1980.

Avoids the extremes of the Women's Liberation movement and inflexible traditionalism and in their place offers a balanced statement of the biblical evidence. 225.8.W84.ST4

**Tidball, Derek.** *The Social Context of the New Testament: A Sociological Analysis.* Grand Rapids: Zondervan Publishing House, Academie Books, 1984.

Introduces the reader to some of the current theories in the area of biblical sociology. Though written for the general reader, the author nonetheless deals adequately with the data. Accomplishes a difficult task with exceptional skill. 225.8.SO1.T43

**\*Turner, Nigel.** *Christian Words.* Edinburgh: T. and T. Clark, 1980.

Delves into the fascinating world of lexical studies and discovers in the usage of some NT words a significance and meaning often passed over in those works that ignore the contribution of Jewish intertestamental studies to an understanding of the NT. 225.848.T85

**Wilkinson, John.** *Health and Healing: Studies in New Testament Principles and Practice.* Edinburgh: Handsel Press, 1980.

A serious attempt on the part of a physician-theologian to come to grips with the NT teaching on health and its counterpart, healing. Provocative. 225.8.H34.W65

**Wimmer, Joseph F.** *Fasting in the New Testament: A Study in Biblical Theology.* New York: Paulist Press, 1982.

Fasting has become a fad in certain Christian circles. Wimmer begins with a discussion of hermeneutics. He then follows up this section with a discussion of fasting in its cultural and historical setting, including the OT, intertestamental, and NT periods. 225.8.F26.W71

**Wueller, Wilhelm H.,** and **Robert C. Leslie.** *The Surprising Gospel: Intriguing Psychological Insights from the New Testament.* Nashville: Abingdon Press, 1984.

†The writers are to be commended for boldly attempting to integrate the Bible and psychology and to highlight the practicality of the teaching of the NT. The exegesis is based on *Redaktiongeschichte,* and this weakens the work. Nevertheless, the writers have set a pattern for evangelicals to follow. 225.8.P95.W95

## BIBLE ATLASES

**\*Aharoni, Yohanan,** and **Michael Avi-Yonah.** *The Macmillan Bible Atlas.* Rev. ed. New York: Macmillan Co., 1977.

First published in 1968, this outstanding atlas covers all aspects of the religious, political, military, and economic life of God's people in OT times, the intertestamental period, and the NT. Two-thirds of the maps have been revised, and this aids in pinpointing with accuracy the places where biblical events took place. An indispensable work. 220.9.AH1 1977

**\*Beitzel, Barry J.** *The Moody Atlas of Bible Lands.* Chicago: Moody Press, 1985.

This is a most useful work. The maps, pictures, and text are unique. It would be difficult to find a more helpful, usable atlas for laypeople. Author and publisher are to be commended for having produced such a handsome work. 229.9.B39

**Grant, Michael.** *Ancient History Atlas.* New York: Macmillan Co., 1971.

Dealing specifically with the ancient Greek and Roman worlds, this atlas provides an important historical survey of eras and epochs that parallel the biblical period. 911.3.G76

**Luedemann, Gerd.** *Paul, Apostle of the Gentiles: Studies in Chronology.* Translated by F. S. Jones. Philadelphia: Fortress Press, 1984.

†This book is a bridge-building work that opens up the way for German NT scholars to enter into an international discussion of Pauline chronology, and at the same time, it challenges all NT scholars who continue to adhere to a chronology based on Acts to reappraise critically their positions. 225.9'24.L96

**May, Herbert G.,** ed. *Oxford Bible Atlas.* 3d ed. Revised by J. Day. New York: Oxford University Press, 1984.

†Few atlases combine the general accuracy and geographic reliability of this one. Extensively indexed, this is a most usable work, marred, however, by the liberal presuppositions of the contributors. 220.9.M45 1983

**\*Monson, J.** *Student Map Manual: Historical Geography of the Bible Lands.* Grand

Rapids: Zondervan Publishing House, 1979.

This map manual contains 865 place names that are coded to slides that can be purchased through the Pictoral Archive, Jerusalem. The maps reveal a painstaking devotion to detail. The index of main names is also cross-indexed to the *Encyclopedia of Archaeological Excavations in the Holy Land,* edited by M. Avi-Yonah and E. Stern. The serious Bible student will find that this work contains a veritable goldmine of information. 220.9.ST9M

## BIBLE GEOGRAPHY

**\*Aharoni, Yohanan.** *The Land of the Bible: A Historical Geography.* Revised and enlarged edition. Translated and edited by A. F. Rainey. Philadelphia: Westminster Press, 1979.

This long-awaited revision will remain the authoritative work in this area of biblical research for many years to come. It deserves careful and repeated reading. 220.91.AH1 1979

**Avi-Yonah, Michael.** *Jerusalem the Holy.* New York: Schocken Books, 1976.

This pictorial survey of Jerusalem consists of a brief historic introduction, a chronology, and photographs (thirty of which are in color) depicting the city as the center of three monotheistic faiths. 956.94′4.AV5

**\*Baly, Alfred Denis.** *The Geography of the Bible.* New and revised edition. New York: Harper & Row, 1974.

A revision of an outstanding work on biblical geography. Includes not only matters of physical geography, but geological formations, climatology, topography, and flora and fauna as well. 220.91.B34 1974

**\*Baxter, Batsell Barrett, and Harold Hazelip.** *A Devotional Guide to Biblical Lands.* Grand Rapids: Baker Book House, 1979.

One of the best guide books ever produced. 913.3.B33

**Bernstein, Burton.** *Sinai: The Great and Terrible Wilderness.* New York: Viking Press, 1979.

Based on personal visits to the isolated, yet strategic, peninsula, Bernstein recreates Israel's past and also provides his readers with an understanding of the present. A blending of historical, social, and cultural facts into a single narrative. Makes interesting reading. 953′.1.B45

**Bruce, Frederick Fyvie.** *Abraham and David: Places They Knew.* Nashville: Thomas Nelson Publishers, 1984.

Drawing on information gleaned from the OT, early church histories, and archaeological findings, Bruce follows Abraham's journey from Ur to his final resting place in the cave of Machpelah. He also traces David's rise from his birth in Bethlehem through his exile in the wilderness of Judah to his enthronement and rule over all Israel. The text is enhanced with numerous color photographs, along with maps, diagrams, and detailed illustrations. The reading of this book will give readers a rich historical perspective and also provide relevant political, agricultural, and military information. 221.91.B83

**deVaux, Roland.** *The Bible and the Ancient Near East.* Translated by Damain McHugh. Garden City, N.Y.: Doubleday and Co., 1971.

A selection of fifteen articles translated from the author's *Bible et Orient.* 221.91.D49B

**Finegan, Jack.** *Archaeological History of the Ancient Middle East.* Boulder, Colo.: Westview Press, 1979.

An indispensable, connected account of events that transpired around the

Mediterranean and throughout the Fertile Crescent from c. 10,000 B.C. to 330 B.C. Illustrated. An essential reference work. 913.031.M46.F49

**Frank, Harry Thomas.** *Discovering the Biblical World.* Maplewood, N.J.: Hammond Corporation, 1977.

Outlines the physical geography of and archaeological discoveries in Bible lands. Well illustrated. 220.91.F85

**\*Harrison, Roland Kenneth, ed.** *Major Cities of the Biblical World.* Nashville: Thomas Nelson Publishers, 1985.

In clear, nontechnical language, twenty-seven Bible scholars discuss thirty-three major cities that flourished in the biblical world. They take well-known sites such as Jerusalem and Jericho, as well as less familiar ones such as Ebla, Ugarit, and Mari, and reconstruct the everyday life of their citizens. Each essay highlights the most significant features of the city, provides readers with its location and geography and the customs and cultural traditions of its inhabitants. Archaeological information is used to further reinforce the point(s) being made. Excellent. 220.91.H24M

**Hoade, Eugene.** *Guide to the Holy Land.* 4th ed. Jerusalem: Franciscan Press, 1971.

An impressive and valuable travel guide. 913.3.H65 1971

**Jones, Clifford M.** *New Testament Illustrations.* The Cambridge Bible Commentary. Cambridge: At the University Press, 1966.

A useful, pictographic record designed to add a new dimension to NT study. 225.91.J71

**Levenson, Jon D.** *Sinai and Zion: An Entry into the Jewish Bible.* Minneapolis: Winston Press, 1985.

Uses the historical-critical method of interpretation to develop an OT theology. Employs as his foci the giving of the law on Mt. Sinai and the establishment of the Holy City on Mt. Zion as the major issues around which may be clustered all of OT history. 221.91.L57

**Pearlman, Moshe,** and **Yaacov Yannai.** *Historical Sites in the Holy Land.* Revised and enlarged edition. Valley Forge, Pa.: Judson Press, 1985.

This book covers all the important sites in Israel. It describes the salient features that visitors to the Holy Land may wish to know about. It introduces the reader to the drama and excitement of the incidents recorded in the Bible with graphic descriptions of people, places, and events. 220.91.P31 1985

**\*Ramsay, William Mitchell.** *The Historical Geography of Asia Minor.* New York: Cooper Square Publishers, 1972.

This outstanding classic has long been out-of-print. It describes the composition of the peoples of ancient Asia Minor, the geographic divisions of the land, and the bishoprics established as Christianity took root. Dated but still valuable. 225.91.R14 1972

**\*Reader's Digest Association.** *Great People of the Bible and How They Lived.* Pleasantville, N.Y.: Reader's Digest Association, 1974.

A beautifully illustrated, comprehensive, and generally reliable portrayal of the customs and culture of Palestine from Abraham to the apostle Paul. 220.91.R22

**Teringo, J. Robert.** *The Land and People Jesus Knew: A Visual Tour of First-Century Palestine.* Minneapolis: Bethany House Publishers, 1985.

Beautifully illustrated with black-and-white drawings, and with each illustration accompanied by an annotation that accurately describes the practice of those who lived in Bible times, this work makes available to users a visual and written analysis of manners and customs of the Jews to A.D. 70 that is remarkable for its reliability. 225.91.T27

**Vilnay, Zev.** *The Guide to Israel.* Cleveland: World Publishing Co., 1971.

Similar in scope to Hoade. Contains modern maps and descriptions, is revised annually, has a strong archaeological emphasis, and is exceptionally helpful. 913.3.V71.

**Vos, Howard Frederick.** *An Introduction to Bible Geography.* Chicago: Moody Press, 1983.

This is a revised edition of the 1973 book entitled *Beginnings in Bible Geography.* A popular presentation that admirably lends itself to use by discussion groups. 220.91.V92

***Wiseman, Donald John, ed.** *Peoples of Old Testament Times.* Oxford: Clarendon Press, 1973.

A brilliant series of essays dealing with those nations in the ancient Near East whose borders or activities impinged on God's chosen people. Each chapter contains a full discussion of the history, religion, customs, and literature of the race under consideration. 221.91.W75

## BIBLE BIOGRAPHY

**Deen, Edith.** *All the Bible's Men of Hope.* Garden City, N.Y.: Doubleday and Co., 1974.

A popularly written work that appropriately draws attention to the hope that motivated those whose lives are forever enshrined in Holy Writ. Shows that this belief (or hope) was not an abstraction, but a powerful, internal dynamic. 220.92.D36

**Hendricks, Jeanne W.** *A Woman for All Seasons.* Nashville: Thomas Nelson Publishers, 1977.

Perceptive studies of nine prominent women of Scripture. After a careful analysis of each personality, the writer applies principles to the needs of wives, mothers, and widows today. 220.92.H38W

**Lutzer, Erwin Wesley.** *When a Good Man Falls.* Wheaton, Ill.: Victor Books, 1985.

Deals with backsliding/self-will/disobedience and clothes ancient biblical accounts of failure in modern garb. These timely studies are ideal for adult discussion groups. 220.92.L97

**Sanders, John Oswald.** *Just Like Us: 21 Character Studies from the Bible.* Chicago: Moody Press, 1985.

Previously published under the title *People Just Like Us,* this edition uses the text of the NASB. The twenty chapters that make up this book reveal the universality of human nature and the relevance of the Word to our lives. 220.92.SA5J 1985

**Vander Velde, Frances.** *Women of the Bible.* Grand Rapids: Kregel Publications, 1983.

First published in 1957 under the title *She Shall Be Called Woman,* this volume has stood the test of time. It contains thirty-one character studies and should be consulted when teaching or preaching on women of the Bible. 220.92.V26 1983

**Wright, J. Stafford.** *Revell's Dictionary of Bible People.* Old Tappan, N.J.: Fleming H. Revell Co., 1978.

Covers Bible personalities from Aaron to Zophar. Each entry is accompanied by the meaning of the name (where known) and a brief summary of the biblical data about the person. This is a handy reference volume. 220.92.W93

OLD TESTAMENT

**Beegle, Dewey M.** *Moses, the Servant of Yahweh.* Grand Rapids: Wm. B. Eerdmans Publishing Co., 1972.

†Combines a study of Moses' personal-

ity with a running commentary on Exodus and occasional excursions into parallel material in the Pentateuch. Of importance for the insights it contains. Manifests a strong reliance on the works of W. F. Albright. The main strength of Beegle's work is his ability to relate the customs and culture of the ancient Near East to his biography of Moses. 221.92.M85.B39

**\*Blaikie, William Garden.** *David, King of Israel: The Divine Plan and Lessons of His Life.* Minneapolis: Klock & Klock Christian Publishers, 1981.

Buried in oblivion for more than a century, this handling of the life of Israel's greatest king abounds with subtle yet suggestive insights into his character. Spurgeon commented, "Dr. Blaikie is a good writer. This 'Life of David' has supplied a great lack." Recommended. 221.92.D28.B57 1981

\*————. *Heroes of Israel.* Minneapolis: Klock & Klock Christian Publishers, 1981.

In a day when many of our leaders are lamenting the passing of heroes from our national life as well as our literature, it is refreshing to take up a work like this one and remind ourselves of those men of God whose words and deeds are a part of our biblical heritage. A valuable acquisition. 221.92.B57 1981

**Briscoe, D. Stuart.** *A Heart for God.* Nashville: Thomas Nelson Publishers, 1984.

Devotional messages covering important aspects of David's life. 22.92.D28.B77

**Carlisle, Thomas John.** *Eve and After: Old Testament Women in Portrait.* Grand Rapids: Wm. B. Eerdmans Publishing Co., 1984.

"Imagination, wit, and love have inspired Carlisle to offer perceptive readings of women in ancient Israel. His gift challenges even as it entertains us"

(Phyllis Trible). 221.92.C19

**Daiches, David.** *Moses: The Man and His Vision.* New York: Praeger Publications, 1975.

†A fresh appraisal of the story of Moses based on the findings of archaeology, anthropology, history, and linguistics. Well illustrated. 221.92.M85.D11

**\*Edersheim, Alfred.** *Practical Truths from Elisha.* Grand Rapids: Kregel Publications, 1982.

Originally published under the title *Elisha the Prophet* (1882), this work differs from the material on Elisha in the author's famous *Bible History.* As with all the works by Edersheim, this book is worthy of diligent reading. Recommended. 221.92.EL4.ED2 1982

**Flynn, Leslie Bruce.** *Joseph: God's Man in Egypt.* Wheaton, Ill.: Victor Books, 1979.

Brief, inspirational messages. Designed for adult discussion groups. 221.92.J77.F67

**Getz, Gene A.** *Abraham: Trials and Triumphs.* Glendale, Calif.: Regal Books, 1976.

These perceptive studies show the greatness and the humanness of the patriarch and our kinship with him in the trials and triumphs of faith. Designed for group discussion. Recommended. 221.92.AB8.G33

————. *Joseph: From Prison to Palace.* Ventura, Calif.: Regal Books, 1983.

Condenses Joseph's life into twelve succinct chapters and succeeds in conveying the essence of this patriarch's life. 221.92.J77.G33

**Gunn, David M.** *The Story of King David: Genre and Interpretation.* Sheffield, England: University of Sheffield Press, 1978.

This well-researched and comprehensively indexed assessment of David's service as king of Israel provides new and important insights into the history of the times, the literary mold in which the narrative of his life is set, and the private and political milieu in which he lived and moved. 221.92.D28.G95

**\*Hamilton, James.** *Moses, the Man of God.* Minneapolis: Klock & Klock Christian Publishers, 1984.

One of the finest reconstructions of the life of Moses ever written. Shows his greatness and reveals his weaknesses. Spurgeon wrote of this work, "Beautiful as a poem, like everything which fell from Dr. Hamilton's pen. It would be impossible to study it without profit." Recommended. 221.92.M85.H18 1984

**Keller, Weldon Philip.** *David: The Time of Saul's Tyranny.* Waco, Tex.: Word Books, 1985.

Keller is a man of many interests, with abilities equal to each of his avocations. His character studies are well-drawn. This one of David's early life is clear and perceptive. Preachers will find that he has much to offer by way of illustration and application. 221.92.D28.K28

**\*Kirk, Thomas.** *The Life of Joseph.* Minneapolis: Klock & Klock Christian Publishers, 1985.

These studies exemplify the art of Bible character preaching. Kirk combines warmth with a wealth of background information, and the result is a work that preachers will want to refer to again and again. Recommended. 221.92.J77.K63 1985

**\*Krummacher, Frederich Wilhelm.** *Elisha: A Prophet for Our Times.* Translated by R. F. Walter. Grand Rapids: Baker Book House, 1976.

First published in 1837, this important biblical biography emphasizes the uniqueness of Elisha's ministry and its relevance to believers today. 221.92.EL4.K94 1976

**\*_____.** *The Last Days of Elisha.* Grand Rapids: Baker Book House, 1981.

First published in the U.S in 1854, this pleasing biographical sketch ties in the life and times of Elisha with the notable personalities whose activities intersected with his own. Ideal as sermon-starters. 221.92.EL4.K94 1981

**\*MacDuff, John Ross.** *Elijah, the Prophet of Fire.* Minneapolis: Klock & Klock Christian Publishers, 1982.

First published in 1861, this work has long been a favorite among Bible students. With deft descriptions and brilliant flashes of insight into human personality, MacDuff recreates the life and times of the herdsman from Gilead. A delightful book. 221.92.EL4.M14 1982

**Pritchard, James Bennett, ed.** *Solomon and Sheba.* London: Phaidon Art Books, 1974.

A scholarly assessment of the various aspects of Sheba's visit to Solomon. Sifts the reality from the legends and provides informative archaeological material substantiating the developments of various traditions. 221.92.SO4.P93

**Sanford, John A.** *King Saul, the Tragic Hero: A Study in Individuation.* New York: Paulist Press, 1985.

To appreciate fully Sanford's treatment of the Old Testament story of Saul from the point of view of individuation, readers need some background in both biblical scholarship and psychology. Sanford supplies both. The first chapter presents the historical situation in Israel at the time of Saul and the findings of biblical scholarship about the story. Sanford then compares three men as he develops his psychological portrait of Saul: Saul, Samuel, and David. His analysis of the personalities of Samuel and David is faulty. His explanation of Saul, however, is helpful. 221.92.SA8.S5

**\*Stedman, Ray C.** *Man of Faith: Learning from the Life of Abraham.* Portland, Oreg.: Multnomah Press, 1985.

Amid the plethora of books on the life

of Abraham, this work must stand as one of the best for general use. In fact, it may well take the place of F. B. Meyer's treatment. Laypeople should buy this work and read it carefully. Every page gives evidence of the author's careful study and personal warmth. It meets a need. 221.92.AB8.ST3

**Tatford, Frederick Albert.** *Prophet from the Euphrates—Balaam and His Parables.* Eastbourne, Sussex, England: Prophetic Witness Publishing House, 1973.

A perceptive work that combines an exposition of Balaam's oracles with an application to the needs of people today. 221.92.B18.T18

\*————. *The Sons of Jacob: The Blessings of the Tribes of Israel.* Eastbourne, Sussex, England: Prophetic Witness Publishing House, 1976.

This exposition of Genesis 49 and Deuteronomy 33 ably blends prophetic and personal characteristics into a work that opens up God's Word to the reader. A rewarding study. 221.92.T18

**Van Seters, John.** *Abraham in History and Tradition.* New Haven, Conn.: Yale University Press, 1975.

†A work marked by critical precision and provocative insights into the patriarchal period. Van Seters also challenges source-critics and form-critics, but his evaluation of the literary context of the Abrahamic tradition needs to be carefully weighed by those engaged in the study of this period of history. 221.92.AB8.V26

**Weisfeld, Israel H.** *David the King.* New York: Block Publishing Co., 1983.

Weisfeld, a prolific writer, provides a vivid description of David as viewed in rabbinic, postrabbinic, Hasidic, Hebrew, and modern literature. Includes a collection of poems that preachers will find helpful. 221.92.D28.W43

**Wiesel, Elie.** *Five Biblical Portraits.*

Notre Dame, Ind.: University of Notre Dame Press, 1981.

Uses his extensive knowledge of Talmudic and Hasidic sources to illumine the lives of Joshua, Saul, Elijah, Jeremiah, and Jonah. Often perceptive, sometimes psychoanalytic, yet historically insightful. 221.92.W63

**Zeligs, Dorothy F.** *Psychoanalysis and the Bible: A Study in Depth of Seven Leaders.* New York: Bloch Publishing Co., 1974.

†An important, though strongly Freudian approach to the lives of Abraham, Jacob, Joseph, Samuel, Saul, David, and Solomon. 221.92.Z3

NEW TESTAMENT

**Barber, Cyril John.** *Vital Encounter: First Century Encounters with Jesus Christ and Their Relevance for Us Today.* San Bernardino, Calif.: Here's Life Publishers, 1979.

Draws principles from the lives of those who came into contact with Christ during His earthly ministry and applies these truths to the lives of present-day believers. Each chapter concludes with open-ended questions to promote discussion. 225.92.B23 1979

**Barclay, William.** *Ambassador for Christ: The Life and Teaching of the Apostle Paul.* Valley Forge, Pa.: Judson Press, 1974.

First published in 1951, this book surveys the travels and ministry of the apostle Paul. 225.92.P28.B23

**Brownrigg, Ronald.** *The Twelve Apostles.* New York: Macmillan Co., 1974.

A well-written but shallow portrayal of the lives and legends of the apostles. Combines the biblical records with historical interpretations and artist's impressions. 225.92.B82

**\*Bruce, Frederick Fyvie.** *Paul: Apostle of the Heart Set Free.* Grand Rapids: Wm.

B. Eerdmans Publishing Co., 1977.

In this work readers are treated to the fruits of a lifetime of study and research. Bruce ably combines history, archaeology, and biography with the biblical text and provides Bible students with a work to which they will repeatedly turn. 225.92.P28.B83

―――. *The Pauline Circle*. Grand Rapids: Wm. B. Eerdmans Publishing Co., 1984.

Surveys the biblical evidence for the stories of those who gathered about the apostle Paul, presents their contribution to the progress of the gospel in light of the background of the first century, and examines the relationships that underlie the NT references. The result is a fascinating look at the men and women who surrounded Paul and influenced the NT church. 225.92.B83C

―――. *Peter, Stephen, James, and John: Studies in Early Non-Pauline Christianity*. Grand Rapids: Wm. B. Eerdmans Publishing Co., 1979.

Assesses the leadership of the men at the helm of affairs, and traces the steps in their rejection of Judaism. 225.92.B83

**Cook, Madison Dale.** *Biographical Concordance of the New Testament*. Neptune, N.J.: Loizeaux Brothers, 1985.

This study seeks to provide a biographical concordance that differs from other similar works. Cook has made available the kind of book that pastors will find most helpful. Recommended. 225.92′2.C77

***Farrar, Frederic William.** *The Life and Work of St. Paul*. 2 vols. Minneapolis: Klock & Klock Christian Publishers, 1981.

Long out of print, these volumes constitute a priceless asset to the preacher who possesses and uses them aright. Includes valuable excurses on special topics ranging from the "man of sin" to

traditional accounts of Paul's personal appearance. 225.92.F24 1981

**Flynn, Leslie Bruce.** *The Twelve*. Wheaton, Ill.: Victor Books, 1982.

Colorful vignettes ably introducing the reader to those whom Christ chose to carry the message of life to the uttermost parts of the earth. Excellent for group discussion. 225.92.AP4.F67

**Grant, Michael.** *Herod the Great*. New York: American Heritage Press, 1971.

A fascinating account of the crafty politician who ruled Judea at the time of Christ's birth. Disappointing in that the writer considers the biblical account of Herod's massacre of the children in Bethlehem a myth. Enhanced by beautiful photographs. 225.92.H43G

―――. *Saint Paul*. New York: Charles Scribner's Sons, 1976.

This handsomely produced, well-illustrated book combines Paul's Grecian, Roman, and Jewish heritages, and assesses the factors that contributed to the success of his ministry. 225.92.P28.G76

**Grassi, Joseph A.** *The Secret of Paul the Apostle*. Maryknoll, N.Y.: Orbis Books, 1978.

Follows the sequence of events that shaped the apostle Paul and gave dynamic impetus and direction to his life. Roman Catholic. 225.92.P28.G76

**Griffith, Arthur Leonard.** *Gospel Characters: The Personalities Around Jesus*. Grand Rapids: Wm. B. Eerdmans Publishing Co., 1976.

Enlightening studies of Bible personalities who prepared the way for Christ, followed Him, were helped by Him, opposed Him, or watched Him die. 225.92.G87 1976

**Grollenberg, Lucas Hendricus.** *Paul*. Translated by J. Bowden. Philadelphia: Westminster Press, 1979.

A brief, scholarly sketch of the apostle's life, ministry, and letters. Insightful. Roman Catholic. 225.92.P28.G89

**\*Hiebert, David Edmond.** *Personalities Around Paul.* Chicago: Moody Press, 1973.

A superb treatment of the men and women who labored with the apostle Paul. Helpful to any preacher desiring to expound the Acts or the Pauline epistles. Excellent. 225.92.H53

**Jewett, Robert.** *A Chronology of Paul's Life.* Philadelphia: Fortress Press, 1979.

†A scholarly assessment of the sources of chronology together with the fixed and discernible dates of Paul's life and ministry. Offers some new ideas and pinpoints with great detail the apostle's travel schedules and missionary activities. 225.92.P28.J55

**\*Jones, John Daniel.** *The Apostles of Christ.* Minneapolis: Klock & Klock Christian Publishers, 1982.

First published in 1904 under the title *The Glorious Company of the Apostles,* these messages are deserving of repeated study, for they show the way in which Christ discipled the twelve. 225'92.AP4.J71 1982

**\*MacDuff, John Ross.** *The Footsteps of St. Peter: Being the Life and Times of the Apostle.* Minneapolis: Klock & Klock Christian Publishers, 1982.

Often overshadowed by writings on the life and accomplishments of the apostle Paul, Peter is also worthy of renewed attention. This study of his conversion and ministry is one of the best and deserves a place in every preacher's library. Recommended. 225.92.P44.M14

**\*Pollock, John.** *The Apostle: A Life of Paul.* Wheaton, Ill.: Victor Books, 1985.

Well written. This book deals adequately with Paul's life and ministry. Pollock's descriptions of the places Paul visited adds graphic color to the biblical text. This is a work that can be read with real profit. 225.92.P28.P76

**Sanders, John Oswald.** *Paul the Leader.* Colorado Springs, Colo.: NavPress, 1984.

This sequel to *Spiritual Leadership* draws from the life of Paul those principles of leadership that, when properly understood and made a part of each Christian's personality, will have the effect of transforming his/her work for the Lord. 225.92.P28.SA5

**\*Turner, George Allen.** *Paul: Apostle for Today.* Wheaton, Ill.: Tyndale House Publishers, 1981.

Ably depicts the life and work of the apostle against the background of his Jewish heritage and the Greco-Roman milieu of the first century A.D. 225.92.P28.T85

## BIBLE ARCHAEOLOGY

**\*Aharoni, Yohanan.** *The Archaeology of the Land of Israel.* Edited by M. Aharoni. Translated by A. F. Rainey. Philadelphia: Westminster Press, 1982.

The summation of years of work in Israel. Provides the student as well as the specialist with the author's final decisions on the location of different cities of antiquity and his judgments regarding the significance of the various findings. Excellent. 220.93.AH1 1982 (Alt. DDC. 933)

**Avigad, Nahman.** *Discovering Jerusalem.* Nashville: Thomas Nelson Publishers, 1980.

A fascinating, well-illustrated account of the history of Jerusalem unearthed by the archaeologist's spade. The pictures—black and white as well as color—and charts lead the reader to a new appreciation of the incidents recorded in the Bible. The text correlates the archaeological findings with the biblical narrative. An excellent work. 220.93.AV5D

**Baez-Camargo, Gonzolo.** *Archaeological Commentary on the Bible.* Garden City, N.Y.: Doubleday and Co., 1984.

As a succinct and valuable summary of archaeological discoveries to date, this volume records findings that have helped scholars understand Bible times and customs with greater accuracy. Documents from OT and NT times are used to give an otherwise unattainable clarity to the customs and thought of people, and several otherwise obscure passages are illumined by the information that the author has made available. 220.93.B14

**\*Blaiklock, Edward Musgrave,** and **R. K. Harrison, eds.** *The New International Dictionary of Biblical Archaeology.* Grand Rapids: Zondervan Publishing House, 1983.

"This very useful and convenient tool will be of immense help to the general reader who wishes to become acquainted with the major persons, places, and products of the biblical and ancient Near Eastern world. Even the scholar will find occasional articles to which he will turn again and again for easy reference. A fine set of maps with complete index to them as well as a good number of full color and black-and-white illustrations add to the value of the publication" *(Bibliotheca Sacra).* 220.93.N42B

**Daniels, Steve,** and **Nicholas David.** *The Archaeology Workbook.* Philadelphia: University of Pennsylvania Press, 1982.

A handy resource showing the neophyte how complex archaeological investigation really is. Explains how faulty conclusions may be drawn from the evidence uncovered. 930.1.D22

**Finegan, Jack.** *Discovering Israel: An Archaeological Guide to the Holy Land.* Grand Rapids: Wm. B. Eerdmans Publishing Co., 1981.

Provides a concise, factually-based account of Palestinian history and the people who have occupied the Holy Land for nearly 4,000 years. 956.94.F49

**Hawkes, Jacquetta, ed.** *Atlas of Ancient Archaeology.* New York: McGraw-Hill Book Co., 1974.

Encompasses the history, geography, and prehistoric background of early civilizations, many of which were directly connected with the unfolding of events recorded in the Bible. 912.1'91.H31

**Kenyon, Kathleen Mary.** *Archaeology in the Holy Land.* 5th ed. Nashville: Thomas Nelson Publishers, 1985.

Designed as a reference for both scholars and neophytes in biblical archaeology, this work outlines the major archaeological sites, what was discovered, and how the different finds have contributed to our knowledge of the Bible and its peoples. Included is a summary of Miss Kenyon's own excavations of Jerusalem between 1961-1967 and their relevance to our understanding of the fall of the Hebrew kingdoms. This edition also traces the development of pre-Israelite hunters and food-gatherers to city-dwellers and the rise of the civilization of the Canaanites and Amorites. 220.93.K42 1985

**\*_____.** *Digging Up Jerusalem.* New York: Praeger Publishers, 1974.

An important work on the history of the Holy City by a renowned archaeologist who, during 1961-1967, excavated portions of Jerusalem. 220.93.J47.K42 (Alt. DDC 913.33)

**\*Kitchen, Kenneth Anderson.** *The Bible in Its World: The Bible and Archaeology Today.* Downers Grove, Ill.: InterVarsity Press, 1978.

A fascinating portrayal of the significance of recent archaeological discoveries for the study of the Bible. Up-to-date. A most important volume. 220.93.K64

**Lawlor, John Irving.** *The Nabataeans in Historical Perspective.* Grand Rapids: Baker Book House, 1974.

A unique volume making available a vast amount of material on these NT inhabitants of OT Edom. 220.93.N11.L42

**\*Millard, Alan Ralph.** *Treasures From Bible Times.* Belleville, Mich.: Lion Publishing Corporation, 1985.

Beautifully illustrated and lavishly produced, this work surveys the whole of Bible history and emphasizes the importance of archaeology in understanding and applying the text. Recommended. 220.93.M61

**Moorey, Roger.** *Excavation in Palestine.* Cities of the Biblical World. Guildford, Surrey, England: Lutterworth Press, 1981.

A delightful introduction to the history of archaeological research in Palestine. Highlights some of the problems and acquaints the interested reader with the benefits of such investigation. 220.93.M78

**\*Thompson, John Arthur.** *The Bible and Archaeology.* 3d ed. rev. Grand Rapids: Wm. B. Eerdmans Publishing Co., 1982.

Designed primarily for students but accessible to general readers as well. This work offers a concise, up-to-date summary of archaeological information as it pertains to the Bible. For this newest edition, Thompson has revised nearly every chapter to incorporate information from the most recent findings. He has also added a new chapter entitled "Cities of Judah and Israel in the Days of the Kings," which provides a picture of everyday life in ancient Israel and examines architecture, places of worship, and art. 220.93.T37 1982

**Yadin, Yigael.** *Hazor: The Rediscovery of a Great Citadel of the Bible.* New York: Random House, 1975.

Based on the author's archaeological digs from 1955 to 1958, this book lays bare more than twenty strata of the city covering three thousand years of occupation. Confirms as well as illumines much of the biblical record. 220.93.Y1

———, ed. *Jerusalem Revealed: Archaeology in the Holy City, 1968-1974.* New Haven, Conn.: Yale University Press, 1976.

Recent archaeological excavations (particularly within the Turkish walls) have revealed more of the city's past than have all the others in the past one hundred years. This well-illustrated volume graphically depicts Jerusalem's history. 956.94'4.Y1

**Yamauchi, Edwin M.** *Men, Methods, and Materials in Biblical Archaeology.* Grand Rapids: Baker Book House, 1972.

Written in nontechnical style, this book ably traces the archaeology of Bible lands and includes a consideration of tomb robbers and scientists, royal palaces and sacred sights, the methodology employed by archaeologists, the greatest discoveries that have been made to date, and detailed consideration of the importance of the Dead Sea Scrolls. 220.93.Y1

OLD TESTAMENT

**Jones, Edgar.** *Discoveries and Documents: An Introduction to the Archaeology of the Old Testament.* London: Epworth Press, 1976.

The subtitle is misleading. This book contains a selection of ancient Near Eastern texts relevant to OT study. Similar to Thomas's *Documents from Old Testament Times,* but more popular and of an introductory nature. 221.93.J71

**Kenyon, Kathleen Mary.** *Royal Cities of the Old Testament.* London: Barrie and Jenkins, 1971.

†This competent archaeological report is comprehensive, well illustrated, and surveys the ancient Jebusite city, as well as Jerusalem during the united and divided kingdom periods, Megiddo,

Hazor, Gezer, and Samaria. 221.93.K42

**Lance, Hubert Darrell.** *The Old Testament and the Archaeologist.* Philadelphia: Fortress Press, 1981.

An introduction to the science of archaeology with a concise statement of the values of such investigation to the study of the OT. Of particular importance is the chapter on the literary output of professional archaeologists and their use by nonprofessionals. 221.93.L22

**Matthiae, Paolo.** *Ebla: An Empire Rediscovered.* Translated by C. Holme. Garden City, N.Y.: Doubleday and Co., 1981.

The eyes of the world have focused on Ebla in N. Syria, and biblical scholars as well as interested laypeople have wondered what these buried archives will yield. Here is one of the first popular books describing how the city was found and what has been uncovered thus far. 939.4.M43

**\*Mazar, Benjamin.** *The Mountain of the Lord.* Garden City, N.Y.: Doubleday and Co., 1975.

Building on archaeological excavations begun in the mid-nineteenth century, Mazar carefully unfolds the saga of Jerusalem and its Temple. In doing so, he provides his readers with an immensely rich and revealing résumé of the history of the Holy City. The text is lavishly illustrated with colored and black-and-white pictures, diagrams, and maps. Indispensable. 956.94′4.M45

**Paul, Shalom M.,** and **William G. Dever, eds.** *Biblical Archaeology.* New York: Quadrangle Books, 1975.

This survey differs from the traditional approach to archaeology in that it is divided according to the type of find. A most useful reference work. 221.93.P28

**Pettinato, Giovanni.** *The Archives of Ebla: An Empire Inscribed in Clay.* Garden City, N.Y.: Doubleday and Co., 1981.

Ebla has been a source of continual excitement and controversy since its discovery. The clay tablets—baked and preserved when the royal palace was destroyed by fire—reveal that Ebla was not the nomadic backwater it was assumed to be, but rather a powerful commercial and cultural link between Mesopotamia and Egypt in the third millennium B.C. Its language, previously unknown and now called Eblaite, is recognized by some as the oldest known Semitic language and is possibly related to biblical Hebrew. Worldwide attention has been focused on the implications of the biblical names and references on the tablets, some of which are found nowhere else except in the Old Testament. 939′.4.P45

**Pritchard, James B., ed.** *The Ancient Near East.* Vol. 2, *A New Anthology of Texts and Pictures.* Princeton, N.J.: Princeton University Press, 1976.

This new volume makes available some of the most important recent discoveries of source material. 221.93.P93T v.2

**Tigay, Jeffrey H.** *The Evolution of the Gilgamesh Epic.* Philadelphia: University of Pennsylvania Press, 1982.

A scholarly study of the history of one of the oldest sagas relating to the origin of the cosmos and the culture of the ancient Near East. Well researched. 892.1.T44

**Yamauchi, Edwin M.** *The Stones and the Scriptures.* Philadelphia: J. P. Lippincott Co., 1972.

A summary of archaeological evidence and its relationship to OT and NT studies. Up to date and informative. 221.93.Y1

NEW TESTAMENT

**\*Blaiklock, Edward Musgrave.** *The Archaeology of the New Testament.* Nashville: Thomas Nelson Publishers, 1984.

Though stating on the cover that this work is revised and updated, the text does not say how extensively or in what way the author revised it prior to his death. The book itself does treat the world of the NT from Christ's parables to the church's persecution and from a Roman emperor's stunning admission of our Lord's empty tomb to an irate father's letter to his prodigal son. The value of this book lies in Blaiklock's interpretation of first-century Christianity in terms of everyday realities. 225.93.B56 1984

**\*Finegan, Jack.** *The Archaeology of the New Testament: The Mediterranean World of the Early Christian Apostles.* Boulder, Colo.: Westview Press, 1981.

The author has endeared himself to a wide following through his other writings, *The Archaeology of the New Testament: The Life of Jesus and the Beginning of the Early Church* and *Archaeological History of the Ancient Middle East.* The latter work describes the river valleys of the Tigris, the Euphrates, and the Nile, and the adjacent lands from Asia Minor in the west to the Iranian plateau in the east, from Urartu in the north to Nubia in the south, and Syria/Palestine, all of which have been rich sources of archaeological information. Most of the materials that have survived are associated with the activities of rulers, priests, scribes, and artists. As a result, political history and religious themes predominate, although there are also intriguing glimpses of the day-to-day life of the common people. This work builds on a carefully established apostolic chronology. Then, intertwined with the narrative of Acts, Finegan describes the milieu of the first century A.D., Paul's travels, the people he encountered, and the reception given his ministry. Well illustrated with photographs, maps, and diagrams, this work will long stand as one of the best contributions ever made on the subject. 225.93.F49M

**\*Yamauchi, Edwin M.** *The Archaeology of New Testament Cities in Western Asia Minor.* Grand Rapids: Baker Book House, 1980.

Popularly written, this handy volume seeks to anchor a preacher's messages in the NT documents and the history of the literature of the Graeco-Roman world. Readers will find Yamauchi's discussion of the churches of Revelation 2-3 insightful and will also have much to learn from his handling of the other important commercial centers. An excellent work. 225.93.Y1

## BIBLE HISTORY

**Avi-Yonah, Michael.** *The Jews Under Roman and Byzantine Rule.* New York: Schocken Books, 1984.

A comprehensive, accurate political history of Palestine from the Bar Kokhba War to the Arab Conquest. Excellent. 956.94.AV5

**Burney, Charles.** *The Ancient Near East.* Ithaca, N.Y.: Cornell University Press, 1977.

A beautifully illustrated portrayal of ancient civilizations from the Neolithic period to the decline of Assyria. Records the facinating saga of mankind's progress and decline. 939.B93

**Cameron, George Glenn.** *History and Early Iran.* New York: Greenwood Press, 1968.

A useful record of Elam, making available to readers a blending of archaeological research with the history of Babylonia, Media, and Persia. Provides a valuable record of those nations often included in the biblical record. 935.C14 1968

**Castel, Francois.** *The History of Israel*

*and Judah in Old Testament Times.* Translated by M. J. O'Connell. New York: Paulist Press, 1985.

†Published in France in 1983, this treatment of OT history deals realistically with the backdrop of the ancient Near East. The author combines biblical, historical, and archaeological information in his presentation. His data is clearly stated and treats the basic issues. Perhaps the most commendable feature of this book is the inclusion of salient information from ancient extrabiblical texts inset conveniently within blocks for easy access. 220.95.C27

**Coleman, William L.** *Today's Handbook of Bible Times and Customs.* Minneapolis: Bethany House Publishers, 1984.

Seeks to supplement other works of a similar nature by leading the reader into a better knowledge of the emotions, mindsets, and life-styles of those who lived in Bible times. For laypeople. Recommended. 220.95.C67

**Crown, Alan David.** *A Bibliography of the Samaritans.* Metuchen, N.J.: Scarecrow Press, 1984.

The Samaritans were an important sect. They have been subjected to scholarly research since the sixteenth century. This has generated a vast body of literature. Writers include historians, biblical scholars, theologians, sociologists, and anthropologists. This bibliography attempts to bring the vast amount of discursive literature under control. Crown makes reference to ancient and medieval sources, ranging from comments on biblical passages to Patristics, information gleaned from German pilgrims to Arab lexicographers. The biblical data is arranged alphabetically and is also indexed by subject. The result is a work that biblical scholars will find well worth consulting. 016.2968.C88

**\*deVaux, Roland.** *The Early History of Israel.* Translated by D. Smith. Philadelphia: Westminster Press, 1978.

†The author, a Roman Catholic priest who spent the greater portion of his life in Palestine, was noted for his meticulous scholarship. This work, published posthumously, contains a mine of valuable material that students of the OT will enjoy for years to come. 220.95.D49 1978

**Ellison, Henry Leopold.** *From Babylon to Bethlehem: The People of God from the Exile to the Messiah.* Atlanta: John Knox Press, 1979.

First published in England in 1976, this important monograph treats the events of the Jews from the Babylonian Captivity, through the intertestamental period, to the coming of Christ. An excellent treatment of the ministries of Nehemiah and Ezra further enhances the usefulness of the brief book. Genealogical tables are included. 933.EL5

**Frank, Harry T.** *Discovering the Biblical World.* New York: Harper & Row, 1975.

Beautifully illustrated, this companion volume to *Bible, Archaeology and Faith* illumines the text and provides a meaningful recounting of archaeological research. 220.95.F84

**Grant, Michael.** *The Ancient Historians.* New York: Charles Scribner's Sons, 1971.

Deals with the techniques, literary goals, and biases of the great classical historians. Important to Bible students because it covers pagan historians who lived in Bible times. 907.2.G76

**Hayes, John H.,** and **J. Maxwell Miller,** eds. *Israelite and Judaean History.* Old Testament Library. Philadelphia: Westminster Press, 1977.

†An exceptional work that approaches the OT not from a historical perspective per se, but rather tackles the whole scope of the OT in terms of its historical development. Though the volume is of value to the evangelical, the contributors fre-

quently intimate their skepticism of the integrity and reliability of the text and the events that took place. 220.95.H32

**Heyerdahl, Thor.** *The Tigris Expedition: In Search of Our Beginnings.* Garden City, N.Y.: Doubleday and Co., 1981.

Traces the trade routes possibly used by merchant sailors during the time of Abraham; visits copper mines used by ancients in Makan; and locates ziggurats where early Sumerians worshiped pagan deities. 913'.035.H51T

**Kramer, Samuel Noah.** *History Begins at Sumer: Thirty-nine Firsts in Man's Recorded History.* Philadelphia: University of Pennsylvania Press, 1981.

Formerly published under the title *From the Tablets of Sumer* (1956), this work documents the rise and development of the Sumerian culture and beliefs. It provides a valuable resource for the study of religious attitudes, domestic relationships, and the like. 935'.01.K86 1981

**\*Lewis, Jack Pearl.** *Historical Backgrounds of Bible History.* Grand Rapids: Baker Book House, 1971.

Presents in readable form the material from archaeological discoveries. Highlights events during the lives of leading biblical personalities and greatly facilitates sermon preparation. 220.95.L58

OLD TESTAMENT

**Aldred, Cyril.** *The Egyptians.* London: Thames and Hudson, 1984.

A beautifully produced, richly illustrated, well-outlined résumé of Egyptology. Chapters set forth the chronology and rediscovery of ancient Egypt and include a journey down the Nile, where the remote past is made to seem compulsively present. Deals with such important sites as Abu Simbel, Thebes, Memphis, and the pyramids. 932.AL2

**Aling, Charles F.** *Egypt and Bible History: From Earliest Times to 1000 B.C.* Grand Rapids: Baker Book House, 1981.

Relates the history of Egypt to the history of God's ancient people, Israel. Provides an excellent synthesis, but with some evident concessions to those who adhere to higher critical theories. 221.95.AL4

**Bartlett, John R.** *Jericho.* Cities of the Biblical World. Guildford, Surrey, England: Lutterworth Press, 1982.

Though adhering to a late date for the conquest of Canaan by the Israelites, this work nevertheless provides a valuable reconstruction of the history of Jericho from the earliest of times to its occupation by the Herodians. 221.95.J47.B28

**Bezemer, M.** *Index to the Biblical References in J. Pedersen's "Israel: Its Life and Culture."* Leiden: E. J. Brill, 1983.

A valuable index, which makes Pedersen's work even more usable. 221.95.P34B

**\*Bright, John.** *A History of Israel.* 3d ed. Philadelphia: Westminster Press, 1981.

†For more than two decades this work has ranked among the finest histories of God's ancient people ever written. It remains an indispensable aid. 221.95.B76 1981

**Budge, Ernest Alfred Thompson Wallis.** *Babylonian Life and History.* New York: AMS Press, 1975.

Reprinted from the second edition, this work ably treats the culture of the ancient Babylonians and correlates their history with the biblical record. 935.02.B85 1975

————. *The Rise and Progress of Assyriology.* New York: AMS Press, 1975.

A companion volume to Budge's work on Babylonia, this treatise makes a significant contribution to the study of these ancient people whose rise to prominence and subsequent decline had such an effect on the history of the Israelites. Reprinted from the 1925 edition. 935.03.B85 1975

**Cogan, Morton.** *Imperialism and Religion: Assyria, Judah and Israel in the Eighth and Seventh Centuries* B.C.E. Missoula, Mont.: Scholar's Press, 1974.

This enlightening volume is based on original source material and focuses on Neo-Assyrian foreign policy. Invaluable in studying the history of Palestine between 750 and 625 B.C. 935.2.C65

**Cook, J. M.** *The Persian Empire.* New York: Schocken Books, 1983.

Fills a need for a modern, reliable treatment of the history of this race whose activities impact much of the OT. The material is recounted in a pleasing manner free from tedious technical data. The result is a rich, rewarding study. 935'.05.C77

**Curtis, Adrian.** *Ugarit (Ras Shamra).* Cities of the Biblical World. Grand Rapids: Wm. B. Eerdmans Publishing Co., 1985.

A very fine résumé of the historical, literary, and archaeological information pertaining to this OT city. Curtis presents the customs and culture of the Canaanites and their religion. In few works can we find such a scholarly synthesis of information. Recommended. 221.95.C94

**\*Davis, John James,** and **John Clement Whitcomb, Jr.** *A History of Israel from Conquest to Exile.* Grand Rapids: Baker Book House, 1980.

A compilation of books covering Israel's history from the period of Joshua and the Judges to the Babylonian Exile. Valuable for its adherence to the text and its correlation of geographical, literary, and political source material with the biblical narrative. Ideal for use with laypeople's discussion groups. 221.95.D29 1980

**Davies, Philip R.** *Qumran.* Cities of the Biblical World. Guildford, Surrey, England: Lutterworth Press, 1982.

Focuses attention on the Essenes of Khirbet Qumran, and chronicles their origin, contribution to the religious beliefs of the Jews, and demise. A stimulating kaleidoscope. 221.95.Q4.D28

**Driver, Geoffrey Rolles,** and **J. C. Miles, eds.** *The Assyrian Laws.* Darnstadt, West Germany: Scientia Verlag Allen, 1975.

Photographically reproduced from the 1935 edition, with supplementary commentary and materials by Driver, this work continues to serve well the needs of OT scholars. 935.AS7 1975

**Grant, Michael.** *The History of Ancient Israel.* New York: Charles Scribner's Sons, 1984.

†"An excellent short history of a land that was and still is the battleground of many great empires. . . . In retelling this epic, Grant raises many provocative issues. His book is sure to send readers back to the [Bible]. Maps, chronology, and index make this a useful biblical reference work" *(Library Journal).* 221.95.G76 (Alt. DDC 933).

**Herm, Gerhard.** *The Phoenicians: The Purple Empire of the Ancient World.* Translated by C. Hillier. London: Victor Gollancz, 1975.

Two thousand years ago Phoenicians exerted immense influence over the Western world. They invented the alphabet, sailed around Africa, and may even have crossed the Atlantic; they engineered a shipping route from the Mediterranean to the Indian Ocean; built temples, fortresses, and docks; and above all constructed ships. As a result of their enterprise, they established a remarkable trade network. Herm has followed the Phoenician trade routes and put together a graphically real picture of their life and work. What emerges from these pages is a cleverly presented mosaic of this ancient people. 933.H42

**\*Hindson, Edward E.** *The Philistines and the Old Testament.* Grand Rapids:

Baker Book House, 1971.

By reconstructing the history, and drawing heavily on recent archaeological excavations, the writer provides an informative picture that highlights the significance of the Philistines in the early history of Israel. 933.H58

*Josephus, Flavius.** The Works of Flavius Josephus. Translated by William Whiston. Grand Rapids: Kregel Publications, 1984.

This classic should be in every Christian's library. Though Josephus was not an accurate historian, what he wrote has survived almost two millennia and serves to elucidate a study of the OT. This is a beautifully produced edition of Josephus's works, and it helps Occidentals come to appreciate the spirit that activates and motivates Orientals in the Middle East. 933.J77 1984

**Kuntz, John Kenneth.** The People of Ancient Israel: An Introduction to Old Testament Literature, History and Thought. New York: Harper & Row, 1974.

†Ably fulfills the intent of the subtitle. Complete with charts, maps, photographs, and bibliography. 221.95.K96

*LaHaye, Tim,** and **John D. Morris.** The Ark on Ararat. Nashville: Thomas Nelson Publishers, 1976.

The release of the motion picture In Search of Noah's Ark awakened new interest in the historicity of the biblical record. This work provides impressive documentation in support of a universal deluge. 221.95.AR4.L13

**Matheson, Sylvia A.** Persia: An Archaeological Guide. 2d ed. London: Faber and Faber, 1979.

Iran has been estimated to have about 250,000 archaeological and historical sites. This book provides a comprehensive introduction to the most important ones. Furnishes incidental, collateral information on places and events highlighted in the OT. 935'.05.M42

**Miller, J. Maxwell.** The Old Testament and the Historian. Philadelphia: Fortress Press, 1976.

Not a history of Israel per se, but an introduction to the historical method: nature of the evidence, methodology, interpretation of data, and problem areas. 221.95.07M61

**Murname, William J.** The Guide to Ancient Egypt. New York: Facts on File Publications, 1983.

A timely, practical, reliable guide for travelers to Egypt. Although modern in the sense that it relates to what travelers are likely to see today, it includes the antiquity of Egypt and the history behind the kings and peoples of dynasties that have long since perished. 916.2.M94

**Payne, David F.** Kingdoms of the Lord: A History of the Hebrew Kingdoms from Saul to the Fall of Jerusalem. Grand Rapids: Wm. B. Eerdmans Publishing Co., 1981.

This history of ancient Israel, from the time of Saul to the Babylonian Exile, is made up of four main parts: (1) the history itself, drawing on the Bible's own record as well as the evidence of archaeology and other ancient documents; (2) a discussion of Israel's enemies, not only foreign, such as the Philistines and Assyrians, but also "the enemy within"; (3) the special role of the prophets in Israel's history; and (4) a section devoted to the faith of Israel as it developed during this major formative period. 221.95.P29

**Pearlman, Moshe.** The Maccabees. New York: Macmillan Co., 1974.

A well-illustrated portrayal of Hebrew history during the intertestamental period. 933.M12.P31

**Schultz, Samuel J.** The Gospel of Moses. New York: Harper & Row, 1974.

A refreshing survey stressing the grace of God in His dealings with Israel in OT times. 221.95.M85.SCH8

**Soggin, J. Alberto.** A History of Ancient

*Israel.* Translated by J. Bowden. Philadelphia: Westminster Press, 1985.

†Subtitled *From the Beginnings to the Bar Kochba Revolt, A.D. 135.* This history draws on tradition, archaeology, and the most recent research to provide a scholarly résumé of Israel's history. 933.SO2

**Stevens, Charles H.** *The Wilderness Journey.* Chicago: Moody Press, 1971.

Discusses the Christian principles illustrated in Israel's wanderings in the desert. 221.95′002.ST4

**Wagner, George.** *Practical Truths from Israel's Wanderings.* Grand Rapids: Kregel Publications, 1982.

A clearly reasoned attempt to draw principles for Christian living from the experiences of the Israelites in the wilderness. First published in 1862. A welcome reprint. 221.95.W12 1982

NEW TESTAMENT

**\*Bruce, Frederick Fyvie.** *New Testament History.* Nelson's Library of Theology. New York: Thomas Nelson and Sons, 1971.

A well-documented, brilliantly written, generally conservative history that covers the entire NT era and will remain a standard for many years. 225.95.B83

**Kee, Howard Clark.** *The New Testament in Context: Sources and Documents.* Englewood Cliffs, N.J.: Prentice-Hall, 1984.

†Treats the outpouring of the Holy Spirit as the fulcrum of NT experience. In light of that, he sees the book of Acts as a pattern for contemporary events and allows for repeated Pentecosts whenever and wherever the occasion requires. 225.95.K24

**Koester, Helmut.** *Introduction to the New Testament.* 2 vols. Philadelphia: Fortress Press, 1982.

Describes the history, culture, and religion of the Hellenistic age as well as the literature of the early Christians. An extensive treatment that serious Bible students will appreciate. 225.95.K81

**Lohse, Eduard.** *The New Testament Environment.* Translated by John E. Steely. Nashville: Abingdon Press, 1976.

†This scholarly treatment succeeds in summarizing the environmental features that are of primary importance in the accurate interpretation of the NT. 225.95.L83

**Malina, Bruce John.** *The New Testament World: Insights from Cultural Anthropology.* Atlanta: John Knox Press, 1981.

Helps the reader explore the literature and sociology of the NT with a view to developing a cultural anthropology. A revealing series of essays. 225.95.M29

**Schurer, Emil.** *The History of the Jewish People in the Age of Jesus Christ.* 3 vols. Revised and edited by Gaza Vermas and Fergus Miller. Edinburgh: T. & T. Clark, 1973-.

This revision of a standard and much-used work is designed to update Schurer's magisterial treatment published between 1890-1891. It is a welcome addition to our knowledge of that period and should be referred to as frequently as its predecessor. 933.SCH8V

**Starr, Chester G.** *The Ancient Romans.* New York: Oxford University Press, 1971.

Includes an analysis of Roman laws and government, human values, and the *Pax Romana.* Enhanced by full color and halftone plates, together with eight maps and six color charts. 937.03.ST2

# 2

# Old Testament

Good commentaries are hard to find, yet they are indispensable to exposition. A good commentary should exhibit the plan, design, and scope of the biblical writer's thought. To produce such a commentary, the commentator must first and foremost be an exegete. Although there are many exegetical commentaries available today, few exhibit a mastery of the theme of the book. They fail to expound the parts in relation to the purpose of the biblical writer. Care, therefore, must be exercised in their selection.

Exegetical commentaries familiarize us with the meaning of words, matters pertaining to syntax and word order, the translation of idiomatic expressions found in the original, and comparative linguistics. Their value should not be ignored. They provide an important first step in the process of expounding and applying the text.

A good commentary must also furnish us with a knowledge of the times in which certain people lived and acquaint us with their customs and culture. History and geography, commerce and industry, all contribute toward an understanding of those we read about in God's inspired Word. In this connection, books on archaeology can be of immense help.

The task of the expository preacher is similar to the role of the commentator. He must possess both exegetical and expository skills. Charles Haddon Spurgeon stated:

> A man to comment well should be able to *read the Bible in the original*. Every minister should aim at a tolerable proficiency both in Hebrew and Greek. These two languages will give him a library at a small expense, an inexhaustible thesaurus, a mine of spiritual wealth. Really, the effort of acquiring a language is not so prodigious that brethren of modest abilities should so frequently shrink from the task.[1]

1. Charles Haddon Spurgeon, *Commenting and Commentaries* (London: Banner of Truth, 1969), p. 47.

The preacher's task is not complete when he has studied the passage in the original language and mastered the theme of the book. Two important additional duties await him: (1) applying the text to the need of his hearers and (2) finding how this portion of God's self-disclosure contributes toward the development of a biblical philosophy of life.

Several impediments stand in the way of accomplishing these goals. First, our experience of life is necessarily limited. Herman H. Horne pointed out that there are some people

> who admire nothing but their own meditations, and who hold all human helps in contempt . . . as tending to found our faith on the opinions of men rather than on the divine oracles: while others, on the contrary, trusting exclusively to the expositions of some favorite commentators, receive as infallible whatever views or opinions they may choose to deliver, as *their* expositions of the Bible.[2]

The shallowness and superficiality of such thinking soon becomes evident. We need to rely on the enlightening ministry of the Holy Spirit and also make use of the learning experiences of others if our application and correlation of truth to life is to be effective.

Second, in selecting commentaries, the expository preacher needs to be aware of the strengths and weaknesses, background and biases, and presuppositions and blind spots of the person whose work he is reading. Some would-be commentators merely rehash what others have written. Others are superficial. Still others avoid controversy and are notoriously evasive when it comes to tackling difficult passages. And then there are those who are enamored with their own scholarship and think the sheer novelty of their position will give them a following. Again, Dr. Horne's comments are worth noting:

> We must not accumulate and read every interpreter or commentator *indiscriminately*, but [we] should select one or two, or a few, at most, of acknowledged character for learning in piety; and by frequent perusal of them, as well as studying their manner of expounding, endeavor to form [or model] ourselves after them until we are completely masters of their method.[3]

It is here that devotional commentaries have both strengths and weaknesses. If the writer has built his exposition on solid exegesis and is so in tune with the needs of the human heart that he can skillfully apply the text, then his writings are to be valued and esteemed for their intrinsic worth. If, however, as is all too often the case, his work does not give evidence of thorough research and reflection, then what he has written will not make any lasting impact.

2. Herman H. Horne, *An Introduction to the Critical Study and Knowledge of the Holy Scriptures*, 5 vols., 8th ed. (Grand Rapids: Baker, 1970), 1:353
3. Ibid., 1:353-54.

A third problem facing the expository preacher concerns the proliferation of commentaries. Each publishing house, it seems, has its own series. That makes it difficult to select works of abiding worth.

In that connection, however, there are some encouraging signs. Two new kinds of commentaries have recently made an appearance. *Malachi: God's Unchanging Love*, by Walter C. Kaiser, Jr., is designed to serve as a prototype of a new series of expositions. The second is in reality the revival of the expositional commentary made famous by the Reformers and their successors. *Genesis* and *The Minor Prophets*, by James Montgomery Boice are illustrative of scholarship being applied to the needs of individuals, and perhaps the same may be said of a recently published work on Ruth. In addition, both kinds contribute toward the development of a biblical theology of life.

In summary, the task of the commentator begins with exegesis, moves through an exposition of the theme of the biblical writer, and concludes with the application of truth to the life of the believer and the development of a coherent and cohesive view of the purpose of God for His people. The needs of the expositor parallel those of the commentator. He needs to be familiar with the original languages and use the knowledge gained from a close examination of the text to draw out the plan of the book and the subtle emphases of the writer. To discharge the duties committed to him, the expositor needs to avail himself of the very best resources that are available. And these, whether introductory works or books on the history, geography, and archaeology of the Bible, all need to be subordinated to the supreme task of preaching the Word.

## HISTORICAL BOOKS

**Clines, David J. A.** *The Theme of the Pentateuch.* Sheffield, England: University of Sheffield Press, 1978.

Advocates the unity of the Pentateuch in its original form. In elaborating on his thesis, Clines challenges the two major tendencies in OT research, atomism and geneticism. Stresses the need for a return to a recognition of the Mosaic authorship of Genesis through Deuteronomy. Recommended. 222.1'06.C61

**\*Hamilton, Victor P.** *Handbook on the Pentateuch.* Grand Rapids: Baker Book House, 1982.

An informative introductory guide that serves to introduce the contents of each book without becoming involved in

higher critical issues. The writer gives evidence of extensive reading and a thorough grasp of the purpose of each book. 222.1'061.H18

**\*Livingstone, George Herbert.** *The Pentateuch in Its Cultural Environment.* Grand Rapids: Baker Book House, 1974.

This informative, well-illustrated book introduces the Bible student to the lives and times of the patriarchs, analyzes the literature of the period, and provides a valuable critique of Near Eastern customs and culture. 222.1'09.L76

**Mackintosh, Charles Henry.** *Genesis to Deuteronomy: Notes on the Pentateuch.* Neptune, N.J.: Loizeaux Brothers, 1974.

Contains all of CHM's *Notes* in one

handy volume. Originally published between 1880-1882. 222.1'07.M21 1974

**Noth, Martin.** *A History of Pentateuchal Traditions.* Translated by Bernhard W. Andersen. Englewood Cliffs, N.J.: Prentice-Hall, 1972.

†Published posthumously, this source-critical work shows no awareness of trends in OT study over the decade prior to the writer's passing. 221.1'066.N81

**\*Thomas, William Henry Griffith.** *Through the Pentateuch Chapter by Chapter.* Grand Rapids: Kregel Publications, 1985.

These chapters are "models of simplicity and clarity that contrive to conceal very cleverly [the author's] massive erudition and spirituality" (R. K. Harrison). 222.1'06.T36 1985

GENESIS

**Aalders, Gerhard Charles.** *Genesis.* 2 vols. Bible Student's Commentary. Translated by W. Heymen. Grand Rapids: Zondervan Publishing House, 1981.

The publication in English of this outstanding Dutch commentary makes available to present-day preachers the exegetical insights of a renowned Bible scholar. Should aid in the exposition of the Word. 222.11'07.AA4

**\*Alford, Henry.** *The Book of Genesis, and Part of the Book of Exodus.* Minneapolis: Klock & Klock Christian Publishers, 1979.

Though accepting a modified form of the documentary hypothesis, Alford succeeds in bringing to his study of the OT the same depth of insight and richness of thought that characterized his treatment of the NT. A rare work; buy it while it is available. 222.11'07.AL2 1979

**Augustinus, Aurelius.** *The Literal Meaning of Genesis.* 2 vols. Translated and annotated by J. H. Taylor. New York: Newman Press, 1982.

Part of the Ancient Christian Writers series. Records Augustine's impressions of Genesis during the years following his conversion. In these volumes we see how he corrected the Manichean heresy that characterized his early beliefs. 222.11'06.AU4

**\*Boice, James Montgomery.** *Genesis: An Expositional Commentary.* In process. Grand Rapids: Zondervan Publishing House, 1982-.

Adequately explains the basic theme, purpose, and theology inherent in Genesis. Deals bravely with critical issues. Champions the cause of biblical creationism. Challenges the thinking of his readers as he deals realistically with the "sons of God" issue, the extent of the Deluge, and similar questions. Succeeds in providing the kind of exposition that may well become the best ever produced on this portion of God's Word. Scheduled for three volumes. Recommended. 222.11'07.B63

**Bonar, Horatius.** *Thoughts on Genesis.* Grand Rapids: Kregel Publications, 1979.

First published in 1875 under the title *Earth's Morning*, these devotional studies of Genesis chaps. 1-6, covering the period from Adam to the Flood, are permeated with practical application of biblical truth to life. 222.11'06.1—6.B64 1979

**Bruggemann, Walter.** *Genesis.* Interpretation, a Bible Commentary for Teaching and Preaching. Atlanta: John Knox Press, 1982.

†Presenting in a popular format the results of higher critical theories, this work succeeds in combining historical, textual, and theological issues in a way that is designed to enrich a preacher's pulpit ministry. 222.11'07.B83

**\*Bush, George.** *Notes on Genesis.* 2 vols. in 1. Minneapolis: Klock & Klock Christian Publishers, 1976.

Although dated archaeologically and historically, Bush more than makes up for these deficiencies with his enriching comments on the text, sidelights drawn from his thorough knowledge of the Arab culture, and devotional application. 222.11'07.B96 1976

**\*Candlish, Robert Smith.** *Studies in Genesis.* Grand Rapids: Kregel Publications, 1979.

First published in 1868. Candlish highlights the doctrinal issues as well as the biographical features contained in this portion of God's Word. In spite of its age, this remains one of the best works for pastors. Recommended. 222.11'06.C16 1979

**Davidson, Robert.** *Genesis 1-11.* Cambridge Bible Commentary on the New English Bible. New York: Cambridge University Press, 1973.

†This "Prologue" to Genesis presents the material in the form of myths within a religious framework and seeks to see extrabiblical tales behind the events of creation, the Fall, the Flood, and the tower of Babel. 222.11'07.1—11.D28

————. *Genesis 12-50.* Cambridge Bible Commentary on the New English Bible. Cambridge: Cambridge University Press, 1979.

If one makes allowance for the writer's use of *Redaktionsgeschichte,* this work has some value for it is rich in historical references and has some occasional exegetical insights. 222.11'07.12—50.D28

**\*Davis, John D.** *Genesis and Semitic Tradition.* Grand Rapids: Baker Book House, 1980.

First published in 1894, this conservative work by a Reformed Bible scholar demonstrates the uniqueness as well as the integrity of the OT when compared with literary material from the ancient Near East. Most valuable. 222.11'06.D29 1980

**\*Davis, John James.** *Paradise to Prison: Studies in Genesis.* Grand Rapids: Baker Book House, 1975.

An indispensable aid to the study of Genesis by one whose archaeological,

historical, and philological expertise places him in the forefront of evangelical scholars today. Recommended. 222.11'06.D29

**Delitzsch, Franz Julius.** *A New Commentary on Genesis.* Translated by S. Taylor. 2 vols. Minneapolis: Klock & Klock Christian Publishers, 1979.

Adopts a moderate approach to the critical theories of authorship. Provides an excellent treatment of the period from Abraham to Joseph. Deserving of careful reading. 222.11

**\*Dillow, Joseph C.** *The Waters Above: Earth's Pre-Flood Vapor Canopy.* Chicago: Moody Press, 1981.

By drawing information from a variety of sources, Dillow provides ample evidence in support of an antediluvian vapor canopy around the earth. His exegesis is thorough and the model he proposes is plausible, explaining thermal and physical phenomena in an understandable manner. Recommended. 222.11'06.D58

**Erdman, Charles Rosenbury.** *The Book of Genesis: An Exposition.* Grand Rapids: Baker Book House, 1982.

First published in 1950, this handy overview of Moses' first book traces the main theme and reveals the relevance of this portion of God's Word through the leading characters. 222.11'06.ER2 1982

**Gibson, John C. L.** *Genesis.* 2 vols. Philadelphia: Westminster Press, 1981-.

†Inspired by William Barclay's NT studies, these OT works seek to follow a similar format. Gibson's scholarship is impeccable, but his reliance on extrabiblical source material and adherence to beliefs long identified with the theological left undermine the value of this commentary. "This is liberal scholarship at its worst. Conservative views of this section of scripture are set aside and often ridiculed. Evangelicals should look elsewhere for insights into this vital portion of the Old Testament" (Donald K.

Campbell). 222.11'07.G35

**\*Green, William Henry.** *The Unity of the Book of Genesis.* Grand Rapids: Baker Book House, 1979.

First published in 1895, this volume answers the adherents of the documentary hypothesis point-by-point. Green maintains the consistency, harmony, unity, and Mosaic authorship of Genesis and succeeds in demolishing higher critical theories with a fairness that is impressive. 222.11'06.G82 1979

**Jacob, Benno.** *The First Book of the Bible: Genesis.* Translated and edited by Ernest I. Jacob and Walter Jacob. New York: Ktav Publishing House, 1974.

After rejecting the documentary hypothesis, the author breaks new ground as he correlates the rich heritage of Judaism with the text of Genesis. 222.11'07.J11 1974

**Jukes, Andrew.** *Types in Genesis.* Grand Rapids: Kregel Publications, 1976.

Reprinted from the eighth (1898) edition, this work concentrates on the spiritual significance of the lives of those mentioned by Moses in his first book. 222.11'06.J93 1976

**Kikawada, Isaac M.,** and **Arthur Quinn.** *Before Abraham Was: The Unity of Genesis 1-11.* Nashville: Abingdon Press, 1985.

After carefully analyzing a century of OT scholarship supporting the documentary hypothesis, these authors affirm the unity of Genesis 1-11. It is hoped that this work will contribute much toward a fresh appreciation of this all-important portion of God's Word. 222.11'06.1—11.K55

**\*Morris, Henry Madison.** *The Genesis Record: A Scientific and Devotional Commentary on the Book of Beginnings.* Grand Rapids: Baker Book House, 1976.

Valuable as corollary reading. Of great importance for the scientific data that has been included in the author's exposition. Should be consulted by all who wish

to be well-informed on the issues alluded to by Moses. 222.11'07.M83

**Schaeffer, Francis August.** *Genesis in Space and Time: The Flow of Biblical History.* Downers Grove, Ill.: InterVarsity Press, 1972.

In grappling with the dilemmas facing modern man, Schaeffer correctly traces their origin to man's rejection of the early chapters of Genesis. The author from L'Abri explains their relevance in contemporary terms. 222.11.1—11.SCH1

**Stedman, Ray C.** *The Beginnings.* Waco, Tex.: Word Books, 1978.

Covering Genesis 4-11, this sequel to *Understanding Man* continues the author's expository studies and treats the major events from the sin of Cain to the tower of Babel. Insightful. 222.11'07.4—11.ST3

**Stigers, Harold G.** *A Commentary on Genesis.* Grand Rapids: Zondervan Publishing House, 1975.

Information from the recently discovered Ebla texts was not available to the author when he worked on the manuscript of this book. Though the treatment is primarily exegetical, the translation of the Hebrew text is helpful, and the handling of the grammar brings out the nuances inherent in the original. The placing of events in their ancient setting is particularly valuable to preachers. Unfortunately, the work is marred by numerous misspellings of Hebrew words (in their transliteration). 222.11'07.ST5

**Westermann, Claus.** *Genesis: A Commentary.* Translated by J. J. Scullion. In process. Minneapolis: Augsburg Publishing House, 1984-.

†Scheduled for three volumes, this painstaking commentary covers all of the issues that undergird the development of a sound biblical theology. Westermann adheres to the usual documentary hypothesis and makes use of *Formgeschichte and Redaktiongeschichte.* Valuable excurses are included in each section.

These help readers gain an invaluable understanding of these chapters of Genesis in the development of theology. 222.11'07.W52

*Whitcomb, John Clement, Jr.* The World That Perished. Grand Rapids: Baker Book House, 1973.

This supplement to *The Genesis Flood* and companion volume of *The Early Earth* brings up to date the author's vast research into the primeval conditions prevailing on the earth before the Deluge, as well as the changes that took place following the Flood. 222.11'06.6—9.W58W

EXODUS

*Bush, George.* Notes on Exodus. 2 vols in 1. Minneapolis: James & Klock Publishing Co., 1976.

Considering the paucity of good works on Exodus, this commentary is a must. Although dated archaeologically and historically, it more than makes up for these deficiencies with its enriching comments on the text. 222.12'07.B96 1976.

**Childs, Brevard S.** *The Book of Exodus.* Philadelphia: Westminster Press, 1974.

Building on the principles laid down in his *Biblical Theology in Crisis,* Childs applies them to the book of Exodus and succeeds in providing his readers with a scholarly work that pastors will find helpful. Needs to be read with discernment. 222.12'07.C43

*Cole, Robert Alan.* Exodus: An Introduction and Commentary. Tyndale Old Testament Commentaries. Downers Grove, Ill.: InterVarsity Press, 1973.

Basing his exposition primarily on the theology of Exodus, the writer succeeds in providing a brief but valuable commentary on the text. 222.12'07.C67

**Courville, Donovan A.** *The Exodus Problem and Its Ramifications.* 2 vols. Loma Linda, Calif.: Challenge Books, 1971.

This critical examination of the chronological problems surrounding the Israelites and their emancipation from Egypt gives evidence of careful inquiry. Deserves careful reading on the part of those interested in the problems. 222.12'06.C83

**Davies, G. I.** *The Way in the Wilderness: A Geographical Study of the Wilderness Itinerary in the Old Testament.* Cambridge: Cambridge University Press, 1979.

Focuses on the Exodus, evaluates the possible routes the Israelites might have taken, and traces the development of the Exodus motif in Jewish, Christian, and Arabic writings. 222.12'095.D28W

**Ellison, Henry Leopold.** *Exodus.* Philadelphia: Westminster Press, 1982.

Based on the text of the RSV, this brief commentary deals with the scope and principal teaching of this part of the Mosaic corpus. 222.12'07.EL5

**Erdman, Charles Rosenbury.** *The Book of Exodus: An Exposition.* Grand Rapids: Baker Book House, 1982.

In his usual balanced and exemplary manner, Erdman deals with the historical events surrounding Israel's emancipation by, and worship of, the Lord. 222.12'07.ER2 1982

**Gisper, Willem Hendrik.** *Exodus.* Bible Student's Commentary. Translated by Ed van der Maas. Grand Rapids: Zondervan Publishing House, 1982.

Describes the Lord's redemption and adoption of Israel and the establishment of the worship of His people. Clear, succinct. Recommended. 222.12'07.G44

**Hyatt, James Philip.** *Exodus.* New Century Bible Commentary. Grand Rapids: Wm. B. Eerdmans Publishing Co., 1980.

Manifests little regard for the integrity of the MT. Reconstructs the history and theology of this era of Israel's history after adopting a late date for the Exodus. First published in 1972. 222.12'07.H99 1980

**Jordan, James B.** *The Law of the Covenant: An Exposition of Exodus 21-23.* Tyler,

Tex.: Institute for Christian Economics, 1984.

The unity of Exodus 20-23 has often been overlooked. Though omitting the Decalogue, "this book [makes] a tremendous contribution. There are fresh insights on every page. It raises the discussion of biblical law to a new level of precision and cogency. . . . It is the most practical piece of biblical theology I've seen in a long time" (John M. Frame). 222.12′06.21—23.J76

**Julien, Tom.** *Spiritual Greatness—Studies in Exodus.* Winona Lake, Ind.: BMH Books, 1979.

A clear, concise, well-outlined study. Designed for use by adult discussion groups. Recommended. 222.12′07.J94

**\*Murphy, James Gracey.** *A Critical and Exegetical Commentary on the Book of Exodus.* Minneapolis: Klock & Klock Christian Publishers, 1980.

This handy volume easily ranks as one of the best general works ever produced on Exodus. It is designed for general readers and should be studied diligently by laypeople in all walks of life. Pastors, however, also stand to gain much from Murphy's learned, judicious, and reverent treatment. 222.12′07.M95 1980

LEVITICUS

**Bush, George.** *Notes, Critical and Practical, on the Book of Leviticus.* Minneapolis: Klock & Klock Christian Publishers, 1981.

First published in 1852, this study of Israel's Levitical code provides an indispensable basis for an examination of the NT book of Hebrews. The teaching is clear and presented in a way that will appeal to laypeople as well as those who shepherd the flock. 222.13′07.B96 1981

**Erdman, Charles Rosenbury.** *The Book of Leviticus: An Exposition.* Grand Rapids: Baker Book House, 1982.

An exemplary discussion of the provi-

sions and principles of proper worship. First published in 1951. 222.13′07.ER2 1982

**\*Harrison, Roland Kenneth.** *Leviticus, an Introduction and Commentary.* Tyndale Old Testament Commentaries. Downers Grove, Ill.: InterVarsity Press, 1980.

A fitting introduction to the regulations and rituals, sacrifices and offerings of the Levitical code. Does not evade interpretative problems and provides a firm basis for the understanding of NT teaching of the atonement of Christ and the priesthood of believers. 222.13′07.H24

**\*Kellogg, Samuel Henry.** *The Book of Leviticus.* 3d ed. Minneapolis: Klock & Klock Christian Publishers, 1978.

Perhaps the finest exposition of this portion of God's Word ever to come from the pen of man. A worthy addition to every minister's library. 222.13′07.K29 1978

**Knight, George Angus Fulton.** *Leviticus.* Philadelphia: Westminster Press, 1981.

†Describes Israel's ancient rites and the abiding lessons to be learned from their ritual. 222.13′07.K74

**Murphy, James Gracey.** *A Critical and Exegetical Commentary on the Book of Leviticus.* Minneapolis: James & Klock Publishing Co., 1976.

Reprinted from the 1874 edition, this able exposition combines sound exegesis with a pleasing and relevant devotional emphasis. 222.13′07.M95 1976

**Noth, Martin.** *Leviticus: A Commentary.* Translated by J. E. Anderson. Rev. ed. Philadelphia: Westminster Press, 1977.

A new translation of a work that first appeared in 1965. Corrects the inaccuracies of the first edition. 222.13′07.N84 1977

**Porter, J. R.** *Leviticus.* Cambridge Bible Commentary. New York: Cambridge University Press, 1976.

Based on the text of the NEB, these

brief notes reveal the author's insights into Israelite customs but offer little to those who minister the Word to others. 222.13′07.P82

**Seiss, Joseph Augustus.** *Gospel in Leviticus.* Grand Rapids: Kregel Publications, 1981.

First published in 1860, these expository lectures relate the teaching of the OT to Christ's high priesthood. Stimulating. 222.13′07.SE4 1981

**Wenham, Gordon J.** *The Book of Leviticus.* New International Commentary on the Old Testament. Grand Rapids: Wm. B. Eerdmans Publishing Co., 1979.

Following a brief introduction and a selective bibliography containing all the best works and journal articles, Wenham settles down to expound the text. Each section is prefaced by a translation of the MT. Following an historical assessment of the teaching of the passage, "the abiding theological value" of the portion of Scripture under consideration is discussed. The result is a valuable contribution to the biblical preacher's library. 222.13′07.W48

### NUMBERS

**Budd, Philip J.** *Word Biblical Commentary: Numbers.* Waco, Tex.: Word Books, 1984.

†Contains an excellent introduction, and the bibliographies at the beginning of each section are most helpful. The translation requires careful attention for its values to become apparent. There are also times when liberties have been taken in handling the MT. As with other books in this series, a heavy reliance is placed on *Redaktionsgeschichte,* and there are also places where definite theological weaknesses occur. This book is of value to the discerning reader. 222.14′07.B85 (Alt. DDC 220.7′07 v.4)

**\*Bush, George.** *Notes, Critical and Practical, on the Book of Numbers.* Minneapolis:

Klock & Klock Christian Publishers, 1981.

Meets a definite need for a thorough work in this sorely neglected area of God's revelation. Can be read with profit by laypeople as well as pastors. Recommended. 222.14′07.B96 1981

**Erdman, Charles Rosenbury.** *The Book of Numbers: An Exposition.* Grand Rapids: Baker Book House, 1982.

An overview of the history of Israel in the wilderness with principles of application drawn from their experiences. 222.14′07.ER2 1982

**Sturdy, John.** *Numbers.* Cambridge Bible Commentary. New York: Cambridge University Press, 1976.

Based on the text of the NEB, this study follows the documentary hypothesis and places the final composition in the reign of David or Solomon. The brief notes supply background information, but are insufficient to meet the needs of the expository preacher. 222.14′07.ST9

**\*Wenham, Gordon J.** *Numbers: An Introduction and Commentary.* Tyndale Old Testament Commentaries. Downers Grove, Ill.: InterVarsity Press, 1981.

Seldom read by Christians, the book of Numbers has been ignored by the majority of the contemporary "lamp-toting children of Diogenes." Now, however, Wenham's excellent treatment not only illumines the text, but also suggests applications to everyday life. 222.14′07.W48

### DEUTERONOMY

**Benjamin, Don C.** *Deuteronomy and City Life: A Form-Criticism of Texts with the Word City ('ir) in Deuteronomy 4:41—26:19.* Lanham, Md.: University Press of America, 1983.

Questions contemporary histories and theologies of ancient Israel that stress the complete nonurban character of the Israelites. Provides some startling and insightful sidelights on this period of Israel's history. 222.15′08.B43

**Carmichael, Calum M.** *The Laws of Deuteronomy.* Ithaca, N.Y.: Cornell University Press, 1974.

†A scholarly study showing that the book of Deuteronomy is a carefully constructed, coherent treatise, written with a definite purpose in mind. 222.15′06.C21

**Craigie, Peter Campbell.** *The Book of Deuteronomy.* New International Commentary on the Old Testament. Grand Rapids: Wm. B. Eerdmans Publishing Co., 1976.

A learned and comprehensive treatment. Craigie shows that he is abreast of the latest trends in literary critical scholarship, yet defends the integrity of the Mosaic writings with discretion and skill. His comments on the text are illuminating, and he enriches his exposition with important historical information and a judicious use of archaeological data. 222.15′07.C84

**Cumming, John.** *Sabbath Morning Readings on the Old Testament: Book of Deuteronomy.* Minneapolis: Klock & Klock Christian Publishers, 1981.

First published in 1856, these expository messages ably unfold the theme and purpose of Moses' last discourses. Of special value due to the fact that there are so few homiletic studies of Deuteronomy. 222.15′07.C91 1981

**Erdman, Charles Rosenbury.** *The Book of Deuteronomy: An Exposition.* Grand Rapids: Baker Book House, 1982.

A clear exposition of the love of God. Excellent for laypeople. 222.15′07.ER2 1982

**Payne, David F.** *Deuteronomy.* Daily Study Bible. Philadelphia: Westminster Press, 1985.

Defends the Mosaic authorship of this book and provides a concise, theologically astute commentary on the text. More conservative than some other

works in this series. 222.15′07.P29

**Ridderbos, Jan.** *Deuteronomy.* Bible Students' Commentary. Translated by E. M. Van der Maas. Grand Rapids: Zondervan Publishing House, Regency Reference Library, 1984.

An admirable, generally conservative commentary that was first published in Dutch in 1950-1951. The writer's treatment of critical problems is judicious without being tedious. His comments on the text are worthy of serious consideration. 222.15′07.R43

**Schultz, Samuel J.** *Deuteronomy: The Gospel of Love.* Everyman's Bible Commentary. Chicago: Moody Press, 1971.

A simple, thought-provoking exposition. 222.15′07.SCH8

———. *The Gospel of Moses.* New York: Harper & Row, 1974.

This intriguing study of Deuteronomy appropriately emphasizes the need to respond to the love of God with a corresponding love for Him. Schultz shows that the concept of loving God "with all your heart . . . and your neighbor as yourself" is not a NT teaching, but has its roots deeply imbedded in the OT. He provides an excellent treatment of a much misunderstood theme. 222.15′06.SCH8

**\*Thompson, John Arthur.** *Deuteronomy.* Tyndale Old Testament Commentaries. Downers Grove, Ill.: InterVarsity Press, 1975.

This work provides all that a Bible student could wish for, and in a handy format. Comparable to the best works ever produced on Deuteronomy. 222.15′07.T37

TEN COMMANDMENTS

**Davidman, Joy.** *Smoke on the Mountain.* Philadelphia: Westminster Press, 1971.

The wife of C. S. Lewis interprets the Ten Commandments and passes on observations she has made concerning those who have attempted to order their lives according to the Decalogue. 222.16′07.D28

**Huffman, John A., Jr.** *Liberating Limits: A Fresh Look at the Ten Commandments.* Waco, Tex.: Word Books, 1980.

Not since Joy Davidman's *Smoke on the Mountain* has a work as interesting and relevant as this one been published. Huffman treats the Decalogue as the sage counsel of God the Father to His children to protect them from their own destructive tendencies. 222.16.H87

**Schaeffer, Edith.** *Lifelines: The Ten Commandments for Today.* Westchester, Ill.: Crossway Books, 1982.

Far from being a relic of outdated legislation, the Decalogue is shown to be remarkably up-to-date. Mrs. Schaeffer's treatment is both stimulating and insightful. 222.16.SCH1

JOSHUA

**Auld, A. Graeme.** *Joshua, Judges, and Ruth.* Daily Study Bible. Philadelphia: Westminster Press, 1984.

†Auld writes out of the conviction that these books are the Bible's prime witness to Israel's early history in Canaan. He expounds the text skillfully and incorporates important historical, linguistic, and archaeological information into his discussion. 222.2′07.AU5

**\*Blaikie, William Garden.** *The Book of Joshua.* Minneapolis: Klock & Klock Christian Publishers, 1978.

One of the finest books ever written on this section of God's Word. Admirably treats Israel's history under Joshua. Filled with practical lessons for everyday living. Recommended. 222.2′07.B57 1978

**Boling, Robert G.** *Joshua.* The Anchor Bible. Garden City, N.Y.: Doubleday and Co., 1982.

This work, with an introduction by the late G. Ernest Wright, gives the reader a lucid and scholarly exposition of the contents of Joshua. A commendable work. 222.2′07.B63

**\*Bush, George.** *Joshua and Judges.* Minneapolis: Klock & Klock Christian Publishers, 1981.

These formerly separate studies have now been combined into one volume. They provide a pleasing synthesis of scholarship and devotion, historical background and relevant exposition. Bible students, whether laypeople or pastors, should eagerly acquire the writings of this fine biblical scholar and for their own edification and enrichment read what he wrote. 222.2′07.B96 1981

**Campbell, Donald Keith.** *No Time for Neutrality.* Wheaton, Ill.: Victor Books, 1981.

A perceptive presentation of the main movements and principal teaching of the book of Joshua. Recommended for adult Bible study groups. 222.2′07.C15

**Garstang, John.** *Joshua—Judges: The Foundations of Bible History.* Grand Rapids: Kregel Publications, 1978.

Reprinted after years of neglect, this epochal work treats history, geography, archaeology, and the settlement of Israel in the land. Though he adheres to a modified form of the documentary hypothesis, Garstang's treatment is nevertheless possessed of a freshness and vitality seldom found in works of this nature. 222.2′07.G28 1978.

**Gray, John.** *Joshua, Judges and Ruth.* New Century Bible. Greenwood, S.C.: Attic Press, 1967.

†A highly critical treatment. 222.2′07.G79

**Hamlin, E. John.** *Inheriting the Land: A Commentary on the Book of Joshua.* International Theological Commentary. Grand Rapids: Wm. B. Eerdmans Publishing Co., 1983.

Well outlined and giving evidence of thorough research, this popular commentary is designed to interpret the events of the conquest of the land from the perspective of the Hebrews. Though containing helpful interpretative ideas, the application of the text is almost exclusively in terms of sociological criteria. 222.2'07.H17

**Sanders, John Oswald.** *Promised Land Living.* Chicago: Moody Press, 1984.

A pleasant devotional treatment of the book of Joshua in which the principles of spiritual victory are applied to the believer today. 222.2'06.SA5

**Scroggie, William Graham.** *Joshua in Light of the New Testament: The Land of Life and Rest.* Grand Rapids: Kregel Publications, 1981.

A brief survey of the message of the book of Joshua in light of the teaching of the NT. 222.2.SC5 1981

**\*Wouldstra, Marten H.** *The Book of Joshua.* New International Commentary of the Old Testament. Grand Rapids: Wm. B. Eerdmans Publishing Co., 1981.

A valuable contribution to this series. Fully abreast of the latest archaeological and philological research. Should be in every pastor's library. Recommended. 222.2'07.W91

JUDGES AND RUTH

**\*Barber, Cyril John.** *Ruth: An Expositional Commentary.* Chicago: Moody Press, 1983.

"Emphasizes the theme of Ruth as exemplifying the grace of God. The author has given us an extremely satisfying exposition of this OT book. . . . [He] has deduced from it many lessons that are pertinent to us in our late twentieth-century circumstances. The references in the appendix indicate the extent of his research and the breadth of his reading, and we are consequently his debtors.

Here is a book that deserves to be read— and then re-read. I wholeheartedly recommend it" (Frederick A. Tatford). 222.3'07.B23

**Boling, Robert G.** *Judges.* The Anchor Bible. Garden City, N.Y.: Doubleday and Co., 1975.

A new translation with scholarly notes and commentary. Neither as helpful to the expository preacher as Fausset's exemplary treatment, nor as abreast of the latest scholarly research as Wood's invaluable work. What is presented, however, is valuable for its correlation of linguistic and historical data. 222.3'07.B63 (Alt. DDC 220.7).

**\*Bush, George.** *Notes on Judges.* Minneapolis: Klock & Klock Christian Publishers, 1976.

This valuable reprint of the 1852 edition makes available the rare and rich homiletic suggestions of this Princeton scholar. 222.3'07.B96 1976

**Campbell, Edward F., Jr.** *Ruth.* The Anchor Bible. Garden City, N.Y.: Doubleday and Co., 1975.

A stimulating and exacting study. It is fully abreast of the latest MS evidence and makes appropriate use of comparative Semitic studies (particularly Ugaritic). Recommended. 222.35'07.C15 (Alt. DDC 220.7).

**\*Cox, Samuel,** and **Thomas Fuller.** *The Book of Ruth.* Minneapolis: Klock & Klock Christian Publishers, 1982.

Combines Cox's devotional studies from *The Expositor* with Fuller's sermons on chapters 1-2. Includes useful appendixes on Christ as the *menuchah* of the World and Christ as the true *goel* of men. Excellent. 222.35'07.C83F 1982

**Enns, Paul P.** *Bible Study Commentary: Judges.* Grand Rapids: Zondervan Publishing House, 1982.

A practical, clearly outlined, conservative treatment. Ideal for laypeople. 222.32'07.EN6

———. *Bible Study Commentary: Ruth.* Grand Rapids: Zondervan Publishing House, 1982.

A brief introductory survey of this important but oft neglected OT book. 222.35'07.EN6

*Fausset, Andrew Robert. *A Critical and Expository Commentary on the Book of Judges.* Minneapolis: James & Klock Publishing Co., 1977.

A work of immeasurable value. Remains one of the finest treatments extant. A must for the expositor. 222.3'07.F27 1977

**Jordan, James B.** *Judges: God's War Against Humanism.* Tyler, Tex.: Geneva Ministries, 1985.

Draws a parallel between OT Baalism and the contemporary allurement of humanism. Relates this to the decline in spirituality. Though Jordan follows a literal interpretation of the text, he resorts to allegorism/symbolism when applying the text. And though his observations are useful, his comments should not be accepted uncritically. On the positive side, Jordan goes a long way toward reviving interest in this OT work, and he challenges our thinking in new and different ways. 222.3'06.J76

*Lang, John Marshall, and Thomas Kirk. *Studies in the Book of Judges.* 2 vols. in 1. Minneapolis: Klock & Klock Christian Publishers, 1983.

Though all conservative believers boldly affirm that the Bible exists in sixty-six books, most relegate the teaching of portions of Judges to the early Sunday school years. Not so with the able Scots who took on the task of explaining the relevancy of this section of Scripture to our lives. Lang concentrates on Gideon, with incidental comments on the other judges. Kirk focuses attention on Samson. Together they provide a satisfying work that covers the material and shows to readers how the incidents of the OT

find a parallel in our day. 222.32'07.L25

**Martin, James D.** *The Book of Judges.* Cambridge Bible Commentary. New York: Cambridge University Press, 1975.

Based on the NEB, this work follows the pattern of the series. The author repeatedly calls in question the historicity of the events, expresses doubt over the Samson narrative, and believes that sun mythology underlies much of what is recorded. Unreliable. 222.3'07.M36

**Mayes, A. D. H.** *Israel in the Period of the Judges.* Studies in Biblical Theology, Second Series. London: SCM Press, 1974.

†This attack on Noth's amphictyonic concept views Israel's unity as purely theoretical. Mayes, however, concludes by admitting that the paucity of materials precludes the possibility of any final judgment. 222.3'06.M45

**Rogers, Richard.** *A Commentary on Judges.* Carlisle, Pa.: Banner of Truth Trust, 1983.

Described by C. H. Spurgeon as "THE work upon Judges," this facsimile of the 1615 edition contains a wealth of practical and relevant material. Throughout his discussion of the events of this book, Rogers reveals a pastor's heart. Though his messages mirror the experience of God's people in England during the time of Sir Francis Drake and the Spanish Armada, their application is to any people facing external threat and the struggle for spiritual, economic, and social freedom. Beautifully reproduced with handsome binding and printed on excellent paper, this is a worthy acquisition— all the more so because it has been unobtainable for more than a century. Recommended. 227.3'06.R63 1983

**Sasson, Jack M.** *Ruth: A New Translation with a Philological Commentary and a Formalist-Folklorist Interpretation.* Baltimore, Md.: Johns Hopkins University Press, 1979.

†Photoduplicated from typed pages.

This technical commentary provides some valuable insights into the text but is disappointing in its interpretation of the theme and purpose of the biblical account. 222.35'07.SA7

**Soggin, J. Alberto.** *Judges, a Commentary.* Old Testament Library. Philadelphia: Westminster Press, 1981.

An able commentary that readily makes available to the busy pastor a wealth of textual material. 222.32'07.SO2

**Wiseman, Luke H.** *Practical Truths from Judges.* Grand Rapids: Kregel Publications, 1985.

Formerly published as *Men of Faith,* this work contains a wealth of practical material; applications are offered to encourage and challenge us today. The author presents a general view of the period of the Judges along with an in-depth study of the lives of Barak, Gideon, Jephthah, and Samson. 222.32.W75

**\*Wood, Leon James.** *Distressing Days of the Judges.* Grand Rapids: Zondervan Publishing House, 1975.

A most important work. It is well researched, reliable, and ideally suited to the needs of the expositor who desires relevant data to support his exposition of the text. Wood makes this colorful period of Israelite history come alive with his apt descriptions and careful use of historical, linguistic, and archaeological material. This book is deserving of a place in every preacher's library. 222.3'06.W81

BOOKS OF SAMUEL

**Ackroyd, Peter R.** *The First Book of Samuel.* Cambridge Bible Commentary. Cambridge: At the University Press, 1971.

†Based on the NEB. This source-critical work by a leading comparative reli-

gionist contains an up-to-date evaluation of the archaeological material relating to the period of Samuel and Saul. Adheres to a modified documentary theory. 222.43'07.AC5

**Ahlstrom, G. W.** *Royal Administration and National Religion in Ancient Palestine.* Leiden: E.J. Brill, 1982.

Sets out to establish the intimate relationship between state and religion in the milieu of ancient Israel. Shows how religion was an expression of the life of the community and therefore constituted a part of the political system. 222.4'06.AH4

**\*Barber, Cyril John,** and **John Daniel Carter.** *Always a Winner: A Commentary for Laymen/I Samuel.* Glendale, Calif.: Regal Books, 1977.

According to a review in *Christian News,* this book is a "readable, yet deeply insightful commentary. [The authors] have written a handbook on handling life's problems by using spiritual resources. As they trace the careers of Samuel, Saul and David, they draw practical applications that everyone can use in the stress and strain of daily life." 222.43'07.B23

**Blaikie, William Garden.** *The First Book of Samuel.* Minneapolis: Klock & Klock Christian Publishers, 1978.

One of the finest devotional commentaries ever produced. First published in 1887 as part of *The Expositor's Bible.* 222.43'07.B57 1978.

_____. *The Second Book of Samuel.* Minneapolis: Klock & Klock Christian Publishers, 1978.

A work that deserves a place in every Bible student's library. Perceptive and enlightening. First published in 1893 as part of *The Expositor's Bible.* 222.44'07.B57 1978

**Campbell, Anthony F.** *The Ark Narrative (I Samuel 4—6; II Samuel 6): A Form-critical and Traditio-historical Study.* Missoula, Mont.: Scholars Press, 1975.

An evaluation of the meaning and message of these two narratives, together with an assessment of their theological import to the Israelites. 222.4.C15

*Deane, William John, and Thomas Kirk. *Studies in the First Book of Samuel.* 2 vols. in 1. Minneapolis: Klock & Klock Christian Publishers, 1983.

In this treatment of the lives of Samuel and Saul, Samuel is shown to possess an inner Godward orientation that motivated all he did. Saul is revealed as being motivated by external considerations. These two men—contemporaries for a time—explain for us the dynamics of success from God's perspective. In explaining 1 Samuel, Deane and Kirk provide the kind of practical application that will delight every devout Bible student. Recommended. 222.43'07.D34 1983

**Gordon, R. P.** *1 and 2 Samuel.* Sheffield, England: Journal for the Study of the Old Testament Press, 1984.

†Serves to introduce the reader to the books of Samuel and prepare him/her for the writer's commentary, which is in the course of preparation. 222.4'06.G65

**Klein, Ralph W.** *I Samuel.* Word Biblical Commentary. Waco, Tex.: Word Books, 1983.

Based on the latest *Redaktionsgeschichte,* this exposition makes a valuable contribution but needs to be used with discernment. The bibliographies at the beginning of each chapter are of the utmost value. Comments on the text are technical, and because Klein feels the text is in poor shape, he relies heavily on the LXX and other critical commentaries. Seminarians and pastors will find Klein's translation helpful, his research impeccable; but his explanation of the theme of 1 Samuel is lacking. However, his overall treatment is one that deserves careful consideration. 222.43'07.K67

**McCarter, P. Kyle, Jr.** *1 Samuel, a New Translation with Introduction, Notes and Commentary.* The Anchor Bible. Garden City, N.Y.: Doubleday and Co., 1980.

†No one who desires to do serious study on this portion of God's Word can afford to neglect this scholarly work. McCarther reconstructs the MT, and that is disappointing to conservative Bible students. However, his handling of the problems is instructive and up-to-date. 222.43'07.M11

————. *II Samuel.* The Anchor Bible. Garden City, N.Y.: Doubleday and Co., 1984.

†Reviews the literary problems presented by the present state of the text and the historical circumstances that gave rise to its composition. Devotes special attention to chapters 9-20, which contain the much-discussed stories of David's adultery with Bathsheba and the political turmoil that was the result. Though it is the first to make full use of the Qumran scrolls, the translation takes liberties with the MT. 222.44'07.M12

**Payne, David F.** *I and II Samuel.* Daily Bible Study. Philadelphia: Westminster Press, 1982.

Combines history and theology in his description of the events surrounding Israel's first two kings. 222.4'07.P29

**Whitelam, Keith W.** *The Just King: Monarchical Judicial Authority in Ancient Israel.* Sheffield, England: University of Sheffield Press, 1979.

Based on the author's dissertation at the University of Manchester. This partial treatment of the Davidic dynasty and the continuation of the theocracy through David's line makes a distinct contribution to OT history as well as the anticipation of the Messiah and the establishment of His kingdom. 222.44'06.W58

*Wood, Leon James. *Israel's United Monarchy.* Grand Rapids: Baker Book House, 1979.

A refreshing excursus into Israel's history, the dawn of the "Golden Age," and the strengths and weaknesses of the first three kings. Excellent. 222.43′09.W85 1979

BOOKS OF KINGS

**DeVries, Simon J.** *1 Kings.* Word Biblical Commentary. Waco, Tex.: Word Books, 1985.
A capable, reasonably conservative treatment of the text. The introduction is most helpful, and the bibliographies are exceedingly valuable. Though pastors will find the critical issues discussed of marginal worth, this is the best commentary on 1 Kings to be produced in many years. 222.53′07.D49 (Alt. DDC 220.7′07.W89 v.12)

**Ellul, Jacques.** *The Politics of God and the Politics of Man.* Grand Rapids: Wm. B. Eerdmans Publishing Co., 1972.
Basing his political theory on the fact that the problems of our times are theological and not sociological, the writer shows from a study of 2 Kings how God has provided a blueprint for self-government in the Bible. Rewarding reading. 222.54′092.EL5

**\*Farrar, Frederick William.** *The First Book of Kings.* Minneapolis: Klock & Klock Christian Publishers, 1981.
A thorough and delightful exposition of this history of Israel from Solomon to Elijah. In places it manifests an unwise dependence on the LXX and follows some higher critical theories in vogue at the time. 222.53′07.F24 1981.

**\*_____.** *The Second Book of Kings.* Minneapolis: Klock & Klock Christian Publishers, 1981.
Treats Israel's history from the ascension of Elijah to the deportation of Judah. Remains one of the most satisfactory works for the expository preacher. 222.54′07.F24 1981

**Gray, John.** *I and II Kings: A Commentary.* Old Testament Library. 2d ed. rev. Philadelphia: Westminster Press, 1971.
†An expansion and revision of the writer's earlier commentary. Includes a vast amount of archaeological and exegetical material, covers every significant verse, and makes a valuable though critical contribution to the study of these books.
222.5′07.G79 1971

**Jones, Gwilym H.** *1 and 2 Kings.* 2 vols. Grand Rapids: Wm. B. Eerdmans Publishing Co., 1984.
Capably introduced. Carefully attends to the history, customs, culture, and etymology of Hebrew words. Deals adequately with the text of these two books. Helpful. 222.5′07.J71

**\*Kirk, Thomas,** and **George Rawlinson.** *Studies in the Books of Kings.* 2 vols. in 1. Minneapolis: Klock & Klock Christian Publishers, 1983.
It is difficult to refrain from speaking eloquently of the value of this work. Kirk's handling of the life of Solomon (1 Kings 1-9) is done so well that it suggests messages by the score and provides, in addition, pertinent areas of application. It is instructive as well as revealing, edifying, and also enlightening. And Rawlinson's handling of the remainder of 1 Kings 10—2 Kings 25 provides one of the finest syntheses of biblical history (set against the background of the ancient Near East) that has ever been written. Rawlinson's chronology is lacking, but this in itself is not sufficient to condemn his work to oblivion. The chronology of other similar treatises was also faulty up to the time Thiele produced his *Mysterious Numbers of the Hebrew Kings.* Any deficiencies, therefore, can easily be corrected by checking Rawlinson against Thiele. What is important is that here we have a work that makes the OT come alive. 222.5′07.K63 1983

*Whitcomb, John Clement, Jr. *Solomon to the Exile: Studies in Kings and Chronicles.* Grand Rapids: Baker Book House, 1971.

An ideal book for discussion groups. Recreates the OT setting, graphically depicts the cause of decline in Israel and Judah, and draws valid lessons from these incidents that are applied to the needs of the present. 222.5'06.W58

BOOKS OF CHRONICLES

**Ackroyd, Peter R.** *I and II Chronicles, Ezra, Nehemiah.* Torch Bible Commentaries. London: SCM Press, 1973.

†Fully abreast of the latest scholarship, these brief studies survey the content of the post-exilic writings and provide occasional helpful insights into problems in the text. 222.6'07.AC5

**Bennett, William Henry.** *An Exposition of the Books of Chronicles.* Minneapolis: Klock & Klock Christian Publishers, 1983.

Commentaries on Chronicles are few and far between. This work meets a need. It is to be regretted, however, that the writer allowed critical presuppositions to enter into his handling of the biblical text. In spite of this weakness, what is presented to the reader is worthy of serious reflection. 222.6'07.B43 1983

**McConville, J. Gordon.** *I and II Chronicles.* Daily Study Bible. Philadelphia: Westminster Press, 1984.

Succinct, pointed comments on each facet of these long-neglected books. Readers will find these pages replete with perceptive hints that can be fleshed out with further study. 222.6'07.M13

**Murphy, James Gracey.** *The Books of Chronicles.* Minneapolis: James & Klock Publishing Company, 1976.

An important reprint that treats briefly, yet fairly, these neglected books. 222.6'07.M95 1976

**Williamson, Hugh Godfrey Maturin.** *Israel in the Books of Chronicles.* New York: Cambridge University Press, 1977.

Challenges the accepted results of modern scholarship and advances the belief that the books of Chronicles and Ezra-Nehemiah bear evidence of separate authorship. Emphasizes that those in Judah after the Exile looked forward to the reunion of all Israel around Jerusalem and its Temple. 226.6'06.W67

EZRA

*Adeney, Walter Frederick. *Ezra and Nehemiah.* Minneapolis: Klock & Klock Christian Publishers, 1980.

One of the best works on this facet of Israel's postexilic history. Can be read with profit by both pastor and layperson. 222.7.AD3 1980

**Clines, David J. A.** *Ezra, Nehemiah, Esther.* New Century Bible Commentary. Grand Rapids: Wm. B. Eerdmans Publishing Co., 1984.

Each book is introduced with care and precision so that the structure and key aspects of each is readily revealed. Helpful biographical notes are interspersed throughout the text. Exegetical accuracy and historical reliability are a hallmark of Clines's studies. This work has much to commend it. 227.7'07.C61

**Coggins, R. J.** *The Books of Ezra and Nehemiah.* Cambridge Bible Commentary. New York: Cambridge University Press, 1976.

Based on the text of the NEB. This work provides readers with the results of modern scholarship, but it does little to illumine or apply the theme of these works or the teaching of the passage under consideration. Sterile. 222.7' 07.C65

*Fensham, Frank Charles. *The Books of Ezra and Nehemiah.* New International Commentary on the New Testament.

Grand Rapids: Wm. B. Eerdmans Publishing Co., 1982.

"A thoroughly competent conservative commentary, well worthy of the series. It will meet the needs of readers at every level. The preacher should be sparked by it to many useful lines of thought about the application of the unchanging Word of God to our modern situation" (Donald J. Wiseman). 222.7'07.F36

**Kidner, Derek.** *Ezra and Nehemiah, an Introduction and Commentary.* Tyndale Old Testament Commentaries. Downers Grove, Ill.: InterVarsity Press, 1979.

All that readers of the author's other expositions have come to expect is true of this one as well. Kidner provides a graphic description of the struggles of the Jews in post-exilic Jerusalem and portrays the lives of Ezra and Nehemiah against the backdrop of their times. He follows the current trend of limiting the size of Jerusalem to "David's City," and this makes the dimensions of Nehemiah's wall (as spelled out in the MT) inaccurate. In spite of this weakness, Kidner's comments are judicious. 222.7'07.K54

**Williamson, H. G. M.** *Ezra, Nehemiah.* Word Biblical Commentary. Waco, Tex.: Word Books, 1985.

†Williamson builds on *Redaktionsgeschichte.* He treats the text of Ezra/Nehemiah capably, and those who value critical works will enjoy this one. Each section is prefaced with a section entitled "Bibliography," and these provide access to valuable resource materials. 222.7.W67 (Alt. DDC 220.7'7 v.16).

NEHEMIAH

***Barber, Cyril John.** *Nehemiah and the Dynamics of Effective Leadership.* Neptune, N.J.: Loizeaux Brothers, 1976.

"An unusual book that is both a commentary on Nehemiah and an excellent handbook on leadership. . . . It is probably the most unique treatment of Nehemiah ever written" (*Ministry in Focus*). 222.8'07.B23

————. *Study Guide to Nehemiah and the Dynamics of Effective Leadership.* Neptune, N.J.: Loizeaux Brothers, 1980.

Designed for individual or group use, and containing twenty additional visuals for transparencies, this study guide is not a quick "how to." Rather "the questions have been designed in such a way as to promote thought and discussion. They relate the teaching of Scripture to contemporary problems and provide a healthy integration of Biblical and managerial principles" (*Journal of Psychology and Theology*). 222.8'06.B23S

**Getz, Gene A.** *Nehemiah: A Man of Prayer and Persistence.* Ventura, Calif.: Regal Books, 1981.

Twelve chapters adequately explaining the subheading. 222.8'07.G33

ESTHER

**Baldwin, Joyce G.** *Esther: An Introduction and Commentary.* Tyndale Old Testament Commentaries. Downers Grove, Ill.: InterVarsity Press, 1984.

Prefaced by an extensive introduction, this work assesses the origin, scope, and purpose of Esther. The commentary is very brief—too brief to be of lasting worth. The "Additional Notes" is helpful. 222.9'07.B19

**Moore, Carey A.** *Esther.* The Anchor Bible. Garden City, N.Y.: Doubleday and Co., 1971.

†A higher critical study. Archaeologically illuminating but intended for the advanced student of Hebrew rather than the pastor. 222.9'07.M78

***Raleigh, Alexander.** *Book of Esther: Its Practical Lessons and Dramatic Scenes.* Minneapolis: Klock & Klock Christian Publishers, 1980.

A refreshing study based on a literal interpretation of the text. Each character is analyzed with "insight approaching genius," to quote one reviewer, and the practical application of Scripture to life is accomplished with rare skill. 222.9′.07.R13 1980

**Whitcomb, John Clement, Jr.** *Esther:*

*The Triumph of God's Sovereignty.* Chicago: Moody Press, 1979.

Intended for laypeople, this devout commentary deals judiciously with the text and explains the events so as to illustrate God's sovereignty. Recommended. 222.9′.07.W58

## POETIC BOOKS

**Bullock, C. Hassell.** *An Introduction to the Old Testament Poetic Books.* Chicago: Moody Press, 1979.

A thorough, well-written introduction to the poetic writings of the OT. Includes a section on the theology of wisdom literature. Will be used repeatedly by teachers in Bible colleges and seminaries. 223′.06.B87

**Crenshaw, James L.** *Old Testament Wisdom: An Introduction.* Atlanta: John Knox Press, 1981.

Examines three aspects of wisdom literature: the nature of ancient wisdom, the literary corpus produced by Israel's sages, and wisdom literature's abiding contributions. The heart of the book is the extensive treatment of each literary product of the sages: Proverbs, Job, Ecclesiastes, Sirach, wisdom psalms, wisdom of Solomon, and other minor texts. Crenshaw considers the central theme of each book, characterizes its chief literary form, and places the book within the larger context of wisdom literature. 223′.06.C86 1981

**Cross, Frank Moore,** and **David Noel Freedman.** *Studies in Ancient Yahwistic Poetry.* Missoula, Mont.: Scholar's Press, 1975.

Building on an earlier work entitled *The Evolution of Early Hebrew Orthography* (1948, rev. 1952), the authors apply to four Yahwistic poems the principles spelled out in the first treatise. This is a

highly technical work, and whatever its merits, pastors will find little in it that is really valuable or aids pulpit exposition. 223′.08.C87

**Kidner, Derek.** *An Introduction to Wisdom Literature: The Wisdom of Proverbs, Job and Ecclesiastes.* Downers Grove, Ill.: InterVarsity Press, 1985.

Kidner's works are appreciated by pastors and Bible students. He provides a sensitive introduction to the form and content of the books mentioned in the subtitle. His summaries of modern criticism are generally helpful. Also worthy of note is Kidner's comparison of the literary genre of the biblical and Apocryphal writings. 223′.06.K54

**Murphy, Roland Edmund.** *Wisdom Literature: Job, Proverbs, Ruth, Canticles, Ecclesiastes, and Esther.* Grand Rapids: Wm. B. Eerdmans Publishing Co., 1981.

The author, a Carmelite monk, makes available the first volume in a series, The Forms of the Old Testament Literature. Though form-critical, the purpose is to lead students of the Scriptures into a first-hand acquaintance with the text. 223′.066.M95

**Sternberg, Meir.** *The Poetics of Biblical Narrative: Ideological Literature and the Drama of Reading.* Bloomington, Ind.: Indiana University Press, 1985.

†Approaches the Scriptures from a literary-critical perspective and seeks to understand the Bible as a work of literature. 809.9.ST4

*Williams, Neal D.* *A Lexicon for the Poetical Books.* Irving, Tex.: Williams and Watrous Publishing Company, 1977.

Follows the MT and provides a verse-by-verse lexicon to the poetical books on the OT, thereby placing at the pastor's fingertips an extensive vocabulary. Word meanings are taken from BDB and Koehler/Baumgartner's *Lexicon in Veteris Testamenti Libros.* Most helpful. 223'.044.W67

## JOB

**Andersen, Francis Ian.** *Job: An Introduction and Commentary.* Downers Grove, Ill.: InterVarsity Press, 1976.

An excellent treatment that maintains a high standard of evangelical scholarship and must take its place among the finest nontechnical expositions ever produced on this enigmatic portion of God's Word. 223.1'07.AN2

**Dhorme, Edouard.** *A Commentary on the Book of Job.* Translated by H. Knight. Nashville: Thomas Nelson Publishers, 1984.

First published in French in 1926 and made available in English in 1967, this work has been reissued with a new preface by F. I. Andersen. Eagerly sought after for its exegetical insights, but readers will be dismayed by Dhorme's frequent emendation of the MT and lack of usage of Near Eastern sources. Though the comments on the text are valuable, the abiding worth of this compendious study lies in the introductory essays. 223.1'07.D53 1984

*Gibson, Edgar Charles Sumner.* *The Book of Job.* Minneapolis: Klock & Klock Christian Publishers, 1978.

A perceptive and edifying study. Contains useful outlines at the beginning of different sections. These are most helpful to expository preachers in preparing biblically based messages on the

grammar of the OT text. The value of this work increases with its use. It should be in every minister's library. 223.1'07.G35 1978

**Gibson, John C. J.** *Job.* Daily Study Bible. Philadelphia: Westminster Press, 1985.

†Contains a mixture of good and not-so-good things. Flashes of insight reveal the writer's pastoral heart. Much of the text is taken up citing the biblical passage with the exposition being proportionately brief. Though this study should not be ignored, other English works are more reliable on critical issues. 223.1'07.G35

*Green, William Henry.* *The Argument of the Book of Job.* Minneapolis: Klock & Klock Christian Publishers, 1981.

Few works are as helpful as this one in tracing the argument of the book, exposing the shallowness of human explanations of suffering, and then revealing the believer's resources. Careful perusal of this book will add depth and new insight into Job. It will enhance any messages preached on this portion of God's word. Recommended. 223.1'07.G82 1981

**Habel, Norman C.** *The Book of Job.* Cambridge Bible Commentary. New York: Cambridge University Press, 1975.

Based on the text of the NEB. This study generally follows the emendations of the Hebrew text adopted by the translators on whose work the series is based. Habel locates the events of Job in the patriarchal period but believes the book was not written until the seventh century. He sees the theme of Job revolving around the conflict between the integrity of God and the integrity of man. What he presents is truly helpful in spite of the weaknesses inherent in his presuppositions. 223.1'07.H11

———. *The Book of Job: A Commentary.* Old Testament Library. Philadelphia: Westminster Press, 1985.

†Not since Dhorme's magisterial work has a treatment as comprehensive as this one been attempted. Habel makes good use of modern research and combines this information into his own contribution. Those who preach on this long-forgotten book of the OT will find Habel's commentary most valuable. 223.1′07.H11

**Rowley, Harold Henry.** *Job.* New Century Bible. Grand Rapids: Wm. B. Eerdmans Publishing Co., 1980.

First published in 1970. This study is not a commentary in the strict sense of the word but rather treats specific words or phrases in different verses. It is insightful and also most useful due to the bibliographic references interspersed throughout the text. 223.1′07.R79 1980

**\*Stedman, Ray C.** *Expository Studies in Job: Behind Suffering.* Waco, Tex.: Word Books, 1981.

With an emphasis on essential values and a word of comfort to those facing the perplexities of suffering, Stedman relates the teaching of the book of Job to the needs of the hour. A most worthy addition to a Bible student's library. 223.1′07.ST3

**Thomas, David.** *Book of Job:* Expository and Homiletical Commentary. Grand Rapids: Kregel Publications, 1982.

First published in the 1870s under the title *Problemata Mundi,* this work outlines and discusses each discourse and unfolds the essential theme of the book. 223.1′07.T36 1982

**Zuck, Roy B.** *Job.* Everyman's Bible Commentary. Chicago: Moody Press, 1978.

In thirteen pertinent, well-written chapters, Zuck explains the theme of Job and the lessons to be learned from his sufferings. This is a masterful condensation of material, and the structure lends itself for use with adult Bible study groups. Recommended. 223.1′07.z8

PSALMS

**Allen, Ronald Barclay.** *Lord of Song: The Messiah Revealed in the Psalms.* Portland, Oreg.: Multnomah Press, 1985.

Grounded in biblical theology and with solid scholarly support, this book champions the cause of worship and warmly and personally urges readers to restudy the Psalms in order to learn the truth of an overflowing heart. Allen also excites our minds to wonderment at how the Psalms anticipate the life of the Messiah and prefigure His earthly ministry. The climax comes as Allen delves into personal experience and calls on us to respond to the Lord of song with our own form of praise. 223.2′06.AL5L

**\*_____.** *Praise! A Matter of Life and Breath.* Nashville: Thomas Nelson Publishers, 1980.

Dissatisfaction with contemporary styles of worship has caused the author of this excellent volume to go to the Bible to find suitable guidelines by which to glorify God. His study of the book of Psalms has yielded some important truths. He boldly breaks out of the mold of commonly held forms of worship and charts a course that is both innovative and exciting. No one can seriously interact with what Allen has presented without being profoundly moved. Highly recommended. 223.2′06.AL5P

**Anderson, Bernard W.** *Out of the Depths: The Psalms Speak for Us Today.* Philadelphia: Westminster Press, 1974.

†Grounded in form-criticism and an existential theology. May nevertheless be read with profit by the discerning reader. 223.2′06.AN2D

**Clarke, Arthur G.** *Analytical Studies in the Psalms.* Grand Rapids: Kregel Publications, 1979.

Written during his imprisonment by the Japanese in North China during World War I, these brief analyses of each psalm breathe the confidence of one whose reliance (regardless of his outward circumstances) was established on the unchanging character of God. The personal element and spiritual triumph contained in these pages will provide many expository preachers with the raw material for sermons on this portion of God's Word. 223.2.C55 1979.

*Cox, Samuel. *The Pilgrim Psalms.* Minneapolis: Klock & Klock Christian Publishers, 1983.

In these chapters Cox focuses attention on the oft neglected psalms of ascent (Psalms 120-134) and in a series of well-reasoned, clear, and relevant messages draws from each portion of Scripture pertinent truths that are then applied in practical ways. James Moffatt paid high tribute to Cox when he wrote, "Dr. Cox was too honest an expositor to intrude his views into his interpretation of Scripture. He was as scrupulous as Calvin himself on this point." The reprinting of this fine work is welcomed. 223.2'07.120—134.C83 1983

*Davis, John James. *The Perfect Shepherd: Studies in the Twenty-Third Psalm.* Winona Lake, Ind.: Brethren Missionary Herald Books, 1979.

A beautifully written, in-depth treatment of this choice psalm. Recommended. 223.2'07.23.D29

Dickson, David. *A Commentary on the Psalms.* 2 vols. Minneapolis: Klock & Klock Christian Publishers, 1980.

First published in 1655, these devout studies of Israel's ancient hymnic literature exhibit a vibrancy of faith and a care in exposition that is refreshing. 223.2'07.D56 1980

Kidner, Derek. *Psalms 1-72.* Tyndale Old Testament Commentaries. Downers Grove, Ill.: InterVarsity Press, 1973.

This small volume condenses the fruit of scholarly inquiry of the past sixty years and presents in layman's language an analysis of the different kinds of hymnic literature and the setting of the worship ritual of the ancient Israelites. 223.2'07.1—72.K53

Kirkpatrick, Alexander Francis. *The Book of Psalms.* Grand Rapids: Baker Book House, 1982.

First published in 1902, this work was part of the Cambridge Bible for Schools and Colleges series. It is a substantive volume that retains its value, even though modern philology has contributed much to our knowledge of ancient hymnic literature. 223.2'07.K63 1982

Knight, George Angus Fulton. *Psalms.* 2 vols. Daily Study Bible. Philadelphia: Westminster Press, 1983.

†Writes to re-create interest in the Psalms. Succeeds in making their message relevant to people's needs but does little to really build them up in the faith. The translation is helpful, but the comments on the text are too brief to be of lasting worth. 223.2'07.K74

*Maclaren, Alexander. *The Psalms.* 3 vols. Minneapolis: Klock & Klock Christian Publishers, 1980.

Until they are replaced by a better work, these volumes by England's prince of expository preachers will remain the best treatment for the expositor. Recommended. 223.2'07.M22 1981

Perowne, John James Stewart. *The Book of Psalms.* 2 vols. Grand Rapids: Zondervan Publishing House, 1976.

Reprinted from the 1878 edition, these conservative studies retain much of their value, even though they need to be supplemented by more up-to-date treatments. 223.2'07.P42 1976

Phillips, John. *Exploring the Psalms. Vol. One: 1-41.* Neptune, N.J.: Loizeaux Brothers, 1985.

These studies are well outlined and provide seed thoughts on each verse or paragraph. Preachers will find this volume ideal for use as a preliminary re-

source for a series of messages.
223.2'07.P53 v.l

**Power, Philip Bennett.** *The "I Wills" of the Psalms.* Carlisle, Pa.: Banner of Truth Trust, 1985.

First published in 1858, this unique book ably fulfills the title and, in doing so, provides believers with a delightful devotional treatise and preachers with a seedbed of useful sermon topics. 223.2'06.P87 1985

**Sabourin, Leopold.** *The Psalms: Their Origin and Meaning.* New York: Alba House, 1974.

A revision in one volume of the author's 1969 introduction to hymnic literature. Sacramental. 223.2'06.SA1 1974

**Westermann, Claus.** *Praise and Lament in the Psalms.* Translated by K. R. Crim and R. N. Soulen. Atlanta: John Knox Press, 1981.

†Praise and lament are two major approaches to God. This work assesses both, and the result is a new understanding of the book of Psalms. Westermann's handling of these aspects of Israel's hymnic literature is helpful and insightful. Future treatments will show their indebtedness to this important volume. 223.2'06.W52P

———. *The Psalms: Structure, Content and Message.* Translated by R. D. Gehrke. Minneapolis: Augsburg Publishing House, 1980.

†Discusses different types of hymnic literature and seeks to relate the message of the Psalms to life today. 223.2'06.W52

**White, Reginald Ernest Oscar.** *A Christian Handbook to the Psalms.* Grand Rapids: Wm. B. Eerdmans Publishing Co., 1984.

†Explains Israel's hymnic literature for today's laypeople. Every chapter gives evidence of a scholar's care. Draws on modern approaches to the literary genre of the times. 223.2'06.W58

PROVERBS

**Arnot, William.** *Studies in Proverbs.* Grand Rapids: Kregel Publications, 1978.

Formerly published under the title *Laws of Heaven for Life on Earth,* these inspirational gems provide both practical instruction and spiritual direction. 223.7'07.AR6 1978

***Bridges, Charles.** *A Modern Study in the Book of Proverbs: Charles Bridges' Classic Revised for Today's Reader by George F. Santa.* Milford, Mich.: Mott Media, 1978.

Rewritten in modern English, using the text of the NASB, and carefully cross-indexed, this modern reissue of Bridges's famous commentary is indispensable to the expository preacher and should stimulate fresh interest in this Puritan work as well as in the book of Proverbs. Recommended. 223.7'07.B76 1978

**Briscoe, Jill.** *Queen of Hearts: The Role of Today's Woman, Based on Proverbs 31.* Old Tappan, N.J.: Fleming H. Revell Co., 1984.

Delightful devotional messages. It is hard to imagine anyone's not being blessed by what Mrs. Briscoe relates. 223.7'06.31.B77

***Lawson, George.** *Exposition of Proverbs.* Grand Rapids: Kregel Publications, 1981.

Those who are fortunate enough to possess a copy of this work will readily testify to the rich rewarding insights to be found in this able Scot's warm devotional exposition. He, in company with very few others, knew the human heart and had the ability to so teach the Word that his hearers and/or readers were continuously blessed by his messages. 223.7'07.L44 1981

**McKane, William.** *Proverbs, A New Approach.* Old Testament Library. Philadelphia: Westminster Press, 1970.

†An informative, but highly critical, study. 223.7'07.M19

**\*Mouser, William E., Jr.** *Walking in Wisdom: Studying the Proverbs of Solomon.* Downers Grove, Ill.: InterVarsity Press, 1983.

"Here is a highly recommended book—a gold-miner's manual for all who want to become spiritually wealthy" (Roy B. Zuck). 223.7'06.M86

**Santa, George F.** *Proverbs: Personalized Studies for Practical Living; for Use with a Modern Study in the Book of Proverbs.* Milford, Mich.: Mott Media, 1978.

A topical summary of the contents of Proverbs with hints on how to study this much-neglected portion of God's Word. (For the work to be used with this handy volume, see under Bridges.) 223.7'06.SA5

**Thomas, David.** *The Book of Proverbs: Expository and Homiletical Commentary.* Grand Rapids: Kregel Publications, 1982.

Reprinted from the 1885 edition, these meditations cover every verse and provide Westerners with an illustration of how this Eastern work may be taught and applied. Based on the text of the KJV. 223.7'07.T36 1982

**\*Wardlaw, Ralph.** *Lectures on the Book of Proverbs.* 3 vols. Edited by J. S. Wardlaw. Minneapolis: Klock & Klock Christian Publishers, 1981.

Highly esteemed by C. H. Spurgeon and other expository preachers, this choice set makes rich, rewarding reading. Buy it while it is still in print. 223.7'07.W12 1981

ECCLESIASTES

**DeHaan, Richard,** and **Herbert Vander Lugt.** *The Art of Staying Off Dead-end Streets.* Wheaton, Ill.: Victor Books, 1974.

A practical study of Ecclesiastes. Ideal for Bible discussion groups. 223.8'07.D36

**\*Kaiser, Walter C., Jr.** *Ecclesiastes: Total Life.* Chicago: Moody Press, 1979.

One of the most satisfying expositions on this portion of Scripture. Highly recommended. 223.8'07.K12

**Kidner, Derek.** *A Time to Mourn, a Time to Dance: Ecclesiastes and the Way of the World.* The Bible Speaks Today. Downers Grove, Ill.: InterVarsity Press, 1976.

Though rejecting Solomonic authorship and struggling with the theme of his book, Kidner nevertheless presents his readers with a fascinating, well-balanced exposition of Qoheleth's thought. His material makes stimulating reading. 223.8'07.K54

**Loader, J. A.** *Polar Structures in the Book of Qohlet.* Berlin: Walter de Gruyter, 1979.

Analyzes the polar structures of Ecclesiastes and uses these to highlight the tensions created in the experience of the author. For use by the well-informed student. 223.8'06.L78

**\*MacDonald, James Madison.** *The Book of Ecclesiastes Explained.* Minneapolis: Klock & Klock Christian Publishers, 1982.

C. H. Spurgeon said of this work, "Thoroughly exegetical, with excellent 'scopes of argument' following each division; to be purchased if found." An excellent work. Buy it. 223.8'07.M14 1982

**Stedman, Ray C.** *Solomon's Secret: Enjoying Life, God's Good Gift.* Portland, Oreg.: Multnomah Press, 1985.

Brief though adequate messages on Ecclesiastes. Opens up this long-ignored book of the OT. Ideal for laypeople's discussion groups. 223.8'07.ST3

**\*Swindoll, Charles Rozell.** *Living on the Ragged Edge: Coming to Terms with Reality.* Waco, Tex.: Word Books, 1985.

Addresses the contemporary milieu; explains from what God chose to reveal through His inspired penman the secret of contentment and the way to enjoy a sense of fulfillment. Each message is at once timely and relevant. The result is a work that deserves widespread circulation. 223.8'06.SW6

*Wardlaw, Ralph. *Exposition of Ecclesiastes.* Minneapolis: Klock & Klock Christian Publishers, 1982.

These sermons, first published in 1868, adequately expound the ethical and practical principles of this portion of God's Word. Readers will find in them a richness of thought and a relevance of application that will reward their inquiry. Recommended. 223.8'07.W21 1982

SONG OF SOLOMON

**Bernard of Clairvaux.** *Song of Solomon.* Translated and edited by S. J. Eales. Minneapolis: Klock & Klock Christian Publishers, 1984.

First published in 1895, these studies by Bernard (c. 1090-1153) are deeply devout and interpret Solomon's Song in terms of the union of Christ and the believer. Well deserving the status of a classic. 223.9'07.B45 1984

**Carr, G. Lloyd.** *The Song of Solomon: An Introduction and Commentary.* Tyndale Old Testament Commentaries. Downers Grove, Ill.: InterVarsity Press, 1984.

Basing his interpretation on a literal approach to Solomon's Song, Carr provides a satisfying introduction to this portion of God's Word. His commentary is ideally suited to lay people. 223.9'07.C23

**Dillow, Joseph C.** *Solomon on Sex.* Nashville: Thomas Nelson, 1977.

A verse-by-verse commentary that unhesitatingly applies the teaching of the Song of Solomon to modern marriages.

In a few places Dillow follows a critical emendation of the MT. 223.9'06.D59

*Durham, James. *Clovis Cantici: or, An Exposition of the Song of Solomon.* Minneapolis: Klock & Klock Christian Publishers, 1981.

Interprets this song as depicting the union between Christ and the believer. Abounds with devotional insights. Heretofore virtually unattainable. 223.9'07.D93 1981

**Falk, Marcia.** *Love Lyrics from the Bible: A Translation and Literary Study of the Song of Songs.* Sheffield, England: Almond Press, 1982.

"Her interpretations of the individual poems are full of interest—the delimiting of each piece, its metaphors, its movement between levels of experience (dream, fantasy, reality). Nothing I have read on these matters speaks so articulately and authoritatively—so easily familiar with the genre of lyric expression—as she" (Moshe Greenberg). 223.9'06.F18

**Fox, Michael V.** *The Song of Songs and the Ancient Egyptian Love Songs.* Madison, Wis.: University of Wisconsin Press, 1985.

This treatise makes available the kind of information not always accessible to preachers and Bible teachers. Though certain parallels between Solomon's Song and ancient Egyptian (and on occasion, Mesopotamian) love songs does indicate a particular mindset, the nature of God's revelation lifts Solomon's reminiscences above the level of the practices of the surrounding nations. 223.9'06.F83

*Glickman, S. Craig. *A Song for Lovers.* Downers Grove, Ill.: InterVarsity Press, 1976.

Glickman gives to his readers a literal interpretation and an intelligent exposition of marital love and sexuality. His excellent handling of Solomon's Song has succeeded in retrieving it from the oblivion to which neglect had relegated it. Recommended. 223.9'06.G49

**Gordis, Robert.** *The Song of Songs and Lamentations: A Study, Modern Translation and Commentary.* Rev. ed. New York: Ktav Publishing House, 1974.

Technical studies, first published in 1954, that interpret these OT writings and provide numerous cultural and linguistic insights. Extensive documentation makes them ideal for the scholar, but their technical nature minimizes their value for the busy pastor. 223.9'06.G65 1974

**Phillips, John.** *Exploring the Song of Solomon.* Neptune, N.J.: Loizeaux Brothers, 1984.

Attempts to avoid controversy over the interpretation of Solomon's Song by adhering to the three-character theory and explaining the theme in relation to Christ and His church. 223.9'07.P54

## PROPHETIC BOOKS

**Miller, Patrick D., Jr.** *Sin and Judgment in the Prophets: A Stylistic and Theological Analysis.* Chico, Calif.: Scholars Press, 1982.

A brief, scholarly assessment of the teaching of Israel's prophets on the consequences of sin and the inevitability of judgment where there is no repentance. 224.'.08.J89.M61

**Newsome, James DuPre.** *The Hebrew Prophets.* Atlanta: John Knox Press, 1984

†The key feature of this introductory volume is its treatment of each of the canonical prophets in chronological order. The teaching of the prophet is subjected to a systematic analysis. Each chapter summarizes key elements in the prophet's message so that readers may gain a basic understanding of the condition of the people as well as the teaching they received. Included is a discussion of each prophet's background with exegetical studies on individual passages. 224.06.N47

**\*Wood, Leon J.** *The Prophets of Israel.* Grand Rapids: Baker Book House, 1979.

A careful and reverent treatment of the place, importance, and teaching of the OT prophets. Should be in every preacher's library. 224'.061.W85

ISAIAH

**\*Alexander, Joseph Addison.** *Isaiah,* *Translated and Explained.* Minneapolis: Klock & Klock Christian Publishers, 1981.

An abridgment of the author's critical treatment of this portion of Scripture. Excellent, nontechnical, ideal for pastors and laypeople. 224.1'07.AL2 1981

**Bultema, Harry.** *Commentary on Isaiah.* Grand Rapids: Kregel Publications, 1981.

Translated from the Dutch, this work treats Isaiah's prophecy chapter-by-chapter. Brief and to the point. 224.1'07.B87

**Clements, Ronald Ernest.** *Isaiah 1-39.* New Century Bible Commentary. Grand Rapids: Wm. B. Eerdmans Publishing Co., 1980.

Treats the text with rare insight and provides readers, if not with a commentary, at least with scholarly comments on selected words and phrases. 224.1'07.C59 1980

**Erdman, Charles Rosenbury.** *The Book of Isaiah: An Exposition.* Grand Rapids: Baker Book House, 1982.

Reprinted from the 1954 edition. Makes available this pulpit master's lucid exposition. A well-balanced treatment. 224.1'07.ER2 1982

**Govett, Robert.** *Isaiah Unfulfilled: Being an Exposition of the Prophet . . .* Miami Springs, Fla.: Conley and Schoettle Publishing Co., 1984.

Replete with studies on the "sons of God" and the "giants of Genesis 6," together with a comparison of Hebrew and Greek texts, this study also focuses attention on each chapter in Isaiah and stresses the unfulfilled prophecies. This feature alone makes this a useful resource tool. Originally published in 1841. Premillennial. 224.1'06.G74 1984

**Kaiser, Otto.** *Isaiah 13-39.* Old Testament Library. Translated by R. A. Wilson. Philadelphia: Westminster Press, 1974.

†An exacting study whose chief value lies in its discussion of the relationship of Jewish expectation to her apocalyptic literature and the eventual removal of her hopes as a nation from the realm of history. 224.1'07.K12

**\*Kelly, William.** *An Exposition of the Book of Isaiah.* 4th ed. Minneapolis: Klock & Klock Christian Publishers, 1979.

Fills a long-standing need for a premillennial commentary. Kelly was a well-informed student of God's Word. His knowledge of eschatology was exacting. He never evaded critical or hard-to-explain sections of Scripture. His sensitivity to the Holy Spirit's thoughts often led him to understand intuitively what later expositors have verified experimentally. This is a work that can be recommended to serious Bible students. It is nontechnical, accurate, and well worth the time spent on mastering its contents. 224.1'07.K28 1979

**Knight, George Angus Fulton.** *The New Israel: A Commentary on the Book of Isaiah 56-66.* International Theological Commentary. Grand Rapids: Wm. B. Eerdmans Publishing Co., 1985.

†A masterful condensation of material that is unhappily marred by adherence to higher critical theories pertaining to the date, composition, and authorship of this portion of God's Word. 224.1'07.K74N

————. *Servant Theology: A Commentary on the Book of Isaiah 40-55.* Grand Rapids:

Wm. B. Eerdmans Publishing Co., 1984.

†First published in 1965, this work approaches Isaiah's work as coming from the hand of a later penman. Justifiable emphasis is placed on the Servant-Messiah concept, and in this respect Knight has much that is commendable. He emphasizes the theology of this portion of Scripture and provides an important discussion of the motifs that are later developed in the NT. 224.1'07.40—55.K74

**\*Leupold, Herbert Carl.** *Exposition of Isaiah.* 2 vols. Grand Rapids: Baker Book House, 1968-1971.

Defends the unity of this prophecy and furnishes a satisfying exposition. Amillennial. 224.1'07.L57

**\*Lindsay, Franklin Duane.** *The Servant Songs: A Study in Isaiah.* Chicago: Moody Press, 1985.

Expounds the Servant Songs of Isaiah in such a way as to provide students of God's Word with the clearest and most complete picture of Christ in the OT. Lindsey's contribution is balanced and well reasoned. Preachers will find this volume to be invaluable. 224.1'07.40—55.L64

**\*MacRae, Allan Alexander.** *The Gospel of Isaiah.* Chicago: Moody Press, 1977.

A brilliant study of the servant motif in Isaiah 40:1—56:8. Opens up the content for examination and discussion. Recommended. 224.1'06.40—56.M24

**\*Martin, Alfred,** and **John A. Martin.** *Isaiah: The Glory of the Messiah.* Chicago: Moody Press, 1983.

Though designed for laypeople, this treatment of the theme of Isaiah can only be described as brilliant. It is a masterful summation of what God chose to reveal through this OT prophet. It is happily free from critical issues and maintains the unity of Isaiah's thought. It builds on a consistent eschatological foundation so that NT truths are brought into harmony with the OT without confusing Israel and the church. 224.1.M36G 1983

**Ridderbos, Jan.** *Isaiah*. Bible Students' Commentary. Translated by J. Vriend. Grand Rapids: Zondervan Publishing House, Regency Reference Library, 1984.

Part of the *Korte Verklaring Der Heilige Schrift*. This study deals adequately and conservatively with the history of the times and the unity of Isaiah's prophecy. Students will find Ridderbos's treatment to be insightfully written and exegetically sound. 224.1'07.R43

**Sawyer, John F. A.** *Isaiah*. Vol. 1, Daily Study Bible. Philadelphia: Westminster Press, 1984.

†Covering chapters 1-32, this well-outlined discussion succeeds in elucidating the main tenets of Isaiah's indictment of Israel. 224.1'07.SA9 v.1

**Watts, John D. W.** *Isaiah 1-33*. Word Biblical Commentary. Waco, Tex.: Word Books, 1985.

Awakens new interest in Isaiah's early prophecies. Describes the change in God's dealings with His people. Important themes are to be found in these pages: the day of the Lord, true servanthood, God's discipline of the nations, and the like. Excurses on theological themes are included. A redactional exposition. 224.1'07.W34 (Alt. DDC 220.7 v.24).

**Whybray, Roger Norman.** *Isaiah 40—66*. Greenwood, S.C.: Attic Press, 1975.

†Accepts the Trito-Isaiah theory and expounds the prophecy as if it were history. Disappointing. 224.1'06.40—66.W62

**Wolf, Herbert M.** *Interpreting Isaiah: The Suffering and Glory of the Messiah*. Grand Rapids: Zondervan Publishing House, Academie Books, 1985.

The many quotations and allusions to Isaiah in the NT provide a vital clue to understanding this prophetic work. Indeed, one of the most fruitful challenges in the preparation of this book was the interpretation of those quotations and allusions, especially the ones that refer to the Person and work of Christ. Wolf's main concern is to explain clearly the meaning of Isaiah's words and concepts and in that way begin to fathom the meaning of his prophecies about the future of God's people in a world that will be judged and then marvelously renewed. 224.1'06.W83

JEREMIAH

**Davidson, Robert.** *Jeremiah*. Vol. 1, Daily Study Bible series. Philadelphia: Westminster Press, 1983.

†Covers chaps. 1-20. Helps to explain the words of the Lord through Jeremiah. Contains insightful thoughts on the autobiographical and theological passages in these chapters. 224.2'07.D28 v.1

**Efird, James M.** *Jeremiah: Prophet Under Seige*. Valley Forge, Pa.: Judson Press, 1979.

Designed for use by laypeople, this topical approach to the life of Jeremiah treats only incidentally the arrangement of the book and the prophet's message. 224.2'06.EF4

**Erdman, Charles Rosenbury.** *The Books of Jeremiah and Lamentations: An Exposition*. Grand Rapids: Baker Book House, 1982.

Serves to introduce laypeople to the theme and purpose of these books. Each is a fine example of practical exposition. 224.2'07.ER2 1982

*****Feinberg, Charles Lee.** *Jeremiah, a Commentary*. Grand Rapids: Zondervan Publishing House, 1982.

A clear, relevant treatment of Jeremiah's life and messages. Calls attention to Judah's demise and self-will. Shows how God was working behind the scenes—with Assyria declining in power and the Neo-Babylonian Empire in its ascendancy—all the while showing to

His people that their only hope lay in a return to honoring the principles of His covenant. We have long needed a good premillennial commentary on this portion of God's Word, and Feinberg's handling of Jeremiah's predictions supplies that need. 224.2'07.F32

**Hamby, Warren C.** *Winds of Change.* Old Tappan, N.J.: Fleming H. Revell Co., 1971.

Sermons based on the book of Jeremiah that deal with finding God's direction in turbulent times. 224.2'07.H17

**Holladay, William Lee.** *Jeremiah: Spokesman Out of Time.* Philadelphia: United Church Press, 1974.

A well-reasoned explanation of the message of Jeremiah. Sheds light on Hebrew word meanings and the puns used by the prophet. In spite of Holladay's reluctance to amend the text, his liberal views are seen in his adherence to certain documentary theories (among them a Deutero-Isaiah). Though designed for laypeople, this generally helpful commentary is better suited to those with a background in OT study. 224.2'07.H71

**Orelli, Hans Conrad von.** *The Prophecies of Jeremiah.* Minneapolis: Klock & Klock Christian Publishers, 1977.

A moderately conservative work that meets a need felt by evangelical pastors. 224.2'07.OR3 1977

**Perdue, Leo G.,** and **Brian W. Kovacs, eds.** *A Prophet to the Nations: Essays in Jeremiah Studies.* Winona Lake, Ind.: Eisenbrauns, 1984.

Deals with the current issues involved in Jeremiah studies. Assesses the call and mission of Jeremiah and the relationship of his writing to the book of Deuteronomy and the reform of Josiah. A pleasing, scholarly study. 224.2'06.P41

**\*Thompson, John Arthur.** *The Book of Jeremiah.* New International Commentary on the Old Testament. Grand Rapids: Wm. B. Eerdmans Publishing Co., 1980.

This highly competent commentary deals thoroughly with every aspect of the prophet's life and ministry and stresses the importance of Judah's covenant relationship with the Lord. Readers are treated to a careful handling of the Hebrew text ably correlated with the DDS. Also they are given a definitive explanation of the backdrop of the times in the Josianic reformation. Recommended. 224.2'07.T37

LAMENTATIONS

**\*Kaiser, Walter Christian, Jr.** *A Biblical Approach to Personal Suffering.* Chicago: Moody Press, 1982.

This study deals clearly and adequately with the problem of personal suffering and provides a definitive exposition of Lamentations. Recommended. 224.3'07.K12

EZEKIEL

**\*Alexander, Ralph.** *Ezekiel.* Everyman's Bible Commentary. Chicago: Moody Press, 1976.

Designed for laypeople, this able work admirably combines learning and devotion. Alexander sheds light on the scope of the prophet's message and does so in a way that brings into focus the purpose of God for His people. 224.4'07.AL2

**\*Fairbairn, Patrick.** *An Exposition of Ezekiel.* Minneapolis: Klock & Klock Christian Publishers, 1979.

Makes judicious use of the Hebrew text but not at the expense of the English reader. Provides a timely exposition that is devotional as well as historical and practical. Recommended. Amillennial. 224.2'07.F15 1979

**Hengstenberg, Ernst Wilhelm.** *The Prophecies of the Prophet Ezekiel.* Translated by A. C. Murphy and J. G. Murphy. Minneapolis: James & Klock Publishing Company, 1976.

A capable exposition by an evangelical Lutheran of a generation past. Reprinted from the 1879 edition. Amillenial. 224.4'07.H38 1976

**Wevers, John W.** *Ezekiel.* New Century Bible Commentary. Grand Rapids: Wm. B. Eerdmans Publishing Co., 1982.

Based on the text of the RSV, this work reveals how often the translators amended the MT. Disappointing. 224.4'07.W54 1982

DANIEL

**Anderson, Robert A.** *Signs and Wonders: A Commentary on the Book of Daniel.* International Theological Commentary. Grand Rapids: Wm. B. Eerdmans Publishing Co., 1984.

Has little to add to what can be gleaned from a careful reading of the text. Disappointing. 224.5'07.AN2

**Baldwin, Joyce G.** *Daniel: An Introduction and Commentary.* Downers Grove, Ill.: InterVarsity Press, 1979.

A capable exposition by a respected OT scholar. Good treatment of textual matters but indifference to prophetic themes minimizes the value of this book. 224.5'07.B18

**Boutflower, Charles.** *In and Around the Book of Daniel.* Grand Rapids: Kregel Publications, 1977.

Reproduced from the 1923 edition. This work is indispensable to a study of the visions and prophecies of Daniel. It sets each incident in the historic context of the times and demonstrates how an understanding of the setting frequently contains the key to the correct interpretation of the passage. Recommended. 224.5'06.B66 1977

**Campbell, Donald Keith.** *Daniel: Decoder of Dreams.* Wheaton, Ill.: Victor Books, 1977.

Thorough in interpretation and practical in application, this treatment of Daniel is ideal for use with laypeople. Premillennial. 224.5'07.C15

**Casey, Maurice.** *Son of Man: The Interpretation and Influence of Daniel 7.* London: Society Promoting Christian Knowledge, 1979.

A comprehensive survey of the interpretation of this passage from apostolic times to the present. Of value for its historical material. Of less value for its messianic teaching. 224.5'07.7.C26

**Culver, Robert Duncan.** *The Histories and Prophecies of Daniel.* Winona Lake, Ind.: BMH Books, 1980.

A fact-filled, biblically based exposition that explains the meaning and message of Daniel's prophecy. An ideal work for home Bible classes and adult Sunday school groups. 224.5'07.C89H

**Feinberg, Charles Lee.** *Daniel: The Man and His Visions.* Chappaqua, N.Y.: Christian Herald Books, 1981.

Written for laypeople, this study adequately expounds the purpose and prophecies of Daniel. Recommended. 224.5'07.F32

**Ford, Desmond.** *Daniel.* Nashville: Southern Publishing Association, 1978.

Employs the text of the RSV. Expounds the text with insight. Displays an awareness of the history of the ancient Near East as well as the political machinations and their prophetic implications. Insightful. Poorly bound. 224.5'07.F75

**Hartman, Louis Francis,** and **Alexander A. DiLella.** *The Book of Daniel.* The Anchor Bible. Garden City, N.Y.: Doubleday and Co., 1978.

In keeping with the format of this series, the authors try to provide background material for their historic interpretation, thus negating the prophetic element. Roman Catholic. 224.5'07.H25

**\*Lang, George Henry.** *The Histories and Prophecies of Daniel.* Grand Rapids: Kregel Publications, 1974.

Based primarily on the RSV, this premillennial, posttribulation work by a leading Plymouth Brethren writer combines extensive research with a comprehensive treatment of the prophetic Scriptures. 224.5'07.L25

**Mickelsen, A. Berkeley.** *Daniel and Revelation: Riddles or Realities.* Nashville: Thomas Nelson Publishers, 1984.

Views these apocalyptic writings topically to discern their view of God, man, sin, human government, holiness, history, and eschatology. Mickelsen avoids dogmatism and provides his readers with food for thought and a fresh understanding of these portions of God's Word. 224.5'06.M58

**Pusey, Edward Bouverie.** *Daniel the Prophet.* Minneapolis: Klock & Klock Christian Publishers, 1978.

Reproduced from the 1885 edition, this volume contains Pusey's lectures delivered at Oxford University. Though superseded by more recent works, the historical and philological strengths of this treatment should be neither neglected nor ignored. Amillennial. 224.5'07.P77 1978

**Russell, David Syme.** *Daniel.* Philadelphia: Westminster Press, 1981.

Inspired by the profound truths contained in this fascinating book, Russell explains the content of each chapter. He emphasizes God's sovereignty but fails to do justice to the eschatological portions. 224.5'07.R91

**\*Tatford, Frederick Albert.** *Daniel and His Prophecy: Studies in the Prophecy of Daniel.* Minneapolis: Klock & Klock Christian Publishers, 1980.

First published in 1953, this study exhibits a balance between extremes. It treats the prophetic word with respect but does not probe minutiae. Instead, the message of Daniel is explained to the enlightenment and edification of the reader. Throughout his exposition, Tatford blends history and theology, practical application and devotional stimulation in a most pleasing manner. Premillennial. 224.5'07.T18 1980

**Towner, Wayne Sibley.** *Daniel.* Interpretation, A Bible Commentary for Teaching and Preaching. Atlanta: John Knox Press, 1984.

†Utilizes form-criticism and redaction-criticism supposedly to lay bare the teaching of the book of Daniel. Helpful historically. The work also contains some insightful exegetical comments. 224.5'07.T66

**\*Walvoord, John Flipse.** *Daniel: The Key to Prophetic Revelation.* Chicago: Moody Press, 1971.

Emphasizes the genuineness of the prophet and his writings, and provides a clear interpretation of the book. Thorough, well outlined, and well documented. Premillennial. 224.5'07.W17

**Whitcomb, John Clement, Jr.** *Daniel.* Everyman's Bible Commentary. Chicago: Moody Press, 1985.

A masterful synthesis of information. Provides a clear overview of the scope of Daniel's prophecy. Well executed, easy to understand. Recommended. 224.5'07.W58

**\*Wilson, Robert Dick.** *Studies in the Book of Daniel.* 2 vols. in 1. Grand Rapids: Baker Book House, 1979.

The reprinting in paperback of an indispensable defense of the accuracy and integrity of the book of Daniel. Highly recommended. Amillennial. 224.5'06.W69 1979

**Wood, Leon James.** *A Commentary on Daniel.* Grand Rapids: Zondervan Publishing House, 1972.

This is a fascinating and enlightening

commentary. It is also an accurate and reliable one. Wood expounds the historic setting of the book, unfolds its prophetic message, and provides his readers with fresh insights into the text. Recommended. Premillennial. 224.5'07.W85

MINOR PROPHETS

**Craigie, Peter Campbell.** *Twelve Prophets.* 2 vols. Daily Study Bible. Philadelphia: Westminster Press, 1984.

†These volumes adequately introduce the writing of each minor prophet. The exposition contains something good on each canonical book. Craigie's writings always give evidence of being well researched, and this study is no exception. Interesting sidelights are to be found on the history and culture of the times. The eschatology of these OT writers is marred, however, by the author's amillennialism. 224.6'07.C84

**DiGangi, Mariano.** *Twelve Prophetic Voices.* Wheaton, Ill.: Victor Books, 1985.

Brief, informative studies for laypeople. Ideal for group discussion. 224.6'07.D56

**Feinberg, Charles Lee.** *The Minor Prophets.* Chicago: Moody Press, 1976.

Formerly published between 1948 and 1952 in a series of volumes under the title *Major Messages on the Minor Prophets,* these studies have served well the needs of laypeople for more than thirty years. 224.6'07.F32 1976

**\*Orelli, Hans Conrad von.** *The Twelve Minor Prophets.* Minneapolis: Klock & Klock Christian Publishers, 1977.

Another valuable reprint in the *Limited Classical Reprint Library.* Ably expounds the teaching of these prophetic writings and provides valuable historical and linguistic data. 224.6'07.OR3 1977

**\*Tatford, Frederick Albert.** *The Minor Prophets.* 3 vols. Minneapolis: Klock & Klock Christian Publishers, 1982.

A masterful exposition ably blending historical facts with a pleasing contemporary application. Worthy of serious consideration. 224.6'07.T18 1982

HOSEA

**Andersen, Francis Ian,** and **David Noel Freedman.** *Hosea, a New Translation with Introduction and Commentary.* The Anchor Bible. Garden City, N.Y.: Doubleday and Co., 1980.

A complete and thorough explanation of the prophet's message with a fascinating interpretation of his life and work. Can be read with profit even by those who would have preferred a more accurate presentation of the eschatological aspects of the book. 224.7'07.AN3

**Emerson, Grace I.** *Hosea: An Israelite Prophet in Judean Perspective.* Sheffield, England: University of Sheffield Press, 1984.

†Provides the conclusions to which the author's critical investigation has led her. Deals with the authenticity, theology, and relevance of Hosea but believes that his indictment is really of Judean origin with prevailing Deuteronomic overtones. 224.7'06.EM6

**Kidner, Derek.** *Love to the Loveless: The Message of Hosea.* The Bible Speaks Today. Downers Grove, Ill.: InterVarsity Press, 1981.

A clear interpretative commentary that deals adequately with the theme and purpose of this portion of God's revelation. 224.7'07.K53

**Morgan, George Campbell.** *Hosea: The Heart and Holiness of God.* Grand Rapids: Baker Book House, 1974.

Morgan was one of the first modern pulpiteers to draw attention to the neglected book of Hosea. On this account his messages deserve consideration. He was breaking new ground as far as popular expository studies were concerned.

His ability to relate the message of this book to the present needs of God's people is evident throughout his work. He provides a clear delineation of the sins of God's people with an equally clear call to repentance. His material is deserving of consideration for his approach to the presentation of difficult issues from the pulpit. Amillennial. 224.7'07.M82 1974

**Riggs, Jack R.** *Hosea's Heartbreak.* Neptune, N.J.: Loizeaux Brothers, 1983.

A careful explanation of the theme of the book of Hosea. Reveals the triumph of Hosea's unquenchable love for Gomer, which is designed to illustrate God's enduring love for His ancient people, Israel. Recommended. 224.7'07.R44

**Tatford, Frederick Albert.** *Prophet of a Broken Home: An Exposition of Hosea.* Eastbourne, Sussex, England: Prophetic Witness Publishing House, 1974.

Now a part of the author's 3-vol. series *The Minor Prophets,* this is a work of merit. Those who would require a minister to resign his pastorate if his wife chooses to leave him should seriously consider the model set by Hosea and the purpose of God in the lives of His people. As with Tatford's other books, this one expounds the personal issues and prophetic content of this canonical work with insight and skill. 224.7'07.T18

**Wolff, Hans Walter.** *Hosea.* Philadelphia: Fortress Press, 1974.

†This form-critical study contains extensive footnotes and a wealth of grammatical insights. It will be of value to serious students of the OT. 224.7'07.W83

JOEL

**Ahlstrom, G. W.** *Joel and the Temple Cult of Jerusalem.* Leiden, The Netherlands: E. J. Brill, 1971.

A scholarly assessment of the historical background and cultural setting of Joel's prophecy. Interspersed throughout the work are important comments on the motifs alluded to by the prophet. 224.8'06.AH4

**Allen, Leslie C.** *The Books of Joel, Obadiah, Jonah, and Micah.* New International Commentary on the Old Testament. Grand Rapids: Wm. B. Eerdmans Publishing Co., 1976.

Extensive research into the historic setting coupled with interesting information on the etymology of certain words makes this book worthy of serious consideration. Other treatments of individual books are fuller and may better meet the needs of the expositor. 224.8'07.AL2

**Wolff, Hans Walter.** *Joel and Amos.* Hermenia. Translated by W. Janzen et al. Edited by S. D. McBride, Jr., Philadelphia: Fortress Press, 1977.

A technical work that makes use of a full range of historical and philological material. 224.8'06.W83

AMOS

**Coote, Robert B.** *Amos Among the Prophets: Composition and Theology.* Philadelphia: Fortress Press, 1981.

Coote makes provision for three stages of composition before beginning to analyze the content and assess the theological importance of this OT prophecy. 224.9'06.C78

**Crenshaw, James L.** *Hymnic Affirmation of Divine Justice: The Doxologies of Amos and Related Texts in the Old Testament.* Missoula, Mont.: Scholars Press, 1975.

A form-critical study that presents the reasons for the presence of these doxologies, suggests who placed them in their present position, and then ascertains their *Sitz im Leben.* 224.9'06.C86

**\*Cripps, Richard S.** *A Commentary on the Book of Amos.* Minneapolis: Klock & Klock Christian Publishers, 1981.

First published in 1929, this work remains one of the finest expositions of Amos's oracles available. Though all readers will not agree with Cripps's interpretation of Amos's eschatology, this commentary is nevertheless deserving of close study. 224.9′07.C86 1981

**Kapelrud, Arvid Schou.** *Central Ideas in Amos.* Oslo, Norway: Aschenhoug, 1971.

A valuable, critical introductory study to the meaning and message of this prophecy. 224.9′06.K14

**Martin-Achard, R., and S. Paul Re'mi.** *A Commentary on the Book of Amos and a Commentary on the Book of Lamentations.* International Theological Commentary. Grand Rapids: Wm. B. Eerdmans Publishing Co., 1984.

Moves beyond a descriptive-historical approach to offer a relevant exegesis of the OT text and expound its theology in light of the social milieu of the prophets. Emphasizes the relevance of these studies in the life of the church today. 224.9′07.M36

***Motyer, John Alexander.*** *The Day of the Lion.* The Voice of the Old Testament. Downers Grove, Ill.: InterVarsity Press, 1974.

A helpful examination of the book of Amos. Relates the message of this OT prophet to the needs of the present day. 224.9′07.M85

**Veldkamp, Herman.** *The Farmer from Tekoa—On the Book of Amos.* Translated by T. Plantenga. St. Catherines, Ontario: Paideia Press, 1977.

A perceptive, eloquent, readable commentary that paints a colorful picture of the cultural setting of Amos's times and relates his message to the needs of people today. 224.9′07.P69

OBADIAH

**Clark, David J., and Norm Mund-**

**henk.** *A Translator's Handbook on the Books of Obadiah and Micah.* Helps for Translators. New York: United Bible Societies, 1982.

A substantive work that will help preachers (as well as translators) come to grips with the essence of the teaching of these two books. Uses the text of the RSV and TEV for comparative purposes, and as neither of these is accurate or reliable, this is a distinct weakness. The writers are also weak in eschatological matters and miss the point of some of the theological discussions. Replete with glossary. 224.91′06.C54

**Coggins, Richard J., and S. Paul Re'emi.** *Esther, Obadiah, Nahum: Israel Among the Nations.* International Theological Commentary. Grand Rapids: Wm. B. Erdmans Publishing Co., 1985.

This commentary follows the aim of the entire series in developing the theological significance of the books under consideration and emphasizing the relevance of each book for the life of the church. Moving beyond the parochialism of Western civilization, the authors are sensitive to issues that are the special problems of those who live outside the Christian West. 224.91′07.C68

JONAH

***Burn, Samuel Clift.*** *The Prophet Jonah.* Minneapolis: Klock & Klock Christian Publishers, 1981.

All things considered, this is one of the best expositions on this OT book for the preacher. 224.92′07.B93 1981

**Ellul, Jacques.** *The Judgment of Jonah.* Grand Rapids: Wm. B. Eerdmans Publishing Co., 1971.

A relevant investigation into the person, mission, and situation of Jonah and the application of the story to the present day. 224.92′07.EL5

***Excell, Joseph Samuel.*** *Practical*

*Truths from Jonah.* Grand Rapids: Kregel Publications, 1982.

A capable devotional commentary that, for all its simplicity, is nonetheless based on sound scholarship. Recommended. 224.92'07.EX2

**Kendall, Robert Tillman.** *Jonah: An Exposition.* Grand Rapids: Zondervan Publishing House, 1978.

Contains expository sermons preached at Westminster Chapel, London. Emphasizes the nature of God as well as the willfulness of His servants. 224.92'07.K33

**\*Kirk, Thomas.** *Jonah: His Life and Mission.* Minneapolis: Klock & Klock Christian Publishers, 1983.

It is difficult to think of any devout Bible student failing to receive blessing from a perusal of this fine work. In these pages we are introduced to new insights and brought into a new relationship with God the Father. We also come to understand more clearly the Lord's hand on our lives. This is not a book for academicians but rather for humble, devout believers who wish to learn the secret of God's grace toward them as well as the path of blessing. 224.92'07.K63 1983

**Kohlenberger, John R., III.** *Jonah and Nahum.* Everyman's Bible Commentary. Chicago: Moody Press, 1984.

A verse-by-verse examination of these two books that have as their point of unification the city of Nineveh. Readily reveals the practical or devotional value of these prophetic writings. Readable, devout, informative. Recommended. 224.92'07.K82

**Lacocque, Andre,** and **Pierre-Emanuel Lacocque.** *The Jonah Complex.* Atlanta: John Knox Press, 1981.

†Two scholars, a theologian and a psychologist, assess the meaning and central message of the book of Jonah. Neither writer treats the text as an authentic piece of history. Rather, their preoccupa-

tion seems to be with symbols and a Jungian form of psychoanalysis. 224.92'07.L11

MICAH

**Hillers, Delbert R.** *Micah.* Hermeneia. Edited by P. D. Hanson and L. Fisher. Philadelphia: Fortress Press, 1984.

†A full and factual, highly critical work. For the specialist. 224.93'07.H55

**Mays, James Luther.** *Micah; A Commentary.* Old Testament Library. Philadelphia: Westminster Press, 1976.

†The author challenges his readers to remedy their neglect of this prophecy. He presents the results of modern critical research, allows for redaction, and provides appropriate comments on the utterance of God's prophet and the Lord's message to His people. 224.93'07.M45

**Smith, Ralph L.** *Word Biblical Commentary: Micah—Malachi.* Waco, Tex.: Word Books, 1984.

The commentaries in this series are not of equal value, but this work contains much to commend it. Smith appears fully abreast of the latest critical data, uses the OT text wisely, and is judicious in his handling of form-criticism and redaction-criticism. 224.93.SMS (Alt. DDC 220.7.W89 v. 32)

NAHUM

**Heflin, J. N. Boo.** *Nahum, Habakkuk, Zephaniah, and Haggai.* Grand Rapids: Lamplighter Books, 1985.

A handy commentary for lay study. Explains the historic circumstances of each book. 224.94'07.H36

**\*Maier, Walter A.** *The Book of Nahum.* Minneapolis: James and Klock Christian Publishers, 1973.

A lengthy, critical commentary in which every word of each verse is evaluated and expounded in light of the theme of the book. Very extensive. 224.94'07.M28 1973

### HABAKKUK

**Barber, Cyril John.** *Habakkuk and Zephaniah.* Everyman's Bible Commentary. Chicago: Moody Press, 1985.

A clear, nontechnical exposition that opens up the problems of injustice and suffering on the one hand and God's plan for the consummation of the age on the other. Designed for laypeople. 224.95'07.B23

**Gowan, Donald E.** *The Triumph of Faith in Habakkuk.* Atlanta: John Knox Press, 1976.

A refreshing study for lay readers. Adequately expounds the prophet's agonizing dilemma. Recommended. 224.95'06.G74

### ZEPHANIAH

See under *Habakkuk.*

### HAGGAI

**Baldwin, Joyce.** *Haggai, Zechariah, Malachi.* Tyndale Old Testament Commentaries. Downers Grove, Ill.: Inter-Varsity Press, 1972.

Brief, scholarly verse-by-verse comments with additional notes interspersed throughout the text. 224.97.B19

**Petersen, David L.** *Haggai and Zechariah 1-8, a Commentary.* Old Testament Library. Philadelphia: Westminster Press, 1984.

†Based on the author's long-standing interest in the post-exilic period of Israel's history. Deals relevantly with the events leading up to the building of the second Temple and ably relates the ministry of Haggai and Zechariah to the life and work of the Jews during this period. 224.97'07.P44

**Wolf, Herbert.** *Haggai and Malachi.* Everyman's Bible Commentary. Chicago: Moody Press, 1976.

Part of the growing corpus of popular commentaries backed by sound evangelical scholarship. Wolf's handling of the writings of these two prophets reveals the timeliness and practical relevance of their message. Recommended. 224.97'07.W83

### ZECHARIAH

**\*Feinberg, Charles Lee.** *God Remembers: A Study of Zechariah.* Portland, Oreg.: Multnomah Press, 1977.

First published in 1950, this work possesses an enduring quality. Ideal for laypeople and of value to pastors as well. Ably expounds the theme of this portion of God's Word. 224.98'07.F32 1977

**Laney, J. Carl.** *Zechariah.* Everyman's Bible Commentary. Chicago: Moody Press, 1984.

Provides masterful coverage of the biblical data. Ties in Zechariah's predictions with the scope of God's prophetic Word. Clear, concise, premillennial. 224.98'07.L24

**\*Leupold, Herbert Carl.** *Exposition of Zechariah.* Grand Rapids: Baker Book House, 1971.

Provides a serious, technical study of the prophetic predictions of Zechariah from an amillennial viewpoint. Very helpful. Originally published in 1956. 224.98'07.L57 1971

**\*Wright, Charles Henry Hamilton.** *Zechariah and His Prophecies, Considered in Relation to Modern Criticism.* Minneapolis: Klock & Klock Christian Publishers, 1980.

Constituting the author's Bampton Lectures at Oxford University in 1878, these extensive studies translate, introduce, and treat the visions of this neglected OT prophet. Amillennial. 224.98'07.W93 1980

### MALACHI

**\*Kaiser, Walter Christian, Jr.** *Malachi: God's Unchanging Love.* Grand Rapids: Baker Book House, 1984.

A work of exceptional merit. Demonstrates the goal of true exposition: the synthesis of scholarship with devotion so that the text of Scripture is clearly and adequately explained. Serves as a model of what commentaries should be like.

Highly recommended. 224.99'07.K12

**\*Morgan, George Campbell.** *Malachi's Message for Today.* Grand Rapids: Baker Book House, 1972.

First published in 1898 under the title *Wherein Have We Robbed God?* Applies the pertinent truths of Malachi's prophecy to the needs of our modern society. 224.99'07.M82

**Oswalt, John.** *Where Are You, God?* Wheaton, Ill.: Victor Books, 1982.

This commentary on the book of Malachi provides a contemporary application that helps modern man through some of the problems confronting our civilization and shows how to uncover God's solutions. 224.99'07.OS9

# 3

# New Testament

There are times when those of us who are preachers and teachers need to be reminded of certain basic facts. Often the instrument God uses to reawaken us is a layperson who places his or her finger on some important truths that we have neglected to emphasize.

We would all agree that the study of God's Word should be exciting. It took Dr. Paul Tournier to remind me of that fact. In his book *The Adventure of Living*, he states:

> The Bible is the book of adventure and must be read as such. Not only adventure of the world and of humanity, but the personal adventure of each man and woman whom God touches, calls and sends into action. In it we find the coming together of adventure and poetry. . . . Children feel this spontaneously, and hence in one sense we are to divest ourselves of our cold intellectualism and become children again. In the Bible we rediscover the deep emotions which rekindle in us the fire of adventure. The Bible also gives adventure its true meaning, for from end to end it reveals what is at stake in all our work, all our choices, and all our self-commitment.[1]

Like those ancient seamen who encountered the equally hazardous alternatives of sailing between Scylla and Charybdis in the Strait of Messina, two problems face the pastor-teacher today. The one extreme is to be so concerned about exegesis that little or no attention is paid to matters of the Spirit. The other is to produce pietistic sermons that are blithely unconcerned about correct interpretation and slight the demands of scholarship.

As the seafarers who plied their trade on the Mediterranean early learned to navigate the treacherous waters separating the toe of Italy from the Island of Sicily, so the expository preacher needs to steer a middle course between

1. Paul Tournier, *The Adventure of Living* (New York: Harper & Row, 1965), p. 82.

these two extremes. Scholarly books need to be read but *never* with the intent of impressing the congregation with our learning. And devotional messages need to be delivered but *not* at the expense of edifying believers and building up people in the faith.

Much is being said and written about redaction-criticism and other approaches to the books of the Bible. When books advocating literary sources for various New Testament documents have been read, however, the resulting benefit is meager compared to what may be gained from those works that build on the more objective historical-textual-cultural approach to God's Word. Only in this way can the excitement of studying God's Word be preserved.

An introductory note in John Kerr's *Introduction to the Study of the Books of the New Testament* reminds us of another important truth.

> The New Testament is far more than a body of literature. It is the Word of God. It is not simply the literary product of the Church of the first age. It is the gift of God to the Church of all ages. Neither in composition of its individual books, nor in the collection of those books into a "canon," can it be justly looked upon as the creation of the literary genius or of the selective instincts of the Church. The books were given one by one by the authoritative founders of the Church—the apostles whom Christ had chosen and whom the Spirit had endowed—to the Church which they founded, as its authoritative Rule of Faith and Practice, its *corpus juris;* and the Book formed itself by this simple fact from all other books or collections of books. The principle of the canon has ever been apostolic gift, never fitness to edify or adaption to the Christian consciousness: authoritativeness is its note. And when a Christian approaches it, he approaches it not merely as a book which he finds spiritually helpful, far less, merely as one which he finds literally interesting, but as the Oracles of God. . . . But they are also the writings of men, and every word of them is a word of man. By a perfect confluence of the divine and human, the one word is at once all divine and all human. So then, for their proper and complete understanding, we must approach each book not only as the Word of God, but also as the words of Peter, or of Paul, or of John. We must seek to understand its human author in his most intimate characteristics, in his trials, experiences, and training, in the special circumstances of joy or sorrow, of straits or deliverance, in which he stood when writing this book, in his relations to his readers, and to the immediate needs and special situation of his readers which gave occasion to his writing . . . in order that we may understand the Word of God [through His servants].[2]

Only as these issues are maintained in balance can we continue to experience the kind of enthusiasm for the study of God's Word that will carry over into our ministry and bless as well as strengthen those to whom we minister. In this respect the dedication of William Tyndale can serve as a useful

2. John Kerr, *Introduction to the Study of the Books of the New Testament* (Chicago: Revell, 1892), pp. ix, x.

reminder of the place and importance of the inspired Scripture in our lives. A letter was recently discovered in the archives of the Council of Brabant, probably addressed to the Marquis of Brabant. It was written in Latin in William Tyndale's own handwriting, penned while he was awaiting execution. In it the great Bible translator and reformer wrote:

> I beg your lordship, and that by the Lord Jesus, that if I am to remain here through the winter, you will request the commissary to have the kindness to send me, from the goods of mine which he has, a warmer cap, for I suffer greatly from cold in the head . . . a warmer coat also, for this one which I have is very thin. . . . But most of all I beg and beseech your clemency to be urgent with the commissary, that he will kindly permit me to have the Hebrew Bible, Hebrew grammar and Hebrew dictionary, that I may pass the time in study.

It requires little imagination to sense William Tyndale's predicament. His words echo those of the apostle Paul in 2 Timothy 4:7-8, 13. His desire for warmer clothing was understandable. Even in his imprisonment, however, he was intent on translating the Bible. His New Testament had already been translated and smuggled into England. His work on the Pentateuch had likewise been published. His translation of the historical books was finished but awaited typesetting. Sensing the urgency of making the Word of God available, he wanted to try to complete his translation of the Old Testament. He was not able to do so. Within six months he was strangled and his body burned. His example, however, serves to inspire us to similar diligence in making the Bible known. Only in this way can we be true "stewards of the mysteries of God" (1 Corinthians 4:1).

**Bratcher, Robert Galveston, ed.** *Old Testament Quotations in the New Testament.* 2d ed. New York: United Bible Societies, 1984.

Brings together in an English translation and in parallel columns quotations found in the NT; also provides the context in which they appear in the OT. A most useful volume. 225.5'2046.B73 1984

**Dunn, James D. G.** *Unity and Diversity in the New Testament: An Inquiry into the Character of Earliest Christianity.* Philadelphia: Westminster Press, 1977.

†Assesses the unity of primitive Christianity's preaching, teaching, organiza-

tion, and worship. Follows up that study with an assessment of the diversity of later Christian movements. Of value to the historian. 225'.08.D91

**\*Hort, Fenton John Anthony, and Arthur Fenton Hort.** *Expository and Exegetical Studies: Compendium of Works Formerly Published Separately.* Minneapolis: Klock & Klock Christian Publishers, 1980.

Includes the hard-to-obtain exegetical and expository studies of Hort and notes on the Greek text of Mark's gospel by his son. Considering the many decades students of the NT have looked in vain for any of Hort's writings to appear on the second-hand book market, the reissuing of all of his biblical works in one handy volume is extremely fortuitous. 225'.06.H78 1980

**Martin, Ralph Philip.** *New Testament Books for Pastors and Teachers.* Philadelphia: Westminster Press, 1984.

†Manifests an unhealthy bias. Martin comments all too briefly on those studies based on the faulty presuppositions that underlie much of the literature using *Formgeschichte, Redaktionsgeschichte,* and critical approaches to the text. Provides virtually no information that is of value to a pastor-teacher. 016.225.M36

**Skilton, John H.,** and **Curtiss A. Ladley, eds.** *The New Testament Student and His Field.* Vol. 5. Phillipsburg, N.J.: Presbyterian and Reformed Publishing Co., 1982.

An excellent work. Deserves careful reading. 225'.07.W52 v.5

**Westerholm, Stephen.** *Jesus and Scribal Authority.* Lund, Sweden: CWK Gleerup, n.d.

†The author's 1978 dissertation, Lund University. Discusses the *Halakhah* in its relationship to the ministry of the Lord Jesus. Provides information that will assist interpreters in grappling with key Marcan passages. 225'.08.AU8.W52

## GOSPELS AND ACTS

**Brown, Raymond E.** *The Critical Meaning of the Bible.* New York: Paulist Press, 1981.

†Brown's scholarship is beyond dispute. He deals with new trends in hermeneutics and seeks to establish a foundation for the understanding of the meaning of Scripture. 226.B81

**Cartlidge, David R.,** and **David L. Dungan.** *Documents for the Study of the Gospels.* Philadelphia: Fortress Press, 1980.

Provides, in a handy format, translations of Gnostic texts relating to the birth, life, and ministry of the Lord Jesus. Details Greek, Jewish, and Roman thought paralleling the gospel records. 226'.06.C24

**Colquhoun, Frank.** *Four Portraits of Jesus: Christ in the Gospels.* Downers Grove, Ill.: InterVarsity Press, 1984.

Reiterates in a refined, positive, and convincing manner what A. Jukes offered in his *Four Views of Christ.* Colquhoun, however, is to be commended for his courage. The information he presents has been rejected by the scholarly community whose adherence to lib-

eral presuppositions pertaining to the authorship and supposed sources of the gospels has led them far afield and away from the truth. This is an excellent discussion, and it is hoped the book will receive widespread circulation. 226'.06.C69

**Farmer, William Reuben.** *Jesus and the Gospel: Tradition, Scripture, and Canon.* Philadelphia: Fortress Press, 1982.

Covering the period from the ministry of Christ to the time of Constantine, Farmer describes the development in the church of the traditions concerning Jesus. 226'.012.F22

**Jukes, Andrew.** *Four Views of Christ.* Edited by J. S. Kiefer. Grand Rapids: Kregel Publications, 1982.

First published in 1853 under the title *Characteristic Differences in the Four Gospels,* this work analyzes the differences in the four gospels and uses the material gleaned from that kind of objective investigation to explain the thematic purpose of each writer. 226'.06.J93 1982

**Kistemacher, Simon J.** *The Gospels in Current Study.* 2d ed. Grand Rapids: Baker Book House, 1980.

First published in 1972, this important volume provides brief, pointed, evangelical responses to the claims of radical critics, who have frequently failed to find their erroneous theories rebutted by a theologically competent NT scholar. Kistemacher provides such a rebuttal. 226'.06.K64 1980

**Montgomery, John Warwick.** *History and Christianity.* Downers Grove, Ill.: InterVarsity Fellowship, 1971.

A scholarly apologetic for the historical reliability of the gospels, particularly as these relate to the testimony concerning Jesus Christ. 226.06.M76

**Tannehill, Robert C.** *The Sword of His Mouth.* Philadelphia: Fortress Press, 1975.

In his study of the "forceful and imaginative language" of Christ there is a great deal to interest the serious student. The detailed analysis of representative texts is likewise helpful. 226'.06'6.T15

**Vermes, Geza.** *Jesus and the World of Judaism.* Philadelphia: Fortress Press, 1984.

†Seeks to show Jesus' ministry *within* Judaism, and as such, makes a sorely needed contribution to the corpus of literature dealing with the life and mission of Christ. 226'.067.V59

HARMONIES AND SYNOPTIC PROBLEM

**Edwards, Richard Alan.** *A Theology of Q: Eschatology, Prophecy, and Wisdom.* Philadelphia: Fortress Press, 1975.

Building his thesis on material found in the supposed Q passages, Edwards reconstructs not only the theology, but also the characteristics of the "Q community." Of interest for the writer's conclusions but unlikely to convince many of the viability of this source material. 226'.06.ED9

**Farmer, William Reuben.** *The Synoptic*

*Problem: A Critical Analysis.* Dillsboro, N.C.: Western North Carolina Press, 1976.

Challenges afresh the traditional acceptance of Q and the priority of Mark to Matthew and Luke. 226.11.F22

***Alexander, Joseph Addison.** *The Gospel According to Matthew.* Lynchburg, Va.: James Family Publishers, 1979.

Published posthumously in 1861 and covering only chapters 1-16, this volume contains the same richness of thought and close attention to detail that is found in Alexander's other commentaries. 226.2'07.1—16.AL2 1979

**Beare, Francis Wright.** *The Gospel According to Matthew: Translation, Introduction and Commentary.* San Francisco: Harper & Row, 1981.

A well-informed commentary that skillfully correlates Matthew's unique presentation of the life and ministry of Jesus, though it adheres to supposed Marcan sources. Has much to commend it. For the discerning reader. 226.2'07.B38

**Brown, Raymond Edward.** *The Birth of the Messiah: A Commentary on the Infancy Narratives in Matthew and Luke.* Garden City, N.Y.: Doubleday and Company, 1977.

†Parallels Leon Morris's *Story of the Christ Child.* Fits Matthean and Lukan accounts into the perceived perspective of each writer. Discusses the basic thrust of the narrative. The treatment, however, is marred by critical views concerning the origin, purpose, and composition of each book. The exegetical insights are of value. Roman Catholic. 226.2'06.B81

**Dickson, David.** *A Brief Exposition of the Evangel of Jesus Christ According to Matthew.* Edinburgh: Banner of Truth Trust, 1981.

Though highly praised by C. H. Spurgeon, this work fails to treat the narrative consecutively or thematically.

There are rich devotional thoughts contained within these pages, but they bear little relationship to the purpose of this gospel. 226.2'07.D56 1981

**Goulder, Michael.** *Midrash and Lection in Matthew.* London: S.P.C.K., 1974.

†Following in the footsteps of Austin Farrer, the author dispenses with Q and attempts to build a case for Matthew's gospel being a midrash of Mark. 226.2'06.G72

**Govett, Robert.** *The Prophecy of Olivet, or Matthew XXIV and XXV Expounded.* Miami Springs, Fla.: Conley and Schoettle Publishing Co., 1985.

This premillennial posttribulational work shows the writer's independence of thought. He diligently subjects Christ's words to the teaching of the totality of Scripture. What emerges is a refreshing, provocative work. 226.2'07.G74 1985

**Green, H. Benedict.** *The Gospel According to Matthew.* New Clarendon Bible. London: Oxford University Press, 1975.

Relying heavily on source criticism, Green provides little more than a summary of modern critical opinion regarding matters of authorship, date, and the like. His comments on the text are of help to the discerning reader, but his failure to expound the theme of this gospel and his handling of Christ's virgin conception, ministry, vicarious death, and resurrection leave much to be desired. 226.2'07.G82

**Gundry, Robert Horton.** *Matthew: A Commentary on His Literary and Theological Art.* Grand Rapids: Wm. B. Eerdmans Publishing Co., 1982.

†Carefully analyzed and clearly outlined, this interpretative commentary treats Matthew's gospel as a Christian midrash. Because that form of literature did not come to the fore in Jewish thinking until much later, Gundry errs in superimposing that literary genre on a first-century document. 226.2'06.G95M

**Hendriksen, William.** *Exposition of the Gospel According to Matthew.* New Testament Commentary. Grand Rapids: Baker Book House, 1973.

Following a comprehensive introduction, the writer treats his readers to 900 pages of detailed exposition. His approach is geographic and his style pedantic. There is an elaborate explanation of the text and a full discussion of varying views. 226.2'07.H38

**Hill, David.** *The Gospel of Matthew.* New Century Bible Commentary. Grand Rapids: Wm. B. Eerdmans Publishing Co., 1981.

†A form-critical study that discusses recent developments in NT scholarship, followed by comments on the text of the RSV. The author does not expound the purpose of this gospel, and his treatment of Matthean theology beclouds the issues. 226.2'07.H55

**MacArthur, John F., Jr.** *Kingdom Living Here and Now.* Chicago: Moody Press, 1980.

Representing exposition at its best, these sermons on the Beatitudes of Matthew 5 will challenge and edify the reader in much the same way they did when MacArthur's congregation first heard them. Recommended. 226.2'07.5.M11

*_____. *Matthew 1-7.* The MacArthur New Testament Commentary. Chicago: Moody Press, 1985.

This pace-setting volume is the first of three on this gospel. It reveals MacArthur's expository method; thorough grasp of the theme of the biblical writer; warm, evangelistic style; and remarkable ability to apply the text to life. No preacher can afford to be without this fine work. 226.2'07.M11 v.1

**Meyer, Frederick Brotherton.** *Inherit the Kingdom: Meditations on the Sermon on the Mount.* Wheaton, Ill.: Victor Books, 1984.

Meyer does not interpret Matthew 5-7 accurately. As a result, this work, though deeply devotional, does not make a lasting contribution. 226.2′07.5—7.M57 1984

**Minear, Paul S.** *Matthew: The Teacher's Gospel.* New York: Pilgrim Press, 1982.

Approaches the gospel from the perspective of the writer as a teacher and shows how what he wrote was designed to strengthen the faith of believers in the early church. 226.2′07.M66

**\*Morison, James.** *A Practical Commentary on the Gospel According to St. Matthew.* Minneapolis: Klock & Klock Christian Publishers, 1981.

A worthy addition to any preacher's library. The practical and devotional thoughts alone are worth many times the cost of the book. 226.2′07.M82 1981

**Morrison, George H.** *Matthew.* 3 vols. Chattanooga, Tenn.: AMG Publishers, 1978.

These eloquent messages expound the meaning of Matthew's gospel with a force that is compelling. 226.2′07.M83 1978

**\*Plummer, Alfred.** *An Exegetical Commentary on the Gospel According to St. Matthew.* Grand Rapids: Baker Book House, 1982.

First published in 1915, this work remains one of the best treatments of Matthew's gospel ever written. 226.2′07.P73 1982

**Senior, Donald P.** *The Passion Narrative According to Matthew.* Leuven, Belgium: Leuven University, 1975.

Based on the latest *Redaktionsgeschichte*, this study of Matthew 26:1—27:56 shows how the Matthean account of the passion differs literally and substantively from the Marcan account. A work for the specialist. 226.2′06.26—27.SE5

**\*Stott, John Robert Walmsey.** *Christian Counter-Culture: The Message of the Sermon on the Mount.* Downers Grove, Ill.: Inter-Varsity Press, 1978.

A work of rare brilliance. Demonstrates the relevance of the Bible to the needs of believers. Should enjoy widespread acceptance. 226.2′07.5—7.ST7

**\*Toussaint, Stanley Dale.** *Behold the King: A Study in Matthew.* Portland, Oreg.: Multnomah Press, 1980.

A work that expounds the theme of Matthew's gospel in the most able manner. Toussaint's exposition is based on a thorough exegesis of the text. He unfolds Matthew's purpose in writing about Jesus as the Messiah and convincingly demonstrates that He is Israel's long-awaited King. The kingdom is shown to be the central theme of Matthew's gospel. It is fair to say that Tousssaint has produced a work that places all Bible-believing Christians in his debt. Recommended. 226.2′07.T64

**Vos, Howard Frederick.** *Matthew: A Study Guide Commentary.* Grand Rapids: Zondervan Publishing House, 1979.

A careful presentation. Of value to lay readers. 226.2′07.V92

**\*Wagner, Gunter, ed.** *An Exegetical Bibliography of the New Testament: Matthew and Mark.* Macon, Ga.: Mercer University Press, 1983.

A work of immense value. Originally published by off-set printing from cards, this work now has the type completely reset. It contains information found in books and 248 journal articles covering every verse in these two gospels. A most important resource tool. 226.2′02.W12

**Walvoord, John Flipse.** *Matthew: Thy Kingdom Come.* Chicago: Moody Press, 1974.

In this book we have a modern attempt to expound Matthew's gospel thematically. Though it lacks a solid introduction, this commentary deserves a place in the library of the expository Bible teacher and preacher. Recommended. 226.2′07.W17

**Watson, Thomas.** *The Beatitudes: An*

*Exposition of Matthew 5:1-12.* New ed. London: Banner of Truth Trust, 1971.

A Puritan work originally published in London in 1660. Deeply devotional but fails to interpret this passage in the light of the writer's theme. 226.2'07.5.W33

**White, Reginald Ernest Oscar.** *The Mind of Matthew.* Philadelphia: Westminster Press, 1979.

Though he uses the form-critical approach to Matthew's gospel, the author nevertheless has grasped the thematic structure of the evangelist's narrative, and he explains the purpose of this canonical book accordingly. 226.2'06.W58

**Wiersbe, Warren Wendell.** *Live Like a King: Making the Beatitudes Work in Daily Life.* Chicago: Moody Press, 1976.

A devotional masterpiece. Practical, relevant, rich in insights, and rewarding in its application of truth to life. This brief work deserves to be read slowly and carefully. 226.2'07.5:1-12.W63

MARK

**\*Alexander, Joseph Addison.** *Commentary on the Gospel of Mark.* Minneapolis: Klock & Klock Christian Publishers, 1980.

An old classic. Still worthy of the busy pastor's time and attention in spite of the passage of years. Devotional. 226.3'07.AL2 1980

**Anderson, Hugh.** *The Gospel of Mark.* New Century Bible Commentary. Grand Rapids: Wm. B. Eerdmans Publishing Co., 1981.

†A learned treatment based on the text of the NEB. Contains excellent exegetical insights but not on a par with the expositions of Hiebert and Lane. 226.3'07.AN2 1981

**Farmer, William Reuben.** *The Last Twelve Verses of Mark.* New York: Cambridge University Press, 1974.

An examination, first of the textual evidence for the omission of the verses and second of the linguistic reasons for their inclusion. Though the author advocates their retention, he leaves numerous questions unanswered. 226.3'06.16:9-20.F22

**Hendriksen, William.** *Exposition of the Gospel According to Mark.* New Testament Commentary. Grand Rapids: Baker Book House, 1975.

Makes its own unique contribution to the study of Mark's gospel. This work will be eagerly sought after by preachers of all persuasions. 226.3'07.H38

**\*Hiebert, David Edmond.** *Mark: A Portrait of the Servant.* Chicago: Moody Press, 1974.

A reverent and insightful treatment that deserves the attention of the Bible teacher and expository preacher. Recommended. 226.3'07.H53

**Kealy, Sean P.** *Mark's Gospel: A History of Its Interpretation from the Beginning Until 1979.* New York: Paulist Press, 1982.

Surveys the history of the interpretation through the centuries and brings to the fore the leading contribution of the great men of the past. Each chapter is filled with insights that provide clues to the interpretation of the Marcan narrative. Instructive. 226.3'06.K19

**Kelber, Werner H., ed.** *The Passion in Mark: Studies on Mark 14-16.* Philadelphia: Fortress Press, 1976.

In this collection of essays the contributors attempt to explain Mark's Passion narrative on the basis of a Marcan theology that is strangely detached from the political milieu and legal system in force at the time of Christ's crucifixion. That has the effect of truncating Mark's message. These studies have merit, but they require considerable time to digest. The results are often disproportionate to the effort expended. 226.3'06.14—16.K27

**Lane, William L.** *The Gospel According to Mark.* New International Commentary on the New Testament. Grand Rapids: Wm. B. Eerdmans Publishing Co., 1974.

Combines the exacting care of a philologist with the expertise of a theologian. Uses moderate redaction-criticism. 226.3'07.L24

**Lightner, Robert Paul.** *Mark: God's Son in Action.* Denver, Colo.: Accent Publications, 1985.

In thirteen brief chapters Lightner opens up Mark's gospel. This book is geared toward adult discussion groups. It ably unfolds the theme of the gospel and applies the principles that are latent in the text. 226.3'07.L62

**Martin, Ralph Philip.** *Mark: Evangelist and Theologian.* Grand Rapids: Zondervan Publishing House, 1973.

A scholarly assessment of the scope of Mark's gospel with a suggestion for a new purpose and *Sitz im leben*. 226.3'06.M36

**Matera, Frank J.** *The Kingship of Jesus: Composition and Theology in Mark 15.* Chico, Calif.: Scholars Press, 1982.

Produced from typewritten pages, this thorough study of Mark 15 seeks to establish Christ's royal office. In addition to his discussion of the text, Matera pursues the theme of Christ's kingship in the Qumran writings as well as in the teaching of the apostolic Fathers. The result is a thorough theological treatise. 226.3'06.15.M41

**\*Morison, James.** *A Practical Commentary on the Gospel According to St. Mark.* Minneapolis: Klock & Klock Christian Publishers, 1981.

A rich, rewarding devotional treatment that possesses some grammatical weaknesses but is nevertheless a commentary all expositors and students of the Word will want to own. Buy it. 226.3'07.M82 1981

**Morrison, George H.** *Mark.* Ridgefield, N.J.: AMG Publishers, 1978.

Morrison was one of the giants of the Scottish pulpit. He was particularly per-suasive when expounding the Scriptures. Few who heard him remained unmoved. These studies are worthy of serious consideration. Quite apart from the light they shed on the gospel narrative, they also exhibit Morrison's homiletic style. 226.3'07.M83 1978

**Nineham, Dennis Eric.** *The Gospel of Saint Mark.* Westminster Pelican Commentaries. Philadelphia: Westminster Press, 1977.

†Manifests a heavy reliance on *Formgeschichte*, so much so that his exposition of the text is impaired. Of value are the nuances of thought drawn from the original. 226.3'07.N62

**Phillips, John Bertram.** *Peter's Portrait of Jesus.* London: Collins Publishing Co., 1976.

The title is misleading. This is really a commentary on Mark's gospel with an exposition of 1 and 2 Peter. Phillips uses his own translation as the basis for his exposition. He regards Mark's gospel as the reminiscences of Peter, believes that 1 Peter was indeed the work of the apostle, but rejects the Petrine authorship of the second epistle. As a commentary, this work lacks any praiseworthy features. 226.3'08.P54

**\*Plummer, Alfred.** *The Gospel According to St. Mark.* Grand Rapids: Baker Book House, 1982.

This study first appeared in 1914 as a part of the *Cambridge Greek Testament*. It deals with the historical and critical values of Mark's gospel but is now very much out of date. 226.3'07.P73 1982

**Ryle, John Charles.** *Expository Thoughts on the Gospel of Mark.* Carlisle, Pa.: Banner of Truth Trust, 1985.

An ideal work for laypeople. Makes rich, rewarding reading. Recommended. 226.3'07.R98 1985

**Scroggie, William Graham.** *The Gospel of Mark.* Grand Rapids: Zondervan Publishing House, 1976.

This timely reprint makes available again this British Baptist's unique and insightful studies. The material is deeply devotional, and Scroggie was an accomplished expositor. Preachers have much to learn from his helpful approach. 226.3′07.SCR5 1976

**\*Stedman, Ray C.** *The Ruler Who Serves.* Waco, Tex.: Word Books, 1976.

A beautiful, thematic exposition of Mark 8:27—16:20. Well deserving of a place in every preacher's library. Warmly recommended. 226.3′07.ST3 v.2

**\*_____.** *The Servant Who Rules.* Waco, Tex.: Word Books, 1976.

An impressive treatment of Mark 1:1—8:26. Stedman stands in the tradition of Merrill Unger when it comes to hermeneutics and the application of the text to life. In this work Christ is presented as the believer's model, and through the unfolding of each scene in the narrative, Stedman shows how that may be accomplished. Recommended. 226.3′07.ST3 v.1

**\*Swete, Henry Barclay.** *Commentary on Mark.* Grand Rapids: Kregel Publications, 1977.

Cambridge scholar and exegete par excellence, Swete placed the Christian world in his debt when he wrote this perceptive study. What he presents is ideal for the student; a must for the pastor. Amillennial. 226.3′07.SW4 1977

**Trocme, Etienne.** *The Formation of the Gospel According to Mark.* Translated by P. Gaughan. Philadelphia: Westminster Press, 1975.

Basing his approach squarely on *Formgeschichte* and the latest literary criticism, Trocme discusses the supposed sources used by Mark. He also outlines Mark's aversions and the causes he espoused. Trocme concludes with an evaluation of the usual introductory matters (authorship, date, etc.) and the possible phases of redaction through which this gospel supposedly passed. 226.3′06.T74

**Vos, Howard Frederick.** *Mark: A Study Guide Commentary.* Grand Rapids: Zondervan Publishing House, 1978.

A well-reasoned, thematic study that proves again that sometimes the most valuable things come in small packages. Of great value to laypeople who desire to obtain a good grasp of this material. 226.3′07.V92

LUKE

**Caird, George Bradford.** *Saint Luke.* Westminster Pelican Commentaries. Philadelphia: Westminster Press, 1977.

One of the better works in this series. Contains numerous references to Jewish literature as well as pertinent comments on the text. Is of value to the preacher. Needs to be read with discernment. 226.4′07.C12

**Conzelmann, Hans.** *The Theology of St. Luke.* Translated by G. Buswell. Philadelphia: Fortress Press, 1982.

†Having first made its appearance more than two decades ago, this work has now been superseded by other theories of Lukan theology. 226.4′008.C76 1982

**Fitzmeyer, Joseph Augustine.** *The Gospel According to Luke.* 2 vols. The Anchor Bible. Garden City, N.Y.: Doubleday and Co., 1981-1985.

†This lengthy, scholarly treatment of the text of Luke's gospel with extensive footnotes containing critical data is ideal for student use. 226.4′07.F58

**Ford, Josephine Massyngbaerde.** *My Enemy Is My Guest: Jesus and Violence in Luke.* Maryknoll, N.Y.: Orbis Books, 1984.

†"This is a very readable and clear exposition of Luke's presentation of Jesus as an advocate of nonviolence. It rests on a profound knowledge of the political background in the first century" (I. Howard Marshall). 226.4′06.F75

**Franklin, Eric.** *Christ the Lord: A Study of the Purpose and Theology of Luke-Acts.*

Philadelphia: Westminster Press, 1975.

Based solidly on *Redaktionsgeschichte*, this work seeks to explain Luke's writings in terms of the imminency of the parousia. Speculative. 226.4'06.F84

**Hendriksen, William.** *Exposition of the Gospel According to Luke.* New Testament Commentary. Grand Rapids: Baker Book House, 1978.

Fills a long-felt need for a comprehensive, scholarly exposition of this neglected gospel. Structures Luke's thematic presentation around Christ's words "the work which Thou gavest Me to do." Treats Christ's ministry in terms of its inauguration, continuation, and consummation. Recommended. 226.4'07.H38

**\*Kelly, William.** *An Exposition of the Gospel of Luke.* Minneapolis: Klock & Klock Christian Publishers, 1981.

An excellent handling of Luke's theme, replete with the author's own translation and an exposition that is at once refreshing and satisfying. 226.4'07.K29 1981

**\*Marshall, I. Howard.** *Luke, Historian and Theologian.* Grand Rapids: Zondervan Publishing House, 1971.

Attempts to bridge the gap between those treatments of Luke's gospel that are solely historical and those that emphasize only the theological importance of his writings. A scholarly, well-documented treatment. 226.4'08.M35

**Mattill, A. J., Jr.** *Luke and the Last Things: A Perspective for the Understanding of Lukan Thought.* Dillsboro, N.C.: Western North Carolina Press, 1979.

†An exacting, technical presentation of Lukan theology. Rich and full. 226.4'06.M43

**\*Morris, Leon Lamb.** *The Gospel According to St. Luke.* Tyndale New Testament Commentaries. Grand Rapids: Wm. B. Eerdmans Publishing Co., 1974.

A clear, forthright presentation of the facts surrounding the authorship and date of this gospel, followed by almost 300 pages of exposition. A handy and helpful volume. 226.4'07.M83

**Morrison, George H.** *Luke.* 2 vols. Chattanooga, Tenn.: AMG Publishers, 1978.

Excellent examples of the art of exposition. Does not cover every verse. 226.4'07.M83

**Reiling, J., and J. L. Swellengrebel.** *A Translator's Handbook on the Gospel of Luke.* Leiden, The Netherlands: E. J. Brill, 1971.

An invaluable work for translators. Helpful to pastors, too, for its hints as to the meaning of words or phrases. 225.4'05.R27

**Schweizer, Eduard.** *Luke: A Challenge to Present Theology.* Atlanta: John Knox Press, 1982.

†Treats the basic theological issues that emerged as a result of working on a critical commentary on Luke's gospel. Draws attention to issues that students may expand into full-length discussions. 226.4'06.SCH9T

**————.** *The Good News According to Luke.* Translated by D. E. Green. Atlanta: John Knox Press, 1984.

†Examines Luke and provides a detailed exposition that will delight the scholar. In Luke, Schweizer sees the Word truly become flesh, in spite of the supposed uncertainties of the historical details. He seeks to sift through the various myths that embody eternal timeless truth in narrative form so as to draw from Luke's writing a picture of Jesus of Nazareth. This work will appeal only to the scholar and offers little to the pastor. 226.4'07.SCH9

**Talbert, Charles H.** *Literary Patterns, Theological Themes, and the Genre of Luke-Acts.* Missoula, Mont.: Scholars Press, 1974.

†This is a scholarly work that also provides readers with a detailed analysis of Luke's style of writing. The search for

Luke's admitted sources leads Talbert to take some unnecessary steps in his handling of this theme. He concludes his discussion by advancing information in support of his hypothesis that Luke organized his material around a balanced architectonic schema. 226.4'06.T14

**Van Doren, William Howard.** *The Gospel of Luke.* Expository and Homiletical Commentary. 2 vols. in 1. Grand Rapids: Kregel Publications, 1981.

First published between 1876-1878 as a *Suggestive Commentary,* this work merited C. H. Spurgeon's approval. He wrote: "Well named 'suggestive'; it is all suggestions. It teems and swarms with homiletic hints." 226.4'06.V26 1981

**Wilcock, Michael.** *The Savior of the World: The Message of Luke's Gospel.* Downers Grove, Ill.: InterVarsity Press, 1979.

A clear evangelical exposition of this gospel. Avoids stereotypes and provides some helpful insights into Luke's special interests and style. 226.4'07.W64

JOHN

**\*Barber, Cyril John.** *Searching for Identity.* Chicago: Moody Press, 1975.

Thirteen studies based on men and women in John's gospel. The writer integrates psychology with theology as he expounds the text. Designed for individual or group use. 226.5'092.B23

**Barrett, Charles Kingsley.** *Essays on John.* Philadelphia: Westminster Press, 1982.

A valuable collection of essays dealing with John's theology and vocabulary. Also discusses his symbolism and relationship to contemporary religious movements. 226.5'06.B27E

\*_____. *The Gospel According to St. John: An Introduction with Commentary and Notes on the Greek Text.* 2d ed. Philadelphia: Westminster Press, 1978.

†An insightful work that must take its place among the best exegetical studies ever written on this portion of God's Word. 226.5'07.B27G 1978

_____. *The Gospel of John and Judaism.* Translated by D. M. Smith. Philadelphia: Fortress Press, 1975.

This English edition of the 1967 Franz Delitzsch Lectures assesses, in the light of modern critical scholarship, the environment, purpose, language, and provenance of John's gospel as seen against the backdrop of Judaism during the first century A.D. 226.5'06.B27

**Benware, Paul N.** *Luke: The Gospel of the Son of Man.* Chicago: Moody Press, 1985.

A brief, informative, and readable exposition—the kind laypeople should be encouraged to master. Helpful. 226.4'07.B44

**\*Bernard, Thomas Dehany.** *The Central Teaching of Christ: A Study of John 13-17.* Minneapolis: Klock & Klock Christian Publishers, 1985.

This work made its debut in 1892. It contains the same "wonderful force and freshness that made *The Progress of Doctrine in the New Testament* justifiably famous. The book gives no sign of hastiness. All seems to be the outcome of years of reverent thought, now brought to light in the clearest, most telling way" *(Cambridge Review).* A *must* for every pastor. 226.5'07.13—17.B45 1985

**Boice, James Montgomery.** *The Gospel of John.* 5 vols. in 1. Grand Rapids: Zondervan Publishing House, 1985.

"Any expositor, beginner or veteran, will find this work useful not only in the realm of interpretation but also in applications, illustrations, and quotations" *(Bibliotheca Sacra).* 226.5'07.B63G 1985

**\*Brown, John.** *Exposition of Our Lord's Intercessory Prayer.* Minneapolis: Klock and Klock Christian Publishers 1979.

The concluding prayer of our Lord's in the Garden here receives sensitive treatment. Brown was a pastor as well as an exegete. His handling of the text is excellent. His exposition serves as a model. Recommended. 226.5′07.17.B81 1979

**Brown, Raymond Edward.** *The Community of the Beloved Disciple.* New York: Paulist Press, 1979.

†This resume of Johannine ecclesiology attempts to reconstruct the church of the first century with a view to gleaning principles that might be applied to the church today. The aim is praiseworthy; the writer's theological presuppositions, however, lead him wide of the truth. 226.5′082.B81

**Bruce, Frederick Fyvie.** *The Gospel of John: Introduction, Exposition and Notes.* Grand Rapids: Wm. B. Eerdmans Publishing Co., 1983.

Designed for the general Christian reader, this work grew out of studies that first appeared in *The Bible Student,* Bangalore, India. The translation is clear, and the comments, though brief, will prove valuable to preachers. 226.5′07.B83

**Carson, Donald A.** *The Farewell Discourse and Final Prayer of Jesus: An Exposition of John 14-17.* Grand Rapids: Baker Book House, 1980.

Brief, pertinent expository studies on a vital section of John's gospel. Combines exegesis with a timely exposition of the truth. 226.5′07.14—17.C23

**\*Cook, W. Robert.** *The Theology of John.* Chicago: Moody Press, 1979.

A detailed examination of Johannine literature covering all the major areas of thought. A worthy contribution to this area of biblical theology. Recommended. 226.5′06.C77

**Cullmann, Oscar.** *The Johannine Circle.* Translated by J. Bowden. Philadelphia: Westminster Press, 1976.

†A new investigation into the origins of John's gospel. Cullmann advances a hypothesis concerning the problems of

the origin, character, and setting of John's writing by suggesting that the "Johannine Circle" stood behind the gospel, influenced its composition, and maintained the concerns expressed by the apostle. 226.5′06.C89

**Culpepper, R. Alan.** *Anatomy of the Fourth Gospel: A Study in Literary Design.* Philadelphia: Fortress Press, 1983.

†Competent interdisciplinary studies in English are rare. This one explores John and makes ample use of modern redactional works to highlight the poetics, narrative structure, and other aspects of the gospel. The result is a stimulating, scholarly work. 226.5′06.C89

**Ellis, Edward Earle.** *The World of St. John: The Gospel and the Epistles.* Grand Rapids: Wm. B. Eerdmans Publishing Co., 1984.

First published in 1965. This brief monograph shows that John was a theologian in his own right with roots in primitive Christianity as deep as Paul's. 226.5′06.EL5 1984

**\*Godet, Frederic Louis.** *Commentary on John's Gospel.* Grand Rapids: Kregel Publications, 1978.

One of the finest expositions of John's gospel ever produced. No preacher should be without it. 226.5′07.G54 1978

**Govett, Robert.** *Govett on John.* 2 vols. in 1. Miami Springs, Fla.: Conley and Schoettle Publishing Co., 1984.

First published in 1891. This careful exposition of approximately 1,000 pages combines sound theology with a clear presentation of the meaning of the text. It remains one of the best works produced during this era. Recommended. 226.5′07.G74 1984

**Haenchen, Ernst.** *John 1: A Commentary on the Gospel of John Chapters 1-6.* Hermenia. Translated by R. W. Funk. Edited by R. W. Funk and U. Busse. Philadelphia: Fortress Press, 1984.

†A work of impeccable scholarship.

The introduction is full and complete. The comments on the text illumine as well as elucidate the theme of the writer. The bibliographies that preface each section are of the utmost value. This is a scholarly work and will be appreciated by the discerning reader. 226.5'07.H11 v.1

**Harvey, Anthony Ernest.** *Jesus on Trial: A Study of the Fourth Gospel.* Atlanta: John Knox Press, 1977.

Uses the trial of Jesus—as conceived through its literary form and in terms of Jewish conventions—to cast light on the theme and composition of the fourth gospel. 226.5'06.H25

**\*Hengstenberg, Ernst Wilhelm.** *Commentary on the Gospel of St. John.* 2 vols. Minneapolis: Klock & Klock Christian Publishers, 1980.

Rich in grammatical and syntactical insights, this reverent and devout work ably treats the life and labors of Christ as recorded in John's gospel. A rewarding work that will handsomely repay the time spent reading it. 226.5'07.H38 1980

**Hughes, R. Kent.** *Behold the Man.* Wheaton, Ill.: Victor Books, 1984.

These studies based on John's gospel (covering chaps. 11-21) provide rich reflections on Christ's concluding months of ministry. The chapters are perceptive and revealing. 226.5'07.11—21.H87

**Kent, Homer Austin, Jr.** *Light in the Darkness: Studies in the Gospel of John.* Grand Rapids: Baker Book House, 1974.

This work adequately expounds the theme and content of John's gospel. Of value for use with groups. 226.5.K41

**Lindars, Barnabas.** *The Gospel of John.* New Century Bible. Greenwood, S.C.: Attic Press, 1973.

†This work is by far the most extensive and also the most radical to have been published in this series thus far. Lindars claims that the only valid interpretation of John's gospel is an existential one. In consequence, he searches for meaning(s)

behind the events recorded but fails to treat the incidents mentioned by John as literal happenings. Disappointing. 226.5'07.L64

**Mahoney, Robert.** *Two Disciples at the Tomb: The Background and Message of John 20, 1-10.* Bern, Switzerland: Herbert Lang, 1974.

A scholarly, critical analysis that treats the burial pericope in the light of the synoptic gospels. Examines John's teaching from the position of later didactic intent rather than from the perspective of history. 226.5'06.20.M27

**Marsh, John.** *Saint John.* Westminster Pelican Commentaries. Philadelphia: Westminster Press, 1977.

First published in England in 1968. This form-critical work contains an extensive introduction, a brief commentary, and evaluative notes covering problems in the text. Judicious. 226.5'07.M35 1977

**\*Morris, Leon Lamb.** *The Gospel According to John.* New International Commentary on the New Testament. Grand Rapids: Wm. B. Eerdmans Publishing Co., 1971.

A work of superlative scholarship that not only replaces the majestic work by Westcott but surpasses Barrett as well. 226.5'07.M83

**Morrison, George H.** *John.* Chattanooga, Tenn.: AMG Publishers, 1978.

Preachers will find these brief expository studies helpful. Each one is a masterpiece of the homiletic art. During his lifetime, Morrison's preaching attracted large crowds, and few who heard him remained unmoved. 226.5'07.M83

**Plummer, Alfred.** *The Gospel According to St. John.* Grand Rapids: Baker Book House, 1981.

Published a century ago, this study of the Greek text of John's gospel first appeared in the *Cambridge Greek Testament.* It has now been superseded by more recent treatments. 226.5'07.P73 1981

**\*Rainsford, Marcus.** *Our Lord Prays for His Own: Thoughts on John 17.* Grand Rapids: Kregel Publications, 1985.

In what is now regarded as "the greatest classic ever written on Christ's high priestly prayer for His people," Marcus Rainsford gives us a true masterpiece—of both devotional and expository literature. The author deals with the "Holy of Holies" of Christ's earthly life. Those who prayerfully read it through will find ample reward in its exposition of doctrine and its application of truth to mind and heart. Here is, indeed, a timely, relevant, and practical exposition of John 17. 226.5'07.17.R13 1985

**\*Rosscup, James E.** *Abiding in Christ: Studies in John 15.* Grand Rapids: Zondervan Publishing House, 1973.

An in-depth discussion of the apostle's teaching on abiding in Christ. Contains a full presentation of the problems and shows clearly the Christian's responsibility to live in love and obedience to the Lord. 226.5'07.15:1-6.R73

**Scroggie, William Graham.** *The Gospel of John.* Grand Rapids: Zondervan Publishing House, 1976.

A clear analysis of John's theme, coupled with a lucid exposition of his purpose. Helpful, but overpriced. 226.5'07.SCR5 1976

**Segovia, Fernando F.** *Love Relationships in the Johannine Tradition: Agape/Agapan in I John and the Fourth Gospel.* Chico, Calif.: Scholars Press, 1982.

An excellent discussion of love and its theology in the Johannine writings (excluding the Apocalypse). A revealing study. 226.5'06.SE3

**Smalley, Stephen S.** *John: Evangelist and Interpreter.* Greenwood, S.C.: Attic Press, 1978.

A scholarly work marked by independence of thought and a tendency to see too much of the Essenes and Gnostics in John's portrayal of Christ. Succeeds in alerting the reader to the depths of spiritual perception in John's writings, and for this reason is worth consulting. 226.5'06.SM1

**Smith, Dwight Moody.** *Johannine Christianity: Essays on its Setting, Sources, and Theology.* Columbia, S.C.: University of South Carolina Press, 1984.

†Scholarly essays dealing with the sources, relation to the synoptics, and theology of the Johannine writings. Each essay is a model of scholarship. 226.5'06.SM5

**\*Stedman, Ray C.** *Secrets of the Spirit.* Old Tappan, N.J.: Fleming H. Revell Co., 1975.

As an exposition of Christ's "last will and testament," these studies of John 14-16 ably treat the events that took place on the eve of the crucifixion. 226.5'07.14—16.ST3

**Van Doren, William Howard.** *Gospel of John.* 2 vols. in 1. Grand Rapids: Kregel Publications, 1981.

"If men who read this volume do not preach the better for so doing, it is not Mr. Van Doren's fault; they must be Van Dolts by nature, though they may ignore the family name" (Charles H. Spurgeon). 226.5'07.V26 1981

**Vanderlip, George.** *Christianity According to John.* Philadelphia: Westminster Press, 1975.

A study of the theology of John's gospel. The author bases his material on recent scholarship but does not maintain a consistent evangelical position. 226.5'08.V28

ACTS

**\*Alexander, Joseph Addison.** *Commentary on the Acts of the Apostles.* 2 vols. in 1. Minneapolis: Klock & Klock Christian Publishers, 1980.

A beautifully produced work that

brings within the reach of the busy pastor the benefits of this commentator's prodigious labors. A warmly devotional treatment. 226.6'07.AL2 1980

**Arnot, William.** *Studies in Acts: The Church in the House.* Grand Rapids: Kregel Publications, 1978.

First published in 1883. These sermons reveal Arnot's thorough awareness of the original text and the milieu of the early church. His material is provocative as well as edifying. Both laypeople and pastors should read this book eagerly in order to better determine the course of the church, its commitments, and the criteria of its fellowship. Recommended. 226.6'07.AR6 1978

**\*Eadie, John.** *The Words of the Apostle Paul.* Minneapolis: Klock & Klock Christian Publishers, 1985.

This companion volume to Steir's *The Words of the Risen Saviour* and *Words of the Apostles* deals with the messages of the apostle Paul in the book of Acts. C. H. Spurgeon said Eadie's work was "designed to give ordinary readers a juster and fuller conception of the doctrine and life-work of the apostle." Recommended. 226.6'06.P28.EA1 1985

**Gasque, Woodrow Ward.** *A History of the Criticism of the Acts of the Apostles.* Grand Rapids: Wm. B. Eerdmans Publishing Co., 1975.

Beginning with F. C. Baur and the Tübingen school, Gasque traces the *Actaforschung* down to the present time. His coverage is remarkably full, and he makes available to students a wealth of material that will guide them in their study of Luke's writings and suggest possible thesis and dissertation topics. 226.6'06.G21

**\*Gloag, Paton James.** *A Critical and Exegetical Commentary on the Acts of the Apostles.* 2 vols. Minneapolis: Klock & Klock Christian Publishers, 1979.

H. B. Hackett wrote appreciatively of this work: "I have examined it with special care. For my purposes I have found it unsurpassed by any similar work in the English language. It shows a thorough mastery of the material, philology, history, and literature pertaining to this range of study, and a skill in the use of this knowledge, which places it in the first class of modern expositions." Warmly recommended. 226.6'07.G51 1979

**\*Harrison, Everett Falconer.** *Acts: The Expanding Church.* Chicago: Moody Press, 1976.

A very readable, conservative exposition that deserves a place in every home. The treatment is clear, and Harrison presents his resume of apostolic history in a most pleasing and acceptable manner. Recommended. 226.6'07.H24

**Hengel, Martin.** *Acts and History of Earliest Christianity.* Translated by J. Bowden. Philadelphia: Fortress Press, 1980.

†Asserts the essential reliability of the book of Acts and examines Luke's historical-theological methodology. 226.6'06.H38

**Kent, Homer Austin, Jr.** *Jerusalem to Rome—Studies in Acts.* Grand Rapids: Baker Book House, 1972.

In recounting the beginning and expansion of the early church, the writer reveals the personal struggles of those who participated in the events recorded by Luke. The inclusion of discussion questions makes this an ideal volume for adult Bible study groups. 226.6'07.K41

**Laurin, Roy L.** *Acts: Life in Action.* Grand Rapids: Kregel Publications, 1985.

In this topical commentary, Laurin brings out practical applications as he shows how these early Christians were filled with the dynamic power of a new life of faith. The chapter outlines are also suggestive of discourses, and these will

be particularly useful to pastors.
226.6'08.L36 1985

**\*Marshall, I. Howard.** *The Acts of the Apostles.* Tyndale New Testament Commentaries. Grand Rapids: Wm. B. Eerdmans Publishing Co., 1981.

Replaces Blaiklock's commentary. Emphasizes the theological importance of this Lukan work. A thorough study. Highly recommended. 226.6'07.M35

**Neil, William.** *Acts.* New Century Bible Commentary. Grand Rapids: Wm. B. Eerdmans Publishing Co., 1981.

†Based on the RSV. This handy commentary does not provide an exposition of the theme but, rather, furnishes readers with perceptive comments on select words or phrases. 226.6'07.N31 1981

**\*Rackham, Richard Belward.** *The Acts of the Apostles.* Grand Rapids: Baker Book House, 1978.

The reissue in an overpriced paperback format of one of the great commentaries on the book of Acts. 226.6'07.R11 1978

**Scroggie, William Graham.** *The Acts of the Apostles.* Grand Rapids: Zondervan Publishing House, 1976.

Reprinted from the 1931 edition. This handy volume abounds in helpful outlines and practical insights. Valuable for lay use, and I hope it enjoys widespread circulation. 226.6'07.SCR5 1976

**\*Stedman, Ray C.** *Acts 21-28. Triumphs of the Body.* Santa Ana, Calif.: Vision House Publishers, 1981.

Brief studies completing the author's trilogy. Recommended. 226.6'07.ST3 v.3

**\*_____.** *Birth of the Body.* Santa Ana, Calif.: Vision House Publishers, 1974.

A vibrant recounting of the early church's beginning and witness. The author shows how the power available to the early Christians is available today. The formula is found in Acts 1-12. 225.6'07.ST3 v.1

**\*_____.** *Growth of the Body.* Santa Ana, Calif.: Vision House Publishers, 1976.

A continuation of the author's exposition of Acts in which he demonstrates from the history of the early church the fallacy of relying solely on man-made programs without making room for the "body life" of believers. 226.6'07.ST3 v.2

**\*Stier, Rudolf Ewald.** *The Words of the Apostles.* Translated by G. H. Venables. Minneapolis: Klock & Klock Christian Publishers, 1981.

Examines the public ministry of the apostles and expounds each message with insight and skill. A must for every student of the book of Acts. 226.6'04.ST5 1981

**\*Vaughan, Charles John.** *Studies in the Book of Acts.* Minneapolis: Klock & Klock Christian Publishers, 1985.

Vaughan achieved justifiable acclaim for his expositional commentaries on Romans, Philippians, and Revelation. C. H. Spurgeon wrote of this work on Acts, "Not only does Dr. Vaughan expound his text in the ablest manner, but he introduces passages of Scripture so aptly that he suggests discourses." This is a work of rare merit, and it will be appreciated by those who use it wisely. 226.6'07.V46 1985

MIRACLES

**\*Bruce, Alexander Balmain.** *The Miracles of Christ.* Minneapolis: Klock & Klock Christian Publishers, 1980.

Vindicates a belief in miracles in the face of the most plausible unbelief. Provides preachers with grist for their homiletic mill, and also defends the miraculous against those who have sought to discredit the accuracy and integrity of the NT text. Will richly reward the discerning user. 226.7'06.B83 1980

**\*Laidlaw, John.** *Studies in the Miracles of Our Lord.* Minneapolis: Klock & Klock

Christian Publishers, 1982.

One of the best presentations of this kind of material for the preacher. Laidlaw was never trite. His material gives evidence of long exposure to the biblical text. Though not intended as an apologetic for the miraculous, what is presented does have apologetic value. The primary purpose, however, is to present Christ's miracles as the means to accrediting His Person and demonstrating the validity of His claims. Highly recommended. 226.7′07.L14 1982

**\*Ryrie, Charles Caldwell.** *The Miracles of Our Lord.* Nashville: Thomas Nelson Publishers, 1984.

Does not attempt to defend or vindicate Christ's miracles as recorded in the gospels, but, rather, to explain them in terms that at once bring out their central message. Ryrie combines exegesis with theology and a thorough knowledge of the major movements in Christ's life. All may profit from this book. Recommended. 226.7′06.R99

**Taylor, William Mackergo.** *Miracles of Our Saviour.* Grand Rapids: Kregel Publications, 1975.

First published in 1890, this present work is a reproduction of the 5th edition of 1906. An excellent example of expository preaching. Recommended. 226.7′07.T21 1975

PARABLES

**Arnot, William.** *Lesser Parables of Our Lord.* Grand Rapids: Kregel Publications, 1981.

True to the title, these sermons deal with the simplicity of faith, the issues of life, and the essence of a Christlike character presented in Christ's parables. A valuable resource. 226.8.AR6L 1981

―――. *Parables of Our Lord.* Grand Rapids: Kregel Publications, 1981.

First published in 1865. These messages on the parables of the gospels of Matthew and Luke explain in non-technical terms Arnot's insights into their meaning and message. Recommended. 226.8.AR6 1981

**\*Bruce, Alexander Balmain.** *The Parables of Christ.* Minneapolis: Klock & Klock Christian Publishers, 1980.

A fresh study of the parables that readily dispenses with the older approaches and establishes new parameters for modern research. A stimulating and rewarding discussion. 226.8′06.B83 1980

**Jones, Peter Rhea.** *The Teaching of the Parables.* Nashville: Broadman Press, 1982.

A scholarly reappraisal of the NT parables with some fresh deductions as to their meaning. Each is seen to expand on some facet of the kingdom. 226.8.J72

**Kissinger, Warren S.** *The Parables of Jesus: A History of Interpretation and Bibliography.* Metuchen, N.J.: Scarecrow Press, 1979.

Begins with a delineation of the chief exponents of the parables from Irenaeus through Dodd and Crossan. Following these instructive and enlightening essays, Kissinger provides a comprehensive bibliography on each parable. This is a most helpful work, one to which all students of Christ's teachings will turn repeatedly. Indexed. 226.8′06.K64

**Kistemacher, Simon J.** *The Parables of Jesus.* Grand Rapids: Baker Book House, 1980.

Written to aid pastors in the preparation of sermons on the parables; gives evidence of careful research. Kistemacher ably illustrates the biblical material from extrabiblical sources (e.g., DDS, Gnostic materials, etc.). Thorough. 226.8.K64

**\*Laidlaw, John.** *Studies in the Parables of Our Lord.* Minneapolis: Klock & Klock Christian Publishers, 1984.

Long out of print. Many will welcome the reappearance of this most valued volume. Laidlaw deals adequately with each parable and illumines the text in ways that add luster to what Christ taught. This is an intriguing work, and it deserves a place in the library of every pastor. Highly recommended. 226.8.L14 1984

**Lang, George Henry.** *Pictures and Parables: Studies in the Parabolic Teaching of Holy Scripture.* Miami Springs, Fla.: Conley and Schoettle Publishing Co., 1985.

Published in the U.K. in 1955 and in the U.S. in 1956 under the title *The Parabolic Teaching of Scripture.* This work treats OT and NT parables and figures of speech. Each discussion is thorough, and there is a timely application of the truth to the life of the believer and the future of the kingdom. 226.8'07.L25. 1985

**Pentecost, John Dwight.** *The Parables of Jesus.* Grand Rapids: Zondervan Publishing House, 1982.

Building on a lifetime of biblical scholarship, Pentecost presents the essence of Jesus' parables. Each parable is introduced in its setting. That is followed by a discussion of the problem(s) associated with its interpretation and a presentation of the solution. Recommended. 226.8.P38

**Taylor, William Mackergo.** *Parables of Our Saviour.* Grand Rapids: Kregel Publications, 1975.

Reproduced from the 1906 edition, this handy volume of expository messages may be consulted with profit by all who schedule a series of sermons on the parables of the NT. Recommended. 226.8'07.T21 1975

BEATITUDES

See under Matthew.

LORD'S PRAYER

***MacArthur, John F., Jr.** Jesus' Pattern of Prayer.* Chicago: Moody Press, 1981.

An in-depth study of the Lord's Prayer. Draws the essence from these verses, and shows how they underscore the true character of prayer. 226.96.M11

***Saphir, Adolph.** Our Lord's Pattern for Prayer.* Grand Rapids: Kregel Publications, 1984.

An outstanding work that is worthy of repeated consultation. Scholarly, devotional, a must for every believer. Recommended. 226.96.SA6 1984

## PAULINE EPISTLES

**Barrett, Charles Kingsley.** *Essays on Paul.* Philadelphia: Westminster Press, 1982.

Scholarly essays by a leading NT exegete. Several of these studies deal with the relationship of Paul to the church at Corinth. Illuminating. 227'.06.B27E

**Beker, J. Christiaan.** *Paul's Apocalyptic Gospel: The Coming Triumph of God.* Philadelphia: Fortress Press, 1982.

Explores the apocalyptic portions of Paul's writings with a view to demonstrating their relevance for the church today.

Sifts through the prevailing theories and shows that Paul's gospel provides motivation for the church here and now in anticipation of the coming triumph of God. 227'.082.B39

**Bradford, Ernle Dusgate Selby.** *Paul the Traveller.* New York: Macmillan Co., 1977.

The author of the popular *Ulysses Found* here traces the journeys of the apostle Paul. He adds little to our knowledge of the theology of Paul or the missionary enterprise he undertook, but he does flesh out considerably the historic, geographic, and social setting in which the apostle worked. 227'.09.B72

**Drane, J. W. Paul:** *Libertine or Legalist?* London: S. P. C. K., 1975.

†Those looking for reassuring answers to confirm their ideas about Paul's stance on either legalism or license should not consult this work. The author engages in an in-depth examination of the Pauline corpus and raises several thorny problems that must be solved before an ethic can be formulated. What is to be found between these covers is a well-reasoned, provocative treatise. 227'.082.D79

**\*Ellicott, Charles John.** *Commentaries, Critical and Grammatical on the Epistles of Saint Paul, with Revised Translations.* 3 vols. Minneapolis: The James Family, 1978.

These handy volumes, covering 1 Corinthians to Philemon, make available in beautiful format and binding the rich exegetical legacy of this nineteenth-century Anglican theologian. 227'.07.EL5 1978

**Fairweather, William.** *The Background of the Epistles.* Minneapolis: Klock & Klock Christian Publishers, 1977.

An indispensable work. Will handsomely repay the busy pastor each time he uses it. Recommended. 229'.09.F16 1977

**Francis, Fred O.,** and **J. Paul Sampley.** *Pauline Parallels.* Philadelphia: Fortress Press, 1975.

Prints each letter of the apostle (excluding the pastorals) side by side with passages from other letters that use similar language or literary forms. The result is a work that scholars and literary critics will welcome. 227'.06'5.F84

**Furnish, Victor Paul.** *The Moral Teaching of Paul.* Nashville: Abingdon Press, 1979.

Fails to ground Paul's ethic in the "fear of the Lord" motif. Deals topically with sex, homosexuality, governments, the place of women in the church, and other topics. Well researched. 227.017.F98

**Godet, Frederic Louis.** *Studies in Paul's Epistles.* Grand Rapids, Mich.: Kregel Publications, 1984.

Another welcome reprint. Originally published in 1889, this volume will be of value to students of the NT who wish to gain a synthetic overview of Paul's letters. Though modern scholarship has enlarged our understanding of Gnosticism and the places in which Paul ministered, this work places the important facts in easy reach. Here is an example of Godet's unadorned and unsophisticated scholarship. 227'.06.G54 1984

**Gunther, John Jacob.** *Paul: Messenger and Exile.* Valley Forge: Judson Press, 1972.

A study in the chronology of Paul's life and letters. Recommended. 227.094.G95

————. *St. Paul's Opponents and Their Background.* Leiden, The Netherlands: E. J. Brill, 1974.

This seminal study finds Paul's opponents closer to Essenism than to any other school or sect (including Pharisaism) in Judaism. 227.08.G95

**Hagner, Donald A.,** and **Murray J. Harris, eds.** *Pauline Studies: Essays Presented to Professor F. F. Bruce on his 70th Birthday.* Grand Rapids: Wm. B. Eerdmans Publishing Co., 1980.

A second festschrift honoring the contribution of Professor Bruce. Part 1 deals with the life and theology of the apostle Paul; Part 2 focuses on the literary and exegetical aspects of the Pauline writings. 227.B83.H12

**Hanson, Anthony Tyrrell.** *Studies in Paul's Technique and Theology.* Grand Rapids: Wm. B. Eerdmans Publishing Co., 1974.

Though not writing for evangelicals, Hanson does provide important insights into Paul's life and thought. The first seven chapters are based on a careful examination of Romans and Galatians. The final two chapters are devoted to a discussion of Paul's hermeneutics. 227'.082.H19

**Holmberg, Bengt.** *Paul and Power: The Structure and Authority of the Primitive Church as Reflected in the Pauline Epistles.* Lund, Sweden: CWK Gleerup, n.d.

†The author's 1978 doctoral dissertation at Lund University. This work treats the issue of power in the Pauline corpus and in the experience of the early church. Very thorough. 227'.08.P87.H73

**Keck, Leander E.** *Paul and His Letters.* Philadelphia: Fortress Press, 1979.

Treats the major issues in Pauline studies. Focuses on Paul's message (apart from the controversies that marked so much of his ministry), and draws from his writings the fundamental issues that he taught and defended. 227.'06.K24

——, and **Victor Paul Furnish.** *The Pauline Letters.* Nashville: Abingdon Press, 1984.

†Takes a new and different approach to the Pauline corpus. Provides interesting sidelights on Paul's Christology, his ethical ideals, and the traditions that have grown up about his writings. 227'.06.K23

**Kim, Seyoon.** *The Origin of Paul's Gospel.* Grand Rapids: Wm. B. Eerdmans Publishing Co., 1982.

In answer to Pauline scholarship that tends to explain the origin of Paul's gospel in Palestinian Judaism, Hellenistic Judaism, mystery cults, or Gnosticism, Kim here argues that the origin lies in Paul's own testimony that he received the gospel from the revelation of Jesus Christ. He begins his investigation of Paul's interpretation of the Damascus event by examining Paul's rabbinic background. He then takes a more detailed look at just what occurred on the Damascus highway and follows this with a thorough discussion of Paul's gospel— its revelation, Christology, and soteriology—keeping in mind at all times how it relates to the event at the time of his conversion. 227'.06.K56

**Knight, George W., III.** *The Faithful Sayings in the Pastoral Letters.* Grand Rapids: Baker Book House, 1979.

This monograph expounds the repeated "this is a faithful saying and worthy of all acceptation" in the pastoral epistles. Knight concludes that these formed the self-conscious creedal/liturgical expression of the early church. Stimulating. 227'.06.K74

**\*Lightfoot, Joseph Barber.** *Notes on the Epistles of St. Paul.* Winona Lake, Ind.: Alpha Publications, 1979.

Covers 1 and 2 Thessalonians, 1 Corinthians 1-7, Romans 1-7, and Ephesians 1. Follows the format of Lightfoot's other monumental works. 227'.07.L62 1979

**\*Loane, Marcus Lawrence.** *Grace and the Gentiles: Expository Studies in Six Pauline Letters.* Edinburgh: Banner of Truth Trust, 1981.

Delightful devotional studies by one of Australia's leading evangelical clergymen. 227'.08.L78

**\*Longenecker, Richard Norman.** *Ministry and Message of Paul.* Grand Rapids: Zondervan Publishing House, 1971.

A clear and concise introduction to the ministry and message of Paul. 227.092.P28.L85

——. *Paul, Apostle of Liberty.* Grand Rapids: Baker Book House, 1976.

A welcome reprint. See *The Minister's Library* (1985), p. 196, for comment. 227'.082.L86 1976

**Lyall, Francis.** *Slaves, Citizens, Sons: Legal Metaphores in the Epistles.* Grand Rapids: Zondervan Publishing House, Academie Books, 1984.

The author, a professor of law at the University of Aberdeen in Scotland, assesses the teaching of the NT on such terms as slaves, freedmen, aliens, citizens, adoption, heirs, and redemption. Clear, direct, valuable—this book deserves an honored place in every Bible student's library. 227'.064.L98

**Moxnes, Halvor.** *Theology in Conflict: Studies in Paul's Understanding of God in Romans.* Leiden, The Netherlands: E. J. Brill, 1980.

†A scholarly discussion of Pauline thought that strikes at the center of the apostle's theology. There is much in this volume that is insightful and stimulating. It does, however, need to be read judiciously. 227'.082.M87

**Pagels, Elaine H.** *The Gnostic Paul.* Philadelphia: Fortress Press, 1975.

†Incorrectly titled and expensive, this brief study concentrates attention on the use that Gnostic writers of the second century made of Paul's letters. Highlights the erroneous concepts of those Gnostic writers. 227'.077.P14

**Ridderbos, Herman N.** *Paul: An Outline of His Theology.* Translated by J. R. DeWitt. Grand Rapids: Wm. B. Eerdmans Publishing Co., 1975.

A comprehensive and learned work by one of the foremost NT scholars of our day. 227'.082.R43

**Sampley, J. Paul.** *Pauline Partnership in Christ: Christian Community and Commitment in Light of Roman Law.* Philadelphia: Fortress Press, 1980.

This vigorous, scholarly discussion of the mission of the church blends history and sociology with an explanation of selected passages from the Pauline corpus. Gives evidence of much originality of thought. 227.SA4P

**Sandmel, Samuel.** *The Genius of Paul.* Philadelphia: Fortress Press, 1979.

First published in 1958. This informative study of a Jew by a Jew reveals an appreciation of the apostle without giving evidence of his faith in Jesus as the Messiah. Sandmel seeks to correct errors he has detected in Davies's book *Paul and Rabbinic Judaism.* 225.92.P28.SA5

**Schmithals, Walter.** *Paul and the Gnostics.* Translated by John E. Steely. Nashville: Abingdon Press, 1972.

†Continuing the author's study begun in *Gnosticism in Corinth*, this work applies his earlier material to conditions of the church and the development of Pauline theology. 227.SCH6

**Stanley, David Michael.** *Boasting in the Lord.* New York: Paulist Press, 1974.

A theological examination of Paul's prayers that probes the heart of Paul's life and reveals not only his personal commitment to the Lord but the secret of his success as well. 227.08.ST2

**Wiles, Gordon P.** *Paul's Intercessory Prayers: The Significance of the Intercessory Prayer Passages in the Letters of St. Paul.* New York: Cambridge University Press, 1974.

A scholarly work limited to an investigation of the supplications by which Paul presented the needs of others to the Lord. Though complicated by the intrusion of "liturgical" material, this book may nevertheless be studied with profit. 227.08.P89.W64

ROMANS

**Achtemeier, Paul J.** *Romans.* Interpretation. Atlanta, Ga.: John Knox Press, 1985.

†Traces Paul's thought as he lays before his readers his understanding of the gospel and describes the power of God to change and transform the believer. The comments on the text seek to make clear Paul's thought, but on occasion the writer's presuppositions mar his exposition. Because Paul's argument is cumulative, Achtemeier has included summaries at strategic places. 227.1'07.AC4

**Black, Matthew.** *Romans.* New Century

Bible Commentary. Grand Rapids: Wm. B. Eerdmans Publishing Co., 1981.

This brief, exegetical commentary's uniqueness lies in its bibliographical notes, which are included in the text. 227.1'07.B56 1981

**\*Brown, John.** *Analytical Exposition of the Epistle of Paul the Apostle to the Romans.* Minneapolis: Klock & Klock Christian Publishers, 1979.

Of all the works by John Brown of Edinburgh, this exposition is without doubt one of the best. It was out of print for so long that many Bible students were unaware of its existence. Now it has been retrieved from oblivion. Buy it. 227.1'07.B81 1979

**Bruce, Frederick Fyvie.** *The Letter of Paul to the Romans.* Rev. ed. Tyndale New Testament Commentaries. Grand Rapids: Wm. B. Eerdmans Publishing Co., 1985.

Little revised from the 1963 edition, this commentary still is worthy of consultation. It is also handy for lay study. 227.1'07.B83 1985

**\*Cranfield, Charles E. B.** *A Critical and Exegetical Commentary on the Epistle to the Romans.* 2 vols. International Critical Commentary. Edinburgh: T. & T. Clark, 1975-1979.

This indispensable work takes its place among the foremost works on Romans. Though it does not displace the renowned contribution by Sanday and Headlam, which has admirably served the needs of students since 1895, Cranfield's magisterial handling of the grammar and syntax is of such quality as to immediately accord these volumes a place in every preacher's library. Those who take the time to study these volumes carefully will find themselves amply rewarded. 221.1'07.C85

**\*_____.** *Romans: A Shorter Commentary.* Grand Rapids: Wm. B. Eerdmans Publishing Co., 1985.

Provides the layperson with an excellent treatment of Paul's theme and the development of his thought. 227.1'07.C85S

**\*Gifford, Edwin Hamilton.** *The Epistle of St. Paul to the Romans, With Notes and Introduction.* Minneapolis: The James Family, 1977.

A worthy reprint. This work has been virtually unobtainable for approximately seventy-five years. The author's exposition is based on a painstaking exegesis. His treatment of chapters 9-11 is from an amillennial perspective. The exposition is judicious and well reasoned. 227.1'07.G36 1977

**\*Godet, Frederic Louis.** *Commentary on Romans.* Grand Rapids: Kregel Publications, 1977.

One of the most satisfying of all the nineteenth-century commentaries on Romans. Recommended. 227.1'07.G54 1977

**Govett, Robert.** *Govett on Romans.* Miami Springs, Fla.: Conley and Schoettle Publishing Co., 1981.

Originally issued in 1891 as *The Righteousness of God the Salvation of the Believer,* this study of Romans presents in an ordered way the development of Paul's thought. Excellent. 227.1'07.G74 1981

**\*Hendriksen, William.** *Exposition of Paul's Epistle to the Romans.* 2 vols. in 1. New Testament Commentary. Grand Rapids: Baker Book House, 1980.

A masterful commentary that will take its place among the leading expositions on this portion of the Pauline corpus. Recommended. 227.1.'H38

**Johnson, Alan F.** *The Freedom Letter.* 2 vols. Chicago: Moody Press, 1985.

A contemporary exposition of the theme and content of Paul's Roman epistle. This edition is an expansion of the single volume 1974 work that proved invaluable to laypeople. 227.1'07.J63 1985

**Kasemann, Ernst.** *Commentary on Romans.* Translated and edited by G. W. Bromiley. Grand Rapids: Wm. B. Eerdmans Publishing Co., 1980.

This clearly outlined and well-documented scholarly commentary expands our awareness of Pauline theology. Reflects an individualism that necessitates care in reading as well as discernment. 227.1'07.K11

**\*Liddon, Henry Parry.** *Explanatory Analysis of St. Paul's Epistle to the Romans.* Minneapolis: James & Klock Publishing Co., 1977.

Only on rare occasions does a student of Scripture come across a work as rich and insightful as this one. Forming as it does the basis of Liddon's expository sermons, it demonstrates how a preacher may approach the text in order to lay bare the thoughts of the writer. As such, it provides a fitting model of the kind of analysis every preacher should engage in prior to attempting to deliver God's Word. 227.1'07.L61 1977

**Lloyd-Jones, David Martyn.** *Romans: Assurance.* London: Banner of Truth Trust, 1971.

An important companion volume to the writer's study on justification and the atonement. Expounds Paul's teaching on sin and grace, hope and faith, redemption and glory. The heartwarming application of the Word of God to the needs of people today will edify preachers and laymen alike. 227.1'07.5.L77

———. *Romans: An Exposition of Chapter 8:5-17; The Sons of God.* Grand Rapids: Zondervan Publishing House, 1975.

Full of new insights and of great importance to all who wish to study the doctrine of sanctification. 227.1'07.8:5-17.L77

———. *Romans: An Exposition of Chapter 8:17-39; The Final Perseverance of the Saints.* Grand Rapids: Zondervan Publishing House, 1976.

A beautiful blending of doctrine and application, of theology and practice. As examples of expository preaching, these must rank among the choicest works of Christendom and should be accorded a place alongside those of Calvin, Jewel, Manton, and Sibbes. Recommended. 227.1'07.8:17-39.L77

———. *Romans: Exposition of Chapters 3:20 to 4:25.* Grand Rapids: Zondervan Publishing House, 1971.

A superb exposition of the doctrines of the atonement and justification. 227.1'07.3—4.L77

\*———. *Romans: An Exposition of Chapters 7:1—8:4; The Law: Its Functions and Limits.* Grand Rapids: Zondervan Publishing House, 1974.

This careful and detailed work is an example of expository preaching at its best. Lloyd-Jones's analysis of carnality and spirituality is designed to expose the reason for the former and the way to acquire the latter. 227.1'07.7:1—8:4.L77

**\*Luther, Martin.** *Commentary on the Epistle to the Romans.* Translated by J. T. Mueller. Grand Rapids: Kregel Publications, 1976.

A reprint of the 1954 edition, this significant commentary deserves repeated consultation. 227.1'07.L97 1976

**\*Moule, Handley Carr Glyn.** *The Epistle to the Romans.* Minneapolis: Klock and Klock Christian Publishers, 1982.

One of the best expositions of Romans ever produced. Ably blends the theology of the epistle with rich devotional insights. Should be read often and studied in a spirit of true devotion. First appeared in The Expositor's Bible. 227.1'07.M86 1982

———. *Studies in Romans.* Grand Rapids: Kregel Publications, 1977.

A capable exegetical study that contains important notes on the text—notes that are of importance to the preacher even though they do not expound Paul's argument. For an exposition of Romans by Moule see his work in The Expositor's Bible. 227.1'07.M86S 1977

**Newman, Barclay,** and **Eugene A. Nida.** *A Translator's Handbook on Paul's Letter to the Romans.* New York: American Bible Society, 1973.

The syntax of this volume is of particular importance, and the authors attempt to resolve some of the problems inherent in the text. As with all volumes in this series, the thrust is to meet the needs of translators. Pastors and seminarians may also find these works helpful. 227.1'06.N46

**Olshausen, Hermann.** *Studies in the Epistle to the Romans.* Minneapolis: Klock & Klock Christian Publishers, 1983.

First published in 1849, this staunch evangelical exposition follows closely Paul's thought and deals adequately with the Greek text. Though adhering to a rigid view of inspiration, Olshausen was a devout and original scholar. His work may still be read with profit. 227.1'07.OL8 1983

**Olyott, Stuart.** *The Gospel As It Really Is; Paul's Epistle to the Romans Simply Explained.* Welwyn, Hertfordshire, England: Evangelical Press, 1979.

Written for laymen. This book provides an explanation of the text and an application of it to the life of the believer. 227.1'07.OL1

**Plumer, William Swan.** *Commentary on Romans.* Grand Rapids: Kregel Publications, 1971.

Contains brief extracts from other commentators together with Plumer's own analysis of the text. Originally published in 1871. 227.1'07.P73 1971

**Pridham, Arthur.** *Notes on Reflections on the Epistle to the Romans.* Grand Rapids: Kregel Publications, 1985.

First published in 1864, this exposition deals with the theme of the epistle and the application of its teaching to the believer as well as to God's people, the Jews. C. H. Spurgeon said that Pridham was sound and gracious. We concur. He has something good on each section. 227.1'07.P93 1985

**Robinson, John Arthur Thomas.** *Wrestling with Romans.* Philadelphia: Westminster Press, 1979.

†A popular presentation that aims at making the apostle Paul's purpose understandable to intelligent laypeople. Uneven in treatment and unreliable in theology. 227.1'07.R56

**\*Shedd, William Greenough Thayer.** *A Critical Commentary on the Epistle of St. Paul to the Romans.* Minneapolis: Klock & Klock Christian Publishers, 1978.

First published in 1879. This work deserves a place alongside the treatments of John Brown, Robert Haldane, and Charles Hodge, 227.1'07.SH3 1978.

**\*Stedman, Ray C.** *From Guilt to Glory.* 2 vols. Waco, Tex.: Word Books, 1978.

A clear exposition of Paul's purpose in writing to the Christians in Rome. Combines doctrinal accuracy with practical relevancy. Highly recommended. 227.1'07.ST3

FIRST CORINTHIANS

**Bratcher, Robert Galveston.** *A Translator's Guide to Paul's First Letter to the Corinthians.* New York: United Bible Societies, 1982.

Advocating TEV and using as well the RSV, Bratcher provides helpful and insightful comments on translating 1 Corinthians into languages other than English for a culture different from our own. 227.2'07.B73

**\*Brown, John.** *The Resurrection of Life: An Exposition of First Corinthians XV, With a Discourse on Our Lord's Resurrection.* Minneapolis: Klock & Klock Christian Publishers, 1979.

Rivals Candlish's *Life in a Risen Saviour*

in expounding this all-important chapter. Remains one of the best discussions extant. Ably combines doctrine with a pleasing exhortation. 227.2'07.15.B81 1979

**Bruce, Frederick Fyvie.** *First and Second Corinthians.* New Century Bible Commentary. Grand Rapids: Wm. B. Eerdmans Publishing Co., 1980.

First published in 1971. This brief, perceptive study aims at the elucidation of words or phrases and pays little or no attention to the theme of the epistle. 227.2'07.B83 1980

**\*Candlish, Robert Smith.** *Life in a Risen Saviour.* Minneapolis: James & Klock Publishing Co., 1977.

As with Candlish's other works (on Genesis, John's first epistle, etc.) this treatment of 1 Corinthians 15 is noteworthy for its clarity, careful exposition of the text, and balanced application of the truth of the passage to the life of the believer. Candlish boldly sets forth the Christian's hope, and his material is both helpful and enlightening. 227.2'07.15.C16 1977

**Conzelmann, Hans.** *I Corinthians: A Commentary on the First Epistle to the Corinthians.* Hermenia. Translated by J. W. Leitch. Philadelphia: Fortress Press, 1975.

†Fails to consistently avoid both mysticism and Gnosticism in his interpretation of the text. Draws attention to what he has chosen to call the biblical writer's "exaltation theology," "exaltation Christology," or "fanaticist eschatology." Grammatically, this work is worthy of serious consideration. 227.2'07.C76

**Davis, James A.** *Wisdom and Spirit: An Investigation of 1 Corinthians 1:18—3:20 Against the Background of Jewish Sapiential Traditions in the Greco-Roman Period.* Lanham, Md.: University Press of America, 1984.

A new investigation of wisdom at Corinth. Argues that the wisdom that Paul opposed in 1 Corinthians 1-3 may be understood against the background of early postbiblical Jewish spaiential traditions. Includes in his presentation a consideration of the book of Sirach, the Qumran scrolls, the Philonic literature, and the book of Wisdom. 227.2'06.1:18—3:20.D29

**\*Edwards, Thomas Charles.** *A Commentary on the First Epistle to the Corinthians.* Minneapolis: Klock & Klock Christian Publishers, 1980.

Combines solid exegesis with satisfying exposition. Exemplifies the commentator's art and at the same time introduces the reader to the nuances of the Greek text. Also explains Paul's theme and provides an excellent statement of the problems the apostle encountered in Corinth. This work is truly meritorious and deserves a place in every pastor's library. 227.2'07.ED9 1980

**\*Godet, Frederic Louis.** *Commentary on First Corinthians.* Grand Rapids: Kregel Publications, 1977.

No preacher should be without this fine work. Godet ably expounds Paul's first letter to the church at Corinth and deftly applies the teaching of the apostle to the needs of the local assembly in our day. Indispensable. 227.1'07.G54 1977

**Govett, Robert.** *The Church of Old in Its Unity, Gifts, and Ministry; An Exposition of 1 Corinthians 12, 13, 14.* Miami Springs, Fla.: Conley and Schoettle Publishing Co., 1985.

A verse by verse exposition, explaining and drawing from these verses the essence and function of the local church. 227.2'07.12—14.G74 1985

**\*Gromacki, Robert Glenn.** *Called to Be Saints: An Exposition of I Corinthians.* Grand Rapids: Baker Book House, 1977.

True to the text, this work expounds Paul's message with clarity and insight. Nontechnical. Ideal for use with adult discussion groups. 227.2'07.G89

**\*Hodge, Charles.** *An Exposition of the First Epistle to the Corinthians.* Grand Rapids: Baker Book House, 1980.

Reprinted from the 1857 edition. This important exposition of the doctrine contained in this epistle explains the essence of church member effectiveness, enlarges on the nature of Christian liberty, and discusses the principles and practice of the Christian assembly. 227.2'07.H66 1980

**Hughes, Robert B.** *First Corinthians.* Everyman's Bible Commentary. Chicago: Moody Press, 1985.

As capable and concise a commentary as can be found. Deals adequately with all the important issues. Excellent for laypeople. 227.2'0.7H87

**Jones, John Daniel.** *An Exposition of First Corinthians 13.* Minneapolis: Klock & Klock Christian Publishers, 1982.

Reverent messages laying bare the truths of this important chapter. A fine example of British preaching. 227.2'07.13.J71 1982

**\*MacArthur, John F., Jr.** *First Corinthians.* The MacArthur New Testament Commentary. Chicago: Moody Press, 1984.

Consistently good, this is *the* modern work for the expository preacher and Bible teacher. MacArthur follows the theme of the epistle with care. His treatment is original without making originality the goal. He adheres loyally to Paul's purpose, and there emerges from his consideration of the text a work that well deserves to stand alongside Godet or Hodge or Lenski. 227.2'07.M11

**Martin, Ralph Philip.** *The Spirit and the Congregation: Studies in 1 Corinthians 12-15.* Grand Rapids: Wm. B. Eerdmans Publishing Co., 1984.

†This is a well-intentioned treatise. Martin believes that the claims of the "charismatics" need to be examined closely in light of the social context, textual issues, and the theological problems in Corinth. He identifies those who were abusing their spiritual gifts as an influential Hellenistic group. He is less clear in his views of the appropriate use of this phenomenon today. What he presents can well be viewed in light of MacArthur's *The Charismatics* and Thomas's *Understanding Spiritual Gifts.* 227.2'07.12—15.M36

**\*Olshausen, Hermann.** *A Commentary on Paul's First and Second Epistles to the Corinthians.* Minneapolis: Klock & Klock Christian Publishers, 1984.

First published in 1855. This highly esteemed exegetical and expository work enlivens the sacred page and enriches the spiritual life of the reader. "Pays careful attention to the theological exposition, entering into the marrow of religious ideas, and introducing the student to the spirit and inward unity of the divine revelation" (Philip Schaff). 227.2'07.OL9 1984

**Orr, William Fridell,** and **James Ar thur Walther.** *I Corinthians.* The Anchc Bible. Garden City, N.Y.: Doubleday an Company, 1976.

Includes a study of the life of Paul. Otherwise uninspiring. 227.2'07.OR7

**\*Prior, David.** *The Message of 1 Corinthians: Life in the Local Church.* The Bible Speaks Today. Downers Grove, Ill.: InterVarsity Press, 1985.

From years of pastoral experience, Prior expounds 1 Corinthians as a tract for our times. He manifests a heavy reliance on C. K. Barrett and does a modest piece of work where the theme of the epistle is concerned. By far the greatest contribution he makes is in the application of the text to the situation facing the local church. In this respect, what he presents is worthy of serious consideration. 227.2'07.P93

**Ruef, John.** *Paul's First Letter to Corinth.*

Westminster Pelican Commentaries. Philadelphia: Westminster Press, 1977.

†First published in England in 1971. This scholarly, critical work is based on the text of the RSV and aims at making modern liberal scholarship acceptable to laymen. Contains some valuable historical insights. 227.2'07.R83 1977

**Smedes, Lewis B.** *Love Within Limits: A Realist's View of I Corinthians 13.* Grand Rapids: Wm. B. Eerdmans Publishing Co., 1978.

An able blending of human and divine love that applies the latter to the needs of the former. Succeeds in showing the transcendence of divine love and the way in which it can transform human relationships. 227.2'07.13.SM33

**Stanley, Arthur Penryn.** *The Epistles of St. Paul to the Corinthians.* 2d ed. Minneapolis: Klock & Klock Christian Publishers, 1981.

A scholarly, critical study of the setting and text of these letters. Follows the format of Lightfoot's studies, with dissertations on different ideas that require extended treatment. Not of the same order as Lightfoot's commentaries, but nonetheless valuable for its insights. 227.2'07.ST2 1981

**\*Stedman, Ray C.** *Expository Studies in I Corinthians: The Deep Things of God.* Waco, Tex.: Word Books, 1981

Excellent examples of biblical exposition, revealing at the same time rich insights into Paul's life and thought. Highly recommended. 227.2'07.ST3

**\*Thomas, Robert L.** *Understanding Spiritual Gifts: The Christian's Special Gifts in the Light of I Corinthians 12-14.* Chicago: Moody Press, 1978.

A well-researched exposition that should clarify much of the misunderstanding surrounding spiritual gifts and, in particular, the charismatic movement. Worthy of highest praise. 227.2'07.12—14.T36

## SECOND CORINTHIANS

**\*Barrett, Charles Kingsley.** *A Commentary on the Second Epistle to the Corinthians.* Harper's New Testament Commentaries. New York: Harper & Row, 1973.

†An exegetical study that will be of help to the expository preacher. Barrett is always worth consulting. 227.3'07.B27

**Baughen, Michael.** *Strengthened by Struggle: The Stress Factor in 2 Corinthians.* Wheaton, Ill.: Harold Shaw Publishers, 1984.

"Baughen has effectively mixed his scholarship and pastoral gifts to bring us fresh insight into St. Paul's remarkable second letter to the Corinthian congregation. What he has demonstrated . . . is that the doctrinal and moral issues that tore at the soul of Corinth are still with us today" (Gordon MacDonald). 227.3'06.B32

**Baumann, J. Daniel.** *Confronted by Love.* Ventura, Calif.: Regal Books, 1985.

A brief exposition of God's principles for daily living from 2 Corinthians. Designed for adult discussion groups. It is to be regretted that this book was published on newsprint. The appearance alone will militate against widespread acceptance. 227.3'06.B32

**Bratcher, Robert Galveston.** *A Translator's Guide to Paul's Second Letter to the Corinthians.* New York: United Bible Societies, 1983.

This work is *not* a full-length commentary but, rather, an exegetical work dealing with problems translators face as they seek to bridge the gap between the world of the first century A.D. and the different cultures in which Paul's "successors" minister today. 227.3'06.B73

**Gromacki, Robert Glenn.** *Stand Firm in the Faith: An Exposition of II Corinthians.* Grand Rapids: Baker Book House, 1979.

A well-balanced exposition using the

text of the KJV. Provides an excellent treatment of Paul's theme. Gives evidence of Gromacki's exemplary use of the original Greek. Recommended. 227.3′07.G89

**\*Hodge, Charles.** *An Exposition of the Second Epistle to the Corinthians.* Grand Rapids: Baker Book House, 1980.

First published in 1859. This doctrinal commentary demonstrates the importance of exegesis in proper biblical exposition. Also reveals the many facets of the apostle Paul's ministry. 227.3′07.H66 1980

**\*Kent, Homer Austin, Jr.** *A Heart Opened Wide: Studies in II Corinthians.* New Testament Studies. Grand Rapids: Baker Book House, 1982.

In his inimitable style, Kent expounds the theme of 2 Corinthians. His material is well researched and presented in a capable manner so that readers may draw maximum benefit from their study of this apostolic letter. 227.3′07.K41

**Laurin, Roy L.** *Second Corinthians: Where Life Endures.* Grand Rapids: Kregel Publications, 1985.

With genuine devotional warmth, Laurin explains how life endures and matures in accordance with the plan and purpose of God. Recommended. 227.3′08.L36 1985

**\*Stedman, Ray C.** *Expository Studies in 2 Corinthians: Power Out of Weakness.* Waco, Tex.: Word Books, 1982.

Fully in keeping with all we have come to expect of this gifted expositor and wise pastor. Explains this epistle in easy-to-understand terms. 227.3.ST3

GALATIANS

**Barrett, Charles Kingsley.** *Freedom and Obligation: A Study of the Epistle to the Galatians.* Philadelphia: Westminster Press, 1985.

Contains the Sanderson Lectures,

Theological Hall, United Church of Australia, 1983. As is always the case with Barrett's works, this book bears the evidence of his lifelong devotion to the NT. His writing is clear and succinct, and his treatment of the issues facing the Galatian church is revealing. 227.4′06.B27

**\*Brown, John.** *An Exposition of the Epistle of Paul the Apostle to the Galatians.* Minneapolis: Klock & Klock Christian Publishers, 1981.

A refreshing treatment of Paul's letter that has been called the Charter of Christian Liberty. By all means buy it. 227.4′07.B81 1981

**Bruce, Frederick Fyvie.** *The Epistle to the Galatians: A Commentary on the Greek Text.* New International Greek Testament Commentary. Grand Rapids: Wm. B. Eerdmans Publishing Co., 1982.

"Fulfills all we have come to expect of [this writer]. Those who are looking for a penetrating study of the Greek text will find this commentary a treasury of information" (Donald Guthrie). 227.4′07.B83

**Cousar, Charles B.** *Galatians.* Interpretation. Atlanta: John Knox Press, 1982.

Of particular value to preachers, this section-by-section commentary is important for its exegetical insights. The hermeneutical approach and literary-historical details need to be read with caution. 227.4′07.C83

**DeWolf, Lotan Harold.** *Galatians: A Letter for Today.* Grand Rapids: Wm. B. Eerdmans Publishing Co., 1971.

†The author's views on the inspiration and authority of the Scriptures are such that he regards the Bible as a "more or less accurate" human document. He does not deal with the historic setting that gave rise to the epistle and yet finds in its teaching the cure for many of America's contemporary ills. 227.4′06.D51

**Ebeling, Gerhard.** *The Truth of the Gos-*

*pel: An Exposition of Galatians.* Translated by D. Green. Philadelphia: Fortress Press, 1985.

†This scholarly work is rich in insights and builds on the author's study of Luther's hermeneutic. It expands the Reformer's contribution, interpreting Paul's epistle in light of modern redaction criticism. Many of Eberling's unique thoughts have come as a result of years of arduous labor, and we are grateful for this lucid English translation. 227.4′06.EB3

**Govett, Robert.** *Govett on Galatians.* Miami Springs, Fla.: Conley Schoettle Publishing Co., 1981.

First published in 1872. This work provides a verse-by-verse study of this important epistle. Insightful and enlightening. Recommended. 227.4′07.G74 1981

**\*Gromacki, Robert Glenn.** *Stand Fast in Liberty: An Exposition of Galatians.* Grand Rapids: Baker Book House, 1979.

Grounded in the historical setting of the people to whom Paul wrote, this study describes in nontechnical language the meaning and message of this letter. Based on the text of the KJV. 227.4′07.G89

**Guthrie, Donald.** *Galatians.* New Century Bible Commentary. Grand Rapids: Wm. B. Eerdmans Publishing Co., 1981.

Based on the RSV. Following a fairly extensive introduction the writer settles down to provide his readers with brief comments on select words and/or phrases in the text. These remarks are of value for the philological and theological light they shed but do not provide the reader with a consecutive exposition of the apostle's thought. 227.4′07.G98

**Howard, George.** *Paul: Crisis in Galatia, a Study in Early Christian Theology.* Cambridge: Cambridge University Press, 1979.

Intertwines Paul's teaching of justifica-

tion by faith with the universal blessings of the Abrahamic Covenant. Identifies Paul's opponents in Galatia as Jewish Christians from Jerusalem and offers some well-researched ideas regarding Paul's view of the Mosaic law and the liberty believers enjoy in Christ. 227.4′06.H13

**\*Kent, Homer Austin, Jr.** *The Freedom of God's Sons: Studies in Galatians.* Grand Rapids: Baker Book House, 1976.

A cogent treatment characterized by exegetical accuracy and an impeccable handling of the original text. 227.4′07.K41

**\*Luther, Martin.** *Commentary on Galatians.* Edited by J. P. Fallowes. Translated by E. Middleton. Grand Rapids: Kregel Publications, 1979.

The reissue of a famous series of lectures delivered at Wittenberg University in 1553. 227.4′07.L97 1979

**McDonald, Hugh Dermot.** *Freedom in Faith.* Old Tappan, N.J.: Fleming H. Revell Co., 1974.

A concise, doctrinally helpful commentary. Clear and to the point. 227.4′07.M14

**\*Ramsay, William Mitchell.** *A Historical Commentary on St. Paul's Epistle to the Galatians.* Minneapolis: Klock & Klock Christian Publishers, 1978.

One of the great commentaries on this portion of Scripture. Deserving of a place in every expository preacher's library. 227.4′07.R14 1978

**Vos, Howard F.** *Galatians: A Call to Christian Liberty.* Everyman's Bible Commentary. Chicago: Moody Press, 1971.

Emphasizing the need for biblical "freedom," the writer expounds Paul's teaching in an understandable manner. 227.4′07.V92

EPHESIANS

**Barth, Markus.** *Ephesians.* The Anchor

Bible. 2 vols. Garden City, N.Y.: Double-day and Co., 1974.

†An extensive, critical exposition combining a careful blend of historical-grammatical exegesis with a down-to-earth application of the truth of the text to the condition of the church today. This is a work of real quality that expository preachers will find most helpful. 227.5'07.B27

**Clark, Gordon Haddon.** *Ephesians.* Jefferson, Md.: Trinity Foundation, 1985.

Fearing that Christianity may be eclipsed in the West, Clark writes to dispel ignorance and champion the cause of biblical Christianity. The result is a work of apologetic value as well as a commentary on the text of this important letter. 227.5'07.C54

**\*Eadie, John.** *Commentary on the Epistle to the Ephesians.* Minneapolis: James & Klock Publishing Co., 1977.

A full exposition that deals at length with the exegetical problems, pays careful attention to the development of Paul's theme, and provides extended discussions on important theological matters that arise as a result of his painstaking analysis of the text. Reprinted from the 1883 edition. 227.5'07.EA2 1977

**\*Getz, Gene A.** *Looking Up When You Feel Down.* Ventura, Calif.: Regal Books, 1985.

These important chapters cover Ephesians chaps. 1-3. The emphasis is on biblical renewal, which Getz has pioneered. Personal, marital, familial, church, and parachurch issues are all included. The format is also new, and the publishers are to be commended for presenting the material in an attractive and highly readable manner. 227.5'07.1—3.G33

**Govett, Robert.** *Govett on Ephesians.* Miami Springs, Fla.: Conley and Schoettle Publishing Co., 1981.

This reprint of the 1889 book entitled *What Is the Church? or The Argument of Ephesians* enables readers to draw much needed refreshment and inspiration from the depths of the apostle's thought. Recommended. 227.5'07.G74 1981

**Houlden, J. L.** *Paul's Letters from Prison.* Westminster Pelican Commentaries. Philadelphia: Westminster Press, 1978.

†Based on the latest literary criticism. These studies provide important comments on the text but without treating the theme of each book. 227.5'07.H81

**\*Kent, Homer Austin, Jr.** *Ephesians: The Glory of the Church.* Chicago: Moody Press, 1971.

An evangelical commentary that ably expounds the theme of this epistle and clearly defines the nature and function of the church. 227.5'07.K41

**\*Lloyd-Jones, David Martyn.** *The Christian Soldier: An Exposition of Ephesians 6:10-20.* Grand Rapids: Baker Book House, 1977.

Full and complete, these sermons by one of the great Bible expositors of all time adequately present the believer's resources, conflict, and reward. Important. 227.5'07.6.L77

**\*_____.** *The Christian Warfare: An Exposition of Ephesians 6:10-13.* Grand Rapids: Baker Book House, 1977.

This very extensive exposition of four verses deals with the character and strategy of the devil and demonstrates how his attacks affect our emotional lives and, eventually, our walk with and work for the Lord. 227.5'07.6:10-13.L77

**\*_____.** *Darkness and Light: An Exposition of Ephesians 4:17—5:17.* Grand Rapids: Baker Book House, 1982.

Ranks among the richest, fullest, and most rewarding of expository studies ever produced. Deals adequately with the way in which believers "grow up into Christ" and the way in which this relationship permeates every area of our being. Reformed. 227.5'07.4—5.L77

―――. *Life in the Spirit, In Marriage, Home and Work: An Exposition of Ephesians 5:18—6:9.* Grand Rapids: Baker Book House, 1975.

An invaluable discussion of the biblical teaching on interpersonal relationships—within the family and on the job—with practical counsel for people in all walks of life. 227.5'07.5:18—6:9.L66

*―――. *God's Ultimate Purpose: An Exposition of Ephesians 1:1-23.* Grand Rapids: Baker Book House, 1979.

In keeping with the author's exceptional gifts as an expositor, this work lifts the reader up and helps him understand God's glorious plan for the church and the destiny of the believer. 227.5'07.1.L77

*―――. *God's Way of Reconciliation: Studies in Ephesians 2.* Grand Rapids: Baker Book House, 1972.

A detailed exposition applying the truth of this passage to man's entire personality—mind, emotions, and will—and showing how, in Christ, God has made full provision for all of his needs. 227.5'07.2.L77

*―――. *The Unsearchable Riches of Christ: An Exposition of Ephesians 3:1-21.* Grand Rapids: Baker Book House, 1980.

Probing deeply into Paul's thought, Lloyd-Jones expounds the essence of the apostle's teaching and explains how Christians may know the true God as opposed to worshiping and serving a god of their own making. 227.5'07.3.L77 1980

**Loane, Marcus Lawrence.** *Three Letters from Prison.* Waco, Tex.: Word Books, 1971.

A topical approach to the study of selected passages from Paul's letters to the Ephesians, Colossians, and Philemon. 227.5'07.L78

**Mitton, Charles Leslie.** *Ephesians.* New

Century Bible Commentary. Grand Rapids: Wm. B. Eerdmans Publishing Co., 1981.

Full of judicious comments on the text. Exhibits rare discernment in the choice of readings. Not as elaborate as M. Barth's treatment, this work nevertheless will merit the student's attention. Based on the RSV. 227.5'07.M69 1981

**Moule, Handley Carr Glyn.** *Studies in Ephesians.* Grand Rapids: Kregel Publications, 1977.

Reprinted from the edition in the Cambridge Bible for Schools and Colleges series. Differs from the author's *Ephesian Studies: Lessons in Faith and Walk.* Designed for English readers, but the notes on the text give evidence of Moule's acquaintance with the original. Biblically sound. 227.5'07.M86S 1977

***Robinson, Joseph Armitage.** *Commentary on Ephesians.* Grand Rapids: Kregel Publications, 1979.

†One of the finest expository and exegetical studies ever written on this epistle. By all means obtain it. 227.5'07.R42 1979

***Stedman, Ray C.** *Riches in Christ.* Waco, Tex.: Word Books, 1976.

Covers Ephesians 1-3. Probes the source of the problems that vex modern man and finds in this section of God's Word the solution to our dilemma. 227.5'07.1—3.ST3

***Stott, John Robert Walmsey.** *God's New Society: The Message of Ephesians.* The Bible Speaks Today. Downers Grove, Ill.: InterVarsity Press, 1979.

A delightful exposition that is at once timely and relevant. It is an example of expository preaching at its best. Buy it and read it often. 227.5'07.ST7

**Van Roon, A.** *The Authenticity of Ephesians.* Leiden, The Netherlands: E. J. Brill, 1975.

A serious, scholarly defense of the

Pauline authorship. Will be welcomed by conservative Bible students. 227.5'07.V35

**Westcott, Brooke Foss.** *St. Paul's Epistle to the Ephesians.* Minneapolis: Klock and Klock Christian Publishers, 1979.

A widely acclaimed work. Complete with introduction, critical notes, vocabulary list, and index of subjects. Deserving of careful study. 227.5'07.W52 1979

PHILIPPIANS

**Cradock, Fred B.** *Philippians.* Interpretation. Atlanta: John Knox Press, 1985.

†This commentary deals with the text as a letter giving us a window on a relationship between a pastor and a church. The purpose is to inform as well as inspire those in the church. The implications of this letter are evident. Cradock uses this as a vehicle for communicating the essence of Paul's epistle to the Philippians. Down-to-earth and helpful. 227.6'07.C84

**\*Eadie, John.** *A Commentary on the Greek Text of the Epistle of Paul to the Philippians.* Minneapolis: James & Klock Publishing Co., 1977.

An important reprint that provides excellent definitions of the meaning of Greek words, contains an extensive discussion of the *kenosis* passage and presents an evaluation of the opinions of leading writers on each crucial point. First published in 1859. 227.6'07.EA2 1977

**Govett, Robert.** *Govett on Philippians.* Miami Springs, Fla.: Conley and Schoettle Publishing Co., 1985.

The late Wilbur M. Smith said, "Govett summarizes what most commentators have attempted to say." He was in the best sense of the word a doctrinal preacher. His handling of the theme of this epistle

is weak, but his presentation of its theology is excellent. 227.6'07.G74 1985

**\*Gromacki, Robert Glenn.** *Stand United in Joy: An Exposition of Philippians.* Grand Rapids: Baker Book House, 1980.

Adheres to the format established in the author's other NT commentaries. Ideal for personal or group use. Nontechnical. 227.6'07.G89

**Houlden, James Leslie.** *Paul's Letters from Prison: Philippians, Colossians, Philemon, and Ephesians.* Westminster Pelican Commentaries. Philadelphia: Westminster Press, 1980.

†An exacting work that approaches matters of authorship, date, and the like critically. Highlights the different purposes of each letter. Of value for its exegetical insights. Must be read with discernment. 227.6'07.H12

**\*Hutchinson, John.** *Exposition of Paul's Epistle to the Philippians.* Minneapolis: Klock & Klock Christian Publishers, 1985.

This expositional commentary traces with care the unfolding of Paul's thought and applies the principles that are laid bare to the needs of believers. Hutchinson deals deftly with the apostle's varying moods and shows how these provide a pattern for the Christian's own growth. This is an excellent volume, perspicuous and practical. 227.6'07.H97 1985

**\*Johnstone, Robert.** *Lectures on the Epistle to the Philippians.* Minneapolis: Klock & Klock Christian Publishers, 1977.

A valued reprint. Deals admirably with the theme of the epistle. Buy it while it is still available. 227.6'07.J65 1977

**Moule, Handley Carr Glyn.** *The Epistle to the Philippians.* Grand Rapids: Baker Book House, 1981.

First published in 1897 as a part of the Cambridge Greek Testament, this insightful study treats the key words and

phrases of this prison epistle.
227.6'07.M86 1981

———. *Studies in Philippians.* Grand Rapids: Kregel Publications, 1977.

First published in 1893 in the Cambridge Bible for Schools and Colleges series. These notes on the text demonstrate the author's perception and sensitivity in handling the apostle Paul's thought processes and theme. Differs from Moule's other work entitled *Philippian Studies: Lessons in Faith and Love.* Evangelical. 227.6'07.M86S 1977

**Pentecost, John Dwight.** *The Joy of Living: A Study of Philippians.* Grand Rapids: Zondervan Publishing House, 1973.

This series of expository messages not only does justice to the apostle's stated purpose but also edifies and enriches the reader as he is led by this master of the pulpit to understand the theme of this epistle. Recommended. 227.6'07.P38

**\*Vaughan, Charles John.** *Epistle to the Philippians.* Minneapolis: Klock & Klock Christian Publishers, 1984.

First published in 1872. These expository studies should be in the library of every pastor. They provide vivid and lasting impressions of the theme of this epistle and of the message Paul intended to convey to his readers. Excellent. 227.6'07.V46 1984

**Walvoord, John Flipse.** *Philippians: Triumph in Christ.* Chicago: Moody Press, 1971.

A brief exposition. Helpful, but does not make a lasting contribution. 227.6'07.W17

COLOSSIANS

**Bruce, Frederick Fyvie.** *The Epistles to the Colossians, to Philemon, and to the Ephesians.* New International Commentary on the New Testament. Grand Rapids: Wm. B. Eerdmans Publishing Co., 1984.

Colossians was the first Pauline epistle

on which Bruce wrote a commentary. Now, thirty years later, he has rewritten this work and added to it entirely new studies on Philemon and Ephesians. He believes that Ephesians *follows* Colossians in thought and that Philemon, with its close association to Colossians, is appropriately included in this group of Paul's writings. Provocative. 227.7'07.B83

**Clark, Gordon Haddon.** *Colossians: Another Commentary on an Inexhaustible Message.* Phillipsburg, N.J.: Presbyterian and Reformed Publishing Co., 1979.

A brief, pertinent exposition refuting various contemporary manifestations of Gnosticism. Excellent in its application of the truth to the needs of the church. 227.7'07.C54

**Demarest, Gary W.** *Colossians: The Mystery of Christ in Us.* Waco, Tex.: Word Books, 1979.

Designed for discussion groups. This study is partly expository and partly sermonic. Does stress the centrality of Christ in Christian experience. 227.7'07.D39

**Francis, Fred O.,** and **Wayne A. Meeks, comps.** *Conflict at Colossae: A Problem in Interpretation of Early Christianity, Illustrated by Selected Modern Studies.* Rev. ed. Missoula, Mont.: Scholars Press, 1975.

Apart from the introduction and epilogue, which were written by the compilers, the other chapters were contributed by J. B. Lightfoot, M. Dibelius, G. Bornkamm, et al. 227.7'06.F85 1975

**\*Govett, Robert.** *Govett on Colossians.* Miami Springs, Fla.: Conley and Schoettle Publishing Co., 1981.

Formerly published under the title *Christ the Head; The Church His Body,* this study was lauded by C. H. Spurgeon, who predicted that a day would come when Govett's work would be treasured. Perhaps that day has finally arrived. 227.7'07.G74 1981

**\*Gromacki, Robert Glenn.** *Stand Per-*

*fect in Wisdom: An Exposition of Colossians and Philemon.* Grand Rapids: Baker Book House, 1981.

Perceptive studies of these letters, adequately explaining the central message of each. Excellent as an aid in personal Bible study. 227.7'07.G89

**Harrison, Everett Falconer.** *Colossians: Christ All-Sufficient.* Chicago: Moody Press, 1971.

Good things frequently come in small packages. This is one of them. 227.7'07.H24

**\*Kent, Homer Austin, Jr.** *Treasures of Wisdom: Studies in Colossians and Philemon.* Grand Rapids: Baker Book House, 1978.

Continues the author's valuable New Testament Studies series. Expounds these letters in the light of their historical situation and then applies their message to the needs of the believer. Recommended. 227.7'07.K41

**Lohse, Edward.** *Colossians and Philemon: A Commentary on the Epistles to the Colossians and Philemon.* Translated by W. R. Poehlmann and R. J. Karris. Edited by H. Koester. Philadelphia: Fortress Press, 1971.

†Basing his approach to the text upon the latest critical data, the writer provides a wealth of information on the meaning of some Greek words and their usage. Good bibliographies. 227.7'07.L83

**Lucas, R. C.** *Fullness and Freedom: The Message of Colossians and Philemon.* The Bible Speaks Today. Downers Grove, Ill.: InterVarsity Press, 1980.

Omits introductory matters and launches straight into an exposition of the text. Designed for expository preachers, but has value for personal lay study as well. 227.7'07.L96

**Martin, Ralph Philip.** *Colossians and Philemon.* New Century Bible Commentary. Grand Rapids: Wm. B. Eerdmans Publishing Co., 1981.

First published in 1973. This work, based on the RSV, contains scholarly

comments on key words or phrases in most of the verses of these epistles. 227.7'07.M36 1981

————. *Colossians: The Church's Lord and the Christian's Liberty.* Grand Rapids: Zondervan Publishing House, 1972.

A modern treatment that bridges the gap between a superficial study and a technical treatise. 227.7'07.M36

**McDonald, Hugh Dermot.** *Commentary on Colossians and Philemon.* Waco, Tex.: Word Books, 1980.

A verse-by-verse, nontechnical treatment that will satisfy the needs of the seminarian and delight the lay Bible student. Accurate, thorough. 227.7'07.M14

**\*Moule, Handley Carr Glyn.** *Colossian and Philemon Studies: Lessons in Faith and Holiness.* Minneapolis: Klock & Klock Christian Publishers, 1981.

One of the most reverent and delightful of expositions extant. By all means, buy it. First published in 1877. 227.7'07.M86 1981

————. *Studies in Colossians and Philemon.* Grand Rapids: Kregel Publications, 1977.

Appearing initially in the Cambridge Bible for Schools and Colleges series, these commentaries on two of Paul's epistles have endeared themselves to evangelical students of the NT since their first appearance in 1893. They should not be confused with the same author's *Colossians and Philemon Studies: Lessons in Faith and Holiness.* 227.7'.M86S 1977

**\*Schweizer, Eduard.** *The Letter to the Colossians: A Commentary.* Translated by Andrew Chester. Minneapolis: Augsburg Publishing House, 1982.

†This commentary is to be commended for its lucid analysis of the theme and purpose of the epistle and for its extensive discussion of the nuances of the text. A series of short theological essays conclude Schweizer's discussion. 227.7'07.SCH9

**Thomas, William Henry Griffith.** *Colossians and Philemon.* Grand Rapids: Baker Book House, 1973.

Based on the notes of this renowned expositor and theologian, these studies serve to stimulate and encourage Bible teachers and pastors, helping them enjoy the blessings made available to them through their union with Christ. 227.7'07.T36

**Westcott, Frederick Brooke.** *Colossians: A Letter to Asia.* Minneapolis: Klock & Klock Christian Publishers, 1981.

Provides an informative paraphrase of the apostle Paul's thought, includes perceptive comments on the text, and succeeds in explaining the essence of this letter in a manner that is both enlightening and edifying. 227.7'07.W52 1981

THESSALONIAN EPISTLES

**Best, Ernest.** *A Commentary on the First and Second Epistles to the Thessalonians.* Harper's New Testament Commentaries. New York: Harper & Row, 1972.

†A critical and in some respects negative commentary. Best's handling of the nuances of the original text, however, are insightful, and preachers will be able to glean some important truths from these pages. 227.81'07.B46

**Bruce, Frederick Fyvie.** *Word Bible Commentary: 1 and 2 Thessalonians.* Waco, Tex.: Word Books, 1982.

A clear, technical, highly competent treatment, replete with introduction, bibliographies, translation, notes, commentary, and explanation. Generally conservative. 227.81'07.B83 (Alt. DDC 220.7'07.W89 v.45)

**Eadie, John.** *A Commentary on the Greek Text of the Epistles of Paul to the Thessalonians.* Minneapolis: James & Klock Publishing Co., 1976.

Reprinted from the 1877 edition. This posthumous work is characterized by Eadie's usual thoroughness in sifting through the views of different writers.

He provides a clear evaluation of each viewpoint. An important essay on the man of sin is valuable for its historical and theological insights. 227.81'07.EA2 1976

**Findlay, George Gillanders.** *The Epistles of Paul the Apostle to the Thessalonians.* Grand Rapids: Baker Book House, 1982.

First published in 1904 as part of the Cambridge Greek Testament. The treatment is clear and concise. Although still of value, this work has now been superseded. 227.81'07.F49 1982

**Govett, Robert.** *Govett on Thessalonians.* Miami Springs, Fla.: Conley and Schoettle Publishing Co., 1985.

First published in 1893. This posttribulational work explains the theme of these letters. Govett's material on the apostasy is typical of his era, but his handling of the material reveals the heart of the apostle Paul. Clear, helpful. 227.81.G74 1985

**\*Hiebert, David Edmond.** *The Thessalonian Epistles.* Chicago: Moody Press, 1971.

An outstanding exposition based on unusually comprehensive and complete exegesis. This work will become a leader among commentaries for accuracy and reliability. Premillennial. 227.81'07.H53

**\*Milligan, George.** *St. Paul's Epistles to the Thessalonians.* Minneapolis: Klock and Klock Christian Publishers, 1980.

A rare work, ably combining scholarship with an explanation of the apostle's theme and purpose. Amillennial. 227.81'07.M62 1980

FIRST TIMOTHY

**\*Bernard, John Henry.** *The Pastoral Epistles.* Grand Rapids: Baker Book House, 1980.

First published in the Cambridge Greek Testament series in 1899, this exegetical study is preceded by a lengthy introduction. A critical edition of the Greek text follows and then a word-by-word or phrase-by-phrase exposition of the text. Excellent. 228.83′07.B45 1980

**Caird, George Bradford.** *Paul's Letters from Prison.* New Clarendon Bible. London: Oxford University Press, 1976.

One of the better works in this series. Of value for its exegetical insights. 227.83′07.C12

**\*Calvin, John.** *Sermons on the Epistles of Timothy and Titus.* Edinburgh, U.K./Carlisle, Pa.: Banner of Truth Trust, 1983.

First published in 1579, this facsimile edition consisting of 1,248 pages of exposition and application contains the great Reformer's messages delivered before the congregation of the Cathedral of St. Peter, Geneva. The messages were taken down in shorthand and were later translated by a person who signed himself "L.T." Spurgeon highly esteemed these messages, and they are now available again in the same format as that which graced the homes of Puritan laypeople three hundred years ago. Their richness and relevance will amply repay the time spent mastering their contents. This is a worthy reprint, beautifully bound, and printed on fine paper. Recommended. 227.83′06.C13 1983

**\*Clark, Gordon Haddon.** *The Pastoral Epistles.* Jefferson, Md.: Trinity Foundation, 1983.

Uses these epistles to address some of the complex problems facing the church today. Provides an informative exposition, and deftly applies the truth of what Paul taught to the needs of believers. Favors the Reformed tradition. 228.83′07.C54

**Dibelius, Martin,** and **Hans Conzelmann.** *The Pastoral Epistles.* Translated by P. Buttolph and A. Yarbro. Edited by H. Koester. Philadelphia: Fortress Press, 1972.

A commentary built on the premise that these epistles are unauthentic and that a form-critical approach is indispensable to exegesis and a proper understanding of their meaning. The handling of the text is thorough and exacting. The work, however, does not give evidence of having any of those features that a pastor will find helpful as he prepares his messages. 227.83′06.D54

**\*Fairbairn, Patrick.** *The Pastoral Epistles.* Minneapolis: Klock & Klock Christian Publishers, 1980.

A particularly appropriate reprint in light of the fact that so many men are leaving the ministry on account of its unusual pressures. Fairbairn provides a delightful example of exegesis aiding the exposition of the text. 227.83′07.F15 1980

**Fernando, Ajith.** *Leadership Lifestyle: A Study of 1 Timothy.* Wheaton, Ill.: Tyndale House Publishers, 1985.

Drawing heavily on other authors for his information on leadership, Fernando deals solely with the English text of 1 Timothy. The result is a work of interest but one that lacks depth and fails to provide the reader with anything of lasting significance. 227.83′06.F39

**\*Gromacki, Robert Glenn.** *Stand True to the Charge: An Exposition of I Timothy.* Grand Rapids: Baker Book House, 1982.

A fine treatment of Paul's message to a young pastor. Describes the essence of the ministry with guidelines for the establishment of local churches. 227.83′07.G89

**Hanson, Anthony Tyrell.** *The Pastoral Epistles.* New Century Bible Commentary. Grand Rapids: Wm. B. Eerdmans Publishing Co., 1982.

This totally new work is not to be confused with Hanson's *Studies in the Pastoral Epistles* (1968). His comments are incisive and worthy of serious consideration. 227.83′07.H19

**Houlden, J. L.** *The Pastoral Epistles: 1 and 2 Timothy, Titus.* Penguin New Testament Commentaries. London: Penguin Books, 1975.

†Exceedingly brief. This well-written but biased interpretation attempts to establish a non-Pauline authorship for

these letters. Its redeeming feature lies in its exegetical insights. In other matters, however, it is unreliable. 227.83'07.H81

*Kent, Homer Austin, Jr.* The Pastoral Epistles: Studies in 1 and 2 Timothy and Titus. Rev. ed. Chicago: Moody Press, 1982.

This exemplary study has stood the test of time. Now, in this new, revised edition, Kent's commentary should continue to enjoy wide-spread acceptance. 227.83'07.K41 1982

*Liddon, Henry Parry.* Explanatory Analysis of St. Paul's First Epistle to Timothy. Minneapolis: Klock & Klock Christian Publishers, 1978.

This "first century message to twentieth century pastors" is a work of rare merit, and we welcome its reappearance. 227.83'07.61 1978

*Rowland, Alfred.* Studies in First Timothy. Minneapolis: Klock & Klock Christian Publishers, 1985.

"We may say it is a work of no ordinary value, and Christians will find it a rich feast. It is needless, of course, to say that [this study] is a work of a scholar; it is also the work of a whole-hearted believer and its design was intended for the use of all who love the Lord in simplicity and truth" *(The English Churchman)*. 227.83'07.R79 1985

### SECOND TIMOTHY

**Moule, Handley Carr Glyn.** *Studies in II Timothy.* Grand Rapids: Kregel Publications, 1977.

A delightful devotional commentary. First published in 1905. 227.84'07.M86S 1977

*Stott, John Robert Walmsey.* Guard the Gospel: The Message of II Timothy. Downers Grove, Ill.: InterVarsity Press, 1973.

The first volume in a new series entitled The Bible Speaks Today. Deserves to be read by all who are interested in living dynamically for Christ. Highly rec-

ommended. 227.84'07.ST7

**Woychuk, Nicholas A.** *Exposition of Second Timothy.* Old Tappan, N.J.: Fleming H. Revell Co., 1974.

An original and creative exposition that abounds in illustrative material. Recommended. 227.84'07.W91

### TITUS

**Getz, Gene A.** *The Measure of a Man: Studies in Titus.* Ventura, Calif.: Regal Books, 1983.

Published first in 1978 by Zondervan. This practical study now takes its place alongside the author's other "Measure of" books. It is a pleasing series of meditations on Paul's letter to his youthful protégé and edifies as well as instructs the reader. 227.85'07.G33 1983

**Taylor, Thomas.** *Exposition of Titus.* Minneapolis: Klock & Klock Christian Publishers, 1980.

A Puritan commentary that readily explores the inner reality of Paul's letter to his youthful associate. 227.85'07.T21 1980

### PHILEMON

*Cox, Samuel,* and **A. H. Drysdale.** The Epistle to Philemon. Minneapolis: Klock & Klock Christian Publishers, 1982.

Contains Cox's *The Private Letters of St. Paul* (1867) and Drysdale's work first published in the Devotional Commentary series in 1897. Both works will delight the Bible class teacher or the lay preacher. 227.86'07.C83 1982

*Scroggie, William Graham.* Studies in Philemon. Grand Rapids: Kregel Publication, 1982.

Formerly entitled *A Note to a Friend* (1927), this work remains one of the best ever written on Paul's letter to Philemon. 227.86'07.SCR5 1982

# GENERAL EPISTLES

**Sidebottom, E. M.** *James, Jude, 2 Peter.* New Century Bible Commentary. Grand Rapids: Wm. B. Eerdmans Publishing Co., 1982.

This study, first published in 1967, is based on the text of the RSV. It provides helpful insights into the background of each letter. The comments on the text, however, leave much to be desired. 227.9′07.SI1 1982

**Wiersbe, Warren Wendell.** *Be Alert.* Wheaton, Ill.: Victor Books, 1984.

A timely treatment of 2 Peter, 2 and 3 John, and Jude. Exposes those who are merchandisers of error, teachers of false doctrine, and deceivers of those whose lack of knowledge of God's Word makes them easy prey to cultists. 227.9.W63

HEBREWS

**Anderson, Robert.** *Types in Hebrews.* Grand Rapids: Kregel Publications, 1978.

A rewarding study that evangelical Christians can ill afford to neglect. 227.87′06.AN2 1978

**Brown, Raymond.** *Christ Above All: The Message of Hebrews.* Downers Grove, Ill.: InterVarsity Press, 1982.

Treats this epistle as a letter of encouragement to those enduring persecution, and turns the eyes of its readers from their problems to the One who fulfills all that the law and the prophets predicted. 227.87′07.B81

**\*Bruce, Alexander Balmain.** *The Epistle to the Hebrews: The First Apology for Christianity; an Exegetical Study.* Minneapolis: Klock & Klock Christian Publishers, 1980.

In twenty-one chapters, Bruce treats the theology and theme of this epistle. He interprets it as Christianity's first apologetic. His work is a masterful com-

bination of sound exegesis and helpful exposition. Preachers will find this a most helpful exposition. 227.87′07.B83 1980

**Bullinger, Ethelbert William.** *Great Cloud of Witnesses in Hebrews Eleven.* Grand Rapids: Kregel Publications, 1979.

A careful exegetical study that succeeds in examining the life and labors, trials and triumphs of those heroes of the faith whose names are forever enshrined in God's Hall of Fame. 227.87′06.11.B87 1979

**\*Delitzsch, Franz Julius.** *Commentary on the Epistle to the Hebrews.* 2 vols. Minneapolis: Klock & Klock Christian Publishers, 1978.

An extremely fine exposition that uses Talmudic source material to highlight the meaning of the text. A valuable acquisition. 227.87′07.D37 1978

**\*Edwards, Thomas Charles.** *The Epistle to the Hebrews.* Minneapolis: Klock & Klock Christian Publishers, 1982.

A masterful explanation of the purpose of this epistle. Serves to give laypeople as well as those looking for a theological development of a central theme exactly what they need. 227.87′07.ED9 1982

**Ellingworth, Paul,** and **Eugene Albert Nida.** *A Translator's Handbook on the Letter to the Hebrews.* New York: United Bible Societies, 1983.

Continues this series of translation aids. Using TEV and the RSV for comparison, Ellingworth and Nida provide useful hints for translators without giving either a sequential commentary on the text or an exposition of the writer's theme. 227.87′06.EL5

**Goudge, William.** *Commentary on Hebrews, Exegetical and Expository.* Grand Rapids: Kregel Publications, 1980.

This is a monumental work and should find its way into all college and seminary libraries. Goudge was a Puritan divine who ministered at Blackfriar's in London for forty-five years. He was also a member of the Westminster Assembly of Divines who drew up the Westminster Confession. The contents of this volume represent his weekly Bible readings over a period of thirty years. Spurgeon esteemed this work "a great prize." 227.87'07.G72 1980

**Govett, Robert.** *Govett on Hebrews.* Miami Springs, Fla.: Conley and Schoettle Publishing Co., 1981.

First published in 1884. This commentary, as Dr. Wilbur M. Smith said, "summarizes what most commentators have attempted to say." A valuable acquisition for those whose time for research is limited. 227.87'07.G74 1981

**Guthrie, Donald.** *The Letter to the Hebrews.* Tyndale New Testament Commentaries. Grand Rapids: Wm. B. Eerdmans Publishing Co., 1983.

Replaces Hewitt's earlier contribution to the series. Believes the recipients were Jews in danger of apostasizing back into Judaism. This is a good treatment but too general when dealing with the problem portions of this letter. 227.87'07.G98 1983

**Hughes, Graham.** *Hebrews and Hermeneutics: The Epistle to the Hebrews as a New Testament Example of Biblical Interpretation.* Cambridge: Cambridge University Press, 1979.

In this important contribution to the difficult subject of biblical interpretation, Hughes builds on the thesis that the author of Hebrews was trying to establish a theological understanding of the relationship between the outmoded forms and institutions of OT ritual and worship and the distinctions of the Person and work of Christ. Interesting but misleading. 227.87'063.H87

**\*Hughes, Philip Edgcumbe.** *A Commentary on the Epistle to the Hebrews.* Grand Rapids: Wm. B. Eerdmans Publishing Co., 1977.

This is an outstanding work and is well deserving of a place in the front rank of expository and exegetical treatments of this epistle. With consummate skill Hughes has marshaled his facts and presented his material in a most pleasing and edifying manner. No preacher should be without this fine study. 227.87'07.H

**Kasemann, Ernst.** *The Wandering People of God: An Investigation of the Letter to the Hebrews.* Translated by R. A. Harrisville and I. L. Sandberg. Minneapolis: Augsburg Publishing House, 1984.

†Deals only with Hebrews 3:7—6:12. Explains the concept embodied in the title in light of Hebraic and Gnostic teachings. Though mind-stretching, the writer's thesis and the development of his central idea is marred by his view of Scripture. 227.87'06.K15

**Lane, William L.** *Call to Commitment: Responding to the Message of Hebrews.* Nashville: Thomas Nelson Publishers, 1985.

In clear, nontechnical language, Lane explains that Hebrews is more a sermon than a letter. It also addresses the same concerns that face the church today: the absence of God, the climate of uncertainty and insecurity, the tension between secular conformity and spiritual maturity, the threat of societal perversion, and the pressure of materialism. This is a challenging book, one that Christians will want to study carefully. 227.87'06.L23

**Lang, George Henry.** *The Epistle to the Hebrews: A Practical Treatise for Plain and Serious Readers.* Miami Springs, Fla.: Conley and Schoettle Publishing Co., 1985.

A rare work that was first published in

1951 and has since been extremely hard to obtain. Deals adequately with the theme of this portion of God's inspired Word. Explains the Christological import of each section. Highly recommended. 227.87.L25 1985

**\*Milligan, George.** *The Theology of the Epistle to the Hebrews, With a Critical Introduction.* Minneapolis: Klock & Klock Christian Publishers, 1978.

First published in 1899, this is one of the most significant works to be reprinted in recent years. It treats concisely matters of introduction and then systematizes the theology of the epistle in light of God's covenants with Israel. 227.87′082.M62 1978

**Neighbour, R. E.** *If They Shall Fall Away: The Epistle to the Hebrews Unveiled.* Miami Springs, Fla.: Conley and Schoettle Publishing Co., 1984.

First published in 1940. This clear, concise study of Hebrews focuses on the debate between Calvinists and Arminians. The discussion is enlightening. The treatment is brief and to the point. 227.87′06.N31 1984

**Peterson, David.** *Hebrews and Perfection: An Examination of the Concept of Perfection in the "Epistle to the Hebrews."* Cambridge: Cambridge University Press, 1982.

Peterson's chosen method of investigation provides a substantial amount of penetrating exegesis as well as an interesting discussion of the concept of perfection. It is safe to say that this is one of the most thorough discussions available in English. 227.87′06.P44

**Turner, George Allen.** *The New and Living Way.* Minneapolis: Bethany Fellowship. 1974.

A brief but thorough explanation of Hebrews, combining helpful word studies with a concise exposition of the text. Arminian. 227.87′07.T85

**\*Wiersbe, Warren Wendell.** *Be Con-*fident: An Expository Study of the Epistle to the Hebrews.* Wheaton, Ill.: Victor Books, 1982.

A challenging and insightful book that should be used extensively by adult Bible study groups. Recommended. 227.87′07.W63C

———. *Be Hopeful.* Wheaton, Ill.: Victor Books, 1982.

A clear-cut, challenging reminder of the importance of a Christocentric lifestyle, if we are to be able to surmount the pressures of contemporary living. Excellent. Ideal for laypeople's discussion groups. 227.87′07.W63H

\*———. *Run with Winners: A Study of the Champions of Hebrews 11.* Wheaton, Ill.: Tyndale House Publishers, 1985.

Clear, direct, relevant messages on the application of truth from the lives of the great men of the past to the life of each believer today. Recommended. 227.87′07.W63

**Wiley, H. Orton.** *The Epistle to the Hebrews.* Edited by M. A. Weigelt. Kansas City, Mo.: Beacon Hill Press of Kansas City, 1984.

Standing in the tradition of the great Arminian theologians, Wiley expounds the epistle to the Hebrews as a "divinely inspired commentary on the Old Testament." 227.87′07.W65 1984

JAMES

**Adamson, James B.** *The Epistle of James.* New International Commentary on the New Testament. Grand Rapids: Wm. B. Eerdmans Publishing Co., 1976.

This careful treatment combines accuracy in exegesis with a concise exposition of the text. Adamson also seeks to emphasize the cohesion of James's thought, something that other writers have seldom attempted. Recommended. 227.91′07.AD1

**Bratcher, Robert Galveston.** *A Trans-*

*lator's Guide to the Letters from James, Peter, and Jude.* New York: United Bible Societies, 1984.

Designed for missionaries, the purpose of this work is to help translators recognize and solve some of the problems that will be encountered in translating these epistles. Though not intended to replace the standard commentaries, this work does help resolve certain difficult issues. 227.91'06.B73

**\*Davids, Peter H.** *The Epistle of James: A Commentary on the Greek Text.* New International Greek Testament Commentary. Grand Rapids: Wm. B. Eerdmans Publishing Co., 1982.

A scholarly work giving evidence of extensive research. The exegesis is sound. Davids establishes his conclusions on viable principles of interpretation. A rewarding volume. 227.91'07.D28

**Doerksen, Vernon D.** *James.* Everyman's Bible Commentary. Chicago: Moody Press, 1983.

Provides a new and original approach to the theme of the book, and then follows this with a capable, readily understandable commentary on the text. Ideal for lay Bible discussion groups. Recommended. 227.91'07.D67

**Getz, Gene A.** *The Measure of a Christian: Studies in James 1.* Ventura, Calif.: Regal Books, 1983.

A clear, well-outlined study of James 1, with pertinent application of the truth to the life of the believer. The format lends itself to adult discussion groups. Recommended. 227.91'07.1.G33

**\*Hiebert, David Edmond.** *The Epistle of James: Tests of a Living Faith.* Chicago: Moody Press, 1979.

The product of mature scholarship, this work explains the intent of the epistle and maintains its unity of purpose. A work at once readable and reliable. 227.91'07.H53

**\*Johnstone, Robert.** *Lectures Exegetical and Practical on the Epistle of James.* Minneapolis: Klock & Klock Christian Publishers, 1978.

One of the few works of its kind. Makes rich, rewarding reading. Suitable for both pastor and informed layperson. 227.91'07.J65 1978

**Laws, Sophie.** *A Commentary on the Epistle of James.* Harper's New Testament Commentaries. San Francisco: Harper & Row, 1980.

†The writer's scholarship is beyond question. She grounds her understanding of the epistle of James in the attitude of Jewish Christians of the time and sees James taking issue with the apostle Paul and Pauline tradition. The helpful exegetical insights are negated by the author's lack of reliability as a theologian. 227.91'07.L44

**\*Mayor, Joseph Bickersteth.** *The Epistle of St. James.* Minneapolis: Klock & Klock Christian Publishers, 1977.

A work of massive scholarship that ranks among the most important exegetical works ever produced on this epistle. 227.91'07.M45 1977

**\*Motyer, J. Alec.** *The Message of James: The Tests of Faith.* The Bible Speaks Today. Downers Grove, Ill.: InterVarsity Press, 1985.

Believing that Christians are "born for battle," Motyer expounds the epistle with a view to preparing believers for conflict. He also points the way by which the church may recover its message and dynamic. This is a fine evangelical treatment, and it is to be warmly recommended. 227.91'07.M85

**\*Stier, Rudolf Ewald.** *The Epistle of James.* Translated by W. B. Pope. Minneapolis: Klock & Klock Christian Publishers, 1982.

First published in English in 1871. This work is of value to preachers as well as laypeople. To the former, the method of exposition is at once informative and instructive. To the latter, the method of application is enriching and edifying. 227.91'07.ST5 1982

FIRST PETER

**\*Barbieri, Louis Albert, Jr.** *First and Second Peter.* Everyman's Bible Commentary. Chicago: Moody Press, 1977.

An excellent volume to place in the hands of laypeople. Barbieri makes available a clear, thematic, biblically sound exposition of the text. 227.92'07.B23

**Best, Ernest.** *I Peter.* New Century Bible Commentary. Grand Rapids: Wm. B. Eerdmans Publishing Co., 1982.

†First published in England in 1971, this competent study has only one major drawback: it is based on the text of the RSV. Users, however, can still keep the Greek text before them as they gain insights from Best's exposition. 227.92'07.B47 1982

**Hamblin, Robert L.** *Triumphant Strangers: A Contemporary Look at First Peter.* Nashville: Broadman Press, 1982.

Contains brief devotional messages. Southern Baptist. 227.92'07.H17

**\*Hiebert, David Edmond.** *First Peter.* Chicago: Moody Press, 1984.

A fine exposition based on a thorough analysis of the Greek text. Hiebert treats each section of the epistle in light of the theme of the book. The result is a work from which all pastors and laypeople may profit. All things considered, this is an excellent commentary. We recommend it warmly. 227.92'07.H53

**\*Hort, Fenton John Anthony.** *The First Epistle of St. Peter, I:1—II:17.* Minneapolis: James & Klock Publishing Co., 1976.

An exceedingly rare work. Hort provides a full, scholarly study based on a careful examination of the Greek text.

First published in 1898. 227.92'07.1:1— 2:17.H78 1976

**\*Johnstone, Robert.** *The First Epistle of Peter.* Minneapolis: The James Family, 1978.

These concise studies faithfully expound the Greek text and provide a solid foundation for a series of relevant messages. Works of this nature are rare and should be obtained and used by every Bible-teaching preacher. 227.92'07.J65 1978

**Kelly, John Norman Davidson.** *A Commentary on the Epistles of Peter and Jude.* Grand Rapids: Baker Book House, 1981.

First published in 1969. This commentary treats the text in a detailed and concise fashion. The thematic unfolding of each writer's material is highly commendable, and the word studies drawn from early Christian and pagan literature enhance the overall value of this commentary. 227.92'07.K29 1981

**Lillie, John.** *Lectures on the First and Second Epistles of Peter.* Minneapolis: Klock & Klock Christian Publishers, 1978.

A full exposition exhibiting the best exegetical skills of the times. 227.92'07.L62 1978

**Luther, Martin.** *Commentary on the Epistles of Peter and Jude.* Edited by J. N. Lenker and P. W. Bennehoff. Grand Rapids: Kregel Publications, 1982.

Issued to commemorate the 500th year of Luther's birth (1483). These studies challenge the spiritual laxity of our times and call us back to the principles that led to the Reformation. Recommended. 227.92'07.L97 1982

**Mounce, Robert H.** *A Living Hope: A Commentary on 1 and 2 Peter.* Grand Rapids: Wm. B. Eerdmans Publishing Co., 1982.

A balanced, effective, and highly readable interpretation of Peter's epistles in which Mounce sees the keynote of the letters as hope but their main purpose as hortatory. That is, they were written "to encourage believers in Asia Minor to expect and endure hardship as a result of their commitment to the Christian faith" and "to stimulate them to wholesome thinking" vis-a-vis false teachers who had risen up within the church itself. 227.92'07.M86

### SECOND PETER

**Brown, John.** *Parting Counsels: An Exposition of 2 Peter 1.* Edinburgh: Banner of Truth Trust, 1980.

First published in 1856. This study was cut short by the author's death. The material covering chapter 1 (more than 300 pages) was published posthumously. It is rich, clear, and worthy of careful attention. 227.93'07.1.B81 1980

**\*Lloyd-Jones, David Martyn.** *Expository Sermons on 2 Peter.* Carlisle, Pa.: Banner of Truth Trust, 1983.

These sermons were first preached at Westminster Chapel in London from 1946-1947. They depict the struggles of the congregation in the post-World War II years. Their relevance to other people in other situations is obvious. 227.93'06.L77

### JOHANNINE EPISTLES

**Boice, James Montgomery.** *The Epistles of John.* Grand Rapids: Zondervan Publishing House, 1979.

Boice finds the theme of 1 John to be Christian assurance rather than fellowship, and he expounds all three epistles from that point of view. His insights are keen, and his presentation is helpful. As with all expositional commentaries, this one applies the text to the life of the believer and makes a valuable contribution to our knowledge of the apostle as

well as his thought. 227.94'07.B63

**\*Brown, Raymond Edward.** *The Epistles of John, Translated with an Introduction, Notes, and Commentary.* The Anchor Bible. Garden City, N.Y.: Doubleday and Co., 1982.

†Meticulous in detail, exhaustive in analysis, persuasive in argument, this study provides the best answers available to questions and controversies that have troubled scholars and nonscholars alike ever since these epistles first saw the light of day. In addition to the superb analysis, Brown also brings to life those to whom these letters were sent, reminding us that the epistles were written by a person for real people of the first century A.D. A model of biblical study. 227.94'07.B81

**Burdick, Donald W.** *The Letters of John the Apostle: An In-Depth Commentary.* Chicago: Moody Press, 1985.

Written for laypeople. This work is designed to lay bare the meaning of John's letters for his own time and ours as well. Clear and cogent. 227.94'07.B89L

**\*Candlish, Robert Smith.** *The First Epistle of John.* Grand Rapids: Kregel Publications, 1979.

A true classic. Rich in insights, it makes rewarding reading. When we consider that these studies were really sermons delivered to the congregation of which Candlish was the pastor, it would be encouraging to see laypeople buying and reading this work today. Reprinted from the 1877 edition. Recommended. 227.94'07.C16 1979

**\*Findlay, George Gillanders.** *Fellowship in the Life Eternal: An Exposition of the Epistles of John.* Minneapolis: James & Klock Publishing Co., 1977.

A fine example of dedicated scholarship ably blended with rich spiritual insights. Well deserving of the status of classic. Preachers will find this study of great value as they prepare their own messages. 227.94'07.F49 1977

**Grayson, Kenneth.** *The Johannine Epis-tles.* New Century Bible Commentary. Grand Rapids: Wm. B. Eerdmans Publishing Co., 1984.

Following a brief but adequate introduction, Grayson reappraises Johannine scholarship, and though some of his views differ from those of others who have written on these epistles, readers are nevertheless treated to a discussion that is spiritually stimulating and culturally apropos. 227.94'07.G79

**Haas, C., M. DeJonge,** and **J. L. Swellengrebel.** *A Translator's Handbook on the Letters of John.* New York: American Bible Society, 1972.

Can be of use to expositors and those whose Greek has become rusty with the passing of time. Users will benefit from the translation hints and syntactical helps. 227.94'06.H11

**Houlden, J. L.** *A Commentary on the Johannine Epistles.* New York: Harper & Row, 1974.

†This scholarly exposition by a British Anglican theologian manifests an awareness of critical scholarship without following the trends set by more liberal Continental writers. 227.94'07.H81

**\*Lias, John James.** *An Exposition of the First Epistle of John.* Minneapolis: Klock & Klock Christian Publishers, 1982.

One of the finest exegetical and expository works for preachers. Provides an excellent basis for a series of sermons. Deserves a place in the library of every minister and lay preacher. 227.94'07.L61 1982

**\*Marshall, I. Howard.** *The Epistles of John.* New International Commentary on the New Testament. Grand Rapids: Wm. B. Eerdmans Publishing Co., 1978.

An extensive introduction that adequately surveys the historical and textual background of these letters is followed by a careful exposition of John's epistles in the order in which they were written.

Provides interested readers with a complete and satisfying treatment. 227.94'07.M35

**Matheson, Roy R.** *Loving God's Family.* Wheaton, Ill.: Victor Books, 1985.

A brief, valuable exposition of John's first epistle. Designed for lay use. 227.94'07.M42

**\*Morgan, James,** and **Samuel Cox.** *The Epistles of John.* Minneapolis: Klock & Klock Christian Publishers, 1982.

Both highly regarded by C. H. Spurgeon, *First John,* by Morgan and *The Private Letters . . . of St John,* by Cox are here combined to treat all three letters in a way that will be of benefit to the expository preacher. A valuable acquisition. 227.94'07.M82 1982

**Pentecost, John Dwight.** *The Joy of Fellowship.* Grand Rapids: Zondervan Publishing House, 1977.

A series of brief messages that unfold the central purpose of the first epistle of John most admirably. 227.94'07.P37

**\*Plummer, Alfred.** *The Epistles of St. John.* Grand Rapids: Baker Book House, 1980.

This reprint of the 1886 commentary from the Cambridge Greek Testament series readily interacts with critical issues raised by the publication of the NT texts of Tischendorf and Tregelles. Plummer then treats these letters in a most commendable way, providing some unique insights into the thought of the apostle and the nuances of the original text. 227.94'07.P73 1980

**Smalley, Stephen S.** *1, 2, 3 John.* Word Biblical Commentary. Waco, Tex.: Word Books, 1984.

This is a scholarly work that is well deserving of careful reading. Following a thorough introduction (pp. xvii-xxxiv), Smalley treats his readers to a word-by-word or phrase-by-phrase exposition. His comments are judicious as well as insightful. This volume, for all its merit, shares the limitations of the series. It is well researched and exegetically helpful but manifests a weakness in treating the theme of these letters and fails to complete what has been begun by applying the teaching of the passage to the life of the reader. 220.7'7.W89 v.51 (Alt. DDC 227.94'07.SM1).

**\*Stedman, Ray C.** *Expository Studies in 1 John: Life by the Son.* Waco, Tex.: Word Books, 1980.

An outstanding exposition that explains the heart of John's message and applies it with verve to the life of believers today. Recommended. 227.94'07.ST3

JUDE

**\*Jenkyn, William.** *An Exposition upon the Epistle of Jude.* Revised by J. Sherman. Minneapolis: James & Klock Christian Publishers, 1976.

Jenkyn structured his exposition on a painstaking grammatical outline of the Greek text. His work is very full. At one time it was unobtainable but now, with this reprinting, all may again have access to it. 227.97'07.J41 1976

**\*Lawlor, George Lawrence.** *Translation and Exposition of the Epistle of Jude.* Nutley, N.J.: Presbyterian and Reformed Publishing Co., 1972.

Includes a basic study of the original text, and then treats Jude's letter in terms of its original purpose. This is a most important study and deserves a place in every expository preacher's library. 227.97'07.L42

**Manton, Thomas.** *An Exposition on the Epistle of Jude.* Minneapolis: Klock & Klock Christian Publishers, 1978.

Originally published in 1658, these messages unfold and apply the message of Jude. Historically, they precede the infamous Act of Uniformity (1662) and, as such, give readers some idea of the circumstances and events that led up to it. 227.97'07.M31 1978

**\*Mayor, Joseph Bickersteth.** *The Epistles of St. Jude and II Peter.* Minneapolis: Klock & Klock Christian Publishers, 1978.

A welcome reprint. Though he denies the Petrine authorship of 2 Peter, Mayor nevertheless is inclined to accept its canonicity. His exposition of both epistles is as full and complete as any work could be. Of immense value for the author's exegetical insights. 227.97'07.M45 1978

**Tatford, Frederick Albert.** *Jude's Apostates: An Exposition of the Epistle of Jude.* Eastbourne, Sussex, England: Upperton Press, 1975.

A concise exposition laying bare the character of those whose false teaching was leading some believers to engage in immorality and other forms of antinomianism. 227.97'06.T18

# REVELATION

**Barnhouse, Donald Grey.** *Revelation: God's Last Word.* Grand Rapids: Zondervan Publishing House, 1971.

Contains articles reprinted from *Revelation* magazine. The last two chapters have been contributed by Ralph Keiper. 228'.07.B26

**Beasley-Murray, George Raymond, Herschel H. Hobbs,** and **Ray Frank Robbins.** *Revelation: Three Viewpoints.* Nashville: Broadman Press, 1977.

Three Southern Baptists, all of whom have written on prophetic themes, discuss the book of Revelation from different points of view. Beasley-Murray is premillennial and approaches John's vision from the perspective of a postribulationist; Hobbs is amillennial; and Robbins focuses attention on the genre of apocalyptic literature. 228′.06.B38 1977

**Bullinger, Ethelbert William.** *Commentary on Revelation.* Grand Rapids: Kregel Publications, 1984.

First published in 1935, this work offers a uniquely different interpretation of the Apocalypse. It follows a premillennial view of the end times and interprets chaps. 2-3 as applying to future Jewish churches in existence at the time God's wrath is poured out on the world. 228′.07.B87 1984

**Cohen, Gary G.** *Understanding Revelation.* Chicago: Moody Press, 1978.

A definitive work that develops a chronological framework for the interpretation of John's Apocalypse. Premillennial. 228′.07.C66

**Coleman, Robert Emerson.** *Songs of Heaven.* Old Tappan, N.J.: Fleming H. Revell Co., 1980.

A unique devotional study of the "songs heard around the throne" in John's vision of the Celestial City in the book of Revelation. Provides a pattern of worship for God's people here on earth. 228′.06.C67

**Court, John M.** *Myth and History in the Book of Revelation.* Atlanta: John Knox Press, 1979.

A brief literary and historical approach to John's Apocalypse. Focuses on the seven key themes of the book, and uses these as a basis for understanding this portion of Scripture. 228′.06.C83

**Eller, Vernard.** *The Most Revealing Book of the Bible: Making Sense Out of Revelation.* Grand Rapids: Wm. B. Eerdmans Publishing Co., 1974.

This scholarly work has value in that the author explains the true nature of apocalyptic literature. It is surprising to note, however, that he denies the possibility of a literal interpretation of the events prefigured by the various literary descriptions. Such a view produces am-

bivalence in the reader and removes the book of Revelation from the realm of prophecy. 228′.07.EL5

**Feinberg, Charles Lee.** *A Commentary on Revelation: The Grand Finale.* Winona Lake, Ind.: Brethren Missionary Herald Press, 1985.

A brief, reliable overview of the Apocalypse. Ideal for laypeople. Should meet with widespread acceptance. 228′.07.F33

**Ford, Desmond.** *Crisis.* 3 vols. Newcastle, Calif.: Desmond Ford Publications, 1982.

"The visions of John . . . have a permanent and universal relevance, especially for readers living in a situation not unlike that in which John and his first readers lived. And Ford's study deserves special commendation because of the clarity with which it brings out that permanent and universal relevance. He has read widely in exegetical literature, as the wealth of quotation in this work shows; yet throughout he has exercised his own judgement on the meaning of the text. Above all, the book of the Revelation emerges from his study as a powerful witness to the authentic biblical gospel" (F. F. Bruce). 228′.07.F75

**Ford, Josephine Massyngberde.** *Revelation.* The Anchor Bible. Garden City, N.Y.: Doubleday and Company, 1975.

This translation and commentary approaches the Apocalypse from the premise that its message emanated from the disciples of John the Baptist, not the apostle John. The treatment is thorough. Though dissonance is caused in the mind of the reader over certain interpretations of phenomena mentioned in the book of Revelation, the writer shows herself to be a master of the apocalyptic genre of literature. 228′.07.F75

**Gager, LeRoy.** *The Second Exodus.* Barnaby, British Columbia: Second Exodus Publications Society, 1981.

This unique approach to the book of Revelation finds parallels between Israel's first exodus from Egypt and the events described in the Apocalypse. Premillennial, mid-Tribulation. 228'.07.G12

**Govett, Robert.** *Govett on Revelation.* 4 vols. in 2. Miami Springs, Fla.: Conley and Schoettle Publishing Co., 1981.

Originally published as *The Apocalypse: Expounded by Scripture* (1861) under the pseudonym Matheetees, this work earned its author justifiable recognition as an expositor. It remains today one of the most eagerly sought after works on this portion of God's Word. Premillennial, posttribulation. 228'.07.G74 1981

**Hobbs, Herschel H.** *The Cosmic Drama: An Exposition of the Book of Revelation.* Waco, Tex.: Waco Books, 1971.

An amillennial interpretation. 228'.07.H65

**\*Hort, Fenton John Anthony.** *The Apocalypse of St. John, I-II.* Minneapolis: James & Klock Publishing Co., 1976.

All of Hort's works have been exceedingly hard to find on the secondhand book market. The reprinting of this 1908 work is most welcome. Hort's careful handling of the text of these two chapters is judicious, and it is wished that he had been spared to give us more of his insights into the background of Revelation and the churches of Asia Minor. 228'.07.1—2.H78 1976

**Kelshaw, Terence.** *Send This Message to My Church: Christ's Words to the Seven Churches of Revelation.* Nashville: Thomas Nelson Publishers, 1984.

After visiting the land in which the churches of Revelation 1-3 were situated, Kelshaw wrote this book showing how the difficulties facing first-century churches in ancient Turkey were essentially the same as those confronting assemblies today. 228'.06.1—3.K29

**Lang, George Henry.** *The Revelation of Jesus Christ: Select Studies.* Miami Springs, Fla.: Conley and Schoettle Publishing Co., 1985.

Lang, a Plymouth Brethren writer, was a man of uncommon spirituality. His life was devoted to the study of God's Word. All of his writings are of the utmost value. Though adhering to a posttribulation return of Christ, Lang had only one ambition, to honor the Lord. This attitude finds itself on every page of this book, where his honesty in investigating even problematic areas of discussion led him into areas where few would dare to tread. 228'.06.L25S 1985

**Lindsey, Hal.** *There's a New World Coming.* Santa Ana, Calif.: Vision House Publishers, 1973.

A popular exposition of the book of Revelation. Some of Lindsey's assertions concerning the manner in which prophetic events are most likely to be fulfilled are questionable. Premillennial. 228.'067.L64

**Loane, Marcus Lawrence.** *They Overcame: An Exposition of the First Three Chapters of Revelation.* Grand Rapids: Baker Book House, 1981.

First published in Australia in 1971. This expository study discusses adequately and with sound common sense the text and teaching of Christ's letters. Recommended. 228'.07.1—3.L78 1981

**Morris, Henry Madison.** *The Revelation Record: A Scientific and Devotional Commentary on the Book of Revelation.* Wheaton, Ill.: Tyndale House Publishers, 1983.

Treating the Apocalypse chapter-by-chapter, Morris provides his readers with numerous sidelights on the text not found in other works. 228'.07.M83

**Mounce, Robert Hayden.** *The Book of Revelation.* New International Commentary on the New Testament. Grand Rapids: Wm. B. Eerdmans Publishing Co., 1977.

A full and detailed commentary containing a great deal of information that will be of particular interest to those who preach on prophetic themes. Mounce is premillenial and views the visions of Revelation as depicting historic events from the first century to the return of Christ. 228'.07.M86

**Phillips, John.** *Exploring Revelation.* Chicago: Moody Press, 1974.

A careful commentary that those who preach through this portion of God's Word will want to consult. Premillennial. 228'.07.P54

**Sweet, John Philip McMurdo.** *Revelation.* Westminster Pelican Commentaries. Philadelphia: Westminster Press, 1979.

Views the contents of John's vision as a series of historically unrelated events— past, present, and future intertwined. Of value for the writer's information on Hebrew imagery. 228'.07.SW3 1979

**Swete, Henry Barclay.** *Commentary on Revelation.* Grand Rapids: Kregel Publications, 1977.

Reprinted from the 3d (1911) edition, this work rivals that of R. H. Charles (2 vols., 1920) for thoroughness. Through an exacting examination of the Greek text, Swete opens up to his readers the rich nuances of the original, and as he discourses on the meaning of each seg-ment of John's unveiling of the future, he does so from an amillennial perspective. 228'.07.SW4 1977

***Tatford, Frederick Albert.** *The Revelation.* Minneapolis: Klock & Klock Christian Publishers, 1985.

This successor to the author's earlier work, *Prophecy's Last Word* (1947), ably correlates the writings of Moses, Balaam, Isaiah, Jeremiah, Ezekiel, and other biblical writers with the text of the book of Revelation. The result is an amazing synthesis of eschatological thought, and one of the finest expositions for laypeople ever written. Recommended. 228'.07.T18R 1985

**Wiersbe, Warren Wendell.** *Be Victorious.* Wheaton, Ill.: Victor Books, 1985.

A clear, easy-to-read, understandable exposition of the book of Revelation. Can be used with profit by individuals or groups. Recommended. 228.W63

**Wilcock, Michael.** *I Saw Heaven Opened: The Message of Revelation.* Downers Grove, Ill.: InterVarsity Press, 1975.

A historical interpretation that explains the symbols and figures of speech in light of the history of the church. Fanciful. 228'.07.W64

## APOCRYPHA AND PSEUDEPIGRAPHA

**Beale, G. K.** *The Use of Daniel in Jewish Apocalyptic Literature and in the Revelation of St. John.* Lanham, Md.: University Press of America, 1984.

A detailed exegetical analysis of various apocalyptic texts that attempts to solve the problem concerned with the method of studying allusive OT material, particularly from Daniel. This study shows how Daniel helped mold the eschatological thinking of both Jews and Christians around the time of Christ. Daniel is seen as the most formative influence on the structure and "realized" eschatological thought of John's Apocalypse. 229.B36

**Bruns, J. Edgar.** *The Forbidden Gospel.* New York: Harper & Row, 1976.

Presents a "portrait" of Jesus showing how the Gnostics reworked the biblical data into the form of a "gospel" narrative. Of historic interest only. 229'.8.B83

**Goldstein, Jonathan A.** *I Maccabees.* The Anchor Bible. Garden City, N.Y.: Doubleday and Co., 1976.

Provides detailed chronological tables, maps, and diagrams. Of help when studying the intertestamental period. 229.7.G57

――――. *II Maccabees.* The Anchor Bible. Garden City, N.Y.: Doubleday and Co., 1983.

Tells the meaning behind the victories for the Jews and of the events that contributed to them. 229'.73.G57

**Morris, Leon Lamb.** *Apocalyptic.* Grand Rapids: Wm. B. Eerdmans Publishing Co., 1972.

A helpful introduction to apocalyptic literature showing its importance in biblical study. 229.94.M83

**Nickelsburg, George William Elmer.** *Jewish Literature Between the Bible and the Mishnah: A Historical and Literary Introduction.* Philadelphia: Fortress Press, 1981.

A comprehensive treatise designed to introduce students to Jewish literature in the intertestamental period. Includes a discussion of works from the late Persian period (c. 400 B.C.) to the Second Revolt (A.D. 140). Well researched. 229'.061.N53

――――, ed. *Studies in the Testament of Joseph.* Missoula, Mont.: Scholars Press, 1975.

A collection of papers on pseudepigraphal literature presented to the Society of Biblical Literature, 1975. 229'.08.ST9 1975

**Russell, David Syme.** *The Method and Message of Jewish Apocalyptic.* Philadelphia: Westminster Press, 1974.

First published in 1964. This work makes an important contribution to our understanding of apocalyptic literature and enhances our knowledge of Judaistic beliefs in the intertestamental period. 229.913.R91

**Sparks, Hedley Frederick Davis, ed.** *The Apocryphal Old Testament.* Oxford: Clarendon Press, 1984.

Sensing the need to update Charles's *Apocrypha and Pseudepigrapha of the Old Testament* and provide a companion volume to James's *The Apocryphal New Testament* Sparks gathered together a team of competent scholars. They combined their skills to produce a small, handy, less expensive volume that parallels James's work in style and format. The task was executed with distinction, and we are grateful for their efforts. 229SP2

# 4

# Doctrinal Theology

In the mid-1950s we witnessed what some scholars have chosen to call the evangelical renaissance. More and more well-trained conservative theologians began applying the benefits of their learning to the study of God's Word. The result was seen in a form of evangelical scholarship that made its presence felt in biblical, historical, theological, and practical areas. The advances of that movement are now evident in books that are of the utmost importance to both the pastor and the people to whom he ministers.

In the 1960s, however, there was also a reaction on the part of university and seminary students to the intellectual detachment that characterized much of their studies. They began clamoring for a form of scholarship that would meet their emotional, physical, and spiritual needs. They no longer wanted to be taught a series of facts but instead wanted to know what the facts meant. Theory, they insisted, must be allied with practice. And so a relational emphasis was added.

As with all movements, there were dangers inherent in the relational theology that began to receive such widespread acceptance. One of the primary dangers was an emphasis on personhood that encouraged Christians to become self-centered. We now realize the extent to which humanism influenced this movement, but lasting damage has been done. The task facing those of us in the ministry is to counteract this trend toward egocentricity with a sound, Christocentric emphasis. To the extent that we are able to do so, our ministry will show the fruit of our endeavors. We will also find that those to whom we minister will begin to respond with new enthusiasm. Their lives will also be marked by a deeper, richer appreciation for the Word of God. Mental *and* emotional needs will be met as well as spiritual ones. Prospects for the future, therefore, appear promising.

There is always a danger that we may revert back to the stifling orthodoxy of the past. Change is threatening, and many still prefer the comfort and security of that which is familiar to them. The need of the present, however, requires that scholarship be united with an awareness of people's needs so that those to whom we minister will be able to develop a truly godly life-style.

Benjamin B. Warfield once pointed out the need for orthodoxy to be wedded to a devout and holy life. Quoting from John Miley's *Systematic Theology* (1:48-49), he said:

> A religious movement with power to lift up souls into a true spiritual life must have its inception and progress in a clear and earnest presentation of the vital doctrines of religion. The order of facts in every such movement in the history of Christianity has been, first, a reformation of doctrine, and then, through the truer doctrine, a higher and better moral and spiritual life. . . . Such has ever been and must forever be the chronological order of these facts, because it is the logical order. When men should move up from a sinful life they must have the necessary reasons and motives for such actions. . . . If we should be consecrated to God in a life of holy obedience and love, it must be for reasons of duty and motives of spiritual well-being which are complete only in the distinctive doctrines of Christianity. These doctrines are not mere intellectual principles or dry abstractions, but living truths which embody all the practical forces of Christianity. The spiritual life takes a higher form under evangelical Christianity than is possible under any other form, whether ritualistic or rationalistic, because therein the great doctrines of Christianity are apprehended in a living faith and act with their transcendent practical force upon all that enters into this life.[1]

This union of scholarship and devotion may be seen in the lives and work of men and women of the caliber of Archibald Alexander, Lancelot Andrews, Horatius and Andrew Bonar, John Brown [of Haddington as well as his grandson, John Brown of Edinburgh], John Calvin, Catherine of Siena, Thomas Chalmers, Jonathan Edwards, Patrick Fairbairn, John W. Fletcher, Thomas Goodwin, Charles Hodge, Julian[a] of Norwich, Samuel Kellogg, William Kelly, Brother Lawrence [Nicholas Herman], Martin Luther, Alexander Maclaren, John Miley, George Milligan and William Milligan, Handley Moule, James Orr, F. W. Robertson, William Romaine, J. C. Ryle, Philip Schaff, W. G. Scroggie, W. G. T. Shedd, P. J. Spener, Jeremy Taylor, W. H. Griffith Thomas, C. J. Vaughan, B. B. Warfield, John and Charles Wesley, B. F. Westcott, Alexander Whyte, Samuel Zwemer, and others, as well as some of our contemporaries.

Let us take to heart, therefore, Dr. Warfield's words:

> It cannot be a matter of indifference, therefore, what doctrines we preach or whether we preach any doctrines at all. We cannot preach at all without preaching doctrine; and the type of religious life which grows up under our preaching will be determined by the nature of the doctrines we preach.[2]

1. B. B. Warfield, *Homiletic Review* (February 1897), pp. 99-105
2. Ibid.

Those are wise words. They strike at the very heart of the present relational revolution that has abandoned sound doctrine for a religion of the senses. By following Warfield's counsel and diligently studying the writings of great men of the past as well as the present, we can add an exciting, *qualitative* dimension to our ministry. The following books should prove helpful.

**Barth, Karl.** *The Doctrine of the Word of God.* Vol. 1, Pt. 1: *Church Dogmatics.* Edited by W. G. Bromily. Edinburgh: T. & T. Clark, 1975.

†A fresh translation demonstrating that, in the forty years since the first English edition, Barth's fame has not waned and his value as a theologian has increased. Neo-orthodox. 230′.41.B28 v.1, pt.1

**Battles, Ford Lewis,** and **John Walchenbach.** *Analysis of the Institutes of the Christian Religion of John Calvin.* Grand Rapids: Baker Book House, 1980.

Based on lectures delivered at the Pittsburgh Theological Seminary. This analysis serves to introduce students to the 1559 edition of Calvin's famous *Institutes.* A worthy acquisition. 230′.42.C13.B31

**Berkhof, Hendrikus.** *Christian Faith: An Introduction to the Study of the Faith.* Translated by S. Woudstra. Grand Rapids: Wm. B. Eerdmans Publishing Co., 1979.

Not a theology in the traditional sense but rather a series of brief, scholarly essays on a variety of theological themes from revelation to eschatology. Includes excurses into the nature of the people of Israel and the "new community." 230′.232.B45 1979

**Bonhoeffer, Dietrich.** *Christ the Center.* Translated by E. H. Robertson. San Francisco: Harper & Row, 1978.

Constructed from lecture notes by Eberhard Bethge, and published in English in 1966. Stimulating, Christocentric, neo-orthodox. 230′.41B64 1978.

**Bromiley, Geoffrey William.** *An Introduction to the Theology of Karl Barth.* Grand Rapids: Wm. B. Eerdmans Publishing Co., 1979.

A valuable introduction to Barth's *Kirchliche Dogmatik.* Balanced and judicious. 230′.41.B28.B78

**Calvin, Jean, et al.** *Calvinism by Calvin: Being the Substance of Discourses Delivered by Calvin and the Ministers of Geneva on the Doctrines of Grace.* Miami Springs, Fla.: Conley and Schoettle Publishing Co., 1984.

Ably introduced by Robert Govett, these studies, though brief, are deserving of careful reading. They provide readers with a clear explanation of election and the grace of God in the life of the believer. 230′.42.C13 1984

**Carey, John J., ed.** *Kairos and Logos: Studies in the Roots and Implications of Tillich's Theology.* Macon, Ga.: Mercer University Press, 1984.

A new approach to Tillich's theology. Provides a scholarly discussion for those interested in this philosopher-theologian's thought. 230′.41.T46.C18

**\*Chafer, Lewis Sperry.** *Major Bible Themes.* Revised by John F. Walvoord. Grand Rapids: Zondervan Publishing House, 1974.

This manual of Christian doctrine retains in the revised edition the clarity and brevity for which the original was noted. Ideal for individual or adult study group use. 230′.51.C34M 1974

**\*Dabney, Robert Lewis.** *Systematic Theology.* Carlisle, Pa.: Banner of Truth Trust, 1985.

Regarded as the finest theologian of his day, Dabney was well suited to produce a work of this nature. Though modern syntactical research has enabled contemporary theologians to achieve greater accuracy in the development of doctrine, Dabney possessed the ability to integrate the teaching of the Bible on theology with his Reformed beliefs, a clear application of truth to civil government, plus a clarion call for Christian involvement in all walks of life. 230′.51.D11 1985

**Davis, John Jefferson.** *Theology Primer: Resources for the Theological Student.* Grand Rapids: Baker Book House, 1981.

Includes guidelines for research, a glossary of terms, brief biographical sketches, an analysis of issues, and an annotated bibliography of the major works on different aspects of theology. 230.D29

**Denney, James.** *Studies in Theology.* Grand Rapids: Baker Book House, 1976.

Reprinted from the 1895 edition. This book makes available to a new generation the author's famous lectures delivered at the Chicago Theological Seminary in 1894. 230′.5.D42 1976

**Elwell, Walter A., ed.** *Evangelical Dictionary of Theology.* Grand Rapids: Baker Book House, 1984.

This work is designed to replace *Baker's Dictionary of Theology* (1960). It contains more than 1,250 articles covering the fields of biblical, historical, philosophical, and systematic theology. It also includes articles on ethics as well as important movements in the history of the church. The scholarly acumen of the contributors is unquestioned. An ecumenical tone pervades the work, and every effort has been made to insure that the varying views of Anabaptists and Lutherans, charismatics and Wesleyans, Pentecostals and Moravians, Mennonites and Calvinists have been fairly presented. The bibliographies are less extensive then in *BDT* but are up-to-date and representative. 230′.03.EV1.EL8

**Fackre, Gabriel.** *The Christian Story: A Narrative Interpretation of Basic Christian Doctrine.* Rev. ed. Grand Rapids: Wm. B. Eerdmans Publishing Co., 1984.

First published in 1976. This revised edition reflects recent theological dialogue as well as the author's own fresh study. Fackre has included a new section on narrative theology in general, an expanded discussion of the role of Scripture in theology, and a revised treatment of eschatology. In addition, the bibliographies have been brought up-to-date. 230′.01.F11 1984.

**\*Ferguson, Sinclair B.** *Know Your Christian Life: A Theological Introduction.* Downers Grove, Ill.: InterVarsity Press, 1981.

Heartily endorsed by J. I. Packer. This biblical approach to Christianity treats each major facet of doctrine with fervency and evangelical zeal. For laypeople. 230.F38

**Furness, John Malcolm.** *Vital Doctrines of the Faith.* Grand Rapids: Wm. B. Eerdmans Publishing Co., 1974.

A brief but important presentation. 230.F98

**Gill, John.** *Complete Body of Doctrinal and Practical Divinity: A System of Evangelical Truths Deduced from the Sacred Scriptures.* 2 vols. Grand Rapids: Baker Book House, 1978.

Reproduced from the 1839 edition, this beautifully bound set makes available Gill's vast learning, deep piety, and perceptive application of the OT to theology. Verbose, but what Gill has to say makes rewarding reading. 230′.61.G41 1978

**Hunter, Archibald Macbride.** *Jesus: Lord and Saviour.* Grand Rapids: Wm. B. Eerdmans Publishing Co., 1978.

Written in a winsome style. This work

focuses on the Bible as God's revelation, the kingdom as the means of entering it, the ministry of the Holy Spirit, and the centrality of Christ for faith. Designed for laypeople. Recommended. 230.H89 1978

**Macquarrie, John.** *Principles of Christian Theology.* 2d ed. New York: Charles Scribner's Sons, 1977.

†A thoroughly revised edition of this survey of doctrine. First published in 1966. Anglican. 230'.3.M24 1977

**Marty, Martin Emil,** and **Dean G. Peerman, eds.** *Handbook of Christian Theologians.* Enlarged ed. Nashville: Abingdon Press, 1984.

Assesses the contribution of thirty-eight prominent thinkers (Catholic as well as Protestant) of the nineteenth and twentieth centuries. Helpful as an introduction to contemporary liberal thought. 230'.09.M36

**Milne, Bruce.** *Know the Truth: A Handbook of Christian Belief.* Downers Grove, Ill.: InterVarsity Press, 1982.

In this one volume there is a careful blending of the Bible's own teaching on the cardinal tenets of the faith together with a historical recounting of the development of those doctrines in the Christian church. A handy volume packed with sound theology. Recommended. 230.M63

**Niesel, Wilhelm.** *The Theology of Calvin.* Translated by H. Knight. Grand Rapids: Baker Book House, 1980.

First published in German in 1938. This detailed study of Calvin's system of theology deals concisely with such topics as the knowledge of God, the Trinity, creation and providence, sin, and the law of God. 230'.42.C13.N55

**Purkister, W. T., Richard S. Taylor,** and **Willard H. Taylor.** *God, Man, and Salvation: A Biblical Theology.* Kansas City, Mo.: Beacon Hill Press, 1977.

An evangelical treatment of the OT and NT teaching on creation, the Godhead, and salvation. Arminian. 230'.99.P97

**\*Ryrie, Charles Caldwell.** *Survey of Bible Doctrine.* Chicago: Moody Press, 1972.

Writing with clarity and insight, the author discusses each aspect of doctrine in his unique and inimitable way. Ideal for discussion groups. 230.R99

**\*_____.** *Understanding Bible Doctrine.* Chicago: Moody Press, 1983.

This expanded version of *A Survey of Bible Doctrine* is designed for laypeople. It ably presents each biblical doctrine and supports each belief with Scripture. It is an excellent resource. Recommended. 230.R99U 1983

**\*Shedd, William Greenough Thayer.** *Dogmatic Theology.* 4 vols. Minneapolis: Klock & Klock Christian Publishers, 1979.

A clear discussion of each doctrine, incorporating biblical, historical, and philosophical information so as to give as accurate and all-encompassing a treatment as possible. The issues Shedd presents have withstood the test of time, and he still is highly regarded among conservative evangelicals. Reformed. 230'.51.SH3 1979

**Thiessen, Henry Clarence.** *Lectures in Systematic Theology.* Edited by V. D. Doerksen. Grand Rapids: Wm. B. Eerdmans Publishing Co., 1979.

First published thirty-five years ago, this introductory study has served the needs of collegians well. The revision retains the same format as the original work with the exception of a new chapter on the Holy Spirit. Many sections have been completely reworked and outmoded material has been eliminated. 230'.5.T34D 1979

**Ziefle, Helmut W.** *Dictionary of Modern Theological German.* Grand Rapids: Baker Book House, 1982.

Contains a list of approximately 10,000 German words with their English equivalents. Includes terms derived from the Bible and Apocrypha. A valuable resource. 830.Z6

## INTRODUCTORY WORKS

**Beversluis, John.** *C. S. Lewis and the Search for Rational Religion.* Grand Rapids: Wm. B. Eerdmans Publishing Co., 1985.

†Beversluis systematically dissects Lewis's arguments and finds them wanting. He believes the British historian's thesis for the existence of God fails to provide a convincing rationale for a belief in God and must be discarded. As to the problem of evil, Beversluis claims that Lewis was guilty of trying to harmonize incompatible philosophical traditions, with like failure. He therefore accentuates what he perceives to be the shortcomings of Lewis's case for Christianity. 230'.01.L58.B46

**\*Blamires, Harry.** *On Christian Truth.* Ann Arbor, Mich.: Servant Books, 1983.

"Offers a fresh and vivid summary of the classical Christian faith. . . . Takes tough theology and makes it clear and understandable" (R. C. Sproul). 111.1.B58

**Brummer, Vincent.** *Theology and Philosophical Inquiry: An Introduction.* Philadelphia: Westminster Press, 1982.

Zeroes in on the conceptual, axiological, epistemological, and ontological aspects of theological research. Warns against the taking of short-cuts if systematic theology is to be truly systematic. 230'.01.B83

**\*Conn, Harry.** *Four Trojan Horses of Humanism.* Milford, Mich.: Mott Media, 1982.

This is one of the most important works to be published on this subject. The recollections brought before the reader of the fall of Troy are intentional. This time, however, it is the citadels of psychology, sociology, politics, and theology that have taken the deceptive "trophy" into their midst. The result is the overthrow of the truth in these disciplines. 144.C76

**Cully, Iris V.,** and **Kendig Brubacker Cully, eds.** *Process and Relationship: Issues in Theology, Philosophy, and Religious Education.* Birmingham, Ala.: Religious Education Press, 1978.

This festschrift honoring Randolph Crump Miller draws attention to the process of communication in religious education, the philosophical presuppositions, and the results. Even though much of what is presented is of interest to religious educators, the basic adherence to process theology that is evident on the part of the contributors undermines the value and lasting significance of this book. 230'.01.C89

**Duncan, Homer.** *Secular Humanism: The Most Dangerous Religion in America.* Lubbock, Tex.: Missionary Crusader, 1980.

"This fact-filled book should alert intelligent Americans concerning the cancer of Secular Humanism. It deals with the cause rather than the symptoms of moral decline" (John F. Walvoord). 144.D91

**Evans, C. Stephen.** *Subjectivity and Religious Belief: An Historical, Critical Study.* Washington, D.C.: University Press of America, 1982.

This book brings us into the heart of long-standing issues of knowledge and belief but does so in a novel and useful way. It is well written and deals adequately with the pertinent issues. For those with a philosophical bent, it will provide the catalyst for reflection as well as debate. 121.6.EV1

**Hitchcock, James.** *What Is Secular Humanism? Why Humanism Became Secular* *and How It Is Changing Our World.* Ann Arbor, Mich.: Servant Books, 1982.

Probes the origins of secularism and assesses its present impact on Western society. Provocative. 144.H63

**Johnston, Robert K., ed.** *The Use of the Bible in Theology/Evangelical Options.* Atlanta: John Knox Press, 1985.

The contributors have laid their finger on the fundamental issues of our time. In this collection of essays they highlight both evangelism's common theological center with regard to Scripture and its theological diversity in approach and perspective. Provocative. 230'.01'8.J63

**Keeley, R., et al, eds.** *Eerdman's Handbook to Christian Belief.* Grand Rapids: Wm. B. Eerdmans Publishing Co., 1982.

Published first in the U.K., this book covers a wide variety of topics: apologetics, Christology, theology proper, creation, and more. Some of the contributors are conservative theologically, others are not. 230.'01.EE7K

**Lang, Gerhard, and George D. Heiss.** *A Practical Guide to Research Methods.* 3d ed. Lanham, Md.: University Press of America, 1984.

Deals adequately with the different methods of research. Ideal for use in colleges and seminaries. The methodologies outlined in this work lend themselves to a variety of disciplines. Recommended. 001.4.L25 1984

**Leon-Dufour, Xavier, ed.** *Dictionary of Biblical Theology.* 2d ed. rev. and enlarged. New York: Seabury Press, 1973.

A widely used Roman Catholic reference work that concentrates on key words and important themes in the Bible. Forty new articles in this revision include "Conscience," "Cupidity," "Predestination," "Providence," "Sexuality," and "Yahweh." 230.03.D56L 1973

**McShane, Philip, ed.** *Searching for Cultural Foundations.* Lanham, Md.: University Press of America, 1984.

An in-depth examination and enlargement of Lonergan's seminal ideas by five leading Lonergan scholars. These essays explore the early suggestions that were made for the renewal of theology and point to fundamental transformations in the disciplines of psychology, economics, political theory, and aesthetics. 110.M24

**Moreland, James Porter.** *Universals, Qualities, and Quality-Instances: A Defense of Realism.* Lanham, Md.: University Press of America, 1985.

"This essay in analytic ontology succeeds in determining the reality of those things which exist, providing ultimate categories of being into which all entities may be classified. I am glad . . . to have this well-researched and intelligent criticism of the doctrine of 'tropes' or quality instances" (D. M. Armstrong). 111.1.M81

**Nash, Ronald H.** *Christian Faith and Historical Understanding.* Grand Rapids: Zondervan Publishing House, 1984.

This apologetic for Christianity grounds the reality of our faith in the historical events surrounding the life and ministry of Christ. Nash tackles squarely the problems posed by existentialism and naturalism, analyzes the relationship of faith and history, deals forthrightly with Bultmann's demythologizing of the NT, and leads readers into an awareness of the uniqueness of the Judeo-Christian religion. Contains a response by Harold W. Hoehner. 901.N17

**\*Southard, Samuel.** *Religious Inquiry: An Introduction to the Why and How.* Nashville: Abingdon Press, 1976.

This slender monograph may well be regarded as indispensable to all D.Min. students as they begin working on their dissertations. It explains the importance of proper research but manifests a weakness in the development of an adequate research design. In general, the points Southard makes are of the utmost value, and it is to be hoped that seminaries across the country will heed the counsel given. 230'.072.SO8

**Taylor, Richard S., ed.** *Beacon Dictionary of Theology.* Kansas City, Mo.: Beacon Hill Press of Kansas City, 1983.

This scholarly Arminian dictionary of theology covers all aspects of history, dogmatics, philosophy, psychology, ecclesiology, and the like. The essays are clear and concise. 230'.03.T21

**Trigg, Joseph Wilson.** *Origen: The Bible and Philosophy in the Third-century Church.* Atlanta: John Knox Press, 1983.

A thorough and comprehensive résumé of the major events in the life of Origen and his contribution to Christianity. 230.13.OR4.T73

**Webber, Robert Eugene.** *God Still Speaks: A Biblical View of Christian Communication.* Nashville: Thomas Nelson Publishers, 1980.

This theological discussion of communication places emphasis on the church, its people, and mission. Techniques of communication are an integral part of Webber's discussion and are based solidly on the teaching of Scripture. Recommended. 230'.01.W38

————. *Secular Humanism: Threat and Challenge:* Grand Rapids: Zondervan Publishing House, 1982.

In this well-produced book, Webber describes the pros and cons of the controversy that presently divides Christendom. Included in this discussion is an assessment of the *Playboy* mentality; the impact of the media on people's beliefs and values; the tensions generated in the classroom over values clarification, creation/evolution, sex education; and politics. An important work. 144.W38

**Wolfe, David L.** *Epistemology: The Justification of Belief.* Downers Grove, Ill.: InterVarsity Press, 1982.

A well-articulated essay on the science of rationality and the credibility of belief.

Ably establishes a viable method for establishing criteria that first test and then provide validity for our beliefs. 121.W83

SPECIAL STUDIES

**Barth, Karl.** *The Theology of Schleiermacher: Lectures at Gottingen, Winter Semester of 1923/24.* Edited by D. Ritschl. Translated by G. W. Bromiley. Grand Rapids: Wm. B. Eerdmans Publishing Co., 1982.

Carefully explains Schleiermacher's teachings before critiquing them. Asserts that the primary emphasis of Schleiermacher's theology found expression in the German scholar's piety and self-consciousness. 230'.044.SCH3.B28

**Campbell, Donald K., ed.** *Walvoord: A Tribute.* Chicago: Moody Press, 1982.

A well-deserved festschrift honoring Walvoord's more than fifty years of theological leadership. The essays are grouped under the headings "Biblical," "Theological," and "Ministry and Communication." 230'.044.W17.C15

**Gollwitzer, Helmut.** *An Introduction to Protestant Theology.* Translated by D. Cairns. Philadelphia: Westminster Press, 1982.

Builds on the theologies of Barth and Bonhoeffer, and traces the developments in theology from World War II to the present. Excellent coverage of the major new tenets. Weak in his consideration of trends in evangelicalism. 230'.044.G58

**Packer, James Innell.** *God's Words: Studies of Key Bible Themes.* Downers Grove, Ill.: InterVarsity Press, 1981.

Discusses seventeen biblical words and the relevance of their meaning in the life of the believer. Includes revelation, Scripture, sin, grace, and reconciliation. Worthy of serious consideration. 230'.04.P12

**Stott, John Robert Walmsey.** *Under-*

*standing Christ: An Enquiry into the Theology of Prepositions.* Grand Rapids: Zondervan Publishing House, 1981.

Discusses the theology of Greek words like *dia, sun, en.* Each is a model of capable exposition. 230'.04.ST7

**Whitehouse, Walter Alexander.** *Creation, Science and Theology: Essays in Response to Karl Barth.* Edited by A. Loades. Grand Rapids: Wm. B. Eerdmans Publishing Co., 1981.

Mediates the tension between theology and the natural sciences. What emerges is a sensitive appreciation of Karl Barth and his theology. Stimulating. 230'.044.W58

## HISTORICAL THEOLOGY

**\*Anderson, James Norman Dalrymple.** *A Lawyer Among the Theologians.* Grand Rapids: Wm. B. Eerdmans Publishing Co., 1974.

A valuable critique of the higher-critical assumptions relating to the "historical Jesus," the atonement, and issues raised in Robinson's book *The Difference in Being a Christian Today.* 230.08.AN2

**Barr, James.** *Fundamentalism.* Philadelphia: Westminster Press, 1978.

†Examines the upsurge of fundamentalism in the church. Discusses the focal point of these movements, namely, the inerrancy of the Bible, and provides a critique of such from his perspective. 230'.08.F95.B27

**Barth, Karl.** *Final Testimonies.* Edited by E. Busch. Translated by W. G. Bromiley. Grand Rapids: Wm. B. Eerdmans Publishing Co., 1977.

Contains a translation of Barth's last five utterances, both formal and informal, and shows the state of his thinking on topics such as Christ, Catholicism, and ecumenism. 230'.08.B28

**\*Berkhof, Louis.** *The History of Christian Doctrines.* Grand Rapids: Baker Book House, 1975.

This introductory text has been reproduced from the 1937 edition. It condenses a wealth of material into succinct chapters. Designed for the beginner. 230'.09.B45 1975

**Bloesch, Donald George.** *Essentials of*

*Evangelical Theology.* 2 vols. San Francisco: Harper & Row, 1979.

This is a scholarly discussion that uses the controversies of the church through the ages as the basis for the development of theological categories. Having dismissed the traditional categories of theology, Bloesch demonstrates his expertise as a historian and theologian by sifting through two millennia of controversy, councils, and creeds to provide a work that has value for dialogue but fails to provide a solid basis for arriving at a knowledge of the truth. 230'.08.B62

**Boice, James Montgomery, ed.** *Our Sovereign God.* Philadelphia Conference on Reformed Theology, 1974-1976. Grand Rapids: Baker Book House, 1977.

Contains addresses delivered at the conference. Excellent content. Will appeal to those of a Reformed persuasion. 230'.08.P53

**\*Bromiley, Geoffrey William.** *Historical Theology: An Introduction.* Grand Rapids: Wm. B. Eerdmans Publishing House, 1978.

An outstanding introduction to the historical development of Christian theology. Generally objective and reliable. If there is any weakness in this fine work it lies in the author's tendency to favor the sacramental segment of the church. This should not dissuade those from other persuasions from reading this handy, well-outlined, scholarly book. What Bro-

miley has presented is excellent.
230′.09.B78

**Butterfield, Herbert.** *Writings on Christianity and History.* Edited by C. T. McIntire. New York: Oxford University Press, 1979.

By limiting himself to data that can be verified by scientific historiography, the author of this collection of essays (written over a period of thirty years) deals with the major movements of Christianity and the people behind them. 230′.09.B98

**Campbell, Dennis M.** *Authority and the Renewal of American Theology.* Philadelphia: United Church Press, 1976.

Aims to show how the question of authority illumines the study of theology. Considers the respective contributions of Jonathan Edwards, Horace Bushnell, William Adams Brown, and H. Richard Niebuhr. Of mixed value.
230′.08.AU8.C15

**Cherry, Conrad.** *Nature and Religious Imagination: From Edwards to Bushnell.* Philadelphia: Fortress Press, 1980.

Absorption with nature during the eighteenth and early nineteenth centuries captured the interest of scholars in all areas of academic pursuit. This work surveys the contribution of theologians to this subject during that period.
230′.08.C42

**Chestnut, Roberta C.** *Three Monophosite Christologies: Severus of Antioch, Philoxenus of Mabbug, and Jacob of Sarug.* New York: Oxford University Press, 1976.

Presents and contrasts the place of Christ in the thought of these three Syrian theologians of the later fifth and sixth centuries, when quarrels of the Ephesus-Chalcedon period were hardening into lasting traditions. 230.16.C42

**Coleman, Richard J.** *Issues of Theological Conflict, Revised: Evangelicals and Liberals.* Grand Rapids: Wm. B. Eerdmans Publishing Co., 1980.

Previously published as *Issues of Theological Warfare* (1972). In its revised format this work continues to provide a forum for discussion between liberals and evangelicals. Its weaknesses, however, though less apparent, are still in evidence. Coleman ignores the Bible's own testimony to the supernatural. The goal of forging middle ground can be accomplished only through compromise on the part of those who sincerely treat God's revelation as the only guide in matters of faith and practice.
230′.08.C67 1980

**Colquhoun, Frank, ed.** *Hard Questions.* Downers Grove, Ill.: InterVarsity Press, 1977.

Concise answers by British evangelical scholars to thirty-one questions relating to doctrine, Christian living, and apologetics. 230′.08.H21C

**Cuncliffe-Jones, Hubert, ed.** *A History of Christian Doctrine.* Edinburgh: T. & T. Clark, 1978.

†Replaces G. P. Fischer's work in the *International Theological Library* series. The superb scholarship of the contributors makes this an ideal book to use in introductory courses in seminaries. The left-wing position of most of them necessitates that this book be used with caution. 230′.09.C91 1978

**Custance, Arthur C.** *The Sovereignty of Grace.* Grand Rapids: Baker Book House, 1979.

A full, historically complete discussion of the five points of Calvinism, with a concluding section in which Custance inveighs against those who only partially adhere to these tenets of Reformed doctrine. 230′.08.C83.C96

**Danielou, Jean.** *The Development of Christian Doctrine Before the Council of Nicaea.* In process. Philadelphia: Westminster Press, 1974-.

Important studies that focus attention on the theology of Jewish Christianity and the reception given the gospel within Hellenism. Roman Catholic. 230.09.D22

**Day, Heather F.** *Protestant Theological Education in America: A Bibliography.* Metuchen, N.J.: Scarecrow Press, 1985.

Protestant theological education is defined broadly to include not only theological seminaries, but also Bible colleges and church and other private institutions. The bibliography has been expanded to make it as comprehensive as possible so as to include works from the 1800s up to the early 1980s. There are no annotations. The index divides materials into four sections: "Background Materials"; "Materials Relating to Theological Education"; "Theological Seminaries and Schools . . ."; and "Individuals of Significance in Theological Education." Ed.D students will find this an indispensable compilation. 016.2'07'73.D33

**\*Dollar, George W.** *A History of Fundamentalism.* Greenville, S.C.: Bob Jones University Press, 1973.

This book surveys the history of fundamentalism in America. Although the author has only words of praise for militant fundamentalists, and is unsparing in his censure of moderate and modified fundamentalists, his contribution to American church history is real. 230.09.F96.D69

**Ferm, Deane William.** *Contemporary American Theologies.* 2 Vols. New York: Seabury Press, 1981-1982.

Well structured and clearly outlined, this work draws attention to the differences among the leading thinkers in each theological camp. Provides an assessment of movements in America during the first six decades of this century. 230'.08.AM3.F38

**Gasper, Louis.** *The Fundamentalist Movement, 1930-1956.* Grand Rapids: Baker Book House, 1981.

†First published in 1963. This vigorous attack on the American Council of Christian Churches and the N.A.E. presents a thorough, though not impartial, appraisal of the Fundamentalist movement. 230'.09.F96.G21 1981

**Gelpi, Donald L.** *Experiencing God: A Theology of Human Emergence.* Ramsey, N.J.: Paulist Press, 1978.

Seeks to develop a foundation for anthropological research and, in turn, to provide a basis for spiritual growth. Misapplies psychology and minimizes the importance of the Scriptures in the renewing of the mind, by which process we come to approve the good and acceptable and perfect will of God. Disappointing. 230'.0834.G8

**Gese, Hartmut.** *Essays on Biblical Theology.* Translated by Keith Crim. Minneapolis: Augsburg Publishing House, 1981.

Following a discussion of the biblical view of Scripture, Gese considers specific themes such as death in the Old Testament, law, atonement, the Lord's Supper, and the Messiah. Stimulating. 230'.08.G33

**Griffin, David R.** *A Process Christology.* Philadelphia: Westminster Press, 1974.

†Standing in the tradition of Cobb, Ogden, Pettinger, and Williams, this book treats "process conceptuality" as a vehicle for the reconception and restatement of the Christian faith. 230.09.G87

**Gundry, Stanley N.,** and **Alan F. Johnson.** *Tensions in Contemporary Theology.* Chicago: Moody Press, 1976.

A competent contribution to present-day developments in theology. Concentrates on trends that have taken place since Barth, Brunner, Bonhoeffer, and Tillich. 230'.09.G95

**Hall, Douglas John.** *Lighten Our Darkness: Towards an Indigenous Theology of the Cross.* Philadelphia: Westminster Press, 1976.

†Writing for success-oriented North

American Christians, Hall claims that the task of theology today is *not* to offer a refuge from darkness but rather to help men and women find meaning and hope through an indigenous theology of the atonement. 230′.08.H14

**Hamilton, Kenneth.** *To Turn from Idols.* Grand Rapids: Wm. B. Eerdmans Publishing Co., 1973.

A forthright analysis of the cults or idols of, for example, relevance and change that plague modern Christendom and detract from the reality of one's experience. 230.08.H18T

**Harris, Horton.** *David Frederich Strauss and His Theology.* Cambridge: At the University Press, 1973.

†Adequate attention is paid to Strauss's radical approach to the life of Christ and his advocacy of a desupernaturalized history of the human Jesus. Harris seeks to leave his readers with the impression that Strauss was right. 230.09.ST8.H24

**Henry, Carl Ferdinand Howard.** *God, Revelation and Authority.* 6 vols. Waco, Tex.: Word Books, 1976-1985.

Building on his years of teaching, lecturing, writing, and meeting with world leaders, Henry propounds a series of theses that he proceeds to debate. These center in bibliology and are crucial to evangelicalism and the achievement of any degree of rapprochement in biblical-theological studies. 230′.08.H38

**Hoedemaker, Libertus A.** *The Theology of H. Richard Niebuhr.* Philadelphia: Pilgrim Press, 1971.

†Evaluates the seminal thought of Niebuhr, and sympathetically comments on the impact of his originality on twentieth-century Christianity. 230′.09.N55.H67

**Hunt, George Laird, ed.** *Twelve Makers of Modern Protestant Thought.* New York: Association Press, 1971.

†Brief sketches of Schweitzer, Rauschenbusch, Kierkegaard, Barth, Niebuhr, Tillich, Bultmann, Buber, Bonhoeffer,

Heidegger, Moltmann, and Whitehead. 230′.0922.H91

**Kantzer, Kenneth S.,** and **Stanley N. Gundry, eds.** *Perspectives on Evangelical Theology.* Grand Rapids: Baker Book House, 1979.

Composed of papers read at the Thirtieth Annual Meeting of the Evangelical Theological Society, these studies treat facets of systematic, biblical, philosophical, and pastoral theology. 230′.08.EV1 1979

**\*Kelly, John Norman Davidson.** *Early Christian Doctrines.* Rev. ed. New York: Harper & Row, 1978.

An indispensable work that readily makes available the results of the author's vast research and ably delineates the manner in which the truth emerged in the era immediately following the apostles. 230′.09.K29 1978

**Kent, John H. S.** *The End of the Line? The Development of Christian Theology in the Last Two Centuries.* Philadelphia: Fortress Press, 1982.

First published in Edinburgh in 1978. This scholarly assessment of theological trends in the eighteenth and nineteenth centuries does everything except evaluate these movements in light of the Scriptures. 230′.09′03.K41

**Klotsche, E. H.** *The History of Doctrine.* Rev. ed. Grand Rapids: Baker Book House, 1979.

First published in 1945. This able Lutheran work traces the development of doctrine from the apostolic age to the present. Well outlined. 230′.09.K69 1979

**Lewis, Clive Staples.** *The Joyful Christian.* New York: Macmillan Co., 1977.

Contains 127 excerpts from Lewis's writings. Should make the works of this British scholar easy to quote in the coming decade. 230′.08.L58 1977

**Lightner, Robert Paul.** *Neoevangelicalism Today.* Schaumburg, Ill.: Regular Baptist Press, 1978.

Previously issued under the title *Neo-*

*evangelicalism* (1965). This is a careful delineation and exposure of a subtle trend within Christendom. No one decries true scholarship, but many neo-evangelicals have made too many concessions for the sake of scholarly acclaim. What Lightner has presented remains an important historical and theological study. 230′.09.L62 1978

**Macleod, John.** *Scottish Theology in Relation to Church History Since the Reformation.* Edinburgh: Banner of Truth Trust, 1974.

There is great need for a work of this nature. It is to be regretted, however, that Macleod's handling of Scottish history and theology is so inadequate. Even though he does provide his readers with a lively chronicle of events and brings to the fore the leading personalities, what he has to say lacks substance. We must wait for some other scholar to give us a wholesome treatment of this subject. 230′.09.M22 1974

**May, Rollo.** *Paulus.* New York: Harper & Row, 1973.

A psychoanalytic evaluation of Paul Tillich, his life and love affairs. Nontheological and mostly sympathetic. 230.09.T46.M45

**Meeks, M. Douglas.** *Origins of the Theology of Hope.* Philadelphia: Fortress Press, 1974.

A full and sympathetic handling of Jurgen Moltmann's theology. 230.09.M73.M47

**Moltmann, Jurgen.** *The Crucified God: The Cross of Christ as the Foundation and Criticism of Christian Theology.* New York: Harper & Row, 1974.

†In the afternoon of his "theology of liberation," the author turns to Christology in a futile attempt to produce a "salvation" that will lead to a political liberation. 230′.09.M73

―――. *The Experiment Hope.* Edited and translated by M. D. Meeks. Philadelphia: Fortress Press, 1975.

This collection of essays provides a possible link between two of Moltmann's earlier works, *Theology of Hope* and his *Crucified God.* It also shows the movement of his thought toward a Trinitarian theology. 230′.08.M73

**Moody, Dale.** *The Word of Truth: A Summary of Christian Doctrine Based on Biblical Revelation.* Grand Rapids: Wm. B. Eerdmans Publishing Co., 1981.

Attempts to relate the best of biblical criticism to Christian doctrine and yet remain within the broadest bounds of evangelical orthodoxy. The book gives evidence of extensive classroom experience. 230′.08.M77

**Nash, Ronald H., ed.** *Liberation Theology.* Milford, Mich.: Mott Media, 1984.

This collection of essays gives the reader a critical overview of liberation theology and related themes. It shows the goal to be "Christian" action on behalf of the poor and the oppressed but not necessarily based on biblical principles taught by Christ or expressed in the NT. 230′.09.N17

**\*Núñez C., Emilio Antonio.** *Liberation Theology.* Translated by P. E. Sywulka. Chicago: Moody Press, 1985.

Liberation theology poses some definite problems for evangelicals. Advocates of the movement have so far paid scant attention to the whole counsel of God. In this work we have a far-ranging yet thorough assessment of the historical and social context of the movement, the development of its doctrine, the theological methodology used, and the need for a strong evangelical emphasis. 230′.09.N49

**Oden, Thomas C.** *Agenda for Theology.* San Francisco: Harper & Row, 1979.

†Discusses the dilemmas facing quasi-orthodox theologians, and challenges them with the need for pastoral and sociological relevance. Makes stimulating reading. 230′.08.OD2

**Pannenberg, Wolfhart.** *Faith and Re-*

*ality.* Translated by J. Maxwell. Philadelphia: Westminster Press, 1977.

This translation of *Glaube und Wirklichkeit* seeks to confront modern Christians with the tension that exists between the tradition of faith and their experience of reality. 230′.08.P19

**Pauck, Wilhelm.** *From Luther to Tillich: The Reformers and Their Heirs.* Edited by M. Pauck. San Francisco: Harper & Row, 1984.

†These essays were published over a fifty year period. They exhibit a remarkable blend of historical description, informed criticism, and theological insight. They also serve as a valuable introduction to the thought of the leaders of the church from the Reformation to the present. 230′.09.P28

**Pelikan, Jaroslav Jon.** *The Christian Tradition: A History of the Development of Doctrine.* In Process. Chicago: University of Chicago Press, 1972-.

Scheduled for five volumes, these studies are valuable in acquiring a comprehensive grasp of the development of theological thought. 230.09.P36

————. *Historical Theology, Continuity, and Change in Christian Doctrine.* Philadelphia: Westminster Press, 1971.

A history of the historical study of doctrine with reflections of the relationships of biblical, historical, and systematic theology. 230.09.P36

**Placher, William Carl.** *A History of Christian Theology.* Philadelphia: Westminster Press, 1983.

A well-documented, capably presented résumé of the history of the development of Christian doctrine. Traces the beginnings of orthodoxy, the conflicts of the various councils, and the thought of the leading theologians. 230′.09.P69

**Ramm, Bernard Lawrence.** *After Fundamentalism: The Future of Evangelistic Theology.* San Francisco: Harper & Row, 1983.

Building on Barth's theology, Ramm seeks to offer evangelicals a basis on which they can unite and put behind them the Modernist-Fundamentalist controversy of the past half century. Unhappily, this work offers little to conservative theologians, for it advocates concessions and compromises to those of more liberal persuasion. 230′.09.B28.R14

**Roark, Dallas M.** *The Christian Faith: An Introduction to Christian Thought.* Grand Rapids: Baker Book House, 1977.

First published in 1969. This historical and philosophical approach to Christianity deals concisely with such topics as the nature of religion, God, and the Trinity. 230′.08.R53

**\*Shedd, William Greenough Thayer.** *A History of Christian Doctrine.* 2 vols. Minneapolis: Klock & Klock Christian Publishers, 1978.

Reprinted from the ninth (1889) edition. This excellent presentation of the growth and development of Christian theology ably confirms that the history of Christianity is a record of disagreements. Shedd concentrates attention on the philosophical presuppositions underlying those disagreements and includes in his discussion apologetics as well as theology proper, Christology and Christian anthropology, soteriology and eschatology. An informative section deals with different confessions of faith. Long out of print, this work should be purchased while it is still available. 230′.09.SH3 1978

**Sponheim, Paul R.** *Faith and Process: The Significance of Process Thought for Christian Faith.* Minneapolis: Augsburg Publishing House, 1979.

†Grounds his thesis in the philosophical views of Alfred North Whitehead and, by availing himself of the contribution of theologians such as Hartshorne, Cobb, Ogden, and others, attempts to integrate metaphysics and theology. 230′.08.S6

**Sproul, Robert Charles, ed.** *Soli Deo Gloria: Essays in Reformed Theology; Festschrift for John H. Gerstner.* Nutley, N.J.: Presbyterian and Reformed Publishing Co., 1976.

Contains fifteen essays by contemporary Reformed theologians covering the areas of Gerstner's specialties. A fitting tribute. 230'.08.G32.SP4

**Stone, Ronald H.** *Reinhold Niebuhr: Prophet to Politicians.* Nashville, Abingdon Press, 1973.

†Stone does not deal with this neo-orthodox theologian's theology, but he does describe his influence on society. Disciples of Niebuhr will welcome this treatise; others will find that the writer's obvious sympathy with Niebuhr minimizes his objectivity. 230.09.N55.ST7

**Stroup, George W.** *The Promise of Narrative Theology: Recovering the Gospel in the Church.* Atlanta: John Knox Press, 1981.

†Considers the implications of narrative theology and, by looking particularly at Deuteronomy and Mark, offers a fresh perspective on biblical interpretation. 230'.08.ST8

**Thielicke, Helmut.** *The Evangelical Faith.* 3 vols. Translated and edited by Geoffrey W. Bromiley. Grand Rapids: William B. Eerdmans Publishing Co., 1974-1984.

This translation of *Der evangelische Glaube* contains much that will cause concern to committed evangelicals. Thielicke, however, does offer some well-reasoned criticisms of modern existentialists and exposes the fallacies inherent in secularism. This set is well deserving of careful reading. 230.09.T34

**Wall, Joe Layton.** *Bob Thieme's Teachings on Christian Living.* Houston: Church Multiplication, Inc., 1982.

Since the appearance of the first edition in 1978, Thieme has changed some of his views and these changes have been included in this printing. This work has been well researched from Thieme's numerous writings and serves as a careful résumé of the Houston pastor's theology and practices. 230'.08.T34.W15

**Welch, Claude.** *Protestant Thought in the Nineteenth Century, 1799-1870.* New Haven: Yale University Press, 1972.

†The decline of neo-orthodoxy is permitting the theological grandsons of liberalism to look at their grandfathers. This backward look is leading to a refurbishing of the reputations and contributions of men such as Schleirmacher, Ritschl, and Troeltsch. Welch's volume forms an enlightening survey of this era of history. 230.09.W44

PRIMITIVE CHURCH

**Hanson, Richard Patrick Crosland.** *The Continuity of Christian Doctrine.* New York: Seabury Press, 1981.

Traces the eras of history when *sola scriptura* was the pervasive trend in the church. Insightful but lacking empathy with true evangelicalism. 230'.01.H19

**Martin, Ralph Philip.** *Reconciliation: A Study of Paul's Theology.* New Foundation Theological Library. Atlanta: John Knox Press, 1981.

Uses the Pauline doctrine of reconciliation as a comprehensive umbrella under which he considers the major elements of Paul's theology. This is a scholarly discussion, but it would have been more accurate to subordinate the different aspects of Pauline thought to God's sovereignty. 230.12.M36

**Nash, Ronald H.** *Christianity and the Hellenistic World.* Grand Rapids: Zondervan Publishing House, 1984.

A discerning investigation of the relationship between Christianity and the pagan religions of the Roman Empire. Well reasoned and well presented. 231.12.N17

ROMAN CATHOLIC

**Gratsch, Edward J., ed.** *Principles of*

*Catholic Theology.* Staten Island, N.Y.: Alba House, 1981.

One of the best syntheses of Catholic theology in the post-Vatican II era. Well documented. 230.2.G77

**Kiwiet, John.** *Hans Kung.* Makers of the Modern Theological Mind. Waco, Tex.: Word Books, 1985.

The author, a Southern Baptist, evaluates Kung's life and thought and finds him to be one of the most provocative leaders in Roman Catholic thought. He praises Kung as a mature scholar, a devoted pastor, and an eloquent speaker. 230.2.K96.K54

**Pelikan, Jaroslav Jon.** *The Emergence of Catholic Tradition.* Chicago: University of Chicago Press, 1971.

The first of five volumes scheduled to appear over the next decade. Surveys the history of the development of doctrine in the Roman Catholic church. 230'.2.P36

**Sheridan, John D.** *The Hungry Sheep: Catholic Doctrine Restated Against Contemporary Attacks.* New Rochelle, N.Y.: Arlington House, 1974.

A trenchant apologetic of the basic doctrines of Roman Catholicism. 230.2.SH5

ANGLICAN

**Faulkner, Robert K.** *Richard Hooker and the Politics of a Christian England.* Berkeley, Calif.: University of California Press, 1981.

A definitive study of Hooker's assessment of the relationship between church and state, and the role of the church in society. 230.3.H76.F27

**Hanson, Richard Patrick Crosland.** *The Attractiveness of God: Essays in Christian Doctrine.* Atlanta: John Knox Press, 1973.

†An attempt to establish Christian doctrine on liberal theological hypotheses. 230.3'08.H19

**Hooker, Richard.** *Of the Laws of Eccle-*

*siastical Polity.* An abridged edition by A. S. McGrade and Brian Vickers. New York: St. Martin's Press, 1976.

This classic on politics, theology, and philosophy in the field of Christian ministry has now been made available in a modern, readable form. It retains the key phrases of Hooker's argument, and the introductions admirably set his work in its philosophical, historical, and literary context. 230.3.H76

**LeMahieu, D. L.** *The Mind of William Paley.* Lincoln, Nebr.: University of Nebraska Press, 1976.

Examines the thought of this eighteenth-century philosopher whose system of apologetics is still followed in certain circles today. 230.3.P17.L54

PROTESTANT DENOMINATIONS— EUROPE

**Balthasar, Hans Urs von.** *The Theology of Karl Barth.* Translated by John Drury. New York: Holt, Rinehart and Winston, 1971.

A heavy work that is not as reliable as Brown's *Karl Barth and the Christian Message* and Hartwell's *Theology of Karl Barth.* 230'.41.B2'7.B21

**Calvin, John.** *Institution of the Christian Religion.* Translated by Ford Lewis Battles. Atlanta: John Knox Press, 1975.

A translation based on the first (1536) edition of Calvin's famous *Institutes.* It is free of the tedious polemic found in Calvin's later editions. The translator has provided a lengthy introduction, copious notes, and seven indexes. 230.42.C13.B32 1975

**Ellul, Jacques.** *The Humiliation of the Word.* Translated by J. M. Hanks. Grand Rapids: Wm. B. Eerdmans Publishing Co., 1985.

"Anyone interested in promoting or communicating the truth in our frantic society will be challenged and assisted by [this book]. Pastors, teachers, parents, and thoughtful people in virtually any vocation will find their work illuminated by an analysis that is both deep and broad ranging in its scope. The translation, preface, and index by Joyce Main Hanks are a superb contribution from one who is expert in both Ellul's thought and in the French language" (D. W. Gill). 230'.42.EL5

――――. *In Season, Out of Season: An Introduction to the Thought of Jacques Ellul.* Based on interviews by M. Garrigou-Lagrange. Translated by L. K. Niles. San Francisco: Harper & Row, 1982.

Contains this Bordeaux University professor's reflections on his long life and the forces that have been influential in shaping his beliefs. 230'.42.EL5G

**Fasching, Darrell J.** *The Thought of Jacques Ellul: A Systematic Exposition.* Toronto Studies in Theology. New York: Edwin Mellen Press, 1981.

Attempts to introduce readers to the total scope of Ellul's works. Explores his sociological theory and apparent opposition to technology. Shows how Ellul's views are directly related to his theology of apocalyptic hope and freedom. 230.42.EL5.F26

**Feil, Ernest.** *The Theology of Dietrich Bonhoeffer.* Translated by M. Rumscheidt. Philadelphia: Fortress Press, 1985.

The purpose of this book is to investigate Bonhoeffer's writings and analyze how he confronted the world and the reasons he was led into compromise. 230'.41.B64.F32

**Galloway, Allan D.** *Wolfhart Pannenberg.* London: Allen and Unwin, 1973.

A survey of Pannenberg's theology based on his writings. 230.41.P19.G13

**Greaves, Richard L.** *Theology and Resolution in the Scottish Reformation: Studies in the Thought of John Knox.* Grand Rapids: Wm. B. Eerdmans Publishing Co., 1980.

Draws attention to John Knox's theol-

ogy but, though elaborating on the major themes undergirding his beliefs, fails to treat all aspects of his thought and influence. In spite of this weakness, these essays are deserving of careful reading. 230'.42.K77.G79

**Helm, Paul.** *Calvin and the Calvinists.* Carlisle, Pa.: Banner of Truth Trust, 1982.

Examines the writings of Calvin and the Puritans and shows that, at the root of their theology, they were one in their beliefs and practices. 230'.42.H36

**Humphrey, James Edward.** *Emil Brunner.* Waco, Tex.: Word Books, 1976.

With Karl Barth, Brunner dominated European theology for nearly fifty years, exposed the inadequacies of theological liberalism, and contributed to the establishment of neo-orthodoxy. This book contains a brief summary of his life and an analysis of his theology. 230.41.B83.H88

**Hyma, Albert.** *Luther's Theological Development from Erfurt to Augsburg.* Landmarks in History. New York: AMS Press, 1971.

An important study by a Lutheran historian. 230'.41.H99

**Lecerf, Auguste.** *An Introduction to Reformed Dogmatics.* Translated by A. Schlemmer. Grand Rapids: Baker Book House, 1981.

This Calvinistic treatise applies the principles of that branch of theology to other disciplines with the result that it has both polemical and apologetic value. 230'.42.L49 1981

**Loewenich, Walther von.** *Luther's Theology of the Cross.* Translated by H. J. A. Bouman. Minneapolis: Augsburg Publishing House, 1976.

A classic on this facet of Luther's theology. 230.41.L97.L82

**Melanchthon, Philip.** *Melanchthon on Christian Doctrine: Loci Communes 1555.* Translated and edited by C. L. Manschreck. Grand Rapids: Baker Book House, 1982.

First published in England in 1965. This fine translation of Melanchthon's theology provides an essential foundation to any understanding of the Reformation. Recommended. 230'.41.M48 1982

**Weber, Otto.** *Foundations of Dogmatics.* 2 vols. Translated by D. L. Guder. Grand Rapids: Wm. B. Eerdmans Publishing House, 1981-1983.

This comprehensive work interacts freely with theologians of the past as well as the present and succeeds in making available to modern theologians a definitive study that consistently subordinates all issues to the authority of the Scriptures. Both publisher and translator are to be commended for producing such an exemplary study. 230'.41.W38

PRESBYTERIAN AND
CONGREGATIONAL CHURCHES IN
AMERICA

**Bloesch, Donald George.** *The Ground of Certainty: Toward an Evangelical Theology of Revelation.* Grand Rapids: Wm. B. Eerdmans Publishing Co., 1971.

A readable, provocative discussion of a current trend in theology. 230'.57.B62

**Cook, James I., ed.** *The Church Speaks.* Historical Series of the Reformed Church in America, 15. Grand Rapids: Wm. B. Eerdmans Publishing Co., 1985.

A collection of major papers presented at the Commission on Theology of the Reformed Church in America over the past twenty-five years. Founded in 1959, the Commission serves the church by articulating its theological understanding of contemporary issues. The papers are arranged under the headings "Scripture," "Faith," "Sacraments," "Ministry," "Witness," and "Sexuality." 230.5'732.C77

**\*Conn, Harvie M.** *Contemporary World Theology: A Layman's Guide.* Nutley, N.J.: Presbyterian and Reformed Publishing Co., 1973.

Provides a clear and concise evangelical assessment of contemporary European theological movements. Includes a critical treatment of dispensationalism, fundamentalism, and neo-fundamentalism. Calvinistic. 230.09.C83

**Dabney, Robert Lewis.** *Discussions.* Vol. 3. Edinburgh: Banner of Truth Trust, 1982.

Represents data culled from vols. 3 and 4 of Dabney's works. Presents those articles on the biblical, historical, and philosophical themes still regarded as viable today. 230'.51.D11 1982

**DeWitt, John Richard.** *What Is the Reformed Faith?* Carlisle, Pa.: Banner of Truth Trust, 1981.

A brief tract on the central tenets of Reformed theology. 230'.5.D51

**Hindson, Edward E., ed.** *Introduction to Puritan Theology: A Reader.* Grand Rapids: Baker Book House, 1976.

These selections from the writings of the Puritans cover the main areas of theology and focus attention primarily on the "Reformed Augustinian stream of thought in the English-speaking world over a period of two centuries." 230.5'9.H58

**Lowrie, Ernest Benson.** *The Shape of the Puritan Mind: The Thought of Samuel Willard.* New Haven, Conn.: Yale University Press, 1974.

This systematic analysis of the writings of Samuel Willard (1640-1707) is based on a comprehensive understanding of the history of prerevolutionary America and the thinking of the people. Lowrie is to be commended for having executed his task with such skill. 230.5'9.W66.L95

**Osterhaven, Maurice Eugene.** *The Faith of the Church: A Reformed Perspective on Its Historical Development.* Grand

Rapids: Wm. B. Eerdmans Publishing Co., 1982.

Has received the accolades of the scholarly community. There is little that we can add other than an endorsement. This work is accurate, readable, and illuminating. 230'.57.S7

**Schaeffer, Francis August.** *The Church Before the Watching World.* London: Inter-Varsity Press, 1971.

Schaeffer's thesis is that the church is constantly on trial before God and the world. The church claims to be God's representative, but its deeds and words seldom substantiate this profession. Schaeffer makes a strong plea for believers to accept the truth as it is contained in the Bible and begin to practice it before the watching world. A sequel to his booklet *The Mark of the Christian.* 230'.51.SCH1

**\*Shedd, William Greenough Thayer.** *Theological Essays.* 2 vols. in 1. Minneapolis: Klock & Klock Christian Publishers, 1981.

Contains the author's *Theological Essays* (1877) and *Orthodoxy and Heterodoxy* (1893). The essays are rich and varied and treat such topics as the preparation for the pastoral ministry as well as infidelity, immortality, the atonement, and personal spiritual disciplines. Recommended. 230'.51.SH3T 1981

**Simonson, Harold Peter.** *Jonathan Edwards: Theologian of the Heart.* Macon, Ga.: Mercer University Press, 1982.

First published in 1974. This volume contradicts the theory of Perry Miller that Lockean epistemology formed the basis of Edwards's thought. Simonson contends instead that the New England theologian's thought was based on Calvin, Augustine, and eventually the Scriptures. He attempts to prove his assertion by quoting from Edwards's sermons and theological writings. 230.58.ED9.SI5 1982

**Stob, Henry.** *Theological Reflections: Essays on Related Themes.* Grand Rapids: Wm. B. Eerdmans Publishing Co., 1981.

Contains essays on science, theology, philosophy, revelation, the church, and education. Deals specifically with issues that have confronted the church in recent years. 230'.57.ST6

**Weddle, David Leroy.** *The Law As Gospel: Revival and Reform in the Theology of Charles G. Finney.* Metuchen, N.J.: Scarecrow Press, 1985.

This is the first book-length critical study of the theology of the nineteenth-century revivalist. Reviews Finney's legal training and dramatic conversion before describing at length his subsequent career as a revivalist, professor of theology, and president of Oberlin College. In the name of "legal order," Finney rejected the "Old School" Calvinist doctrines of original sin, vicarious atonement, and irresistible grace, and instead developed a new approach based on his experiences as a preacher of the gospel in seeing people come to Christ through his ministry. His writings show the extent to which Finney insisted on not only the possibility but also the duty of attaining moral perfection through disciplined obedience to the law of love in both personal conduct and social action. His consistent emphasis on the principles of legal responsibility as the foundation for interpreting the gospel is shown by Weddle to be the key to understanding the effectiveness of his life as well as the system of doctrine he propounded. 230.5'8.F49.W39

**Wells, David F., ed.** *Reformed Theology in America: A History of Its Modern Development.* Grand Rapids: Wm. B. Eerdmans Publishing Co., 1985.

Seeks to remedy a lack in the literature and at the same time to make Americans aware of this neglected aspect of their heritage. Sections of this book focus on Princeton and Westminster schools of theology, the contribution of Dutch Reformed seminaries, the Southern tradition, and the contribution of neo-orthodoxy. 230'.5.AM3.W44

## BAPTIST

*Hobbs, Herschel H., and Edgar Young Mullins. The Axioms of Religion. Rev. ed. Nashville: Broadman Press, 1978.

A revision of Mullins's 1908 work on Baptist polity. Valuable for its adherence to the principles of nonconformity and the independent church movement. Should be read by all who cherish religious freedom, whether they are baptistic in their persuasion or not. 230.6.H65 1978

Jaehn, Klaus Juergen. Rauschenbusch: The Formative Years. Valley Forge, Pa.: Judson Press, 1976.

Makes use of previously unpublished sources, and thereby provides new insights into the development of Rauschenbusch's social gospel. 230.61.R19.J16

## METHODISTS

Carter, Charles Webb, R. Duane Thompson, and Charles R. Wilson, eds. A Contemporary Wesleyan Theology: Biblical, Systematic, and Practical. 2 vols. Grand Rapids: Francis Asbury Press, 1983.

Produced to meet the need of those whose interest in John Wesley has led to a desire for a modern theology expounding the principles that have become a part of the Wesleyan tradition. The usual theological structures are treated in vol.

1, but the emphasis is on a historical-theological-political approach. Vol. 2 contains eleven lengthy essays covering a variety of themes. This is a challenging, stimulating, evangelical work. 230'.7.C24

Greathouse, William M., and H. Ray Dunning. An Introduction to Wesleyan Theology. Kansas City, Mo.: Beacon Hill Press of Kansas City, 1982.

A brief compendium of theology covering the Trinity, anthropology, and the Christian life. A brief epilogue covers the issue of eschatology. 230'.77.G769

Russell, Colin A. Cross-currents: Interactions Between Science and Faith. Grand Rapids: Wm. B. Eerdmans Publishing Co., 1985.

Examines the strange ways in which science has developed over the years and, in particular, how it has interacted with biblical Christianity. Russell sees no reason for science and Christianity to be in conflict and advocates a view that makes use of the values of both systems of thought. 509.R91

## OTHER DENOMINATIONS AND SECTS

Baker, Charles F. A Dispensational Theology. Grand Rapids: Grace Bible College Publishers, 1971.

This work by an ultradispensationalist dates the beginning of the church with Paul's ministry in the middle of Acts. Avoids the extreme view of Bullinger, saves the Pauline epistles from oblivion, retains the Bread and the Cup as a church ordinance, but rejects water baptism. Unreliable. 230'.99.B17D

# THE GODHEAD

*Bavinck, Herman. The Doctrine of God. Translated by W. Hendriksen. Edinburgh: Banner of Truth Trust, 1977.

First published in English in 1951. This perceptive excerpt from the author's

Gereformeerde Dogmatik provides readers with a clear and enriching study of the nature and attributes of God. Recommended. 231.B32 1977

Baxter, James Sidlow. Majesty: The God

*You Should Know.* San Bernardino, Calif.: Here's Life Publishers, 1984.

Contains lectures delivered at Grace Theological Seminary in Winona Lake, Indiana. This book introduces readers to the things God has chosen to reveal about Himself in the OT and NT. Everything that is to be found between these covers is of the utmost importance. Recommended. 231.B33

**\*Boice, James Montgomery.** *The Sovereign God.* Vol. 1: Foundations of the Christian Faith. Downers Grove, Ill.: InterVarsity Press, 1978.

An important introduction to, and discussion of, the Person of God and the revelation of His will to mankind. Boice's treatment is thorough without being tedious. What he presents illustrates doctrinal preaching at its best. This volume, and the others in this series, are warmly recommended. 231.B63

**Charnock, Stephen.** *The Knowledge of God.* Vol. 4: The Works of Stephen Charnock. Carlisle, Pa.: Banner of Truth Trust, 1985.

This is perhaps Charnock's most famous work. It incorporates a study of the nature of unbelief and the atonement, together with some enlightening material on the Lord's Supper. When it is remembered that the material in this volume originally consisted of sermons, then some indication may be gleaned of the content given from the pulpit in years gone by as well as the appreciation of people for sound doctrine. It is to be hoped that the publishers will make available the other volumes in this series. Reprinted from the 1865 edition. 283.C38 v.4

**\*Clark, Gordon Haddon.** *The Trinity.* Jefferson, Md.: Trinity Foundation, 1985.

A clear, historically and theologically accurate assessment of the teaching of Scripture on the Trinity and how this doctrine has been understood during the past two millennia. Recommended. 231.C54

**Connoly, John R.** *Dimensions of Belief and Unbelief.* Washington, D.C.: University Press of America, 1980.

Closely reasoned, this historical and theological treatise discusses the philosophical and psychological aspects of faith. Attempts to correlate the theoretical and existential poles that many writers believe constitute a never-ending tension. 231'.042.C76

**Fortman, Edmund J.** *The Triune God: A Historical Study of the Doctrine of the Trinity.* Grand Rapids: Baker Book House, 1982.

First published in 1972. This Roman Catholic study of the Christian church's belief in the Trinity organizes and presents a vast amount of material in a most pleasing manner. 231.F77

**Hogan, Ronald F.** *The God of Glory.* Neptune, N.J.: Loizeaux Brothers, 1984.

Traces the self-revelation of God through the Bible, champions the evangelical doctrine of trinitarianism, and succeeds in providing readers with a concise statement that blends a doxological approach to theology with a devout appeal to believers to live in light of God's nature and glory. 231.H67

**Holloway, Richard.** *Beyond Belief: The Christian Encounter with God.* Grand Rapids: Wm. B. Eerdmans Publishing Co., 1981.

Disenchanted with externalism in religious profession, Holloway draws attention to the forms of belief rather than the object; and though there is much in what he says that is truly commendable, he confines his remarks to the church as a corporate body rather than Christians as individuals. 231'.08.H72

**Lampe, Geoffrey William Hugo.** *God a Spirit.* New York: Oxford University Press, 1978.

†Probes the biblical record and the teaching of the early church Fathers and concludes that these support a belief in

the deity of Christ, His preexistence, and His continuing presence. Lampe, however, believes that the Holy Spirit should not be spoken of as the third Person of the Trinity but as "God" in relationship to "His creation." 231.L19 1978

**Lightner, Robert Paul.** *The God of the Bible: An Introduction to the Doctrine of God.* Grand Rapids: Baker Book House, 1978.

A handy, well-outlined study that covers all of the essential aspects of theology proper. Ideal for use in adult study groups. 231.L64 1978

**Macquarrie, John.** *Thinking About God.* New York: Harper & Row, 1975.

†Based in part on the author's lectures at the University of Oxford, these chapters treat his theological method, concepts of deity, and basis for belief in God; they provide as well an evaluation of various religious thinkers. 231.M24

**Malik, Charles Habib.** *The Wonder of Being.* Waco, Tex.: Word Books, 1974.

A penetrating examination of the cosmological argument by one who is philosophically and theologically competent to discuss the subject. 231'.042.M29

**Nash, Ronald Herman.** *The Word of God and the Mind of Man.* Grand Rapids: Zondervan Publishing House, 1982.

A post-World War II critique of modern man's understanding of divine revelation and his ability to receive propositional truth. Of value for its historical summary. 231'.042.N17

**Ott, Heinrich.** *God.* Philadelphia: Fortress Press, 1974.

†This study by Karl Barth's successor at the University of Basel seeks to provide a creditable rationale for the existential approaches of Buber and Tillich. Antitrinitarian. 231.OT8

**\*Packer, James Innel.** *Knowing God.* Downers Grove, Ill.: InterVarsity Press, 1973.

These essays describe the kind of relationship redeemed man may enjoy with God—"a relationship calculated to thrill a man's heart." Part I deals with the blessings and benefits of knowing God; Part II with who God is; and Part III with the effect these truths should have on our lives. 231.P12

**\*Sproul, Robert Charles.** *The Holiness of God.* Wheaton, Ill.: Tyndale House Publishers, 1985.

"The foundation of all Christian behavior is the holiness of God. If the church doesn't understand this most basic of all issues, its perspective in every other area will be adversely affected. In this important study R. C. Sproul gives clear biblical insight with a refreshing and infectious enthusiasm" (John F. MacArthur, Jr). 231.SP8

**Toon, Peter.** *God Here and Now: The Christian View of God.* Wheaton, Ill.: Tyndale House Publishers, 1979.

Builds on an understanding of God's attributes and describes the process whereby the Christian, having been brought by God into a relationship with Him, may now enjoy continuing fellowship with Him. Recommended. 231.T61

_____, and **James D. Spiceland, eds.** *One God in Trinity.* Westchester, Ill.: Cornerstone Books, 1980.

Contains lectures delivered at the British Tyndale Fellowship, Durham, 1978. These chapters focus on the Trinity and the contribution of leading contemporary theologians to this doctrine. 231.T61G

GOD THE FATHER

**\*Culver, Robert Duncan.** *The Living God.* Wheaton, Ill.: Victor Books, 1978.

This is an excellent work. It is ideal for adult discussion groups. Culver's sage counsel strengthens believers in the faith and grounds their relationship with the Lord squarely on the Scriptures. Recommended. 231.1.C89

**\*France, R. T.** *The Living God.* Downers Grove, Ill.: InterVarsity Press, 1973.

This popular study centers in what the Bible teaches about God and His dealings with men. 231.1.F84

**Hocking, David Lee.** *The Nature of God in Plain Language.* Waco, Tex.: Word Books, 1984.

A handy and helpful book for laypeople. Deals with God's nature and seeks to answer the kind of questions people are asking. Extended discussions focus on God's omniscience, omnipotence, and omnipresence. 231.1.H66

**Law, Peter W.** *A Portrait of My Father: The Wonder of Knowing God.* Portland, Oreg.: Multnomah Press, 1985.

"In this day when God is obscured by the lengthening shadows of man, [Law] gives us a glimpse of Jehovah that is desperately needed and gratefully received" (Don Baker). 231.1.L41

**Lightner, Robert Paul.** *The First Fundamental: God.* Nashville: Thomas Nelson Publishers, 1973.

Beginning with a concise presentation of the historic arguments for the existence of God, the author then concentrates on the heart of theology—the being and nature of God. The inclusion of charts enhances the usefulness of the book for general readers. 231.1.L62

**Macquarrie, John.** *The Humility of God.* Philadelphia: Westminster Press, 1978.

†Consists of addresses given at Christ Church Cathedral, Oxford. Defines humility as God's "down-to-earthness" and involvement with His creatures. Existential; neo-liberal. 231'.1.M24

**Smail, Thomas Allan.** *The Forgotten Father.* Grand Rapids: Wm. B. Eerdmans Publishing Co., 1981.

Recent decades have witnessed a revival of interest in Christ, the Son, in the Jesus movement, and in the Holy Spirit in the charismatic movement. By contrast, as Smail points out, God the Father has been forgotten. He, therefore, emphasizes the importance of a believer's relationship to the first Person of the Trinity. Stimulating. 231.1.SM1

**\*Varghese, Roy Abraham, ed.** *The Intellectuals Speak Out About God: A Handbook for the Christian Student in a Secular Society.* Chicago: Regnery Gateway, 1984.

This book reaffirms the need for character, personal integrity, spiritual depth, and moral standards that are essential if education is to remain viable and democracy survive. The essays that make up this book are stimulating, and it is a work that can be heartily recommended. 231.1.V42

### GOD THE HOLY SPIRIT

**Biederwolf, William Edward.** *Study of the Holy Spirit.* Grand Rapids: Kregel Publications, 1985.

First published in 1903, this brief, conservative study covers the important aspects of the Paraclete's person and work. Recommended. 231.3.B47 1985

**Bullinger, Ethelbert William.** *The Giver and His Gifts, or the Holy Spirit and His Work.* Grand Rapids: Kregel Publications, 1979.

Building his theology on a careful investigation of the Hebrew and Greek words for "spirit," Bullinger provides a penetrating study of the biblical teaching. Ultradispensational. 231.3.B87 1979

**Fitch, William.** *The Ministry of the Holy Spirit.* Grand Rapids: Zondervan Publishing House, 1974.

Geared to the needs of the individual and the congregational life of the church. Warns against a "unitarianism of the Son" to the neglect of the Spirit.

Provides a helpful section on the gifts of the Spirit and a critique of Pentecostalism, past and present. Calvinistic. 231.3.F55

**Gaffin, Richard Birch, Jr.** *Perspectives on Pentecost: Studies in the New Testament Teaching on the Gifts of the Holy Spirit.* Grand Rapids: Baker Book House, 1979.

A scholarly study of the historicity of spiritual gifts, glossolalia, and the ministry of the Spirit in the life of the believer. Reformed. 231.3.G12

**Graham, William Franklin.** *The Holy Spirit.* Waco, Tex.: Word Books, 1978.

Popular, well-illustrated essays on the ministry of the Paraclete in the life of the believer. Makes stimulating reading. 231.3.G76

**\*Green, Edward Michael Bankes.** *I Believe in the Holy Spirit.* Grand Rapids: Wm. B. Eerdmans Publishing Co., 1975.

A competent survey of the biblical teaching on the Holy Spirit. Though easy to read, this study nevertheless reflects considerable research and the kind of mature reflection that warms the heart and edifies the spirit. Recommended. 231.3.G82

**Kirkpatrick, Don, ed.** *The Holy Spirit.* Nashville: Tidings Publications, 1974.

†Contains papers presented at the Fifth Session of the Oxford Institute of Methodist Theological Studies held at Lincoln College in the summer of 1973. The themes treated include the theology of the Holy Spirit, His work in the world, and a reassessment of modern Pentecostalism. 231.3.OX2K

**Lloyd-Jones, David Martyn.** *Joy Unspeakable: Power and Renewal in the Holy Spirit.* Wheaton, Ill.: Harold Shaw Publishers, 1984.

Christopher Catherwood in his Introduction to his grandfather's book writes: "'The Doctor' as he was called by evangelical Christians . . . was one of the men primarily responsible for the resurrection of interest in reformed doctrine

in Britain. . . . He believed passionately in the baptism with the Holy Spirit as a distinct, post-conversion experience. But he equally realized that it was a filling with power that made those who received it better witnesses for Christ." 231.3.L77 1985

**\*Morgan, James.** *The Biblical Doctrine of the Holy Spirit.* Minneapolis: Klock & Klock Christian Publishers, 1985.

First published in 1865. This is a work of solid erudition. Though written initially for intelligent laypeople wanting a definitive work laying bare the progressive revelation of God's Word on the Person and work of the Holy Spirit, today Morgan's book needs close attention if its truths are to be mastered. "Controversy and criticism are avoided. Scripture ideas are unfolded in a clear and popular way, so as not only to inform the judgment, but also to purify the heart" (*Evangelical Christian*). 231.3.M82 1984

**Moule, Charles Francis Digby.** *The Holy Spirit.* Grand Rapids: Wm. B. Eerdmans Publishing Co., 1979.

Characterized by the wisdom and spiritual insight that we have come to expect of the author, these seven chapters provide a contemporary discussion of the relationship of the Holy Spirit to specific areas of theology and ministry. A final chapter deals with the charismatic question. 231.3.M86

**\*Moule, Handley Carr Glyn.** *Person and Work of the Holy Spirit.* Grand Rapids: Kregel Publications, 1977.

A reverent, scholarly study that appropriately relates the Paraclete's ministry to the needs of the believer. Timely and practical. 231.3.M86 1977

**\*Packer, James Innell.** *Keep in Step with the Spirit.* Old Tappan, N.J.: Fleming H. Revell Co., 1984.

Packer believes that in order to live in the Spirit we must not only open up our lives to Him but also clearly understand Him and His work. In explaining the

Bible's teaching on the Holy Spirit as the agent of change, Packer lays justifiable stress on practical issues. His treatment is especially valuable for its forthright discussion of difficult and controversial issues. 231.3.P12

**Ramsey, Arthur Michael.** *Holy Spirit: A Biblical Study.* Grand Rapids: Wm. B. Eerdmans Publishing Co., 1977.

An examination of the experience of the first-century Christians and the theology linked with their beliefs and practices. 231.3.R14

**Rosanto, Philip J.** *The Spirit as Lord: The Pneumatology of Karl Barth.* Edinburgh: T. & T. Clark, 1981.

Advances the thesis that Barth was essentially a theologian of the Holy Spirit. Probes his letters and theological writing for verification of this belief. 231.3.B28.R71

**Schweizer, Eduard.** *The Holy Spirit.* Translated by R. H. and I. Fuller. Philadelphia: Fortress Press, 1980. ·

†Avoids treating the Paraclete as a person. Investigates the roles of the Spirit in both Testaments and in the intertestamental period. 231'.3.SCH9

**\*Unger, Merrill Frederick.** *The Baptism and Gifts of the Holy Spirit.* Chicago: Moody Press, 1974.

This revision of *The Baptizing Work of the Holy Spirit* updates the earlier material and provides a helpful guide in the midst of confusion over the charismatic movement. 231.3.UN3 1974

**Walvoord, John Flipse.** *The Holy Spirit at Work Today.* Chicago: Moody Press, 1973.

A contemporary discussion of the mission of the Paraclete, including His ministry as the revealer of truth and the agent of spiritual renewal. 231.3.W17T

**White, Reginald Ernest Oscar.** *The Answer Is the Spirit.* Philadelphia: Westminster Press, 1979.

In keeping with the form-critical approach used in the writer's other books, this treatment of the teaching on the ministry of the Holy Spirit gives evidence of the extent to which this British Baptist has been influenced by Bultmannian form-criticism. 231.3.W58

ATTRIBUTES OF GOD

**DeHaan, Dan.** *The God You Can Know.* Chicago: Moody Press, 1982.

Written by a layman, the chapters of this book nevertheless reverberate with a passion and unction seldom found in modern works. They treat the essence and existence of God in a way that makes his presence real so that He may become a motivating force in one's life. 231.4.D36

**\*Hook, H. Philip.** *Who Art in Heaven.* Grand Rapids: Zondervan Publishing House, 1979.

With devotion and skill the author discusses the attributes of God and then applies the truths gleaned from Scripture to the relationship of the believer with the members of the Godhead. Ideal for adult discussion groups. 231.4.H76

LOVE AND WISDOM

**MacGregor, John Geddes.** *He Who Lets Us Be: A Theology of Love.* New York: Seabury Press, 1976.

An exacting study of the *kenosis*. This philosophical/biblical statement of "God is love" is challenging, disturbing (owing to some imprecision in the author's theology), and enlightening. 231.6.M17

SOVEREIGNTY, KINGDOM OF GOD, REVELATION

**Bahnsen, Greg L.** *By This Standard: The Authority of God's Law Today.* Tyler, Tex.: Institute for Christian Economics, 1985.

This Reformed study looks at God's law as Christianity's tool of dominion. Bahnsen presents a case for Christ's rulership over the earth. The key, he believes, is the Christian's adherence to and advocacy of God's law. The author has some helpful insights on the Abrahamic covenant, and his treatment of Christian activism is excellent. His confusion of certain elements kept distinct in Scripture leads to an unfortunate equation of Israel and the church. This work, however, should be read even by those who differ with Bahnsen's hermeneutics and eschatology. 231.72.B14

**\*Borland, James A.** *Christ in the Old Testament.* Chicago: Moody Press, 1978.

A brilliant theological discussion of the theophanies and appearances of the Angel of Yahweh in the OT. A most valuable treatise. 231.74.B64

**Brown, Colin.** *That You May Believe: Miracles and Faith Then and Now.* Grand Rapids: Wm. B. Eerdmans Publishing Co., 1985.

In this book Brown provides his readers with another treatise on miracles. He avoids detailed philosophical discussion and clearly lays out the arguments for the reader who is not trained in polemic debate. Those who have ever questioned the viability of miracles or their place in Christian belief will find this discussion refreshing. 231.7.B81T

**\*Carson, Donald A.** *Divine Sovereignty and Human Responsibility: Biblical Perspectives in Tension.* New Foundations Theological Library. Atlanta: John Knox Press, 1981.

A masterful treatment of all the doctrinal issues (e.g., biblical anthropology, the providence and government of God, the history of doctrine, etc.) that compose the study of free will and determinism. 231.7.C23

**Chittick, Donald E.** *The Controversy: Roots of the Creation-Evolution Conflict.* Portland, Oreg.: Multnomah Press, 1984.

The author approaches creation from two perspectives: the first, involving a discussion of the contemporary debate; and the second, a presentation of the scientific data relating to the controversy that has developed. 231.7'65.C49

**\*Demarest, Bruce A.** *General Revelation: Historical Views and Contemporary Issues.* Grand Rapids: Zondervan Publishing House, 1982.

This lengthy, in-depth presentation of the witness of general revelation to the Person of God provides a comprehensive treatment of the development of the doctrine throughout the history of the church. Informative. 231.7'4.D39

**DeVries, Simon.** *Yesterday, Today and Tomorrow.* Grand Rapids: Wm. B. Eerdmans Publishing Co., 1975.

Examines the words *day, today,* and the *day of Yahweh* with a view to determining their meaning and relation to the nature of time and the future. 231.7.D49

**Evans, William Glyn.** *Beloved Adversary: Our Complex Relationship with a Loving God.* Grand Rapids: Daybreak Books, 1985.

The author contends that struggles between God and man are inevitable because of the great contrast between God's perfect and infinite nature and our imperfect and finite one. In layman's terms, Evans addresses the issues of alienation, the struggle of the will, and adversarial roles of God and man in prayer. 231.7.EV1

**Foster, Roger T.,** and **V. Paul Marston.** *God's Strategy in Human History.* Minneapolis: Bethany House Publishers, 1984.

Deals with the biblical evidence for determining God's strategy throughout history. Uses reference as well as inference as material is culled from the scriptural record. Examines carefully the continuing conflict between good and evil as well as the relationship of truth to life. This is an important, scholarly work that deserves careful reading. 231.76.F77

**\*Gaebelein, Arno Clemens.** *The Conflict of the Ages.* Revised by D. A. Rausch. Neptune, N.J.: Loizeaux Brothers, n.d.

Shows the development of the conflict between God and the devil, good and evil. Succeeds in providing a fine example of the biblical doctrine of theodicy. 231.7.G11

**\*Geisler, Norman Leo.** *Miracles and Modern Thought.* Grand Rapids: Zondervan Publishing House, 1982.

A forthright rebuttal of Kantian metaphysics and agnostic speculation. Establishes a rational basis for belief in miracles as recorded in the Bible. Provocative. 231.7′3.G27

**Govett, Robert.** *The Kingdom of God Future.* Miami Springs, Fla.: Conley and Schoettle Publishing Co., 1985.

Contains messages covering a variety of themes dealing with the kingdom, from its present mystery form to its future consummation. 231.7.G74 1985

**Harkness, Georgia Elma.** *Understanding the Kingdom of God.* Nashville: Abingdon Press, 1974.

†Aiming at providing an understanding of the personal and social relevance of the kingdom, this work focuses attention on new movements and the growth of conservative churches. Lacking in evangelical emphasis. 231.7.H22

**Helm, Paul.** *Divine Revelation: The Basic Issues.* Foundations for Faith. Westchester, Ill.: Crossway Books, 1982.

A substantive work covering natural (or, general) and special revelation, the issues surrounding revelation and objectivity, infallibility, certainty, and the unity of knowledge. Informative. 231.7′4.H36

**\*Houston, James M.** *I Believe in the Creator.* Grand Rapids: Wm. B. Eerdmans Publishing Co., 1980.

Though all evangelicals will not agree with everything Houston says, he has made a fine contribution to an understanding of the doctrine of creation,

Christ's role as originator and sustainer of the universe, and the relationship of His creatures to Himself. 231.7.H81

**Lang, George Henry.** *God at Work on His Own Lines.* Miami Springs, Fla.: Conley and Schoettle Publishing Co., 1985.

Describes the things the author had seen in various lands in the late nineteenth and early twentieth centuries. Challenging. 231.7.L25 1985

**McDonald, Hugh Dermott.** *Theories of Revelation: An Historical Study, 1700-1960.* Grand Rapids: Baker Book House, 1979.

Composed of two previously published books, *Ideas of Revelation* (1959) and *Theories of Revelation* (1963). Contains an excellent historical and theological discussion. 231.7′09.M14T 1979

**McIntire, C. T.,** and **Ronald A. Wells,** eds. *History and Historical Understanding.* Grand Rapids: Wm. B. Eerdmans Publishing Co., 1984.

†This collection of essays explores what insight Christian faith may bring to an understanding of history and historical study. The authors go beyond the usual themes of the theology of history— providence, *Heilsgeschichte,* meaning in history—and instead ground their analysis in an unadorned approach that is free of outside influences and other people's ideas as to its flow and meaning. It is this ordinary approach that they seek to adorn and explain. 231.76.M18

**Mitton, Charles Leslie.** *Your Kingdom Come.* Grand Rapids: Wm. B. Eerdmans Publishing Co., 1978.

A well-reasoned biblical study of the concept of the kingdom of God in the NT. Avoids both amillennial and premillennial molds. Attempts to uncover what Christ *really* taught. Speculative, but makes interesting reading. 231.7.M69

**Murray, Andrew.** *The Believer's New Covenant.* Minneapolis: Bethany House Publishers, 1984.

This edition of Murray's earlier work

on the Old and New Covenants has been modernized for today's readers. The teaching of this work is relevant and intended to aid in the believer's growth toward maturity. Recommended. 231.7'6.M96 1984

**Perrin, Norman.** *Jesus and the Language of the Kingdom.* London: S.C.M. Press, 1976.

†Explores the historical understanding of Christ's use of the phrase *kingdom of God* and attempts to explain its possible relevance to people today. 231.7.P41

**\*Roper, David H.** *The New Covenant in the Old Testament.* Waco, Tex.: Word Books, 1976.

An informative and instructive study showing how the New Covenant relationship was anticipated and "mirrored" in the OT, and how in the gospels, in the writings of Paul, and in the epistle to the Hebrews we have an explanation of the way in which believers in Christ may benefit from its soteriological blessings. 231.7.R68

**Shorter, Aylward.** *Revelation and Its Interpretation: Introducing Catholic Thought.* London: Geoffrey Chapman; Minneapolis: Winston Press, 1983.

A readable textbook that draws on contemporary hermeneutics as well as Catholic tradition to provide an informative discussion of the nature of revealed religion in the contemporary world together with the content of OT revelation. 231.7'4.SH8

**Snyder, Howard A.** *The Community of the King.* Downers Grove, Ill.: InterVarsity Press, 1977.

†A sequel to *The Problem of Wineskins* (1975). Makes a strong case for the involvement of the laity and the use of God-given gifts in their ministry. The author is to be commended for his ability to communicate effectively. The shortcoming of this work is that, as with its predecessor, it lacks a truly biblical foundation. 231.7.SN9

**Torrance, Thomas Forsyth.** *Reality and Evangelical Theology.* Philadelphia: Westminster Press, 1982.

Presented as the Payton Lectures, Fuller Theological Seminary, 1981, these chapters have little to do with evangelicalism per se, but do treat the nature of theological and biblical interpretation of revelation. 231.74.T63

**Willard, Dallas.** *In Search of Guidance: Developing a Conversational Relationship with God.* Ventura, Calif.: Regal Books, 1984.

By combining a discussion of the providence of God with His guidance of His children, Willard shows how God has revealed His will in the past and still guides today. Provocative. 231.7.W66

**\*Wilson, Clifford A.,** and **Donald W. McKeon.** *The Language Gap.* Grand Rapids: Zondervan Publishing House, 1984.

This monograph, which contains a response by Marvin K. Mayers, focuses on the gap between animals and man and shows by implication the logical impossibility of evolution. Excellently reasoned. 231.7'65.W69

**Young, Davis A.** *Christianity and the Age of the Earth.* Grand Rapids: Zondervan Publishing House, 1982.

In dealing with the Bible and geology, Young advances the claim that the earth is much older than creationists have believed. His evidence is impressive and his material well documented. He does not explain the possibility of God's creating the earth with apparent age, even as He did Adam and Eve. 231.7'65.Y8

JUSTICE AND GOODNESS

**Clarkson, Margaret.** *Destined for Glory: The Meaning of Suffering.* Grand Rapids:

Wm. B. Eerdmans Publishing Co., 1983.

"Margaret Clarkson knows her Bible well, and from painful personal experience she knows suffering well too. Her determination in her new book is to relate one to the other. It is this which gives it strength and integrity. . . . Above all, it is a wholesome book, avoiding glibness and extravagance, and returning again and again to the sovereign God's eternal and loving purpose to make us like Christ" (John R. W. Stott). 231.8.C56

**Crenshaw, James L., ed.** *Theodicy in the Old Testament.* Issues in Religion and Theology. Philadelphia: Fortress Press, 1983.

†These chapters by renowned OT scholars focus attention on Job, Ecclesiastes, Psalm 73, and certain Apocryphal books with a view to establishing a basis for understanding the tension between good and evil. At times insightful, but also disappointing because many of the contributors have such a low view of Scripture as God's Word. 231.8.C86

**Doughty, Flavian, ed.** *The Meaning of Human Suffering.* New York: Human Sciences Press, 1982.

†Suffering is mankind's most persistent problem. Its manifestations are innumerable. This volume is composed of papers read at the International Ecumenical Congress on the Meaning of Human Suffering, 1979. They are of mixed value, but almost always provocative. 231.8.D74

**Plantiga, Theodore.** *Learning to Live with Evil.* Grand Rapids: Wm. B. Eerdmans Publishing Co., 1982.

After discussing the three major types of evil (natural, moral, and demonic), the author surveys four major conceptions of evil—evil as ultimate (Manichaeism), evil as necessary (Hegel, Schleiermacher, and others), evil as nonbeing (Platonism), and evil as alienation from God (Augustine and Calvin). Then, taking his stand within the framework of Augustinian and Calvinistic theology, he poses a series of practical and existential questions that he answers out of the theological framework he has chosen. 231.8.P69

**Wenham, John William.** *The Enigma of Evil: Can We Believe in the Goodness of God?* Grand Rapids: Zondervan Publishing House, Academie Books, 1985.

Formerly titled *The Goodness of God*, this book treats the doctrine of theodicy and shows God in all His fullness dealing justly (through a perfect blend of His kindness and severity) with His creatures. In the process of expounding on this doctrine, Wenham takes up the moral problems of the Bible and explains them in light of a biblical theism. 231.8.W48 1985

**\*Wiersbe, Warren Wendell.** *Why Us? When Bad Things Happen to God's People.* Old Tappan, N.J.: Fleming H. Revell Co., 1984.

"More than just a theological treatise or a philosophical stab at secondary issues, *Why Us?* answers the tough questions with a biblical, emphatic pen. It is my hope that this book will be read and internalized by many" (John F. MacArthur, Jr.). 231.8.W63

**\*Wilder-Smith, A. E.** *The Paradox of Pain.* Wheaton, Ill.: Harold Shaw Publishers, 1971.

A detailed consideration of the problem of suffering, theodicy, and the providence of God. 231.8.W64

**Woods, Robert William.** *Christians in Pain: Perspectives on Suffering.* Grand Rapids: Baker Book House, 1982.

First published in 1974 under the title *Understanding Suffering*, this book seeks to provide support and comfort to those enduring a variety of mental, physical, and emotional pain. 231.8.W87

## CHRISTOLOGY

**Berkhof, Hendrikus.** *Christ, the Meaning of History.* Translated by L. Buurman. Grand Rapids: Baker Book House, 1979.

Grapples realistically with the relationship between faith and history. Of limited value. 232.B45 1979

**Blaiklock, Edward Musgrave.** *Jesus Christ, Man or Myth?* Nashville: Thomas Nelson Publishers, 1984.

Presents the testimony of pagan writers to the historicity of Christ and examines and refutes the theories of those who doubt His messiahship. First published in 1974 under the title *Who Was Jesus?* 232'.09.57 1984

**Cobb, John B.** *Christ in a Pluralistic Age.* Philadelphia: Westminster Press, 1975.

†This study of Christology is based on process theology and develops a view of Christ's person and work that rejects both liberal and conservative views. Cobb believes that through an understanding of the incarnation, Christian faith is able to achieve its own transformation through its openness to all faiths. 232.C63

**\*Coleman, Robert Emerson.** *The Mind of the Master.* Old Tappan, N.J.: Fleming H. Revell Co., 1977.

Six perceptive essays that take the reader into the thoughts of Christ and demonstrate His love and concern for the unsaved. A great stimulus for evangelism. 232.C67M

**Dunn, James D. G.** *Jesus and the Spirit: A Study of the Religious and Charismatic Experience of Jesus.* Philadelphia: Westminster Press, 1975.

†A scholarly work that, in many areas of interpretation, goes far beyond the biblical evidence. 232.D92

**Frei, Hans W.** *The Identity of Jesus Christ: The Hermeneutical Bases of Dogmatic Theology.* Philadelphia: Fortress Press, 1975.

†This mature study has some commendable features. The author states that "knowing [Christ's] identity is identical with having him present or being in his presence." He affirms that knowing Christ's identity helps a believer know his own identity. Frei, however, does not credit this knowledge to the work of regeneration or the process of sanctification. 232.F88

**\*Lawlor, George.** *When God Became Man.* Chicago: Moody Press, 1978.

A remarkable, though brief, treatise on the Person and work of Christ. Recommended. 232.L41

**Lindars, Barnabas.** *Jesus Son of Man: A Fresh Examination of the Son of Man Sayings in the Gospels in Light of Recent Research.* Grand Rapids: Wm. B. Eerdmans Publishing Co., 1984.

†The use and meaning of the term *Son of Man* has been the cause of endless controversy. In this monograph, Lindars attempts to break the deadlock. He offers a complete reappraisal of the phrase and reviews linguistic usage of similar expressions in Aramaic. He concludes that Jesus used this term to indicate His identification with the human person. 232.L64

**Marshall, I. Howard.** *The Origins of New Testament Christology.* Downers Grove, Ill.: InterVarsity Press, 1976.

Explores the NT teaching concerning the Person of Christ and explains what the church thought about Him. 232.M35N

**\*_____.** *The Work of Christ.* Palm Springs, Calif.: Ronald N. Haynes Publishers, 1981.

First published in 1969. This study surveys the teaching of the NT on the various aspects of the life and ministry of Christ. Recommended. 232.M35 1981

**\*Martin, Hugh.** *The Abiding Presence.* Grand Rapids: Zondervan Publishing House, 1984.

Focuses on the presence of Christ in the world and in the believer. These deeply devotional studies expound a facet of Christology and illustrate the way in which a believer is conformed to the image of Christ. 232.M36 1984

**Michaels, John Ramsey.** *Servant and Son: Jesus in Parable and Gospel.* Atlanta: John Knox Press, 1981.

Building on the supposed priority of Mark's gospel and making allowance for the existence of Q, Michaels reappraises the teachings and ministry of Christ, believing that it was what He Himself learned from God the Father and from human experience that motivated His actions. 232.M58

**Moule, Charles Francis Digby.** *The Origin of Christology.* New York: Cambridge University Press, 1977.

An important excursus treating some of the names of Jesus (e.g., figures of speech ["body," "temple," etc.] used to describe the union of believers with Christ) and the extent of the atonement. Like Moule's other works, this one shows the depth as well as the richness of his thought. Marred by adherence to certain liberal presuppositions. 232'.09.M86C

**Neill, Stephen Charles.** *The Supremacy of Jesus.* Downers Grove, Ill.: InterVarsity Press, 1984.

More theologically conservative than Neill's earlier works. In this book he shows the uniqueness and supremacy of Jesus over the salvation-claims of other faiths. Deserves careful reading for its apologetic values. 232'.08.N31

**Pannenberg, Wolfhart.** *Jesus: God and Man.* Translated by L. L. Wilkins and D. A. Priebe. 2d ed. Philadelphia: Westminster Press, 1977.

An important, though controversial contribution to Christology. 232.P19J 1977

**Preus, Jacob Aall Ottesen.** *It Is Written.* St. Louis: Concordia Publishing House, 1971.

An examination of the attitude of Jesus Christ toward the OT. 232.01.P92

**Robinson, John Arthur Thomas.** *The Human Face of God.* Philadelphia: Westminster Press, 1973.

†This book is an example of what happens after a person has thrown off all submission to the authority of divine revelation. Though some critics of contemporary theology regard this work as an autobiography of Robinson's struggles to date, others view it as an advanced form of apostasy. 232.R56

**Schoonover, Melvin E.** *What If We Really Did Follow Jesus?* Valley Forge, Pa.: Judson Press, 1978.

Concentrates on Christ's ministry in the towns and villages of Palestine and attempts to develop a methodology for Christian ministry in the city as well as the suburbs today. A seminal work. 232.SCH8

**Stanton, G. N.** *Jesus of Nazareth in New Testament Preaching.* New York: Cambridge University Press, 1974.

Demonstrates from Luke and Acts that the early church preached the life and character of the earthly Jesus as well as proclaimed Him as the risen Lord. Stanton ably defends his thesis against those who hold to a demythologizing of the records. At the same time he shows how tenuous and speculative is the nature of much NT scholarship today. Recommended. 232.ST1

**Stott, John Robert Walmsey.** *The Authentic Jesus: The Centrality of Christ in a Skeptical World.* Downers Grove, Ill.: InterVarsity Press, 1985.

A brief, valuable apologetic covering the Person and offices of Christ. Answers such critiques of Christianity as *The Myth of God Incarnate* (1977) and *Towards a Theology of InterFaith Dialogue* (1984). 232.ST7A

**Sykes, S. W., and J. P. Clayton.** *Christ, Faith and History:* Cambridge Studies in Christology. Cambridge: At the University Press, 1972.

†A learned collection of essays on the Person and work of Christ, His origin, and His place in history and theology. 232.SY4

**Tenney, Merrill Chapin.** *Who's Boss?* Wheaton, Ill.: Victor Books, 1980.

Zeroes in on the questions Christ asked during His ministry and shows how they deal with the issues of life that still are of concern to people today. 232'.09.T25

**Toon, Peter.** *Jesus Christ Is Lord.* Valley Forge, Pa.: Judson Press, 1979.

A popular presentation of the exaltation of Jesus Christ as Lord. Makes Christology easy to understand. Of great value to laypeople. 232.T61

PERSON AND WORK OF CHRIST

**\*Anderson, James Norman Dalrymple.** *The Mystery of the Incarnation.* Downers Grove, Ill.: InterVarsity Press, 1978.

With his usual wit and wisdom, Sir Norman surveys the present theological malaise, probes the issues surrounding the unwillingness of some theologians to allow for the supernatural, and then offers some of his own insights into the mystery of Christ's humanity. The reading of this book is a theological necessity. 232.1.AN2

**Anderson, Robert.** *The Lord from Heaven.* Grand Rapids: Kregel Publications, 1978.

A refreshing study of Christ's deity with special emphasis on His messiahship. Ably correlates the teaching of both Testaments. 232.1.AN2L 1978

**Barnes, Albert.** *The Atonement.* Minneapolis: Bethany Fellowship, 1980.

Published in 1860, this logically reasoned, biblically based discussion of the atonement answers objections and demonstrates clearly the imperative necessity of Christ's death. Lacks Scripture, subject, and author indexes. Presbyterian. 232.2.B26 1980

**\*Custance, Arthur C.** *Two Men Called Adam: A Fresh Look at the Creation/Evolution Controversy.* Brockville, Ontario: Doorway Publications, 1983.

With his usual precision, Custance assesses the issues surrounding the creation of the body. He also treats the incarnation of Christ, and, based on His death and resurrection, draws a valid parallel to the resurrection of believers. He then relates the biology of the body to man's original special creation. After painstaking induction in different disciplines, Custance deduces that if the early chapters of Genesis are mythical (as many modern scholars affirm) and if mankind ascended some evolutionary ladder of development, then Christ could *not* have borne the kind of identity to mankind that the writers of the NT Scripture (especially Paul) set forth. An excellent discussion. 232.1.C95

**Delitzsch, Franz Julius,** and **Paton John Gloag.** *The Messianic Prophecies of Christ.* 2 vols in 1. Minneapolis: Klock & Klock Christian Publishers, 1983.

These two books, here issued together, make available works that were virtually unobtainable. Delitzsch's famous lectures entitled *The Messianic Prophecies in Historical Succession* is sufficient to reawaken interest in some long-neglected OT Scriptures. As always, what he presents is of the utmost value. Gloag's *Messianic Prophecies* composed his equally famous Baird Lectures delivered at the University of Glasgow. Together they place in the hands of the busy pastor a wealth of material hitherto found only in footnotes. 232.1.D37 1983

**\*Denney, James.** *The Death of Christ.* Minneapolis: Klock & Klock Christian Publishers, 1982.

A complete, unabridged reprint of Denney's magnum opus. Worthy of serious study. 232.3.D41 1982

**Douty, Norman F.** *The Death of Christ.* Rev. ed. Irving, Tex.: Williams and

Watrous Publishing Co., 1978.

Seeks to refute the limited atonement theory. Deals adequately with the biblical data. Douty's presentation gives evidence of being well researched, and it is well written. 232.3.D74 1978

**\*Gifford, Edwin Hamilton,** and **Samuel James Andrews.** *The Incarnation of Christ.* 2 vols. in 1. Minneapolis: Klock & Klock Christian Publishers, 1981.

Contains Gifford's famous discussion of Philippians 2:5-11 and Andrew's *Man and the Incarnation.* Both works complement each other. Gifford treats the *kenosis* with rare theological acumen, and Andrews discourses on the necessity of Christ's humanity. Indispensable to a minister's library. 232.1.G36 1981

**Goulder, Michael, ed.** *Incarnation and Myth.* Grand Rapids: Wm. B. Eerdmans Publishing Co., 1979.

Furthers the discussion begun in *The Myth of God Incarnate* (1977). Evangelical contributors are conspicuous by their absence. Each of the essays bears the marks of scholarship, but the liberal presuppositions of each writer minimize the value of this work. 232.1.IN2 1979.

**Hengel, Martin.** *The Atonement: The Origins of the Doctrine in the New Testament.* Philadelphia: Fortress Press, 1981.

A careful examination of the development of the doctrine of the atonement. Offers some surprising correctives to current liberal teaching. 232.3.H38

**\*Hindson, Edward E.** *Isaiah's Immanuel: A Sign of His Times, or the Sign of the Ages?* Grand Rapids: Baker Book House, 1978.

In no way duplicates the material covered by Lawlor in *Almah . . . Virgin or Young Woman,* or Gromacki in *The Virgin Birth.* Treats cogently and well the difficulties of Isaiah 7 and applies the teaching of the text in the best evangelical tradition. 232.1.H58

**\*Liddon, Henry Parry.** *The Divinity of Our Lord and Saviour Jesus Christ.* Minne-apolis: Klock & Klock Christian Publishers, 1978.

Constituting Liddon's famous Bampton lectures, Oxford University, these chapters deal adequately with Christ's unique person. His deity is explained as fully as possible, and the information presented is of such a nature that it strengthens the reader's faith and also grounds his belief in the "impregnable rock of Holy Scripture." Recommended. 232.1.L61 1978

**\*Lightner, Robert Paul.** *The Death Christ Died: A Case for Unlimited Atonement.* Schaumburg, Ill.: Regular Baptist Press, 1983.

First issued in 1967. This fine study of the atonement of Christ is thoroughly conservative and stands in the finest evangelical tradition. Lightner interacts with all viewpoints as he makes a case for unlimited atonement. 232.3.L62 1983

**Martin, Ernest L.** *The Birth of Christ Recalculated.* 2d ed. Pasadena, Calif.: Foundation for Biblical Research, 1981.

Extensive research went into the publication of this work. The author presents evidence in support of Christ's birth three or four years later than has been generally claimed. Deserves to be considered alongside the works of Ramsay and others. 232.1.M36

**McDonald, Hugh Dermot.** *Salvation.* Westchester, Ill.: Crossway Books, 1982.

Stresses the soteriological (as opposed to a doxological) approach to the teaching of Scripture on the purpose of life. Provides a good discussion of salvation in both Testaments before enlarging our understanding of the benefits of God's grace. Excellent. 232.4.M14

**McDowell, Josh,** and **Bart Larson.** *Jesus: A Biblical Defense of His Deity.* San Bernardino, Calif.: Here's Life Publishers, 1983.

This apologetic lends itself for use with collegians. Each chapter is simply outlined, cogently reasoned, and ably supported by Scripture. The result is the kind of study manual that can confidently be placed in the hands of college students. 232.1.M14J

*Morris, Leon Lamb. *Glory in the Cross: A Study in Atonement.* Grand Rapids: Baker Book House, 1979.

Expounds the significance of Christ's death as the central tenet of the Christian faith. Thoroughly evangelical. Recommended. 232.3.M83G 1979

Robinson, John Arthur Thomas. *Jesus and His Coming.* Philadelphia: Westminster Press, 1979.

Published in England in 1957, this treatment of *parousia* in the NT has a great deal to offer. Unfortunately, it has been written from a highly critical perspective and interprets the eschatological expectations of Christ and Paul in light of an assumed evolution of the theology of the early church. Disappointing. 232.6.R56 1979

Rudisill, Dorus Paul. *The Doctrine of the Atonement in Jonathan Edwards and His Successors.* New York: Poseidon Books, 1971.

A helpful contribution. 232.3.R83

Smeaton, George. *The Doctrine of the Atonement as Taught by Christ Himself.* Winona Lake, Ind.: Alpha Publications, 1979.

First published in 1871. This exegetical work by a British Reformed scholar contains a substantive treatment of Christ's own teaching on His death, the application of the benefits of His atonement to the church, and the effects of the atonement on the saved and unsaved. 232.3.S3C 1979.

Torrance, Thomas Forsyth. *The Mediation of Christ.* Grand Rapids: Wm. B. Eerdmans Publishing Co., 1983.

Scholarly essays portraying Christ as both God and Man, and as such, as an ideal mediator between God and man. 232.8.T63

*Vine, William Edwy. *The Divine Sonship of Christ.* 2 vols. in 1. Minneapolis: Klock & Klock Christian Publishers, 1984.

Contains *Christ's Eternal Sonship* (n.d.) and *The First and the Last* (n.d.). These studies in Christology draw information from both Testaments and relate the information to the nature of Christ, His work, and the benefits of the believer's union with Him. Stimulating. Recommended. 231.2.V73 1984

Wallace, Ronald. *The Atoning Death of Christ.* Foundations for Faith. Westchester, Ill.: Crossway Books, 1981.

Popularly written, this work nevertheless is based on sound scholarship. The historical understanding of the Christian church is a particularly noteworthy feature of this book. 232.3.W15

LIFE OF CHRIST

Anderson, James Norman Dalrymple. *Jesus Christ: The Witness of History.* Downers Grove, Ill.: InterVarsity Press, 1984.

Believing that the Christian faith rests squarely on existential as well as historical grounds, Sir Norman deals with the uniqueness of Christ's person and mission. Each essay is important for its apologetic value as well as for its theological acumen. The result is a work that is deserving of close attention. 232.9'08.AN2

Baird, William. *The Quest for the Christ of Faith: Reflections on the Bultmann Era.* Waco, Tex.: Word Books, 1977.

Examines the legacy of Bultmann and attempts to synthesize the main dilemmas facing NT scholars in the wake of negative form-criticism. 232.9'08.B16

Barclay, William. *Jesus of Nazareth.* Nashville: Thomas Nelson Publishers, 1981.

The simplicity and drama of the gospel is beautifully and breathtakingly re-told with the aid of 124 full-color photo-graphs selected from among 5,000 scenes that formed the basis of Franco Zeffirelli's film *Jesus of Nazareth*. Barclay's clear and direct narrative captures the mood of the times, the emotion that attended Christ's miracles, and the enor-mity of His earthly mission. Recom-mended. 232.95.B23

**Blaikie, William Gardner.** *The Public Ministry of Christ.* Minneapolis: Klock & Klock Christian Publishers, 1984.

Contains Blaikie's lectures delivered to his students in the New College, Edin-burgh. By probing into the method of Christ, Blaikie was able to deduce vital information that is as relevant to the ministry of a pastor today as when these studies were first presented. The entire treatment is reverent and devout. We are glad that this volume is available again so that it can direct the activities of a new generation of pastor-teachers. 232.9.B57 1984

*_____, and **Robert Law.** *The Inner Life of Christ.* 2 vols. in 1. Minneapolis: Klock & Klock Christian Publishers, 1982.

Combines the rare work by Blaikie entitled *Glimpses of the Inner Life of Our Lord* with Law's indispensable study *The Emotions of Jesus*. Each work makes a unique contribution to our knowledge of the life of Christ, and together they make rich, rewarding reading. 232.95.B57 1982

**Boa, Kenneth,** and **William Proctor.** *The Return of the Star of Bethlehem.* Grand Rapids: Zondervan Publishing House, 1985.

Deals with Christ's two advents. Fur-nishes interesting information on the star the Magi saw before dealing with modern views of certain phenomena. Concludes with a powerful apologetic of the events leading up to Christ's return.

A welcome volume. Should be in every preacher's library. 232.9'2.B63

*****Boice, James Montgomery.** *The Christ of the Empty Tomb.* Chicago: Moody Press, 1985.

Easter messages that rejoice in Christ's victory, glory in His grace, and celebrate His resurrection, knowing that on the first Easter Sunday morning He accom-plished the redemption of those who place their trust in Him. 232.97.B63 (Alt. DDC 252'.63)

**Bowker, John.** *Jesus and the Pharisees.* Cambridge: At the University Press, 1973.

Briefly annotated translations of passages from Josephus, the Mishnah, Tosefta, and the Talmuds, shedding light on the Pharisees and their conflict with Jesus Christ. Of value to the student of the NT. For some of the materials in-cluded in this volume, there is no other standard English version available. 232.9'5.B67

**Brown, Colin.** *Miracles and the Critical Mind.* Grand Rapids: Wm. B. Eerdmans Publishing Co., 1984.

Makes a fresh examination of the ar-guments about the miracles of Christ and their place in faith today. Integrates philosophical, theological, and critical considerations into a workable apolo-getic. Also provides a survey of the at-titudes of people throughout church his-tory to the miraculous and covers in his examination the prescientific age, the rise of skepticism, the legacy of the Enlightenment, the ongoing debate of critics, and finally, a reappraisal of the evidence in light of the truth-claims of the NT. 232.9'55.B81

**Brown, Raymond Edward.** *The Vir-ginal Conception and Bodily Resurrection of Jesus.* New York: Paulist Press, 1973.

†In dealing with the relation between history and dogma, Brown attempts to reconcile the world of the Bible student

with the traditions of the Roman Catholic church. He is an able and articulate form-critic and seeks to relate the results of this approach to the Scriptures with the teaching of the Bible and the church. 232.9'21.B81

**Bruce, Frederick Fyvie.** *Jesus and Christian Origins Outside the New Testament.* Grand Rapids: Wm. B. Eerdmans Publishing Co., 1974.

Contains pertinent data from pagan sources—Josephus, the rabbis, the apocryphal gospels, Islam, and archaeology—relating to the Person and work of Christ and the origin of Christianity. 232.9'08.B83

————. *What the Bible Teaches About What Jesus Did.* Wheaton, Ill.: Tyndale House Publishers, 1979.

Designed for laypeople, this slender volume covers the important events in Christ's life and ministry and discusses their relevance to the believer. 232.95.B83

**Buell, Jon A.,** and **O. Quentin Hyder.** *Jesus: God, Ghost or Guru?* Grand Rapids: Zondervan Publishing House, 1978.

A careful inquiry into Jesus' claims to be the Messiah. Well reasoned. Of apologetic value. 232.954.B86

**\*Chandler, Walter M.** *The Trial of Jesus: From a Lawyer's Standpoint.* Atlanta: Harrison Company, 1972.

First published in two volumes in 1908. This unabridged one-volume edition contains a lawyer's analysis and evaluation of Christ's Jewish and Roman trials. Insightful. Should be in every preacher's library. 232.9'62.C36

**Cohn, Haim.** *The Trial and Death of Jesus.* New York: Harper & Row, 1971.

†Cohn, a justice of the Israeli Supreme Court, brings his legal training to bear on the problem of the trial and death of Christ. Attempts to vindicate the Sanhedrin for meeting at night on the grounds that they were not trying to prosecute or even examine Jesus but rather to save Him from the Romans. Fails to provide a worthwhile contribution to the subject. 232.962.C66

**Conzelmann, Hans.** *Jesus.* Edited by J. Reumann. Translated by J. R. Lord. Philadelphia: Fortress Press, 1973.

†This material first appeared as an article in *Die Religion in Geschichte und Gegenwart* at the height of the "new quest" movement (which Conzelmann has since abandoned). Its translation into English makes available to NT scholars a work otherwise relatively unknown in the United States. 232.9'08.C76

**\*Culver, Robert Duncan.** *The Life of Christ.* Grand Rapids: Baker Book House, 1976.

This is a refreshing, original, thematic approach to the life of Christ, and it deserves careful reading. Culver is never trite. His material epitomizes the biblical and systematic theologian's art. His grasp of the issues is at once incisive and revealing. His work is highly recommended. 232.9.C90

**\*Dalman, Gustaf Hermann.** *Jesus-Jeshua, Studies in the Gospels.* Translated by Paul T. Levertoff. New York: Ktav Publishing House, 1971.

Reprinted from the 1929 edition. This exemplary study illuminates the Jewish background and environment of Jesus. 232.95.D16 1971

\*————. *The Words of Christ.* Translated by D. M. Kay. Minneapolis: Klock & Klock Christian Publishers, 1981.

Eighty years have passed since this work was first translated into English, and its value has increased with age. It still provides the busy pastor with one of the best treatments of the Aramaic background of the gospels extant. Recommended. 232.9'01.D16 1981

**Dawe, Donald G.** *Jesus: The Death and Resurrection of God.* Atlanta: John Knox Press, 1985.

Struggles to present a faith in the biblical record brought to fruition and finding expression within a modern theological tradition. Integrates history and theology as these relate to the death and resurrection of Christ. Applies the effects of these events in a way that is relevant to the Christian community. 232.97.D32

*\*Farrar, Frederick William.* The Life of Christ. Minneapolis: Klock & Klock Christian Publishers, 1982.

One of the finest and, from a literary point of view, one of the best treatments of Christ's life and ministry ever written. Spurgeon said it was "THE WORK ON THE SUBJECT." Farrar's treatment is ideal for devotional reading as well as for serious study. 232.9′01.F24 1982

*\*France, Richard T.* I Came to Set the Earth on Fire: A Portrait of Jesus. Downers Grove, Ill.: InterVarsity Press, 1975.

Well organized, stimulating, and readable, this thoroughly biblical assessment of the impact of Christ's life deserves careful reading. 232.9.F84

*\*Fraser, Donald.* The Metaphores of Christ. Minneapolis: Klock & Klock Christian Publishers, 1985.

This work by one of Scotland's great pulpit masters was first published one hundred years ago. Fraser makes a unique contribution to the study of Christology and also provides unique insights into Christ's teachings. A *must* for all who desire to know how Christ used metaphors to communicate truth to His hearers. This study may well serve as a model of good communication even today. Excellent. 232.9′54.F85 1985

**Govett, Robert.** Christ's Resurrection and Ours: 1 Corinthians XV. Miami Springs, Fla.: Conley and Schoettle Publishing Co., 1985.

Govett divides the material into eight parts and discourses on the importance of the resurrection as well as the nature of the resurrection body. His material is stimulating and edifying. 232.5.G74 1985

**Green, Edward Michael Bankes.** The Day Death Died. Downers Grove, Ill.: InterVarsity Press, 1982.

The author correctly points to the bodily resurrection of Christ as the central tenet of NT theology. In true apologetic style he defends this doctrine against the blandishments of those who would detract from it. Recommended. 232.963.G82

————. The Empty Tomb of Jesus. Downers Grove, Ill.: InterVarsity Press, 1984.

Recent scholarship has focused attention on the bodily resurrection of Christ. This book takes a fresh look at some of the controversial issues. What emerges is a timely apologetic that also unfolds the mystery of the Christian faith. An excellent treatment. 232.97.G82

**Griffiths, Michael.** The Example of Jesus. Downers Grove, Ill.: InterVarsity Press, 1985.

After paying tribute to the epochal works of Thomas á Kempis and James Stalker, Griffiths provides a fresh, original, closely reasoned, edifying study that evangelicals will welcome. Readers will particularly appreciate the last four chapters of the book, which deal with the distinctives of Christ's life and work. Recommended. 232.9′04.G87E

**Grollenberg, Lucas Hendricus.** Jesus. Translated by J. Bowden. Philadelphia: Westminster Press, 1978.

This work by a Roman Catholic scholar applies principles from the life of Christ to the experience of the maturing Christian. Provocative. 232.95.G89

*\*Gromacki, Robert Glenn.* The Virgin Birth: Doctrine of Deity. Nashville: Thomas Nelson Publishers, 1974.

A masterful statement that dispels popular misinterpretations of Christ's conception and birth. Gromacki adequately answers critics of the doctrine and soundly trounces the liberal views of J. A. T. Robinson, William Barclay, and others. All things considered, this is an important contribution, and it deserves to be placed alongside the magisterial work of Machen. 232.9′1.G89

**Habermas, Gary R.** *Ancient Evidence for the Life of Jesus.* Nashville: Thomas Nelson Publishers, 1984.

This book is chiefly an effort to examine the life, death, and resurrection of Jesus from another and somewhat different perspective. It is largely concerned with prebiblical and nonbiblical evidence for these events. In other words, the main body of this book is devoted to a study of sources that date from before, during, and just after the NT itself. What Habermas presents is both fascinating and largely unknown because much of Christian scholarship and apologetics has neglected these areas of investigation. 232.9′08.H11

————. *The Resurrection of Jesus.* Lanham, Md.: University Press of America, 1984.

This book, originally published in 1980, is an argument from the historical resurrection of Jesus to several major tenets of Christian theism. It asserts that by utilizing the techniques of skeptical historians, the bodily resurrection of Christ can be proved and that this event becomes the crux of Christian theology. A serious, sobering study. 232.97.H11

**Harney, Anthony Ernest.** *Jesus and the Constraints of History.* Philadelphia: Westminster Press, 1982.

Denies the integrity and reliability of the gospel records; interprets their composition and message as arising out of the milieu of the second or third century. With this as a premise, Harvey assesses what may be "known" about the Jesus of history. Disappointing. 232.9′08.H26

**\*Harris, John.** *The Teaching Methods of Christ.* Minneapolis: Klock & Klock Christian Publishers, 1984.

Formerly appearing under the title *The Great Teacher,* this work can only be described as indispensable. The pedagogical truths that Harris draws from the pages of the NT are deserving of careful study and close emulation. All pastors and teachers should be thoroughly familiar with this book. 232.9′54.H24 1984

**Hengel, Martin.** *Crucifixion in the Ancient World and the Folly of the Message of the Cross.* Philadelphia: Fortress Press, 1977.

†Expanded version of an article that appeared in a festschrift in honor of Ernst Kasemann. Examines the way in which this "most vile death" was regarded in the ancient Roman world. 364.6′6.H38

**\*Hoehner, Harold Walter.** *Chronological Aspects of the Life of Christ.* Grand Rapids: Zondervan Publishing House, 1977.

A brilliant, reverent treatise that unravels many perplexing problems relating to the life of Christ and dates as accurately as possible the important events of His life. Recommended. 232.9′01.H43

**\*Hoskins, Edwyn Clement,** and **Francis Noel Davey.** *Crucifixion—Resurrection: The Pattern of the Theology and Ethics of the New Testament.* London: Society Promoting Christian Knowledge, 1981.

This sequel to *The Riddle of the New Testament* is concerned, as the subtitle indicates, with the theology and ethics of the NT. The authors provide a detailed exposition of select passages dealing with Christ's death and resurrection. Provocative; profound. 232.96.H79

**Hultgren, Arland J.** *Jesus and His Adversaries: The Form and Function of the Conflict Stories in the Synoptic Tradition.* Minneapolis: Augsburg Publishing House, 1979.

†This scholarly form-critical work draws attention to the confrontations of Christ with the Pharisees, Sadducees, and others. Although the author has a great deal to offer, so much stress is placed on the literary form that the historical significance and the importance of the events in the life of Christ are obscured. 232.9.H87

**Hunter, Archibald Macbride.** *Christ and the Kingdom.* Ann Arbor, Mich.: Servant Books, 1980.

Probes the essence of the theocracy in the teaching of Jesus and points out that those belonging to the kingdom should be characterized by a radically different life-style. 232.954.H91

**\*Innes, Alexander Taylor,** and **Frank John Powell.** *The Trial of Christ.* 2 vols. in 1. Minneapolis: Klock & Klock Christian Publishers, 1982.

Two British barristers examine the trials of Jesus Christ from different, yet complementary, points of view. The result is a pair of legal monographs that are deserving of a place in every zealous Christian's library. Highly recommended. 232.962.IN6 1982

**Jeremias, Joachim.** *The Prayers of Jesus.* Philadelphia: Fortress Press, 1978.

This form-critical work identifies the main elements of Christ's prayers—His attitude to and relationship with the Father, the basis of His petitions, and the pattern for prayer that He established for His followers. It is valuable for its insights. 232.9.J47

**King, Geoffrey R.** *The Forty Days.* 4th ed. London: Henry E. Walter, 1983.

"It is astonishing that so many books on the Atonement have been content to stop short at the Cross, or have brought in the Resurrection only as an epilogue, an appendix to the story of the sacrifice of Jesus. It cannot be said too emphatically that there is no salvation from the distracted and bewildered world in a theology that ends at Calvary. 'If Christ be not raised, your faith is vain'" (James S. Stewart). 232.97.K58 1983

**Klooster, Fred H.** *Quests for the Historical Jesus.* Grand Rapids: Baker Book House, 1977.

Chronicles the historical developments since Schweitzer and describes the changes in liberal, neo-liberal, and neo-orthodox theology. Concludes with an assessment of Pannenberg's contribution to Christology. 232.9'08.K69

**\*Liddon, Henry Parry,** and **James Orr.** *The Birth of Christ.* 2 vols. in 1. Minneapolis: Klock & Klock Christian Publishers, 1980.

Combines Liddon's exposition of Luke 1 with Orr's fine study of the virgin conception of Christ. These works ably complement each other. Preachers will have occasion to refer to this book often. 232.921.L61 1980.

**Lindars, Barnabas,** and **S. S. Smalley, eds.** *Christ and Spirit in the New Testament: Studies in Honour of Charles F. D. Moule.* Cambridge: At the University Press, 1973.

This festschrift contains twenty-seven essays by world-renowned scholars. Their reading will prove to be a mind-stretching experience even to those who do not agree with the viewpoints adhered to by the contributors. 232.9.M86.C46

**\*Maclaren, Alexander,** and **Henry Barclay Swete.** *The Post-Resurrection Ministry of Christ.* 2 vols. in 1. Minneapolis: Klock & Klock Christian Publishers, 1985.

These studies, originally published separately, are deserving of careful consideration. They have variously been described as "brilliant and effective," evidencing "mastery of the subject matter," and being representative of the finest scholarly and suggestive material ever written on this long-neglected aspect of

Christ's ministry. Together these books will provide ministers of the Word with an abundance of resource material for a series of telling messages. 232.97.M22 1985

**\*Marshall, I. Howard.** *I Believe in the Historical Jesus.* Grand Rapids: Wm. B. Eerdmans Publishing Co., 1977.

This author's writings are always abreast of the latest scholarship and demonstrate his ability to interact fairly with critical issues without compromising his theological beliefs. In this volume, Marshall evaluates the contribution of those who have preceded him and then lays a foundation for the future study of this important subject. 232.9'08.M35

**\*_____.** *Last Supper and Lord's Supper.* Grand Rapids: Wm. B. Eerdmans Publishing Co., 1981.

An easy-to-understand, comprehensive survey of the NT teaching concerning Christ's institution of the New Covenant. Excellent. 232.9'57.M35

**McDowell, Josh.** *The Resurrection Factor.* San Bernardino, Calif.: Here's Life Publishers, 1981.

Tackles the criticisms commonly leveled against the bodily resurrection of Christ. Ably defends the biblical account—and that *after* answering all questions and criticisms. An excellent, convincing apologetic. 232.971.M14

**McHugh, John.** *The Mother of Jesus in the New Testament.* Garden City, N.Y.: Doubleday and Co., 1975.

A scholarly study that investigates the historicity of the virgin conception and birth of Christ, the question of the brothers of Jesus, and the circumstances surrounding the marriage of Joseph and Mary. 232.9.M18

**McKenna, David L.** *The Jesus Model.* Waco, Tex.: Word Books, 1977.

A valiant and, in many respects, successful attempt to probe the principles the Lord Jesus used in His life and ministry and to show how these may become the basis of our own conduct and service. Recommended. 232.9'03.M19

**Miguens, Manuel.** *The Virgin Birth: An Evaluation of the Scriptural Evidence.* Westminster, Md.: Christian Classics, 1975.

A brief, scholarly analysis of the NT documentary evidence. Seeks to determine what the gospel writers and early Christians believed about Christ's conception and deity. Roman Catholic. 232.92'1.M58

**Milligan, William.** *The Ascension of Christ.* Minneapolis: Klock & Klock Christian Publishers, 1980.

Combines excellence in presentation with accuracy in interpretation to make this study of Christ's postresurrection and present heavenly ministries a book that all Christians will enjoy reading. 232.973.M62 1980.

**Minear, Paul Sevier.** *Commands of Christ: Authority and Implications.* Nashville: Abingdon Press, 1972.

†This scholarly volume draws attention to a subject frequently overlooked in NT scholarship. It considers the commands of Jesus rather than His assertions, invectives, or interrogations. Claims that Christ's commands clearly point to His authority and that they form the basis of salvation history. 232.9'54.M66

**\*Moule, Handley Carr Glyn,** and **James Orr.** *The Resurrection of Christ.* 2 vols. in 1. Minneapolis: Klock & Klock Christian Publishers, 1980.

Combines Moule's inimitable exposition of John 20-21 with Orr's theological treatise. Together these works provide pastors and students with a rare combination of excellence in exposition coupled with a clear enunciation of theological truth. 232.97.M86 1980

**Neil, William,** and **Stephen H. Travis.** *More Difficult Sayings of Jesus.* Grand Rapids: Wm. B. Eerdmans Publishing Co., 1981.

This sequel to *What Jesus Really Meant* (1975) continues Neil's discussion of the teachings of Jesus as found in His parables and discourses. Brief, devotional. 232.9′54.N31M

**O'Collins, Gerald.** *The Resurrection of Jesus Christ.* Valley Forge, Pa.: Judson Press, 1973.

A concise summary of contemporary European theories relating to Christ's resurrection. Avoids the extreme of skepticism, but the writer fails to come out strongly in favor of the bodily resurrection of Jesus. Roman Catholic. 232.97.OC5

**Pentecost, John Dwight.** *The Words and Works of Jesus Christ: A Study of the Life of Christ.* Grand Rapids: Zondervan Publishing House, 1981.

Traces the stages of Christ's earthly life thematically, and shows how He was the fulfillment of all that the OT predicted. In His being rejected, His ministry underwent a change, and this change in the kingdom program is discussed cogently and with a thorough understanding of God's plan for the future realization of the messianic prophecies. An excellent work. 232.9′01.P38

**Pollock, John.** *The Master: A Life of Christ.* Wheaton, Ill.: Victor Books, 1985.

"Sketches, with love, faithfulness, and sensitivity, the life of the One whose mandates have compelled those he has profiled to live their obedient lives of faith" (Charles W. Colson). 232.95.P76

**Sanders, E. P.** *Jesus and Judaism.* Philadelphia: Fortress Press, 1985.

†This unique work approaches Christ's life and ministry from the perspective of His attitude toward Judaism. Sanders, however, does not see anything distinctively different in Christ's teaching, nor does he conclude that Christianity has anything to offer that is/was not available within Judaism. Though Christians cannot agree with Sanders's conclusions, he has supplied us with an impor-

tant, scholarly contribution explaining the way Jews view Jesus. 232.9.SA5

**Sanders, John Oswald.** *The Incomparable Christ.* Chicago: Moody Press, 1971.

A devotional study of the Person, work, and leadership qualities of Christ. First published in 1952. 232.95.SA51 1971

**Schonfield, Hugh Joseph.** *The Jesus Party.* New York: Macmillan Co., 1974.

†Writing with greater reserve and paying more attention to historical data than was true in *The Passover Plot*, Schonfield attempts to analyze the Jewish-Christian group of the early church. He continues to brand them as revolutionary nationalists and claims that they tried to make their message palatable to Gentiles by blaming the Jews for the crucifixion of Jesus. Highly speculative and antisupernaturalistic. 232.9.SCH7

**Schweizer, Eduard.** *Jesus.* Translated by D. E. Green. Philadelphia: John Knox Press, 1971.

†Based on the 1968 German edition. This work draws attention to the various perspectives on Jesus that find expression throughout the NT. Of particular significance is the chapter "Jesus: The Man Who Fits No Formula." 232.9.SCH9

**Stier, Rudolf Ewald.** *Words of the Risen Christ.* Minneapolis: Klock & Klock Christian Publishers, 1982.

A delightful study of the words of the Lord Jesus during His postresurrection ministry, appearances to the apostles in the book of Acts, and letters to the seven churches of Revelation 2-3. Abounds in suggestive material for a series of sermons. 232.97.ST5S 1982

**Toon, Peter.** *The Ascension of Our Lord.* Nashville: Thomas Nelson Publishers, 1984.

This is a landmark work in which the author explores fully all aspects of Christ's ascension—its foreshadowing in the OT, accounts of it in the New, and the teaching of the church through the ages.

Drawing on the work of the most respected theologians, Toon shows that "the Ascension inaugurates a new age" in which Christ began a new ministry as "King, Priest, and Prophet." His work is marked by clarity and penetrating insight. It is a valuable resource for pastors as well as seminarians. Includes notes, appendixes, and a complete bibliography. 232.97.T61

*Wenham, John. *Easter Enigma*. Grand Rapids: Zondervan Publishing House, Academie Books, 1984.

A bold and discerning work in which Wenham "clearly and deliberately refuses to play the critical game according to the accepted rules, and is for that reason . . . refreshing and deserving of notice" (Richard T. France). 232.9'7.W48

**White, Reginald Ernest Oscar.** *The Night He Was Betrayed*. Grand Rapids: Wm. B. Eerdmans Publishing Co., 1982.

A "profoundly spiritual, yet scholarly book . . . [that] takes us through John 13-17 with a view to deepening our appreciation of what Jesus did for us" (Walter A. Elwell). 232.96.W58

## ANTHROPOLOGY

**Allen, Ronald Barclay.** *The Majesty of Man: The Dignity of Being Human*. Portland, Oreg.: Multnomah Press, 1984.

The author's aim is to help his readers reaffirm the biblical dignity of man in an age of confusion about his being. Using Psalm 8 as his foundational text, Allen answers the question, "What is man?" with a strong affirmative biblical apologetic for the *imago Dei*. This is a fine treatise and well-deserving of careful attention. 233.AL5

**Anderson, Ray Sherman.** *On Being Human: Essays in Theological Anthropology*. Grand Rapids: Wm. B. Eerdmans Publishing Co., 1982.

A scholarly, biblically grounded work that deals effectively with man's nature but is sufficiently free from humanism to provide a definitive assessment of the form and function of man. 233.AN2

*Berkouwer, Gerrit Cornelis. *Sin*. Studies in Dogmatics. Translated by Phillip C. Holtrop. Grand Rapids: Wm. B. Eerdmans Publishing Co., 1971.

Stresses the fact of guilt, and shows that only through true confession can man be truly forgiven. Destined to take its place as one of the most authoritative works of its kind. 233.2.B45

**Brand, Paul,** and **Philip Yancey.** *Fearfully and Wonderfully Made*. Grand Rapids: Zondervan Publishing House, 1980.

Discusses the marvels of God's handiwork in the human body. C. Everett Koop said this work is "a unique book . . . that alternates from dazzling descriptions of the function of various parts of the human body in layman's terms to analyses of the form and function of the Body of Christ . . . an enthralling edifying book which I wish I had had the insight to write." Recommended. 233.B73

**Carey, George.** *I Believe in Man*. Grand Rapids: Wm. B. Eerdmans Publishing Co., 1977.

This important work covers both old and new ground. The author demonstrates his acquaintance with those writers who have preceded him and then goes on to emphasize some aspects of biblical anthropology that have long been neglected. 233.C18

**Clark, Gordon Haddon.** *The Biblical Doctrine of Man*. Jefferson, Md.: Trinity Foundation, 1984.

In this volume Christian and humanist views of man are compared. Clark, a philosopher par excellence, ably defends the biblical doctrine and also provides a refutation of current erroneous theories. Reformed. 233.C54

**Collins, Gary R.** *The Magnificent Mind.* Waco, Tex.: Word Books, 1985. Seeks to answer many questions about behavior. Also helps to understand why people act the way they do, why some are characterized by "double mindedness," and why some are inefficient. Recommended. 233'.5.C69

**Cosgrove, Mark P.** *The Essence of Human Nature.* Grand Rapids: Zondervan Publishing House, 1977. Sponsored by Probe Ministries, Inc., this book is part of a growing corpus of material that endeavors to extricate certain Christian doctrines or beliefs from the limbo to which modern scholarship has confined them. In this case the doctrine is anthropology. The treatment ably combines psychology and theology into a harmonious synthesis and advances our knowledge of man as the apex of God's creative handiwork. 150'.1.C82E

**Culliton, Joseph T.** *Personal Presence: Its Effects on Honesty and Truthfulness.* Lanham, Md.: University Press of America, 1985. Presents psychological, philosophical, and religious insights into various forms of personal presence and shows how these different forms affect honesty and truthfulness. Highlights the consequences of our present behavior; suggests ways of improving various kinds of relationships, including the enrichment of community and family life; and discusses how to promote a deepening of religious experience. 233'.5.C89

**Dokecki, Paul R.,** and **O. Hobart Mowrer,** eds. *Conscience, Contract, and Social Reality: Theory and Research in Behavioral Science.* New York: Holt, Rinehart and Winston, 1972. Essays by social critics and psychol-

ogists providing an in-depth discussion of the relationship of the conscience to guilt, shame, crime, moral judgment, and more. 154.2.C74

**\*Fiske, Samuel.** *Divine Sovereignty and Human Freedom.* Neptune, N.J.: Loizeaux Brothers, 1973. A forthright attempt to bring these complementary truths into focus and to discuss the biblical teaching supporting each view. Clarifies much of the confusion surrounding predestination and preterition. 233.7.F54

**Flynn, Leslie Bruce.** *Man: Ruined and Restored.* Wheaton, Ill.: Victor Books, 1978. In twelve chapters the author explains the essence of biblical anthropology. Designed for church discussion groups. Recommended. 233.F67

**\*Geisler, Norman Leo.** *Is Man the Measure: An Examination of Contemporary Humanism.* Grand Rapids: Baker Book House, 1983. One of the best exposés of philosophical humanism to have been published to date. Geisler shows himself a master of the material, and pastors as well as students should consult his work before reading any other. 233.G27

**\*Gilpin, Richard.** *Daemonologia Sacra; or, A Treatise on Satan's Temptations.* Minneapolis: Klock & Klock Christian Publishers, 1982. Originally published in 1677 and now reissued under the new title *Biblical Demonology,* this collection of sermons ably explores Satan's person and work. It is of particular value for Gilpin's analysis of the way Satan tempts the saints. A rare and edifying study. 233.2.G42 1982

**\*Harris, Robert Laird.** *Man: God's Eternal Creation.* Chicago: Moody Press, 1971. Explores man's culture during OT times, emphasizes the uniqueness of the divinely appointed worship patterns, stresses the importance of God's revelation pertaining to social controls, and explains the military struggles of God's people. A very thorough, biblical study. 233.H24

**Hocking, David Lee.** *Who Am I and What Difference Does It Make?* Portland, Oreg.: Multnomah Press, 1985.

This book was written "for those who think and act on most issues from a selfish and individualistic viewpoint—those who have been captured by the spirit of the age with its existential, experiential and narcissistic reasoning." Hocking notes a general dissatisfaction with present philosophies about human life and values and claims that there is a desire on the part of many for clear thinking and reliable answers. His book seeks to meet this need by applying biblical principles to pressing problems. Recommended. 233.H66

**Jaki, Stanley, L.** *Angels, Apes, and Men.* LaSalle, Ill.: Sherwood Sugden and Co., 1983.

Jaki has written extensively in areas integrating theology and physics. The present volume combines a knowledge of philosophy and history with these other disciplines in an endeavor to assess the nature of man, his unique creation, and the failure of modern philosophies (Newtonian, Kantian, Hegelian, Darwinian, etc.) to reach a proper understanding of the *imago Dei.* Jaki also assesses man's potential as the highest created earthly being, interacts with various cosmological issues, and discusses Einstein's cosmology. The result is a stimulating, mind-stretching apologetic for biblical anthropology that is deserving of careful reading. 233.J21

**Keyes, Richard.** *Beyond Identity: Finding Your Self in the Image and Character of God.* Ann Arbor, Mich.: Servant Books, 1984.

A wholesome work that seeks to estab-lish a biblical basis for the development of a sound identity. This work is a fine blend of philosophy, psychology, and theology. 233.K52

**\*Lee, Francis Nigel.** *The Origin and Destiny of Man.* Nutley, N.J.: Presbyterian and Reformed Publishing Co., 1974.

Five brief, biblical lectures delivered at the inauguration of the Christian Studies Center, Memphis. Reformed. 233.L51

**MacKay, Donald M.** *Human Science and Human Dignity.* Downers Grove, Ill.: InterVarsity Press, 1979.

This plea for an authentic humanness penetrates through the "froth and bubble" of behaviorism, humanism, and genetic manipulation. Develops a unique interdisciplinary view of the *imago Dei.* 233.M19

**Maddi, Salvatore R.** *Personality Theories: A Comparative Analysis.* Rev. ed. Homewood, Ill.: Dorsey Press, 1972.

This secular approach to the nature of man is of value for its evaluation of prevailing psychological theories. Maddi does not support a biblical view of man, but his disenchantment with the theories of Freudians, behaviorists, and others brings the reader to see the value of the biblical model. 155.2.M26 1972

**McDonald, Hugh Dermot.** *The Christian View of Man.* Foundations for Faith. Westchester, Ill.: Crossway Books, 1981.

Distills a vast amount from the writings of leaders in the history of the Christian church, and presents a thoroughly evangelical assessment of the nature of man. An important synthesis. 233.M14

**\*Menninger, Karl.** *Whatever Became of Sin?* New York: Hawthorn Books, 1973.

†The author is a psychiatrist, not a theologian, and as such, views sin existentially and is primarily concerned about its effect on human behavior. In spite of this perspective, he effectively traces the semantic game we have played

with sin and calls on preachers to reassert their authority in exposing its many forms. 233.2.M52

**Miles, Margaret R.** *Fullness of Life: Historical Foundations for a New Asceticism.* Philadelphia: Westminster Press, 1981.

Explores the history of asceticism and the Christian church's teaching on the human body. The writer's purpose is to bring believers into a new appreciation of what it is to be alive. 233.5.M59

**Moltmann, Jurgen.** *Man: Christian Anthropology in the Conflicts of the Present.* Philadelphia: Fortress Press, 1974.

†Although the author's ethical principles are of value, he is unable to deal adequately with the *imago Dei* because of his adherence to universalism and his unorthodox approach to the Person and work of Christ. 233.M73

**Narramore, Stanley Bruce,** and **William M. Counts.** *Freedom from Guilt.* Irvine, Calif.: Harvest House Publications, 1976.

Formerly published under the title *Guilt and Freedom,* this work clarifies the different forms of guilt. The authors also provide insights that make clear the Bible's teaching on the emotions. That helps reconcile our inner experiences. The discussion of forgiveness is misleading and either needs to be restated or dropped from the book. 233.2.N16 1976

**Packer, James Innell.** *Knowing Man.* Westchester, Ill.: Cornerstone Books, 1979.

In a series of direct, pointed messages, Packer treats the true humanity of man in his relation to God, society, and others. Clarifies much of the confusion interjected into the discussion of anthropology by those who do not adhere to biblical revelation. 233.P12

**Pannenberg, Wolfhart.** *Anthropology in Theological Perspective.* Translated by J. O'Connell. Philadelphia: Westminster Press, 1985.

†This is an eclectic book. It combines biology, psychology, anthropology, sociology, and history in its development of a systematic anthropology. Pannenberg tries to avoid ego-centricity, but his humanistic philosophy betrays his good intentions. In spite of this weakness, he has made available to his readers a reasoned treatise that will be referred to continually by all engaged in the study of the biblical doctrine of man. 233.P19 1985

**Ruby, Jay, ed.** *A Crack in the Mirror: Reflexive Perspectives in Anthropology.* Philadelphia: University of Pennsylvania Press, 1982.

Takes a fresh look at anthropological theories of personality, exposes the ruts in which current thought has tended to run, and provides a fresh approach to new theoretical developments. 306.R82

**\*Stowell, Joseph M., III.** *Kingdom Conflict.* Wheaton, Ill.: Victor Books, 1985.

This is a brave and timely treatise. Years ago G. Campbell Morgan gave to the world *The Voice of the Devil.* This exposition of the Bible's teaching on temptation is better. It applies the teaching of the Word to the mind, the emotions, and the will of each individual. Recommended. 233.7.ST7

**Thielicke, Helmut.** *Being Human . . . Becoming Human: An Essay in Christian Anthropology.* Translated by G. W. Bromiley. Garden City, N.Y.: Doubleday and Co., 1984.

Calling on seminal figures in Western culture—among them Goethe, Darwin, Kierkegaard, Nietzche, Freud, Teilhard, and Barth—Thielicke helps sift the various views of these writers, evaluates the influences propeling them in their investigation, and seeks to provide a reasoned statement of belief that is consistent with anthropology, biology, medicine, psychology, sociology, and technology. 233.T34

**Vandervelde, G.** *Original Sin: Two Ma-*

jor Trends in Contemporary Roman Catholic Interpretation. Amsterdam, The Netherlands: Rodopi N. V., 1975.

A detailed study that ably fulfills the subtitle. The one viewpoint interprets original sin as historical, the other as personal. 233.14.V28

**Wolff, Hans Walter.** *Anthropology of the Old Testament.* Translated by M. Kohl. Philadelphia: Fortress Press, 1975.

†Outlines the basic anthropological concepts of the OT; traces the physical, intellectual, and psychological makeup of both men and women, and draws attention to the activities and social relationships in which people were involved. 233.W83

SALVATION

**\*Anderson, Robert.** *The Gospel and Its Ministry.* Grand Rapids: Kregel Publications, 1978.

Sir Robert was for many years director of Scotland Yard in England. He was a devout and knowledgeable Christian. In his books, his astute legal training was coupled with a thorough mastery of theology, and he left behind him numerous important studies that laypeople as well as pastors still find eminently usable. This important volume surveys the major tenets of Bible doctrine and provides clear, accurate definitions of terms, together with explanations of what the Bible teaches. 234.AN2G 1978

———. *Redemption Truths.* Grand Rapids: Kregel Publications, 1980.

Published soon after the turn of the century under the title *For Us Men*, these chapters unfold the doctrine of salvation, showing, as well as man can, the marvels of God's plan for our redemption. Well done; stimulating. 234.AN2R 1980

**Babcock, Neil.** *A Search for Charismatic Reality: One Man's Pilgrimage.* Portland, Oreg.: Multnomah Press, 1985.

"This book is not for the insincere or dishonest. It is for those who earnestly search for spiritual reality. It is the result of the honest and fruitful search of a charismatic pastor for the reality of Christ in and through the gift of tongues" (Norman L. Geisler). 234.8.B11

**Banks, Robert, ed.** *Reconciliation and Hope: New Testament Essays on Atonement and Eschatology Presented to L. L. Morris.* Grand Rapids: Wm. B. Eerdmans Publishing Co., 1974.

A festschrift honoring the distinguished career of Leon Morris. The essays reflect evangelical thinking on important Christological themes. Stimulating. 234.R24

**Barker, Harold.** *Secure Forever.* Neptune, N.J.: Loizeaux Brothers, 1974.

Surveys the teaching of the Bible on the subject of eternal security and then seeks to answer the criticisms leveled against the doctrine. 234.18.B24

**Baxter, James Sidlow.** *Christian Holiness: Restudied and Restated.* Grand Rapids: Zondervan Publishing House, 1977.

This work brings together the author's thoughts on and heartfelt concern for the individual Christian's conformity to the image of Christ. Mediating. 234.8.B33 1977

**\*Boice, James Montgomery.** *Awakening to God.* Vol. III, Foundations of the Christian Life. Downers Grove, Ill.: InterVarsity Press, 1979.

Continues the series of doctrinal issues for laypeople. Discusses the work of the Holy Spirit in the salvation of the repentant sinner and provides an excellent treatment of such key issues as justification, adoption, and sanctification. Recommended. 234.B63

**Bray, Gerald Lewis.** *Holiness and the Will of God: Perspectives on the Theology of Tertullian.* Atlanta: John Knox Press, 1979.

Emphasizes the theme of holiness.

This survey of Tertullian's teaching on the subject serves to bring into perspective the historic setting that gave rise to his views. An excellent treatment. 234.8'09.T27.B73

**Bray, John S.** *Theodore Beza's Doctrine of Predestination.* Nieukoop, The Netherlands: DeGraff Publishers, 1975.

Carefully researched. This historical study analyzes Beza's theology to determine whether he defended and promoted Calvin's views or, in altering them, paved the way for a Protestant scholasticism. Bray advances evidence in support of his thesis that Beza adopted a mediating position. 234.9.B73

**Bridge, Donald,** and **David Phypers.** *The Water That Divides.* Downers Grove, Ill.: InterVarsity Press, 1977.

The writers discuss the views of their respective churches on the subject of water baptism. They do not provide any new insights but instead seek to explore possible common ground for cooperation and union. Thorough and objective. 234.161.B76

***Buchanan, James.** *The Doctrine of Justification: An Outline of Its History in the Church and of Its Exposition from Scripture.* Carlisle, Pa.: Banner of Truth Trust, 1984.

A valuable book that every evangelical preacher should study carefully. 234.7.B85 1984

**Burkhardt, Helmut.** *The Biblical Doctrine of Regeneration.* Translated by O. R. Johnston, Downers Grove, Ill.: InterVarsity Press, 1978.

Builds on the meaning of the biblical terminology and notes that his doctrine is seldom considered by contemporary theologians. Traces the history of the concept of regeneration and its importance in the teaching of evangelical churches. 234.4.B91

**Clark, Gordon Haddon.** *Faith and Saving Faith.* Jefferson, Md.: Trinity Foundation, 1983.

Writing out of a heart of concern for the lost and with the conviction that most conservative preachers today preach a watered-down gospel, Clark sets out to provide a definitive explanation of the message of salvation. 234.2.C54

**Denney, James.** *The Biblical Doctrine of Reconciliation.* Minneapolis: Klock & Klock Christian Publishers, 1985.

Denney was both a pastor and a theologian. He defines and describes the biblical doctine of reconciliation and demonstrates that the essence of Christianity lies in its message of grace. Well conceived and well executed. This book deserves careful reading. 234.7.D41 1985

***Edgar, Thomas R.** *Miraculous Gifts, Are They for Today?* Neptune, N.J.: Loizeaux Brothers, 1983.

Probes the NT teaching on spiritual gifts and compares modern phenomena to the biblical record. Well reasoned, up-to-date. Recommended. 234'.12.ED3

**Ellul, Jacques.** *Hope in Time of Abandonment.* Translated by C. E. Hopkin. New York: Seabury Press, 1973.

Written with conviction and insight, this book exposes a host of false hopes that are common to our age. It warns against a false optimism and urges readers to place their confidence solely in God's lovingkindness and providence. Recommended. 234.2.EL5H

————. *Living Faith: Belief and Doubt in a Perilous World.* Translated by P. Heinegg. San Francisco: Harper & Row, 1983.

Like all the works from the pen of this lawyer-theologian, this one is lucid and at the same time provocative. He asks hard questions and then gives astonishingly optimistic answers. The distinction that Ellul draws between the authentic and the spurious in matters of religious belief is astonishing. Recommended. 234.2.EL5

**Erickson, Millard John,** ed. *The New Life: Readings in Christian Theology.* Grand

Rapids: Baker Book House, 1979.

This valuable anthology is designed to serve as a companion volume to *The Living God* and *Man's Need and God's Gift.* Contains essays by a wide variety of post-Reformation scholars. 234.ER4

———. *Salvation: God's Amazing Plan.* Wheaton, Ill.: Victor Books, 1978.

A clear, concise résumé. Intended for adult discussion groups. The author does not necessarily present any new material, but what is to be found within these covers is perfectly adequate for the purpose for which the book was designed. Recommended. 234.ER4

**Fenhagen, James C.** *Invitation to Holiness.* San Francisco: Harper & Row, 1985.

†Seeks to unite the personal quest for wholeness with a justifiable emphasis on holiness. Provides a useful paradigm by which both goals may be achieved. 234.8.F35

**Finney, Charles Grandison.** *Principles of Holiness.* Compiled and edited by L. G. Parkhurst, Jr. Minneapolis: Bethany House Publishers, 1984.

A valuable compendium of Finney's views on sanctification. Arminian. 234.8.F49P 1984

**Fowler, James W.** *Stages of Faith: The Psychology of Human Development and the Quest for Meaning.* San Francisco: Harper & Row, 1981.

Quite apart from religious belief, the author probes the issue of personal confidence and the way in which this is developed through the various stages of life. Fowler then provides his readers with valuable information on the way in which values, goals, and commitments are inculcated and developed. Provocative. 234.2.F82

**Gillespie, Virgil Bailey.** *Religious Conversion and Personal Identity: How and Why People Change.* Birmingham, Ala.: Religious Education Press, 1979.

Gillespie does not hold to an evangelical view of conversion. He treats the social, familial, theological, philosophical, or psychological reasons for religious change. 234.G41

**Govett, Robert.** *Is Sanctification Perfect Here Below? or Romans VI-VIII Expounded.* Miami Springs, Fla.: Conley and Schoettle Publishing Co., 1985.

This is a handy work on sanctification. It begins with a presentation of the teaching of Romans 1-5. Govett then discusses at length in chaps. 6-8 the essence of the doctrine of sanctification. He draws from the text Paul's teaching on the Christian life. He then evaluates the doctrinal distinctives of two leading exponents holding differing views of Romans 7. Those who read Govett's presentation will find his material well reasoned and helpful. 234.8.G74 1985

**Graham, William Franklin.** *Peace with God.* Revised and expanded edition. Waco, Tex.: Word Books, 1984.

First published in 1953. These sermons deal with the message of the gospel, how it is received, the way in which people may be sure of their salvation, and the dynamics of spiritual growth. Well written and replete with down-to-earth illustrations, this book is assured of wide readership. 234.G76 1984

**Green, Edward Michael Bankes.** *Faith for the Nonreligious.* Wheaton, Ill.: Tyndale House Publishers, 1979.

Deals with the typical excuses of the unsaved. Provides practical sidelights on how people in the church may deal with those whom they meet. 234.2.G82

***Gromacki, Robert Glenn.** *Salvation Is Forever.* Chicago: Moody Press, 1974.

A scholarly treatment relating the doctrine of eternal security to other facets of theology (e.g., sanctification, perseverance, etc.). Treats those passages of Scripture that seem to teach a contrary view with fairness and discernment. 234.18.G89

**Harran, Marilyn J.** *Luther on Conversion: The Early Years.* Ithaca, N.Y.: Cornell University Press, 1983.

"While many scholars have analyzed Luther's description of his own conversion, Harran's book is the first full-length study in English of his theological considerations of conversion . . . shows that Luther's development of the concept of conversion parallels his development from a scholastic to a 'reformer'" (Denis Janz). 234'.09.H23

**Hebblethwaite, Brian.** *The Christian Hope.* Grand Rapids: Wm. B. Eerdmans Publishing Co., 1985.

This is a definitive work. It looks at the background of Christian hope in the OT and NT. Important facts are drawn from incidents beginning with the faith of Abraham all the way through to the teaching of Christ. Hebblethwaite also culls from church history the attitudes of people toward the future. The survey concludes with particular attention being drawn to the modern period and the phenomenal scientific advances being made. By means of this the writer hopes to show what affect this will have on the future of our world. 234.2.H35

**Heppenstall, Edward.** *Salvation Unlimited: Perspectives in Righteousness by Faith.* Washington, D.C.: Review and Herald Publishing Co., 1974.

An evangelical's clear presentation of righteousness by faith. Aimed at a "personal living relationship with Christ through His Holy Spirit." Seventh Day Adventist. 234.H41

**Hordern, William.** *Living by Grace.* Philadelphia: Westminster Press, 1975.

A critical examination of Protestant churches that boldly announce their belief in the theology of grace but are so works oriented that their practice belies their profession. 234'.7.H78

**Horn, Robert M.** *Go Free!* Downers Grove, Ill.: InterVarsity Press, 1976.

An exceptionally fine treatment of the doctrine of justification. Recommended. 234'.7.H78

**Jewett, Paul King.** *Election and Predestination.* Grand Rapids: Wm. B. Eerdmans Publishing Co., 1985.

In this study Jewett, a Reformed Baptist, "takes on the most difficult problems facing Christian theology—God's sovereignty and the fact of evil, God's love and his judgment, grace and human freedom. In dialogue with the best that the church has given us on the problems, he makes Scripture his criterion and concludes that there is an element of mystery that must be recognized and honored. . . . For accuracy, clarity, and competency, this is the best modern discussion of the subject that I know" (M. Eugene Osterhaven). 234.J55

**Kendall, Robert Tillman.** *Once Saved, Always Saved.* Chicago: Moody Press, 1985.

A comprehensive, convincing discussion of the hotly debated topic of eternal security. Gives both sides of the argument. A work of this quality deserves a more durable quality of paper. It is feared that would-be purchasers might be dissuaded from purchasing it on account of its appearance. 234.18.K33

**Leaver, Robin A.** *Luther on Justification.* St. Louis: Concordia Publishing House, 1975.

Treats fairly the controversies in which Luther became embroiled and highlights these incidents with quotations from the Reformer's own writings. 234'.7.L97

**Macquarrie, John.** *Christian Hope.* New York: Seabury Press, 1978.

†Beginning with the universal presence of hope in mankind, the author

treats the subject both doctrinally and historically. 234.2.M24

**McRae, William J.** *The Dynamics of Spiritual Gifts.* Grand Rapids: Zondervan Publishing House, 1976.

A biblically based presentation of the distribution, discovery, and development of spiritual gifts, ably distinguishing those that were temporary from those that are permanent. 234'.1.M24

**Murray, Andrew.** *The Believer's Secret of Holiness.* Minneapolis: Bethany House Publishers, 1984.

Beautifully produced, and now in a series designed to update Murray's message, this reissue of *Holy in Christ* is worthy of prolonged reflection. 234.8.M96H 1984

**Pink, Arthur Walkington.** *The Doctrine of Salvation.* Grand Rapids: Baker Book House, 1975.

A strongly Calvinistic exposition of the doctrine of soteriology, including in its treatment the practical aspects of growing in grace. 234.P65 1975

**Pinnock, Clark H., ed.** *Grace Unlimited.* Minneapolis: Bethany Fellowship, 1975.

Thirteen essays by Arminian theologians stressing man's authentic freedom and rebutting Calvinistic doctrines such as God's foreknowledge and His decree. Ephemeral. 234.P65G

**\*Prior, Kenneth.** *The Way of Holiness: A Study in Christian Growth.* Downers Grove, Ill.: InterVarsity Press, 1982.

One of the best discussions of sanctification to be published in recent years. Formerly published in England, this work treats such topics as spiritual renewal, perfectionism, Christian growth, the filling of the Holy Spirit, and mortification of the flesh. Excellent. 234.8.P93 1982

**Schaeffer, Francis August.** *True Spirituality.* Wheaton, Ill.: Tyndale House Publishers, 1971.

Comes to grips with the problem of reality and the all-sufficiency of Christ. Presents the gospel as the only message to meet the needs of men and women today. 234.8.SCH1

**Schwab, Richard C.** *Let the Bible Speak . . . About Tongues.* Grand Rapids: Kregel Publications, 1983.

"This book represents the finest balance between careful scholarship and practical application that I have seen on the subject. . . . If I were to pick one book to give to a person to read [about tongues] that is THE book" (Earl D. Radmacher). 234'.13.SCH9

**Shank, Robert.** *Elect in the Son: A Study of the Doctrine of Election.* Springfield, Mo.: Westcott Publishers, 1971.

A sequel to *Life in the Son.* Attempts to demonstrate that Calvin's doctrine of unconditional election and reprobation is without foundation in Scripture. Arminian. 234.9.SH1E

**\*Smedes, Lewis B.** *Forgive and Forget: Healing the Hurts We Don't Deserve.* Cambridge: Harper & Row, 1984.

"There are some hurts we can all ignore . . . some old pains do not wash out so easily; they remain like stubborn stains in the fabric of our own memories. Deep hurts we never deserved flow from a dead past into our living present. . . . Forgiveness is God's invention for coming to terms with a world in which, despite their best intentions, people are unfair to each other and hurt each other deeply. He began by forgiving us. And he invites us all to forgive each other" (Preface). 234.5.SM3

**Tyrell, Francis Martin.** *Man: Believer and Unbeliever.* Staten Island, N.Y.: Alba House, 1974.

†A humanistic approach to anthropology. Attempts to retain the normative status of Christian revelation while adhering to principles totally at variance with the biblical record. Roman Catholic. 234.T98

**Vander Lugt, Herbert.** *God's Plan in All*

*the Ages.* Grand Rapids: Zondervan Publishing House, 1979.

Blends God's soteriological purpose for mankind with His theocracy. Informative. Designed for laypeople. Of value for adult study groups. 234.V2

**Yohn, Richard N.** *Discover Your Spiritual Gift and Use It.* Wheaton, Ill.: Tyndale House Publishers, 1974.

A timely and practical treatise on the development and use of gifts within the Body of Christ. Recommended for discussion groups. 234.1.Y7

**Ziesler, J. A.** *The Meaning of Righteousness in Paul: A Linguistic and Theological Enquiry.* New York: Cambridge University Press, 1972.

A study reflecting the writer's desire to come to grips with this facet of Pauline theology. His goal is to overcome categorical difficulties underlying much of the present debate. He shows that *dikaioo* is used relatively, often with the meaning "to acquit" and that *dikaios* frequently has a behavioral meaning. 234.7.Z6

ANGELOLOGY

**Alexander, Ben.** *Out from Darkness.* Joplin, Mo.: College Press Publishing Co., 1985.

This book contains the true story of Ben Alexander, who turned from witchcraft and Satan worship to Christ. Apart from the human interest, the recounting of this odyssey reveals the inner working of covens and the way occultism is spreading. 131.AL2

**Alexander, William Menzies.** *Demonic Possession in the New Testament: Its Historical, Medical, and Theological Aspects.* Grand Rapids: Baker Book House, 1980.

First published in 1902. This work by a man holding doctorates in medicine, science, and theology is valuable for its realistic appraisal of the teaching of the NT and particularly for its insights into the increasing prevalence of the "powers

of darkness" today. 235.4.AL2 1980

**\*Andrews, Samuel J.** *Christianity and Anti-Christianity in Their Final Conflict.* Minneapolis: Klock & Klock Christian Publishers, 1981.

Highly acclaimed, yet long out-of-print, this work deserves to be studied by every professing Bible student. 235.48.AN2 1981

**\*Dickason, C. Fred.** *Angels, Elect and Evil.* Chicago: Moody Press, 1975.

One of the most comprehensive discussions to appear to date. Of value as a supplement to most systematic theologies. 235.3.D55

**Drury, Nevill.** *Dictionary of Mysticism and the Occult.* San Francisco: Harper & Row, 1985.

Contains brief, comprehensive explanations of terms and practices that are characteristic of Satanism and spiritism. 133'03.D84

**Graham, William Franklin.** *Angels: God's Secret Agents.* Garden City, N.Y.: Doubleday and Co., 1975.

To fill a hiatus in literature on spirit beings, Graham researched material on good angels and here presents his findings. The result is a heartwarming account of the Bible's teaching presented in a way that should bring encouragement to all believers. 235.3.G76

**Green, Edward Michael Bankes.** *I Believe in Satan's Downfall.* Grand Rapids: Wm. B. Eerdmans Publishing Co., 1981.

In opposition to the tendency to dismiss Satan and Satanism as a carryover of medieval superstition into the church's theology, Green deals factually with Satan-worship, fascination with the occult, black and white magic, astrology and horoscopes, seances and tarot cards, and the like. He shows these to be on the increase. And despite the professed skepticism and supposedly scientific outlook of the modern world, most people are naively responsive to any new religion that comes along. Green takes a fresh look at the biblical account of evil and the possibility of its defeat. He then calls Christians to take seriously the spiritual battle in which followers of Christ are necessarily engaged, recognizing both the strength of the devil and the greater strength of the living God. He also cautions against involvement—even at the trivial level—in spiritism and the occult. Recommended. 235.G82

**Hill, John Edward Christofer.** *Anti-Christ in Seventeenth Century England.* New York: Oxford University Press, 1971.

These lectures, delivered at the University of Newcastle-on-Tyne in 1969, survey the history of the development of the doctrine of the Antichrist, with excursions into the religious thought of England during the seventeenth century. 235.48'09.H55

**Koch, Kurt E.** *Satan's Devices.* Translated by M. Freeman. Grand Rapids: Kregel Publications, 1978.

Brief, informative chapters on the forms and effects of spiritualistic beliefs and practices. A *must* for those who work with teens and those in college. Should be in every church library. 133.K81S

**\*Lindsey, Hal,** and **Carole C. Carlson.** *Satan Is Alive and Well on Planet Earth.* Grand Rapids: Zondervan Publishing House, 1972.

Following a dramatic first chapter, the writers settle down to analyzing the modern preoccupation with the occult and synthesizing the data they have gathered into a systematic treatment of Satanism. 235.47.L64

**\*Pink, Arthur Walkington.** *The Antichrist.* Minneapolis: Klock & Klock Christian Publishers, 1979.

First published in 1923. These chapters provide one of the finest and most comprehensive overviews of the origin and identity, character and destination of the Man of Sin available. 235.48.P65 1979.

**Russell, Jeffrey Burton.** *Satan: The Early Christian Tradition.* Ithaca, N.Y.: Cornell University Press, 1981.

The author of *The Devil: Perceptions of Evil from Antiquity to Primitive Christianity* here provides his readers with an assessment of the views of leaders in the early church to Augustine. Unfortunately Russell's contribution is marred by his mistaken views of God as well as "his infernal majesty." 235.47.R91

**Strauss, Lehman.** *Demons Yes—But Thank God for Good Angels.* Neptune, N.J.: Loizeaux Brothers, 1976.

A study—predominantly of Satan and demons—that relates the biblical material to Christian living, world governments, and the future. 235.4.ST8

**Tatford, Frederick Albert.** *The Prince of Darkness.* Eastbourne, Sussex, England: Prophetic Witness Publishing House, n.d.

A compact survey of Satan's rejection of God's right to rule and his struggle against His authority. Incidental light is shed on such subjects as the "sons of God" in Genesis 6 and the spiritual conflict in heavenly places. 235.47.T18

**\*Unger, Merrill Frederick.** *Demons in the World Today: A Study of Occultism in the Light of God's Word.* Wheaton, Ill.: Tyndale House Publishers, 1971.

A well-known Semitic scholar and theologian examines the subject of demonism from a biblical point of view and provides a detailed analysis of its present activity. Recommended. 133.4.UN3

————. *The Haunting of Bishop Pike: A Christian View of the Other Side.* Wheaton, Ill.: Tyndale House Publishers, 1971.

Unger brings his vast training to bear on the psychic experiences of the late Bishop James Pike, revealing Pike's own misguided beliefs as well as his dabbling with the occult. An illuminating, helpful work. 133.3.UN3H

———. *What Demons Can Do to Saints.* Chicago: Moody Press, 1977.

Books on demonology glut the market. Many are superficial. This one is different. A specialist in the field, Unger addresses himself to the issues others have either ignored or neglected. His treatment of Satanic influence on believers is at once relevant and biblical. This is a most important book. 235.4.UN3W

**Wiersbe, Warren Wendell.** *The Strategy of Satan: How to Detect and Defeat Him.* Wheaton, Ill.: Tyndale House Publishers, 1979.

Insightful chapters on Satan's personality, strategies, plans, and destiny. 235.47.W63

ESCHATOLOGY

**\*Boice, James Montgomery.** *God and History.* Vol. 4, Foundations of the Christian Faith. Downers Grove, Ill.: InterVarsity Press, 1981.

Blends an awareness of time with future eschatological events and shows how the church, through its ministry, is able to meet the needs of the present while preparing for the future. 236.B63

**Bultema, Harry.** *Maranatha! A Study of Unfulfilled Prophecy.* Translated by C. Lambregtsk. Grand Rapids: Kregel Publications, 1985.

These studies by a Christian Reformed church pastor make a strong case for the premillennial return of Christ. The author's use of the writings of the early church Fathers as well as his synthesis of the Bible's teaching are commendable. Bultema has some excellent comments on the first resurrection, the rapture of believers, the distinction between Israel and the church, and the reign of Christ during the Millennium. All things considered, this is an important treatise, which Bible students of all

persuasions will appreciate. 236.B87 1985

**Chilton, David.** *Paradise Restored: A Biblical Theology of Dominion.* Tyler, Tex.: Reconstruction Press, 1985.

In this well-reasoned, Reformed treatise, Chilton points the way to economic prosperity. The problem lies in persuading apathetic Christians of the viability of the theocracy today. Though readers will not agree with all that Chilton presents, the gravest danger lies in dismissing *Paradise Restored* without giving it due consideration. Of particular value is the linking of a dynamic Christian activism with world-wide evangelism. Postmillennial. 236.C43

**Erickson, Millard John.** *Contemporary Options in Eschatology: A Study in the Millennium.* Grand Rapids: Baker Book House, 1977.

Surveys the various schools of eschatology and evaluates each in light of history and current debate. 236.ER4

**Feinberg, Charles Lee, ed.** *Jesus the King Is Coming.* Chicago: Moody Press, 1975.

In this symposium the writers tackle some important and difficult themes— all of which pertain to the role and responsibility of the church in the world at the present time. 236.F32

**Hanson, Paul D.** *The Dawn of Apocalyptic.* Philadelphia: Fortress Press, 1975.

Examines the roots of Jewish apocalyptic literature, corrects mistaken impressions that this genre only arose in the intertestamental period, and clarifies the issues between prophetic and apocalyptic writings. 236.H19

**Hoekema, Anthony Andrew.** *The Bible and the Future.* Grand Rapids: Wm. B. Eerdmans Publishing Co., 1979.

A scholarly reconstruction of the history of eschatology with a deft application of biblical teaching to future events. Amillennial. 236.H67B

**Ironside, Henry Allan,** and **Ford C. Ottman.** *Studies in Biblical Eschatology.* 2 vols. in 1. Minneapolis: Klock & Klock Christian Publishers, 1983.

A detailed discussion of such passages as Daniel 9:24-27; Isaiah 61:2,3; Matthew 24-25; and Acts 15:7-29. These studies show the imperative necessity for a literal fulfillment of prophecy. They also build on fulfilled Bible prophecy and demonstrate that the events took place exactly as predicted. Based on that, they make a convincing case for a hermeneutic that interprets all portions of Scripture consistently. 236.IR6 1983

**Ladd, George Eldon.** *The Presence of the Future.* Grand Rapids: Wm. B. Eerdmans Publishing Co., 1974.

A revision of *Jesus and the Kingdom.* In contrast to the former work, which was mildly premillennial, there is nothing in this revision that would prevent Ladd's being classified as an amillennarian. 236.L12P

**\*Mason, Clarence E., Jr.** *Prophetic Problems, with Alternate Solutions.* Chicago: Moody Press, 1973.

The writer has long been recognized for his ability to break out of traditional molds and do his own thinking. An original contribution on a variety of important eschatological themes. 236.M37

**Murray, Iain Hamish.** *The Puritan Hope: A Study of Renewal and the Interpretation of Prophecy.* London: Banner of Truth Trust, 1971.

A significant study of the eschatology of those Puritans who expected revivals before Christ came to bring in the eternal state. 236.M96

**Payne, J. Barton.** *Encyclopedia of Biblical Prophecy.* New York: Harper & Row, 1973.

Of value for its introduction to the interpretation of prophecy, but disappointing in that the author fails to apply some of these principles to the passages he discusses and overlooks several important prophetic chapters in the Bible. 236'.03.P29

**Pember, George Hawkins.** *The Great Prophecies Concerning the Church.* Miami Springs, Fla.: Conley and Schoettle Publishing Co., 1984.

Widely regarded as a standard work since its first appearance in 1909, this study admirably bridges the gap between the OT and the New. It treats the nature and scope of the gospel of Matthew, highlighting prophetic elements that are of importance to all students of God's Word. Appended is a brief analysis of the scope of the book of Revelation with special emphasis being placed on the letters to the seven churches. This is an excellent, far-ranging posttribulational treatment. 236.P36C 1984

————. *The Great Prophecies Concerning the Gentiles, the Jews, and the Church of God.* 4th ed. Miami Springs, Fla.: Conley and Schoettle Publishing Co., 1984.

Originally published in 1887. This work provides a very thorough assessment of the three topics mentioned in the title. Pember links Scripture with Scripture to furnish his readers with an important mosaic of God's prophetic word. Premillennial. 236.P36G 1984

————. *The Great Prophecies of the Centuries Concerning Israel and the Gentiles.* 7th ed. Miami Springs, Fla.: Conley and Schoettle Publishing Co., 1984.

Another volume long overdue for republication. Pember favors a posttribulational return of Christ and expounds various Scriptures pertaining to the promises made to Abraham, Moses, Balaam, Daniel, and others in a practical and meaningful manner. 236.P36I 1984

**\*Peters, George Nathaniel Henry.** *The Theocratic Kingdom of Our Lord Jesus the Christ, as Covenanted in the Old Testament and Presented in the New Testament.* 3 vols. Grand Rapids: Kregel Publications, 1979.

Originally published in 1884. This

work ranks as one of the greatest studies on the interpretation of the prophetic word ever produced. Appears to favor a partial, mid-Tribulation rapture. Discourses at length on the theocratic kingdom concept in both testaments. Indispensable and highly recommended. 236.P44 1979

**\*Price, Walter K.** *The Coming Antichrist.* Neptune, N.J.: Loizeaux Brothers, 1985.

A comprehensive biblical and historical study of the doctrine of the Antichrist. 236.P93

**Russell, David Syme.** *Apocalyptic: Ancient and Modern.* Philadelphia: Fortress Press, 1978.

These lectures cover the historical situation of the apocalyptic writers, their methodology, and their place in the literature of the early church. 236.R89

**Ryrie, Charles Caldwell.** *The Final Countdown.* Wheaton, Ill.: Victor Books, 1982.

Originally published as *The Bible and Tomorrow's News,* this concise résumé of prophetic truth can be read with profit by all who are interested in the future. 236.R99F

**Sneen, Donald.** *Visions of Hope: Apocalyptic Themes from Biblical Times.* Minneapolis: Augsburg Publishing House, 1978.

Introductory survey of Hebrew apocalyptic literature. Treats Daniel, 1 Enoch, the Qumran Documents, Mark 13, and Revelation. 236.SN2

**Strauss, Lehman.** *Prophetic Mysteries Revealed.* Neptune, N.J.: Loizeaux Brothers, 1980.

Contains studies on Matthew 13 and Revelation 2-3. Premillennial. The excellence of these expository studies, in part, is minimized by the omission of a similar study covering Matthew 24-25 and Romans 9-11. Stimulating. 236.ST8

**\*Tan, Paul Lee.** *The Interpretation of Prophecy.* Winona Lake, Ind.: Brethren Missionary Herald Books, 1974.

A cogent argument for the literal method of interpreting prophecy that satisfactorily grapples with the problem. 236'.06.T15

**Travis, Stephen H.** *Christian Hope and the Future.* Downers Grove, Ill.: InterVarsity Press, 1980.

Directs the attention of readers to the leading issues of the last two decades. Probes the parousia, the resurrection of the dead, immortality, and related topics, and discusses the contributions of modern thinkers to eschatology. 236.T69

**Vos, Geerhardus.** *The Pauline Eschatology.* Grand Rapids: Baker Book House, 1979.

First published in 1930. This sequel to *The Kingdom and the Church* (1903) continues the author's treatment of redemptive history as found in Scripture and seeks to elucidate Paul's eschatology. Amillennial. 235.V92 1979

**Wood, Leon James.** *The Bible and Future Events: An Introductory Survey of Last-Day Events.* Grand Rapids: Zondervan Publishing House, 1973.

An overview of God's prophetic program. Significant because it deals with eschatology from the viewpoint of a Semitic scholar. Provides an entirely new perspective on many old, timeworn themes. Premillennial. 236.W81

OLD TESTAMENT PROPHECY

**De Haan, Richard W.** *Israel and the Nations in Prophecy.* Grand Rapids: Zondervan Publishing House, 1967.

Combines trends in the Middle East with a biblical perspective on prophecy. 236.1.D36

**Goldberg, Louis.** *Turbulence over the Middle East.* Neptune, N.J.: Loizeaux Brothers, 1982.

Evaluates and interprets the events taking place in the Middle East in light of the eschatological "shadows" case in the OT. 236.1.G56

**Gray, John.** *The Biblical Doctrine of the Reign of God.* Edinburgh: T. & T. Clark, 1979.

†A detailed, scholarly discussion of the enthronement psalms and the messianic teaching of the postexilic prophets. Traces the idea of the theocracy through the intertestamental period and the ministry of Jesus and concludes with the reign of God in the church. For the discerning reader. 236.1.G79

NEW TESTAMENT PROPHECY

**Hill, David.** *New Testament Prophecy.* Atlanta: John Knox Press, 1979.

Of value for its historic treatment of Jewish apocalyptic literature. Hill bases his assessment of NT prophecy on a form of *Redaktionsgeschichte* that undermines the divine authority of the text. He has perceptive comments on the eschatological views of the different NT writers but is not able to integrate the evidence into a consistent pattern of thought. 236.2.H55

END OF THE CHURCH AGE, SIGNS OF THE TIMES

**Anderson, Robert.** *Forgotten Truths.* Grand Rapids: Kregel Publications, 1980.

First published in 1914. This study directs the attention of readers to Israel, God's chosen people, and describes their role in the prophetic scriptures. Insightful. 236.3.AN2 1980

**Govett, Robert.** *The Locusts, the Euphratean Horsemen and the Two Witnesses.* Miami Springs, Fla.: Conley and Schoettle Publishing Co., 1985.

Writing more than a century before Hal Lindsey, Govett sought to interpret certain phenomena in light of the knowledge of his times. He was justifiably

cautious and sought to find fulfillment of these predictions in light of historic events. We may disagree with Govett (as well as with Lindsey), but the fact remains that he attempted to explain what many others were afraid to handle. 236.3.G74 1985

**Jewett, Robert.** *Jesus Against the Rapture: Seven Unexpected Prophecies.* Philadelphia: Westminster Press, 1979.

A vigorous rebuttal of tribulationalism, with a denunciation of Carl McIntyre, Hal Lindsay, Kenneth Kantzer, and others who look for Christ's return and the inauguration of His millennial reign. Jewett bases his views on seven NT passages. 236.3.J55

**Weber, Timothy P.** *Living in the Shadow of the Second Coming: American Premillennialism, 1879-1925.* New York: Oxford University Press, 1979.

Based on the author's doctoral dissertation, University of Chicago Divinity School, this scholarly, though biased, study purports to find the origins of premillennial thought in the Civil War and identifies adherents to the movement with a socioeconomic group rather than the Scriptures. 236.3.AM3.W38

**White, John Wesley.** *Arming for Armageddon.* Milford, Mich.: Mott Media, 1983.

Traces the tremendous arming for war that characterizes the nations at this time. Expresses the view that this is in fulfillment of Scripture, leading up to the final war, Armageddon. Appears to hold to a posttribulation return of Christ. His illustrative material is helpful. 236.3.W58

**Yamauchi, Edwin M.** *Foes from the Northern Frontiers: Invading Hordes from the Russian Steppes.* Grand Rapids: Baker Book House, 1982.

Discusses the biblical significance of Russia and the reference in the sacred text to the territory and its peoples. Will cause some exponents of prophetic truth to revise their ideas. Well documented. 236.3.Y1

SECOND ADVENT, RAPTURE

**Govett, Robert.** *The Saints' Rapture to the Presence of the Lord Jesus.* Miami Springs, Fla.: Conley and Schoettle Publishing Co., 1984.

C. H. Spurgeon said of this work: "[He] wrote a hundred years before his time, and the day will come when his works will be treasured as sifted gold." Premillennial. 236.4.G74 1984

**Gundry, Robert H.** *The Church and the Tribulation.* Grand Rapids: Zondervan Publishing House, 1973.

A vigorous and technical rejection of pretribulationism by a NT scholar who is convinced of the posttribulational position. Weak in dealing with the material in the gospels. Gundry places his emphasis on data from the epistles. This book will become one of the main supports of posttribulationism. 236.4.G95

**Hughes, Philip Edgcumbe.** *Interpreting Prophecy: An Essay in Biblical Perspectives.* Grand Rapids: Wm. B. Eerdmans Publishing Co., 1976.

Surveys biblical prophecy from the protoevangelium to the book of Revelation. Evaluates the strengths and weaknesses of each school. Provides a clear apologetic for amillennialism. 236.4.H87 (Alt. DDC 220.15)

**Kimball, William R.** *The Rapture: A Question of Timing.* Joplin, Mo.: College Press Publishing Co., 1985.

Those who reject the pretribulation return of Christ will welcome this book. Kimball seeks to discredit pretribulationism on historical grounds. His attack is similar to that of Alexander Reece, and he deals more with the position of Hal Lindsey or the works of W. E. Blackstone,

G. B. Fletcher, W. E. Vine, and C. I. Scofield than with the Scriptures. Disappointing. 236.4.K56

**Lang, George Henry.** *Firstfruits and Harvest: A Study in Resurrection and Rapture.* 3d ed. Miami Springs, Fla.: Conley and Schoettle Publishing Co., 1985.

Focuses attention on the resurrection of believers, the events surrounding the rapture, and the judgment seat of Christ. Makes available informative material on 1 Thessalonians 4 and 1 Corinthians 15. 236.4.L25 1985

**MacPherson, David.** *The Great Rapture Hoax.* Fletcher, N.C.: New Puritan Library, 1983.

Attempts to prove that the doctrine of premillennialism (and a pretribulation return of Christ) originated with Margaret MacDonald and Edward Irving. Ironically, neither were pretribulationists—a point overlooked by the author of this book. Historically, this work lacks substance; biblically, it is deficient; and the writer's phenomenal journalistic skills cannot and do not make up for the inadequacies inherent in this book. 236.4.M24

**Pink, Arthur Walkington.** *The Redeemer's Return.* Ashland, Ky.: Calvary Baptist Church, n.d.

Written shortly before World War I. This book contains a clear exposition of Pink's premillennialism. Readers will find that he also espoused pretribulationism. This position was later abandoned in favor of amillennialism. In the preface, John R. Gilpin, an intimate friend, states that at the time of his death Pink was "on the verge of turning back to his original position" as set forth in this book. 236.4.P65

**Reese, Alexander.** *The Approaching Advent of Christ.* Grand Rapids: Grand Rapids International Publications, 1975.

Long out of print and difficult to procure, this work has now been made available again. It embodies a critical examination of the teachings of J. N. Darby by an ardent posttribulationist. 236.4.R25 1975

**Ryrie, Charles Caldwell.** *What You Should Know About the Rapture.* Chicago: Moody Press, 1981.

In a simple, yet plausible way, Ryrie explains the Bible's teaching regarding Christ's second coming. After reading these chapters no one need ever be in doubt again. 236.4.R99

**Sanders, John Oswald.** *Certainties of Christ's Coming.* Wheaton, Ill.: Harold Shaw Publishers, 1984.

"Promotes deep understanding and enthusiasm about our Lord's return" (Warren W. Wiersbe). 236.4.SA5 1984

**Sproule, John A.** *In Defense of Pretribulationism.* Winona Lake, Ind.: BMH Books, 1981.

A highly commendable critique of Gundry's *The Church and the Tribulation.* Exposes the weaknesses in Gundry's approach, which, of course, assists all readers to come that much closer to the truth. 236.4.SP8

**Travis, Stephen.** *I Believe in the Second Coming of Jesus.* Grand Rapids: Wm. B. Eerdmans Publishing Co., 1982.

Of this scholarly work, Joel Nederhood had this to say: "[It is] a helpful, sober, and up-to-date examination of current eschatological speculation in the light of the full range of biblical material . . . material which leaves the reader with great expectations for the future and a sense of the extreme necessity of proclaiming the gospel of the kingdom." Amillennial. 236.4.T68

**Walvoord, John Flipse.** *The Rapture Question.* Rev. and enl. ed. Grand Rapids: Zondervan Publishing House, 1979.

A clear, definitive presentation of the biblical data pointing to a pretribulation rapture. This revised edition answers briefly and concisely some of the issues raised by Gundry in *The Church and the Tribulation.* 236.4.W17R 1979

MILLENNIUM, KINGDOM AGE

**Feinberg, Charles Lee.** *Millennialism: The Two Major Views.* 3d enl. ed. Chicago: Moody Press, 1980.

Constrasts the premillennial and amillennial systems of interpretation and critiques their eschatological strengths and weaknesses. 236.6.F32 1980

**Govett, Robert.** *Entrance into the Kingdom, or Reward According to Works.* Miami Springs, Fla.: Conley and Schoettle Publishing Co., 1978.

Reprinted from the 1853 edition. This theological treatise discusses the position of the elect of God, the privileges of service, and the reward of their inheritance in Christ. 236.6.G74 1978

**Lang, George Henry.** *The Last Assize: A Review of Universal Restoration, Annihilation, and Punishment.* Miami Springs, Fla.: Conley and Schoettle Publishing Co., 1985.

Contains brief chapters adequately explaining the Bible's teaching on the subject of mankind's accountability to God. Deals specifically with the fate of the unsaved, and presents in clear, understandable terms the theological truths concerning unconfessed sin. Provides preachers with a variety of seed thoughts for a series of messages. 236.6.L25 1985

**Schweitzer, Albert.** *The Mystery of the Kingdom of God: The Secret of Jesus' Messiahship and Passion.* Translated by W. Lowrie. Buffalo, N.Y.: Prometheus Books, 1985.

First published in 1914. This seminal work has had an impact upon German eschatology. Like his *Quest for the Historical Jesus,* this one probes the teaching of Jesus on the kingdom and enhances our understanding of the gospel narratives.

A welcome reprint. 236.6.SCH1 1985

**Tatford, Frederick Albert.** *Will There Be a Millennium?* Eastbourne, Sussex, England: Prophetic Witness Publishing House, 1982.

Basing his treatment of the biblical data on a consistent hermeneutic, Tat-ford deals at length with the different views. He also expounds passages of Scripture relating to the establishment of Christ's kingdom. The task he has undertaken is well-executed. This is a work that can be recommended with confidence. 236.6.T18

## FUTURE STATE

**Winter, David.** *Hereafter: What Happens After Death.* Wheaton, Ill.: Harold Shaw Publishers, 1973.

A brief, scripturally based book that draws on paranormal research to show the reasonableness of the Christian belief in life after death and the expectation of a bodily resurrection. Worthy of serious consideration. 237.1.W68

**Wolff, Richard.** *The Last Enemy.* Grand Rapids: Baker Book House, 1974.

A survey of different attitudes toward death showing that only in Christianity can there be any certainty of a blessed future state. 237.1.W83

### DEATH

**Bailey, Lloyd R.** *Biblical Perspectives on Death.* Philadelphia: Fortress Press, 1979.

Surveys the variety of views on mortality found in the literature of the ancient Near East, the OT, the intertestamental period, and the NT. Evaluates the biblical perspectives and applies the results to present-day circumstances. 237.1.B15

**Custance, Arthur C.** *Journey Out of Time.* Brockville, Ontario: Doorway Publications, 1981.

Written by one of the ablest Christian anthropologists of our day, this work handles very capably the biblical evidence for the difference between time and eternity and of the interval between death and the resurrection of the body. A most valuable treatise. 237.11.C96

**Holden, Douglas T.** *Death Shall Have No Dominion.* St. Louis: Bethany Press, 1971.

A study of the concept of death as found in the synoptic gospels, the Pauline epistles, and the Johannine writings. Thorough, illuminating, and provides a basis for future study. 237.1.H71

**\*Morey, Robert A.** *Death and the Afterlife.* Minneapolis: Bethany House Publishers, 1984.

"[This] work provides an extensive examination of the biblical language related to human destiny beyond death and a careful discussion of the passages of canonical scripture in which the future condition of the lost is considered. The lucid style and the very careful organization of the material make the work readily understandable for a lay audience as well as pastors and Bible scholars" (Roger Nicole). 237.1.M81

### IMMORTALITY

**Harris, Murray J.** *Raised Immortal: Resurrection and Immortality in the New Testament.* Grand Rapids: Wm. B. Eerdmans Publishing Co., 1983.

A thorough work of rare exegetical merit. Harris here continues to develop his thesis that Paul, in dealing with the resurrection, changed his mind between the writing of 1 Corinthians 15 and 2 Corinthians 5. 237.2.H24

**Kelsey, Morton T.** *Afterlife: The Other Side of Dying.* New York: Paulist Press, 1979.

†This full, extensively researched, moderately psychoanalytic, antisupernaturalistic treatise has been written in the wake of the plethora of out-of-the-body experiences recorded by those who "died," only to be resuscitated. The author attempts to walk a theological tightrope between modern parapsychology and the Scriptures. His material is presented well but lacks conviction, particularly when dealing with heaven and hell. 237.2.K29

**Lightner, Robert Paul.** *Heaven for Those Who Can't Believe.* Schaumberg, Ill.: Regular Baptist Press, 1977.

What happens to those who die before they are able to personally trust in Christ? This book gives the answer. It is thorough, adequate, and reliable. It is the kind of work that pastors and counselors can give to parents who are concerned about the eternal state of their deceased or retarded child. 237.2.L62

**\*Salmond, Stewart Dingwall Fordyce.** *The Biblical Doctrine of Immortality.* Minneapolis: Klock & Klock Christian Publishers, 1984.

This "excellent study deserves an honored place in every Christian's library. What [Salmond] has written underscores the believer's hope. His work, therefore, should be studied by all who wish to be faithfully instructed in the Bible's teaching on this important subject" (Foreword). 237.2.SA3 1984

### JUDGMENT, DESTINY OF THE WICKED

**Fudge, Edward William.** *The Fire That Consumes: A Biblical and Historical Study of Final Punishment.* Houston: Providential Press, 1982.

Advocates a temporary duration of "eternal" punishment. "The doctrine of hell and the final judgment of the wicked is much neglected in the modern church. Fudge attributes this in part to the traditional understanding of hell as eternal conscious torment. In a thorough reexamination of the biblical data on this subject, the author concludes that God intends to destroy the wicked rather than make them suffer forever. In this extensive and effective book, Fudge seriously challenges the popular assumption, more Greek than scriptural, that God plans to raise the wicked to immortality in order to inflict upon them everlasting pain. I hope this book will rekindle interest in an important biblical theme which should not be neglected. I know of no book which answers Fudge's powerful case for conditional immortality" (Clark H. Pinnock). 237.4.F95

**Shedd, William Greenough Thayer.** *The Doctrine of Endless Punishment.* Minneapolis: Klock & Klock Christian Publishers, 1980.

A well-reasoned, theologically accurate statement of the doctrine that treats fully, yet concisely, the data contained in the Scriptures. 237.4.SH3 1980

## APOLOGETICS

**Bloesch, Donald George.** *Faith and Its Counterfeits.* Downers Grove, Ill.: InterVarsity Press, 1981.

Examines legalism, formalism, humanitarianism, and the like and shows how and why these are substitutes for genuine religious belief and practice. 239'.08.B62

**Bruce, Frederick Fyvie.** *The Defense of the Gospel in the New Testament.* Rev. ed. Grand Rapids: Wm. B. Eerdmans Publishing Co., 1977.

For an explanation of the value of this work see *The Minister's Library*, vol. 1 (1985), p. 281. This book has retained its popularity despite the passing of the years. 239.B83 1977

**Bush, L. Russ.** *Classical Readings in Christian Apologetics*, A.D. 100-1800. Grand Rapids: Zondervan Publishing House, Academie Books, 1983.

An important collection of the most valuable apologetic works from Justin Martyr to William Paley. Ideal for use with college students. Handy, compact. 239.B96

**Craig, William Lane.** *Apologetics: An Introduction:* Chicago: Moody Press, 1984.

Craig has correctly assessed the contemporary American climate as fundamentally anti-Christian. Given that context, Christians need to be aware of how to present their faith. And that is where Craig's book comes in. It is easy to read, reliable, and provides a powerful apologetic for biblical Christianity. Recommended. 239.C84

**Dyrness, William.** *Christian Apologetics in a World Community.* Downers Grove, Ill.: InterVarsity Press, 1983.

With characteristic thoroughness, Dyrness outlines the path to be followed in the development of a twentieth-century apologetic. The particular strength of Dyrness's approach is his development of a working premise for dealing with non-Christian religions. 239.D84

**\*Eusebius Pamphili.** *Preparation for the Gospel.* 2 vols. Translated by E. H. Gifford. Grand Rapids: Baker Book House, 1981.

Historically, this is one of the finest of the apologetic works of antiquity. Its translation was beset by many difficulties. However, once completed, it placed in the hands of theologians a wealth of information. These volumes, now reprinted for the first time in nearly eighty years, are deserving of careful consideration. 239.EU7 1981

**Evans, C. Stephen.** *Existentialism: The Philosophy of Despair and the Quest for Hope.* With a Response by W. L. Craig. Grand Rapids: Zondervan Publishing House, 1984.

Designed as a treatise in theological apologetics, this work replaces the author's earlier book *Despair: A Moment or a Way of Life.* Pages 92-93 show poor editing. Evans delineates the great lack of existentialism and demonstrates how it is the end of the road for mankind. By contrast, only in biblical Christianity is there a satisfactory explanation of life, the solution to man's quest for meaning, and provision for hope to sustain the heart through all the vicissitudes of life. 239.9.EV1 1984

**Green, Edward Michael Bankes.** *Running from Reality: Is Christianity Just Another Escape?* Downers Grove, Ill.: InterVarsity Press, 1983.

A discerning treatise on contemporary "escapism" in our twentieth-century society, coupled with a persuasive apologetic for Christianity. Helpful. 239.G82

―――. *What Is Christianity?* Nashville: Abingdon Press, 1981.

Well illustrated. This work contains the author's pithy statements about the need for, and the relevancy of, a biblically oriented faith. 239.G82

**\*Hanna, Mark M.** *Crucial Questions in Apologetics.* Grand Rapids: Baker Book House, 1981.

Seeks to resolve the deadlock between presuppositionism and verificationism by developing an epistemological approach to the search for truth that preserves the distinctiveness of special revelation. 239.H19

**\*Howe, Frederic R.** *Challenge and Response: A Handbook of Christian Apologetics.* Grand Rapids: Zondervan Publishing House, 1982.

This introduction to apologetics and Christian evidences is at once biblically and historically valuable. Philosophical speculation is subordinated to the author's primary intent to (1) develop a system of apologetics, (2) focus attention on crucial areas, and (3) challenge believers with the reality of God's self-revelation through Scripture and in Christ. 239.H83

**\*Jeremiah, David.** *Before It's Too Late.* Nashville: Thomas Nelson Publishers, 1982.

Deals with the issues facing the home and the nation. Jeremiah shows how secularism has eroded the foundations of our social and national structure. He points realistically to the only solution, a return to those principles that made this nation great. 239'.4.J47

**\*Keith, Alexander.** *Christian Evidences: Fulfilled Bible Prophecy.* Minneapolis: Klock & Klock Christian Publishers, 1984.

This unique volume was first published in 1831. Thomas Chalmers said of it, "It is recognized in our halls of theology as holding a high place in sacred literature, and it is found in almost every home and known as a household word throughout the land." 239.K26 1984

**Kung, Hans.** *On Being a Christian.* Translated by E. Quinn. Garden City, N.Y.: Doubleday and Co., 1976.

This important, radical Roman Catholic work honestly and courageously presents an *apologia* for a new brand of Christianity that Kung sees taking place in the church. 239.K96

**\*Lewis, Gordon R.** *Testing Christianity's Truth Claims: Approaches to Christian Apologetics.* Chicago: Moody Press, 1976.

An important history of apologetics that not only analyzes the major schools of thought but provides for the development of a distinctively biblical approach to this important aspect of theology. 239.L58

**Mayers, Ronald B.** *Both/And: A Balanced Apologetic.* Chicago: Moody Press, 1984.

Believing that Christianity has been divided over evidentialism and presuppositionalism, Mayers attempts to bring both methodologies together. His success is evident, for he builds his apologetic on a sound exegetical foundation before providing historical illustration and verification for his thesis. 239.M45

**McDowell, Josh,** and **Dale E. Bellis.** *Examining Misconceptions About Christianity.* San Bernardino, Calif.: Here's Life Publishers, 1983.

A practical, well-designed workbook. Provides variety as well as accuracy so that users can virtually teach themselves apologetics. 239.M14M

**\*_____, comp.** *Evidence That Demands a Verdict: Historical Evidences for the Christian Faith.* Rev. ed. San Bernardino, Calif.: Here's Life Publishers, 1979.

A handy work covering bibliology, Christology, eschatology, and human experience. Provides ready access to a variety of source materials. 239.M14 1979.

**_____, and Don Stewart.** *Reasons Skeptics Should Consider Christianity.* San Bernardino, Calif.: Here's Life Publishers, 1981.

Tackles issues pertaining to the Scriptures, the ark, and evolution. Follows a question and answer format. Makes available the kind of information those young in the faith will appreciate as they seek for a secure, rational faith. 239.M14R

**\*Morris, Henry Madison.** *Many Infallible Proofs.* San Diego: Creation-Life Publishers, 1974.

Building on Christianity's historic reliability, the author develops a strong case for supernaturalism. He combines his mastery of scientific data with a careful evaluation of the biblical material. An important work on Christian evidences. 239.M83

**Morris, Thomas V.** *Francis Schaeffer's Apologetics: A Critique.* Chicago: Moody Press, 1976.

Draws attention to weaknesses in Schaeffer's presuppositions—epistemological, metaphysical, cosmological—and though not detracting from his influence, strengthens the foundation for those who wish to build on Schaeffer's system of apologetics. 239'.08.SCH1.M83

**North, Gary, ed.** *Foundations of Christian Scholarship: Essays in the Van Til Perspective.* Vallecito, Calif.: Ross House Books, 1979.

This valuable compilation of essays represents an attempt to apply the philosophical teachings of Van Til to different academic disciplines. Though each chapter makes a distinct contribution to the development of apologetics, some may find Van Tillianism too confining. In spite of this, readers will appreciate the stand taken by the writers, and their contribution is well-deserving of careful reading. Recommended. 239.N75F

*\_\_\_\_\_. *Seventy-five Bible Questions Your Instructors Pray You Won't Ask.* Tyler, Tex.: Spurgeon Press, 1984.

This is an excellent book for high school and college-bound young people to use in group discussions. North adopts a proactive approach and poses questions for discussion that atheists and agnostics find impossible to answer apart from a biblical faith. Bibliographies at the end of each question also direct readers to reliable resource material, thus adding to the benefit of this book. Recommended. 239.N81

**Pratt, Richard L., Jr.** *Every Thought Captive: A Study Manual for the Defense of Christian Truth.* Phillipsburg, N.J.: Presbyterian and Reformed Publishing Co., 1979.

In the Van Tillian tradition. This book fulfills the subtitle by providing a workbook for young laypeople. Pratt has succeeded in making available the kind of practical work that should prove useful in discussion groups. 239.P88

**Purtill, Richard L.** *C. S. Lewis's Case for the Christian Faith.* San Francisco: Harper & Row, 1981.

The author culls information from Lewis's works to provide this impressive introduction to his thought. The result is a fresh and envigorating apologetic for Christianity. 239.L58.P97

*\***Sproul, Robert Charles.** *Objections Answered.* Glendale, Calif.: Regal Books, 1978.

Treats fairly and incisively the evidences of Christianity. The content of this work is excellent, and it should be made available to all inquiring minds. Written in a popular style. 239.SP8

\_\_\_\_\_. *The Psychology of Atheism.* Minneapolis: Bethany Fellowship, 1974.

A powerful apologetic for a biblical faith. Answers the charge that a Christian's belief is motivated by his psychological needs, and shows that an atheist's "faith" is a direct result of his unwillingness to submit to the claims of Christ. 239.7.S7

*\***Wilder-Smith, A. E.** *He Who Thinks Has to Believe.* Translated by P. Wilder-Smith. San Diego, Calif.: Master Books, 1981.

This writer never disappoints us. His material always gives evidence of being well reasoned. Readers will find that this work has distinct apologetic value. 160.W64

# 5

# Devotional Literature

The Christian has to wage a continuous battle between the flesh and the spirit, between the public world and the private world, between the sphere of meetings and deadlines, production schedules and the tyranny of the urgent, and the pursuit of a quiet, godly life. Few people have captured the essence of this kind of tension more eloquently than Anne Morrow Lindberg. As the wife of the famous aviator Charles Lindberg, Anne found it necessary to jealously guard her private world. She wrote:

> I want first of all . . . to be at peace with myself. I want a singleness of eye, a purity of intention, a central core to my life that will enable me to carry out these obligations and activities as well as I can. I want, in fact—to borrow from the language of the saints—to live "in grace" as much of the time as possible. I am not using the term in a strictly theological sense. By grace I mean an inner harmony, essentially spiritual, which can be translated into outward harmony. . . . I would like to achieve a state of inner spiritual grace from which I could function and give as I was meant to in the eye of God.[1]

There are healthy signs in different segments of the Christian community. There is evidence of a turn from externalism to the development of an internal God-consciousness. James Packer's *Knowing God* met a genuine need, and the publication of books by men and women like John MacArthur, Chuck Colson, Jill and Stuart Briscoe, Gordon and Gail MacDonald, Ray Stedman, John Stott, and Chuck Swindoll are beginning to make a difference. Furthermore, the reprinting of works like Bernard of Clairvaux's *The Love of God*, Jonathan Edwards's *Religious Affections*, Teresa of Avila's *Life of Prayer*, and William Wilberforce's *Real Christianity* enable believers in all walks of life to learn from the experiences of those who have preceded them.

1. Anne Morrow Lindberg, *The Gift from the Sea* (New York: Random House, 1978), pp. 23-24.

These works provide the kind of substantive teaching that undergirds our faith and delivers us from the trite, superficial, ephemeral kinds of books that have been produced in such abundance in recent years.

There still remains a need for certain important issues to be addressed. These include:

1. A study of the "fear of the Lord" motif and its relationship to ethics
2. A fresh investigation of the Psalms and their contribution to a deeper, richer, and fuller understanding of the spiritual life
3. The production of a qualitatively different kind of book that can be used in neighborhood Bible studies to the enhancement of the lives of those who participate and to the development of truly caring relationships
4. A fresh understanding of the teaching of *all* of Scripture on the home and a more comprehensive discussion of biblical principles that can be applied to dual-career families
5. The development of biblical derived beliefs, values, and goals that can be applied to all age groups, from children in the home to the specific needs of the elderly

The challenge before us is great. Never before have our resources been so plentiful. Change, however, must always be in accordance with the principles of God's Word. It is only through the renewing of our minds that we come progressively to approve the "good, and acceptable, and perfect will of God" (Romans 12:2).

**Branson, Mark Law.** *The Reader's Guide to the Best Evangelical Books.* San Francisco: Harper & Row, 1982.

A carefully prepared book designed to introduce readers to the writings of others. Covers a variety of subjects of interest to Christians of all denominations. Brief annotations accompany many of the entries. 016.2.B73

**LaHaye, Timothy F.** *The Battle for the Mind.* Old Tappan, N.J.: Fleming H. Revell Co., 1980.

Building on the scriptural teaching about the mind, and ably blending this teaching with an awareness of history and the dangers of humanism, LaHaye gives to his readers a positive statement of the blessings as well as the dangers facing each one of us. 240.L13

**McKinley, John.** *Group Development Through Participation Training.* New York: Paulist Press, 1980.

Complete with a student's manual, this description of groups and the way in which they work also points out the need for and importance of acceptance, support, and growth. 301.1.M21

**McMahon, J. J.** *Between You and You.* New York: Paulist Press, 1980.

Dispenses with the traditional approaches to psychotherapy and concentrates instead on one's inner thought processes. Enables readers to tap into these concepts and provides guidelines on what to look for. Explains the significance of one's inner verbalizations, what they indicate about up-and-coming behavior, and what can be done now to correct it. Moderately psychoanalytic. 158.1.M22

**Skoglund, Elizabeth R.** *To Anger with Love.* New York: Harper & Row, 1977.

Offers sane counsel and encouragement on how to deal with hostility. This is a helpful book to use in lay counselor training. Deals realistically with the ways to handle anger. 152.4.SK4

**\*Sproul, Robert Charles.** *In Search of Dignity.* Ventura, Calif.: Regal Books, 1983.

"As Christians, we see full well the overwhelming spiritual bankruptcy of our society—but the real question is, What do we do about it? This book gives those answers, applying biblical perspectives on worth and value to the home, the workplace, the church, the hospital, the prison. In doing so, Sproul has sounded a call for our times; he has joined the battle between humanist myth and Christian dignity" (Charles W. Colson). 240.SP8

**\*Strauss, Richard L.** *Win the Battle for Your Mind.* Wheaton, Ill.: Victor Books, 1980.

A biblical and theological study of the place and importance of the mind in the life and spiritual growth of the Christian. Also exposes the social forces that, through appeals to the mind, seek to subvert the senses and conform believers to the world's standards and system of values. 248.27.ST8

**Swindoll, Charles Rozell.** *Second Wind: A Fresh Run at Life.* Portland, Oreg.: Multnomah Press, 1977.

Brief, dynamic messages expounding Hebrews 12:1-3. 242.2.SW5S

**Twerski, Abraham J.** *Like Yourself, and Others Will Too.* Englewood Cliffs, N.J.: Prentice-Hall, 1978.

Written by a psychiatrist, this book advocates self-help for a wide variety of common problems. It concludes with a section on when to seek professional help. 158.1.T91

## ETHICS, MORAL THEOLOGY

**Aldrich, Joseph C.** *Love for All Your Worth: A Quest for Personal Value and Lovability.* Portland, Oreg.: Multnomah Press, 1985.

Encourages his readers to embark on a quest to develop a true, God-given lovability that will bring out the best in each one of us. Each chapter is based on a careful exposition of Scripture. This is a challenging book that is deserving of careful reading. 241.4.AL2

**Allen, Joseph L.** *Love and Conflict: A Covenantal Model of Christian Ethics.* Nashville: Abingdon Press, 1984.

†This is an important book. Allen defines "love" in terms of loyalty, steadfastness, and the like and sees conflict as an integral part of working together to resolve differences. He identifies four kinds of conflict in dealing with moral

issues and treats decisively the forms of deception that hinder the resolution of difficulties. Thought-provoking. 241.AL5

**\*Anderson, James Norman Dalrymple.** *Issues of Life and Death.* London: Hodder and Stoughton, 1976.

In this work Sir Norman presents his "Lectures on Contemporary Christianity," University of London, 1975. He establishes his thesis for the development of ethical principles squarely on the sacredness of human life as presented in the Bible. While on the one hand this treatise is a valuable corrective to Ward's *The Divine Image,* on the other it is a bold attempt to provide a rational defense for a viable system of ethics. In this we believe Anderson has been most successful. 171.1.AN2

*_____. *Morality, Law and Grace.* London: Tyndale Press, 1971.

Faces the pressing problems of the present day and provides perceptive counsel and sane solutions to the moral confusion of our contemporary society. Also underscores the relevancy of the Christian message, the uniqueness of its ethic, and the richness of its liberty. An admirable blending of scientific logic, legal expertise, and biblical knowledge. 170.AN2

**Bahnsen, Greg L.** *Theonomy in Christian Ethics.* Exp. ed. Phillipsburg, N.J.: Presbyterian and Reformed Publishing Co., 1984.

Vigorously attacks antinomianism and in doing so seeks to establish law as an antidote to lawlessness. 241.B14 1984

**Barry, Vincent.** *Applying Ethics: A Test with Readings.* Belmont, Calif.: Wadsworth Publishing Co., 1982.

Previously published as *Personal and Social Ethics* (1978). This work underscores the importance of ethics in social relationships. Also treats such topics as sex outside marriage, pornography, abortion, euthanasia, and capital punishment. Secular. 170.B27 1982

**\*Barth, Karl.** *The Christian Life.* Church Dogmatics IV. 4: Lecture Fragments. Translated by G. W. Bromiley. Grand Rapids: Wm. B. Eerdmans Publishing Co., 1981.

Barth's *Church Dogmatics* was left unfinished. Of the projected five volumes, only the first three were completed. Three chapters of the fourth were published, and a final chapter on the ethics of reconciliation was left undone. This book throws considerable light on the political and social trends of Barth's thought. 241.B32

*_____ *Ethics.* Edited by D. Braun. Translated by G. W. Bromiley. New York: Seabury Press, 1981.

Containing lectures delivered at the University of Munster, 1928-1929, these studies expose the timeworn theme of ethics, bring to the fore new problems, and reach some astonishing conclusions. Excellent. 241.B28E

**Beauchamp, T. L.,** and **Norman E. Bowie, eds.** *Ethical Theory and Business.* Englewood Cliffs, N.J.: Prentice-Hall, 1979.

Reviews representative viewpoints on currently controversial topics in business ethics, and takes a fresh look at certain long-forgotten themes. 174.4.ET3B

**Bell, Robert R.** *Contemporary Social Problems.* Homewood, Ill.: Dorsey Press, 1981.

A fitting introduction to the plethora of problems plaguing society today. The topics discussed include those issues spawned by institutions, matters concerning the family, problems related to health, and those connected with crime. Provocative, valuable, enlightening. 362'.042.B41

**Benson, George C. S.** *Business Ethics in America.* Lexington, Mass.: D. C. Heath & Co., 1982.

In the wake of the moral interregnum in America, this work, written from a secular point of view, attempts to provide a basis for the development and implementation of ethical principles in business. 174.4.AM3.B44

**Borgman, Paul.** *TV: Friend or Foe?* Elgin, Ill.: David C. Cook Publishing Co., 1979.

Designed for parents, this work will help them understand their children's needs and experiences and will explain why they so frequently become absorbed with certain programs. 791.42.B64

**Brown, Harold O. J.** *Death Before Birth.* Nashville: Thomas Nelson Publishers, 1977.

A philosophical and historical assessment of the ethics of abortion. Brown directs some difficult questions at the pro-abortion forces. His material is well reasoned, and those who desire to be informed on the issues would do well to read this book. 179.76.B81

**\*Buscaglia, Leo F.** *Living, Loving and Learning.* Edited by S. Short. New York: Holt, Rinehart and Winston, 1982.

Writing with contageous enthusiasm, Buscaglia talks about love and describes how it can be demonstrated, its benefit to the giver and the receiver, and the way to overcome self-defeating forms of behavior. Recommended. 155.2.B96

―――. *Love.* New York: Fawcett Crest, 1978.

Nauseated by superficiality, Buscaglia writes of "love" as a means of enriching our interpersonal relationships and, indeed, our lives. His material is carefully reasoned, and he is never trite. He emphasizes the fact that love *grows,* and describes the process, the possible pitfalls, and also the rewards. Indispensable. 177.7.B96L

**Bustanoby, Andre.** *Can Men and Women Be Just Friends?* Grand Rapids: Pyranee Books, 1985.

Friendships among the ancients were strong and durable. Such, however, is no longer the case. Shallowness, "warm fuzzies," or inhibition prevail today. Understanding and a willingness to be vulnerable are what is needed. To this end Bustanoby has produced a helpful guidebook. Though omitting the reason for the present malaise (described so effectively in D. Reisman's *The Lonely Crowd*), and lacking the optimism of Leo Buscaglia's numerous works, this book nonetheless is deserving of careful reading. 302.3′4.B96C

**Cahn, Edmond.** *The Moral Decision: Right and Wrong in the Light of American Law.* Bloomington, Ind.: Indiana University Press, 1981.

Assesses the connection between the rights of the legal system and the responsibilities of human conduct. 340′.112.C11 1981

**Catherwood, Henry Frederick Ross.** *First Things First: The Ten Commandments in the 20th Century.* Downers Grove, Ill.: InterVarsity Press, 1979.

These studies by a British politician demonstrate not only the abiding relevance of the Decalogue but also illustrate the necessity of men and nations living in accordance with its teaching. 241.52.C28

**Christoff, Nicholas B.** *Saturday Night, Sunday Morning: Singles and the Church.* San Francisco: Harper & Row, 1978.

Draws attention to the neglect felt by singles in churches today and points out ways in which their needs may be met. Christoff has done his research well. He has found out what those in single fellowships think, say, and do. The results are startling. They point to the need for a totally different approach—one in which old clichés and staid moralisms are cast aside and a new approach is adopted based upon a clearer understanding of the example of Christ. 241′.63.C46

**Conn, Walter Eugene.** *Conscience: Development and Self-Transcendence.* Birmingham, Ala.: Religious Education Press, 1981.

Introduces his theme by relating the role of conscience to ethics. Then, describes the place of conscience in human development and self-transcendence. 241.1.C76

**Cosby, Michael R.** *Sex in the Bible: An Introduction to What the Scriptures Teach Us About Sexuality.* Englewood Cliffs, N.J.: Prentice-Hall, 1984.

†A learned, erudite study that ably condenses a vast amount of information into eight fact-filled chapters. 241′.66.C82

**\*Cottrell, Jack.** *Tough Questions—Biblical Answers.* Joplin, Mo.: College Press Publishing Co., 1985.

Believing that the Bible is God's inerrant word, Cottrell applies the teaching of Scripture to such topics as marriage, sex, homosexuality, divorce and remarriage, work, labor, strikes, leisure, capitalism, poverty, and ecology. Excellent. 241.C82

**Davis, John Jefferson.** *Abortion and the Christian: What Every Believer Should Know.* Phillipsburg, N.J.: Presbyterian and Reformed Publishing Co., 1984.

This work on ethics reflects the tensions and conflicts felt by all who are involved in unwanted pregnancies. It tackles the complex social problems while also dealing with intricate philosophical and psychological issues. It succeeds in making Christians aware of what is happening to those caught up in the web of unwanted and unhappy events. 363.4'6.D29

————. *Evangelical Ethics: Issues Facing the Church Today.* Phillipsburg, N.J.: Presbyterian and Reformed Publishing Co., 1985.

Tackles realistically the major issues of our day: birth control, biological engineering, divorce/remarriage, homosexuality, abortion. Provides a well-reasoned discussion on each topic. 241'.04.D29E

**\*Dayton, Edward Risedorph,** and **Theodore Wilhelm Engstrom.** *Strategy for Living.* Glendale, Calif.: Regal Books, 1976.

An important work outlining how anyone may make his life more effective. Advances a unique and insightful key to organizing one's time and harnessing one's resources. Highly recommended. 241.D33 1976

**deWolf, Lotan Harold.** *Responsible Freedom: Guidelines for Christian Action.* New York: Harper & Row, 1971.

A study of Christian ethics from a liberal perspective. Valuable for the sense of responsibility placed on individuals operating within society. Unreliable in some of the conclusions reached. 241.D51

**Diamond, Eugene F.,** and **Rosemary Diamond.** *The Positive Values of Chastity.* Chicago: Franciscan Herald Press, 1983.

This husband-wife team treat chastity as a necessary prerequisite to committed love. Each chapter is clearly reasoned and concise. The difficulty lies in convincing young people within our society to accept the viability of the position presented in this treatise. 241.66.D54

**Dominian, Jack.** *The Growth of Love and Sex.* Grand Rapids: Wm. B. Eerdmans Publishing Co., 1984.

Written by a British psychiatrist, this brief though valuable book reassesses the role of sexuality within a Christian context. He points out the reasons for as well as the fallacies of the liberation movement of the 1960s and shows how one's sexual identity continues to grow throughout life. 241'.66.D66

**Donagan, Alan.** *The Theory of Morality.* Chicago: University of Chicago Press, 1977.

A comprehensive analysis of contemporary morality. Philosophical rather than theological, even though the author ultimately does make a case for the establishment of ethics based on Hebrew-Christian values. 170.D71

**Donnelly, Dody H.** *Radical Love: An Approach to Sexual Spirituality.* Minneapolis: Winston Press, 1984.

"An authentic, deeply-needed prophetic voice, Donnelly understands how the split between body-spirit and male-female rends asunder social peace. Spirituality must be sexual in order to be human" (Malcolm Boyd). 241.4.D71

**Dyck, Arthur J.** *On Human Care: An Introduction to Ethics.* Nashville: Abingdon Press, 1977.

A provocative work that proposes that

ethical principles be taught as a discipline so that people may have a basis for moral choices. 170.D99

**Eidsmoe, John.** *The Christian Legal Advisor.* Milford, Mich.: Mott Media, 1984.

This book "is a delight from start to finish. Without agreeing on all points, I found his analyses excellent, and his perspective and account rich enough to provide one with alternate conclusions. This is a work of major importance, and a must for pastors, churches, lawyers, Christian schools and Christians generally. This is a book on how Christians and their churches can stay alive and active in the days ahead" (R. J. Rushdoony). 241.2.EI2

**\*Ellul, Jacques.** *The Ethics of Freedom.* Translated and edited by W. G. Bromiley. Grand Rapids: Wm. B. Eerdmans Publishing Co., 1976.

The first volume of a projected three-volume series based on Paul's theological virtues. Ellul believes that ethics is, above all, eschatological in character and is based on the principles of Christ's coming kingdom. What he presents is most helpful and deserving of careful reading. 241.EL5

**Evans, Donald.** *Struggle and Fulfillment: The Inner Dynamics of Religion and Morality.* Philadelphia: Fortress Press, 1979.

Designed to bridge the gap between religious belief and moral practice, this book discusses eight traits that, when transformed into virtues, have the ability to guide and govern one's conduct. 241.EV1

**Fitch, William.** *Christian Perspectives on Sex and Marriage.* Grand Rapids: Wm. B. Eerdmans Publishing Co., 1971.

Lifts the subject of sex out of the morass of contemporary literature, exalts it as God's gift to man, and enlarges on the unifying and perfecting aspects of sex in the strengthening of the marriage bond. 241.1.F55

**Fletcher, Joseph.** *The Ethics of Genetic Control: Ending Reproductive Roulette.* Garden City, N.Y.: Doubleday and Co., 1974.

†Pushes situation ethics to new extremes and shows again the depths to which a person may sink after abandoning belief in God's authoritative revelation. 176.F63E

**Forell, George Wolfgang.** *History of Christian Ethics.* Vol. 1: *From the New Testament to Augustine.* Minneapolis: Augsburg Publishing House, 1979.

Commendable for its survey of the development of ethical theories. The reader is left with the impression that Forell's neo-orthodoxy has beclouded the issues and led to the development of a quasi-sophisticated theory in which the teaching of Scripture, even on the part of the early church Fathers, is now distorted to fit a preconceived point of view. Disappointing. 241′.09.F76 v.1

**Foster, Richard J.** *Money, Sex and Power.* New York: Harper & Row, 1985.

This sequel to *Celebration of Discipline* and *Freedom of Simplicity* fails to live up to the expectations created by the earlier works. Some insightful and challenging thoughts are shared with readers, but *Money, Sex and Power* is not as much of a pace-setter as Foster's followers had hoped for. 241.4.F81M

**Frazier, Claude A., ed.** *Should Doctors Play God?* Nashville: Broadman Press, 1971.

Should doctors perform abortions? This work considers the complexity of the problem. Does not offer simplistic solutions. 179.7.F86

**Fromm, Erich.** *The Anatomy of Human Destructiveness.* New York: Holt, Rinehart and Winston, 1973.

Within these pages we have another important discussion that leads the reader into a greater understanding of himself/herself and at the same time opens up new areas of investigation. Fromm's heurism affirms the possibility of self-actualization, and this is a positive departure from Freud's pessimistic prognosis. His humanism is also evident on every page. Although this can be detrimental if taken to extremes, the discussion may help some whose idea of Christianity is marked by passivity to take responsible action. Fromm's personal awareness of the course of violence, coupled with his keen awareness of our American character, makes this book particularly relevant to our generation. Preachers will also find his analysis of human nature to be most insightful and may glean useful quotations or illustrations from his material. 152.5.F91

**Gallagher, John.** *The Basis for Christian Ethics.* New York: Paulist Press, 1985.

Gallagher has long been interested in the process of the acquisition of knowledge and how individuals come to know the truth. He posits four questions in this treatise on ethics: Can human reason discover a basis for moral judgment, or does it lead to ethical relativism? In what way is Scripture a basis of Christian ethics? In applying general norms to a particular situation, how can we arrive at the truth? And, What is the role of the magisterium and the believing community in forming moral judgments? A good discussion. Roman Catholic. 241.G13

**Gamson, William A., Bruce Fireman,** and **Steven Rytina.** *Encounters with Unjust Authority.* Homewood, Ill.: Dorsey Press, 1982.

A book that every pastor and counselor has wanted to obtain so that he could place it in the hands of those confronting situations and pressures brought about by unethical managers, politicians, or shift bosses. 174.G14

**Ganz, Richard L., ed.** *Thou Shalt Not Kill: The Christian Case Against Abortion.* New Rochelle, N.Y.: Arlington House, 1978.

Essays in which deeply commited evangelicals repudiate the permissiveness of our society that allows for abortion on demand, and point the way to a viable, biblical alternative. Deserving of careful reading. 179.76.G15

**Gardner, Reginald Frank Robert.** *Abortion: The Personal Dilemma.* Grand Rapids: Wm. B. Eerdmans Publishing Co., 1972.

This is one of the best books on the subject of abortion. All who are engaged in pastoral or clinical counseling should become thoroughly familiar with what Gardner has written. He tackles openly and honestly the many and varied facets of abortion and discusses the emotional problems as well as the ethical issues that are involved. For those wanting a truly humane discussion, this work is highly recommended. 301.G17

**\*Geisler, Norman Leo.** *Options in Contemporary Christian Ethics.* Grand Rapids: Baker Book House, 1981.

This is an excellent work. Geisler discusses relativism, revelation, and unqualified and conflicting and graded absolutism, but the most important aspect of his book is its powerful critique of the subtle inroads of existentialism and pragmatism and the effect of these fallacious views on the making of ethical decisions. Recommended. 241.G27

**Gill, David W.** *The Word of God in the Ethics of Jacques Ellul.* Metuchen, N.J.: Scarecrow Press, 1984.

This book analyzes the contribution of Jacques Ellul, one of the pioneer social critics of technological society and a prolific writer on theology and ethics. After reviewing the current debate about the role of Scripture and Jesus Christ in ethics, this study presents and critiques

Ellul's views of the Word of God, his basic presuppositions in the development of his ethical theory, and how he applies principles to our modern political and urban-technological milieu. 241.2.EL5.G41

**Goodloe, Alfred, Jane Bensahel,** and **John Kelly.** *Managing Yourself: How to Control Emotion, Stress, and Time.* New York: Franklin Watts, 1984.

The authors advocate a three-step process to effective work habits. They begin by describing the essentials that are necessary for the control of our emotions and show how to make them work for us. The information shared with readers demonstrates how each of us may handle stress and also redeem the time. Their recommendations are helpful and can easily be put into practice. 658.4.G61

**Grant, Brian W.** *From Sin to Wholeness.* Philadelphia: Westminster Press, 1982.

Relates the seven deadly sins to characteristic stages of growth. Reveals insights that come only after carefully integrating psychological and theological truth. Both, however, as man-made disciplines, need to be related to the teaching of the Word of God and regulated by it. 241.3.G76

**Groeschel, Benedict J.** *The Courage to Be Chaste.* New York: Paulist Press, 1985.

Chastity is a much maligned and neglected virtue in our times of moral upheaval and social expectation. Yet for a growing number, it is an appealing alternative to a life of lassitude and indignity. Though tending toward celibacy, this book nonetheless offers some plausible and patent reasons for sexual purity. 241.4.G89

**Gustafson, James Moody.** *Can Ethics Be Christian?* Chicago: University of Chicago Press, 1975.

An analysis of the relationship between moral behavior and Christian belief. Stops short of affirming that a distinctive Christian ethic can be derived only from a commitment to live under the authority of God's revelation of His will to man. 241.G97

**Hamilton, Michael, ed.** *The New Genetics and the Future of Man.* Grand Rapids: Wm. B. Eerdmans Publishing Co., 1972.

Concentrating on the ramifications of genetic engineering (e.g., artificial insemination), the contributors discuss "New Beginnings of Life," "Genetic Therapy," and "Pollution and Health." Kass, Ramsey, and Epstein present well-reasoned papers calling for caution. The other contributors are of a more liberal orientation, and their essays demand careful evaluation. 575.1.H18

**Hampshire, Stuart.** *Thought and Action.* Notre Dame, Ind.: University of Notre Dame Press, 1982.

Hampshire believes that our observations of the world and our intentions to act within it are complementary and interconnected aspects of our lives as human beings. Similarly, he argues against theories of ethics that imagine that a person's moral sentiments are merely expressions of preference—or of universal prescriptions that exist quite apart from the physical, social, and cultural environments in which they are made. He provides a challenging discussion, which those who are of a philosophical bent will appreciate. 170.H17

**Hass, Aaron.** *Teenage Sexuality: A Survey of Teenage Sexual Behavior:* New York: Macmillan Co., 1979.

A recent and, from all accounts, reliable assessment of teenage sexual mores. Based on extensive experimental research, what Hass presents makes sobering reading. Though it is easy for pastors to denounce current social practices—and with good biblical warrant—research has revealed that many teenagers leave the church on account of their inability to correlate the burgeoning sexual awareness with the teaching they receive in church. Moralisms are out of place. What is needed is a new, healthy understanding of sexuality coupled with the ability of those in the church to meet the emotional needs of the young with such love and acceptance that their desire to expresss their sexuality in unac ceptable ways can be controlled. Hass helps pastors realize the dangers of peer pressure (which often results in the kind of behavior described in this book), so as to implement healthy ways to cope with the young person's growth toward maturity. 305.23.H27

**Hauerwas, Stanley.** *Character and the Christian Life: A Study in Theological Ethics.* San Antonio, Tex.: Trinity University Press, 1985.

First published in 1975. This work aims at the establishment of Christian virtues and the formulation of a distinctive Christian ethic. Hauerwas interacts with theological and philosophical issues and in particular treats the theories of Bultmann and Barth and finally Joseph Fletcher. The aim of the book is praiseworthy, but the treatment lacks a sound biblical base. 241.H29 1985

**Hebblethwaite, Brian.** *Christian Ethics in the Modern Age.* Philadelphia: Westminster Press, 1982.

A review of ethical theories culminating with a defense of Christian ethics and a vindication of theological belief rooted in Christian tradition. 241.H35

**Hekman, Randall J.** *Justice for the Unborn: Why We Have "Legal" Abortion, and How We Can Stop It.* Ann Arbor, Mich.: Servant Books, 1984.

Tells the story of his conflict with the Supreme Court over abortion and the consequences that followed. Exposes the moral injustice of abortion on demand. A fine exposé. 363.4′6.H36

**Herron, Orley R.** *A Christian Executive in a Secular World.* Nashville: Thomas Nelson Publishers, 1979.

Develops a biblical philosophy of life for Christian leaders in all spheres of work and service. The counsel he gives is practical and relevant, and the principles he offers for maintaining ethical norms, though also aiming for success, are ones that all can follow. 303.34.H43

**Hollis, Harry, Jr., ed.** *A Matter of Life and Death: Christian Perspectives.* Nashville: Broadman Press, 1977.

Contains lectures on biomedical ethics. Includes in the coverage a treatment of such controversial issues as euthanasia, behavior control, abortion, and genetic engineering. 709.22.H72

**Huggett, Joyce.** *Dating, Sex and Friendship: An Open and Honest Guide to Healthy Relationships.* Downers Grove, Ill.: Inter-Varsity Press, 1985.

Addressed to young people, this practical book seeks to break the stalemate many Christians face when they seek to move in the direction of marriage. Deals realistically with sexual, emotional, and relational issues. Recommended. 241′.66.H87

**Hughes, Gerald J.** *Authority in Morals: An Essay in Christian Morals.* Washington, D.C.: Georgetown University Press, 1978.

Sensing that the moral convictions of Christians are at a low ebb, Hughes sets out to provide a clarion call for a return to a NT morality. Roman Catholic. 241.H87

**\*Hughes, Philip Edgcumbe.** *Christian Ethics in a Secular Society.* Grand Rapids: Baker Book House, 1983.

Believing that Christian ethics is essentially theological in nature, Hughes treats each issue from the sure foundation of the Word of God. As a result, even philosophical matters are brought into conformity with the truth. Excellent. 241.H87

————. *The Control of Human Life.* Grand Rapids: Baker Book House, 1971. Explores the ethical ramifications of birth control from a biblical point of view. 176.4.H87

**\*Inrig, Gary.** *Quality Friendship.* Chicago: Moody Press, 1981. True friendship is a priceless asset. Its costs and rewards are ably described by the author with an abundance of biblical support. 241.6.IN7

**Jones, D. Gareth.** *Brave New People: Ethical Issues at the Commencement of Life.* Grand Rapids: Wm. B. Eerdmans Publishing Co., 1985.

†This book makes a serious attempt to discover what principles are important in making decisions about human life around the time of its inception. Originally published in 1984, the book was later withdrawn from the U.S. market owing to the controversy that it aroused. Though still controversial, it has now been republished in the belief that those responsible for making these tough ethical decisions need to be aware of all sides of the argument. This slightly revised edition contains the author's responses to some of the criticisms leveled against the earlier edition. What is presented here is intended for those who desire to be well-informed. It is *not* designed for neophytes. 174.2.J71 1985

**Jones, Donald G., ed.** *Business, Religion, and Ethics: Inquiry and Encounter.* Cambridge, Mass.: Oelgeschlager, Gunn and Hain, 1982.

These essays portray the tensions that presently exist between the world of business and the church. The writers are cognizant of the problems and apply various philosophical approaches in an attempt to reduce the distance separating these two areas of man's life. Insightful even if they do not suggest a viable model. 174.4.J71

————, **ed.** *Doing Ethics in Business:* *New Ventures in Management Development.* Cambridge, Mass.: Oelgeschlager, Gunn and Hain, 1982.

Reports on some of the unusual new management development programs in ethics training and discusses current business mores. Strikes an important balance between theory and practice. 174.4.J71D

**Joy, Donald M., ed.** *Moral Development Foundations: Judeo-Christian Alternatives to Piaget/Kohlberg.* Nashville: Abingdon Press, 1983.

This well-researched study treats the issues of moral development from a theological point of view and provides readers with a well-integrated assessment of the theories of Jean Piaget and Lawrence Kohlberg, with some interesting alternatives. Recommended. 155.2′5.J84

**Justice, Blair,** and **Rita Justice.** *The Broken Taboo.* New York: Human Sciences Press, 1983.

Treats the problem of incest that, as most pastors and counselors know, is becoming more and more prevalent. Describes the causes and effect on offender and subject. A must for those on the pastoral staff. 306.7.J98

**Kalish, Richard A.,** and **Kenneth W. Collier.** *Exploring Human Values: Psychological and Philosophical Considerations.* Monterey, Calif.: Brooks/Cole Publishing Co., 1981.

Focusing on personal and social values, the authors discuss the different philosophical and psychological issues that undergird human behavior and mental health. Their discussion is stimulating and helpful. 128.K12

**Kirk, Jerry R.** *The Mind Polluters.* Nashville: Thomas Nelson Publishers, 1985.

Charles Colson described this book as "a discerning, well-founded view on the insidious evil of pornography." Kirk discusses the severity of the problem in order to alert those who have not been exposed to serious pornography and may not realize its impact on our society. He believes that through quiet submission or noninvolvement in moral issues we have allowed a small minority to dictate and legislate what is seen in theaters or on television or sold in bookstores. He carefully details the rise of pornography in America, reports on its effects, and then outlines specific steps that individuals and churches can take to fight it. 241'.667.K63

**\*Klotz, John William.** *A Christian View of Abortion.* St. Louis: Concordia Publishing House, 1973.

A candid discussion of the issues and alternatives to abortion. Judicious and conservative. 241'.697.K69

**\*Koop, C. Everett.** *The Right to Live, the Right to Die.* Wheaton, Ill.: Tyndale House Publishers, 1976.

A courageous examination of two contemporary ethical concerns—abortion and euthanasia—by an M.D. who asserts the need for a truly Christian morality. 174.2.K83

**Kunkel, Frances Leo.** *Passion and the Passion: Sex and Religion in Modern Literature.* Philadelphia: Westminster Press, 1975.

Examines the work of sixteen twentieth-century writers, and shows how they have grappled with the seeming polarities of Christ and/or religion and the mystery of sex. 823'.03.K96

**LaHaye, Tim.** *The Hidden Censors.* Old Tappan, N.J.: Fleming H. Revell Co., 1984.

Illustrates the pervasiveness and alarming influence of secular humanism. Exposes the media and the mind-blowing role it plays in forming our opinions, tastes, and beliefs. Shows how the media is controlled by an elite group of liberal, secular, humanist thinkers who seem to be at odds with the values that made America great, such as democracy, Christianity, the family, and tradi-

tional moral absolutes. Having virtually usurped the place of God in our country, those behind the scenes raise up whomsoever they will and put down all who oppose them. This is a timely and important book. 144.AM3.L13

**Lande, Nathaniel,** and **Afton Slade.** *Stages: Understanding How You Make Your Moral Decisions.* San Francisco: Harper & Row, 1979.

Describes the process by which ethical decisions are made and how a person may know right from wrong. Secular. 170.1'9.L23

**Lipmann, Walter.** *A Preface to Morals.* New Brunswick, N.J.: Transaction Books, 1982.

First published in 1929, this work presents the author's alternative to ethics. His work has much to commend it, yet in the final analysis the position advocated by Lippmann is the logical outgrowth of his rejection of the church as he understood it, not of biblical Christianity, which he improperly understood. 170.4'2.L66 1982

**\*Mains, Karen Burton.** *Open Heart, Open Home.* Elgin, Ill.: David C. Cook Publishing Co., 1978.

A rare work that has the power to break down the walls of personal isolation and bring into the lives of believers the *koinonia* fellowship about which we have heard so much. An excellent work for pastors, elders, deacons, their wives, Christians in general, and church libraries. 177.1.M28 1978

**Marston, George W.** *The Voice of Authority.* Vallecito, Calif.: Ross House Books, 1978.

A valuable work setting forth an apologetic for a genuine biblical authority. Uses principles drawn from Scripture as a basis for deciding what is true or false, right or wrong, good or bad. Points the way to certainty in matters of personal conduct. 241.2.M35

**Maston, Thomas Bufford.** *The Con-*

*science of a Christian.* Waco, Tex.: Word Books, 1971.

A well-written treatise on Christian ethics. Abounds in usable illustrations. 241.M39

**Meilaender, Gilbert.** *Friendship: A Study in Theological Ethics.* Notre Dame, Ind.: University of Notre Dame Press, 1981.

Reflects on the place of friendship in philosophical and historical writers of the past, and traces the shift from friendship to work (and its attendant depersonalizing influence) in Western society. A valuable treatise. 241'.676.M47

**\*Murray, Andrew.** *The Believer's Secret of Obedience.* Minneapolis: Bethany House Publishers, 1982.

The reprint of Murray's 1935 classic. 241.4.M96 1982

**Nathansen, Bernard N.,** and **Richard N. Ostling.** *Aborting America.* Garden City, N.Y.: Doubleday and Co., 1979.

Re-examines the abortion controversy, the abortion law, the theories behind the pro-abortionist lobby, and exposes the flagrant abuses being practiced in America today. Highlights the fact that socially this indicates a diminished respect for human life. Challenging. 301.N19

**Neall, Beatrice S.** *The Concept of Character in the Apocalypse with Implications for Character Education.* Washington, D.C.: University Press of America, 1983.

Advocates a return from subjectivity to objective moral values, from secular humanism to a morality rooted in the book of Revelation. For those who have never regarded the Apocalypse as an educational "manual," there is more. Neall champions the cause of biblical absolutes but sees them applied only within the framework of the God-man relationship. There is much that is of value in this treatise. For example, based on truths gleaned from the text, Neall helps man find his identity, his origin, and his destiny. This integrative work is welcomed as

another means whereby some of our inhibited thinking might be stretched to consider portions of Scripture normally overlooked in the formulation of ethics or moral values. 144.3.N25

**Niebuhr, Reinhold.** *An Interpretation of Christian Ethics.* New York: Seabury Press, 1979.

†First published in 1935, this approach to ethics continually warrants attention, even by evangelicals. Niebuhr explores the tension between the "love of Jesus" and the conflicts encountered in a sinful world. Though the writer's points are made carefully and well, the reader cannot but be impressed by the fact that Niebuhr is working from a disadvantaged position. He pays scant attention to Scripture, is ignorant of the theocracy and so cannot properly mediate the conflict between good and evil, and, as with many of his liberal colleagues, emphasizes "love" and ignores God's other attributes. 241.N55 1979

**Oden, Thomas C.** *Should Treatment Be Terminated?* New York: Harper & Row, 1976.

An attempt to develop moral guidelines that will help families and counselors determine whether life-sustaining medical treatment should be terminated. Tackles a difficult and potentially volatile topic with skill and understanding. 174.2.OD2

**Otten, Terry.** *After Innocence: Visions of the Fall in Modern Literature.* Pittsburgh: University of Pittsburgh Press, 1982.

†Dismisses the Genesis account of the Fall as a myth. Treats the concept of lost innocence in contemporary novels. Of value to theologians for its collection and review of relevant information. 809'.9.OT8

**Owen, John.** *Sin and Temptation: The Challenge to Personal Godliness.* Abr. and ed. by J. M. Houston. Portland, Oreg.: Multnomah Press, 1983.

A beautifully produced book that

presents in a popular and pleasing manner the essence of Owen's magisterial work. 241.3.OW2 1983

**Packer, James Innell.** *I Want to Be a Christian.* Wheaton, Ill.: Tyndale House Publishers, 1977.

With the brilliance we have come to expect of this author, Packer expounds the Apostle's Creed, the meaning and significance of baptism (from an Anglican/Episcopal viewpoint), the Lord's Prayer, and the Ten Commandments. Appropriate application is made to the life of the believer. Recommended. 241.52.P12

**Pannenberg, Wolfhart.** *Ethics.* Translated by K. Crim. Philadelphia: Westminster Press, 1981.

†Relates ethics to society and Christianity, theology and law. Deals with the theories of contemporary ethicists as well as issues involving world peace and the unity of mankind. 241.P19

**Pinson, W. M., Jr., comp.** *An Approach to Christian Ethics: The Life, Contribution, and Thought of T. B. Maston.* Nashville: Broadman Press, 1979.

Essays by twenty-three Southern Baptists who comment on the influence of Thomas Bufford Maston on themselves, others, churches, and the denomination. 241.B22A

**Plekker, Robert J.** *Divorce and the Christian: What the Bible Teaches.* Wheaton, Ill.: Tyndale House Publishers, 1980.

A compassionate discussion that grapples with the hard questions and ably applies biblical truth to life's enigmatic questions. This is a good book to place in the church library. 173.1.P71

**Ramm, Bernard Lawrence.** *The Right, the Good and the Happy.* Waco, Tex.: Word Books, 1971.

Cuts across traditional mores and the ethical beliefs held by the conservative wing of the Christian church. Offers solutions that are both pragmatic and existential. Leaves several issues unanswered and openly states that there are some dilemmas the Bible does not address. 241.R14

**\*Reagan, Ronald.** *Abortion and the Conscience of the Nation.* Nashville: Thomas Nelson Publishers, 1984.

During the decade immediately following the *Roe v. Wade* Supreme Court decision in 1973, more than fifteen million unborn children were legally aborted. When one considers that this figure is ten times greater than the loss of all Americans in all of the nation's wars, some understanding of the enormity of the problem becomes apparent. In an unprecedented effort to make the public aware of the importance of the situation, President Reagan addressed the volatile subject of abortion. "Afterwords" were supplied by the Surgeon General, C. Everett Koop, and Malcolm Muggeridge. 363.4'6.AM3.R22

**Roberts, Deborah.** *Raped.* Grand Rapids: Zondervan Publishing House, 1981.

Mrs. Roberts recounts her own experience and then with discretion and understanding describes how rape victims may be helped. 362.8'8.R54

**Rokeach, Milton.** *Understanding Human Values: Individual and Societal.* New York: Free Press, 1979.

In his discussion of desirable core concepts, Rokeach provides an interdisciplinary evaluation of human values and their place in our everyday lives. He furnishes readers with an important forum against which to compare their own ideas. His discussion abounds in illustrative materials. This is a stimulating book that should be of value to the pastor as he seeks to reawaken interest in some long-forgotten virtues. 301.2'1.R63

**Rudnick, Milton L.** *Christian Ethics for Today: An Evangelical Approach.* Grand Rapids: Baker Book House, 1979.

Logical but not necessarily biblical. This book traces the origin of the breakdown in ethical standards, the need for absolutes, and how the Christian community might regain the ground lost over the past four decades. Insightful. 241.R83

**\*Rushdoony, Rousas J.** *The Politics of Pornography.* New York: Arlington House, 1974.

A detailed exposé of pornography with important chapters on such matters as its history and legal battles. Rushdoony probes the foundations of the problem and shows why it has grown to such proportions. He includes in his discussion an examination of the underlying philosophical presuppositions, the pagan origin of the movement, and the violence that it fosters. This is a book that is deserving of widespread circulation. 301.21.R89

**Rychlak, Joseph F.** *Discovering Free Will and Personal Responsibility.* New York: Oxford University Press, 1979.

Emphasizes the importance of free will in the development of a healthy personality. Explains the areas in which growth may be experienced. A good, necessary book. 155.2'34.R96

**\*Ryrie, Charles Caldwell.** *What You Should Know About Social Responsibility.* Chicago: Moody Press, 1982.

Discusses ethical issues and the way in which Christians may impact the milieu in which they live. Ideal for discussion groups. 170.R99

**Sanders, E. P.** *Paul, the Law, and the Jewish People.* Philadelphia: Fortress Press, 1983.

Provides important insights from a Jewish perspective on key passages in the epistles to the Galatians and Romans and argues that a clear understanding of *nomos* cannot be based on Pauline usage, but rather demands a comprehensive view of the OT Scriptures. 241.2.SA5

**Schaeffer, Francis August.** *How Should We Then Live? The Rise and Decline of Western Thought and Culture.* Old Tappan, N.J.: Fleming H. Revell Co., 1976.

Drawing on material found in his earlier works, Schaeffer examines the breakdown of our modern society—in philosophy, theology, art, music, literature, films, and morals—and the crumbling of Christian culture. He pinpoints the reason for the present moral relativity and loss of meaning and calls his readers back to the Bible as the revelation of God's will to man and the only sure foundation on which to build a meaningful future. Recommended. 909.SCH1

**\*_____, and C. Everett Koop.** *Whatever Happened to the Human Race?* Old Tappan, N.J.: Fleming H. Revell Co., 1979.

Assesses the prevalence of, and reasons given for, abortion, infanticide, and euthanasia. Sees in the disregard for life a symptom of advanced breakdown of our social order. This is an important treatise, and Christians in all walks of life should thoroughly master its teaching. 241.SCH1 1979

**Shannon, Thomas A., and James J. DiGiacomo.** *An Introduction to Bioethics.* New York: Paulist Press, 1979.

Contains pointed chapters on hotly debated topics, such as technology, abortion, genetic engineering, and euthanasia. Stimulating. 174.2.SH1

**Simmons, Paul D., ed.** *Issues in Christian Ethics.* Nashville: Broadman Press, 1980.

Essays by leading Southern Baptists. Well researched, informative. 241.SI4 1980

**\*Small, Dwight Hervey.** *Christian: Celebrate Your Sexuality.* Old Tappan, N.J.: Fleming H. Revell Co., 1974.

Grounded in the historic tradition of the Judeo-Christian ethic, this book explains sex as being, first and foremost, God's idea and His gift to mankind. The presentation is both judicious and wholesome, and Christians cannot do other than benefit from Small's discussion. Recommended. 241.6'6.SM1

**Smedes, Lewis B.** *Mere Morality: What God Expects from Ordinary People.* Grand Rapids: Wm. B. Eerdmans Publishing Co., 1983.

Believing that there is inherent in all people a moral principle, Smedes seeks to uncover it and lay bare its essence and function. In doing so he takes ethics out of the realm of Christian mysticism and stresses instead its reasonableness and application to everyday situations. 241.SM3

**Southard, Samuel.** *Ethics for Executives.* Nashville: Thomas Nelson Publishers, 1975.

Writing in a popular style, the author demonstrates how ethics is not only essential to the task of management but influences efficiency as well. He believes that the ancient virtues on which the superstructure of ethics is built are prudence, fortitude, and temperance—the *sine qua non* of sound administrative practice today. 174.S8

**Stafford, Tim.** *A Love Story.* Grand Rapids: Zondervan Publishing House, 1977.

A candid presentation of sexual ethics. Deals with such personal aspects of sexuality as petting, masturbation, and homosexuality. Recommended. 241.ST16L

**\*Steele, Paul E.,** and **Charles C. Ryrie.** *Meant to Last.* Wheaton, Ill.: Victor Books, 1983.

Designed for use in adult Bible study groups, this work treats effectively God's design for marriage and the permanence of the relationship into which a couple enters at the time they exchange their vows. 241.ST3

**Stevens, Edward.** *Business Ethics.* New York: Paulist Press, 1979.

Traces the rise of modern ethical theory from Darwin's "Age of Survival," through Machiavelli's "Rule of Expediency," to the present. Historically this work is of great significance. It lacks a solid biblical base, however, and that militates against its general acceptance. 174.4.ST4

**Stout, Jeffrey.** *The Flight from Authority: Religion, Morality, and the Quest for Autonomy.* Notre Dame, Ind.: University of Notre Dame Press, 1981.

A scholarly reassessment of neo-Hegelian presuppositions with a view to determining an autonomy of morals that is free from religious trappings. 170'.42.ST7

**Tengbom, Mildred.** *Talking Together About Love and Sexuality.* Minneapolis: Bethany House Publishers, 1985.

Following a question and answer format, this work has been written for teens. It succeeds in covering the issues uppermost in the minds of young people and, all things considered, is the kind of book that should be placed in the hands of today's youth. 241'.66.T25

**Thayer, Lee, comp. and ed.** *Ethics, Morality, and the Media: Reflections on American Culture.* New York: Hastings House, 1980.

Answers the question about the impact of mass media on morals and values. Includes a consideration of economic and cultural issues as perceived by experts and sociologists. Explores the major moral issues and their impact on society, standards of journalism, and public taste. 301.16.AM3.ET3

**Tournier, Paul.** *The Violence Within.* Translated by E. Hudson. New York: Harper & Row, 1978.

A clear, definitive explanation of the origin and various manifestations of anger. Well written, stimulating, informative. Recommended. 241.T64V

**Van Tatenhove, Frederick C.** *Ambition: Friend or Enemy?* Philadelphia: Westminster Press, 1984.

†This provocative book meets a need. In it the author assesses the reasons for as well as the characteristics of ambition. He deals mainly with the horizontal issues and does not treat adequately the need for a strong Godward relationship. In spite of this weakness, his discussion is timely and necessary. 155.2'32.V36

**Vincent, Meville O.** *God, Sex and You.* Philadelphia: A. J. Holman Co., 1971.

Grapples with the problems of permissiveness, exposes the fallacies of the *Playboy* philosophy, and seeks to liberate sex from the legalism that surrounds it in so many Christian communities. In addition, Vincent (who is an M.D.) provides practical counsel for both single and married people. His entire discussion is wholesome, objective, and responsible, and what he has written is to be warmly commended. 301.41.V74

**Ward, Edward.** *Values Begin at Home.* Wheaton, Ill.: Victor Books, 1979.

Ideal for adult discussion groups. This work by an outstanding educator and father lays down solid principles for the inculcation of moral values. Excellent. By all means read it, and then introduce it to your church. 249.W21

**Ward, Keith.** *The Divine Image.* London: S. P. C. K., 1976.

Attempts to establish a distinctively Christian foundation for morality based on philosophical presuppositions. Con-

spicuously absent is a solid biblical foundation. 241.W21

**White, John.** *Eros Defiled: The Christian and Sexual Sin.* Downers Grove, Ill.: InterVarsity Press, 1977.

The author, a Christian psychiatrist, tackles in depth and detail the ramifications of premarital and extramarital sex, masturbation, and other forms of deviant sexual behavior. 241.W58

**White, Reginald Ernest Oscar.** *Christian Ethics: The Historical Development.* Atlanta: John Knox Press, 1981.

This sequel to the author's *Biblical Ethics* brings the debate from the first century down to the present time. Assesses the contribution of the leading men together with a critique of their theory and theological/philosophical presuppositions. 241.W58

**Wilson, Jerry B.** *Death by Decision: The Medical, Moral and Legal Dilemmas of Euthanasia.* Philadelphia: Westminster Press, 1975.

Explores the medical alternatives to and legal ramifications of euthanasia. Justifies "death by decision," provided proper legal precautions are taken. 174'.24.W69

**Winward, Stephen F.** *Fruit of the Spirit.* Grand Rapids: Wm. B. Eerdmans Publishing Co., 1984.

Because the fruit of the Spirit is the reproducing in the life of the believer the virtues of Christ, Winward begins by outlining Christ's character. He then seeks to show how the nine traits of the Spirit's control can be cultivated. 241.4.W73

## DAILY MEDITATIONS

**Bennett, Arthur, ed.** *The Valley of Vision: A Collection of Puritan Prayers and Devotions.* Edinburgh: Banner of Truth Trust, 1975.

Contains a wealth of insight into the practical application of Puritan theology to the Christian life. Challenging. 242.3.B43

**Davis, Ron Lee,** and **James D. Denney.** *Gold in the Making.* Nashville: Thomas Nelson Publishers, 1983.

Similar in theme to Kushner's *Why Bad Things Happen to Good People.* Breathes hope and encouragement to those grappling with the pain of grief and the agonizing questions that seem to defy a logical answer. Well done. 242.2.D29

**Drescher, John M.** *Spirit Fruit.* Scottdale, Pa.: Herald Press, 1975.

Preachers will welcome this full discussion of Galatians 5:22-23. Drescher expounds, illustrates, and applies (with good stories and helpful anecdotes) Paul's teaching on the fruit of the Spirit. 242.D81

**Hunt, Gladys M.** *The Christian Way of Death.* Grand Rapids: Zondervan Publishing House, 1971.

An intimate book containing consolation for the bereaved, together with thoughtful preparation for those who face death in the family. 242.4.H91

**Israel, Martin.** *The Pain That Heals: The Place of Suffering in the Growth of the Person.* New York: Crossroad Publications, 1982.

The basic thesis of this book is that pain awakens people to deeper levels of the meaning of their existence. It also, incidentally, provides illumination on the biblical teaching regarding suffering. A commendable work. 242.4.IS7

**Lang, George Henry.** *Firstborn Sons, Their Rights and Risks.* Miami Springs, Fla.: Conley and Schoettle Publishing Co., 1984.

This "inquiry" into the "privileges and perils of the members of the Church of God" ably correlates the place of believers in the program of God. Clear and devout and cogently reasoned, it is deserving of serious study. Recommended. 242.L25 1984

**\*Law, William.** *Christian Perfection.* Edited and abridged by E. P. Rudolph. Carol Stream, Ill.: Creation House, 1975.

A devotional classic that was first published in 1726. Recommended. 242.L61 1975

**Linn, Mary Jane, Matthew Linn,** and **Dennis Linn.** *Healing the Dying: Releasing People to Die.* New York: Paulist Press, 1979.

Using the seven final acts and words of Christ on the cross, these dedicated Roman Catholics discuss the kind of care that can and, indeed, should be extended to those who are dying and to their families. This is a truly compassionate book and offers much to those who can look beyond the sacramentalism of the authors. 242.4.L64

**Llewelyn, Robert.** *All Shall Be Well: The Spirituality of Julian of Norwich for Today.* New York: Paulist Press, 1984.

Based on *Revelations of Divine Love,* this assessment of Julian's teaching on prayer evaluates her devotional life, probes her understanding of spiritual communion, discusses her understanding of prayer as a discipline, and lays bare other aspects of her unique spirituality that may in time prompt others to take a closer look at her writings. All things considered, this is a valuable introduction of Julian's life and thought. 282.42.J94.L77

**Maston, Thomas Bufford.** *God Speaks Through Suffering.* Waco, Tex.: Word Books, 1977.

An important work for counselors as well as those experiencing pain and misfortune. Assures readers of the continuous love of God and imparts a message of hope to replace discouragement or despair. 242.2.M39S

**Schaeffer, Edith.** *Affliction.* Old Tappan, N.J.: Fleming H. Revell Co., 1978.

A discerning volume on the reasons for and responses to tribulation. Excellent. 242'.4.SCH1

**Scroggie, William Graham.** *Paul's Prison Prayers.* Grand Rapids: Kregel Publications, 1981.

Brief devotional studies. Recommended. 242.5.SC5 1981

**\*Swindoll, Charles Rozell.** *Come Before Winter . . . and Share My Hope.* Portland, Oreg.: Multnomah Press, 1985.

These bold, challenging meditations focus on the trials and vicissitudes of life, deal realistically with the enigma of suffering, provide hope in the midst of disillusionment, and always leave the reader confident that God is in control. At times humorous, and on occasion bringing tears to the eyes, these chapters never fail to challenge and encourage. Indexed. 242.SW6C

————. *For Those Who Hurt.* Portland, Oreg.: Multnomah Press, 1977.

Based on 2 Corinthians 1:3-11, these exhortations are designed to bring comfort to the hearts of those who have suffered loss. 242.2.SW5

\*————. *Growing Strong in the Seasons of Life.* Portland, Oreg.: Multnomah Press, 1983.

We are wont to speak of "the seasons of life" and in this way describe the epochs from the cradle to the grave. The chapters in this unique book follow that approach. They deal with winter, the "Season of Reverence"; spring, the "Season of Renewal"; summer, the "Season of Rest"; and autumn, the "Season of Reflection." As devotional gems, these brief chapters are comparable to the best that came from the pen of V. Raymond Edman or any other noted modern writer. 242.SW6

**Wiersbe, Warren Wendell, ed.** *Giant Steps: Daily Devotions from Spiritual Giants of the Past.* Grand Rapids: Baker Book House, 1982.

Contains well-selected excerpts from the messages of fifty-two great pulpiteers of the past. Rich, insightful. 242.2.W63

## EVANGELICAL WRITINGS

**\*Stott, John Robert Walmsey.** *Balanced Christianity.* Downers Grove, Ill.: InterVarsity Press, 1975.

A brief but dynamic discussion of the dilemma facing evangelicals who polarize intellect vs. emotion, conservatism vs.

radicalism, form vs. freedom, and evangelicalism vs. social action. As usual, Stott challenges our thinking, shows the superficiality of much that passes as Christian, and charts a course for the future. Recommended. 243.ST6

## HYMNOLOGY

**Osbeck, Kenneth W.** *One Hundred and One More Hymn Stories.* Grand Rapids: Kregel Publications, 1985.

All the major movements of the Spirit through history have been accompanied by a renewed interest in sacred song. Osbeck discusses different songs and the eras from which they came. His handling of the material is excellent. This book makes delightful devotional reading. Preachers will also find that the material presented can be used to enhance the worship service. We are grateful to him

for his research and for making the benefits of his study available in such a pleasing format. 245.OS1M

**Peters, Dan,** and **Steve Peters.** *Rock's Hidden Persuader: The Truth About Backmasking.* Minneapolis: Bethany House Publishers, 1985.

Deals with the subliminal messages latent in rock groups and their songs. Exposes the issues and describes the effects on the gullible, adoring, easily led public. 780.9.R59.P44

## RELIGIOUS DRAMA, ART, ICONS, SYMBOLS

*Schaeffer, Edith. *Hidden Art.* Wheaton, Ill.: Tyndale House Publishers, 1971.

Believing that Christians should be more rather than less creative than non-Christians, Mrs. Schaeffer shows how we may develop the potential with which God has endowed us. 246.SCH1H

## PERSONAL RELIGION

*Edwards, Jonathan. *Religious Affections.* Classics of Faith and Devotion. Portland, Oreg.: Multnomah Press, 1984.

This well-edited reprinting of *A Treatise on Religious Affections* serves to expose the falsity of modern religiosity that is rooted in self-love and a carnal externalism. Edwards describes a true "heart for God" and how a dynamic internal Godward orientation can be maintained. An excellent treatise; warmly commended. 248.2.ED9 1984

**Martin, Walter Ralston.** *Screwtape Rides Again.* Santa Ana, Calif.: Vision House Publishers, 1975.

Writing in the vein of C. S. Lewis, Martin comments on some modern forms of temptation. He explains certain illusions of our culture and deals with the supposed maxim of the underworld "If you can't convince them, confuse them." 248.2.M36

**Warnke, Michael, David Balsiger,** and **Les Jones.** *The Satan-seller.* Plainfield, N.J.: Logos International, 1972.

An interesting and highly personal odyssey that exposes the dangers of Satan worship. Deserves to be read by every parent and teenager. 248.2.W24

PRAYER, PERSONAL WORSHIP

*Allen, Ronald Barclay,** and **Gordon Lamar Borror.** *Worship: Rediscovering the Missing Jewel.* Portland, Oreg.: Multnomah Press, 1982.

In this refreshing book worship is defined and analyzed, and the biblical teaching is expounded. It could revolutionize each Christian's relationship with the living God. Recommended. 248.3.AL5W

**Barth, Karl.** *Prayer.* 2d ed. Edited by D. E. Saliers. Philadelphia: Westminster Press, 1985.

In his straightforward exposition on prayer, Barth creates a striking interpretation of the Lord's Prayer that freshly restates the principles of the Reformers —Calvin, Luther, and the authors of the Heidelberg Catechism—for our times. 248.3'2.B28 1985

**Bloesch, Donald George.** *The Struggle of Prayer.* San Francisco: Harper & Row, 1980.

A neo-evangelical approach to prayer that, in spite of certain inherent weaknesses, seriously confronts the lack of prayer on the part of believers. Bloesch offers some concrete suggestions to remedy the deplorable situation, and his discussion of prayer itself is not tinged with the usual evangelical bromides that mask underlying problems. 248.3'2.B62

**Bryant, David.** *With Concerts of Prayer: Christians Join for Spiritual Awakening and World Evangelism.* Ventura, Calif.: Regal Books, 1984.

"This present volume combines the historical with the practical interest, not only calling to mind the wonderful works of God, as the Psalmist has told us to do, but also offering sound advice on how to promote concerts of prayer" (J. Edwin Orr). 248.3'2.B84

**\*Clowney, Edmund Prosper.** *CM: Christian Meditation.* Nutley, N.J.: Craig Press, 1979.

An important apologetic for genuine meditation. Refutes the false forms current today. Most helpful. 248.3.C62

**Dunlop, Laurence.** *Patterns of Prayer in the Psalms.* New York: Seabury Press, 1982.

†Grounds his approach to the psalms in the Hebrew tendency to emotive forms of ritual and worship and the unity of body and soul. Then discusses prayer in relation to the emotions, memory, awe, and the like. Contains a strong liturgical bias. Roman Catholic. 248.3.D92

**Eims, LeRoy.** *Prayer: More Than Words.* Colorado Springs, Colo.: NavPress, 1982.

Uncovers ways in which believers today may tap the divine resources and experience joy, excitement, and the power of God in their lives. Excellent. 248.3.EI5

**Freer, Harold Wiley,** and **Francis B. Hall.** *Two or Three Together: A Manual for Prayer Groups.* New York: Harper & Row, 1977.

First published in 1954, this book lays emphasis on small groups at prayer. It stresses the ways in which church members may develop a sense of community through small group interaction and participation. 248.3.F87 1977

**Getz, Gene A.** *Praying for One Another.* Wheaton, Ill.: Victor Books, 1982.

Differs from most books on prayer in that it draws attention to the place, importance, and reward of praying with and for others. 248.3.G33P

**Guest, John.** *Only a Prayer Away: Finding Deeper Intimacy with God.* Ann Arbor, Mich.: Servant Publications, 1985.

This is an important, timely book. It

describes prayer as a relationship. "Prayer offers us a link to ultimate fellowship with God. Here is where we find what the saints call 'mystic sweet communion.' One need not be a mystic to enjoy this sweet communion. Prayer is access to God. He hears . . . He responds . . . [He] encourages" (R. C. Sproul). 248.3.G93

**Lockyer, Herbert.** *The Power of Prayer.* Nashville: Thomas Nelson Publishers, 1982.

By ably combining biblical examples of prayer with historical illustrations of those whose prayers moved God to action, Lockyer demonstrates the importance of the Bible's injunctions to pray. Recommended. 248.3'2.L81

**\*MacArthur, John F., Jr.** *The Ultimate Priority: John MacArthur, Jr., on Worship.* Chicago: Moody Press, 1983.

Addressed to individual believers, this timely book on worship reawakens interest and points the way to enjoying these times of intimate fellowship. This is a pace-setting book and deserves careful reading. 248.3.M11W

**Mitchell, Curtis G.** *Praying Jesus' Way: A New Approach to Personal Prayer.* Old Tappan, N.J.: Fleming H. Revell Co., 1977.

An excellent series of expository messages setting forth the principles and practice of effective prayer. Deserves careful reading by every pastor. Can be recommended with confidence. 248.3.M69

**Morgan, George Campbell.** *The Practice of Prayer.* Grand Rapids: Baker Book House, 1971.

Messages containing a vital challenge for believers to return to a vigorous, effective prayer life. Reprinted from the 1906 edition. 248.3.M82 1971

**\*Murray, Andrew.** *The Believer's School of Prayer.* Minneapolis: Bethany House Publishers, 1982.

First published in 1885 under the title

*With Christ in the School of Prayer,* this work deserves to be read and reread by every generation. It is a must for each church library. 248.3′2.M96 1982

**\*Myers, Warren,** and **Ruth Myers.** *Pray: How to Be Effective in Prayer.* Colorado Springs, Colo.: NavPress, 1983.

One of the best works of its kind to appear in many years. Worthy of careful reading. 248.3.M99

**Ray, David.** *The Art of Christian Meditation: A Guide to Your Personal Awareness of God.* Wheaton, Ill.: Tyndale House Publishers, 1977.

A plain, practical guide showing how personal communion with God can become a dynamic force in one's daily life. 248.3.R19

**Sanders, John Oswald.** *Prayer Power Unlimited.* Chicago: Moody Press, 1977.

Following in the steps of Andrew Murray, the writer challenges believers to become active in prayer, particularly in prayer for others. A valuable restatement of the biblical principles. 248.3.SA5

**Scroggie, William Graham.** *How to Pray.* Grand Rapids: Kregel Publications, 1981.

Reprinted from the 1955 edition. Deals effectively with such topics as adoration, confession, petition, intercession, and thanksgiving. 248.3′2.SC5 1981

**\*Stedman, Ray C.** *Talking to My Father: What Jesus Teaches About Prayer.* Portland, Oreg.: Multnomah Press, 1984.

Growing out of his commitment to biblical exposition, these messages ably unfold each passage of Scripture in which the Lord Jesus either illustrated or taught about prayer. The application is timely and relevant. Stands in the tradition of Andrew Murray. Recommended. 248.32.ST3 1984

**Teresa of Avila.** *A Life of Prayer.* Abridged and edited by J. M. Houston. Portland, Oreg.: Multnomah Press, 1983.

Prayer was once described as the "Christian's vital breath." Today few know its secrets, and fewer still know its power. This book draws on the devotional writings of a person whose beliefs are respected by believers of all persuasions. Teresa's symbolism as well as devotion continue to challenge and inspire. This abridgement of her treatise on prayer is most welcome. 248.3′2.T27H 1983

CHRISTIAN LIFE AND PRACTICE

**Allen, Blaine.** *When God Says No.* Nashville, Tenn.: Thomas Nelson Publishers, 1981.

Timely, biblically based studies of the ways in which we may know and do the will of God. Some of the lessons Allen discusses are hard to learn. Their importance, however, may be seen from the fact that failure on our part frequently hinders God's work in our lives. 248.4.AL5

**Allison, Joseph D.** *Setting Goals That Count: A Christian Perspective.* Grand Rapids: Chosen Books, 1984.

A concise statement of the "how to" of setting goals and working toward objectives. What needs clarifying is that beliefs and values precede the establishment of worthy goals. 248.4.AL5

**Applewhite, Barry.** *Christlike.* Chicago: Moody Press, 1984.

Devotional books are plentiful. Their very number can be a deterrent to the earnest Christian who wants something worthwhile but does not have the time or the expertise to sift through the plethora of titles that are available. This book is worthy of a second glance. The author combines sound exposition with a capable handling of the relevant issues. The result is a work that deserves reflective reading. Recommended. 248.4.AP5

**Augsburger, David,** and **John Faul.** *Beyond Assertiveness.* Waco, Tex.: Word Books, 1980.

In the wake of books like *How to Win Through Intimidation,* two Christian psychologists show that there is more to being appropriately assertive than mastering a few techniques. Personal security is needed. This coverage of the issues is a decided step in the right direction. 158.1.AU4

————. *Caring Enough to Forgive/Caring Enough Not to Forgive.* Ventura, Calif.: Regal Books, 1981.

Containing two books in one, this work deals convincingly with true and false forgiveness and covers a whole range of human emotions and situations in the process. 248.4.AU4

**Backus, William.** *Telling Each Other the Truth.* Minneapolis: Bethany House Publishers, 1985.

Applying Paul's admonition to "speak the truth in love," Backus lays down principles for healthy, honest communication. He explains what to say, how to say it, and when the time is right. Recommended. 248.4.B12

**\*Baughen, Michael.** *The Moses Principle: Leadership and the Venture of Faith.* Wheaton, Ill.: Harold Shaw Publishers, 1979.

Discusses the spiritual and administrative skills that made Moses a man of God and the emancipator of the people of Israel. 248.4.B32

**Baumann, J. Daniel.** *Extraordinary Living for Ordinary People.* Irvine, Calif.: Harvest House Publishers, 1978.

Explains in lay terms the process of spiritual change. The messages are based on Galatians 5:22-23. 248.4.B32

**Baxter, James Sidlow.** *Does God Still Guide?* Grand Rapids: Zondervan Publishing House, 1971.

Examines the biblical evidence relating to guidance, considers the requirements, and provides a vigorous rebuttal to the notion that God no longer responds to the needs of His people. 248.4.B33

**Benson, George A.** *What to Do When You're Depressed.* Minneapolis: Augsburg Publishing House, 1975.

Analyzes the causes of depression and helps readers come to an understanding of their own internal dynamics. Then provides sane counsel to help them deal with the issues they have uncovered. 248.4.B43

**\*Bernard of Clairvaux.** *The Love of God and Spiritual Friendship.* Abridged and edited by J. M. Houston. Portland, Oreg.: Multnomah Press, 1983.

Believing that most readers are unacquainted with the great classical writings of the past, Houston provides his readers with a careful introduction to the times of Bernard and his importance in the history of the Christian church. He then furnishes a carefully edited version of this great devotional treatise on the love of God. This is a valuable acquisition. We are indebted to the reviser and the publisher for making it available again. It should be in every Christian home. 248.4.B43 1983

**Blamires, Harry.** *Words Made Flesh: God Speaks to Us in the Ordinary Things of Life.* Ann Arbor, Mich.: Servant Books, 1985.

This is a fine work. It contains a unique blend of spiritual insight coupled with the kind of literary acumen that is the delight of those who have come to appreciate a thoughtful presentation of a worthy theme. 248.4.B58

**\*Bliss, Edwin C.** *Doing It Now: A Twelve-Step Program for Curing Procrastination and Achieving Your Goals.* New York: Charles Scribner's Sons, 1983.

Although procrastination is the primary reason for failing to achieve a rich, fulfilling life, fear of success, depression, shyness, inadequate information, indecision, clutter, disorganization, and stress all lead us to put off until tomorrow what should be done today. Through procrastination goals are not established, timetables are not set, and our full potential is never realized. That is why we need this book. It is based on proved methods, and its helpful question-and-answer format makes it easy to read. 158.1.B61

**Boice, James Montgomery.** *How to Live the Christian Life.* Chicago: Moody Press, 1982.

First published in 1973 under the title *How to Really Live It Up,* this study of the basic truths of Christianity provides practical pointers for earnest Christians. The book has been well written and lends itself for use by church discussion groups. 248.48.B63 1982

**\*Booher, Dianna Daniels.** *Getting Along with People Who Don't Get Along.* Nashville: Broadman Press, 1984.

A helpful book treating interpersonal relationships and interpersonal communication in the church. 302.3'4.B63

**Bowman, George M.** *Clock Wise.* Old Tappan, N.J.: Fleming H. Revell Co., 1979.

Discusses the way in which believers may plan their lives, work, and recreation so as to make the most of the time God has given them. 248.4.B67C

**Bramson, Robert M.** *Coping with Difficult People.* Garden City, N.Y.: Doubleday and Co., 1981.

Written for those in business, this work provides helpful clues to working with difficult people. Many of the principles explained by the author apply to those in the church as well. 658.3.B73

**Brenner, Charles.** *The Mind in Conflict.* New York: International Universities Press, 1982.

Explains in understandable terms the complex dynamics underlying mental and emotional conflict. Comprehensive, lucid. 150.19.B75

**Briscoe, D. Stuart.** *Spirit Life.* Old Tappan, N.J.: Fleming H. Revell Co., 1983.

Messages on the fruit of the Spirit (Galatians 5). Each discussion draws on the whole range of Scripture so that the explanation of the manner in which each virtue is developed is well rounded. The truth is then applied to life situations in practical ways. 248.4.B77

**Brown, Douglas Charles, comp.** *The Enduring Legacy: Biblical Dimensions in Modern Literature.* New York: Charles Scribner's Sons, 1975.

Contains a sampling of biblical material as well as selections of poetry, drama, fiction, and songs from modern literature that reflect the influence of the Bible. 820.8'038.B81

**\*Brownback, Paul.** *The Danger of Self-love.* Chicago: Moody Press, 1982.

Corrects modern concepts of self-love and grounds a proper understanding of love in the Scriptures. This carefully reasoned, perceptive treatise is warmly recommended. 248.4.B81

**Bubeck, Mark I.** *Overcoming the Adversary.* Chicago: Moody Press, 1984.

These contemporary messages reveal the writer's awareness of the various modern manifestations of Satanism, spiritism, and occultism. His exposition of Ephesians 6:10-18 is timely. 248.4'861.B85

**Buckingham, Jamie.** *A Way Through the Wilderness.* Grand Rapids: Chosen Books, 1983.

Though it dates the Exodus in the period of Ramses II, this work does help to put that portion of Israel's history into perspective. Buckingham, who has led tours along the route of the Exodus, vividly recreates the events and then deftly applies the truth to the life of the believer. This is a delightful, well-illustrated book, and we heartily recommend it. 248.4.B85

**Buscaglia, Leo F.** *Loving Each Other: The Challenge of Human Relationships.* New York: Holt, Rinehart and Winston, 1984.

It is ironic that a book on loving, interpersonal relationships between men and women had to come from the pen of an academician/philosopher rather than a theologian/pastor. But that is what has happened, and we are grateful. Though not purporting to be an explanation of *agape* love, Buscaglia has invested "love" with the dignity it deserves, and he has also shown us its absolute necessity. We are indebted to him for this valuable, informative, and discerning study. 302.3′4.B96L

**Calabrese, Alphonse.** *Rx: The Christian Love Treatment.* Garden City, N.Y.: Doubleday and Co., 1976.

A dramatic recounting of an agnostic psychoanalyst's conversion with an explanation of how his new-found values have influenced his outlook on life and his therapeutic practice. 248.4.C12

**Carlson, Dwight L.** *Living God's Will.* Old Tappan, N.J.: Fleming H. Revell Co., 1976.

A stimulating book that avoids the kind of simplistic overgeneralizations so common today. Instead, it gives practical principles from the Bible that assist the reader to come to a knowledge of the will of the Lord. 248.4.C19

**Carter, W. Leslie, Paul D. Meier,** and **Frank B. Minirth.** *Why Be Lonely? A Guide to Meaningful Relationships.* Grand Rapids: Baker Book House, 1982.

Probes the symptoms, causes, and cures of loneliness, and shows the ways in which those who lack a meaningful relationship with another person may develop their spiritual resources as they build bridges to others. 152.4.C24

**Cavanagh, Michael E.** *Make Your Tomorrow Better.* New York: Paulist Press, 1980.

Part of the growing corpus of books designed to help people understand themselves better by becoming more aware of their emotions. Helpful. 158.1.C31

**Christenson, Laurence.** *The Renewed Mind.* Minneapolis: Bethany Fellowship, 1974.

Basing his study squarely on the teaching of the Word of God, Christenson shows us how we may bridge the gap between what we are and what God intends us to be. 248.4.C46

**Coleman, Robert E.** *The New Covenant.* Colorado Springs, Colo.: NavPress, 1984.

Coleman, author of *The Master Plan of Evangelism*, begins his treatment of spirituality by developing a relationship between the blood of Christ and holiness of life. He draws special attention to the sacrifice our Lord made and illustrates the nature of the atonement from the Passover. He also highlights the close relationship between the Word and the blood as a covenant—the blood witnesses to the Word and seals its testimony. Finally, he considers the results of Christ's sacrifice as it applies to the believer's identification with Him in His death and resurrection. This is a warm, devotional book, and it deserves careful reading. 248.4.C68

**Collins, Gary R.** *Calm Down.* Chappaqua, N.Y.: Christian Herald Books, 1981.

From this prolific author comes a book treating briefly, yet perceptively, the causes of tension and anxiety. Recommended. 248.4.C69C

———. *You Can Profit from Stress.* Santa Ana, Calif.: Vision House Publishers, 1977.

The author discusses three different forms of worry, or anxiety, and shows how these create inner distress. He also points out how this state of tension may be turned into opportunities for growth and further personal development. 152.4.C69

**Colson, Charles W.** *Loving God.* Grand Rapids: Zondervan Publishing House, 1983.

In the wake of *Born Again* and *Life*

*Sentence,* Colson probes the love of God and discusses the kind of life-style that should flow from such a realization. His thesis is ably illustrated by references to the writings of Augustine, Calvin, Bonhoeffer, Mother Theresa, and others. 248.4.C71

**Condon, John C., Jr.** *Interpersonal Communication.* New York: Macmillan Co., 1977.

A practical treatise that pastors and educators will do well to read and then apply. 158.2.C75

**Crabb, Lawrence J., Jr., and Dan B. Allender.** *Encouragement: The Key to Caring.* Grand Rapids: Zondervan Publishing House, 1984.

Divided into two parts, this timely treatise deals with the nature of encouragement before discussing the ways in which encouragement may be demonstrated. The result is a valuable work that all pastors should read and that should be in all church libraries. 248.4.C84

**Crane, Thomas E.** *Patterns of Biblical Spirituality.* Denville, N.J.: Dimension Books, 1979.

This brief introduction to biblical spirituality begins with some general guidelines and then studies the experiences of men like Abraham, Moses, Jeremiah, the psalmists, Paul, and Mary. Stimulating. Roman Catholic. 248.4.C85

**Daniels, Madeline M.** *Living Your Religion in the Real World.* Englewood Cliffs, N.J.: Prentice-Hall, 1985.

†This represents an honest attempt to explore the "inner" world and apply religious beliefs to specific situations. The do-it-yourself exercises show a boldness that is refreshing. 248.4.D22

**Davis, Creath.** *Beyond This God Cannot Go.* Palm Springs, Calif.: Ronald N. Haynes Publishing, Inc. 1981.

The precursor of *Lord, If I Ever Needed You It's Now!* Deals realistically with the ways in which persons may come to understand themselves. Stimulating. First published in 1971. 248.4.D29B 1981

————. *Lord, If I Ever Needed You It's Now!* Palm Springs, Calif.: Ronald N. Haynes Publishers, Inc., 1981.

Designed to show how Christians may cope with emotional problems. Insightful. 248.4.D29 1981

**Deffner, Donald.** *You Say You're Depressed.* Nashville: Abingdon Press, 1976.

Another timely self-help book dealing with depression. Offers counsel on how to develop faith, minimize fears, and replace destructive thoughts with positive attitudes and an unselfish concern for others. 248.48.D36

**DeHaan, Richard W.** *Happiness Is Not an Accident.* Grand Rapids: Zondervan Publishing House, 1971.

A discussion of God's plan for a meaningful life. 248.4.D36

**Dobson, James Clayton, Jr.** *Emotions: Can You Trust Them?* Ventura, Calif.: Regal Books, 1980.

The excellence we have come to associate with this writer's books is not in evidence here. Biblically, a case could have been made for two primary emotions: love and fear. A discussion of the negative relational emotions stemming from fear (anxiety, guilt, and hostility) could have provided grist for Dobson's mill. Guilt and anger do find a place in his discussion, but without an adequate biblical foundation. Disappointing. 152.4.D65

**\*Douty, Norman F.** *Union with Christ.* Swengel, Pa.: Reiner Publications, 1973.

Written by an evangelical who is well grounded in theology, this study of one of the central themes of the NT deserves careful reading by all who wish to know more of God's provision for them. 248.4.D74

**DuBrin, Andrew J.** *Bouncing Back:*

*How to Handle Setbacks in Your Work and Personal Life.* Englewood Cliffs, N.J.: Prentice-Hall, 1982.

Though secular in its orientation, this work abounds with practical counsel. It can be read with profit by laypeople, and it is also ideal for use by pastoral counselors. Recommended. 158.1.D85

**Durham, Charles.** *When You're Feeling Lonely: Finding a Way Out.* Downers Grove, Ill.: InterVarsity Press, 1984.

Discusses a common emotion and succeeds in making available some unique insights into the resources—personal and spiritual—that all can develop. 248.4'6.D93

**\*Eims, LeRoy.** *Disciples in Action.* Colorado Springs, Colo.: NavPress, 1981.

Subtitled "A Study of the Apostles' Ministry from Acts." In twenty-eight chapters Eims outlines the way to make disciples so that they in turn will go out to win others also. 248.4.EI5

———. *No Magic Formula.* Colorado Springs, Colo.: NavPress, 1977.

By building on the teaching of the OT, the writer establishes principles that believers may use in the spiritual warfare that faces them each day. 248.4.EI5N

———. *Wisdom from Above for Living Here Below.* Wheaton, Ill.: Victor Books, 1978.

The author's title is reminiscent of William Arnot's work on Proverbs, *Laws of Heaven for Life on Earth.* In this treatment of Proverbs chaps. 1-9, Eims avoids the obvious implication of father-son counsel. Instead of developing a manual on parenting, he applies the text to the lives of believers. The practical content of this book is undenied. Its interpretation and application need careful consideration. 248.4.EI5W

**Emmons, Michael L.,** and **David Richardson.** *The Assertive Christian.* Minneapolis: Winston Press, 1981.

Christians have had impressed on them the need for meekness and have equated this evidence of the Spirit's work in their lives with passivity. Emmons tries to reverse that trend by developing a basis for appropriate self-assertion. 248.4.EM6

**Engstrom, Theodore Wilhelm.** *The Pursuit of Excellence.* Grand Rapids: Zondervan Publishing House, 1982.

Though designed as a tract for the times and aimed at challenging believers in Christ to live up to their full potential, avoid mediocrity, and lead a fulfilling life, this book manifests a lack of creativity as well as originality. 248.4.EN3

———, and **David J. Juroe.** *The Work Trap.* Old Tappan, N.J.: Fleming H. Revell Co., 1979.

This psychological and practical analysis of "workaholism" gives to readers an understanding of its different forms and also shows business people how they can achieve their work goals without sacrificing family, friends, health, and happiness. 248.4.EN3W

**Exel, Godfrey W.** *Live Happily with the Woman You Love.* Chicago: Moody Press, 1977.

Contains pointed admonitions to husbands based on the teachings of the NT. Inspirational. 248.48.EX3

**Faricy, Robert.** *Praying for Inner Healing.* New York: Paulist Press, 1979.

A part of a growing body of literature designed to foster a sense of general well-being. Deals with some very necessary but sorely neglected areas of spirituality. Helpful. Roman Catholic. 248.4.F22

**Ferguson, Sinclair B.** *A Heart for God.* Colorado Springs, Colo.: NavPress, 1985.

"Practical, pastoral, and profound. All who wish to grow in grace should read this superb devotional study. Our debt to [Ferguson] increases with every sentence he writes" (J. I. Packer). 248.4.F38

**Finney, Charles Grandison.** *The Promise of the Spirit.* Compiled and edited by T. L. Smith. Minneapolis: Bethany Fellowship, 1980.

Reveals the essence of holiness teaching that received impetus from Finney's remarkable ministry. 248.4.F49S 1980

**\*Foster, Timothy.** *How to Deal with Depression.* Wheaton, Ill.: Victor Books, 1984.

Defines depression, and then discusses the specific conflicts generated by it. Concludes by describing how this malady may be cured. Insightful and helpful. 152.4.F81

**Gardner, John W.** *Morale.* New York: W. W. Norton and Co., 1978.

The best-selling author of *Excellence* and *Self-Renewal* here provides a discerning discussion of motivation. He addresses himself vigorously to the apathy that characterizes a large segment of the American population and clearly delineates the path to a recovery of national values. 302.3.G17M

**Gendlin, Eugene T.** *Focusing.* New York: Everest House, 1978.

A specialist in actualization therapy, Gendlin shares with his readers those principles that bring about change in one's personality. This is a valuable book for both pastors and counselors, and it is to be hoped that the information contained between these covers will be read and applied. 158.1.G28

**\*Getz, Gene A.** *Serving One Another.* Wheaton, Ill.: Victor Books, 1984.

Directs the attention of readers to the issues involved in spiritual renewal and, in particular, to the teaching of the Bible on servanthood. Getz believes that only as Christians "serve one another" will they be able to maintain an effective witness in the world. Excellent. 248.4.G33S

**Glasser, William.** *Stations of the Mind:*

*New Directions for Reality Therapy.* New York: Harper & Row, 1981.

Basing his approach on Control System Psychology, Glasser develops a thesis for behavior control that helps people achieve a sense of belonging, worth, fun, and freedom. A provocative treatise. 158.1.G46

**Glickman, S. Craig** *Knowing Christ.* Chicago: Moody Press, 1980.

Well-written chapters accurately unfolding the dynamic of "Christ in you, the hope of glory." Recommended. 248.4.G49

**Griffth, Harry C.** *Adventure in Discipleship.* Grand Rapids: Zondervan Publishing House, 1978.

Designed for lay discussion groups, this book treats briefly topics germane to spiritual growth. Will admirably serve the ends for which it was intended. 248.4.G87

**Harcum, Eugene Rae.** *Psychology for Daily Living: Simple Guidance in Human Relations for Parents, Teachers, and Others.* Chicago: Nelson-Hall, 1979.

Describes the basics of human behavior, the kinds of reactions to problems and situations that characterize different kinds of people. Can readily be understood by the average reader. 158.2.H21

**Harrison, Allen F.,** and **Robert M. Bramson.** *Styles of Thinking: Strategies for Asking Questions, Making Decisions, and Solving Problems.* Garden City, N.Y.: Doubleday and Co., 1982.

An epochal work designed to help readers better understand themselves and one another by assisting in recognizing the strengths and weaknesses of each style of thinking and developing strategies for influencing others in the most effective way. Secular. 153.4'3.H24

**\*Hart, Archibald D.** *The Success Factor.* Old Tappan, N.J.: Fleming H. Revell Co., 1984.

Levels a severe yet well-justified critique against the PMA cultists. Shows how their emphasis on positive thinking leads to disillusionment, frustration, and eventual despair. In place of the popular, though empty, illusion associated with "possibility thinking," Hart provides a holistic view based on the Bible. This is an important contribution, and I hope that this book will receive widespread reception. 248.4.H25

**Hauck, Paul A.** *Overcoming Jealousy and Possessiveness.* Philadelphia: Westminster Press, 1981.

This psychodynamic study offers some excellent insights into the nature of jealousy and its effect on the individual. Also shows how those who suffer from either jealousy or possessiveness may overcome these self-centered, destructive, and self-defeating desires. 179.8.H29J

*_____. *The Three Faces of Love.* Philadelphia: Westminster Press, 1984.

†Deals with appreciation, forgiveness, and firmness. Discusses the place of honesty, empathy, and "tough love" in relationships, and, using the principles of RET (Rational-Emotive Therapy), shows how these characteristics may be developed to the enhancement of one's contacts with other people. 158.2.H29

**Hawkins, O. S.** *Tracing the Rainbow Through the Rain.* Nashville: Thomas Nelson Publishers, 1985.

Containing brief sermons on suffering, these studies provide readers with considerable comfort and pastors with valuable illustrations. 248.4′8.H31

**Hendricks, Howard George.** *Taking a Stand: What God Can Do Through Ordinary You!* Portland, Oreg.: Multnomah Press, 1983.

Based on the life of Elijah, these messages challenge, encourage, and direct the believer as he/she progresses through failure to a life of fulfillment. 248.4.H38 1983

**Hocking, David Lee.** *Pleasing God.* San Bernardino, Calif.: Here's Life Publishers, 1984.

A very necessary book showing readers how to reorient their lives, develop a God-centered life-style, and embark on a course of growth that will result in a life of wholeness and dynamic witness. 248.4.H65

**\*Hodge, Melvin Bryant.** *Your Fear of Love.* Garden City, N.Y.: Doubleday and Co., 1967.

The worth of this book cannot be calculated. Though he is writing ostensibly for non-Christians, sound biblical principles undergird all that Hodge has to say. He provides an excellent discussion of the effects of rejection and also lays bare the reasons that some people are unable to establish close relationships. This book should be studied slowly and carefully by all pastors and counselors. 152.4′42.H66

**Hoekema, Anthony A.** *The Christian Looks at Himself.* Grand Rapids: Wm. B. Eerdmans Publishing Co., 1975.

The author is well able to apply psychological and theological concepts to the study of the nature of man and the problem of individual esteem. Though some readers will object to his handling of Romans 7, in the final analysis Hoekema has made an invaluable contribution to the study of the *imago Dei.* 248.4.H67

**\*Howard, J. Grant.** *Balancing Life's Demands: A New Perspective on Priorities.* Portland, Oreg.: Multnomah Press, 1983.

An innovative approach that dispenses with stereotypes and seeks instead to review the biblical teaching on priorities in ways that make sense to harried men and women today. 248.4.H83B

*_____. *Knowing God's Will and Doing It.* Grand Rapids: Zondervan Publishing House, 1976.

A popular exposition of the concept of

the will from a biblical perspective with a fresh and vital look at the practical ramifications of what it means to do the will of God from the heart. 248.4.H83

**Howell, Frank M.,** and **Wolfgang Frese.** *Making Life Plans: Race, Gender and Career Decisions.* Washington, D.C.: University Press of America, 1982.

A work that pastoral counselors will find helpful as they counsel young people in their churches regarding the major decisions of life. 305.9.H83

**Huggett, Joyce.** *Creative Conflict: How to Confront and Stay Friends.* Downers Grove, Ill.: InterVarsity Press, 1984.

Conflict afflicts marriages, including Christian ones. It batters friendships, fellowships, and families. It has a nasty habit of tearing people apart emotionally, leaving behind it a trail of destruction, loneliness, and deep-seated hurt. It is to correct this trend that Huggett has written this perceptive and timely book. All couples should take time to read it and discuss the application of the truth presented to their own lives and their relationship with their children. Only through good modeling can this trend begin to be reversed. 248.4.H87

**Hulme, William Edward.** *Creative Loneliness: A Christian Counselor Helps You Live with Yourself and Others.* Minneapolis: Augsburg Publishing House, 1977.

Designed for those who are single or suffering from the loss of a loved one. This work also treats the problems of those who are lonely in a crowd. Each chapter is filled with important insights, and this book deserves to be read by pastoral counselors as well as those for whom it was written. 248.4.H87

**Hyder, O. Quentin, ed.** *The Whole Book of Health.* Old Tappan, N.J.: Fleming H. Revell Co., 1985.

This compendium by authorities in the areas of exercise and nutrition, self-destructive habits like smoking or imbibing alcohol, the relation of stress to heart attacks, the emotions that stem from mankind's insecurities, the need for relaxation and sleep, and the importance of spiritual growth deserves a place in every home and library. 613.H99

*_____. Don't Blame the Devil.* Old Tappan, N.J.: Fleming H. Revell Co., 1984.

This work applies psychiatric principles to Christian living and discusses at length fourteen of the commonest problems encountered by those who seek to help people grapple realistically with their difficulties. This book is a must for every church library. 248.4.H99D 1984

**Jabay, Earl.** *The God-Players.* Grand Rapids: Zondervan Publishing House, 1970.

Shows the inherent ugliness of a self-controlled life and prescribes the only cure—a life given over to God and lived under the power of the Holy Spirit. 248.4.J11

**Jackson, Edgar Newman.** *Understanding Loneliness.* Philadelphia: Fortress Press, 1981.

Giving evidence of a sensitivity to human need, this work describes the pain of loneliness as well as the ways its anguish may be assuaged. Recommended to all pastoral counselors. 158.2.J13

**Jenkins, Daniel Thomas.** *Christian Maturity and Christian Success.* Philadelphia: Fortress Press, 1982.

An examination of success and failure, power and impotence in Christian living. Uses the life and ministry of Christ to point the way to maturity. 248.4.J41

**Jones, Cliff C.** *Winning Through Integrity.* Nashville: Abingdon Press, 1985.

Disproves the slogans Nice Guys Finish Last and Don't Get Mad; Get Even. Shows how genuine biblical ethics leads to success. 248.4.J71

**Kennedy, Eugene C.** *On Being a Friend.* New York: Continuum Publishing Co., 1982.

In face of the isolation and depersonalization of our era, Kennedy stresses the need for each person to develop meaningful friendships with others. In doing so, he shows how we may become good friends in return. 158.25.K38

**Ketterman, Grace H.** *You Can Win over Worry.* Old Tappan, N.J.: Fleming H. Revell Co., 1984.

Written by a Christian psychiatrist, this work explains the origin and dynamics of worry (or anxiety), before dealing with the specific ways in which the victory over worry may be obtained. 152.4.K51

**\*Klug, Ronald.** *How to Keep a Spiritual Journal.* Nashville: Thomas Nelson Publishers, 1982.

This rewarding volume deals with one of the most important aids yet devised for one's spiritual growth. It provides complete questions, ideas, and the materials needed. Excellent. 248.4'6.K71

**Knapp, Martin Wells.** *Impressions.* Wheaton, Ill.: Tyndale House Publishers, 1984.

First published in 1892. This Arminian discussion of the ways to determine the will of God is as relevant today as when it was first published. The author helps believers distinguish between the true and the false in matters of guidance. 248.4.K72 1984

**Kuiper, Ralph L.** *The Power of Biblical Thinking.* Old Tappan, N.J.: Fleming H. Revell Co., 1977.

Portrays the spiritual struggles of select Bible characters. Delightfully told. Uplifting. 248.4.K26

**LaHaye, Tim,** and **Bob Phillips.** *Anger Is a Choice.* Grand Rapids: Zondervan Publishing House, 1982.

Deals with an emotion common to all of us. Interprets the way in which anger manifests itself in light of the four temperaments devised by Hippocrates. Provides some insightful information, but lacks a sound psychological basis. 152.4.L13A

**Lang, George Henry.** *The Clean Heart.*

Miami Springs, Fla.: Conley and Schoettle Publishing Co., 1985.

Lang ministered throughout Europe and, indeed, around the world. His messages were always well received. What is to be found in this slender volume is a series of messages on the need for purity of life. Recommended. 248.4.L25 1985

———, ed. *The Disciple.* Miami Springs, Fla.: Conley and Schoettle Publishing Co., 1984.

Lang was highly esteemed as a man of God. F. F. Bruce said, "By all these writings, as by his spoken ministry and private correspondence and conversation . . . [G. H. Lang was] for many of us 'an interpreter, one among a thousand.'" Exhaustive, challenging. 248.4.L25 1984

———. *Divine Guidance: Its Reality, Methods, Conditions.* Miami Springs, Fla.: Conley and Schoettle Publishing Co., 1985.

How does God lead? Surely nothing needs to be written on this subject. Wrong. In this book Lang handles the subject of divine guidance with verve and insight. As always, his material is thoroughly biblical. He does not neglect the devotional aspects of his topic but provides the teaching of Scripture on the specific issues encountered in everyday life. 248.4.L25D 1985

**Larson, Bruce.** *The Relational Revolution: An Invitation to Discover an Exciting Future for Our life Together.* Waco, Tex.: Word Books, 1976.

By "hitching his wagon" to changing Christian mores (which have largely turned away from the doctrinal distinctives of the past in favor of that which is experience centered), Larson now finds himself in the van of contemporary evangelicalism. His emphasis is clear. The issues he raises are valid. His treatment, however, lacks a sound foundation, and in spite of its good points, it cannot long survive. 248.48'51.L32R

**Legaut, Marcel.** *True Humanity: Look-*

ing at *Our Desire for Material Things, Love, and Human Solidarity.* Translated by D. Smith. New York: Paulist Press, 1982.

Ably fulfilling the subtitle, this book discusses the essence of life and assists the reader in distinguishing between the transitory and the permanent. Humanistic, but makes for stimulating reading. 248.4.L52

**LeMaire, H. Paul.** *Personal Decisions.* Washington, D.C.: University Press of America, 1982.

Discusses the issues involved in decision-making and interacts with the theories presently in vogue. 153.83.L54

**Lewis, Hywel D.** *The Elusive Self.* Philadelphia: Westminster Press, 1982.

Based on the Gifford Lectures, University of Edinburgh, 1966-1968. Lewis approaches the question of personal identity from philosophical and theological points of view. 126.L58

**Lightner, Robert Paul.** *Truth for the Good Life.* Denver, Colo.: Accent Books, 1978.

"Points out [that] the good life is good because it comes from God and He is good. It is life based upon truth and lived according to the truth" (John W. Peterson). 248.4.L62

**\*Lovelace, Richard F.** *Dynamics of Spiritual Life: An Evangelical Theology of Renewal.* Downers Grove, Ill.: InterVarsity Press, 1979.

Provides a history of spiritual renewal that isolates doctrinal distinctives from those elements that produce spiritual growth. Also deals with the reasons why revivals were shortlived and the results meager. Indexed. 248.4.L94

————. *Renewal as a Way of Life: A Guidebook for Spiritual Growth.* Downers Grove, Ill.: InterVarsity Press, 1985.

Focuses on the need to develop a God-centered, kingdom-centered life-style, and charts a course that he believes will result in growth toward spiritual maturity. 248.4.L94

**\*MacArthur, John F., Jr.** *Keys to Spiritual Growth.* Old Tappan, N.J.: Fleming H. Revell Co., 1976.

A refreshing study covering the major areas of spiritual growth. MacArthur deals with the issues surrounding the place and importance of confession in a unique and wholesome manner. Recommended. 248.4.M11

**\*MacDonald, Gordon.** *Facing Turbulent Times: Dimensions of a Whole Person for These Challenging Days.* Wheaton, Ill.: Tyndale House Publishers, 1981.

Using incidents from the lives of Joseph and Isaiah, MacDonald draws parallels between their respective milieus and our own. He directs the attention of his readers away from the economic and political comparisons and social and interpersonal injustices to the way in which believers may demonstrate a godly authenticity in their attitude and conduct. 248.4.M14

\*————. *Ordering Your Private World.* Nashville: Thomas Nelson Publishers, 1985.

Exhorts his readers with the difference the lordship of Christ can make in their lives. Contains an excellent chapter, "Recapturing My Time." Shows how to order one's spiritual world so as to avoid the traps of externalism. Highly recommended. 248.4.M14

**Machen, John Gresham.** *God Transcendent.* Edited by N. B. Stonehouse. Edinburgh: Banner of Truth Trust. 1982.

First published in 1949. These messages expound the greatness and glory of God and radiate a faith seldom met with today. Recommended. 248.4.M18 1982

**Madden, Myron C.** *Claim Your Heritage.* Philadelphia: Westminster Press, 1984.

This book urges believers to fully live up to their potential by becoming comfortable within the context of their own history. Illustrated with biblical and literary allusions as well as personal examples, it offers fresh understanding of life's experiences and points toward growth that is mental and emotional, spiritual and relational. A healthy emphasis is placed on coming to terms with the way in which we were reared without blaming our parents for our problems. Instead, by maturely assessing the past as well as the present, we are encouraged to embrace our limitations, resolve the problems that may exist, and make meaningful plans for the future. 248.4.M26

**Madow, Leo.** *Love: How to Understand and Enjoy It.* New York: Charles Scribner's Sons, 1982.

Discusses the phases through which love grows as well as some of its aberrations. A clear, psychological analysis. Secular. 158.2.M26

**Mallory, James D., Jr.** *The Kink and I.* Wheaton, Ill.: Victor Books, 1973.

A valiant attempt to integrate psychological principles with a biblical way of life. Each chapter is complete with fresh insights, and the book makes rewarding reading. 248.4.M29

**Martin, Grant L.** *Transformed by Thorns.* Wheaton, Ill.: Victor Books, 1985.

Deals with some of the harsh realities of life and demonstrates how the trials we face can result in personal growth. This is a welcome, practical guide that Christians of all persuasions will come to appreciate as they allow its truths to affect their lives. 248.4.M36

**Maston, Thomas Bufford.** *Why Live the Christian Life?* Nashville: Thomas Nelson Publishers, 1974.

Based on a life-long interest in and an absorption with ethics, Maston demonstrates the superiority of a biblically based model. He does not treat the "fear of the Lord" motif that, according to the OT and NT, is the essence of right conduct. 248.48'61.M37

**Mattson, Ralph,** and **Arthur Miller.** *Finding a Job You Can Love.* Nashville: Thomas Nelson Publishers, 1982.

A practical manual showing how those between jobs or looking for their first one may each assess his gifts, personality, way of doing things, and manner of relating to people. Helps one analyze his strengths and weaknesses and come to a decision on what kind of job to seek. Of help, too, to pastors engaged in counseling youth and the unemployed in their churches. 248.4.M43

**Maxwell, John C.** *Your Attitude: Key to Success.* San Bernardino, Calif.: Here's Life Publishers, 1984.

Contains a series of messages covering an analysis of different outlooks on life, the way to construct positive thought patterns, and the best manner to change wrong thoughts and hurtful behavior. 248.4.M45

**May, Gerald G.** *Will and Spirit: A Contemplative Psychology.* San Francisco: Harper & Row, 1982.

"Provides us with a quantum leap in the understanding of spirituality and psychology. It is the first major work to carefully root the whole human development process in a mature contemplative awareness. The book does wonders in cutting through the confusions and complexities of both the language and content of spirituality and psychology, giving us a lucid and fresh understanding of their relationship" (Tilden H. Edwards, Jr.). 150.19.M45

**Middlemann, Udo.** *Pro-existence.* Downers Grove, Ill.: InterVarsity Press, 1974.

An associate of the late Francis Schaeffer deals objectively with such topics as creativity, work, property, and selfishness. His analysis of our contemporary society forms the basis of his eloquent plea for Christlike living. 248.4.M58

**Mitchell, Curtis G.** *Let's Live! Christ in Everyday Life.* Old Tappan, N.J.: Fleming H. Revell Co., 1975.

An important devotional book that edifies the reader and makes him aware of his spiritual heritage. Recommended. 248.4.M69

**Mostrom, Donald G.** *Intimacy with God.* Wheaton, Ill.: Tyndale House Publishers, 1984.

Seeks to formulate a biblical theology to express the dynamics of the spiritual life. Relates the principles uncovered from his inductive research to the Monday-to-Friday activities of Christian laypeople. 248.4.M85

**Murray, Andrew.** *The Believer's New Life.* Translated by L. P. Lilley. Minneapolis: Bethany House Publishers, 1984.

This new edition, "updated for today's reader" (dustcover), contains all of Murray's *The New Life*. It is valuable as a work of devotion, and it is hoped that this new printing will stimulate believers of all denominations to avail themselves of the benefits of their life in Christ. 248.4.M96N 1984

———. *The Believer's Secret of Living Like Christ.* Minneapolis: Bethany House Publishers, 1985.

This rewritten edition of *Like Christ* should appeal to today's readers. The sensitivity and wise counsel that made Murray a household word have been retained. His depth of spirituality and love for the Lord still are conveyed on every page, and the simple style of writing and deft application of truth to life makes each chapter one that believers will want to savor. 248.4.M96L 1985

**Osborne, Cecil G.** *The Art of Becoming a Whole Person.* Waco, Tex.: Word Books, 1978.

Popular essays dealing with the emotions. Contains good illustrations. Otherwise of minimal help due to the fact that the information presented lacks a sound theological foundation. 248.48′61.OS1

**Osgood, Donald W.** *Pressure Points.* Chappaqua, N.Y.: Christian Herald Books, 1978.

A delightful, practical book outlining in easy-to-read chapters how people can handle stress without coming "unglued." Shows how the techniques advocated in this book will bring about a personal self-awareness that will result in improved health and enhanced relationships. Recommended. 248.4.OS3

**Packer, James Innell.** *Beyond the Battle for the Bible.* Westchester, Ill.: Cornerstone Books, 1980.

Though not as stimulating as *Knowing God*, this work reminds believers of the importance of Christian *living* if the gospel is to spread and the world be evangelized. Packer's reviews of Berkouwer's *Holy Scripture*, Lindsell's *The Bible in the Balance*, and Rogers and McKim's *Authority and Interpretation of the Bible* are included in the appendix. 248.4.P12

**Palau, Luis.** *Heart After God.* Portland, Oreg.: Multnomah Press, 1978.

Vibrant messages based on the spiritual qualities of David, king of Israel. 248.4.P17

**\*Pentecost, John Dwight.** *The Glory of God.* Portland, Oreg.: Multnomah Press, 1978.

An important series of expository messages ably treating the theme of the title. Deserves careful reading by every believer. 248.4.P37

**Peterson, Eugene H.** *A Long Obedience in the Same Direction: Discipleship in an Instant Society.* Downers Grove, Ill.: InterVarsity Press, 1980.

A work like this was inevitable. Based primarily on the book of psalms, these studies explore personal growth and social problems and show that progress in Christian life and service is a long-term project. This is a valuable treatise. Read it. 248.4.P44

———. *Traveling Light: Reflections on the Free Life.* Downers Grove, Ill.: InterVarsity Press, 1982.

Using Galatians as the basis for his elaboration of the theology of freedom,

Peterson expounds the dynamics of a life-style that is at once different and effective. 248.4.P44

**Phillips, Keith W.** *The Making of a Disciple.* Old Tappan, N.J.: Fleming H. Revell Co., 1981.

Helps believers come to grips with Christ's principles of discipleship. 248.4.P54

**Pink, Arthur Walkington.** *Spiritual Growth: Growth in Grace, or Christian Progress.* Grand Rapids: Baker Book House, 1972.

A meaty volume dealing with timeless truths. 248.4.P65 1972

**Porter, Mark.** *The Time of Your Life.* Wheaton, Ill.: Victor Books, 1983.

A clear statement of the ways in which each believer may establish his goals, analyze his progress, and plan for the future. An important contribution. 248.4.P83

**Powell, John.** *Unconditional Love.* Niles, Ill.: Argus Communications, 1978.

Powell states that "there is nothing else that can expand the human soul, actualize the human potential for growth, or bring a person into the full possession of life more than love which is unconditional." He then explains this love in terms of its stages. 248.4.P87

**Pruitt, Carl W.** *What the Bible Says About God's Answers to Personal Problems.* Joplin, Mo.: College Press Publishing Co., 1982.

In thirteen chapters the author covers the teaching of the Bible on the major topics of interest to pastoral counselors. A valuable distillation of the biblical teaching. 248.4.P95

**Raunch, Gerry.** *Handling Conflict: Taking the Tension Out of Difficult Relationships.* Ann Arbor, Calif.: Servant Books, 1985.

This practical book deals realistically with human relationships and the tensions that inevitably arise. Deserves careful reading. 248.4.R19

**Richards, Lawrence O.** *When It Hurts Too Much to Wait: Understanding God's Timing.* Waco, Tex.: Word Books, 1985.

Deals sensitively with painful times spent in the "waiting rooms" of life. Focuses on the believer's experience while waiting for God to act. Provides strong support to those caught in the vicissitudes of life and compares as well as contrasts their desires with the desires of others—biblical characters as well as people Richards has known—and the process through which they passed. Gives to each reader hope in time of painful delay. Recommended. 248.4.R39

**Roberts, Robert C.** *Spirituality and Human Emotions.* Grand Rapids: Wm. B. Eerdmans Publishing Co., 1982.

A bold attempt to correlate the emotional responses of the child of God with the doctrine of the faith he or she professes to believe. Provocative. 248.4.R54

**Rubenstein, Carin,** and **Philip Shaver.** *In Search of Intimacy.* New York: Delacorte Press, 1982.

"Loneliness is both a cause and a consequence of many problems in modern life. The authors of this finely crafted exploration into the dynamics of loneliness provide us with a proper blend of new information, personal insights, and practical suggestions for understanding and repairing this tear in the human fabric" (Philip Zimbardo). 158.2.R82

**Sanders, Randolph K.,** and **H. Newton Malony.** *Speak Up! Christian Assertiveness.* Philadelphia: Westminster Press, 1985.

"This is a helpful and practical book, well-written in an easy-to-read style, enlivened with interesting case histories and 'how-to-do-it' exercises. I especially like the authors' emphasis that assertiveness is *not* the same as selfishness, aggressiveness, or an excuse to manipulate others. Instead, Christian assertiveness is a skillful means of communicating our feelings and desires without hurting or showing disrespect for others.

This book puts assertiveness training in a perspective that is easy to accept and easy to apply" (Gary R. Collins). 248.4.SA5

**Schmidt, Jerry.** *You Can Help Yourself.* Eugene, Oreg.: Harvest House Publishers, 1978.

The use of newsprint and the unprofessional production of this book will militate against its general acceptance. What Schmidt presents, however, is well deserving of widespread circulation. 158.1.SCH5Y

**Seamands, David.** *Putting Away Childish Things.* Wheaton, Ill.: Victor Books, 1982.

A study of the meaning and use of *katargeo* that shows how a Christian may be victorious. Childish things, as Seamands reminds us, do not simply fall away by themselves. They need to be "put away," and this book shows us how. 248.4.SE1P

**Sheehy, Gail.** *Pathfinders.* New York: Wm. Morrow and Co., 1981.

This successor to *Passages* (1976) concentrates on people at the crossroads of life and furnishes readers with information that will help them make decisions without losing the courage to explore new paths and new possibilities. Makes rewarding reading, even though the model of success presented leaves everything to be desired. 305.2'4.SH3P

**Shostrom, Everett L.** *Man, the Manipulator: The Inner Journey from Manipulation to Actualization.* Nashville: Abingdon Press, 1977.

A most valuable work that readily exposes our all-too-human tendencies, then points away from the habits of the past and the coping mechanisms that we have developed to the kind of growth that will result in greater strength and personal fulfillment. 150.13.SH8

**Silverman, Lloyd H., Frank M. Lachmann,** and **Robert H. Milich.** *The Search for Oneness.* New York: International Universities Press, 1982.

An unusually rich volume treating the issues of child development and discussing the problems of psychotic and nonpsychotic children. 616.89.S3

**Simmons, Dale D.** *Personal Valuing: An Introduction.* Chicago: Nelson-Hall, 1982.

A philosophical and psychological inquiry into the attitudes underlying our values and the manner in which these are developed. Good for reviewing the theories of the leading researchers. Lacks a biblical base. 155.2.SI4

**Stedman, Ray C.** *Authentic Christianity: A Fresh Grip on Life.* Portland, Oreg.: Multnomah Press, 1984.

Dealing with what Stedman refers to as "the very heart of the gospel," these messages unfold the dynamics of personal spiritual development. There is no other book quite like this one for clarity, simplicity, and relevance. It is deserving of prolonged study. 248.4.ST3A 1984

*\_\_\_\_\_. Spiritual Warfare: Winning the Daily Battle with Satan.* Portland, Oreg.: Multnomah Press, 1984.

A clear, definitive exposition of Ephesians 6:10-20, laying out precisely and accurately the resources God in Christ has made available to His own. These studies are free of all sectarianism (such as books on holiness frequently exhibit), and readers may safely and confidently rely on this pastor/author's wise exposition. A *must* for every earnest Christian. 248.4.ST3S 1984

**Stendahl, Brita.** *Sabbatical Reflections: The Ten Commandments in a New Day.* Philadelphia: Fortress Press, 1980.

A candid and refreshing discussion of the relevance of the Decalogue for life today. Though not written from an evangelical point of view, these studies may nevertheless be read with profit. 248.4.ST4

*****Stott, John Robert Walmsey.** *Focus on Christ.* London: Wm. Collins Publishers, 1979.

Eight expository messages stressing

the centrality and sufficiency of Christ in the believer's life. 248.4.ST7

*_____. *Your Mind Matters: The Place of the Mind in the Christian Life.* Downers Grove, Ill.: InterVarsity Press, 1972.

A brilliant treatise emphasizing the importance of proper cognitive development in the life and experience of every believer. 248.4.ST7

**Stowell, Joseph M., III.** *Tongue in Cheek.* Wheaton, Ill.: Victor Books, 1983.

A concise exposition of the teaching of Scripture on the use and abuse of the tongue. Recommended. 248.4.ST7

**Strauss, Richard L.** *Getting Along with Each Other.* San Bernardino, Calif.: Here's Life Publishers, 1985.

These messages deal with the reasons for broken relationships, the need to restore friendships, the importance of being honest with one another, the value of learning how to be supportive, and the wisdom behind "keeping your cool" when enduring slander, criticism, or misunderstanding. 248.4.ST8G

**Swindoll, Charles Rozell.** *Dropping Your Guard: The Value of Open Relationships.* Waco, Tex.: Word Books, 1983.

Believing in the need for an authentic and genuine life-style, Swindoll describes many of the masks we wear and shows how these have isolated us from others. The result has been loneliness, fear, and depression. Building on the Scriptures, he treats the ways in which Christians may recover their authenticity. Recommended. 248.4.SW5D

_____. *Killing Giants, Pulling Thorns.* Portland, Oreg.: Multnomah Press, 1978.

Beautifully illustrated, this excellent volume applies biblical principles to the walk and warfare of the believer. 248.4.SW5K

*_____. *Strengthening Your Grip: Essentials in an Aimless World.* Waco, Tex.: Word Books, 1982.

A challenging work expressing in prophetic tones the issues facing us and what we need to do about the present moral and spiritual interregnum. 248.4'899.SW6G

*_____. *Three Steps Forward, Two Steps Back.* Nashville: Thomas Nelson Publishers, 1980.

This devotional work is unique. It focuses attention on the development of Christian character. In these chapters Swindoll describes typical situations in life and shows how believers may grow spiritually by working through the problems they face. Recommended. 248.4.SW6F

**Talbot, Gordon.** *The Breakdown of Authority.* Old Tappan, N.J.: Fleming H. Revell Co., 1976.

A disarmingly simple yet profound assessment of the cause of misery and hurt in the world. Shows that the only realistic and truly rational recourse open to mankind is to acknowledge and willingly submit to God's authority. Recommended. 248.4.T14

**Taylor, Jeremy.** *Holy Living.* New York: Harper & Row, 1971.

An abridgment of the classic *Rules and Exercises for Holy Living,* which was first published in 1650. Spells out the entire duty of man with emphasis on the fact that holiness in life is a condition of wholeness. 248.4.T21 1971

**Tenney, Merrill Chapin.** *Roads a Christian Must Travel: Fresh Insights into the Principles of Christian Experience.* Wheaton, Ill.: Tyndale House Publishers, 1979.

Takes account of certain journeys mentioned in the NT and gleans from them spiritual principles for believers in their Christian pilgrimage. 248.4.T25

*****Thomas, William Henry Griffith.** *Grace and Power.* Nashville: Thomas Nelson Publishers, 1984.

This is one of the *great* books of Christendom. It deals concisely with the problems Christians face in every age: how to make time for prayer, why we often hinder our spiritual growth, the manner in which we may develop our inner resources so as to be able to meet the contingencies of life, and the means God has provided for the development of the spiritual life. Written with clarity and conviction, this book has sustained several generations of readers and brought renewed perspective to the enigmas often encountered in our Christian pilgrimage. 248.4.T36 1984

**Timmons, Howard E.** *Loneliness Is Not a Disease.* Eugene, Oreg.: Harvest House Publishers, 1981.

Exposes the cause of loneliness and shows what people may do to overcome it. A good book, poorly produced on newsprint, however. 248.4.T48L

————. *Maximum Living in a Pressure-cooker World.* Waco, Tex.: Word Books, 1979.

A devotional book that combines biblical orthodoxy with twentieth-century relevancy. 248.4.T48L

**Toon, Peter.** *Free to Obey: The Real Meaning of Authority.* Wheaton, Ill.: Tyndale House Publishers, 1979.

Treats clearly and concisely the fact of sin and the enslavement of mankind to it. Explains the only path to perfect freedom. Recommended. 248.4.T61

————. *Your Conscience As Your Guide.* Wilton, Conn.: Moorehouse-Barlow, 1984.

Meets a felt need for a reliable work that adheres to the Scriptures and at the same time interacts with non-Christian and anti-Christian systems of thought. Recommended. 248.4.T61

**Tournier, Paul.** *The Gift of Feeling.* Translated by E. Hudson. Atlanta: John Knox Press, 1981.

This translation of Tournier's 1979 *La Mission de la femme* discusses the relationship and development of specific emotions to personal growth and one's ability to develop and maintain interpersonal communication. In relating his thesis to the NT, Tournier believes that the Lord Jesus was better understood by the women of His day. 302.T64G

**Tubbs, Stewart L.,** and **Sylvia Moss.** *Interpersonal Communication.* 2d ed. New York: Random House, 1981.

Written as a practical introduction to the dynamics of interpersonal communication. This work treats, in a nontechnical way, all the areas of importance to church members in their relationships with one another. Pastors can also profit from the sage counsel contained in this book. Secular. 153.6.T79 1981.

**Tyrrell, Bernard J.** *Christotherapy II: The Fasting and Feasting Heart.* New York: Paulist Press, 1982.

Like a good disciple, Tyrrell presents the reader with "things old and new." Even the old, however, is set forth in a new light. The result is a fine attempt to synthesize psychology and theology. A provocative treatise. 248.4.T98

**Valdes, Juan de,** and **Don Benedetto.** *The Benefit of Christ: Living Justified Because of Christ's Death.* Abridged and edited by J. M. Houston. Portland, Oreg.: Multnomah Press, 1984.

These Italian Reformers disclose the conviction that burned in their hearts and describe the benefits of justification by faith. They exalt the cross of Christ as the ground of the atonement and the essence of the Christian life. Excellent. 248.4.V23 1984

**Van Kaam, Adrian L.** *Dynamics of Spiritual Self-Direction.* Denville, N.J.: Dimension Books, 1976.

This sequel to *In Search of Spiritual Identity* seeks to apply the spiritual principles of the former work to day-to-day living. Roman Catholic. 248.4.V32D

————. *Living Creatively.* Denville, N.J.:

Dimension Books, 1972.

Formerly published under the title *Envy and Originality*, this humanistic study centers on the manner in which people in all walks of life may discover their sources of originality and achieve self-directed motivation. 248.4.V32L

———. *In Search of Spiritual Identity*. Denville, N.J.: Dimension Books, 1975.

The author, a humanistic scholar of considerable erudition, has already written several important works integrating theology and psychology. In this study he tackles the problem of ego identity. At times he appears to be thoroughly in sympathy with the evangelical beliefs. This book, in spite of differences in terminology, is designed to guide the believer to a place of self-realization through a vital relationship with God. 248.4.V32S

———. *Spirituality and the Gentle Life*. Denville, N.J.: Dimension Books, 1974.

Van Kaam, one of the leading integrationists of psychology and theology in America today, here discusses one manifestation of the fruit of the Spirit and in doing so opens up to his readers the facilitating condition embodied in gentleness. Although steeped in humanism, this work may nonetheless be read with profit. 248.4.V32G

**Wagner, C. Peter.** *Your Spiritual Gifts Can Help Your Church Grow*. Glendale, Calif.: Regal Books, 1979.

Differs from other books on spiritual gifts in that it relates the use of gifts to the building up of the Body of Christ. Subtly presents the principles of church growth. 248.48.W12

***Wagner, Maurice E.** *Put It All Together: Developing Inner Security*. Grand Rapids: Zondervan Publishing House, 1974.

A masterful blending of psychology and theology into a cohesive system of thought that readily reveals how wholeness may be achieved and a poor sense of esteem (Wagner uses the humanistic term "self-esteem"), damaged emotions, and inadequate human relations may be corrected. 158.1.W12

**Waitley, Denis.** *The Double Win*. Old Tappan, N.J.: Fleming H. Revell Co., 1985.

Believing that "success is a two-way street," Waitley provides a distinctively different approach. In this sequel to *Secrets of Greatness* he describes the internal dynamics of what makes people winners. Recommended. 158.1.W13D

**Warlick, Harold C., Jr.** *Conquering Loneliness*. Waco, Tex.: Word Books, 1979.

†Based on the Lentz Lectures, Harvard Divinity School. Demonstrates extensive research and an awareness of human needs. Provides important clues on how to help the lonely find meaningful satisfaction in service and in their relationships. 248.48'61.W24

**Watson, David.** *Called and Committed: World-Changing Discipleship*. Wheaton, Ill.: Harold Shaw Publishers, 1982.

"Transparently clear and ruthlessly straightforward in facing the Bible's often upsetting and bewildering challenges" (J. I. Packer). 248.4.W33

***White, Jerry,** and **Mary White.** *Friends and Friendship: The Secrets of Drawing Closer*. Colorado Springs, Colo.: NavPress, 1982.

Designed to define and motivate the development of biblical friendship. Uncovers principles of friendship latent in the Scriptures with practical suggestions to help the reader cultivate rewarding relationships. A *must* for every church library. 248.4.W58

**Wiseman, James A., trans.** *John Ruusbroec: The Spiritual Espousals and Other Works*. Classics of Western Spirituality. New York: Paulist Press, 1985.

These translations are especially important because Ruusbroec wrote in the fairly obscure language of the Brabantine dialect of Middle Dutch. Evelyn Underhill regarded him as "perhaps the greatest of the mystics of the Church." Now, for the first time in a single volume, some of his more noteworthy writings are available. 248.4.R94W

**\*Woodbridge, John D., ed.** *Renewing Your Mind in a Secular World.* Chicago: Moody Press, 1985.

Despite the evangelical renaissance of the 1950s and 1960s, there is widespread evidence for concern. Believers in all walks of life are struggling to maintain their identity in a world gone awry. The subtle attacks against authority, and in particular biblical authority, have taken a toll. This book assesses the issues and summons Christians to return to a distinctive life-style in which the Word of God is known and its truth applied to all areas of life. Recommended. 248.4.W85

**Woods, C. Stacey.** *Some Ways of God.* Downers Grove, Ill.: InterVarsity Press, 1975.

A wholesome book that, on the one hand, shows the bankruptcy of experientialism, "Madison Avenue" evangelism, and high-powered, statistically minded church-growth techniques and, on the other, calls people back to the plain, simple message of the gospel delivered in the power of the Holy Spirit. 248.4.W86

**Wright, Harry Norman.** *The Christian Use of Emotional Power.* Old Tappan, N.J.: Fleming H. Revell Co., 1974.

An easy-to-read discussion of hostility and anxiety, showing how a believer may attain a better understanding of his emotions and cope with the tensions of everyday living. 248.4.W93

**\*_____.** *Making Peace with Your Past.* Old Tappan, N.J.: Fleming H. Revell Co., 1985.

Similar in scope to Melanie Klein's *Your*

*Inner Child of the Past,* this work reveals how a person may erase the negative effects of the way in which he was reared and change past weaknesses into present strengths. 248.4.W93

**Yankelovich, Daniel.** *New Rules: Searching for Self-Fulfillment in a World Turned Upside Down.* New York: Random House, 1981.

A secular description of modern man's search for fulfillment in an era of changing values and economic uncertainty. Stimulating and very revealing. 973.Y1

WITNESSING

**Eims, LeRoy.** *The Lost Art of Disciple Making.* Grand Rapids: Zondervan Publishing House, 1978.

A valuable book that should be an integral part of every seminarian's training. Highly recommended. 248.5.EI5L

**\*Hartman, Douglas,** and **Douglas Sutherland.** *Guidebook to Discipleship.* Irvine, Calif.: Harvest House Publishers, 1976.

This valuable book describes the principles of disciple-making that the authors have tried and found to be effective. The treatment is biblically sound, and all Christian workers will find the information helpful. 248.5.H25

**Hauck, Kenneth C.** *Christian Caregiving: A Way of Life.* Minneapolis: Augsburg Publishing House, 1984.

Outlines a course of action for the training of laypeople. Demonstrates how they can be used to meet the needs of those who hurt. 248.5.H29

**Hendricks, Howard George,** and **Ted Miller.** *Say It with Love.* Wheaton, Ill.: Victor Books, 1973.

An important, *new* approach to personal evangelism. Ideal for use in group training sessions. 248.5.H38

**Johnson, Ron, Joseph W. Hinkle,** and **Charles M. Lowry.** *Oikos: A Practical Ap-*

*proach to Family Evangelism.* Nashville: Broadman Press, 1982.

Points the way to using one's home for evangelistic purposes. Shows how this strengthens a family and serves as a vital arm of the outreach ministry of the church. 248.5.J63

**Kromminga, Carl G.** *Bringing Good News to Neighbors.* Grand Rapids: Baker Book House, 1975.

Grapples with the issue of lay witnessing in the NT and in the history of the church. Practical, relevant. Reformed. 248.5.K92

**Mayhall, Jack.** *Discipleship: The Price and the Prize.* Wheaton, Ill.: Victor Books, 1984.

Explains in clear, concise terms the way in which a believer may grow in grace and become a true follower of Christ. Recommended. 248.5.M45

**McDill, Wayne.** *Making Friends for Christ.* Nashville: Broadman Press, 1979.

Capitalizes on human need for relationship and shows how believers may use their homes to establish friendships with a view to winning people to Christ. 248.5.M14

**Metzger, Will.** *Tell the Truth: The Whole Gospel to the Whole Person by Whole People.* Downers Grove, Ill.: InterVarsity Press, 1981.

An important contribution to the whole issue of witness bearing. Covers the bases in a wholesome way, emphasizes the important aspects of both the message and the methods of witnessing, and succeeds in showing how one can do all that Christ commanded in the gospels. 248.5.M56

**Moore, Waylon B.** *Multiplying Disciples: The New Testament Method for Church Growth.* Colorado Springs, Colo.: NavPress, 1981.

One of the best books on the subject. Places adequate stress on the discipling process as a means of multiplication.

248.5.M78

**\*Thompson, W. Oscar, Jr.** *Concentric Circles of Concern.* Nashville: Broadman Press, 1981.

Published posthumously, this work provides a fresh approach to evangelism through exercising a caring ministry within each believer's community. Excellent, sorely needed. A must for every church member. 248.5.T37

**White, John.** *The Race: Discipleship for the Long Run.* Downers Grove, Ill.: InterVarsity Press, 1984.

Applies doctrine to issues relating to the Christian life and witness. 248.5.W58

GUIDES FOR SPECIAL
CIRCUMSTANCES

**Andrews, Gini.** *Your Half of the Apple.* Grand Rapids: Zondervan Publishing House, 1972.

A realistic treatment of the problems as well as the opportunities facing single people in a couple's world. Insightful. 248.8'43.AN2

**Andrus, Paul F.** *Why Me? Why Mine?* Nashville, Abingdon Press, 1975.

Attempts to understand suffering and points those who are suffering to the one who alone is able to sustain them in the midst of their trials. Comforting counsel. 248.8'6.AN2

**Ausbel, David P.** *What Every Well-Informed Person Should Know About Drug Addiction.* 2d ed. Chicago: Nelson-Hall, Inc., 1980.

First published in 1958. This work has justified its place in the book market for its description of the problems that bring on drug addiction, the effects of drugs on users, and how drug users may be helped. 613.8'3.AU7 1980

**Baker, Yvonne G.** *Successfully Single.* Denver, Colo.: Accent, 1985.

Another classic—restated in modern English—but retaining its verve and value for contemporary Christians.

248.4.M96S 1985

*A Guide to Christian Colleges: Christian College Coalition.* Grand Rapids: Wm. B. Eerdmans Publishing Co., 1982.

This is the best available guide to information about Christian higher education in this country. It provides essential information on many of the most highly esteemed liberal arts colleges. It is a valuable resource tool and should be in every church library. 378.73.G94

**Banks, Robert J.** *The Tyranny of Time: When 24 Hours Is NOT Enough.* Downers Grove, Ill.: InterVarsity Press, 1983.

Writing for those laboring under the tyranny of the urgent, Banks seeks to draw believers back to the kind of work ethic that leaves time for living and the enjoyment of the things that really count. This is an important book. 640'.43.B22

**Birkey, Verna.** *You Are Very Special.* Old Tappan, N.J.: Fleming H. Revell Company, 1977.

A clear affirmation of a believer's worth. Blends psychology with the Scriptures to produce a work from which men and women may profit. 248.8'43.B53

**Brammer, Lawrence M., Patricia A. Nolen,** and **Margaret F. Pratt.** *Joys and Challenges of Middle Age.* Chicago: Nelson-Hall, 1982.

A detailed development of the problems men encounter as they reach middle age and find that the dreams of youth and the aspirations of their early working years are not being realized. Provides helpful suggestions that enable readers to enjoy fulfillment and establish reasonable goals for the future. 305.2'44.B73

**Brandt, Catherine.** *Forgotten People.* Chicago: Moody Press, 1978.

Deals with the "other" generation—the aged—and explains how the Christian community can reach out and meet their special needs. Recommended. 248.8'5.B73

**Bustanoby, Andre.** *Being a Single Parent.* Grand Rapids: Pyranee Books, 1985.

Addresses a growing need, long-felt by single parents, for a treatment of the problems they face that will help them fulfill the three vitally important aspects of parenting: involvement, modeling, and instruction. 306.8'56.B96

**\*Carson, Herbert M.** *Facing Suffering: A Christian Response.* Welwyn, Hertfordshire, England: Evangelical Press, 1978.

A well-reasoned exposition of the purpose of suffering and how the believer in Christ may respond to it. 248.8'6.C23

**Chelune, Gordon J., ed.** *Self-Disclosure: Origins, Patterns, and Implications of Openness in Interpersonal Relations.* San Francisco: Jossey-Bass Publishers, 1979.

Pastors will be interested in this volume for its practical emphasis on personal growth and the dynamics of fellowship, much of which parallels the teaching of Scripture on the Body of Christ. 301.11.SE4

**Clark, Martin Elliott.** *Choosing Your Career: The Christian's Decision Manual.* Phillipsburg, N.J.: Presbyterian and Reformed Publishing Co., 1981.

Decidophobia? That's what this book is about. Clark establishes a basis for decision-making squarely on the Scriptures, but he only incidentally relates the problem of making decisions to those whose personalities and insecurities cause them to be reactive as opposed to proactive. 658.311.C54

**Clarkson, Margaret.** *So You're Single!* Wheaton, Ill.: Harold Shaw Publishers, 1978.

One of the best works on the subject of aloneness. Deserves widespread circulation. 248.8'3.C56

**Coleman, William L.** *Earning Your Wings.* Minneapolis: Bethany House Publishers, 1984.

This book is intended for teenagers. It is designed to prepare young people for life on their own. The chapters are clear, relevant, and contain sage counsel. 248.8′4.C79

**Collins, Gary R.** *The Joy of Caring.* Waco, Tex.: Word Books, 1980.

Collins treats the emotional responses common to all of us and points to the need for developing a caring community. He then shows how Christians may develop a genuine concern for others and avoid the pitfalls of those who minister to others in order to meet a felt need of their own. 152.4.C69J

\*_____. *A Psychologist Looks at Life.* Wheaton, Ill.: Key Publications, 1971.

A biblical approach to the problem of unconquered human passions and unhealthy attitudes that frequently mar Christian relationships. 248.8.C69

**Cosgrove, Mark P.,** and **James D. Mallory, Jr.** *Mental Health: A Christian Approach.* Grand Rapids: Zondervan Publishing House, 1977.

Treats the dynamics of personality and points the way to sound mental health and emotional stability. Psychoanalytic. 616.89.C82M

**Cox-Gedmark, Jan.** *Coping with Physical Disability.* Philadelphia: Westminster Press, 1980.

Continues the Christian Care Books series. Treats the problems and perplexities of the handicapped and shows how those in the church may reach out with love and acceptance. Should be in every church library. 248.8′6.C83

\***Demarest, Daniel, Marilyn Sexton,** and **Jerry Sexton.** *Marriage Encounter: A Guide to Sharing.* New York: Carillon Books, 1977.

An analysis of the origin, aims, and procedures of the Marriage Encounter movement, complete with details on the ways these principles may be implemented in the local church. Roman Catholic. 248.84.D39

**Duckworth, Marion.** *Becoming Complete: Embracing Your Biblical Image.* Port-

land, Oreg.: Multnomah Press, 1985.

Duckworth recounts her own search for unity in her personality and for significance in daily living. Along the way, she has learned lessons for all women on overcoming feelings of inferiority, fear, and lack of identity. 248.8′43.D85

**Dunlap, Philip W., Sidney F. Austin,** and **Thomas J. McEneaney.** *Career Development for the College Student.* 5th ed. Cranston, R.I.: Carroll Press, 1981.

A handy guide for those who minister to young people. 378′.194.D92

**Elliot, Elisabeth.** *Let Me Be a Woman.* Wheaton, Ill.: Tyndale House Publishers, 1976.

A timely book. Contains letters the author wrote to her recently engaged daughter, Valerie. Mrs. Elliot stresses the need for a loving hierarchy in a Christian marriage and provides the kind of counsel that can come only from a Christian wife and mother. Recommended. 248.8′43.EL5

**Ellison, Craig W.** *Loneliness: The Search for Intimacy.* Chappaqua, N.Y.: Christian Herald Press, 1980.

Directs the attention of readers to one of the leading problems of our day. Ably correlates biblical principles on the subject with the latest psychological research. Provides perceptive guidelines that pastors and counselors will find helpful. 248.8′6.EL5

**Evening, Margaret.** *Who Walk Alone: A Consideration of the Single Life.* Downers Grove, Ill.: InterVarsity Press, 1974.

A bold attempt to come to grips with singleness, particularly on the part of those in their twenties. Deals factually with the matter of sexuality, the risks of love, and the dilemma of loneliness. Though designed for those who have never married, this book can also be read with profit by the widowed and the divorced. 248.8′43.EV2

**Fanning, Marilyn.** *The Not So Golden*

*Years.* Wheaton, Ill.: Victor Books, 1984.

Designed for use as an elective text in the church's educational program. (There are some who will validly question that use.) This book evokes sympathy as well as understanding. It can be read with profit and deserves widespread circulation. 248.8'5.F21

**\*Fecher, Vincent John, comp.** *Religion and Aging: An Annotated Bibliography.* San Antonio, Tex.: Trinity University Press, 1982.

A *must* for those in the ministry. Provides access to more than 500 books and journal articles dealing with the church's ministry to the aged. Excellent. 248.8'6.F31

**Fischer, Kathleen R.** *Winter Grace: Spirituality for the Later Years.* New York: Paulist Press, 1985.

Looks at the Christian meaning of the key experiences of the later years: memories, dependence and independence, love and sexuality, humor and hope, loss, dying, and resurrection. Challenges many of the stereotypes and offers a positive image of old age. 248.8'5.F53

**Forisha-Kovach, Barbara.** *Power and Love: How to Work for Success and Still Care for Others.* Englewood Cliffs, N.J.: Prentice-Hall, 1982.

Shows how those caught up in the demands of staying abreast of affairs in their ever-changing professions may nevertheless improve their interpersonal relations at work and at home. Insightful. 158.F76

**Fowler, James W.** *Becoming Adult, Becoming Christian: Adult Development and Christian Faith.* San Francisco: Harper & Row, 1984.

†A major new book on the interface of faith-development research and the particularity of the Christian calling. Fowler lays bare many new and important areas for fuller investigation, and the information he imparts is vitally important in

today's churches. This book should also serve as a valuable resource for Christian educators in that it describes the needs of the growing adult. 248.8'4.F82

**Frey, William H., II,** and **Muriel Langseth.** *Crying: The Mystery of Tears.* Minneapolis: Winston Press, 1985.

Frey, a biochemist, and his associate here discuss the blessing of tears and its place as well as its importance in the life of the healthy individual. An important contribution to a greatly neglected topic. 152.4.F89

**\*Getz, Gene A.** *Encouraging One Another.* Wheaton, Ill.: Victor Books, 1981.

Zeroes in on one of the most important themes in the NT. Illustrates and applies the truth from the lives of Bible characters as well as didactic portions of the epistles. Insightful. 248.8.G33E

————. *The Measure of a Man.* Glendale, Calif.: Regal Books, 1974.

Basing each chapter on a facet of Paul's teaching in 1 Timothy 3 and Titus 1, Getz encourages his readers to pursue God's ideal and prepare for leadership in the church. Good illustrations and personal projects make each chapter ideal for men's discussion groups. Getz, however, stretches the teaching of these chapters to fit the title of the book. 248.8'32.G33M

————. *The Measure of a Woman.* Glendale, Calif.: Regal Books, 1977.

A companion volume to *The Measure of a Man,* this work describes fourteen ways in which a woman can live a fulfilled and effective life. 305.4.G33W

**Gilhuis, Cornelius.** *Conversations on Growing Older.* Translated by C. W. Barendrecht. Grand Rapids: Wm. B. Eerdmans Publishing Co., 1977.

The emphasis on the "now" generation of the 1960s has shifted to "self" and the needs individuals feel. That is true, too, of older people. Because a large segment of the population is over sixty-five, the last few years have seen a growing number of books on the problems of the elderly (sometimes referred to as "the fourth generation"). Gilhuis's work deserves to be read by those who are growing older as well as by those who may one day be called on to care for them. And then pastoral counselors also need to be aware of the contents of this book so as to be able to use these insights in their ministries. 248.8'6.G37

**Gillies, John.** *A Guide to Compassionate Care of the Aging.* Nashville: Thomas Nelson Publishers, 1985.

This invaluable guidebook offers several alternatives to the traditional retirement home—programs for compassionate care that are already in effect and can be easily duplicated or modified for specific situations. Gillies discusses these innovative approaches and includes an assessment of activity centers, educational services, medical needs, transportation, and meal services. Excellent. 362.7.AM3.G41

**Graham, William Franklin.** *Till Armageddon: A Perspective on Suffering.* Waco, Tex.: Word Books, 1981.

Attempts "to show something of what the future life is going to be like. In so doing [Graham says] we are going to see how the glory which lies ahead is far greater than any suffering we might endure here" (Preface). 248.8'6.G76

**Green, Wendy.** *The Long Road Home.* Belleville, Mich.: Lion Publishing Corporation, 1985.

"[A] poignant tale of a journey we all must make at some point in time. [The author] has written honestly, simply, and yet profoundly, of the real thoughts and feelings that accompany the trauma of watching your husband die. I was delighted with her droll sense of humor—and yes, I cried with her too. But I never felt that she was asking for my sympathy. The underlying girth of this book is that

God is able, and Wendy contrasts beautifully our weakness with His undomitable strength" (Karen Burton Mains). 306.8'8.G82

**Hatfield, Mark O.** *Conflict and Conscience.* Waco, Tex.: Word Books, 1971.

The senator from Oregon shares his personal experiences and explains how Christianity demands an involvement in social and political spheres. 248.8.H28

**Hendricks, Jeanne W.** *Afternoon: For Women at the Heart of Life.* Nashville: Thomas Nelson Publishers, 1979.

Directing the attention of her readers to "the most joyful, the most productive, the most leisurely years of a woman's life," Mrs. Hendricks discusses the challenges of mid-life and shows how, by investing one's self in people, the "afternoon" of life can be rewarding and fulfilling. 248'.843.H38

**Hepburn, Daisy.** *Lead, Follow or Get Out of the Way!* Ventura, Calif.: Regal Books, 1982.

In dealing with the "Decade of the Woman" (i.e., the 1980s), Mrs. Hepburn discusses ways in which her gender may lead fulfilling lives. This book includes an excellent application of "servant leadership" to the role of women today. 248.8'43.H41

**Horton, Marilee,** and **Walter Byrd.** *Keeping Your Balance.* Waco, Tex.: Word Books, 1984.

Subtitled "A Woman's Guide to Physical, Emotional, and Spiritual Well-being." The content fits these descriptors, and the information provided is practical and relevant. As a self-help book, this one should be well received by those who wish to be all they were meant to be. 248.8'43.H78

**Huyck, Margaret H.,** and **William J. Hoyer.** *Adult Development and Aging.* Belmont, Calif.: Wadsworth Publishing Co., 1982.

Based on a developmental approach to

aging, this work draws on a wide range of material from other disciplines and deals adequately with the psysiological and psychological changes taking place during these years. A valuable treatment. 305.2′4.H98

**Hybels, Bill.** *Christians in the Marketplace.* Wheaton, Ill.: Victor Books, 1982.

Designed for use in adult discussion groups. This issue-oriented work deals realistically with the ethical and spiritual problems facing Christians in a secular society. 248.8.H99

**Jourard, Sidney M.** *Self-disclosure: An Experimental Analysis of the Transparent Self.* Huntington, N.Y.: Robert E. Krieger Publishing Company, 1979.

An analysis of human behavior and the means of communication, both verbal and nonverbal, that disclose to others how we think and feel. Complete with questionnaires and appendixes. 155.2′8.J83

**Kalish, Richard A.** *Late Adulthood: Perspectives on Human Development.* 2d ed. Monterey, Calif.: Brooks/Cole Publishing Company, 1982.

Deals candidly with a situation that faces all of us. Helps those involved with the aged understand them and channel their skills and abilities into creative pursuits. 305.2′6.K12 1982

**Karssen, Giel.** *Getting the Most Out of Being Single: The Gift of Single Womanhood.* Colorado Springs, Colo.: NavPress, 1982.

Believing that nothing has to be wasted in the life of a Christian single woman, Karssen explores such emotionally laden topics as finding God's will, discovering one's gifts, overcoming loneliness, work, preparing for marriage and widowhood. Worthy of serious consideration. 248.8.K14 1982

**Ketterman, Grace H.** *Before and After the Wedding Night.* Old Tappan, N.J.: Fleming H. Revell Co., 1984.

The section addressed to prenuptial couples talks about family myths, personality quirks, psychological freedom, physical relationships, sexuality, and the need for adequate information about our bodies. Engaged and married couples will be interested in the author's observations about common marital problems, such as communication breakdown, deep-seated fears, and painful misunderstandings. According to Ketterman, marriage is a continuous learning process, and when certain basic principles are observed, it can be fun. 248.8′4.K51

**Kopp, Ruth Lewshenia,** and **Stephen Sorenson.** *When Someone You Love Is Dying: A Handbook for Counselors and Those Who Care.* Grand Rapids: Zondervan Publishing House, Ministry Resources Library, 1985.

This remarkable book was first published in 1980 under the title *Encounter with Terminal Illness.* As Haddon W. Robinson pointed out, "All life is terminal. Some arrive at the terminal before they know it. Others hear an announcement and anticipate death's coming. For such men and women going to death themselves, or travelling with others, Dr. Kopp provides practical counsel about how to make the journey." 248.8′.6.K83 1985

**Lee, James Michael, ed.** *The Spirituality of the Religious Educator.* Birmingham, Ala.: Religious Education Press, 1985.

†A scholarly volume treating (1) how the process of education deepens the teacher's own spiritual life and (2) the manner in which what is taught contributes to the spiritual growth of those in the class. 248.8′9.L51

**Lee, Mark Wilcox.** *Who Am I and What Am I Doing Here?* Milford, Mich.: Mott Media, 1982.

These addresses zero in on the basic

questions being asked by those in high school and college. This book is must reading for all who work with these age groups. 248.8'L51

**LeTourneau, Richard.** *Management Plus: The Spiritual Dimension in Leadership.* Grand Rapids: Zondervan Publishing House, 1973.

Geared to the needs of Christians in business who wish that their lives and ideas would make a greater impact on those around them. Helpful. 658.4.L56

**Linn, Matthew,** and **Dennis Linn.** *Healing Life's Hurts: Healing the Memories Through Five Stages of Forgiveness.* New York: Paulist Press, 1978.

The authors, charismatic Roman Catholic priests, approach the emotions psychologically and theologically and point the way to sound mental and emotional health. Their information on the need for forgiveness is given in a direct and helpful manner. The information is made easy to follow by case histories that are interspersed throughout the book. The result is a unique and helpful treatise on the need for forgiveness. 248.8'6.L64

————, and **Sheila Fabricant.** *Healing the Greatest Hurt.* New York: Paulist Press, 1985.

Deals with death and the process of recovery. Shows how the loss of a loved one can trigger other problems that may complicate the process of grief. Throughout, the counsel given is practical and easy to implement. 248.8'6.L64

**McDonald, Gordon.** *Living at High Noon: Reflections on the Dramas of Mid-Life.* Old Tappan, N.J.: Fleming H. Revell Co., 1985.

This pastor-author shares his views on the dramas, challenges, and opportunities of mid-life. He sees that period as a time for growth toward maturity and the chance for significant service. An excel-

lent, forthright discussion that restores one's perspective on this period of life. 248.8'4.M14 1985

***Mace, David Robert.** *Getting Ready for Marriage.* Rev. ed. Nashville: Abingdon Press, 1985.

As with all of Mace's works, this one is well worth careful attention. It treats the education of young people for marriage, and as such can be used to good advantage in courses for those in their late teens and early twenties. 62.8'2.M15G 1985

**Maitland, David J.** *Looking Both Ways: A Theology of Mid-Life.* Atlanta: John Knox Press, 1985.

Maitland has developed a theology of living based on the premise that it is by God's fashioning that our experiences from infancy to old age are to be considered. He also develops his thesis in a way that focuses on the kind of questions that people should be asking as they reach the mid-life years. He notes that this period is particularly characterized by an experience of brokenness and a desire for greater wholeness. It is to develop these ideas that he wrote this book. 248.8'4.M28

**McGinnis, Marilyn.** *Single.* Old Tappan, N.J.: Fleming H. Revell Co., 1974.

A positive statement of the qualities that make the difference between the lonely, bitter, self-pitying, depressed, and depressing young adult and those who have learned to rise above their circumstances and lead happy, meaningful lives. Should be in every church library. 248.8'43.M17

**McMinn, Gordon,** and **Larry Libby.** *Choosing to Be Close: Fill Your Life with Rewarding Relationships.* Portland, Oreg.: Multnomah Press, 1984.

Explains the resources we need to build better relationships, and how they may be developed. Timely, practical, helpful. 158.2.M22

**Mitchell, Marcia.** *Spiritually Single.* Minneapolis: Bethany House Publishers, 1984.

Written for those with unsaved mates. Provides practical, wise counsel on a wide variety of issues. Most helpful. 248.8'4.M69

**Morgan, Richard Lyon.** *Is There Life After Divorce in the Church?* Atlanta: John Knox Press, 1985.

A counselee once remarked, "Adultery and murder are forgivable, but not the 'sin' of divorce." He had in mind the attitude of people in the church toward those who have gone through the humiliation and suffering of divorce. This work addresses the issue. Morgan deals with the sense of pain as well as failure that overtakes those whose marriage has floundered onto the rocks, describes and then deals with their feeling of rejection, and seeks to provide some comfort to those who experience the addition of hurt imposed on them by the very people they look to for compassion and some token of kindness. 248.8'6.M82

**Neale, Robert E.** *Loneliness, Solitude, and Companionship.* Philadelphia: Westminster Press, 1984.

Deals with each aspect of the title and passes on to readers the positive and negative experiences associated with loneliness, solitude, and the quest for meaningful relationships. Meets a need. 248.8'6.N25

————. *The Art of Dying.* New York: Harper & Row, 1973.

Covers the subject of death systematically. The inclusion of questionnaires and other aids makes this work ideal for use in group discussions. Though not an answer book, its objectivity enables an individual or group to interact with the issues. 128'.5.N25

**Norman, William H., and Thomas J.**

**Scaramella.** *Mid-Life: Developmental and Clinical Issues.* New York: Brunner/Mazel Publishers, 1980.

This symposium draws attention to nine separate facets of the so-called midlife crisis. The contributors explain the strains and challenges of those in this period of life. They also explain what is happening, and why, and share with their readers what can be done about it. This is a helpful treatise that offers balance to much of the unwise information that has circulated concerning this phenomenon. 616.89.M58

**Osterweis, Marian, Frederic Solomon,** and **Morris Green,** eds. *Bereavement: Reactions, Consequences, and Care.* Washington, D.C.: National Academy Press, 1984.

Studies the effects of death on survivors of all ages. Correlates and then applies scientific and psychological, physiological and sociological data to the needs of the bereaved. Provides material for clinicians as well as those in the helping professions. The information contained between these covers should impact counseling and research for years to come. 155.9'37.OS7

**Pierson, Robert H.** *How to Become a Successful Christian Leader.* Mountain View, Calif.: Pacific Press Publishing Association, 1978.

Abounds with practical pointers on how to be more successful in dealing with others. Contains sage counsel for those in the ministry as well. 158.4.P61

**Potts, Nancy.** *Loneliness: Living Between the Times.* Wheaton, Ill.: Victor Books, 1978.

Written by a marriage counselor, this book takes a candid look at the problem of loneliness, who suffers from it, and why. Includes what Christians may do to alleviate the suffering of others. 248.8.P85

**Powers, Bruce P.** *Christian Leadership.*

Nashville: Broadman Press, 1979.

One of the best works on leadership to appear in recent years. Stresses the importance of the process of leadership rather than the techniques or skills. The valuable principles in this book are, unfortunately, accompanied by inaccuracies in handling Scripture. 158.4.P87

**Rando, Therese A.** *Grief, Dying, and Death: Clinical Interventions for Caregivers.* Champaign, Ill.: Research Press Company, 1984.

†Based on twenty years of research, this work deals concisely with the issues of bereavement and provides helpful counsel to all who are called on to visit or help the terminally ill and their families. This is a truly valuable secular work. 616.89.R15

**Rank, Maureen.** *Free to Grieve.* Minneapolis: Bethany House Publishers, 1985.

A sorely needed book. Deals with the process of healing and encouragement of those who have experienced the physical, mental, and emotional trauma of miscarriage or a stillbirth. 155.9′37.R15

**Ryrie, Charles Caldwell.** *Making the Most of Life.* Wheaton, Ill.: Victor Books, 1982.

Deals realistically with common Christian fallacies frequently substituted for genuine spirituality. 248.83.R99 1982

**Seamands, David.** *Healing for Damaged Emotions.* Wheaton, Ill.: Victor Books, 1981.

Designed to make people more aware of their emotions and to show them how to achieve inner healing. 152.42.SE1

———. *Healing of Memories.* Wheaton, Ill.: Victor Books, 1985.

The tragedy of hurtful memories is the lingering emotional pain that dogs the steps and debilitates the life of the sufferer. Because the pain is intense, we often learn wrong ways of coping, and this, in turn, develops poor patterns of relating to others. Seamands deals directly and wholesomely with the need for forgiveness and at the same time charts a course that can eventuate in the healing of the memories. 248.8.SE2M

**Simenauer, Jacqueline,** and **David Carroll.** *Singles: The New Americans.* New York: Simon & Schuster, 1982.

The result of a nation-wide survey, this work treats candidly and compassionately the major problems confronting singles in America today. Also discusses the issues related to dating, mating, and the like. Secular. 305.SI4

**Smith, David W.** *The Friendless American Male.* Ventura, Calif.: Regal Books, 1983.

Explores the problems of the friendless American male and concludes that there is a remedy. Smith provides counsel on the causes leading up to isolation and suggestions on how to develop lasting relationships. Insightful. 248.8′4.SM5

**Stowell, Joseph M., III.** *Through the Fire.* Wheaton, Ill.: Victor Books, 1985.

These simple, direct, biblical studies focus adequately yet realistically on the process and purpose of pain. Though designed for adult discussion groups, this work can also be read by individuals. Each page breathes the kind of comfort that can only be gleaned from a careful study of Scripture. 248.8′6.ST7

**Swindoll, Lucille.** *Wide My World, Narrow My Bed.* Portland, Oreg.: Multnomah Press, 1982.

A candid discussion of singleness. Points the way from frustration and dejection to hope through a vital relationship with Christ. Timely. 305′.90652.SW6W

**Switzer, David K.** *The Dynamics of Grief.* Nashville: Abingdon Press, 1970.

†Focuses attention on the grieving person rather than on the one who is dying, and helps the individual understand the

inner process of grief. Meets a long-felt need for a reliable guide into the dynamics of suffering. 248.8'6.SW6

**Talley, James A., and Leslie H. Stobbe.** *Reconcilable Differences.* Nashville: Thomas Nelson Publishers, 1985.

Deals with the trauma of divorce and the fact that most separated couples are prepared to work toward reconciliation if someone would only show them how to handle the feelings of anger and bitterness and the resentment they feel as a result of past injuries and injustices. This book makes an important contribution. 248.8'6.T14R

**Tournier, Paul.** *Learn to Grow Old.* Translated by E. Hudson. New York: Harper & Row, 1974.

"Prepare early for retirement," is Tournier's advice. Having said that, he is quick to point out that one should not do so with a view to relaxing and leading a life of leisure but of preparing for a different role—one of injecting into society a sense of personal humanity through involvement in programs that bring help and happiness to others. 306.88.T64

**Towns, Elmer L.** *Ministry to the Young Single Adult.* Grand Rapids: Baker Book House, 1971.

Of help to single adults as well as pastors. Contains insights into the problems and needs of unmarried persons in the church and directs them toward positive, meaningful service for Christ. 248.8'4.T66

**Troup, Stanley B., and William A. Greene, eds.** *The Patient, Death, and the Family.* New York: Charles Scribner's Sons, 1974.

Of particular value to those engaged in counseling. The contributors discuss death from nearly every point of view. Missing, however, is a clear, biblical perspective. In spite of this weakness, there are numerous hints throughout this work that those ministering to the dying will find helpful. 306.88.T75

**White, Jerry E., and Mary Ann Knudson White.** *Your Job: Survival or Satisfaction.* Grand Rapids: Zondervan Publishing House, 1977.

An astronaut who once served as mission controller at Cape Kennedy teams up with his wife to provide a down-to-earth book for Christians. Their treatment runs the gamut from the development of a biblical philosophy of work to committing one's life to a specific task. Included is practical counsel on choosing and preparing for a career. Interspersed is sage advice on seeking a new job and finding satisfaction in one's work. 248.88.W58

**Whitehead, Evelyn Eaton, and James D. Whitehead.** *Christian Life Patterns: The Psychological Challenges and Religious Invitations of Adult Life.* Garden City, N.Y.: Doubleday and Co., 1979.

The authors attempt to reconstruct a contemporary approach to spirituality based on Eriksonian stages of development. Of value is their discussion of "adult encounters" and the often disguised "religious invitations" that are present in specific developmental stages. This book has been thoughtfully written, and whether or not the reader agrees with the premise of the authors, the fact remains that what they have communicated can be read with profit. 248.84.W58

**Wiebe, Katie F.** *Alone: A Widow's Search for Joy.* Wheaton, Ill.: Tyndale House Publishers, 1976.

A touching, practical, helpful book that awakens an empathic response in readers. Mrs. Wiebe deals with the loss of her husband and the things both she and her children did to adjust to their changed circumstances and still find meaning and fulfillment in life. Recommended. 248.8.W63

**Wilson, John Oliver.** *After Affluence: Economics and Human Needs.* San Francisco: Harper & Row, 1980.

Tracing the American middle-class dream to the era following World War II, the realization of the value of a good education, and hard work as the means of achieving economic security, Wilson describes the erosion of the dream and the bureaucratic, political, and economic factors affecting our contemporary society. Pastors will find Wilson's material most helpful as they seek to relate the message of the Bible to the present-day needs of people. He has succeeded in providing a challenging analysis of our modern milieu. 248.8.UN3.W69

**Wright, Harry Norman.** *Into the High Country.* Portland, Oreg.: Multnomah Press, 1979.

Deals with the specifics that will help young people chart a course for their marriage and keep it on track. Beautifully illustrated. 248.84.W93H

**Wylie, Betty Jane.** *The Survival Guide for Widows.* New York: Ballantine Books, 1984.

At age forty the author found herself a widow. She was unprepared for the difficulties that were suddenly thrust on her. To help other widows, Mrs. Wylie has written this book. In part, it chronicles her experiences. It is a helpful treatise. 248.8'6.W97 1984

## CHRISTIAN HOME

**Ackerman, Paul R.,** and **Murray M. Kappelman.** *Signals: What Your Child Is Really Telling You.* New York: Dial Press, 1978.

Discusses the methods of nonverbal communication used by children—the voiceless signals often misinterpreted by parents—and explains their meaning. Also provides suggestions as to how the child's felt needs may be met. 249.AC5

**Adams, Gerald R.,** and **Thomas Gullotta.** *Adolescent Life Experiences.* Monterey, Calif.: Brooks/Cole Publishing Co., 1983.

The field of adolescent development has increasingly become more complex. Now, through the cooperative efforts of specialists, it has also become interdisciplinary. This book is an example of the kind happily becoming more common. Parents seldom know how to cope with their teenager, and the life-changes through which our children pass seem to be reached with increasing rapidity. This book will help both pastors and parents understand the why and how of these changes. The treatment is thorough and yet not so technical that it requires specialized training to understand all the ramifications that are presented. 305.2'35.AD1

**\*Adams, Jay Edward.** *Christian Living in the Home.* Nutley, N.J.: Presbyterian and Reformed Publishing Co., 1972.

Here is a warm, compassionate, and understanding application of the teaching of Scripture on the difficulties many Christians face as they seek to establish their own homes. Recommended. 249.AD1

**Alexander, Olive J.** *Developing Spiritually Sensitive Children.* Minneapolis: Bethany Fellowship, 1980.

Seeks to pass on to parents the skills by which they may develop a strong internal, and therefore personal, faith in their children. 649'.7.AL2

**\*Allen, Ronald Barclay,** and **Beverly Allen.** *Liberated Traditionalism: Men and Women in Balance.* Portland, Oreg.: Multnomah Press, 1985.

This husband-wife team assesses the facts behind the slogans and provides a definitive, biblical approach to the traditional battle of the sexes. The result is a work of significant value to all who are interested in the truth. Heartily recommended. Perhaps it will dispel some of the antagonism that is evident in certain quarters. 305.4'2.AL5

**Altherr, Thomas L., ed.** *Procreation or Pleasure? Sexual Attitudes in American History.* Malabar, Fla.: Robert E. Krieger Publishing Co., 1983.

An important work on the history of sexual attitudes that provides readers with a reliable condensation of information so that a system of ethics can be established that is both morally sound and ethically responsible. 306.7.AM3.AL7

**Ames, Louise Bates, et al.** *The Gesell Institute's Child from One to Six: Evaluating the Behavior of the Preschool Child.* New Haven, Conn.: Yale University Press, 1979.

An updated version of the famous work by Gesell entitled *The First Years of Life* (1940) and the equally valuable treatment by Gesell and Ilg titled *Child Development* (1949). In this newer work the authors describe for parents the dynamics of physical growth and personality development. Their treatment is thorough but without being tedious. What they share with their readers can be taken and adapted to a variety of home situations. Their work is highly recommended. 155.4'22.G33 1979

**Andelin, Aubrey P.** *Man of Steel and Velvet.* Santa Barbara, Calif.: Pacific Press, 1973.

The counterpart to Helen Andelin's *Fascinating Woman*, contains some dos and don'ts for men that, if followed, will result in happier homes, more secure wives, and healthier environments in which to rear children. 306.87.AN2M

**Andelin, Helen B.** *All About Raising Children.* Santa Barbara, Calif.: Pacific Press, 1981.

Mother of eight, grandmother of thirty-three, Mrs. Andelin speaks from experience. In this book she shares her ideas on child-rearing and succeeds in pinpointing ways in which parents may produce moral, responsible, successful offspring. 649'.1.AN2 1981

**Anderson, Ray S., and Dennis B. Guernsey.** *On Being Family: A Social Theology of the Family.* Grand Rapids: Wm. B. Eerdmans Publishing Co., 1985.

The book is divided into six parts. Each writer contributes one essay to each part. Together they "have provided a brilliant and seminal contribution to the literature on the theology of the family. Their work reflects mature scholarship and makes excellent use of the Bible, theology, philosophy, the behavioral sciences, and human experience as sources for constructing family theology" (Myron R. Chartier). 306.8.AN2

***Anderson, Wayne J.** *How to Explain Sex to Children.* Minneapolis: T. D. Denison and Co., 1971.

Gives parents some needed guidelines as well as practical answers to youth's questions about sex. 249.AN2

**Atkin, Edith.** *In Praise of Marriage.* New York: Vanguard Press, 1982.

Contains "the distillation of a wise and good mind in love with its subject. I recommend it for everybody, those who are only thinking of marriage or who have gone through the pain of divorce as well as those who are mid-stream in their marriages or are widowed and looking back on the richness of it all" (John Killinger). 249.AT5

**Attwood, William.** *Making It Through Middle Age: Notes While in Transit.* New York: Atheneum Press, 1982.

On the grounds that he has probably moved around and seen more than most people, Attwood offers a personal refutation of what is commonly called a mid-life crisis and shows that the middle years can be the most rewarding of our lives. Drawing on his immensely varied experiences, he provides valuable advice on a variety of subjects: for example, the importance of our choice ("it's never too late to start out on a new track"), what to do in illnesses (it has given him a keen appreciation of life), the enjoyment of sex, marriage ("about half way through middle age you begin to appreciate it"), children, work (the key to fulfillment), the corporate world, serenity, retirement, and death. 158.1.AT8

**Augsburger, A. Don, ed.** *Marriages That Work.* Scottdale, Pa.: Herald Press, 1984.

Authorities who are well-respected in Christian circles contribute chapters on their own courtships and the kinds of problems they have faced throughout the decades of their marriages. The approach is realistic. Their self-disclosure adds authenticity to what is presented. No two experiences are alike. Young married couples as well as those looking forward to marriage should be encouraged to read this book. It is a must for the church library. 249.AU4M

**Augsburger, David W.** *Cherishable: Love and Marriage.* Scottdale, Pa.: Herald Press, 1973.

This book has a variety of uses. One of them is with discussion groups. It may also serve as a guide for a couple in developing a creative marital relationship. 249.AU4C

**August, Eugene R.** *Men's Studies: A Selected and Annotated Interdisciplinary Bibliography.* Littleton, Colo.: Libraries Unlimited, 1985.

Provides a starting point for those pursuing further research. Makes available a means for assessing the literature by and about men and gives to those familiar with women's studies a comprehensive view of the other half of society's "gender revolution." The bibliography will prove useful to D.Min. students involved in pastoral counseling as well as to those in evangelism who seek to chart a course for the church in the closing decades of this century. The information treats outreach, as well as the needs of men in school, public life, academia, institutions, and, in fact, all walks of life. 016.3.M31.AU4

**\*Barber, Cyril John,** and **Aldyth Ayleen Barber.** *You Can Have a Happy Marriage: Biblical Principles of Marriage.* Grand Rapids: Kregel Publications, 1984.

Whereas in *Your Marriage Has Real Possibilities* the authors discussed the essence of a strong, stable relationship, in this volume they lay stress upon the dynamics of a happy marriage by treating the importance of mutual maturity, the development of unity, and the achievement of sexual compatibility. "In the midst of many volumes written for married couples, there is a refreshing quality to this work . . . The analysis and insights derived from couples in the Bible will be welcomed by the reader, and the discussion questions lend an added benefit to a study of this work. The book has been written in a very readable style, and it is far more biblical in its content than many others which have been completed before" (H. Norman Wright). 249.B23H

**\*\_\_\_\_\_.** *Your Marriage Has Real Possibilities: Biblical Principles for a Successful Marriage.* Grand Rapids: Kregel Publications, 1984.

Contains thirteen biblically based studies of marriage and family life. Paula Ibach, writing in the *Grace Theological Journal* said: "[They] have given us a thoroughly biblical look at the marriage relationship in a style conducive to personal/couple devotional study or use by a group. They present Bible couples as models to emulate or avoid, including interaction questions to stimulate thought and discussion. Readers expecting the topical how-to approach found in many volumes on marriage will be surprised by this deeper, principle-oriented treatment." A healthy marriage is based on the meeting of the security needs of the husband and wife. If they enjoy a sense of *belonging, worth,* and *competence* in their relationship with one another, then they will be able to rear strong children. No other work presently in print deals with marriage in quite the same way. How to have these needs met is the purpose of this book. 249.B23Y

*_____, and **Gary (Gerhard) Henry Strauss.** *The Effective Parent: Biblical Principles of Parenting Based upon the Model of God the Father.* San Bernardino, Calif.: Here's Life Publishers, 1980.

Described by Dan Baumann in the Foreword as a "happy blend of thoughtfulness and helpfulness . . .; appeal[ing] to both my rationality and my need for a faith that fleshes out in the marketplace." Designed for individual or group use. The authors draw practical lessons from the way in which God *the Father* dealt with His recalcitrant son, Jonah. 249.B23E

**Barnes, Robert G., Jr.** *Single Parenting: A Wilderness Journey.* Wheaton, Ill.: Tyndale House Publishers, 1984.

Believes that 90 percent of single parents are women. Deals directly with such problems as loneliness, anger, rejection, discipline, and the need to build relationships. Treats realistically the issues faced by those who try to fulfill the role of both father and mother and offers what counsel he can. This book is recommended to those who minister to this growing segment of society. 249.B26

**Bartusis, Mary Ann.** *Every Other Man.* New York: E. P. Dutton, 1978.

Subtitled "How to Cope with Infidelity and Keep Your Relationship Whole." Apparently half the men in a national survey said that they had cheated on their wives. This book was written for betrayed wives with a view to preserving the marriage. Secular. 301.73.B28

**Belsky, Jay, Richard M. Lerner,** and **Graham B. Spanier.** *The Child in the Family.* Reading, Mass.: Addison-Wesley Publishing Co., 1984.

We live in a time of great change. This work provides a retrospective look at previous approaches to socialization and updates parents and teachers on the dynamics presently in operation within our culture. 306.8'74.B41

**Benson, Daniel.** *The Total Man.* Wheaton, Ill.: Tyndale House Publishers, 1977.

The title of this book is misleading. It is not the male counterpart to Morgan's *The Total Woman.* Instead, it is an honest statement of how a man may be a man and find fulfillment in a woman's world. The treatment is shallow, but the issues covered are of vital importance to all husbands/fathers. 305.3.B43

**Berger, Brigitte,** and **Peter L. Berger.** *The War over the Family: Capturing the Middle Ground.* Garden City, N.Y.: Doubleday and Co., 1983.

The subtitle of this book sounds like something from Tolkien. It is not. The authors approach the subject of the family from an essentially secular perspective, but this work is professional in every sense of the word. It treats the sources of tension that frequently disrupt families and offers practical counsel on how to resolve long-standing difficulties. 306.8'5'B45

**Berger, Evelyn Miller.** *Triangle: The Betrayed Wife.* Chicago: Nelson-Hall, n.d.

Infidelity has become commonplace in our society, but what emotional effect does it have on those who are cheated? This book exposes the causes leading up to extramarital affairs and, though it tends to exonerate the wife from culpability, it nevertheless assesses the issues and provides some sane counsel. 306.8.B45

**Bier, William C., ed.** *Aging: Its Challenge to the Individual and to Society.* New York: Fordham University Press, 1974.

These papers by Roman Catholics discuss with discernment and understanding the historical, cultural, religious, social, and psychological aspects of aging. They offer some practical suggestions on what to do with the aged and how to make their declining years meaningful. 306.88.B47

**Bird, Joseph,** and **Lois Bird.** *To Live As Family: An Experience of Love and Bonding.* New York: Doubleday and Co., 1982.

Making allowance for such common disruptions of family life as illness, sibling rivalry, favoritism, and jealousy, the Birds provide practical counsel on the ways in which unity may be developed and the divisive pressures of society withstood. Recommended. 306.8.B53T

**Blackwell, William L.,** and **Muriel F. Blackwell.** *Working Partners, Working Parents.* Nashville: Broadman Press, 1979.

A social worker and his wife write of the problems that arise when both parents follow their chosen careers. They make an important contribution to our understanding of these pressures. 306.87.B56

**Blitchington, W. Peter.** *Sex Roles and the Christian Family.* Wheaton, Ill.: Tyndale House Publishers, 1980.

This capable study probes the natural laws of growth and sexuality and shows how these contribute to the complexion of the family unit. The book is instructive and may be read with profit by pastoral counselors as well as parents. 306.87.B61

**Bloomfield, Harold H.,** and **Leonard Felder.** *Making Peace with Your Parents.* New York: Random House, 1983.

Deals with an important stage in the growth of adolescents. The counsel in this work provides helpful insights into the growth of interpersonal relationships within the family circle. 306.8'74.B62

***Bower, Robert K.** Solving Problems in Marriage: Guidelines for Christian Couples.* Grand Rapids: Wm. B. Eerdmans Publishing Co., 1971.

Spells out ways in which husbands and wives can find solutions to the problems that arise in the normal course of everyday living. Practical. 249.B67

**Boyer, Ruth G.** *The Happy Adolescent.* Palo Alto, Calif.: R. and E. Research Associates, 1981.

Adolescence is not normally a happy period of life. This psychoanalytic approach charts a course whereby adolescents may make the most of this formative era. 155.5.B69

**Branden, Nathaniel,** and **E. Devers Branden.** *The Romantic Love Question and Answer Book.* Boston: Houghton, Mifflin Co., 1982.

This sequel to *The Psychology of Romantic Love* follows a question-and-answer format. The issues discussed include an analysis of romantic love, communication of emotion, intimacy and sex, jealousy and infidelity, stress, children, and a host of other topics that are relevant to the happiness of the couple and the health of their relationship. Recommended. 646.7'7.B73R

**Bricklin, Barry,** and **Patricia M. Bricklin.** *Strong Family, Strong Child: The Art of Working Together to Develop a Healthy Child.* New York: Delacorte Press, 1970.

By combining their skills as psychologists and their experience as parents, the authors provide valuable counsel and practical guidelines for rearing strong, mature, emotionally healthy children. 306.87.B76

**Bridges, William.** *Transitions: Making Sense of Life's Changes.* Reading, Mass.: Addison-Wesley Publishing Co., 1980.

This practical treatise assesses the

need for change and identifies the crucial stages of life when such changes take place. Provides counsel on how people may cope without having their lives disrupted by the strange tensions they feel inwardly. 306.8.B76

**Briggs, Dorothy Corkille.** *Your Child's Self-Esteem: The Key to Life.* Garden City, N.Y.: Doubleday and Co., 1975.

This is a most important work. The author's humanism is evident, but the fact remains that she has touched on a vital and much neglected area of child-rearing. What she has to say, therefore, is deserving of every parent's careful consideration. The appearance of this book immediately touched off a host of similar ones by Christians. The problem is that those by believers were not nearly as good. 649.1.B76

**Broderick, Carlfred.** *Couples: How to Confront Problems and Maintain Loving Relationships.* New York: Simon & Schuster, 1979.

A leading authority on marriage shares with his readers important principles that will strengthen interpersonal relationships. His material is most judicious and well deserves careful reading. All pastors and counselors should master the contents of this book. 306.87.B78C

**Brown, Stanley C.** *God's Plan for Marriage.* Philadelphia: Westminster Press, 1977.

A return to the Scriptures for a blueprint on marriage is welcome. In this book, Brown discusses common problems and difficulties and the fulfillment that a marital union should bring. He is not prescriptive in his dealing with possible solutions, but rather points the way whereby couples can work through their difficulties and so achieve marital harmony. 249.B81

**\*Buffam, C. John.** *The Life and Times of an MK.* Pasadena, Calif.: William Carey Library, 1985.

"This book, while not attempting to give all the answers, will introduce the reader to the variety of situations, some relevant factors to be considered, and the range of choices for missionary parents at critical periods in the growth and development of their children" (George M. Cowan). 649.1'0882.M86

**Burkett, Larry.** *What Husbands Wish Their Wives Knew About Money.* Wheaton, Ill.: Victor Books, 1977.

Contains practical counsel on financial management. Designed for use in women's discussion groups. Can easily be incorporated into the church's educational program. 332'.024.B92

**Bustanoby, Andre.** *But I Didn't Want a Divorce: Putting Your Life Back Together.* Grand Rapids: Zondervan Publishing House, 1978.

Behaviorally based counseling for those recovering from the trauma of rejection and divorce. Offers practical help. 306.89.B96

———, and **Fay Bustanoby.** *Just Talk to Me: The Principles and Practice of Communication in Marriage.* Grand Rapids: Zondervan Publishing House, 1981.

A timely, practical manual designed to help couples surmount the hurdles to proper communication in their marriages. 306.8'7.B96

———. *The Readymade Family.* Grand Rapids: Zondervan Publishing House, 1982.

The rise in the rate of divorce and remarriage has brought about an increase in stepparenting. In this work, Bustanoby treats the complexities of rearing other people's children. His discussion is seminal and can be read with profit by all who are called on to nurture the victims of broken marriages. 646.7'8.B96

**\*Campbell, Ross.** *How to Really Love Your Teenager.* Wheaton, Ill.: Victor Books, 1981.

Highly acclaimed as a work to reawaken a parent's sense of values and reestablish communication with one's teenager through unconditional love and acceptance. Recommended. 155.5.C15

**Carroll, Anne Kristen.** *From the Brink of Divorce: An Evangelical Marriage Counselor's Advice on How to Step Back and Start Over.* Garden City, N.Y.: Doubleday and Co., 1978.

A book for all church members—men and women alike. Shows how marriages can be both saved and strengthened. Outlines biblical principles for the development of true unity. Recommended. 306.89.C23

————. *Together Forever.* Grand Rapids: Zondervan Publishing House, 1982.

"I have found [this book] to be a valuable tool in my own counseling practice. The author's message, both as an evangelical marriage counselor and as a wife, is communicated with understanding and sympathy. I appreciate her strong biblical viewpoint and her focus on biblical solutions which can bring about dynamic transformations even in seemingly hopeless situations" (Ed Wheat, M.D.). 249.C23

**Carroll, David.** *Living with Dying: A Loving Guide for Family and Close Friends.* New York: McGraw-Hill Book Co., 1985.

How do you know what to say to a person who is dying? How can you avoid saying the wrong things? Carroll provides answers to these difficult situations and does so in the order in which they are likely to occur. His work is "thoroughly impressive," according to Norman Cousins. 306.9.C23

**Carter, Velma Thorne,** and **J. Lynn Leavenworth.** *Caught in the Middle: Children of Divorce.* Valley Forge, Pa.: Judson Press, 1985.

Growing out of their counseling experience, the authors tackle the plight of children who are literally caught in the middle and torn apart emotionally when their parents divorce. Their realistic approach and courage in tackling this unpleasant issue is welcomed. Theirs is a revealing and necessary book. It should be read before taking action to legally end a marriage. Then counsel can be sought to help resolve the difficulties and restore the marriage. 306.8'9.C24

**\*Cedar, Paul A.** *Seven Keys to Maximum Communication.* Wheaton, Ill.: Tyndale House Publishers, 1980.

Treats in simple terms the negative and positive feelings we all share that either erect walls between us or build bridges toward one another. Most helpful. 001.C32

**Chapman, Gary D.** *Hope for the Separated.* Chicago: Moody Press, 1982.

A compassionate treatment of the moral and religious issues facing the divorced and separated. Recommends a process that would lead to eventual reconcilation. 306.8'9.C36

**Christenson, Laurence,** and **Nordis Christenson.** *The Christian Couple.* Minneapolis: Bethany Fellowship, 1977.

In the midst of the clamor for liberation and the cry for individual rights, this Christian couple takes a hard look at marriage from God's perspective. They succeed in charting a course for couples that is at once sensible and scriptural. Recommended. 306.8.C46C

**\*Clark, Stephen B.** *Man and Woman in Christ: An Examination of the Roles of Men and Women in Light of Scripture and the Social Sciences.* Ann Arbor, Mich.: Servant Books, 1980.

A thorough examination of the institution of marriage, the nature of the family, and the roles of husbands and wives. Makes a serious attempt to ground each facet of his presentation in the Scriptures. The author is an evangelical Roman Catholic. 261.8'343.C54

**Cohen, Stephen Z.,** and **Bruce Michael Gains.** *The Other Generation Gap: The Middle-Aged and Their Aging Parents.* Chicago: Follett Publishing Co., 1978.

Deals factually with the problems of the middle-aged and their aging parents. Offers practical solutions. Avoids trite, simplistic answers. Seeks to be both practical and relevant. Pastors will find this book replete with information on what the trials and difficulties of both groups are and how to minister to them. 306.87.C66

*Coleman, William L. *Making TV Work for Your Family.* Minneapolis: Bethany House Publishers, 1983.

A balanced approach to cultivating creativity in children while instilling autonomy and a sense of discipline in them as well. 306.8'5.C67

Collins, Gary R., ed. *Make More of Your Marriage.* Waco, Tex.: Word Books, 1976.

Contains addresses delivered at the Continental Congress on the Family held in St. Louis in 1976. Commendable for its emphasis on marriage but inconsistent and therefore unreliable in its counsel. 362.8'2.C76

Conway, James. *Men in Mid-Life Crisis.* Elgin, Ill.: David C. Cook Publishing Co., 1978.

This book took the Christian world by storm. Building on his own experience, Conway developed a theory of mid-life crisis. He diagnosed the needs of males within this age span and sought to provide guidelines that would help them cope with their sudden, unexpected emotional problems. 155.6.C76

Conway, Sally. *You and Your Husband's Mid-Life Crisis.* Elgin, Ill.: David C. Cook Publishing Co., 1980.

Providing a wife's perspective on the mid-life crisis of her husband, this complement to *Men in Mid-Life Crisis* describes her experiences and shows other women how to cope with the problems peculiar to this period of life. 612'.665.C76Y

Cook, Barbara. *How to Raise Good Kids.* Minneapolis: Bethany Fellowship, 1978.

Ideal for young mothers. Realistically evaluates what can be done to rear happy, creative, well-balanced children. Offers some innovative ideas. 649'.7.C77

Cook, Jerry, and Barbara Cook. *Choosing to Love.* Ventura, Calif.: Regal Books, 1982.

A plain, practical account of a ho-hum marriage and how, through hard work and following some time-worn biblical principles, the Cooks turned it into an exciting adventure of discovering each other and the closeness this brought. 249.C77

Cooper, John C., and R. C. Wahlberg. *Your Exciting Middle Years.* Waco, Tex.: Word Books, 1976.

Designed as an "exciting journey of self-discovery," this practical book unfortunately bogs down where many couples do—in the frustrations, disappointments, fears, and unfulfilled hopes of the middle years. It does treat, however, the problems of "middlescence" realistically, and it is a work that deserves careful reading. 306.87.C78

Costales, Claire, and Jo Berry. *Staying Dry: A Workable Solution to the Problem of Alcohol Abuse.* Ventura, Calif.: Regal Books, 1983.

Formerly published under the title *Alcoholism: The Way Back to Reality,* this recounting of Claire Costales's personal odyssey offers hope and encouragement to those afflicted with this disease. 362.9.C82

*Crabb, Lawrence J., Jr. *The Marriage Builder: A Blueprint for Couples and Counselors.* Grand Rapids: Zondervan Publishing House, 1982.

Zeroes in on the need for unity in the marital relationship. Discusses in a clear, accurate way the steps each couple may take to strengthen their marriage. Valuable for those who are married as well as for counselors in churches and Christian

counseling centers. Recommended.
249.C84

**Crook, Roger H.** *An Open Book to the Christian Divorcee.* Nashville: Broadman Press, 1974.

After arguing that divorce should be a last resort, the author deals with a variety of problems that may lead up to divorce. He then discusses the ways a transition from married to single life can be made and calls for maturity on the part of both parties. This is a compassionate, well-intentioned book. 249.C87

**Cully, Iris V.** *Christian Child Development.* San Francisco: Harper & Row, 1979.

Applies contemporary psychological research in learning theory to Christian child rearing. Relates the findings of Erikson, Piaget, Kohlberg, and others to a child's intellectual, emotional, moral, and spiritual development. 249.B89C

**Curran, Dolores.** *Traits of a Healthy Family: Fifteen Traits Commonly Found in Healthy Families by Those Who Work with Them.* Minneapolis: Winston Press, 1983.

Curran discusses all of the highly ranked traits, adding her own commentary on the hallmarks of each characteristic. She is well equipped for the task, for her own counseling practice served as a resource for much of the material, and her syndicated column, "Talks with Parents" (read by more than four-and-a-half million people each week) has given her a phenomenal understanding of Americans and the homes they establish. Curran deals directly with the disruptive forces at work within our society and spells out the need of each member for the kinds of nurturance and support that are conducive to growth. Though secular in approach, this is a book that emphasizes basic biblical virtues such as respect, open communication, sharing, and affirming. 306.8.C93

**Dahl, Gerald L.** *Why Christian Mar-*

*riages Are Breaking Up.* Nashville: Thomas Nelson Publishers, 1979.

Confronts the rising tide of divorce among Christians and offers a blueprint whereby clogged channels of communication can be reopened and happiness restored. 249.D13

**Dicks, Henry V.** *Marital Tensions: Clinical Studies Towards a Psychological Theory of Interaction.* London: Routledge and Kegan Paul, 1983.

First published in 1967, the relevance of this work has increased with the passing of time. Dicks treats the philosophical concepts as well as the practical ways in which tension may be released and open communication restored. An excellent book. 306.87.D56 1983

**Dillow, Linda.** *Creative Counterpart.* Nashville: Thomas Nelson Publishers, 1977.

A choice book by a wife and mother who enjoys her vocation and has learned from experience how to handle the ups and downs of life without losing sight of her priorities. This is the kind of book every married man wishes his wife would read. 249.D59

**\*Dittes, James E.** *The Male Predicament: On Being a Man Today.* San Francisco: Harper & Row, 1985.

This is an insightful book. Dittes tackles realistically the plight of being a man in a woman's world. He dispenses with stereotypes and deals instead with the kinds of males who find themselves stymied by or who overreact to the situations they face. Pastors, counselors, and husbands/fathers need to read this work carefully. 305.3'1.D63

**Dobbert, John.** *The Love Diet.* Old Tappan, N.J.: Fleming H. Revell Co., 1977.

"Diets don't work," as most overweight people know, but love (caring, empathy, concern) within the family can and does provide the basis for effective weight loss. James Dobson wrote the Foreword and recommended this book highly. 613.25.D65

**Dobbins, Richard D.** *Venturing into a Child's World.* Old Tappan, N.J.: Fleming H. Revell Co., 1985.

This book provides each reader with an introduction to the mental, moral, spiritual, vocational, and physical dimensions of growth. The information should help parents nurture each child in terms of his/her age and stage of growth. Recommended. 249.D65

**Dobson, James Clayton, Jr.** *Dr. Dobson Answers Your Questions.* Wheaton, Ill.: Tyndale House Publishers, 1982.

An encyclopedic work that follows a question-and-answer method. Covers all aspects of marriage and child-rearing. Handy as a reference volume. 158.1.D65A

_____. *Hide or Seek.* Old Tappan, N.J.: Fleming H. Revell Co., 1974.

This book, by the author of *Dare to Discipline,* contains numerous practical suggestions for building a child's self-esteem. Dobson blends the teaching of Scripture with sound psychological principles to form a model that Christian parents may well follow. 649.1′019.D65

_____. *Love Must Be Tough: New Hope for Families in Crisis.* Waco, Tex.: Word Books, 1983.

Deals forthrightly with the need for appropriate assertion but fails to do justice to the theme of love because that important relational quality is not defined. The illustrations used to emphasize the various points are not explained with sufficient clarity, and the author's Arminian theology makes it easy for offended spouses to divorce their husbands/wives on the grounds that they lost their salvation and are to be classified as pagan. There is a place for tough love, but it must be exercised within the sphere of sound theology. 249.D65L

_____. *Preparing for Adolescence.* Santa Ana, Calif.: Vision House Publishers, 1978.

Seeks to answer questions teens and their parents are asking. This is a good book to prepare parents for the tumultuous years from thirteen through nineteen (and sometimes beyond), and it is a useful book for pastors as well. 155.5.D65P

_____. *Straight Talk to Men and Their Wives.* Waco, Tex.: Word Books, 1980.

In part a tribute to the author's father, this book concentrates on those issues that relate to one's identity from Christian and psychological points of view. 306.87.D65S

_____. *The Strong-willed Child: Birth Through Adolescence.* Wheaton, Ill.: Tyndale House Publishers, 1978.

Describes the trials and joys, peculiar hazards and rewards, of rearing precocious children. 649.1.D65S

_____. *What Wives Wish Their Husbands Knew About Women.* Wheaton, Ill.: Tyndale House Publishers, 1975.

Contains invaluable insights into problem areas of life. Will prove helpful to all who read it—men and women alike. Should be placed in the church library. 306.87.D65W

**Dollar, Truman E.,** and **Grace H. Ketterman.** *Teenage Rebellion.* Old Tappan, N.J.: Fleming H. Revell Co., 1980.

Though working from a very small sample, and therefore offering at best only tentative conclusions, these authors combine their understanding of the psychology of child development with a discussion of the problems of adolescents. 305.2.D69

**Doyle, James A.** *The Male Experience.* Dubuque, Iowa: Wm. C. Brown Publishers, 1984.

This work constitutes a new departure from the traditional approach to masculinity. The author combines insights from different disciplines to provide readers with an integrated understanding of "the male experience." 306.8'2.D77

**Drakeford, John W.** *Marriage: How to Keep a Good Thing Growing.* Nashville: Impact Books, 1979.

Amid the plethora of books on marriage and marital counseling, this one, advocating DMA—Decisive Motivational Action—outlines strategies that are designed to build, and then strengthen, the relationship of the couple. Though he follows certain tenets of behavioral modification, what Drakeford has presented is deserving of serious consideration. 249.D78M

**Duvall, Evelyn Ruth (Millis).** *Parent and Teenager: Living and Loving.* Nashville: Broadman Press, 1976.

Abounds with practical suggestions explaining how parents may maximize the benefits and minimize the tensions of the teenage years. 306.87.D95P

\*_____, and **Brent C. Miller.** *Marriage and Family Development.* 6th ed. New York: Harper & Row, 1985.

Approaches marriage from a developmental point of view. Deals admirably with modern trends within our complex American society. The coverage is excellent, and this work is worthy of repeated consultation. 306.8.D95M 1985

**Edens, David.** *Marriage: How to Have It the Way You Want It.* Englewood Cliffs, N.J.: Prentice-Hall, 1982.

This secular work, by an experienced clinical psychologist, is based in part on the author's marriage of more than thirty years. Edens's handling of contemporary issues is at once helpful and thought-provoking. He includes questionnaires, and these give some indication of the topics involved in his research and the scope covered by the book. 306.8.ED2

**Eichenlaub, John E.** *New Approaches to Sex in Marriage.* North Hollywood, Calif.: Wilshire Book Co., 1977.

The author of the popular *Marriage Art* here provides an important postscript to his earlier work by treating sexual problems and instructing couples as to what to do about them. Recommended. 249.EI2 1977

**Elkind, David.** *The Hurried Child: Growing Up Too Fast Too Soon.* Reading, Mass.: Addison-Wesley Publishing Co., 1981.

Believing that today's young people are "hurried children" who feel an intense pressure to achieve and a corresponding fear of failure, Elkind makes an urgent plea to parents not to push them too hard. Well researched. A valuable treatment. 305.2'3.EL5

**Fairfield, James G. T.** *When You Don't Agree.* Scottdale, Pa.: Herald Press, 1977.

A helpful and practical guide for resolving marital conflicts. This is the kind of book that can be read with profit by couples, and pastoral counselors can recommend it with confidence. 158.24.F15

**Figley, C. R.,** and **H. I. McCubbin,** eds. *Stress and the Family.* Vol. II: *Coping with Catastrophe.* New York: Brunner/Mazel, Publishers, 1983.

Introduces readers to the latest research in the area of stress and its effects on the family. Distinguishes between the sudden, unexpected, and overwhelming catastrophic kinds of stress and the kind that gradually increases over a period of time. A well-researched volume that will be of great help to counselors. 306.8'5.ST8F v.2

**Finch, Janet.** *Married to the Job: Wives' Incorporation in Men's Work.* London: George Allen and Unwin, 1983.

Examines an important but neglected area of the marital relationship—a wife's involvement in her husband's work (as executive, diplomat, clergyman, politician, etc.)—and stresses the need for her to see her role as a vital part of her marriage. An insightful discussion. 306.8.F49

**Flack, Frederic F.** *A New Marriage, A New Life.* New York: McGraw-Hill Book Co., 1978.

A practical, optimistic, self-help book for those who have recently remarried or who are contemplating a second marriage. Of primary value is the author's discussion of how human emotions may be turned to constructive use. 306.8.F59

**Florio, Anthony.** *Two to Get Ready.* Old Tappan, N.J.: Fleming H. Revell Co., 1974.

A basic, readable guide to emotional maturity. Florio gears his material for those in their twenties who are contemplating marriage. He provides sage counsel for would-be-weds and lays down principles for a lifetime of commitment to Christ and to each other. 306.8.F65

**Fooshee, George, Jr.** *You Can Be Financially Free.* Old Tappan, N.J.: Fleming H. Revell Co., 1976.

A practical, and in many respects excellent, book on financial management with an emphasis on being a good steward of the resources God has entrusted to us. 332'.024.F73

**Ford, Edward E.** *Choosing to Love: A New Way to Respond.* Minneapolis: Winston Press, 1983.

This important study, based on Glasser's *Reality Therapy,* takes a good, hard look at marriage and provides those facing marital deadlock with principles that ground their expectations in the bedrock of reality without necessarily sacrificing the ideals that make such a union worthwhile. 249.F75

**Forrest, Gary G.** *How to Cope with a Teenage Drinker: New Alternatives and Hope for Parents and Families.* New York: Athenium Press, 1983.

Believing that alcoholism is a family disease, Forrest maintains that whenever one family member has a serious problem, other members become vulnerable to a host of problems ranging from guilt to depression, anger, headaches, stomach problems, and a variety of psychosomatic disorders. It is for this reason that parents as well as siblings must totally commit themselves to the recovery process. Helpful. 362.8.F77

**Foster, Timothy.** *Dare to Lead.* Glendale, Calif.: Regal Books, 1977.

Challenges fathers to fulfill their God-appointed role and model maturity as well as spiritual and vocational values for their children. 155.2.F81

**Freeman, Carroll B.** *The Senior Adult Years: A Christian Psychology of Aging.* Nashville: Broadman Press, 1979.

This work exhibits an understanding of the problems of the aged and provides guidelines so that those who work with them may make their declining years fulfilling. Recommended. 155.67.F87

**Gabler, Mel, Norma Gabler,** and **James C. Hefley.** *What Are They Teaching Our Children?* Wheaton, Ill.: Victor Books, 1984.

The Gablers have engaged in a crusade to return well-identified values back to the schools. Theirs has not been a rabid attack on humanism but a diligent and intelligent approach. They have documented the dangers inherent in modern curricula, and the result is a timely book with an urgent message. It deserves close, careful reading. 371.32.G11

**Gage, Joy P.** *Broken Boundaries, Broken Lives.* Denver: Accent Books, 1981.

Tackles the tension between the rights of parents and the responsibilities of parents. The erosion of authority coupled with peer pressure has made the task of rearing one's children doubly difficult. Gage sets out to help parents cope and provides guidelines for them to follow. This is a perceptive and very necessary work. 249.G12

**\*Gangel, Kenneth Otto.** *The Family First.* Rev. ed. Winona Lake, Ind.: BMH Books, 1979.

The reissue of a popular book that places long-neglected emphasis on the centrality of the family and seeks to provide couples with clear guidelines for the establishment of proper, appropriate priorities. Recommended. 249.G15 1979

**Gerstel, Naomi,** and **Harriett Gross.** *Commuter Marriage: A Study of Work and Family.* New York: Guildford Press, 1984.

Keeping pace with growing economic and career opportunities for women is the incidence of commuter, or dual-career, dual-residence, marriages. As these marriages attest, coresidence, once taken to be the cornerstone of marriage, is no longer the sine qua non of a viable intimate relationship. This book provides a novel response to an old problem commuter marriages represent: they are at once a radical departure from the conventional husband-breadwinner/wife-homemaker arrangement and an affirmation of two of society's most abiding values—the commitment to individual career achievement and the commitment to family. 306.81.AM3.G32

**\*Getz, Gene A.** *The Measure of a Family.* Glendale, Calif.: Regal Books, 1976.

A clear presentation of the role and relationships of those within the Christian home. Excellent. 249.G33F

———. *The Measure of Marriage.* Glendale, Calif.: Regal Books, 1980.

Packed with practical information, outlines, and exercises, this handy book lends itself for use in adult discussion groups. It should be read by those who are married as well as by those who contemplate marriage. 306.8.G33

**Gillies, John.** *A Guide to Caring for and Coping with Aging Parents.* Nashville: Thomas Nelson Publishers, 1981.

A sensitive, loving, and practical approach to the issues that face the middle-aged whose parents can no longer lead independent lives. 646.7'8.G41

**Goldstein, Sonja,** and **Albert J. Solnit.** *Divorce and Your Child: Practical Suggestions for Parents.* New Haven, Conn.: Yale University Press, 1984.

"This book is simply and clearly written and covers practically every conceivable physical and psychological problem that can arise in custody cases. The section on finding and using a lawyer is hard-hitting and sound" (Sanford N. Katz). 646.78.G57

**Goodwin, Jean, et al.** *Sexual Abuse: Incest Victims and Their Families.* Boston: John Wright/PSG Inc., 1982.

Drawing on the experiences of a variety of professionals, Goodwin and her associates describe the rise in the incidents of incest, its cause, and what counselors, clergy, and those in the medical profession may do about it. 306.7.G63

**Gottman, John Mordecai.** *Marital Interaction: Experimental Investigations.* New York: Academic Press, 1979.

The English-speaking world has come to respect the writings of this esteemed social psychologist. In this work he discusses the results of his research into contemporary forms of marital communication—with some interesting discoveries. Pastors may validly apply the truths Gottman uncovers to the needs of some of those in their congregations. 306.87.G71M

**Greenfield, Guy.** *The Wounded Parent: Coping with Parental Discouragement.* Grand Rapids: Baker Book House, 1982.

Tackles the problems of child-rearing and offers both short-term and long-range help. Deals constructively with such topics as managing emotions, overcoming discouragement, and restoring communication. 306.87.G83

**\*Guernsey, Dennis B.** *Thoroughly Married.* Waco, Tex.: Word Books, 1976.

A clear delineation of the way in which

a proper understanding of the Bible's teaching on marriage contributes toward the development of a stable life-style, a healthier sex life, and a happier home. 306.8.G93

**Gundry, Patricia.** *Heirs Together.* Grand Rapids: Zondervan Publishing House, 1980.

A courageous description of marriage, its privileges, limitations, and reciprocal responsibilities, with a logical, balanced discussion of mutual submission. 306.87.G85H

**Gurman, Alan S.,** and **David G. Rice, eds.** *Couples in Conflict.* New York: Jason Aronson, 1975.

Well written, and containing chapters by psychologists, sociologists, and social workers, this objective, innovative approach to the problems married couples face challenges those in the helping professions and at the same time clarifies what counselors can and cannot do to help them. Valuable. 306.8.G96

**Halverson, Kaye,** and **Karen M. Hess.** *The Wedded Unmother.* Minneapolis: Augsburg Publishing House, 1980.

A sympathetic discussion of the plight of the childless wife. Shares her hurts and provides comforting counsel for those trying to overcome infertility. 306.85.H16

**Hamilton, Marshall L.** *Father's Influence on Children.* Chicago: Nelson-Hall, 1977.

Unlike other psychological studies, this book does more than provide an analysis of statistics. It describes how the absence of the father affects the home, how he influences his sons and daughters, and how he may increase his effectiveness. Stimulating. Secular. 306.87.H18

**Hancock, Maxine.** *The Forever Principle,* Old Tappan, N.J.: Fleming H. Revell Co., 1980.

Develops a persuasive apologetic for a firm commitment on the part of those entering into marriage. Describes the benefits that accrue to the couple and the way in which such a commitment forms the basis for all work toward meaningful solutions to interpersonal problems, resulting in satisfaction from the relationship. 306.8.H19

**Hardisty, George,** and **Margaret Hardisty.** *Honest Questions—Honest Answers to Enrich Your Marriage.* Irvine, Calif.: Harvest House Publishers, 1977.

This sequel to *Forever My Love* deals with the questions people have asked in seminars conducted by this husband-wife team. 261.8.H21Q

**Hardisty, Margaret.** *Forever My Love.* Irvine, Calif.: Harvest House Publishers, 1975.

What constitutes the "feminine mystique"? The subtitle on the cover of the book supplies the answer. The autho explains what women wish their hus bands knew about them and at the same time provides a helpful prescription for renewing love in marriage. 249.H21

**Harnik, Bernard.** *Risk and Chance in Marriage.* Waco, Tex.: Word Books, 1975.

Of value for its clarity and depth of perception into the motives and behavioral patterns established by married couples. Most helpful. 306.8.H22

**Hart, Thomas N.,** and **Kathleen Fischer Hart.** *The First Two Years of Marriage: Foundations for a Life Together.* New York: Paulist Press, 1983.

Believing that the first two years of marriage are crucial, the authors assess areas of conflict, possible stagnation, and the difficulties of developing true unity. The approach of the Harts is practical and designed to bring vitality to the relationship. A must for newlyweds. 249.H25

**\*Heiderbrecht, Paul,** and **Jerry Rohrbach.** *Fathering a Son.* Chicago: Moody Press, 1979.

Without heaping guilt on absent fathers and working mothers, the authors demonstrate the importance of the father-son relationship and describe practical ways in which quality time may be spent with one's children. 649.1′32.H36

**Heim, Pamela.** *The Art of Married Love.* Irvine, Calif.: Harvest House Publishers, 1978.

Imperfect people make imperfect spouses and have imperfect marriages. This book shows how a couple may create a harmonious atmosphere in which to work on their respective failings. 249.H36

**\*Hendricks, Howard George.** *Heaven Help the Home.* Wheaton, Ill.: Victor Books, 1973.

A refreshingly candid analysis of the pressures brought to bear on homemakers. Shows how stress may be handled without losing sight of one's priorities or goals. A valuable guide for newlyweds. 249.H38

**Henslin, James M., ed.** *Marriage and Family in a Changing Society.* New York: The Free Press, 1980.

In forty-two brief chapters the contributors discuss all aspects of the interpersonal process, from courtship and the romantic ideal to marital adjustments and the future of the family. 306.8.H39

**Herron, Orley.** *Who Controls Your Child?* Nashville: Thomas Nelson Publishers, 1980.

Sobering in his revelation of the destructive forces surrounding children and youth today, Herron nevertheless is able to challenge parents with a realistic plan of action. He shows them how the home may constructively offset the impact of a secular, godless society and build into each child those strengths that will enable him/her to withstand the pressures that are destructive of the finer things in life. A must for all parents. 649′.1.H43

**Heth, William A.,** and **Gordon J. Wenham.** *Jesus and Divorce: The Problem with the Evangelical Consensus.* Nashville:

Thomas Nelson Publishers, 1984.

Divorce and remarriage remain among the most divisive issues in evangelical circles today, even though the general consensus has existed since the Reformation that it is permissible to remarry in instances where adultery has ruptured the relationship. The authors subject this statement to close scrutiny and find serious flaws in the popular understanding of Christ's teaching in Matthew 19:9. They deal convincingly with the NT evidence and in every respect give to readers a wealth of factual information. What is needed now is a comparable work on the OT, for a valid inference of the Bible's teaching cannot be based on partial evidence. 306.8′9.H47

**\*Hindson, Edward E.** *The Total Family.* Wheaton, Ill.: Tyndale House Publishers, 1980.

Drawing information from many sources, Hindson integrates his material with the Scriptures and presents to his readers practical guidelines for the enrichment of family life and the enabling of each member to achieve his/her full potential. Recommended. 306.8.H58

**Hobbs, Nicholas, et al.** *Strengthening Families.* San Francisco: Jossey-Bass Publishers, 1984.

Because America is experiencing a revolution in work and family life, guidelines need to be developed to strengthen family relationships. This book provides counsel that points out ways to fulfill human development needs and at the same time build family strengths. Hobbs also assesses many of the ingredients involved in child care and parent education. 306.8.AM3.H65

**Hof, Larry,** and **William Ross Miller.** *Marriage Enrichment: Philosophy, Process, and Program.* Bowie, Md.: Robert J. Brady Co., 1981.

Tackles the issue of marital fulfillment

from basic philosophical issues to the expression of affection. Well researched, clear, concise. 301.42.H67

**Holland, John M., ed.** *Religion and Sexuality: Judaic-Christian Viewpoints in the USA.* San Francisco: Association of Sexologists, 1981.

Containing six essays relating to Jewish, Catholic, and Protestant sexual mores, this work seeks to establish a basis for future dialogue. Letha Scanzoni, the only woman contributor, represents the Protestant position inadequately and from a liberal perspective. 306.6.H71

**Holmes, Deborah Lott, and Frederick J. Morrison.** *The Child: An Introduction to Developmental Psychology.* Monterey, Calif.: Brooks/Cole Publishing Co., 1979.

Assists parents in keeping pace with the changes that have taken place over the past twenty years, instructs babysitters on how to respond to cases of child abuse, and provides counsel on what to say and how to deal with neighborhood young people who come wanting counsel. This book will also prove useful to pastors who need a brief manual on the way in which a child's developmental needs impact the church's educational program. For both parents and pastoral staff, this work makes available an abundance of useful material that will help encourage and instruct children in accordance with their growth. 155.4.H73

**Hooker, Susan.** *Caring for Elderly People.* 2d ed. London: Routledge and Kegan Paul, 1981.

More than just another book on the aging process and the care of the elderly, this book also focuses on various types of disability—physical, mental, psychological—and offers constructive counsel on how to diagnose and treat these complex issues. An excellent work. 649.8.H76 1981

**Hudson, Robert Lofton.** *Til Divorce Do Us Part.* Nashville: Thomas Nelson Publishers, 1973.

There is much to learn about compassion in this book, but it is to be regretted that the heart-wrenching experiences of his clients has colored the author's approach to the Scriptures. He sets aside the normal understanding of biblical passages dealing with divorce as literalistic and an impediment to counseling and adopts, instead, a permissive stance by concluding that the Bible permits divorce and remarriage for believers on grounds other than infidelity. 306.89.H86

**Hyder, O. Quentin.** *The People You Live With.* Old Tappan, N.J.: Fleming H. Revell Co., 1975.

A lucid discussion of the different kinds of interpersonal relationships that operate within the family circle. Abounds with useful, practical insights. 306.87.H99 (Alt. DDC 261.8′34)

**\*Ilg, Frances Lillian, Louise Bates Ames, and Sidney M. Baker.** *Child Behavior.* Rev. ed. New York: Harper & Row, 1981.

Members of the Gesell Institute of Human Development share with their readers the counsel they have given parents on how they may rear their children. Excellent. 649′.1.IL4

**James, Muriel.** *Breaking Free: Self-Reparenting for a New Life.* Reading, Mass.: Addison-Wesley Publishing Co., 1981.

Based on TA, this competent handling of one of the keys to personal maturity is worthy of careful consideration. 158.1.J23

**Jenkins, Peggy Davison.** *A Child of God: Activities for Teaching Spiritual Values to Children of All Ages.* Englewood Cliffs, N.J.: Prentice-Hall, 1984.

†The goal of this book is to help young people start believing the things that are true about themselves. The lessons are simple. The ideals will need to be adapted, however, for evangelicals. The practical object lessons and other forms of visual communication are easy-to-use

and excellent as educational aids. 249.J41

**Jensen, Larry Cyril,** and **Janet Mitchell Jensen.** *Stepping into Stepparenting: A Practical Guide.* Palo Alto, Calif.: R. and E. Research Associates, 1981.

With FMs marrying and rearing their new spouse's children, the issues of stepparenting have come to the fore. This book highlights the problems as well as the opportunities. 306.87.J45

**Johnson, James L.** *What Every Woman Should Know About a Man.* Grand Rapids: Zondervan Publishing House, 1977.

The author is a journalist, not a sociologist. He gives evidence of being well read in the area of marriage and family relations. The advice he gives is well intentioned and may help some marriages. Other couples, however, will need more insightful assistance if they are to be helped over the hurdles that lie in their path. 249.J63

**Johnson, Rex.** *Communication: Key to Your Parents.* Irvine, Calif.: Harvest House Publications, 1978.

Tackles the problems of adolescents (and their parents), and offers helpful suggestions that will enable young people to better understand their fathers and mothers and also have a clearer understanding of the change that is taking place in their lives. 249.J63

**\*Johnston, Olaf Raymond.** *Who Needs the Family?* Downers Grove, Ill.: InterVarsity Press, 1979.

Biblically and sociologically sound, this astute discussion of changes taking place in modern marriages not only assesses the past but points the way to reconstruction so that children may have a viable future. 306.8.J64

**Jolly, Hugh.** *The First Five Years: Answers Questions from Parents.* Minneapolis: Winston Press, 1984.

A book that aims at authenticity and practicality and makes available to parents a beautifully illustrated, reliable guide on rearing children from birth to five. A must. 306.8'7.J68

**Jones, John Edward,** and **John D. Boneck.** *Reconciliation.* Minneapolis: Bethany House Publishers, 1984.

A brief, empathic statement of the place of reconciliation in human relationships. Recommended. 249.J71

**Kaye, Evelyn.** *The Family Guide to Children's Television.* New York: Random House, 1974.

Though written from a non-Christian perspective, this book presents an aspect of child-rearing that every parent has encountered in one form or another. The brief evaluations of then-current TV shows is now dated, but the criteria that went into making a determination as to their respective merit may help parents assess the worth of modern serial entertainment. 791.455.K18

**Kelly, Robert K.** *Courtship, Marriage, and the Family.* 3d ed. New York: Harcourt, Brace and Jovanovich, 1979.

A complete coverage of marriage from patterns of courtship to old age. Includes important chapters on such topics as pairing, the problems of premarital relations, changing roles, marriage expectations, dual careers, sexual adjustment, the place of religion, children or childlessness, and adoption. Ideal for those who work with young peole and/or couples in the church. 306.8.K28 1979

**Kendall, Earline Doak,** and **Betty Doak Elder.** *Train Up Your Child . . .: A Guide for Christian Parents.* Nashville: Abingdon Press, 1980.

Two sisters, both married with families of their own, team up to write on the importance of nurturing children in the way of the Lord. In a series of important chapters they describe the process, the problems, and the rewards. 649.7.K33

**\*Kenny, James Andrew,** and **Mary Kenny.** *Whole-Life Parenting.* New York: Continuum Publishers, 1984.

A vigorous challenge to parents to

build into the lives of their children the kind of beliefs, values, and goals that will prepare them for life. Surveys each stage of a child's growth and shows how parents may develop positive traits in their offspring. Recommended. 649'.1.K39

**Kesler, Jay,** and **Ronald A. Beers.** *Parents and Teenagers.* Wheaton, Ill.: Victor Books, 1984.

This book of almost 700 pages is a potpourri of information covering everything from the roles and responsibilities of parents to the handling of different values in teenage development. All the leading "authorities" are represented. The problem with this almanac is that each chapter is too brief to be truly helpful. Parents will derive little lasting benefit from this work. Those who are most likely to use it are preachers who are often asked to address parents on the task of rearing children in an age when peer pressure has replaced the home as the arena in which beliefs, values, and goals are forged. They will find in this book pithy statements and the names of authorities that will lend weight to the material they may choose to quote. 155.5.K48

**\*Kiev, Ari.** *How to Keep Love Alive.* New York: Harper & Row, 1982.

This is an excellent book. Kiev shows how couples may use conflict to effect change and make love grow. His counsel is wise, his insights into human experience are valid, and his ability to communicate what he wants his readers to know is remarkable. Recommended. 646.7'8.K54

**Kiley, Dan.** *The Peter Pan Syndrome: Men Who Have Never Grown Up.* New York: Dodd, Mead and Co., 1983.

Uses the story of Peter Pan to illustrate the rise of passivity and immaturity in grown men. Kiley does not relate this phenomenon to the matriarchal system of child-rearing or identify it as a possible

consequence of some single-parent families, but his analysis of the psychosocial manifestations of immaturity is accurate. The challenge of this book to those in the ministry is to recognize the problem and meet the emptiness and aimlessness of immature males in appropriate God-directed ways. 155.6'32.K55

————. *The Wendy Dilemma: When Women Stop Mothering Their Men.* New York: Arbor House, 1984.

This is a bold, and in some respects, daring approach to the kinds of changes a woman is likely to face when she stops being a mother to the man she married. There are dangers involved in implementing the changes Kiley suggests, but as a wise counselor, he prepares his readers for the difficulties they are likely to encounter. 155.6.K55W

**\*Kilgore, James E.** *Being a Man in a Woman's World.* Irvine, Calif.: Harvest House Publishers, 1976.

In the hope that the furor over "Women's Lib" and ERA is finally dying down, Kilgore draws attention to a long ignored fact. He writes to help the husband/father recover his fallen image and sadly shattered sense of esteem. His counsel is balanced and timely. It contains the kind of information that men (from their late teens onwards) need to read, and reread. 306.87.K55

————. *The Intimate Man.* Nashville: Abingdon Press, 1984.

Written for men, this work bears a subtitle on the cover that explains the purpose of the book: "Intimacy and Masculinity in the 80s." Having previously written on how to be a man in a woman's world, Kilgore knows what men need to hear. His counsel is sane and balanced. 305.3.K55

————. *Dollars and Sense: Family Strength Through Financial Education.* Nashville: Abingdon Press, 1982.

An invaluable guide for husbands and

wives, showing how they may use their resources wisely. This is a good work to use in premarital and marital counseling. 332'.024.K55

———. *Try Marriage Before Divorce.* Waco, Tex.: Word Books, 1978.

This is a good book. True to its title, it recommends that couples give marriage a good try and avoid taking the "easy way" out of their difficulties. Kilgore shows how marital problems can be handled openly and honestly, before they become full-blown predicaments that require the services of a professional counselor to unravel. 306.87.K55T

**Kizziar, Janet, and Judy Hagehorn.** *Search for Acceptance: The Adolescent and Self-esteem.* Chicago: Nelson-Hall, 1979.

A sensitive introduction to the developmental nature and needs of adolescents. Should be in every youth pastor's library. 155.5.K65

**Klimek, David.** *Beneath Mate Selection and Marriage: The Unconscious Motives in Human Pairing.* New York: Van Nostrand Reinhold Co., 1979.

This helpful manual will be welcomed by all youth pastors and those involved in premarital counseling. It describes the maturation process and the origin of character traits that lead young people to instinctively select a certain type of spouse, frequently with unhappy results. The careful study of this book is recommended. It will be of particular value in helping to prevent problems from arising rather than seeking to remedy them after they have developed. 306.82.K68B

**Knight, Bryan M.** *Enjoying Single Parenthood.* New York: Van Nostrand Reinhold Co., 1980.

†Deals with a wide variety of single-parent situations and experiences. Provides practical guidance and a positive approach to the challenges as well as the difficulties involved. Good principles may be culled from this book without

adopting its seemingly permissive morality. 362.8'2.K74

**Knox, David.** *Marriage Happiness: A Behavioral Approach to Counseling.* Champaign, Ill.: Research Press 1971.

An analysis of the cause and cure of marital problems. Of value in premarital and postmarital counseling. Secular in its orientation. 249.K77

**Kohlberg, Lawrence.** *Essays on Moral Development.* In process. Cambridge: Harper & Row, 1981-.

Scheduled for three volumes, these essays, grouped under the various stages of the development of moral values, provide an excellent discussion from which Christian educators and parents may gain valuable insights. 155.2'34.K82

**Kohn, Jane Burgess, and Willard K. Kohn.** *The Widower.* Boston: Beacon Press, 1978.

An important, secular work. "A welcome corrective to the erroneous popular concept that widowers have an easier time of things than do widows. . . . [Contains] sections dealing with grief, coming to grips with loneliness, and, most important, coping with problems arising from children left without maternal care" *(Library Journal).* 155.9'37.K82

**Kubler-Ross, Elisabeth.** *On Children and Death.* New York: Macmillan Publishing Co., 1983.

A thorough treatment of the ways children may be prepared for death as well as the best methods parents may use to prepare themselves for the eventual loss of a terminally ill child. 155.9'37.K95C

**LaHaye, Beverly.** *How to Develop Your Child's Temperament.* Irvine, Calif.: Harvest House Publishers, 1977.

Popularly written, this book gives evidence of the author's experience. Its counsel is particularly apropos to young mothers, and it may also be used by women in church groups. 649;1.L13

**LaHaye, Tim.** *The Battle for the Family.*

Old Tappan, N.J.: Fleming H. Revell Co., 1982.

Evaluates the positive and negative forces being brought to bear on the family today. Points the way to the restoration of moral and spiritual values in the home. Recommended. 306.8.L13

————. *The Battle for the Public Schools.* Old Tappan, N.J.: Fleming H. Revell Co., 1983.

Subtitled "Humanism's Threat to Our Children," this fine, popular exposé of the antibiblical influence of secular humanism on education deserves an honored place in the home of every concerned parent and teacher. A must for the church library. 371'.01.AM3.L13

**Lamm, Maurice.** *The Jewish Way in Love and Marriage.* San Francisco: Harper & Row, 1980.

Though not of the order of Neufeld's *Ancient Hebrew Marriage Laws* or Epstein's numerous works on Jewish marriage customs, this excellent treatment of the history, traditions, and practices associated with Jewish marital rites meets a felt need and provides valuable insights. 306.8.L18

**Laney, J. Carl.** *The Divorce Myth.* Minneapolis: Bethany House Publishers, 1981.

Tackles bravely and with conviction the issue of divorce. Grapples realistically with each passage of Scripture and concludes that marriage is for life and cannot be terminated. Would-be divorcees as well as pastoral counselors need to be familiar with this book. 306.8'9.L24

**Lauer, Robert H.,** and **Jeanette C. Lauer.** *The Spirit and the Flesh: Sex in Utopian Communities.* Metuchen, N.J.: Scarecrow Press, 1983.

This book probes American culture and popular sexual mores. It focuses attention on supposedly utopian societies and provides a clear analysis of the aims and motives of these groups. 306.7.L36

**Lee, Francis Nigel.** *The Central Significance of Culture.* Nutley, N.J.: Presbyterian and Reformed Publishing Co., 1976.

Contains five lectures and three appendixes. Traces the origin of culture and the way it impacts society. Reformed. 301.2.L51

**Lee, Mark Wilcox.** *Creative Christian Marriage.* Glendale, Calif.: Regal Books, 1977.

A candid rehearsal of the major trouble spots of marriage—with one notable omission, in-laws. Fulfills the author's aim of assisting families in their development and in the easing of tensions within the family circle. 249.L51

————. *How to Have a Good Marriage Before and After the Wedding.* Chappaqua, N.Y.: Christian Herald Books, 1978.

The bulk of this book consists of fifty questions and answers that the author believes will prepare a couple for marriage. 306.8.L51H

**Lee, Robert,** and **Marjorie Casebier.** *The Spouse Gap: Weathering the Marriage Crisis During Middlescence.* Nashville: Abingdon Press, 1971.

A realistic approach to the problems of those who think they have weathered all the storms of marriage only to find themselves caught in what some have termed the mid-life crisis. Advises readers what to expect. Provides clear guidelines on what to do. Contains the kind of help that may well save many marriages. Recommended. 306.87.L51

**Leman, Kevin.** *The Birth Order Book: Why You Are the Way You Are.* Old Tappan, N.J.: Fleming H. Revell Co., 1984.

Contains a wealth of information that Leman hopes will help us improve our interpersonal relationships, appreciate our strengths, and overcome our weaknesses. Of value to parents as well as people in all walks of life. 155.9.L54

**LeMasters, E. E.** *Parents in Modern America.* 3d ed. Homewood, Ill.: Dorsey Press, 1977.

An attempt to define parental roles within our modern American milieu. Seeks to restore some of the authority taken from parents by social institutions like the church, schools, mass media, and government. 306.87.L54

**Leslie, Robert Campbell,** and **Margaret G. Alter.** *Sustaining Intimacy.* Nashville: Abingdon Press, 1978.

A substantive work from which newlyweds as well as those in the mid-life malaise may profit. 306.87.L56

**Lewis, Kay Oliver.** *The Complete Handbook for Planning Your Christian Wedding.* Old Tappan, N.J.: Fleming H. Revell Co., 1981.

Not as complete as the title suggests but certainly a most helpful work that will assist the bride in planning a distinctive Christian wedding. Recommended for church libraries. 392.5.L58

**Lewis, Margaret M.,** and **Gregg A. Lewis.** *The Hurting Parent.* Grand Rapids: Zondervan Publishing House, 1980.

This mother-son team writes empathetically of the problems of child-rearing and the differences a vital Godward relationship can make. Recommended for church libraries. 248.8′6.L58

**Lief, Nina R.,** and **M. E. Fahs.** *The Second Year of Life: A Guide for Parenting.* New York: Dodd, Mead and Co., 1984.

A full and comprehensive assessment of the challenges two-year-olds pose as well as the needs they have. It is a work that should be read by all parents as well as pastors and counselors. Recommended. 649′.122.L62

**Linthorst, Ann Tremaine.** *A Gift of Love: Marriage as a Spiritual Journey.* New York: Paulist Press, 1979.

Written by a marriage and family counselor, this treatment covers both old and new ground. It reasserts some long-held basic beliefs about marriage and applies spiritual principles to the everyday problems married couples encounter. 249.L65

**Little, Marilyn.** *Family Breakup.* San Francisco: Jossey-Bass Publishers, 1982.

Studies the causes, patterns, and effects of marital problems and the mediating of child custody decisions. Draws information from a variety of interviews and shares her insights on the dynamics of adjustment. 306.8′9.L72

**\*Lockerbie, D. Bruce.** *Fatherlove: Learning to Give the Best You've Got.* Garden City, N.Y.: Doubleday and Co., 1981.

Shares his experiences with those called to the high and solemn responsibility of being a parent. Excellent. 649′.1.L79

_____. *Who Educates Your Child? A Book for Parents.* Garden City, N.Y.: Doubleday and Co., 1980.

Fully cognizant of the current dilemma facing Christian parents, Lockerbie cuts through the intellectual, political, and emotional confusion. By placing the responsibility squarely where it belongs, he provides wise counsel for parents as well as educators. Recommended. 370.1.L79W

**Love, Vicky.** *Childless Is Not Less.* Minneapolis: Bethany House Publishers, 1984.

Ably introduced by Ann Kiemel Anderson, this poignant book offers comfort and consolation to all infertile married women and their husbands. It is to be recommended for the comfort it brings those who suffer from an inability to bear children. 304.6′6.L94

**Ludwig, David J.** *The Spirit of Your Marriage.* Minneapolis: Augsburg Publishing House, 1979.

Describes ways in which Christian couples can create a richer and more fulfilling environment for the cultivation of their marital relationship. 249.L96

**\*MacArthur, John F., Jr.** *The Family.* Chicago: Moody Press, 1982.

Brief, pointed messages on the patterns established by God for our interpersonal relationships. Ably expounds

Ephesians 5:18—6:4, and concludes with chapters on divorce and remarriage. Recommended. 249.M11

**Macaulay, Susan Schaeffer.** *For the Children's Sake: Foundations of Education for Home and School.* Westchester, Ill.: Crossway Books 1984.

Born out of the author's experience, this book adapts and applies the educational theories of Charlotte Mason to education of children in the home and in the school. A competent, timely, and important work. 370'.01.M11

**MacDonald, Gordon.** *The Effective Father.* Wheaton, Ill.: Tyndale House Publishers, 1977.

An excellent discussion of one of the most important and demanding roles in any society. This timely book should be read by all fathers and the principles enunciated by the author should be put into practice with consistency. 249.M14

**\*Mace, Donald Robert.** *Close Companions: The Marriage Enrichment Handbook.* New York: Continuum, 1982.

A clear, authoritative discussion of marriage past and present, with enlightening chapters detailing the ways in which husbands and wives bring fresh vitality to their relationships. An excellent discussion. 646.7'8.M15C

\*———. *Love and Anger in Marriage.* Grand Rapids: Zondervan Publishing House, 1982.

Written by the dean of marriage and family specialists, this work deals with the way to handle anger while maintaining close, intimate relations with your spouse. Recommended. 306.8'1.M15L

\*———. *Whom God Hath Joined.* Rev. ed. Philadelphia: Westminster Press, 1973.

A valuable and, in some respects, indispensable book. Excellent. 301.42'7.M15 1973

\*———, and **Vera Mace.** *How to Have a Happy Marriage: A Step-by-Step Guide to an*

*Enriched Relationship.* Nashville: Abingdon Press, 1977.

An excellent discussion of interpersonal relationships within the marital dyad. Recommended. 306.8.M15H

———. *We Can Have Better Marriages If We Really Want Them.* Nashville: Abingdon Press, 1974.

One of the better books to be published on this subject in recent years. Focuses attention on the causes of contention, the way in which difficulties may be resolved, and the best means for achieving lasting enrichment from the marital relationship. 306.8.M15W

**Mahan, Sue.** *Unfit Mothers.* Palo Alto, Calif.: R. and E. Research Associates, 1982.

A penetrating assessment of the causes leading up to the failure of some mothers. Perceptive. Should be read by all pastoral counselors. 306.7.M27

**Martin, Ralph.** *Husbands, Wives, Parents, Children: Foundations for the Christian Family.* Ann Arbor, Mich.: Servant Books, 1983.

The author, a Roman Catholic layman, has produced a work that deserves wide reading. Larry Christensen calls it "a wise and practical book." 249.M36

**Mason, John M.** *The Fourth Generation.* Minneapolis: Augsburg Publishing House, 1978.

A candid look at the personal dilemmas of the aged. Offers practical suggestions to those who must care for them. Shows how their declining years may be made meaningful. 305.26.M38

**Master, William H.,** and **Virginia E. Masters (Johnson).** *The Pleasure Bond: A New Look at Sexuality and Commitment.* Boston: Little, Brown and Co., 1975.

Answers many questions that have long plagued married couples and marriage and family counselors. An important strength of this book lies in the emphasis the authors place on loyalty to one's marriage partner as the only basis for proper communication and lasting intimacy. 306.87.M39

**Mattson, Lloyd, and Elsie Mattson.** *Rediscover Your Family Outdoors.* Wheaton, Ill.: Victor Books, 1980.

A reminder of the ways in which families may achieve a sense of togetherness through one-day excursions from the home or through travel, hiking, and camping. A practical book filled with sage suggestions. 796.54.M43R

**Mayfield, James L.** *Up with Marriage: A Positive Adventure in Marriage Enrichment Through Improved Communication.* Independence, Mo.: Herald Publishing House, 1979.

The author places his finger on the number one cause of marital breakdown and describes steps that couples may take to insure that the channels of communication are kept open. Recommended. 306.87.M45

**Mayhall, Jack, and Carol Mayhall.** *Marriage Takes More Than Love.* Colorado Springs, Colo.: NavPress, 1978.

Writing from a background rich in personal experience, the Mayhalls zero in on the distinctive facets of a Christian marriage and challenge their readers with both the precepts and the practice of a happy, rewarding relationship. 306.8.M45M

**McCoy, Kathleen.** *Coping with Teenage Depression: A Parent's Guide.* New York: New American Library, 1982.

Enters the world of the teenager and traces the cause of much of the frustration and disillusionment experienced by America's youth. An important resource. 616.85.M13

**McCubbin, H. I., and C. R. Figley, eds.** *Stress and the Family.* Vol. I: *Coping with Normative Transitions.* New York: Brunner/Mazel, Publishers, 1983.

Focuses on extraordinary stress situations that suddenly strike families and have a devastating effect on all members. Incorporates the latest research, theories of treatment, and therapeutic techniques into the kind of book that can be read with profit by all who are involved in the situation. Makes an important contribution. 306.8'5.ST8 v.1

**\*McDonald, Cleveland.** *Creating a Successful Christian Marriage.* Grand Rapids: Baker Book House, 1975.

This is an important sociological treatment and is well deserving of serious consideration. McDonald ably integrates psychology and sociology with the Scriptures. 306.8.M14

**McDowell, Josh.** *The Secret of Loving: How a Lasting Intimate Relationship Can Be Yours.* San Bernardino, Calif.: Here's Life Publishers, 1985.

Places responsibility for change squarely on the couple. Describes how growth in all areas of the relationship may take place. Demonstrates how mature love can make the difference and lead to the enjoyment of mutually lasting satisfaction. 249.M14S

**McGill, Michael E.** *The McGill Report on Male Intimacy.* New York: Holt, Rinehart and Winston, 1985.

The writer's findings have led him to conclude that "the American male seems incapable of establishing relationships with his spouse, family and friends." Based on more than a decade of research, in which more than 5,000 men and women were surveyed, McGill uncovered vast differences in male-female caring behavior. He then set about explaining the cause. The results are revealing. Among other things he discovered information that "the other woman" is often a nonsexual relationship in which the traditional expectation of adultery is absent, that men in so-called mid-life often collapse in anomie and despair, and that certain men use a variety of means to avoid intimacy with family and friends. There are many sentiments expressed in these pages that others may not consider normative, but McGill has succeeded in providing a valuable analysis of contemporary male problems with interpersonal relationships. 155.6′32.M17

**McGuire, Paula.** *It Won't Happen to Me: Teenagers Talk About Pregnancy.* New York: Delacorte Press, 1983.

Printed on inferior quality paper, this work is one to which pastoral counselors will want to refer again and again. McGuire uses case histories to illumine the points she wishes to make, and her handling of the delicate issues is tasteful and discreet. Excellent. 306.7.M17

***McMillan, Sim I.** None of These Diseases.* Revised and expanded by D. E. Stern. Old Tappan, N.J.: Fleming H. Revell Co., 1984.

This epochal work, when first published in 1963, drew attention to the biblical teaching on health and the care of the body. Now updated with information on modern diseases, it is even more valuable than when it broke new ground two decades ago. 613.M22 1984

**McRoberts, Darlene.** *Second Marriage: The Promise and the Challenge.* Minneapolis: Augsburg Publishing House, 1978.

This sequel to *The Hurt and Healing of Divorce* deals with the problems of a second marriage. It is also a well-researched, practical guide that others in a similar situation may read with profit. 306.8.M24S

**Meier, Paul D.** *Christian Child-Rearing and Personality Development.* Grand Rapids: Baker Book House, 1977.

A straightforward enunciation of the developmental phases of childhood, with practical counsel on how parents may assure the sound emotional growth of their children. Moderately Freudian. 649.1.M48C

**Meredith, Donald.** *Becoming One.* Nashville: Thomas Nelson Publishers, 1979.

Treats five common pitfalls of marriage, and explains in concise terms what couples can do to strengthen their union. One would like to commend this book, but it unhappily exhibits a shallowness that is disappointing—particularly when treating such topics as role relationships, sex, and finances—and all too often the counsel given is trite. About all one can say that is positive is that this book may be of help to courting couples who have come from very sheltered environments. 306.8.M54

**Merrill, Dean,** and **Grace Merrill.** *Together at Home: 100 Proven Ways to Nurture Your Child's Faith.* Nashville: Thomas Nelson Publishers, 1985.

A sensitive book that provides Christian parents with a valuable resource that can serve to focus family time together and make it a rewarding experience. "I find this book a refreshing alternative to sitting around the TV set" (Ruth Senter). 249.M55

***Messenger, David L.,** and **John C. Souter.** Dr. Messenger's Guide to Better Health.* Old Tappan, N.J.: Fleming H. Revell Co., 1981.

Writing in the wake of bestsellers advocating different kinds of diets, Messenger spells out a sane, sensible approach to sound health. In the process he ably integrates the teaching of Scripture with principles of nutrition and how indigestion, excessive weight, fatigue, anxiety, and the like may be eliminated. 613.M56

**Messinger, Lillian.** *Remarriage: A Family Affair.* New York: Plenum Press, 1984.

Breaks new ground and provides counselors as well as couples with an abundance of wise, practical counsel. This book is worthy of serious consideration. Recommended. 306.8′4.M56

**Miles, Herbert J.** *Singles, Sex and Marriage.* Waco, Tex.: Word Books, 1983.

What should single Christians do about their normal, natural sex drives? Miles provides the answer. He sensitively discusses the issues and also talks candidly about sex before marriage, live-in relationships, sexual fantasies, and related topics. All things considered, we find in this book the kind of treatment that is wholesome and Bible centered. Miles has made an important contribution. 306.7.M59S

**Mitchell, Ann.** *Children in the Middle: Living Through Divorce.* London: Tavistock Publications, 1985.

Based on interviews over a five-year period, this revealing study describes the feelings of children as well as their experiences when their parents separated and were later divorced. It is an important work that pastors and professional counselors will welcome. 306.8′9.M69

**Mussen, Paul Henry, John Janeway Conger,** and **Jerome Kagan.** *Child Development and Personality.* 5th ed. New York: Harper & Row, 1979.

As the attention of parents, pastors, and teachers focuses more and more on the importance of proper child development, this welcome text condenses into a single volume a wealth of practical material. Well indexed. 155.4′18.M97 1979

**Narramore, Stanley Bruce.** *Adolescence Is Not an Illness.* Old Tappan, N.J.: Fleming H. Revell Co., 1980.

Deals with the fluctuating moods and problems of adolescents and offers parents creative alternatives to teenage negativism, peer pressure, discipline, and other problems associated with their growth toward maturity. 306.87.N16A

————. *An Ounce of Prevention: A Parent's Guide to Moral and Spiritual Growth of Children.* Grand Rapids: Zondervan Publishing House, 1973.

Well illustrated with line drawings by Diane Head, this handy volume lays down sound principles for the pur-poseful, planned development of a child's moral sensibilities. Questions are included at the end of each chapter to help parents work through problem areas. 649.1.N16

————. *Why Children Misbehave.* Grand Rapids: Zondervan Publishing House, 1980.

Counsels parents on how to prevent problems arising in the lives of their children and describes the causes of bad behavior. Also directs parents on how to implement change in the attitudes of their children. 649′.1.N16W

**Neff, Pauline.** *Tough Love: How Parents Can Deal with Drug Abuse.* Nashville: Abingdon Press, 1982.

Contains case studies of drug abuse and shows what parents may do if their children become hooked on drugs. 362.2′9386.N29

**Neidig, Peter H.,** and **Dale H. Friedman.** *Spouse Abuse: A Treatment Program for Couples.* Champaign, Ill.: Research Press Co., 1984.

One of the best works for pastoral counselors. Deals candidly and sympathetically with the rising incidence of spouse abuse in America. Provides sage information for a family systems approach to the problem of violence, emotionally repressed anger, stress, good communication, and the causes of conflict. Practical, helpful. Recommended. 306.8′7.N31

**Neville, Helen,** and **Mona Halaby.** *No-Fault Parenting.* New York: Facts on File Publications, 1984.

This is *not* another pop-psychology primer written by academic scientists and filled with conflicting, abstract theories. The emphasis here is on offering parents a full menu of practical, parent-tested ways to solve all the common problems of child rearing. Both authors are mothers and so combine practical experience with their research. This is a sane, upbeat book, and readers will find its information helpful. 649.1.N41

**O'Reilly, Sean.** *The Image of God: A Guide to Sex Education for Parents.* Middleburg, Va.: Notre Dame Institute Press, 1974.

A helpful book designed to assist parents in combating modern perverted ideas about sex. Emphasizes the Bible's teaching on sexuality as well as the teaching of the Roman Catholic church. 306.7.OR3

**Orthner, Dennis K.** *Intimate Relationships: An Introduction to Marriage and the Family.* Reading, Mass.: Addison-Wesley Publishing Co., 1981.

The outgrowth of the author's lectures on marriage and family living, this one differs from other texts in its emphasis on the importance of interpersonal relationships within family dyads. 306.8.OR8

**Ortlund, Anne.** *Children Are Wet Cement: Make the Right Impression in Their Lives.* Old Tappan, N.J.: Fleming H. Revell Co., 1981.

Aims to bridge the generation gap. Emphasizes the values that should be instilled in children during their impressionable years. 649.1.OR8

**Otto, Herbert A., ed.** *Marriage and Family Enrichment: New Perspectives and Programs.* Nashville: Abingdon Press, 1976.

The editor surveys trends in marriage and family enrichment seminars and presents the results of his evaluation of nineteen separate programs. 362.8′2.M34

**Packard, Vance.** *Our Endangered Children: Growing Up in a Changing World.* Boston: Little, Brown and Co., 1983.

The author, who gave us *The Hidden Persuaders, The Status Seekers,* and *The Pyramid Climbers,* together with a half dozen other important works, here tackles the dilemma of change faced by our children. As always, Packard's mate-

rial is well researched and right on target. This is a book all who are involved with children in home, church, or school will want to read. Recommended. 649.1.AM3.P12

**Parker, Gordon.** *Parental Overprotection: A Risk Factor in Psychosocial Development.* New York: Grune and Stratton, 1983.

The effects of parental overprotection have been largely overlooked by sociologists and psychologists. This study traces the reasons for it and assesses its effects upon the children. Parker provides an excellent discussion which should be of value to all who work with young people. 306.87.P22

**Patterson, Gerald R.** *Families: Applications of Social Learning to Family Life.* Champaign, Ill.: Research Press 1971.

A behavioristic approach to family life and its problems with particular emphasis being placed on the rearing of children. 249.P27

**Peale, Ruth (Stafford).** *The Adventure of Being a Wife.* Englewood Cliffs, N.J.: Prentice-Hall, 1971.

A scintillating book. Provides a helpful and healthy approach to the frequently misunderstood role of a wife in today's culture. 249.P31

**Peck, Ellen,** and **William Granzig.** *The Parent Test: How to Measure and Develop Your Talent for Parenthood.* New York: G. P. Putnam's Sons, 1978.

Probes the demands of parenthood and offers sage counsel on how to prepare for the arrival of children. Unfortunately this book does not have much to say about rearing them. 306.87.P33P

**Peck, Morgan Scott.** *The Road Less Travelled: A New Psychology of Love, Traditional Values and Spiritual Growth.* New York: Simon and Schuster, 1978.

Takes a new and innovative look at maturation. Traces difficulties back to each person's formative years when inner "road maps" were formed. Then shows how these may be redrawn. An important, provocative guide to personal maturity. 158.1.P33

**Pedrick, Robert.** *The Confident Parent.* Elgin, Ill.: David C. Cook Publishing Co., 1979.

Deals with the art of good parenting. Concentrates on the development of trust, open communication, and the inculcation of values. Worth reading again and again. 306.87.P34

**Peterson, J. Allan, ed.** *The Marriage Affair.* Wheaton, Ill.: Tyndale House Publishers, 1971.

A manual of brief, helpful chapters on marriage by ministers and counselors, physicians and psychiatrists, housewives and film stars, college presidents and Bible teachers, missionaries and evangelists. Contains leading articles from *Time* magazine and other public bodies. 249.P44

**Phillips, Michael.** *Building Respect, Responsibility and Spiritual Values in Your Child.* Minneapolis: Bethany House Publishers, 1981.

Deals capably with the importance of an appropriate sense of esteem, the inculcation of spiritual values, and the development of appropriate attitudes. Underemphasizes the importance of modeling and, perhaps unwittingly, uses humanistic terminology. 649.7.P54

**Pines, Ayala M., Elliott Aronson,** and **Ditsa Kafry.** *Burnout: from Tedium to Personal Growth.* New York: Free Press, 1981.

Deals with the basic issues of fulfillment through work and the causes of tedium, sleeplessness, or burnout. Discusses the physical, emotional, and mental antecedents of this sense of hopelessness and helplessness. 158.7.P65

**Renshaw, Harold D.** *Caring for Kids.* Palo Alto, Calif.: R. and E. Research Associates, 1982.

Writing out of concern for children in institutions or shunted from one foster home to another, Renshaw develops a strong case for an alternate model for dealing with their problems—one that incorporates trust, love, care, and a place to belong. 362.7.R29

**Rhodes, Sonya,** and **Josleen Wilson.** *Surviving Family Life.* New York: G. P. Putnam's Sons, 1981.

By following the human life cycle, the authors are able to focus on, define, and then treat the problems that emerge during these stages. 306.8.R34

**Rice, David G.** *Dual-Career Marriage: Conflict and Treatment.* New York: Free Press, 1979.

With the virtual disappearance of the nuclear family and the emergence of a group who wish to be more than working wives, a book such as this one becomes essential. In nontechnical terms Rice discusses the problems, trade-offs, pitfalls, and potential of this new phenomenon. A clear, secular discussion. 306.8.R36

**Rice, F. Philip.** *Sexual Problems in Marriage: Help from a Counselor.* Philadelphia: Westminster Press, 1978.

A clear analysis of the causes, symptoms, and treatment of sexual dysfunction. Though written for those plagued by some maladjustment, this work can be read by couples for its valuable insights and used by pastors as a resource tool. 613.9′5.R36

**Richards, Lawrence O.** *Remarriage: A Healing Gift from God.* Waco, Tex.: Word Books, 1981.

Discusses the biblical data relating to divorce and concludes that God's grace is great enough to cover human mistakes and errors, even permitting remarriage after divorce. Deserving of careful reading. 306.8′9.R39

**Rickerson, Wayne E.** *Getting Your Family Together: A Guidebook to Christian Parenting.* Glendale, Calif.: Regal Books, 1977.

A handy guide for couples' classes in the church. Each chapter contains brief, pointed suggestions. Does not offer much substance, but the seminal ideas will prove helpful. 249.R42G

_____. *We Never Have Time for Just Us.* Ventura, Calif.: Regal Books, 1982.

Deals with six vital areas of "togetherness," or ways in which a couple may develop and maintain unity in their relationship. Excellent. Ideal for adult study groups in home or church. 249.R42W

**Rinehart, Stacey,** and **Paula Rinehart.** *Choices: Finding God's Way in Dating, Sex, Singleness, and Marriage.* Colorado Springs, Colo.: NavPress, 1982.

In reacting to contemporary social mores, this couple shows that true *liberation* (i.e., freedom) lies in adhering to God's principles, which, in turn, results in personal happiness and the enjoyment of the things He designed for our good. Recommended. 249.R47

**Roberts, Betty Holroyd.** *Middle-Aged Career Dropouts.* Cambridge, Mass.: Schenkman Publishing Co., 1980.

Challenges readers with the problems of the middle-aged and in particular directs attention to those who have lost their jobs through mergers or the advance of technology (which left them behind). Outlines what can be done to make such people productive members of society once more. 306.3.R54

**Robey, Harriet.** *An Ordinary Marriage.* Boston: Little, Brown and Co., 1984.

This is a tender, insightful recounting of Harriet's marriage to Alec, their trials, incompatibilities, problems, and how they worked together, enjoyed their careers, and reared their children. Breathes encouragement on every page. 306.8'1.R54

**Robison, James.** *In Search of a Father.* Life's Answer series. Wheaton, Ill.: Tyndale House Publishers, 1980.

Zeroes in on fatherhood and describes what fathers should be like as well as what their children expect of them. 306.87.R56

_____, and **Jimmie Cox.** *The Right Mate.* Wheaton, Ill.: Tyndale House Publishers, 1979.

Designed for teenagers, this oversimplified book on love, dating, and marriage is supposed to help those who think they are in love to discern between sentimentality and agape love and prepare themselves for the future. 306.82.R56

**Rogers, Carl Ransom.** *Becoming Partners: Marriage and Its Alternatives.* New York: Delacorte Press, 1972.

In an era of liberation and new lifestyles, and with many preferring to live together without undergoing the formality of marriage, this critique of the personality changes of those who struggle to become partners is most revealing. Though secular in its approach, there is a great deal in this book that tacitly confirms the superiority of God's design for marriage laid down in the book of Genesis. 306.87.R63

**Rogers, Dorothy.** *The Adult Years: An Introduction to Aging.* Englewood Cliffs, N.J.: Prentice-Hall, 1982.

A thorough assessment of adulthood from the early twenties to old age. Deals with the situation of singles, the mid-life crisis, and the characteristics and needs of older adults. May be read with profit by pastoral counselors. 155.6.R63

_____. *Life-Span Human Development.* Monterey, Calif.: Brooks/Cole Publishing Co., 1982.

Follows a similar format to Duvall's *Family Development,* though more up-to-date and less centered in the family. Deals graphically with each stage of physical growth, and shows how each phase may lead to greater personal maturity. 155.R63

**Roggow, Linda,** and **Carolyn Owens.** *Handbook for Pregnant Teenagers.* Grand Rapids: Pyranee Books, 1984.

A practical book that meets a need. Counselors as well as parents will value this clear, candid discussion of the issues. 362.8.R63

**Roleder, George.** *Marriage Means Encounter.* 2d ed. Dubuque, Iowa: Wm. C. Brown Co. Publishers, 1979.

An anthology of articles from a wide variety of sources. Explores proposed alternatives to marriage and then focuses on the problems married couples face. Does not provide a reliable guide. 306.8.R64

**Rowatt, G. Wade,** and **Mary Jo Rowatt.** *The Two-Career Marriage.* Philadelphia: Westminster Press, 1980.

In the wake of the demise of the traditional family and the emergence of dual-career families, this practical book brings into focus the problems that have been created. Provides guidelines on the ways to handle pressure and the best means for keeping love alive. A practical manual. 306.87.R78

**Roy, Maria, ed.** *The Abusive Partner: An Analysis of Domestic Battering.* New York: Van Nostrand Reinhold Co., 1982.

This sequel to *Battered Women* provides a thorough analysis of abusers and is replete with ways to counsel them. 362.8′3.R81

**Rubin, Lillian B.** *Women of a Certain Age: The Middle Search for Self.* New York: Harper & Row, 1979.

Though non-Christian in orientation, this work can assist women to better understand their mid-life crisis. Only incidentally does Rubin provide pastors and counselors with insights as to how to minister to women of this age. 612′.665.R82

**Rush, Myron D.** *Richer Relationships.* Wheaton, Ill.: Victor Books, 1983.

Rush first diagnoses the reason for poor relationships among Christians before suggesting how believers may set about establishing lasting friendships. He provides his readers with a whole-some, healthy discussion. 158.2.R89

**Rushford, Patricia H.** *The Help, Hope and Cope Book for People with Aging Parents.* Old Tappan, N.J.: Fleming H. Revell Co., 1985.

Mid-life brims with challenges—mortgages, career changes, rebellious teenagers, and aging parents. Success in coping with any problem requires planning. This book discusses the alternatives and the strategies for handling different situations, and it does so without providing pat answers. Mrs. Rushford is a registered nurse and is sensitive to the emotional turmoil involved when aged parents move in while teenagers, not ready for life on their own, want to move out. Her treatment is one from which all married couples can profit. Recommended. 646.7′8.R89

**Sanford, Ruth.** *The First Years Together: Encouragement and Advice for the Newly Married Woman.* Ann Arbor, Mich.: Servant Books, 1983.

Writing from a woman's perspective, Mrs. Sanford helps new brides cope with the adjustments that must be made if true unity and compatibilty are to be developed. 249.SA5

**Saul, Leon J.** *The Childhood Emotional Pattern in Marriage.* New York: Van Nostrand Reinhold Co., 1979.

A companion volume to *The Childhood Emotional Pattern and Maturity,* this study takes the author's research a step further. On the one hand, it explains why the divorce-to-marriage ratio is so high, and on the other, it offers practical guidelines on how parents may prepare their children for marriage. Both of Saul's works are valuable resource tools, and counselors should lose no time in becoming familiar with them. 306.82.SA8M

_____. *The Childhood Emotional Pattern and Maturity.* New York: Van Nostrand Reinhold Co., 1979.

This, Saul's twelfth book on personality development, points out that emotional maturity is the key to a happy, meaningful life. In order to apply this theory of child development, Saul explains how fight-flight reaction, feelings of inferiority, and other traits are developed, and how through an emotionally unhealthy childhood, neurotic tendencies become normative. Secular. 155.4'18.SA8C

**Scanzoni, John.** *Love and Negotiate: Creative Conflict in Marriage.* Waco, Tex.: Word Books, 1979.

Contends that we live in a male-dominated society. Fails to address the rise of a matriarchy since World War II. Emphasizes mutual submission and a democratic approach to family living. Outlines ways in which a dyadic discussion can be implemented. 306.8.SC1L

**Schaefer, Charles E.** *How to Influence Children: A Complete Guide for Becoming a Better Parent.* 2d ed. Revised and expanded. New York: Van Nostrand Reinhold Co., 1982.

This book has already established itself as a classic in the field of child-rearing. The first edition has been widely used by both professionals and parents. Now this updated and fully expanded second edition provides the most current developments in childrearing practices. Offers step-by-step details on how to resolve conflicts, praise children most effectively, criticize children constructively, talk to children so they will listen, and be firm in giving orders to children. Practical suggestions are given on how to meet a child's need for discipline, love, and guidance—the three basic parenting tasks. 649'.1.SCH1 1982

**Schenk, Quentin F.,** and **Emmy Lou Schenk.** *Pulling Up Roots: For Young Adults and Their Parents—Letting Go and Getting Free.* Englewood Cliffs, N.J.: Prentice-Hall, 1978.

Explains what adolescents and their parents need to know and do in order to make the transition from dependence to independence less traumatic and more fulfilling. Contains wise counsel that can be implemented in a logical way so that there is continuity to the transitions that must eventually take place. 305.24.SCH2

**Schwartz, Roslyn,** and **Leonard J. Schwartz.** *Becoming a Couple.* Englewood Cliffs, N.J.: Prentice-Hall, 1980.

Though there is nothing new about the subject, this couple, a psychiatrist and a psychologist respectively, explore the dynamics of interpersonal relationships from dating through marriage to the rearing of children and old age. Insightful. 306.8.SCH9

**Shafner, Evelyn.** *When Mothers Work.* Santa Barbara, Calif.: Pacific Press, 1972.

A perceptive, readable treatment of the tensions that arise when a wife and mother finds it necessary to work outside the home. Some sections of this book may instill guilt in the hearts of readers (and this is to be regretted, for some wives have no alternative), but for the most part, the counsel given is worthwhile. 306.85.SH1

**Sheehy, Gail.** *Passages: Predictable Crises of Adult Life.* New York: E. P. Dutton, 1976.

†Drawing on the research of others, Sheehy makes available a sensitive, lucid account of the varying stages adults pass through. Some of her suggestions (e.g., the virtual necessity of going through a divorce in order to learn more about oneself) are based on her own experience and should not be regarded as normative. In spite of some inherent weaknesses, what we find between these covers is of value to all who work with adults in the church. 305.24.SH3

**Short, Ray E.** *Sex, Love, or Infatuation: How Can I Really Know?* Minneapolis: Augsburg Publishing House, 1978.

A must for young peoples' groups in churches. Offers candid counsel and important guidelines that will aid those in their early and mid-teen years obtain a sound understanding of the biblical view of love and eventual marriage. 306.8'2.SH8S

**Shorter, Edward.** *The Making of the Modern Family.* London: William Collins, 1976.

A helpful, secular survey of the history of marriage from pre-eighteenth-century traditional society to the present. The author concludes that the nuclear family is crumbling and being replaced by a free-floating dyadic relationship characterized by short-term stability. Now, a decade after his book came out, we can see how accurate was his prediction. 306.8.SH8

**Silberman, Melvin L.,** and **Susan A. Wheelan.** *How to Discipline Without Feeling Guilty: Assertive Relationships with Children.* Champaign, Ill.: Research Press, 1981.

Emphasizes the attitude of parents toward discipline as much as the goal to be accomplished. Thoroughly practical. 306.87.SI3

**Skyuner, Robin,** and **John Cleese.** *Families and How to Survive Them.* New York: Oxford University Press, 1983.

With humor and insight, and using case histories as well as experience, the authors answer some of the most frequently asked questions and provide helpful guidelines for all married couples. 306.8.SK9

**Slonaker, David F.** *Teenagers Ahead.* Chicago: Nelson-Hall, 1980.

Written for parents, this practical primer contains pointers showing how they may relate to their children, keep open the lines of communication, and allow them freedom to make decisions, accept responsibility, stress the positive in their lives and relationships, and grow toward maturity. 649.1.SL5

**Small, Dwight Hervey.** *How Shall I Love You?* San Francisco: Harper & Row, 1979.

This indispensable work ably distinguishes between infatuation and love, romance and caring. Corrects the emphasis in today's society that mistakenly stresses the ephemeral and the sensational, leaving young people and their elders to flounder through marriage, vainly expecting their experience to square with their misguided ideals. Recommended. 249.SM1H

————. *The Right to Remarry.* Old Tappan, N.J.: Fleming H. Revell Co., 1975.

After favoring the Christian world with several excellent books on marriage, Small addresses himself to the subject of remarriage following divorce. In doing so he seeks to build on a biblical foundation. He resorts to "dispensational distinctives" and totally distorts what dispensationalists have characteristically believed. He "uses subjective rationalizations . . . [and] his conclusions are a real threat to the stability of Christian homes. He reasons that since in the OT, divorce and remarriage were permitted for nearly any reason at all . . . [now that] we are in a period of grace, the exceptions for which Christians are permitted to divorce should be even more lenient" (from a review by Paul D. Meier, quoted by permission of *Moody Monthly*). 306.89.SM1

**\*Smalley, Gary,** and **Steve Scott.** *For Better or for Best.* Grand Rapids: Zondervan Publishing House, 1979.

An excellent work that makes available to every married couple a handy, helpful treatment of the dynamics of a happy, healthy marriage. 646.7'8.SM1

**Smith, Harold Ivan.** *A Part of Me Is Missing.* Irvine, Calif.: Harvest House Publishers, 1979.

Printed on newsprint, this handbook addresses itself to the needs of an ever-growing group of Americans—8.1 million at last count—who have been divorced and have not remarried. It also provides practical pointers for those in the church, demonstrating how they can minister to this important segment of society. 306.88.SM5

**Smoke, James.** *Growing Through Divorce.* Irvine, Calif.: Harvest House Publishers, 1976.

In this book the minister to single adults at the Garden Grove Community Church in California outlines his program for those who have experienced divorce. Smoke is to be commended for his practical approach, even though exception can justifiably be taken to certain attitudes expressed in the book. 306.89.SM7

**Spray, Pauline E.** *the Autumn Years: How to Approach Retirement.* Kansas City, Mo.: Beacon Hill Press, 1979.

A practical guidebook for those approaching their retirement. Will be appreciated by all who work with the aged. Shows how this segment of life can be filled with fun and meaning. 305.26.SP7

**\*Stedman, Ray C., et al.** *Family Life: God's View of Relationships.* Waco, Tex.: Word Books, 1976.

A lucid presentation of the biblical teaching on human relationships and the various dyads within the home. Combines practical insights with the needs of the human heart, and shows how these needs may be met. Recommended. 249.ST3F

**Stinett, Nick, Barbara Chesser,** and **John DeFain.** *Building Family Strengths: Blueprints for Action.* Lincoln, Nebr.: University of Nebraska Press, 1979.

Chapters include "Perspective on Family Strengths," "Family Enrichment and Counseling," "Strengthening Families Through More Effective Parenting," "Parenting Children with Special Needs," and "Emerging Family Lifestyles." Contains a wealth of information those who minister to families will find usable. Secular. 306.8.B86S

————, and **John DeFrain.** *Secrets of Strong Families.* Boston: Little, Brown and Co., 1985.

"Here is a book full of wisdom for every family, troubled or untroubled. A careful reading will promote family richness and valuable character development in children" (Vance Packard). 306.8.AM3.ST5

**Stollack, Gary E.** *Until We Are Six: Toward Actualization of Our Children's Human Potential.* Huntington, N.Y.: Robert E. Krieger Publishing Co., 1978.

An important work for all who are engaged in the vital task of rearing their children during their most formative years. 155.4.ST6

**Stout, Martha.** *Without Child: A Compassionate Look at Infertility.* Grand Rapids: Zondervan Publishing House, 1985.

"[The author] has provided hope for those who feel the despair of infertility. As the mother of two, I was transplanted to another world by [her] vivid descriptions of fact and feeling" (Ruth Senter). 616.1'78.ST7

**Strauss, Richard L.** *Confident Children and How They Grow.* Wheaton, Ill.: Tyndale Publishers, 1975.

Practical messages based solidly on Scripture and highlighting areas of personal and familial growth. Recommended. 649.1.ST8

————. *Living in Love: Secrets from Bible Marriages.* Wheaton, Ill.: Tyndale House Publishers, 1978.

Sermons on Bible characters showing how responsibility may be shared and growth maintained. Highlights the benefits of godliness as well as the pitfalls of incompatibility. 249.ST8

————. *Marriage Is for Love.* Wheaton, Ill.: Tyndale House Publishers, 1973.

These thirteen chapters deal with the

most commonly encountered aspects of marriage. The treatment is biblical, and the material can easily be adapted for group discussions in home or church. 249.ST8

**\*Strommen, Merton.** *Five Cries of Youth.* New York: Harper & Row, 1974.

Based on data drawn from an extensive survey, this book tabulates and then discusses the most urgent needs of young people today. No pastor can afford to neglect this timely, helpful work. 170.2′02.ST8

————, and **A. Irene Strommen.** *Five Cries of Parents.* San Francisco: Harper & Row, 1985.

Based on interviews with more than 18,000 parents and adolescents who spoke frankly about their frustrations, crises, hopes, and fears. The Strommens blended these stories as well as the statistics into a provocative summary of the issues that trouble families the most. They show the essence of tension to revolve around the need for understanding between parents and adolescents, a close family life, moral behavior, a shared faith, and outside help in times of crisis. 649.1.ST8P

**Stuart, Irving R.,** and **Carl F. Wells,** eds. *Pregnancy in Adolescence: Needs, Problems, and Management.* New York: Van Nostrand Reinhold Co., 1982.

Because teenage pregnancy has grown to such alarming proportions, counselors have long needed a manual that describes the different approaches to therapy, the legal conflicts, status of adolescent mothers, and the rights of their illegitimate children. Now we have one. 362.7′96.ST9

**\*Swindoll, Charles Rozell.** *Home, Where Life Makes Up Its Mind.* Portland, Oreg.: Multnomah Press, 1979.

Beautifully illustrated, this book contains brief, perceptive chapters that zero in on the pressure points of contemporary family living. Perceptive. 249.SW6H

**\***————. *Strike the Original Match.* Portland, Oreg.: Multnomah Press, 1980.

Prophetlike in his call to return to biblical principles, Swindoll exposes the fallacious thinking of our times and challenges Christians with the responsibilities and privileges of marriage. Recommended. 249.SW6S

**\***————. *You and Your Child.* Nashville: Thomas Nelson Publishers, 1977.

A most valuable and practical discussion of the important aspects of childrearing. Sets forth the dynamics involved as well as the reciprocal responsibilities of parents and children. Highly recommended. 649.1.SW5Y

**Talley, James A.,** and **Bobbie Reed.** *Too Close, Too Soon.* Nashville: Thomas Nelson Publishers, 1982.

Practical and experience-tested, this handbook provides guidelines for the development of quality interpersonal relationships. Shows how to avoid loneliness, rejection, and the heartbreak of premature intimacy. Points the way toward significant, lasting unions. 362′.8286.T14

**Tetlow, Elisabeth Meier,** and **Louis Mulry Tetlow.** *Partners in Service: Toward a Biblical Theology of Christian Marriage.* Lanham, Md.: University Press of America, 1983.

In this work the authors attempt to work toward a positive theology of Christian marriage. To do so they use a biblical methodology and ground their beliefs squarely in what they conceive to be a scriptural mandate. They discuss in detail the Bible's teaching on the man-woman dyad and seek to establish solid parameters for husband-wife mutuality in all areas of life, including serving the church together. Roman Catholic. 249.T29

**Thatcher, Floyd,** and **Harriett Thatcher.** *Long Term Marriage: A Search*

*for the Ingredients of a Lifetime Partnership.*
Waco, Tex.: Word Books, 1980.

Following careful research, the Thatchers provide insights into marriage that couples can adopt and apply to their own relationships. They assist husbands as well as wives to develop realistic expectations, enhance their commitment to one another, use conflict to strengthen their marriage, and develop real unity in their relationship. Eminently practical. 306.88.T32

**Thomas, David M.** *Family Life and the Church.* New York: Paulist Press, 1979.

Written by a Roman Catholic, this brief book deals with the basic issues that undergird all marital relationships. Provides practical insights that should help most couples. 249.T36

**Thornburg, Hershel D.** *Development in Adolescence.* 2d ed. Monterey, Calif.: Brooks/Cole Publishing Co., 1982.

A definitive assessment of adolescent development including all facets of growth, peer relationships, education, socialization, and aspirations. Of value to those in the church who work with this age group. Secular. 305.2'3.T39

**\*Timmons, Howard E.** *Maximum Marriage.* Old Tappan, N.J.: Fleming H. Revell Co., 1976.

A clear, concise discussion of the ways husband and wife may work together to enrich their marriage. 306.8.T48

**Travis, Patricia Y.,** and **Robert P. Travis.** *Vitalizing Intimacy in Marriage (VIM).* Chicago: Nelson-Hall, 1979.

Succeeds in spelling out how couples who really want to, can put vitality back into their marital relationship. Emphasizes the prevention of problems rather than their cure. 306.88.T69

**Tufte, Virginia,** and **Barbara Myerhoff, eds.** *Changing Images of the Family.* New Haven, Conn.: Yale University Press, 1979.

In this book the authors discuss comprehensively and yet concisely the social pressures and practical tensions being experienced by families today. Includes a discussion of the influence of literature, art, and mass media. 306.8.C36

**Vann, Roger,** and **Donna Vann.** *Secrets of a Growing Marriage: Building Our Commitment of Love.* San Bernardino, Calif.: Here's Life Publications, 1985.

Designed as a workbook, this personal guide highlights passages of Scripture to study together, emphasizes matters to discuss, provides working exercises, and draws attention to things a couple may put into practice. Most helpful. 249.V33

**Vernon, Robert,** and **C. C. Carlson.** *The Married Man.* Old Tappan, N.J.: Fleming H. Revell Co., 1980.

Written by the assistant chief of police in Los Angeles, California, this book outlines the servant leadership of the husband and father as he fulfills the roles of family head and chief communicator. Practical. Recommended. 155.6.V58

**Visher, Emily B.,** and **John S. Visher.** *Step-families: A Guide to Working with Stepparents and Stepchildren.* New York: Brunner/Mazel Publishers, 1983.

First published in 1979. This book builds on two decades of research with stepfamilies and introduces readers to the norms, tensions, conflicts, and stages that are all a part of the stepfamily process. 301.42'7.V82

**Voshell, Dorothy.** *Whom Shall I Marry? A Question of Vital Concern to Young Christians, Their Parents and the Church.* Phillipsburg, N.J.: Presbyterian and Reformed Publishing Co., 1979.

A careful examination of the consequences of one's marriage for oneself, one's children, and one's church. Though she touches on important issues and reminds readers of the consequences of their choices—not only to themselves but also to others—the author does little to impart new truths or provide fresh insights. 306.82.V92

**Vredevelt, Pam W.** *Empty Arms.* Portland, Oreg.: Multnomah Press, 1984.

Subtitled "Emotional Support for Those Who Have Suffered Miscarriage or Stillbirth." This is a sensitive, compassionate work. It deals with the pain of disappointment that both husband and wife must endure. It is the kind of book that can be given with confidence to those who face the baffling and frustrating possibility of childlessness. 155.9'37.V95

**Wagemaker, Herbert.** *Why Can't I Understand My Kids?* Grand Rapids: Zondervan Publishing House, 1973.

These short chapters aim at providing guidelines that will help parents bridge the generation gap. 306.87.W12

**Wakefield, Norman G.** *You Can Have a Happier Family.* Glendale, Calif.: Regal Books, 1977.

Builds on five biblically based, psychologically sound principles that, when put into practice, are guaranteed to enhance one's family and overall life-style. Ideal for adult discussion groups. 249.W12

**Wald, Esther.** *The Remarried Family: Challenge and Response.* New York: Family Service Association of America, 1981.

A secular work replete with case histories and suggestions on how to integrate current awareness of the problems with practical counsel on stepparenting. 306.8'7.W14

**Warren, Thomas B., ed.** *Your Marriage Can Be Great!* Jonesboro, Ark.: National Christian Press, 1978.

A symposium of ninety-seven chapters by sixty-one writers, treating the major areas of marriage and family living. Biblically based, each of the twelve major sections deals with aspects of counseling that pastors encounter continually. Most

of the contributors are associated with the Church of Christ. This work can be read with profit by all engaged in ministering to families. 306.8.W25

**Watts, Virginia.** *The Single Parent.* Old Tappan, N.J.: Fleming H. Revell Co., 1976.

Bereavement, separation, or divorce cause problems for children as well as their parent(s). This work draws attention to these problem areas and outlines the ways and means whereby the trauma can be reduced, and social, sexual, financial, occupational, and spiritual adjustments made. 306.87.W34

**Wells, J. Gipson, ed.** *Current Issues in Marriage and the Family.* 3d ed. New York: Macmillan Publishing Co., 1983.

Makes no pretense at advocating a Christian morality. Wells and the other contributors nonetheless deal with issues like marriage versus cohabitation and come out in favor of marriage and marital fidelity. They also discuss the changing roles within the family and offer some important observations that will be of interest to those who seek to keep their finger on the pulse of our ever-changing social mores. 306.7.W46

**Welter, Paul.** *Learning from Children.* Wheaton, Ill.: Tyndale House Publishers, 1984.

Designed to stimulate a renewal in the abilities of children by presenting them as model helpers, creative and expressive, caring and friendly, easy to reach, forgiving and dedicated, sensitive, and examples of faith in action. Excellent. 249.W46L

**White, John.** *Parents in Pain: A Book of Comfort and Counsel.* Downers Grove, Ill.: InterVarsity Press, 1979.

Deals forthrightly with the problems many families face. Explores the origins of tension with one's children, gives a rationale for the predicaments that have arisen, and offers realistic counsel on what may now be done to bring about a degree of harmony in the home. Breathes comfort, and this is what hurting parents will appreciate most. 249.W58

**Whitehead, Evelyn Eaton,** and **James D. Whitehead.** *Marrying Well: Possibilities in Christian Marriage Today.* Garden City, N.Y.: Doubleday and Co., 1981.

The authors state their purpose clearly: "Our conviction is that Christian marriage exists most concretely in the thousands of couples who are attempting to realize the joys and responsibilities of their lives together, as believers, far more than themselves." They grapple realistically with the spiritual issues of marriage. Roman Catholic. 306.8.W58

**Whitehead, John W.,** and **Wendell R. Bird.** *Home Education and Constitutional Liberties: The Historical and Constitutional Arguments in Support of Home Instruction.* Westchester, Ill.: Crossway Books, 1984.

Written to explain the legal precedents for and advantages of educating one's children in the home. Provides some surprising data. In an era of drugs and poor teaching in public schools, more and more parents have considered teaching their children at home. This is a worthy treatment and is well-deserving of a place in every church library. 371'.02.W58

**Wildmon, Donald E.** *The Home Invaders.* Wheaton, Ill.: Victor Books, 1985.

Wildmon believes that there is an intentional effort among many of the leaders of our media to reshape our society and replace the biblical view of man with a humanistic one. His book deals primarily with television, even though he admits that the problem is by no means confined to this medium. He concentrates on TV because he sees it as the most powerful educator in our society. This is a timely work that demands consideration by all thinking people. 175.1.W63

**Wohl, Agnes,** and **Bobbie Kaufman.** *Silent Screams and Hidden Cries: An Interpretation of Artwork by Children from Violent Homes.* New York: Brunner/Mazel, Publishers, 1985.

With a dramatic rise in incidents of child abuse, this book is a must. It provides case histories of those who have suffered abuse, and the net result is a manual that is at once revealing and helpful. This book is of particular interest to pastoral counselors and those in the mental health professions. 618.92′89.W82

**Wood, Bobbye,** and **Britton Wood.** *Marriage Readiness.* Nashville: Broadman Press, 1983.

Written for those who are single, the authors provide sage counsel on how to prepare for marriage. 306.81.W82

**\*Wright, Harry Norman.** *In-Laws, Outlaws: Building Better Relationships.* Irvine, Calif.: Harvest House Publications, 1977.

An excellently written, practical book by an experienced counselor. Includes informative case studies to show how twentieth-century couples may relate to their parents in mature, meaningful ways, without sacrificing their autonomy. Recommended. 306.8.W93I

**\***_____. *The Pillars of Marriage.* Glendale, Calif.: Regal Books, 1979.

Treats eight vital supports of a healthy marriage. Provides helpful suggestions that will strengthen a couple's relationship. Recommended. 306.8.W93P

**\***_____. *So You're Getting Married.* Ventura, Calif.: Regal Books, 1985.

Written for engaged couples. This handy book deals with the basic issues that need to be faced by those planning on a lifetime of commitment to one another. Wright discussses the need for freedom from the past and freedom to choose, change, and resolve conflicts. Each chapter is replete with wise counsel that would-be newlyweds would do well to read together before their wedding. 249.W93S

*——. *Seasons of a Marriage.* Ventura, Calif.: Regal Books, 1982.

In this book a veteran marriage counselor tackles specific areas of marital development not normally discussed in books of this nature. Prepares readers for the challenges that confront all married couples. 306.81.W93

——, and **Marvin N. Inmon.** *Preparing for Parenthood.* Ventura, Calif.: Regal Books, 1980.

Brief but forthright chapters on the issues surrounding parenthood, the expectations of the parents, and the best ways to prepare for the arrival of a new member of the family. 306.83.W93

——. *Preparing Youth for Dating, Courtship and Marriage.* Irvine, Calif.: Harvest House Publishers, 1978.

An important production. Ideal for use with teens and those in their early twenties. Comes complete with twelve overhead transparencies and four reproducible masters. Highly recommended. 646.77.W93Y

——, and **Rex Johnson.** *Building Positive Parent-Teen Relationships.* Irvine, Calif.: Harvest House Publishers, 1977.

Complete with twelve overhead transparencies and an equal number of reproducible masters, this teaching guide contains all that a busy pastor or DCE will need to know in order to teach parents and teens the reasons for as well as the ways to improve poor interpersonal relationships. 306.87.W93T

**Wright, Rusty,** and **Linda Raney Wright.** *Beyond Technique: Unlocking the Secret to Love and Dynamic Sex.* San Bernardino, Calif.: Here's Life Publishers, 1979.

Too few wholesome books like this one are available for pastors and church workers to give away to those in need. This inexpensive paperback is ideal for that purpose. It is also a valuable resource for those preparing for marriage. It discusses the principles, attitudes, and kind of relationship that lies at the bases of a satisfying life. 613.95.W93B

**Young, James J.** *Divorcing, Believing, Belonging.* New York: Paulist Press, 1984.

Follows the process of divorce from the trauma of rejection and a broken marriage, through the struggle to believe, and the process of finding a new sense of belonging. 306.89.Y8

*****Zuck, Roy B.,** and **Gene A. Getz, eds.** *Ventures in Family Living.* Chicago: Moody Press, 1971.

Emphasizes the strategic importance of the home, and furnishes a biblical, practical, and contemporary how-to manual on Christian education in the home. 249.Z8

# 6

# Pastoral Theology

Several respected writers have warned us that we face uncertain times. Peter Drucker, Gordon MacDonald, Alvin Toffler, and James Nesbitt have all sought to present a resumé of what we may expect in the future. Perhaps Dr. Arnold K. Weinstein stated it best, however, in one of the last issues of the *University of Michigan Business Review.* He wrote:

> As a tumultuous decade draws to a close, American executives would be wise to resist the temptation to sigh with relief. Patterns already visible forewarn of coming decades filled with challenges more complex and fundamental than those faced in the past. Political, social, economic and technological changes already underway suggest that our free market system is threatened with obsolescence. Both the assumptions executives have been using to arrive at decisions and the "rules" of the business game are now under attack and undergoing their metamorphosis. The strategic implications of this changed and changing environment will be the major challenge executives are going to face in the coming decades.[1]

An era of such uncertainty presents tremendous possibilities to the man of God. By faithfully declaring the Word of God, he can both channel and direct those who find their way impeded by obstacles hitherto unknown.

What professor Weinstein alluded to has now become an observable fact. The church, however, has been caught up in these changes. The future seems to give promise of developing a small, elite upper-class of wealthy people (who have capitalized on developing technology) with a corresponding diminution of middle-class Americans and a large, ever-growing body who are struggling or underprivileged. If that is so, then changes need to be implemented *now* to

1. Arnold K. Weinstein, "Management Issues for the Coming Decade," *University of Michigan Business Review* (September 1979), p. 29.

modify our theological education so as to be able to meet the needs of the future. Books of the Bible seldom referred to will be found to contain much practical wisdom. They are replete with the kind of principles that can be applied to the coming political, social, and economic world that learned writers have described for us.

It is to help us understand what is happening that we need to take a closer look at some of the books that have been included in this chapter. We also need to be forewarned that some Christian writers, lacking originality, have been quick to latch on to current, secular themes, and then issue their own restatement of the principles suitably sprinkled with personal anecdotes and Bible verses. The inclusion of Scripture does not suddenly make these treatments Christian. Such books make little lasting contribution.

On the other hand, we also need to be aware that some lesser known authors have made a significant contribution. It is hoped that in the following enumeration, pastors and church leaders will be led to choose those works that will be of most help to them in their particular spheres of ministry. It should never be forgotten that *an informed ministry still constitutes one of the most potent forces within our society.*

**Blackwood, Andrew Watterson.** *Pastoral Work.* Grand Rapids: Baker Book House, 1971.

A helpful, inspiring treatise on how the pastor can meet the demands of his office. Reprinted from the 1945 edition. 250.B56P 1971

**Hiltner, Seward.** *Preface to Pastoral The-*ology. Nashville: Abingdon Press, 1979.

†First published in 1958, this book created a new trend in practical theology. Hiltner makes a strong case for including that discipline under theology and stresses the importance of the "shepherding" role of the pastor. 250.SH4.H56 1979

## HOMILETICS, SERMONS, ILLUSTRATIONS

**Achtermeier, Elizabeth.** *Creative Preaching: Finding the Words.* Nashville: Abingdon Press, 1980.

Of value to novice and veteran alike, this handbook on the art of homiletics stresses the importance of language. Topics discussed are style, logic, mental images, principles of effective communication, and motivation. Achtermeier underscores the importance of creativity and lays due emphasis on the place of the Bible in the ministry. 251.AC4

**Alexander, James W.** *Thoughts on Preaching.* Carlisle, Pa.: Banner of Truth Trust, 1975.

Direct and challenging. This important volume calls on preachers to evaluate their messages and determine whether their once finely honed ability has become dull with the passing of time. Included is a practical section showing how to avoid discouragement. 251.AL2

**\*Andersen, Kenneth E.** *Persuasion: Theory and Practice.* Boston: Allyn and Bacon, 1971.

A secular work on preaching. Handles the subject of persuasion from every point of view. A particularly helpful treatment. 251.AN2

**Bartlett, John.** *Familiar Quotations.* Edited by E. M. Beck. 15th ed. Boston: Little, Brown and Co., 1980.

Considerably enlarged and brought up-to-date, this resource retains its well-deserved popularity. Pastors will find it invaluable in sermon preparation as well as in writing. 808.88.B28 1980

**Best, Ernest.** *From Text to Sermon: Responsible Use of the New Testament in Preaching.* Atlanta: John Knox Press, 1978.

Shows how preachers may derive the true message from a given passage and develop it into a dynamic sermon. Prescriptive, helpful. 251′.01.B46

**Bishop, George S.** *The Doctrines of Grace.* Grand Rapids: Baker Book House, 1977.

A reprint of messages delivered at the turn of the century. Concerned mainly with bibliology and the tension between sovereign election and limited atonement. Reformed. 252.B54

**Boice, James Montgomery.** *The Christ of Christmas.* Chicago: Moody Press, 1983.

Insightful messages based on Matthew 2 and Luke 2. Redirects the attention of readers from the sentimentality of the season to the theological reality of Christ's first advent. 252′.51.B63C

**Braga, James.** *How to Prepare Bible Messages.* Rev. ed. Portland, Oreg.: Multnomah Press, 1981.

An extensive and exceedingly practical manual that every young pastor should make time to read. 251′.01.B73

**Browne, Robert Eric Charles.** *The Ministry of the Word.* Philadelphia: Fortress Press, 1976.

Few preachers will lay down this book without experiencing a twinge of unhappiness as they reflect on their own ministry. But equally few will lay it down without a sense of awe as they contemplate the mystery and splendor of their task and of the gospel they have been commissioned to preach. 251.B81

**Cherry, Conrad, ed.** *Horace Bushnell:*

*Sermons.* Sources of American Spirituality. New York: Paulist Press, 1985.

†After introducing readers to Bushnell and his times, Cherry provides fifteen sermons that illustrate his thought. They serve to show Bushnell's brilliance as well as his doctrinal abberations. 252.C42

**Coleman, Richard.** *Gospel-Telling: The Art and Theology of Children's Sermons.* Grand Rapids: Wm. B. Eerdmans Publishing Co., 1982.

Helps pastors and other Christian educators overcome any weaknesses in preparing and delivering sermons for children. Offers an insightful methodology and provides a collection of sample sermons. These illustrate the principles developed earlier and provide refreshing, spiritually substantive models that will spark the creativity of all who are charged with nurturing and challenging a child's faith. 251.C43.C67

**Colquhoun, Frank.** *Christ's Ambassadors: The Priority of Preaching.* Grand Rapids: Baker Book House, 1979.

First published in 1965, this handy monograph provides a powerful apologetic for a vigorous pulpit ministry. 251′.01.C71 1979

**Cory, Lloyd, comp.** *Quotable Quotes.* Wheaton, Ill.: Victor Books, 1985.

This book is designed for use by communicators—teachers, preachers, emcees, writers, speakers—who wish to add color, depth, and insight to whatever they say or do. The material is divided into 1,007 subjects. Because those quoted include a predominance of modern personalities, this material is highly usable and not necessarily found in other sources. No index. 251.C81

**Coulter, Carol, et al.** *Winning Words: A New Approach to Developing Effective Speaking Skills.* Boston: CBI Publishing Co., 1982.

In clear, well-illustrated chapters, the

writers discuss the Mitterling method of public speaking. Contains informative principles from which preachers may profit. 808.5′1.C83

**Cow, Charles Norton.** *Shakespeare's Village.* New York: AMS Press, 1976.

Do not be misled by the title. This handy little volume contains numerous illustrations for those who use literary references in their sermons. 822.33.C65 1976

**Daane, James.** *Preaching with Confidence: A Theological Essay on the Power of the Pulpit.* Grand Rapids: Wm. B. Eerdmans Publishing Co., 1980.

Believing that when God's Word is preached with confidence people change, Daane sets out to describe the fundamental task of every preacher. His material is provocative, and he challenges preachers to be diligent in their preparation if they are to speak with authority. 251.D11

**Demaray, Donald E.** *Proclaiming the Truth: Guides to Scriptural Preaching.* Grand Rapids: Baker Book House, 1979.

Contains material not found in other works. Covers the areas of orientation, preparation, and communication. Includes an appendix entitled "One Hundred Books for the Preacher's Library." 251′.01.D39

**Dodd, Charles Harold.** *The Apostolic Preaching and Its Developments, With an Appendix on Eschatology and History.* Grand Rapids: Baker Book House, 1980.

An epochal series of lectures that when first delivered at King's College, London, in 1935 started a new trend in homiletics. Stimulating. 251′.008.D66 1980

**Fant, Clyde E., Jr.,** and **William M. Pinson, Jr.** *Twenty Centuries of Great Preaching: An Encyclopedia of Preaching.* 13 vols. Waco, Tex.: Word Books, 1971.

Contains sermons of men of all denominations and periods of history.

Extensive, but of little help to expositors. 252′.008.F21

**Fisher, Wallace E.** *Who Dares to Preach? The Challenge of Biblical Preaching.* Minneapolis: Augsburg Publishing House, 1979.

A veteran in the art and science of homiletics reveals the basic principles and philosophy that has molded his own approach to the ministry of the pulpit. Challenging. 251′.01.F53

**Ford, D. W. Cleverley.** *The Ministry of the Word.* Grand Rapids: Wm. B. Eerdmans Publishing Co., 1979.

Treats the sermons of the Bible, the opportunities and responsibilities of modern preachers of the Word, and the methodology for preparing biblical sermons with insight and skill. Recommended. 251′.01.F75M

**Forsyth, Peter Taylor.** *Positive Preaching and the Modern Mind.* Grand Rapids: Baker Book House, 1980.

Comprising the Lyman Beecher Lectures on Preaching, Yale University, 1907, this volume contains Forsyth's explication of the minister's charge and authority, and the manner and means of effective communication. Readers of this book have the opportunity to learn from the experiences of a man whose ministry had an impact throughout the English-speaking world. 251′.01.F77 1980

**Fuller, Reginald Horace.** *The Use of the Bible in Preaching.* Philadelphia: Fortress Press, 1981.

†Working within the framework of theological liberalism, Fuller felt it necessary to defend the usefulness of the Bible against the reaction of those whom he and others were training for the ministry who were inclined to disregard the Bible. In this treatise he asserts that the Bible has not lost its authority and that its message can still be made relevant to the needs of modern man.

**Govett, Robert.** *Gospel Analogies and Other Sermons.* Miami Springs, Fla.: Conley and Schoettle Publishing Co., 1985.

Few men could equal Govett for originality of thought. He also possessed a well-ordered, disciplined mind. He could trace a theme through Scripture with unerring logic. All of these features are exemplified in this present series of messages. Recommended. 252.G74 1985

**Hall, John.** *God's Word Through Preaching.* Grand Rapids: Baker Book House, 1979.

Contains the Lyman Beecher Lectures, Yale Divinity School, 1875. Far ranging in its scope. The major emphasis of these messages is the need for adequate preparation. 251′.01.H14 1979

**Hefley, James C.** *Dictionary of Illustrations.* Grand Rapids: Zondervan Publishing House, 1971.

An up-to-date collection of contemporary illustrative material. 251′.08′03.H36

**Jackson, Benjamin Franklin, Jr., ed.** *You and Communication in the Church: Skills and Techniques.* Waco, Tex.: Word Books, 1974.

Emphasizing the need for effective communication—whether written, visual, or spoken—the contributors to this volume show how the necessary skills may be developed and then used. 001.54.J13

**Jackson, Edgar Newman.** *A Psychology for Preaching.* New York: Harper & Row, 1981.

First published in 1961, this work applies the principles of Freudian psychoanalysis to the ministry of the pulpit. There are some valuable seed thoughts to be found in this work, but readers should be warned against accepting the writer's ideas uncritically. 251.J13 1981

**Johnson, Samuel.** *Sermons.* Edited by J. Hagestrom and J. Gray. New Haven,

Conn.: Yale University Press, 1978.

The first scholarly edition of Johnson's sermons. Will please students of homiletics. 252.J63 1981

**Keck, Leander E.** *The Bible in the Pulpit: The Renewal of Biblical Preaching.* Nashville: Abingdon Press, 1978.

In addition to the standard fare on sermon preparation, Keck also discusses the role of the preacher in addressing social needs and trends. He makes a strong apologetic for the pulpit still being a powerful force in the community. 251.K23

**Kroll, Woodrow Michael.** *Prescription for Preaching.* Grand Rapids: Baker Book House, 1980.

Differing from other works on homiletics, this treatment of the theory and practice of public speaking aims at excellence in delivery as a result of thorough, intelligent, meaningful preparation. Worthy of careful consideration. 251′.03.K85

**Lewis, Ralph L.,** and **Gregg Lewis.** *Inductive Preaching: Helping People Listen.* Westchester, Ill.: Crossway Books, 1983.

Insightful and practical, this work aims at improving the interest level of churchgoers who have become immune to sermons and their delivery. A valuable, challenging treatise. 251′.01.L58

**Liefeld, Walter L.** *New Testament Exposition: From Text to Sermon.* Grand Rapids: Zondervan Publishing House. Ministry Resources Library, 1984.

Challenged to integrate exegesis with a dynamic form of exposition, Liefeld has succeeded in providing a practical and biblical guide to the declaration of God's Word. 251.L62

**\*Litfin, A. Duane.** *Public Speaking: A Handbook for Christians:* Grand Rapids: Baker Book House, 1981.

An excellent, simply written introduction to the dynamics of communication and the influence of the spoken word in challenging and motivating the behavior of others. Recommended. 251'.01.L71

**Lloyd-Jones, David Martyn.** *Evangelistic Sermons at Aberavon.* Carlisle, Pa.: Banner of Truth Trust, 1983.

Containing sermons preached at Aberavon, 1927-1938, these messages provide interesting insights into Lloyd-Jones's early homiletic style, content, and method of application. 252.L77

**Marcel, Pierre Charles.** *The Relevance of Preaching.* Translated by R. R. McGregor. Grand Rapids: Baker Book House, 1977.

Originally prepared for the regional and national synods of the Reformed Church of France, 1951-1952, this work sets forth the importance of the *kerygma* and the method to be used in communicating it. Helpful. 251'.01.M33 1977

**\*McLaughlin, Raymond W.** *The Ethics of Persuasive Preaching.* Grand Rapids: Baker Book House, 1979.

This long-awaited monograph deals admirably with the ethics of persuasion and its use in preaching. The counsel given is balanced and biblical. 251'.008.E19.M22

**Ortlund, Raymond C.** *Intersections: With Christ at the Crossroads of Life.* Waco, Tex.: Word Books, 1978.

Treats the epochal events in the life of a believer—birth, baptism, facing temptation, choosing friends—from a biblical perspective. Omits marriage and choice of a place to worship. Each message is warm, tender, and filled with sage counsel from a true "shepherd." 252'.58.OR8

**Osbeck, Kenneth W.** *101 Hymn Stories.* Grand Rapids: Kregel Publications, 1982.

Unravels the fascination of hymn lore and provides a handy manual that hymnologists will welcome and from which preachers will derive numerous illustrations. 783.9'09.OS1H

**Palmer, Alan,** and **Veronica Palmer.** *Quotations in History: A Dictionary of Historical Quotations. c. 800 A.D. to the Present.* New York: Harper & Row, 1977.

A gold mine of pithy, pertinent sayings that preachers who use historical illustrations will find invaluable. 082.P17

**Pendleton, Winston K.** *Handbook of Inspirational and Motivational Stories, Anecdotes and Humor.* West Nyack, N.Y.: Parker Publishing Co., 1982.

Pastors and teachers will find in this book a fresh series of usable material to spice up their sermons and lecture material. 082.P37

**Perry, Lloyd Merle,** and **John R. Strubhar.** *Evangelistic Preaching.* Chicago: Moody Press, 1979.

A clear presentation of the difference between homiletic sermonizing and true evangelistic preaching. Surveys trends in evangelistic preaching from the earliest times to the present. 251'.01.P42E

**Pierson, Arthur Tappan.** *The Gospel: Its Heart, Heights, and Hopes.* Grand Rapids: Baker Book House, 1978.

In spite of the somewhat hackneyed title, these messages are of historic importance. They were preached in the famous Metropolitan Tabernacle in London after the passing of Charles Haddon Spurgeon, during the two years Pierson was the interim pastor. As such, they serve as a partial model for others who are called on to assume the pulpit under similar circumstances. 252'.051.P59 1978

**Prochnow, Herbert Victor.** *Toastmaster's Quips and Stories, and How to Use Them.* New York: Sterling Publishing Co., 1982.

This veteran raconteur and speechmaker shows how politicians, lawyers, ministers, club presidents, school principals, and Sunday school teachers may use humor to get their point across or reinforce the point they are making.

This volume is replete with jokes, humorous stories, epigrams, proverbs, and amusing definitions. Handy. Well indexed. 808.88′2.P94T

————, and Herbert V. Prochnow, Jr. *The Toastmaster's Treasure Chest.* New York: Harper & Row, 1979.

A valuable resource for pastors. May be used either to spice up one's sermons, introduce a visiting speaker, or enliven a conversation. 080′.24.P94 1979

**Purdy, Dwight Hilliard.** *Joseph Conrad's Bible.* Norman, Okla.: University of Oklahoma Press, 1984.

Describes Conrad's response to the gospels and his obsession with the "end times." Maintains that he (Polish by birth) learned English from the Bible and that he never deserted Scripture's normative value. Reveals a dimension to Conrad's work that serves as a key to unlocking much of the writer's thought. Notes Conrad's reliance on scriptural metaphors, biblical allusions, and the use of parody that came directly from his interaction with the inspired text. Also describes Conrad's view of suffering and how his understanding of the OT found expression in his novels. Contains numerous insights for preachers and should prove of illustrative merit. 823.912.C76.P97

**\*Robinson, Haddon W.** *Biblical Preaching: The Development and Delivery of Expository Messages.* Grand Rapids: Baker Book House, 1980.

Drawing on his extensive experience as a preacher and homiletics professor, Robinson describes the way in which preachers may make their messages clear, direct, vivid, and convincing. This is an excellent presentation and deserves to be considered alongside the other major treatises on this important subject. 251.3.R56

**Ross, Raymond S.,** and **Mark G. Ross.** *Understanding Persuasion.* Englewood Cliffs, N.J.: Prentice-Hall, 1981.

A handy overview of the dynamics of persuasion. Ideal for pastors who do not have time to wade waist-deep through verbiage. 001.51.R73

**Ryckman, W. G.** *What Do You Mean By That? The Art of Speaking and Writing Clearly.* Homewood, Ill.: Dow Jones-Irwin, 1981.

Deals with the techniques of personal communication—from persuasive speaking to good writing. Recommended. 808.R92

**\*Ryle, John Charles.** *The True Christian.* Grand Rapids: Baker Book House, 1978.

Originally published under the title *The Christian Race* (1900), these messages cover a variety of themes. They are deeply moving and, as with Ryle's other works, are also deeply devotional. They make rewarding reading. 252′.03.R98 1978

**Sarnoff, Dorothy.** *Make the Most of Your Best: A Complete Program for Presenting Yourself and Your Ideas with Confidence and Authority.* Garden City, N.Y.: Doubleday and Co., 1981.

This secular approach to oral communication contains some excellent ideas for those who wish to improve their public speaking ability. 001.54.S7

**Scherer, Paul.** *The Word of God Sent.* Grand Rapids: Baker Book House, 1977.

First published in 1965. This book on homiletics explains how preachers today may effectively communicate the truth of Scripture. 251′.01.SCH2 1977

**Shedd, William Greenough Thayer.** *Sermons on the Natural Man.* Edinburgh: Banner of Truth Trust, 1977.

These century-old messages are of historical significance. They reveal Shedd's theological acumen in the pulpit, provide insights into his generation, and at the same time deal with timeless truths like the nature of man and the power and purpose of God. 252′.051.SH3 1977

**Sproule, J. Michael.** *Communication Today.* Glenview, Ill.: Scott, Foresman and Co., 1981.

This assessment of oral communication treats concisely the process and principles by which people share their thoughts and ideas, the fundamentals of interpersonal interaction, speech-making, and the context in which decisions are made. Timely, practical. 001.54'2.SP8

**\*Stott, John Robert Walmsey.** *Between Two Worlds: The Art of Preaching in the Twentieth Century.* Grand Rapids: Wm. B. Eerdmans Publishing Co., 1982.

Of this excellent work Warren W. Wiersbe said, "This is the most comprehensive book on preaching I have seen in a long time. It is almost a course in Pastoral Theology! The concise survey of the history of preaching certainly magnifies 'the glory of preaching.' I especially like the way Dr. Stott lays the theological foundation before presenting the practical matters. No book can make any man a preacher, but if a man will put into practice the principles explained in this volume, he cannot help but become a better preacher and a more fulfilled servant of God." By all means, buy it and read it. 251.ST7B

**Tan, Paul Lee.** *Encyclopedia of 7,700 Illustrations.* Rockville, Md.: Assurance Publishers, 1979.

As a general rule, books of illustrations are seldom worth purchasing. This work is an exception. "Of all the books of illustrations currently available, this *Encyclopedia* stands alone. Despite reservations one must always have regarding such works, this one can be confidently recommended" *(Bibliotheca Sacra).* 251'.08.T15

**Van der Geest, Hans.** *Presence in the Pulpit: The Impact of Personality in Preaching.* Translated by D. W. Stott. Atlanta: John Knox Press, 1981.

This is a mind-expanding book. It contains valid and valuable principles for both preacher and parishioner: to the former it shows how sermons may be made more challenging and relevant; and to the latter it explains how messages should be listened to and followed. 251.V26

**Vines, Jerry.** *A Practical Guide to Sermon Preparation.* Chicago: Moody Press, 1985.

Preachers "will appreciate the blueprint that [Vines] shares for effective expository preaching. He has done both his homework and his heartwork, and he is not afraid to chronicle his own mistakes and frustrations. He has summarized for us the principles and procedures that govern effective expository preaching. No matter how long a man has been ministering, he ought to review these principles and procedures regularly" (Warren W. Wiersbe). 251'.01.V75

**Von Rad, Gerhard.** *Biblical Interpretations in Preaching.* Translated by J. E. Steely. Nashville: Abingdon Press, 1977.

These essays combine exegesis with suggestions on sermon construction. They were written over a twenty-year period (1946-1966) and that accounts for their variety as well as their uneven value. 251'.01.R11

**Wesley, John.** *The Works of John Wesley.* Edited by A. C. Outler. In process. Nashville: Abingdon Press, 1984-.

With a fitting preface introducing readers to the career of Wesley, his theological method, and the best way to read his sermons, Outler then provides for the first time in two centuries the text of Wesley's messages, replete with extensive annotations. Beautifully produced, this set gives promise of surpassing all others in excellence of production and general usefulness. Indexed. 252'.07.W51

**Whitefield, George.** *Select Sermons of George Whitefield.* Carlisle, Pa.: Banner of Truth Trust, 1985.

First published in 1958. Contains a biographical sketch by J. C. Ryle and a summary of Whitefield's doctrine by R. Elliott. The six messages that make up the bulk of this book bear eloquent testimony to Whitefield's persuasiveness as a preacher. 252.W58 1985

**Wiersbe, Warren Wendell, comp.** *Classic Sermons on Faith and Doubt.* Grand Rapids: Kregel Publications, 1985.

This collection of messages by some of the great pulpiteers of the past—A. C. Dixon, J. H. Jowett, D. Martyn Lloyd-Jones, G. Campbell Morgan—is one from which laypeople can obtain edification and preachers can receive exhortation. Recommended. 252.W63F

*————. *Listening to Giants: A Guide to Good Reading and Great Preaching.* Grand Rapids: Baker Book House, 1980.

A delightful book that adequately sketches the life and contribution of some of the world's greatest preachers and then supplies one of their sermons to illustrate their homiletic style. *Includes an important chapter entitled "A Basic Library" for every pastor.* Recommended. 251'.009.W63L

## PASTORAL DUTIES

**Abercrombie, Clarence L., III.** *The Military Chaplain.* Beverly Hills, Calif.: Sage Publications, 1977.

Compares the roles of military chaplains with their civilian counterparts. Offers some needed insights into the unique demands of the chaplaincy. 355.3'47'01.AB3

**Adams, Jay Edward.** *Shepherding God's Flock.* Nutley, N.J.: Presbyterian and Reformed Publishing Co., 1974.

In this volume Adams draws attention to the pastor's personal life and his ministry of visitation. Warmly recommended. 253.AD1S

***Anderson, Robert C.** *The Effective Pastor.* Chicago: Moody Press, 1985.

The author, a pastor and seminary professor, challenges those "called upon to preach, teach, counsel, conduct weddings and funerals, baptize, dedicate babies, serve Communion, visit the sick, win the lost, provide leadership, and give direction to the flock to which God has sent them" with the duties of their office. Realizing that much of what passes for seminary education today ill-prepares a person to minister, Anderson shows how these many aspects of the ministry may be performed efficiently. Paying his debt to the book by Homer Kent, Sr., *The Pastor and His Work*, Anderson states, "Even though I have tried to cover every major subject I believed was possible, I feel the same sense of frustration that Kent felt in the early sixties." In spite of this admission, what is presented here is a work of singular merit. Highly recommended. 253.AN2

**Armstong, Ben.** *The Electric Church.* Nashville: Thomas Nelson Publishers, 1979.

Surveys the origins and development of religious radio and television. Discusses the problems raised by the widespread use of media and its impact on the future of the church. 253.7'8.AR5

***Baxter, Richard,** *The Reformed Pastor: A Pattern for Personal Growth and Ministry.* Abridged and edited by J. M. Houston. Portland, Oreg.: Multnomah Press, 1982.

An indispensable work that everyone in the pastoral ministry should read—and read again. 253.B33 1982

**Biagi, Shirley.** *A Writer's Guide to Word Processors.* Englewood Cliffs, N.J.: Prentice-Hall, 1984.

With more and more churches acquiring word processors, this book becomes a must. It contains a comprehensive survey of the models available and the functions performed by these diverse kinds of machines. Helpful. 652.B47

**\*Boa, Kenneth, and Larry Moody.** *I'm Glad You Asked*. Wheaton, Ill.: Victor Books, 1982.

A carefully reasoned, in-depth assessment of some difficult questions frequently asked those who share their faith with others. Commendable. 253.4.B63

**Borchert, Gerald L., and Andrew D. Lester, eds.** *Spiritual Dimensions of Pastoral Care: Witness to the Ministry of Wayne E. Oates*. Philadelphia: Westminster Press, 1985.

This festschrift by leading therapists surveys each of the major facets of pastoral counseling and provides a valuable synthesis of different methodologies for modern students of this subject. 253.B64

**Brekke, Milo L., Merton P. Strommen, and Dorothy L. Williams.** *Ten Faces of Ministry: Perspectives on Pastoral and Congregational Effectiveness Based Upon a Survey of 5,000 Lutherans*. Minneapolis: Augsburg Publishing House, 1979.

The extensive research that went into the producing of this book is evident on every page. The message of the book extends beyond the boundaries of the three Lutheran church bodies who sponsored the survey. The findings contain some dos and don'ts that pastors will do well to heed. All things considered, this is a book that deserves widespread circulation. 253.B74

**Capps, Donald.** *Pastoral Care: A Thematic Approach*. Philadelphia: Westminster Press, 1979.

Combines a psychosocial approach to the ministry with an existential theology. Offers much practical wisdom in dealing with different cases, but is lacking when it comes to the leading of the Holy Spirit and having Him as a model for the

establishment of a truly caring relationship. 253.C17

**\*Chadwick, William Edward.** *Pastoral Teaching of Paul*. Grand Rapids: Kregel Publications, 1984.

The reader is not expected to agree with everything Chadwick presents, but this is a rare and valuable volume that every minister should own and refer to repeatedly. Warren W. Wiersbe said of it, "I know of no volume that treats the 'images' of the minister as this one does—the workman, the servant, the herald, the steward, etc." Recommended. 253.C34 1984

**Clements, William M.** *Ministry with the Aging*. San Francisco: Harper & Row, 1981.

Building on the solid research of gerontologists, psychologists, historians, and theologians, Clements applies the truths gleaned to the problems of the aged and the way in which the church can meet their needs. 259'.3.C59

**Collins, Gary R.** *Man in Transition: The Psychology of Human Development*. Psychology for Church Leaders. Carol Stream, Ill.: Creation House, 1971.

Written specifically for church leaders and those training for church leadership. Provides insights into the various aspects of growth and development. 155.2.C69

**Cook, J. Keith.** *The First Parish: A Pastor's Survival Manual*. Philadelphia: Westminster Press, 1983.

This is an excellent work, even though it was not written by an evangelical. It deals with all the things a recent seminary graduate needs to know as he takes his first pastoral charge. The material is well presented. 253.C77

**Criswell, Wallie Amos.** *Criswell's Guidebook for Pastors*. Nashville: Broadman Press, 1980.

This compendium of pastoral counsel provides pithy comments on virtually every aspect of the ministry: the preacher's call, his rewards, preparation for the pulpit, the administration of ceremonies and ordinances, staff relations, and personal life. 253.C86 1980

**Dale, Robert D.** *Surviving Difficult Church Members.* Creative Leadership Series. Nashville: Abingdon Press, 1984.

One is constantly impressed with the perceptive insights of the writer. Though he does not deal with personalities—and this is a decided weakness of his book—he does treat different issues and discusses the ways in which pastors may deal with them. A must for every minister's library. 253.D15

**Dittes, James E.** *When People Say No: Conflict and the Call to the Ministry.* New York: Harper & Row, 1979.

Tackles the hard questions of what a minister is to do when confronted by opposition from the congregation he serves. Shows how frustrations may be the beginning of a healthy relationship. 253.D63

**Donnelly, Dorothy.** *TEAM: Theory and Practice of Team Ministry.* Ramsey, N.J.: Paulist Press, 1977.

Presents the case that a team parish ministry is the most hopeful model for the future advance of the church. Roman Catholic. 253.D61

**Ehrlich, Eugene, et al, eds. and comps.** *Oxford American Dictionary.* New York: Oxford University Press, 1980.

Building on the distinguished tradition of Oxford dictionaries, this work contains all the words one is likely to hear or read. It features American spelling, pronunciation, usage, and idioms. It emphasizes concise and precise definitions, and does not use synonyms to define words unless they distinguish shades of meaning. Pastors will find this dictionary most helpful. 423.OX2A 1980

**Eims, LeRoy.** *Be the Leader You Were Meant to Be: What the Bible Says About Leadership.* Wheaton, Ill.: Victor Books, 1975.

A timely work that readily makes available some of the Bible's rich insights into the nature and scope of effective leadership. Recommended. 253.EI5B

**\*Engel, James F.** *Contemporary Christian Communications: Its Theory and Practice.* Nashville: Thomas Nelson Publishers, 1979.

This book meets a definite need in that it distinguishes between witnessing and evangelism, and shows how both may become an integral part of a believer's life-style. Applies the basic principles of communication to people in all areas of the ministry. Recommended. 253.7.EN3

**\*Gillespie, Gerald Whiteman.** *The Empty Pulpit.* Chicago: Moody Press, 1974.

This sequel to *The Restless Pastor* establishes guidelines for the pulpit committee and suggests ways in which they may screen a prospective candidate. Highly recommended. 253.G41E

**Gilmore, Alec.** *Tomorrow's Pulpit.* Valley Forge, Pa.: Judson Press, 1975.

Composed of the Edwin Stephen Griffith Memorial Lectures on Preaching, Cardiff Baptist College, Wales, 1973, these chapters assess the task of the ministry in light of the needs of the closing decades of this century. 253.G42

**Griffith, Leonard.** *We Have This Ministry.* Waco, Tex.: Word Books, 1974.

Drawing on a wealth of practical pastoral experience on both sides of the Atlantic, Griffith challenges as well as counsels his younger colleagues to be true to their mission as ministers of God. 253.G87

**Hicks, H. Beecher, Jr.** *Images of the Black Preacher: The Man Nobody Knows.* Valley Forge, Pa.: Judson Press, 1977.

A forthright presentation of the place, importance, problems, and opportunities of black preachers in America. 253.H52

**Hiltner, Seward.** *The Christian Shepherd: Some Aspects of Pastoral Care.* Nashville: Abingdon Press, 1980.

First published in 1959. This pioneer work in the field of modern pastoral theory and practice remains one of the most innovative and helpful works ever written. 253.H56 1980

**Holifield, E. Brooks.** *A History of Pastoral Care in America: From Salvation to Self-Realization.* Nashville: Abingdon Press, 1983.

Examines the "private side of clerical activity as a mirror to the broader pattern of change in American religion." Also chronicles the interplay between theology, psychology, and changing social mores as these are affected by economic realities. 253'.09.H71

**Kerr, Horace L.** *How to Minister to Senior Adults in Your Church.* Nashville: Broadman Press, 1980.

One of the most comprehensive manuals of this facet of the church's ministry. A vitally important discussion. 259.K46

**Killinger, John.** *The Tender Shepherd.* Nashville: Abingdon Press, 1984.

†Deals with the issues Killinger confronted when he returned to the pastorate after an absence of fifteen years. Because he could not find a work that covered these changes, he decided to write one. The result is a treatise that pastors will find most helpful. 253.K55

**Kruse, Colin G.** *New Testament Models for Ministry: Jesus and Paul.* Nashville: Thomas Nelson Publishers, 1983.

A bold attempt at reaching a biblical theology of ministry. Adheres to progressive revelation and furnishes an admirable synthesis of the information needed to establish a viable ministry. Although Kruse adheres to certain critical presuppositions, this does not unduly impair the material he presents. 253.L94

**Lindgren, Alvin J.,** and **Norman Shawchuk.** *Let My People Go: Empowering Laity for Ministry.* Nashville: Abingdon Press, 1980.

Well reasoned and on target, this discussion of the potential of laypeople comes like a breath of fresh air to those engaged in the ministry. Recommended. 253.L64L

**Peterson, Eugene H.** *Five Small Stones for Pastoral Work.* Atlanta: John Knox Press, 1980.

This provocative book takes the *Megilloth* and applies these writings (used in Israel's feasts) to the needs of the church. To Peterson, "pastoral work is that aspect of the Christian ministry which specializes in the ordinary. It is the pragmatic application of religion in the present. It has a horror of detachment, neutrality, studious isolation, or theoretical otherworldliness." His work challenges our thinking and forces us to reevaluate our beliefs, values, and goals. 253.P44

**Poling, James N.,** and **Donald E. Miller.** *Foundations for a Practical Theology of Ministry.* Nashville: Abingdon Press, 1985.

†A provocative work that makes an important contribution through its presentation of the historic developments of pastoral care. 253.P75

**Raines, Robert A.** *New Life in the Church.* Rev. ed. San Francisco: Harper & Row, 1980.

Emphasizing a relational approach to the ministry of the church, Raines describes the benefits and impact of small groups in the church. His thesis is well-founded. Small groups do add new life to the church. 253.7.R13 1980

**\*Richards, Lawrence O.,** and **Gib Martin.** *A Theology of Personal Ministry.* Grand Rapids: Zondervan Publishing House, 1981.

In keeping with the title, the first part

of this book develops a theological foundation for personal ministry. From this premise the authors expound the practical implications of the fact that the head of the church has called each believer to a personal ministry. All things considered, this is an excellent work. 253.R39P

**Rouch, Mark A.** *Competent Ministry: A Guide to Effective Continuing Education.* Nashville: Abingdon Press, 1974.

Sage counsel for those who are in the ministry or preparing for it. Shows how pastors, through careful, judicious reading, can keep abreast of developments in all areas of life and continue to grow throughout their lives. Such growth will not only benefit them but also the churches they serve. Should also be read by laypeople on church boards. 253.R75

**Schaller, Lyle E.** *Activating the Passive Church.* Nashville: Abingdon Press, 1981.

Tackles the perplexing issues of church renewal. Offers a diagnosis of the causes of passivity, and then discusses ways in which apathy may be replaced with new purpose. 253.SCH1A

———. *The Multiple Staff and the Larger Church.* Nashville: Abingdon Press, 1980.

Written for larger churches, this book discusses the many alternatives of staffing churches. Includes the place and use of volunteers as well as the duties that can be carried out by others. 253.SCH1M

**Schillebeeckx, Edward.** *Ministry: Leadership in the Community of Jesus Christ.* Translated by J. Bowron. New York: Crossroad Publishing Co., 1981.

†Containing the author's reflection on the ministry over twenty-five years, this work provides insight into the work of the priesthood during changing times. Provocative. Roman Catholic. 253.SCH3

**Schmitt, Abraham.** *The Art of Listening with Love.* Waco, Tex.: Word Books, 1977.

This book describes the importance of learning how to listen. It is well illustrated with information drawn from Schmitt's counseling practice. The pastor who reads this work carefully may well have his interpersonal ministry revolutionized. 158.2.SCH4

**Shawchuck, Norman,** and **Lloyd M. Perry.** *Revitalizing the Twentieth-Century Church.* Chicago: Moody Press, 1982.

This sequel to *Getting the Church on Target* deals in part with mobilizing the church for action and in part with church renewal. 253.SH2

**Smith, Wilbur Moorehead.** *The Minister in His Study.* Chicago: Moody Press, 1973.

Contains Smith's addresses to the faculty and students of the Trinity Evangelical Divinity School, Illinois. Highlights the importance of the pastor's *sanctum sanctorum*. Makes effective use of quotations drawn from the writings of great men of the past. 253.SM6

**Stevens, R. Paul.** *Liberating the Laity: Equipping All the Saints for Ministry.* Downers Grove, Ill.: InterVarsity Press, 1985.

Seeks to abolish the distinction between clergy and laity and to elevate believers to their true dignity as ministers of Christ. Stevens is not an anticleric. His iconoclasm is of a different order; and his goal is the mobilization of the people of God to do the work He desires. Challenging. 253.ST4

**\*Stogdill, Ralph M.** *Leadership: Abstracts and Bibliography, 1904-1974.* Columbus, Ohio: Ohio State University Press, 1977.

Up to the time of his death, Stogdill was one of the leading men in the country on the subject of leadership. This bibliography covers seventy years of publications in the areas allied with planning, organizing, controlling, and directing the activities of others. Containing only experimental research articles and papers (with 3,700 entries in all), the material in this volume surveys virtually every facet of leadership. Not all entries are of equal value. Pastors pursuing D. Min. degree programs in leadership administration will find a wealth of usable material here. No college or seminary library can afford to be without this valuable bibliography. 016.3.ST6

**Sugden, Howard F.,** and **Warren W. Wiersbe.** *When Pastors Wonder How.* Chicago: Moody Press, 1973.

Arranged in question-and-answer format. These veteran pastors share their experiences with others either in, or preparing for, the ministry. Their counsel is both wise and witty. The information is of particular value and importance to those preparing for the pastorate. 253.SU3

**Taylor, William Mackergo.** *The Ministry of the Word.* Grand Rapids: Baker Book House, 1975.

Reprinted from the 1876 edition. These Lyman Beecher lectures at Yale deal not only with the preacher's task but also with the pastoral ministry as a whole. Well indexed. 253.T21 1975

**Willimon, William H.,** and **Robert Leroy Wilson.** *Preaching and Worship in the Small Church.* Nashville: Abingdon Press, 1980.

Shows how "small" can be beautiful, and how a small church can have a dynamic fellowship. Lamentably focuses on externals as opposed to fellowship. Nonetheless insightful. 253.W67

**\*Zunin, Leonard,** and **Natalie Zunin.** *Contact: The First Four Minutes.* New York: Ballantine Books, 1976.

This is one of the most important books a pastoral counselor will ever read. Its uses, however, are not confined to counseling. When meeting people socially for the first time, interviewing, doing visitation, and the like, the principles spelled out by this gifted couple can, and indeed should be put to use. 158.2.Z8

## PERSONAL LIFE

**Bailey, Robert W.,** and **Mary Frances Bailey.** *Coping with Stress in the Minister's Home.* Nashville: Broadman Press, 1979.

Without complaint or criticism the authors treat the peculiar pressures of the pastor's wife and deal practically with the physical, emotional, and social issues she faces. They offer some guidelines whereby the minister's family can creatively cope with stress. 253.2.B15

**Bouma, Mary LaGrand.** *Divorce in the Parsonage.* Minneapolis: Bethany Fellowship, 1979.

Takes a candid look at the occupational hazards of those in or entering the ministry. Shares with readers preventive measures that will help them avoid deterioration in their marital relationship. 253.2.B66

**Bratcher, Edward B.** *The Walk-On-Water Syndrome.* Waco, Tex.: Word Books, 1984.

Written by a Southern Baptist pastor, this book warns against the hazard of vocational burnout. Bratcher seeks to answer questions those in the ministry are asking and furnishes his readers with practical counsel based on his years of experience. 252.2.B73

**Demaray, Donald E.** *Preacher Aflame.* Grand Rapids: Baker Book House, 1972.

A brief reminder of the kind of excitement that accompanies a preacher's realization of his high calling. Of particular value to seminarians. 253.2.D39

**Dyer, Wayne P.** *Pulling Your Own Strings.* New York: Thomas Y. Crowell Co., 1978.

Presents appropriate assertiveness as the secret to better emotional health and eventual success. Provides positive suggestions for developing a new kind of life-style. 158.1.D98P

**Engstrom, Theodore Wilhelm,** and

**Edward Risedorph Dayton.** *The Christian Executive.* Waco, Tex.: Word Books, 1979.

Aimed at Christian leaders, this work seeks to assess the problems and opportunities of those whose values and manner of life is different from the unsaved. Each chapter, however, builds on secular theories and pays little attention to the Scriptures. Practical, but there is little that is original in this work. 301.15.EN3C

**Faulkner, Brooks R.** *Burnout in Ministry.* Nashville: Broadman Press, 1981.

Deals factually with a common problem facing men in the ministry. Describes the causes, and then helps pastors and their wives discern the onset of the symptoms. Should be studied by all seminarians. 253.2.F27

**Figler, Homer R.** *Overcoming Executive Midlife Crisis.* New York: John Wiley and Sons, 1978.

Faces squarely the unique problems of executives in their forties and assesses ways and means for limiting the factors that bring on those various crises. Because the situation of a corporate executive differs little from that of the pastor, the information contained in this book can prove insightful. 658.4'07.F46

**Frew, David R.** *Management of Stress.* Chicago: Nelson-Hall, 1977.

Applies the principles of TM to anxiety and the tensions generated by everyday living. Illustrates the ways in which true meditation can, and indeed should, be put to use by the Christian. 158.7.F89

**\*Gillespie, Gerald Whiteman.** *The Restless Pastor.* Chicago: Moody Press. 1974.

This practical book deals honestly and objectively with a problem nearly every pastor faces at one time or another: "Should I remain where I am, or move to another pastorate?" Among the aspects not dealt with by Gillespie are the average cost of living in the new area, schools for children, and where to buy a home.

Information about these vital issues has been handled in *The Minister's Library*, vol. 1, pp. 322-23. 253.2.G41

**Godin, Andre.** *The Psychology of Religious Vocations: Problems of the Religious Life.* Translated and edited by L. A. Wauck. Lanham, Md.: University Press of America, 1983.

An expanded and updated edition of the original French work that made its appearance in 1975. Includes more than thirty new references as well as an expansion of the statistical tables. Unexpected trends have emerged, which Godin treats in the text. He sharply pinpoints reasons behind the current crisis in vocations. Roman Catholic. 253.2.G54 1983

**\*Gordon, Thomas.** *Leadership Effectiveness Training.* New York: Wyden Books, 1977.

As with the author's earlier works on parenting and teaching, this one on leadership is plain, practical, and to the point. The principles of leadership are clearly spelled out, as are the ways in which administrators can develop executive ability. Pastors have much to learn from this simple yet provocative and informative book. 158.4.G65

**Harbaugh, Gary L.** *Pastor as Person.* Minneapolis: Augsburg Publishing House, 1984.

Assesses the needs of the pastor and provides a structured approach that will ensure his professional competency while retaining his personal sanity. 253.2.H21

**Hensley, Dennis E.** *Writing for Profit.* Nashville: Thomas Nelson Publishers, 1985.

With more people than ever aspiring to sell their free-lance writings, this book could not be more timely. The author shares his keys to success in a clear, informative style that is easily understood and serves as a suitable model of effective communication. 808'.02.H39

**Holck, Manfred.** *Making It on a Pastor's*

*Pay.* Nashville: Abingdon Press, 1974.

A practical treatise from which many people in vocational Christian service can draw needed counsel. 253.2.H69 (Alt. DDC 332.024)

**Hulme, William Edward.** *Managing Stress in Ministry.* San Francisco: Harper & Row, 1985.

The pressures of the pastorate have taken their toll. In part, the congregation is to blame. Pastors need to enjoy a sense of belonging, worth, and competence as much as do individuals who join the church. In this book Hulme mediates the kind of problems that arise and shows both the pastor and the people how to confront the difficulties that, when unresolved, lead to discouragement and a distortion of the issues. This book is a valuable sequel to *Your Pastor's Problems.* 253.2.H87M

**Jones, G. Curtis.** *The Naked Shepherd: A Pastor Shares His Private Feelings About Living, Working, and Growing Together in the Church.* Waco, Tex.: Word Books, 1979.

Four things the author believes are indispensable to longevity in a given pastorate: the ability to change, the ability to work with people and develop healthy interpersonal relationships, the ability to grow, and the ability to preserve the sparkle of romance in one's own marriage. Jones explains how these things may be achieved. 253.2.J71

**Keating, Charles J.** *The Leadership Book.* New York: Paulist Press, 1978.

Examines the theories of administrative leadership and applies the results to the oversight of the church. Helpful. 253.2.K21

**Kemper, Robert G.** *Beginning a New Pastorate.* Nashville: Abingdon Press, 1978.

Catalogs an array of practical matters a pastor should keep in mind if he is to be successful in a new charge. 253.2.K32

**\*Lauderdale, Michael.** *Burnout: Strategies for Personal and Organizational Life.* Speculations on Evolving Paradigms. San Diego: University Associates, 1982.

A thorough assessment of the various causes of burnout. The effect on the individual and those near him/her is likewise depicted: confusion, frustration, despair. Treatment is then described with painstaking skill. This book is particularly helpful to those in the ministry. It shows how they may avoid burnout themselves and detect it and treat it in others. Secular. 658.3.L36

**Mace, David Robert,** and **Vera Mace.** *What's Happening to Clergy Marriages?* Nashville: Abingdon Press, 1980.

Discusses the occupational hazards of the ministry and shows how the pressures generated can lead to a breakdown in one's marriage. This is a welcome treatise and deals fairly with a long-neglected aspect of the ministry. 253.2.M26W

**Maslach, Christina.** *Burnout, the Cost of Caring.* Englewood Cliffs, N.J.: Prentice-Hall, 1982.

Recognized as an authority on stress, Maslach offers her readers help in understanding the causes and symptoms of burnout. A valuable, insightful work. 158.7.M37

**\*McBurney, Louis.** *Every Pastor Needs a Pastor.* Waco, Tex.: Word Books, 1977.

Intensified interest in interpersonal relationships has resulted in people caring for and supporting one another. Few, however, are able to empathize with the pastor or his wife. In this timely book McBurney explains how those in the ministry may be included in the caring community. 253.2.M12

**Merrill, Dean.** *Clergy Couples in Crisis: The Impact of Stress on Pastoral Marriages.* Leadership Library, no. 3. Waco, Tex.: Word Books, 1985.

This work is a part of the Christianity

Today Institute monographs on timely and important topics. It focuses on stress, and by using case histories, Merrill portrays the kinds of problems that wreak havoc on one's interpersonal relationships and ability to function effectively. Though it does not provide the answer to the psychological and physiological causes, this book does serve a useful purpose. It should be read in light of Hart's works on depression as well as his recent study on adrenalin and stress. 253.2.M55

**Moremen, William M.** *Developing Spiritually and Professionally.* Philadelphia: Westminster Press, 1984.

Shows that the spiritual life is the very core of existence and through it the professional life is motivated and transformed. Each chapter contrasts these two dimensions of life and provides concrete advice for their mutual development. Moremen explores the holistic relationship between the pastor's spiritual and professional life and shows, through such topics as upgrading skills and deepening awareness, studying and meditating, planning and praying, using time wisely and attending meetings so as to gain the most from them, being attentive to the Spirit and developing intellectually as well as emotionally, how these two interdependent dimensions can grow in pace with one another. 253.2.M81

**\*Nordland, Frances.** *The Unprivate Life of a Pastor's Wife.* Chicago: Moody Press, 1972.

Candid reflections on the trials and joys of those who accompany their husbands into the pastoral ministry. 253.22.N75

**Olson, Robert Wallace.** *The Art of Creative Thinking.* New York: Barnes and Noble, 1980.

Not since Osborne's *Applied Imagination* (1963) has a work as practical as this one been published. Olson shows how to cultivate one's imagination and then put this newly acquired skill to good use. Recommended. 153.3'5.OL8

**Parker, Rolland S.** *Effective Decisions and Emotional Fulfillment.* Chicago: Nelson-Hall, 1977.

Though not written for pastors, this book is one that ministers will want to read. The author's aim is twofold: to introduce people to the way in which effective decisions are made, and then to show them how to grow so as to achieve their full potential. 153.8'3.P22

**Poynter, Daniel.** *The Self-Publishing Manual: How to Write, Print and Sell Your Own Book.* 3d ed. Santa Barbara, Calif.: Para Publishing, 1984.

With "cookbook-like instructions" Poynter shows how housewives and mothers, business executives and preachers, and in fact, people in all walks of life, can gather material, write, publish, and sell their articles and/or books. He explains that those who publish themselves not only get to market sooner, but they make three or four times more than standard royalties. The reading of this book leads to an increased understanding of the publishing process and warns that whether you are only the author, or both the author and the publisher, it is up to you to promote your book. The counsel contained in these pages is excellent for pastors, even if all they begin with is a newsletter. 070.5.P87

————, and **Melinda W. Bingham.** *Is There a Book Inside You?* Edited by S. Stryker. Santa Barbara, Calif.: Para Publishing, 1985.

The authors issue their readers an invitation to join the ranks of those who shape our society. They distinguish between being an author and being a writer. Perhaps this is a commentary on the illiteracy produced by our educational system. In any event, this book will bring hope and encouragement to many. 808'.02.P87

**Ragsdale, Ray W.** *The Mid-Life Crises of the Minister.* Waco, Tex.: Word Books, 1978.

Focuses attention on the problems—personal, professional, marital—of those between thirty-five and fifty-five. Exposes areas where additional research is needed (where D.Min. dissertation students may profitably apply their skills), and seeks in every way possible to help those in the ministry to weather the storms they are likely to face. 253.2.R12

**Rassieur, Charles L.** *Stress Management for Ministers.* Philadelphia: Westminster Press, 1982.

A psychological assessment of the causes of stress, with counsel on how to handle anger and conflict and other sources of tension in the ministry. 253.2.R18

**Ryken, Leland.** *Windows to the World: Literature in Christian Perspective.* Grand Rapids: Zondervan Publishing House, 1985.

It is Ryken's observation that the biases Christians bring to literature can either prove helpful in opening up a whole new vista of understanding or becloud the issues and perpetuate a shallow experience of reality. In this book he examines such topics as truth, morality, and imagination in literature and then places these concepts within a Christian framework. His book is written for both Christians and non-Christians. It will be of particular value to pastors, however, for it shows how the rich resources of literature can be used to enhance messages and add relevance and interest to the teaching of God's Word. It is also a useful tool for better understanding and increasing the enjoyment received from reading good books. 809'.8922.R99

**Schaller, Lyle E., ed.** *Women as Pastors.* Nashville: Abingdon Press, 1982.

Chapters written by women who discuss the problems being encountered by those who seek to enter the ministry. 253.2.SCH1W

**Schuller, David, et al.** *Readiness for Ministry.* In process. Vandalia, Ohio: Association of Theological Schools in the United States and Canada, 1975-.

Each volume in this projected series of essays is intended to draw attention to some specific facet of ministry (e.g., criteria in vol. 1; the uniqueness of ministry in vol. 2; etc.). Included is an explanation of the methodology used in reaching the conclusions presented. This data should serve a valid secondary purpose by providing samples of research design for D.Min. students. 253.2.R22 v.1

**\*Sire, James W.** *How to Read Slowly: A Christian Guide to Reading with the Mind.* Downers Grove, Ill.: InterVarsity Press, 1978.

An indispensable guide to the techniques of reading different kinds of literature, stretching one's mind, and enriching one's life. This book can be of value to pastors, for it opens up a variety of subject areas. That will result in greater depth as well as breadth in their messages. Recommended. 028.9.SI7

**Spencer, Sue.** *Write on Target.* Waco, Tex.: Word Books, 1976.

An excellent book on the art of written communication. Of value to all who are interested in publishing articles, sermons, or books. 808.'042.S3

**Stewart, Charles William.** *Person and Profession: Career Development in the Ministry.* Nashville: Abingdon Press, 1974.

Designed to focus attention on the pastor's humanness. Shows how to make the necessary adjustments in order to survive the pressures of the ministry. Lays justifiable stress on the pastor's need for reading and staying abreast of developments in different areas of life. 253.2.ST4P

**Swets, Paul W.** *The Art of Talking So That People Will Listen.* Englewood Cliffs, N.J.: Prentice-Hall, 1983.

An excellent book—well designed and well executed—that makes a valuable contribution to the subject of personal effectiveness in oral communication. 158.2.SW4

**Switzer, David Karl.** *Pastor, Preacher, Person: Developing a Pastoral Ministry in Depth.* Nashville: Abingdon Press, 1979.

An important sequel to *The Minister as Crisis Counselor.* Helps direct the pastor's energies while he maintains his own personal and professional growth. Insightful. Meets a need. 253.2.SW6

**Truman, Ruth.** *Underground Manual for Ministers' Wives.* Nashville: Abingdon Press, 1974.

Directs attention to the practical needs of pastors' wives and the brides of seminarians. The discussion includes such relevant subjects as sex, other women, caring for children, and the importance of maintaining one's own spiritual life. A most helpful book. 253.22.T77

**Turnbull, Ralph G.** *A Minister's Opportunities.* Grand Rapids: Baker Book House, 1979.

This companion volume to *The Minister's Obstacles* challenges each pastor with the possibility of becoming all that God meant him to be. It is a down-to-earth, practical book containing sage advice from a senior minister. 253.2.T84M

## PASTORAL COUNSELING

**Adams, Jay Edward.** *Competent to Counsel.* Nutley, N.J.: Presbyterian and Reformed Publishing Co., 1970.

This book took the Christian world by storm. Its strengths are obvious; what are regarded as its weaknesses are not as readily discernible. The author traces all personality problems to sin and makes no provision for physiological, psychological, or sociological factors that may have a determining factor. He also advocates a model of counseling based on a *nouthetic* rather than a *paracletic* ministry of the gifts of helps. The former is too restrictive, as a careful consideration of the usage of the word will readily reveal. Though well-meaning, Adams has placed in the hands of would-be counselors an excuse to "admonish" or "reprove" all with whom they are in disagreement, or who are in disagreement with them. This has resulted in an accentuation of the emotional pain of those truly in need of help. There is also an obscuring of the role of the Holy Spirit and the place that a careful study of pneumatology might play in the counseling process. 253.5.AD1C

_____. *Insight and Creativity in Christian Counseling: A Study of the Usual and the Unique.* Phillipsburg, N.J.: Presbyterian and Reformed Publishing Co., 1982.

Expands on two aspects of counseling—insight and creativity—that the author had only alluded to in earlier works. Stimulating. Integrates the psychology of behaviorism with the Scriptures. 253.5.AD1I

_____. *More Than Redemption: A Theology of Christian Counseling.* Grand Rapids: Baker Book House, 1979.

From this prolific author comes a work relating the different areas of theology to counseling. Though informative, there are times when Adams's material gives every evidence of being forced or contrived. Areas of practical usefulness, however, include habits, prayer, suffering, new converts, and good works. Adams is always warm and exhibits genuine concern for those to whom he ministers. 253.5.AD1M

**Akins, Faren R., Dianna L. Akins,** and **Gillian S. Mace.** *Parent-Child Separation: Psychosocial Effects on Development.* An Abstracted Bibliography. New York: IFI/Plenum, 1981.

Part of the growing corpus of resources that helps make research easy. Provides 690 references with copious annotations. Directs the pastoral counselor to up-to-date information on the effects of single parent families and related topics. Most helpful. 016.306′8.AK5 1981

**Anderson, Herbert.** *The Family and Pastoral Care.* Philadelphia: Fortress Press, 1984.

†Part of the series entitled *Theology and Pastoral Care.* Adopts a systems approach to family care, counseling, and intervention. Anderson shows that strong and healthy families are those with flexible roles, consistent and fair rules, and integrated rituals 253.5.AN2

**Anderson, Joseph.** *Counseling Through Group Process.* New York: Springer Publishing Co., 1984.

One of the best works of its kind. The coverage of each area is both adequate and helpful. Though secular in its orientation, pastors and Christian workers will find in this treatment good usable principles for a variety of church settings. Recommended. 158.3.AN2

**Arnold, William V.** *Introduction to Pastoral Care.* Philadelphia: Westminster Press, 1982.

Arnold distinguishes between *care* and *counseling.* His introductory work therefore differs from the traditional approach to pastoral counseling. The two areas are closely allied, and therefore the principles found here will be treated in other works as well. 253.5.AR66

**Backus, William.** *Telling the Truth to Troubled People.* Minneapolis: Bethany House Publishers, 1985.

The title of this book is disarming. In actuality, what we have here is an important manual that lends itself for use in the training of lay counselors. It covers such issues as discernment and diagnosis, as well as how to deal with common disorders. 253.5.B12T

**Bailey, Robert W.** *Ministering to the Grieving.* Grand Rapids: Zondervan Publishing House, 1980.

A handy manual for pastor and counselor. Follows the reality-orientation model of therapy. 253.5.B15

**Barker, Robert L.** *Treating Couples in Crisis: Fundamentals and Practice of Marital Therapy.* New York: The Free Press, 1984.

Featuring frequent case histories, this book stresses practical problem-solving procedures. At a time when divorce rates continue to climb, and when our understanding of marriage must continually be reassessed and revised, *Treating Couples in Crisis* provides a much-needed resource for marital and family therapists and counselors. 616.89.B24

**Beavers, W. Robert.** *Successful Marriage: A Family Systems Approach to Couples Therapy.* New York: W. W. Norton and Co., 1985.

Marriage has been described as a beleagured fortress with those on the inside trying to get out and those on the outside struggling to get in. The integrative approach in this book to the counseling of couples is based on an understanding of emotional distress and the kinds of marital disharmony that such distress precipitates. Though written for clinical therapists, there is much here that can be put to good use by pastoral counselors as well. 616.89.B38

**Blackburn, William.** *What You Should Know About Suicide.* Waco, Tex.: Word Books, 1982.

Suicide is a leading cause of death among adolescents in the U.S. Suicidal people are confronting those in the helping professions with increasing regularity. This book details what to look for in potential suicides and how to counsel those who might commit suicide. 261.8'33.B56

**Block, Donald,** and **Robert Simon, eds.** *The Strength of Family Therapy: Selected Papers of Nathan W. Ackerman.* New York: Brunner/Mazel Publishers, 1982.

Divided into nine sections, this collection of essays by Nathan Ward Ackerman covers the research of that noted psychiatrist from 1937 to his death in 1971. His research is impressive, and readers will appreciate having this compilation of his published writings. 616.89'15.AC5

**Bobgan, Martin,** and **Deidre Bobgan.** *How to Counsel from Scripture.* Chicago: Moody Press, 1985.

The authors address their remarks to Christian psychologists. They propose a nonfee-charging, Scripturally based model of counseling. They also challenge Christians in the church to assume their God-given responsibility to help, nurture, and succor those who are hurting. The key to the success of any counseling lies in the counselor's understanding of the nature of man and the counselee's willingness to change, and herein lies the weakness of the book. The Bobgans have advocated a radical approach. Theirs is a brave and commendable treatise and is deserving of careful reading. 253.5.B63

**Bower, Robert K., ed.** *Biblical and Psychological Perspectives for Christian Counselors.* South Pasadena, Calif.: Publishers Services, 1974.

A pioneer work of considerable merit. Ably fulfills the title and makes available the research of others for interaction and discussion. 253.5.B47

**Buchanan, Duncan.** *The Counseling of Jesus.* Downers Grove, Ill.: InterVarsity Press, 1985.

This is a well-reasoned, perceptive, but not necessarily definitive work. Buchanan answers many often-asked questions about Christ's life and ministry but does not give evidence of having established a biblical model of counseling based on a clear understanding of the nature of man. His work has merit but does not deserve landmark status. We still await that kind of explicit study. 253.5.B85

**Bufford, Rodger K.** *The Human Reflex: Behavioral Psychology in Biblical Perspective.* San Francisco: Harper & Row, 1981.

Summarizes the findings of behaviorism and applies principles to individuals as well as society at large. A vigorous attempt has been made to integrate the teaching of this branch of psychology with the Scriptures. 150.19.B86

**Capps, Donald.** *Biblical Approaches to Pastoral Counseling.* Philadelphia: Westminster Press, 1981.

In four extensive chapters the writer discusses the place of the Bible in counseling and shows how principles may be developed based on Psalms, Proverbs, and the parables. Practical and suggestive. 253.5.C17

————. *Cycle Theory and Pastoral Care.* Philadelphia: Fortress Press, 1983.

Building on Erikson's stages of psychological development, and demonstrating how these may impact pastoral care, counseling, and ministry, Capps provides an innovative approach to the ministry. His work lacks a theological basis, and one is hardpressed to find biblical warrant for much of the material found in this work. 253.5.C17C

**\*Carkhuff, Robert R., R. M. Pierce,** and **J. R. Cannon.** *The Art of Helping, IV.*

Amherst, Mass.: Human Resource Development Press, 1980.

Most informative and practical. Ideal for all who are in the helping professions. 253.5.C19 1980

**Cavanagh, Michael E.** *The Counseling Experience: A Theoretical and Practical Approach.* Monterey, Calif.: Brooks/Cole Publishing Company, 1982.

This introductory approach deals with the behavioral dynamics of counseling, a theoretical approach to modes of counseling, and the practical results of the merger of these two dimensions. 158.3.C31

**Clements, William M.** *Care and Counseling for the Aging.* Philadelphia: Fortress Press, 1979.

Focuses on geriatrics and the personal problems of the aging. Seeks to integrate the problems faced by senior citizens with the down-to-earth realities of ministry to older people. 253.5.C59

**Clinebell, Howard John, Jr.** *Basic Types of Pastoral Care and Counseling: Resources for the Ministry of Healing and Growth.* Revised and enlarged edition. Nashville: Abingdon Press, 1984.

Having discarded the Rogerian and neo-Freudian methods of counseling, and having worked through various other eclectic modalities, Clinebell has now developed his own *holistic* liberation-growth paradigm. He does not hesitate to incorporate Eastern mysticism into his approach and the use of Scripture is noticeably absent. 253.5.C49 1984

_____. *Contemporary Growth Therapies: Resources for Actualizing Human Wholeness.* Nashville: Abingdon Press, 1980.

This companion volume to *Growth Counseling: Hope-Centered Methods for Actualizing Human Wholeness* (1979) is a departure from Freudian psychoanalysis and concentrates on different models of therapy with a view to helping the counselor develop skills that will facilitate the growth of the counselee. 616.89′14.C61C

_____. *Growth Counseling for Mid-Years Couples.* Philadelphia: Fortress Press, 1977.

†Focuses on the problems of middlescence, and offers timely suggestions that emphasize growing through the difficulties together. 253.5.C61C

_____. *Growth Counseling: Hope-Centered Methods of Actualizing Human Wholeness.* Nashville: Abingdon Press, 1979.

A further elaboration of the author's growth counseling model of therapy. Though eclectic, and lacking a thorough theological foundation, Clinebell does achieve a measure of success through focusing on the potentials of the individual rather than discussing his emotions or advocating change through behavior modification. In this book Clinebell describes the principles, methods, and theological presuppositions of his system. 253.5.C61G 1979

**Cobb, John C., Jr.** *Theology and Pastoral Care.* Philadelphia: Fortress Press, 1977.

†Clear, insightful, and problem oriented, this book could have made a greater contribution if it had not been written from the perspective of applying process theology to the issues of pastoral care. 253.5.V63

**Coleman, Sandra B., ed.** *Failures in Family Therapy.* New York: Guildford Press, 1985.

A unique and very important book. Honestly appraises failure in therapy and probes the reasons. Twelve chapters chronicle the difficulties encountered, and a final chapter draws principles from the case histories discussed in this book. Counselors have much to learn from this candid work. 616.89.C67

**Coleman, William L.** *Understanding Suicide.* Elgin, Ill.: David C. Cook Publishing Co., 1979.

Treats suicide from the point of view of the potential victim. Lays bare the causes and shows pastors how to handle this kind of situation should one arise in the church. Recommended. 362.2.C67

**Collins, Gary R.** *Christian Counseling: A Comprehensive Guide.* Waco, Tex.: Word Books, 1980.

Nearly five hundred pages in length, this is Collins's most exhaustive work to date. He treats all of the major areas of personality and their dysfunction. For those who lack training in counseling, this manual will prove indispensable. 253.5.C69C 1980

————. *Fractured Personalities.* Carol Stream, Ill.: Creation House, 1972.

Writing for laymen, Collins discusses abnormal psychology, shows how to diagnose its varied forms, and then suggests various forms of treatment. 157.C69

**Corey, Gerald.** *Theory and Practice of Counseling and Psychotherapy.* 2d ed. Monterey, Calif.: Brooks/Cole Publishing Co., 1981.

Having proved its usefulness in many schools where it has been used as a text, this work sets the stage by tracing the history of various psychological theories then illustrates the model of neo-Freudian therapy espoused by the author. 158.3.C81 1981

————., **Marianne Schneider Cory,** and **Patrick Callahan.** *Issues and Ethics in the Helping Professions.* 2d ed. Monterey, Calif.: Brooks/Cole Publishing Co., 1984.

An essential work for pastoral counselors. Deserves wide-spread circulation. 174.2.C81 1984

**Coulson, William.** *Groups, Gimmicks, and Instant Gurus.* New York: Harper & Row, 1973.

This provocative work explores the values and weaknesses of encounter groups. It restores a much-needed balance to group therapy—the kind of balance that has been lost in the present-day proliferation of techniques. 253.5.C83

**Crabb, Lawrence J.** *Basic Principles of Biblical Counseling.* Grand Rapids: Zondervan Publishing House, 1975.

Crabb started out his counseling career as a neo-Freudian. He later found that this method of dealing with people and their problems did not work. He, therefore, began modifying his approach and in the process corrected Freud's erroneous view of the nature of man. From this came Crabb's own approach to counseling, which, with a few changes, may be of help to pastors with little or no training in this area of the ministry. 253.5.C84

————. *Effective Biblical Counseling.* Grand Rapids: Zondervan Publishing House, 1977.

With a plethora of books on counseling flooding the market, it is refreshing to turn to one by a Christian clinician and to learn from him how to sharpen one's counseling skills. 253.C84E

**D'Angelli, Anthony R., Judith Frankel D'Angelli,** and **Steven J. Danish.** *Helping Others.* Monterey, Calif.: Brooks/Cole Publishing Co., 1981.

A most valuable discussion, simply narrated but backed by solid scholarship. It is the kind of book that pastors can use in training those in their churches to develop helping skills. 158.3.D21

**Dayringer, Richard, ed.** *Pastor and Patient: A Handbook for Clergy Who Visit the Sick.* New York: Jason Aronson, 1982.

In twenty-seven chapters the contributors deal with a variety of facets involved in ministry to the sick. A fine symposium. 253.5.D33

**Dean, Alfred, ed.** *Depression in Multidisciplinary Perspective.* New York: Brunner/Mazel, Inc., 1985.

Depression is a major health problem. People from all walks of life suffer from it. Its forms and complexities boggle the mind. "This book more than fulfills the promise of its title. It is a credit to the editor that he has let it stand this multidisciplinary perspective without ideological barriers" (Myrna M. Weissman). 661.85.D34

**Drakeford, John W.** *The Awesome Power of the Healing Thought.* Nashville: Broadman Press, 1981.

A powerful presentation of the dynamics of one's thoughts, how they affect our lives, and what each person may do to achieve proper mental health. Commendable. 158.1.D78A

**Driscoll, Richard.** *Pragmatic Psychotherapy:* New York: Van Nostrand Reinhold Co., 1984.

This eclectic approach offers procedural guidelines for effective interventions and draws parallels to the techniques of other therapeutic orientations. Useful suggestions help readers achieve and maintain a good therapeutic relationship with their clients. Helpful information is included on the need for a healthy alliance, credibility, and the sharing of responsibility for improvement. 616.89.D83

**DuPont, Robert L., ed.** *Phobia: A Comprehensive Summary of Modern Treatments.* New York: Brunner/Mazel Publishers, 1982.

Fear cripples us and is the cause of all sorts of physical and mental disorders. This book deals with the causes as well as the cure of these disorders. 253.5.D92 (Alt. DDC 616.85)

**Edelwich, Jerry, and Archie Brodsky.** *Sexual Dilemmas for the Helping Professional.* New York: Brunner/Mazel Publishers, 1982.

This well-balanced, informative book deals with virtually every facet of sex therapy. It includes a discussion of such topics as seduction, power, vulnerability, self-interest, morality, and sexual harassment. 616.89'14.ED2

**Ericson, Marilyn T.** *Child Psychopathology: Behavior Disorders and Develop-*

*mental Disabilities.* Englewood Cliffs, N.J.: Prentice-Hall, 1982.

Pastoral counselors will find this work to be a handy introduction to assessing and treating the behavioral and emotional problems of children who may be referred to them. The author provides a full-ranging discussion of the theory, research, and clinical practice of psychotherapy. Secular. 618.92'89.ER4 1982

**Everstine, Diana Sullivan, and Louis Everstine.** *People in Crisis: Strategic Therapeutic Interventions.* New York: Brunner/Mazel Publishers, 1983.

"This is a book on how to deal with 'hard cases,' the true psychological emergency cases—the volatile situation, the violent person, and victims of violence" (Margaret Thaler Singer). 616.85.EV1

**Fairchild, Roy W.** *Finding Hope Again: A Pastor's Guide to Counseling Depresssed People.* San Francisco: Harper & Row, 1980.

Focuses on the causes of depression and advises pastors how to counsel depressed people. An excellent guide. 253.5.F16

**Feigenberg, Loma.** *Terminal Care: Friendship Contacts with Dying Cancer Patients.* Translated by P. Hort. New York: Brunner/Mazel Publishers, 1980.

After a lifetime of work in the area of thanatology, the author shares her insights into the most productive way to work with terminally ill patients. Hers is a compassionate, humane, and truly helpful approach. 616'.028.F32

**Figley, Charles R., ed.** *Trauma and Its Wake: The Study and Treatment of Posttraumatic Stress Disorder.* New York: Brunner/Mazel Publishers, 1985.

"After the war, after the crime, after the fire or flood, the emotional wounds remain. Figley and his collaborators, sensitive and skilled clinicians and research scientists, have compiled an outstanding array of insights to help clinicians address the problems of post-traumatic stress. The search presses forward, with efforts such as this book, to help us understand how we hurt and how we can heal without propelling violence and destruction into future generations" (Frank M. Ochberg). 616.89'21.F46

**Fisch, Richard, John H. Weakland, and Lynn Segal.** *The Tactics of Change: Doing Therapy Briefly.* San Francisco: Jossey-Bass Publishers, 1982.

A full discussion of short-term counseling and the ways in which pastors may bring about change through therapeutic intervention. 616.89.F52

**Franken, Robert E.** *Human Motivation.* Monterey, Calif.: Brooks/Cole Publishing Co., 1982.

An in-depth analysis of the causes of certain kinds of behavior, including the antecedents of drug addiction, sleeplessness, obesity, and sexual deviation. Of help to pastoral counselors. Secular. 153.8.F85

**Fretz, Bruce R., and David H. Mills.** *Licensing and Certification of Psychologists and Counselors: A Guide to Current Policies, Procedures, and Legislation.* San Francisco: Jossey-Bass Publishers, 1980.

Ably fulfills the subtitle. Provides essential information for those engaged in structuring ministerial counseling programs. 351.82.F89

**Garland, Diana S. Richmond.** *Working with Couples for Marriage Enrichment.* San Francisco: Jossey-Bass Publishers, 1983.

As the divorce rate continues to climb, therapists and counselors increasingly realize the need to help couples develop skills for resolving conflicts and strengthening their relationships before problems cause serious damage within the marriage. Marriage enrichment is an effective method of helping couples improve their abilities to communicate openly, solve problems, manage conflicts, make decisions, emphathize, and

much more. This book shows how. 362.8'286.G18

**Goldenberg, Irene, and Herbert Goldenberg.** *Family Therapy: An Overview.* Monterey, Calif.: Brooks/Cole Publishing Co., 1980.

Designed for use in courses on marital counseling, this work provides a comprehensive survey of the major theories of therapy, including evolving viewpoints, perspectives, values, intervention techniques, and goals. 616.89.G64

**Goldstein, Gerald, and Michel Hersen, eds.** *Handbook of Psychological Assessment.* New York: Pergamon Press, 1984.

Focusing on the specialized area of assessment, the contributors cover each aspect (e.g., psychometric foundations, intelligence, achievement, etc.) clearly and efficiently. In view of the complexities involved, the result is a work of remarkable usefulness. 150.28'7.G57

**Gong, Victor, ed.** *Understanding AIDS: A Comprehensive Guide.* New Brunswick, N.J.: Rutgers University Press, 1985.

AIDS (Acquired Immune Deficiency Syndrome) has haunted mankind throughout history. Only since 1979 have doctors become aware of the specific syndrome of the disease. This book is a valuable tool explaining the facts about AIDS in understandable terms. It is the kind of work every well-informed pastoral counselor will want to read. 616.9.G58

**Greenstone, James L., and Sharon C. Leviton.** *Crisis Intervention: A Handbook for Interviewers.* Dubuque, Iowa: Kendall/Hunt Publishing House, 1982.

A handbook for all who are in the helping professions. Describes the anatomy of various kinds of crises and explains how to deal with them. Practical. 616.89.G85

**Guntrip, Henry James Samuel.** *Psychology for Ministers and Social Workers.* 3d ed. rev. London: George Allen and Unwin, 1971.

The outgrowth of the author's personal struggle to integrate his psychological training with his Christian commitments. In the process of his struggle he repudiated Freud's biological approach to psychotherapy in favor of a personal view based on his own theological beliefs and extensive study of Scripture. The result is a book that is distinctive and well deserving of a place in every preacher's library. Provocative. 253.5.G95 1971

**Gurman, Alan S., ed.** *Casebook of Marital Therapy.* New York: Guildford Press, 1985.

"Takes a step forward by not only recognizing marital therapy as a discipline in its own right, but by presenting case histories of marital treatment by experienced clinicians" (James L. Framo). 616.89.G96

_____. *Questions and Answers in the Practice of Family Therapy.* 2 vols. New York: Brunner/Mazel Publishers, 1980-1982.

These volumes contain timely essays by leading theorists. Their research and reflection will be found helpful by all who work with troubled family members. "A smorgasbord of concise discussion of practical family therapy, and thereby offers the reader a wonderful opportunity for creative integration. The discussions are generally clear, interesting, and useful, albeit brief and concise" (*Journal of Marital and Family Therapy*). 253.5.G96 (Alt. DDC 616.89)

**Hahlweg, Kurt,** and **Neil S. Jacobson, eds.** *Marital Interaction: Analysis and Modification.* New York: Guildford Press, 1984.

This volume is the outgrowth of the First International Conference on Behavioral Marital Therapy, 1981. It investigates the different kinds of distress to which marriage may be subjected and

evidences behaviorists' growing awareness of the dynamics of a happy, healthy marriage. 616.89.H12

**Hansen, James C., ed.** *Sexual Issues in Family Therapy.* Rockville, Md.: Aspen Systems Corporation, 1983.

Covers everything from human sexuality in the family life cycle to the ethical and legal aspects of sexual issues. Includes essays on the sexuality of divorced couples. Secular. Well researched and well presented. 616.89.H19

**\*Hart, Archibald D.** *Children and Divorce: What to Expect, How to Help.* Waco, Tex.: Word Books, 1982.

Works systematically through the emotions and reactions of children caught in the quagmire of their parent's divorce—a situation in which everyone loses. 253.5.H25

_____. *Depression: Coping and Caring.* Arcadia, Calif.: Cope Publications, 1981.

Offers professional counsel to pastors on how to handle the emotional stress of the ministry. Most helpful. 616.85'27.H25

_____. *The Hidden Link Between Adrenalin and Stress.* Waco, Tex.: Word Books, 1985.

Books on stress and stress management are legion. Hart points to adrenalin as the key to maintaining physical well-being. He relates the results of his clinical research and demonstrates how individuals may begin to take charge of their lives. 613.H25S

**Hauck, Paul A.** *Brief Counseling with RET.* Philadelphia: Westminster Press, 1980.

Describes the fundamentals of effective, short-term counseling with RET (Rational Emotive Therapy). Included is a description of how various problems and personality disorders may be treated. Pastors will find the discussion highly informative. 616.89.H29B

**Headington, Bonnie Joy.** *Communica-*

*tion in the Counseling Relationship.* Cranston, R.I.: Carroll Press, 1979.

Combining theory with practice, Headington comes to grips with this fundamental issue of counseling: communication. She then explains the principles of effective counselor-counselee communication with sensitivity and skill. Recommended. 253.5.H34

**Hersen, Michel, Alan E. Kazdin,** and **Alan S. Bellack, eds.** *The Clinical Psychology Handbook.* New York: Pergamon Press, 1983.

This is a *big* book covering varying models of personality, research issues, assessment, diagnosis, and treatment. Contains excellent bibliographies that should prove invaluable to all pastoral interns and those taking advanced courses in counseling. 616.89.H43

**Hoffman, John Charles.** *Ethical Confrontation in Counseling.* Chicago: University of Chicago Press, 1979.

Appeals for a "more consistent and enthusiastic moral witness at the very heart of the psychotherapeutic process." Secular in approach, but greatly needed. 253.5.H67

**Horne, Arthur M.,** and **Merle M. Ohlsen, eds.** *Family Counseling and Therapy.* Itasca, Ill.: F. E. Peacock Publishers, 1982.

Contributors provide chapters on such different approaches to family counseling as Gestalt, RET, and TA. Insightful and of value to pastoral counselors who are confronted with a never-ending array of problematical cases. 253.5.H78 (Alt. DDC 362.828'6)

**Hulme, William Edward.** *How to Start Counseling.* Nashville: Abingdon Press, 1979.

Originally published in 1955, this introductory work is ideally suited to the needs of the beginner with no formal training in counseling. Hulme handles both the difficulties and the dangers

skillfully. His insights are deeply appreciated, and his encouragements along the way are most welcome. 253.5.H87 1979

————. *Pastoral Care and Counseling: Using the Unique Resources of the Christian Tradition.* Minneapolis: Augsburg Publishing House, 1981.

Sounds a clarion call to pastors to turn from an uncritical acceptance of modern therapeutic approaches to counseling to those methodologies grounded in God's revelation. 253.5.H87P

**Irion, Paul E.** *The Funeral and the Mourners: Pastoral Care of the Bereaved.* Nashville: Abingdon Press, 1979.

This book first appeared a quarter century ago. It is a complete, helpful, and sound introduction to the funeral, from first telephone call to follow-up counseling. Contains an excellent discussion of the psychology of grief. 253.5.IR4 1979

**Irwin, Paul B.** *The Care and Counseling of Youth in the Church.* Philadelphia: Fortress Press, 1975.

Building on modern psychotherapy and tending toward an eclecticism in treating certain problems, Irwin approaches the dilemmas of youth from an intensely practical (but not necessarily biblical) point of view. 253.5.IR9

**Jacobson, Neil S.,** and **Gayla Margolin.** *Marital Therapy: Strategies Based on Social Learning and Behavior Exchange Principles.* New York: Brunner/Mazel Publishers, 1979.

The authors show how "behavior exchange principles" can be employed to alter communication patterns and no-win situations, and how they can assist in the resolving of marital problems. Recommended. 253.5.J15

**Janis, Irving L.** *Short-term Counseling: Guidelines Based on Recent Research.* New Haven, Conn.: Yale University Press, 1983.

All pastors are called on, at one time or

another, to serve in crisis situations and offer short-term counseling. This work—a thoroughly professional treatise—is packed with insightful information. What is presented within these pages may well become normative as fees for counseling continue to escalate. Most helpful. 158.3.J25

―――, **ed.** *Counseling on Personal Decisions: Theory and Research on Short-Term Helping Relationships.* New Haven, Conn.: Yale University Press, 1982.

This comprehensive manual is designed to assist those in the counseling professions to be more effective in dealing with the different facets of each client's problems and needs. 158.3.C83J

**Johnson, Stephen M.** *Characteriological Transformation: The Hard Work Miracle.* New York: W. W. Norton and Co., 1985.

Applies object relations theory to neo-Freudianism and develops an approach to character change that Johnson has found to achieve the desired results. This is indeed a breakthrough as far as psychology is concerned, and this book offers some unique insights for Christians as well. 616.89.J63

**Justice, William G.** *Don't Sit on the Bed.* Nashville: Broadman Press, 1973.

Brief, pointed chapters describing the dos and don'ts of visiting the sick. 253.5.J98

**Kaufman, Edward.** *Substance Abuse and Family Therapy.* Orlando, Fla.: Grune and Stratton, 1984.

Distinguishing between the motivations of male and female users of alcohol and drugs, Kaufman makes available to counselors and therapists a handy, informative analysis of his own findings. At the same time he provides a wealth of usable information in the treatment of these kinds of abuse. Recommended. 616.86.K16S

―――, **ed.** *Power to Change: Family Case Studies in the Treatment of Alcoholism.* New York: Gardner Press, 1984.

Alcoholism is becoming one of the major problems in the church today. The help the alcoholic needs lies in part within family therapy. This volume makes available to pastoral counselors the experience of other therapists. Different modes of treatment are described and the case studies will prove helpful to those who read this important work. No one methodology is advocated, but rather, through the different presentations, readers are exposed to structural, strategic, and behavioral approaches to the treatment of alcoholism. 616.87.K16

**Kelly, Mary.** *Post-Partum Document.* London: Routledge and Kegan Paul, 1985.

Using art as a means of ascertaining the feelings of those suffering from postpartum blues, Kelly charts the stages of depression. In the process she reveals the longings and frustrations, the organic origins of the feelings as well as the fantasies and fetishes of the individual experiences. There is some doubt as to the wisdom of this book's being read by mothers-to-be, but the information can be used by counselors in dealing with this particular malady. 306.8'743.K29

**Kelly, William E., ed.** *Post-Traumatic Stress Disorder and the War Veteran Patient.* New York: Brunner/Mazel, 1985.

Provides counselors and therapists with a comprehensive blueprint for conceptualizing and treating war veterans' stress disorders. Concludes with the most comprehensive reading list on this subject yet assembled. Excellent coverage. 616.85'212.K29

**Kiev, Ari.** *Recovery from Depression: A Self-Help Strategy.* New York: E. P. Dutton, 1982.

For the millions of Americans who suffer the debilitating symptoms of chronic depression, and for those who suffer less serious bouts with the blues, the author provides practical tips for the sometimes-awesome job of getting through the day. These include setting up a daily schedule of activities, reviewing the day's events, avoiding over-commitment, dealing with mistakes and failures, and learning to put one's self into one's plans. He also urges the reader to change self-destructive behavior patterns and provides techniques for restructuring relationships with friends and relatives to minimize stress, disagreements, and feelings of resentment and martyrdom. 616.85.K54

**Kubler-Ross, Elisabeth.** *On Death and Dying.* New York: Macmillan Co., 1969.

In retrospect, the Christian world has come to appreciate this European physician's remarkable insights. She discusses fairly and fully the five stages through which the dying person characteristically passes. This book is a must for counselors. 155.93.K95

**Kutash, Irwin L., Louis B. Schlesinger, and Associates.** *Handbook on Stress and Anxiety.* San Francisco: Jossey-Bass Publishers, 1980.

Treats the dramatic upward spiral of stress and anxiety cases in commerce and industry, and describes how counselors may play a part in reducing these destructive tendencies. 152.4.K96

**L'Abate, Lucciano,** and **Sherry McHenry.** *Handbook of Marital Interventions.* New York: Grune and Stratton, 1983.

Concerned over the work done by marital therapists, these two qualified counselors assess the techniques and assumptions of those in the field. Well-researched and practical. This is an excellent text to use in the training of pastoral counselors. 616.89.L11

**Laufer, Moses,** and **M. Egle Laufer.** *Adolescence and Developmental Breakdown: A Psychoanalytic View.* New Haven, Conn.: Yale University Press, 1984.

For many years the Laufers have worked at an adolescent center where they have had experience with young people who have come for help because of attempted suicide, severe depression, sudden academic failure, sexual abnormality, or behavior that represented a tenuous link with reality. In this book they provide an analysis of their counseling techniques. What they have to say will be of interest to all who work intimately with this age group. 616.89.L36

**Leehan, James,** and **Laura Pistone Wilson.** *Grown-up Abused Children.* Springfield, Ill.: Charles C. Thomas Publishers, 1985.

The authors have dealt with college-age students for many years. They are in an excellent position to assess the long-term damage that child abuse can cause. How to help these sufferers is the purpose of their book. Because the incidence of child abuse—verbal, emotional, physical, sexual—mushroomed in the late 1970s and early 1980s, pastors and counselors need to know how to recognize the symptoms and what to do to help the victim. 616.89.L51

**Lester, Andrew D.** *Pastoral Care with Children in Crisis.* Philadelphia: Westminster Press, 1985.

Providing an enlightening overview of the major reasons pastors tend to neglect their duties to children in the church, Lester urges them to equip themselves with the knowledge and techniques that will enable them successfully to shape the spiritual development of their young charges—young people who one day will be the leaders in the church. Using such means as play, art, story-telling, and writing techniques, he stimulates the thinking of his readers and at the same time opens up a variety of creative ways to involve those from ages five through twelve. 253.5.L56

**Lester, David.** *Why People Kill Themselves: A 1980s Summary of Research Findings on Suicidal Behavior.* 2d ed. Springfield, Ill.: Charles C. Thomas Publishers, 1983.

First published in 1972. Focuses on *why* people take their own lives. It deals with the predisposition of those who commit suicide, as well as what those who work with such people may do to facilitate therapy. 616.85.L56W 1983

**Levant, Ronald F.** *Family Therapy: A Comprehensive Overview.* Englewood Cliffs, N.J.: Prentice-Hall, 1984.

Growing out of the author's lectures to graduate students, this work focuses primarily on conceptual models and empirical research. Only secondarily does this study touch on the practical application of these models to therapy. 616.89.L57

***Levinson, Daniel J.,** and **Charlotte N. Darrow.** *The Seasons of a Man's Life.* New York: Alfred A. Knopf, 1978.

Readers of *Passages* by Gail Sheehy will welcome this volume. It deals clearly and candidly with the adult life-cycle and explains the periods of growth, plateaus, crises, only to be followed by fresh periods of growth, and so forth. Also demonstrates that the so called mid-life crisis is merely one stage of many in life that is marked by crisis. This book is highly informative and very revealing. It is a book pastors should read to be better able to minister to men in their different stages of growth. This is the kind of book one will wish to refer to again and again. 155.6'32.L57

**Madanes, Cloe.** *Strategic Family Therapy.* San Francisco: Jossey-Bass Publishers, 1981.

A detailed guide to the theory and application of psychoanalytic principles to the practice of "strategic family therapy." Describes intervention strategies and how destructive patterns of behavior may be changed. 616.89'156.M26

**Marshall, Eldon K.,** and **O. David Kurtz, eds.** *Interpersonal Helping Skills.* San Francisco: Jossey-Bass Publishers, 1982.

A careful presentation of the different models used in counseling by different helping professions. Treats the ways in which certain skills may be developed, the form and process of training programs, how group leadership skills are developed, and how programs may be evaluated for effectiveness. Insightful. 302.3.M35

**Masterson, James F.** *The Real Self: A Developmental, Self, and Object Relations Approach.* New York: Brunner/Mazel, Publishers, 1985.

Provides a unique synthesis of theory and clinical expertise that succeeds in filling in the gap in developmental ideas and object relations as these combine to meet the need for a more creative and effective psychotherapy. 616.89.M39

**Matheny, Kenneth B.,** and **Richard J. Riordan.** *Therapy American Style: Person Power Through Self-Help.* Chicago: Nelson-Hall, 1979.

More than just another self-help book, this work lays a foundation for personal change through a practical approach to therapy and actualization that paves the way for growth, the reduction of stress, and the opening of the channels of communication. 158.1.M42

**McCary, James Leslie,** and **Stephen P. McCary.** *McCary's Human Sexuality.* 4th ed. Belmont, Calif.: Wadsworth Publishing Co., 1982.

A thorough discussion of the issues of male and female sexuality. Of value to pastors in premarital counseling as well as in dealing with sexual dysfunction in marital counseling. 253.5.M12 1982 (Alt. DDC 613.9'5)

**McLemore, Clinton W.** *Clergyman's Psychological Handbook.* Grand Rapids: Wm. B. Eerdmans Publishing Co., 1974.

This summary of the major functional and organic disorders pastors encounter in their counseling ministry is of particular value in determining when to refer someone to a psychologist or, on rare occasions, to a psychiatrist. 253.5.M22

————. *The Scandal of Psychotherapy: A Guide to Resolving the Tensions Between Faith and Counseling.* Wheaton, Ill.: Tyndale House Publishers, 1982.

Addresses the contemporary milieu in which more and more pastors are resorting to psychological techniques in the pulpit and following psychoanalytic theories in their counseling. Assesses the reason for this phenomenon and attempts to provide a solution to the resolution of the tension that has arisen. 616.89.M22

**Meiburg, Albert L.** *Sound Body/Sound Mind.* Philadelphia: Westminster Press, 1984.

†Healthy-mindedness is equated in Scripture with the practice of sound doctrine. This volume purports to lead the way to personal "wellness," but Meiburg does little more than encourage his readers to take charge of their own lives, restructure their ways of thinking, and develop new patterns of relating. Each of these areas is necessary to an overall sense of well-being, but the material presented falls short of a truly viable statement of the pattern *and* the process. In spite of this weakness, what Meiburg has presented may well be regarded as of ground-breaking significance. 613.M47

**Meier, Paul D., Frank B. Minirth,** and **Frank Wichern.** *Introduction to Psychology and Counseling: Christian Perspectives and Applications.* Grand Rapids: Baker Book House, 1982.

Treats human development from biblical and psychological perspectives. Then relates the dynamics of personality to the counseling process. A basic resource guide. 150.M47

**Millman, Howard L., Jack T. Huber,** and **Dean R. Diggins.** *Therapies for Adults.* San Francisco: Jossey-Bass Publishers. 1982.

Dealing with depression, anxiety, and personality disorders, this work applies psychoanalytic techniques and theories

to a wide variety of mental and emotional states. 616.89′14.M62

***Minirth, Frank B.** *Christian Psychiatry.* Old Tappan, N.J.: Fleming H. Revell Co., 1977.

Combines a balanced approach to psychotherapy with biblical insights to form a practical manual for pastors and counselors. 616.8′9.M66

**Mitman, John L. C.** *Premarital Counseling: A Manual for Clergy and Counselors.* Minneapolis: Seabury Press, 1980.

A concise digest that helps pastors evaluate a couple's readiness for marriage. Provides guidelines designed to help those in positions of responsibility prepare young people for the future. 253.5.M69

**Morawetz, Anita,** and **Gillian Walker.** *Brief Therapy with Single-Parent Families.* New York: Brunner/Mazel Publishers, 1984.

Examines the myths and realities of single-parent families. Uses a systems framework. Assesses virtually every aspect of the single-parent experience. Provides essential reading for all pastoral counselors. 616.89.M79

**Morrison, Helen L.,** ed. *Children of Depressed Parents: Risk, Identification, and Intervention.* New York: Grune and Stratton, 1983.

Assesses the general climate in America today and notes the rising incidence of depression among all classes of people. Describes the effect of such emotional stress and insecurity on children born to these people. 618.92.M83

**Newman, Philip R.,** and **Barbara M. Newman.** *Living: The Process of Adjustment.* Homewood, Ill.: Dorsey Press, 1981.

The authors, who wrote *Development Through Life,* here provide us with the basic issues about human adjustment in childhood and adolescence, adulthood and mid-life, and describe how change may be facilitated through each stage of growth and development. 158'.1.N46

**Nichols, Michael P.** *Family Therapy: Concepts and Methods.* New York: Gardner Press, 1984.

Begins fittingly with an analysis of the context of family therapy, then explores its history, theoretical framework, and contemporary setting. Includes a thoughtful discussion of such conceptual issues as circular causality and pathological triangles, and makes useful suggestions about literature that can be used in the therapeutic process and in training centers. Also highlights the core principles and techniques of family therapy and makes available to readers and mental health professionals a wealth of usable material. Recommended. 616.89.N51

**Noyce, Gaylord.** *The Art of Pastoral Conversation.* Atlanta: John Knox Press, 1982.

Brief and to-the-point. This work offers practical suggestions on the ways in which pastoral counseling may be made more effective. 253.5.N87

**Oates, Wayne Edward.** *Pastoral Care and Counseling in Grief and Separation.* Philadelphia: Fortress Press, 1976.

Discusses the ways in which the resources of the church can make grief and separation an avenue of constructive growth. 253.5.OA8

**Oden, Thomas C.** *Care of Souls in the Classical Tradition.* Theology and Pastoral Care. Philadelphia: Fortress Press, 1984.

This work, the latest in a new series, falls back on the example of Gregory the Great (A.D. 540-604), and helps modern pastoral counselors benefit from Gregory's insights. As valuable as this treatment is, and Oden has uncovered many new and interesting details that have practical relevance to the ministry, there is a conspicuous absence of Scripture. 253.5.G81.OD2

———. *Kerygma and Counseling: Toward a Covenant Ontology for Secular Psychotherapy.* San Francisco: Harper & Row, 1978.

First published in 1966, this epochal work attempts to provide a common ground for the integration of theology and psychotherapy. Though in large measure successful, Oden fails in his task because of his liberal theological presuppositions. 253.5.OD2 1978

**Oglesby, William B., Jr.** *Referral in Pastoral Counseling.* Nashville: Abingdon Press, 1978.

A practical guidebook. Designed for those who minister to people with deep emotional hurts. 253.5.OG1

**Okun, Barbara F.** *Effective Helping: Interviewing and Counseling Techniques.* 2d ed. Monterey, Calif.: Brooks/Cole Publishing Co., 1982.

By utilizing some of the principles of TA, Okun explains how people may help others, communicate more effectively, and develop healthy relationships. A helpful counseling manual. 158.3.OK7

**\*Olson, G. Keith.** *Counseling Teenagers: The Complete Christian Guide to Understanding and Helping Adolescents.* Loveland, Colo.: Group Books, 1984.

There is a wide variety of books on parenting teenagers. These volumes are primarily oriented to parents. Then, in the area of clinical psychology, there are several important monographs on adolescent psychology and counseling. These have been written from secular as well as Christian perspectives. This work offers a threefold integration. It combines Christian convictions with psychological insights; it offers several counseling theories with specific guidelines; and it shows that any success with any modality necessitates an understanding of the counselee. This is a book that pastoral counselors should obtain and read with care. 253.5.OL8

**Olson, Richard P.,** and **Carole Della Pia-Terry.** *Help for Remarried Couples and*

*Families.* Valley Forge, Pa.: Judson Press, 1984.

Tackles an area commonly ignored by most writers, and is not afraid to discuss issues pertaining to the special problems facing those who desire to remarry. This is an important treatment and is a worthy companion volume to *Ministry with Remarried Persons.* 306.84.OL8H

**Osborne, Cecil G.** *Understanding Your Past, Key to Your Future.* Waco, Tex.: Word Books, 1980.

Though differing from Misseldine's *Your Inner Child of the Past* in certain respects, this work uses some of the same principles. The application here, however, is Osborne's PIT (Primal Integration Therapy). He also explains how counselors may tap into the long-repressed feelings of their counselees. 248.4.OS3

**Patton, John.** *Pastoral Counseling: A Ministry of the Church.* Nashville: Abingdon Press, 1983.

†Deals with the *what* of counseling. Provides a solid basis for pastoral intervention. 253.5.P27

**Peck, Morgan Scott.** *People of the Lie: The Hope for Healing the Human Spirit.* New York: Simon and Schuster, 1983.

As with Peck's earlier work, *The Road Less Travelled,* this one promises to be controversial. In it he attempts a synthesis between the doctrine of theodicy and contemporary examples of human suffering. The value of Peck's treatment lies in his courage to explore new ideas, even if these prove to be wrong. 616.89.P31

**Perez, Joseph Francis.** *Family Counseling: Theory and Practice.* New York: D. Van Nostrand Co., 1979.

Combines both an historical introduction to family counseling and a treatment of theoretical issues and techniques. This work could be used in seminary counseling programs. 616.89.P41

**Phillips, Ewing Lakin.** *A Guide for*

*Therapists and Patients to Short-term Psychotherapy.* Springfield, Ill.: Charles C. Thomas Publishers, 1985.

The rising cost of psychological services has made short-term counseling a necessity. In this book Phillips deals with different methodologies and shows how they may be adapted to counseling over a limited time span. What the writer presents may well become normative within the next few decades. 616.89.P54

*The Process of Child Therapy.* New York: Brunner/Mazel Publishers, 1982.

In a particularly sensitive manner, this work discusses the many ramifications of treatment, emphasizing the identification of its historical roots, the persons involved, the stages of development at which children and adolescents undergo therapy, the kind of therapy, and how it works. The process is further illustrated with cases and dialogues from actual therapeutic sessions dealing with a variety of childhood mental disorders. 616.89.G91

**Pruyser, Paul W.** *The Minister as Diagnostician: Personal Problems in Pastoral Perspective.* Philadelphia: Westminster Press, 1976.

Writing out of concern that pastoral care not become another facet of psychological counseling, the author, a clinical therapist, calls attention to the skills pastors need to develop in order to become better diagnosticians. 253.5.P95

**Puryear, Douglas A.** *Helping People in Crisis.* San Francisco: Jossey-Bass Publishers, 1979.

Of value to paraprofessionals in the ministry of counseling. Treats the interview step by step, from first contact to cessation of therapy. Valuable for its insights. 616.89'915.P97

**Rassieur, Charles L.** *The Problem Clergymen Don't Talk About.* Philadelphia: Westminster Press, 1976.

The theme of this book is the sexual

response of clergymen to the women they counsel. This candid discussion provides sage advice as well as some practical precautions. 253.5.R18

**Robins, Lee N., ed.** *Studying Drug Abuse.* New Brunswick, N.J.: Rutgers University Press, 1985.

This book, a part of the series on psychosocial epistemology, evaluates different therapeutic modalities to the treatment of drug abuse. Several variables are included to assess which modality is the best. The chapters have been contributed by sociologists, biologists, physicians, psychiatrists, and psychologists. This is the kind of scholarly symposium that is of great value to counselors and therapists because of its synthesis of the material. 362.2′93.R55

**\*Roe, John.** *A Consumer's Guide to Christian Counseling.* Nashville: Abingdon Press, 1982.

Assesses the emotional, physical, spiritual, intellectual, and social issues that in time require professional help. 158.3.R62

**Rowe, Dorothy.** *Depression: The Way Out of Your Prison.* London: Routledge and Kegan Paul, 1983.

Explores the causes as well as the cure of depression. Deals forthrightly with problems associated with shame and guilt, fear and courage, forgiveness and revenge, anger, jealousy, hate, and love. 616.89.R79

**Russell, Mary Nomme.** *Skills in Counseling Women: The Feminist Approach.* Springfield, Ill.: Charles C. Thomas, 1984.

The goal of this book is to provide counselors with a specific explanation of feminism and the needs of feminists. In achieving her ends, Russell analyzes the components and skills relevant to those of the feminist persuasion. 158.3.R91

**Rychman, Richard M.** *Theories of Personality.* 2d ed. Monterey, Calif.: Brooks/ Cole Publishing Co., 1982.

One of the finest introductions to the study of human personality. Provides an excellent analysis of the different approaches. Biblical anthropologists will find much in this book to stimulate their thinking. 155.2.R96 1982

**Sager, Clifford J., et al.** *Treating the Remarried Family.* New York: Brunner/ Mazel Publishers, 1983.

Sager and his associates present both their theory and clinical techniques within the framework of a commonly shared theoretical perspective. They interrelate their material on three levels: the family system, individual and family life cycles, and the development of intrapsychic dynamics of each family member. 326.8′286.SA1

**Satir, Virginia,** and **Michele Baldwin.** *Satir, Step-by-Step: A Guide to Creating Change in Families.* Palo Alto, Calif.: Science and Behavior Books, 1983.

This sequel to *Conjoint Family Therapy* is an intimate expression of Satir's pioneering work filtered through the academic acuity of an experienced clinical psychologist. 616.89.SA8B

**Schaefer, Charles E., James M. Briesmeister,** and **Maureen E. Fitton.** *Family Therapy Techniques for Problem Behaviors of Children and Teenagers.* San Francisco: Jossey-Bass Publishers, 1984.

Intended to serve as a practical and comprehensive handbook on different kinds of therapies for children and teenagers. Provides effective, though highly diverse, forms of counseling modalities. Users will need to be skilled in the dynamics involved in order to be able to use these approaches with any degree of success. 616.89.SCH1

————, **Lynette Johnson,** and **Jeffrey N. Wherry.** *Group Therapies for Children and Youth.* San Francisco: Jossey-Bass Publishers, 1982.

Deals with therapeutic approaches to group counseling (including TA, behavioral approaches, diagnosis, and treatment) and work with specific kinds of children and adolescents. Insightful. Of value to all who work with these age groups. 618.92.SCH1

**Schlesinger, Benjamin.** *Sexual Abuse of Children: A Resource Guide and Annotated Bibliography.* Toronto: University of Toronto Press, 1982.

An informative guide to the literature covering all aspects of sexual molestation—including profiles of parents and siblings. 016.3627.SCH3

**Schlossberg, Nancy K.** *Counseling Adults in Transition: Linking Practice with Theory.* New York: Springer Publishing Co., 1984.

With people changing careers three or four times during a lifetime, this work becomes an essential resource for pastoral counselors, who must often guide people through these transitions. Timely, helpful. 158.3.SCH3

**Schmidt, Paul F.** *Coping with Difficult People.* Philadelphia: Westminster Press, 1980.

A brief introduction to different types of personality disorders. Ideal for those in the church with little or no previous training in personality theory. 616.85.SCH5

**Schneider, John.** *Stress, Loss, and Grief: Understanding Their Origins and Growth Potential.* Baltimore: University Park Press, 1984.

A fascinating, time-tested, and reliable approach to bereavement, grief, and the process of recovery. Avoids simplistic answers, yet deals holistically with the needs of the individual. Recommended. 155.9′37.SCH1

**Schuckit, Marc A., ed.** *Alcohol Patterns and Problems.* New Brunswick, N.J.: Rutgers University Press, 1985.

Alcoholism and alcohol abuse are two of the world's leading social problems. Alcoholism has wide-reaching effects on all body systems. This symposium by respected authorities will acquaint pastors

and counselors with the causes as well as the possible cure(s) of this disease. 362.2′922.SCH7

**Seligman, Linda.** *Assessment in Developmental Career Counseling.* Cranston, R.I.: Carroll Press, 1980.

A helpful book for the pastoral counselor who works with young people. 650.1′4.SE4

**Sell, Kenneth D., comp.** *Divorce in the 70's: A Subject Bibliography.* Phoenix: Oryx Press, 1981.

This work documents the social and behavioral, legal, religious, popular, and nonprint materials on divorce published in the 1970s. A valuable resource for research, although it lacks annotations. 016.306′8.SE4

**Smith, Robert L., and Ann M. Alexander.** *Counseling Couples in Groups—A Manual for Improving Troubled Relationships.* Springfield, Ill. Charles C. Thomas, 1974.

Designed "for the neophyte in couple group leadership . . . with explicit directions, plus suggestions, for conducting each session." Brief but helpful. 301.18′5.ST6

**Sourkes, Barbara M.** *The Deepening Shade: Psychological Aspects of Life-Threatening Illness.* Pittsburgh: University of Pittsburgh Press, 1982.

A handy manual for all of those who work with the terminally ill. The insights are valuable, and therapy with those suffering from cancer is particularly helpful. 616.SO8

**Spero, Moshe Halevi, ed.** *Psychotherapy of the Religious Patient.* Springfield, Ill.: Charles C. Thomas Publishers, 1985.

Compiled from mental health practitioners, this work deals with the religious commitments of those who come from Jewish, Catholic, and Protestant orientations. Though not written either to or for evangelicals, there are practical pointers that will prove helpful to pastors in a college or university town. 616.89.SP3

*Spickard, Anderson, and Barbara R. Thompson. *Dying for a Drink: What You Should Know About Alcoholism.* Waco, Tex.: Word Books, 1985.

"Undoubtedly the best book on alcoholism from a Christian perspective I have ever read" (Archibald D. Hart). 616.86′1.SP4

Stahmann, Robert F., and William J. Hiebert. *Premarital Counseling.* Lexington, Mass.: Lexington Books, 1980.

Written by two members of the American Association of Marriage and Family Therapy, this slender but helpful volume covers the foundations of marriage, conjoint counseling of engaged couples, group premarital counseling, and topics of special interest to counselors. An excellent introduction. 253.5.ST1

Stein, Michael D., and J. Kent Davis. *Therapies for Adolescents.* San Francisco: Jossey-Bass Publishers, 1982.

Presented in a ready-reference format, this work provides the user with a wide range of information about adolescents. Of value to pastoral counselors. 616.89′14.ST3

Stern, E. Mark, ed. *Psychotherapy and the Religiously Committed Patient.* New York: Haworth Press, 1985.

This collection of articles views the psychotherapeutic process as a means of enhancing religious commitment rather than merely as a way of abrogating pain and emotional discomfort. Therapeutic intervention, therefore, is seen as a means of focusing on the functions of faith and hope in the improvement of the quality of life of the counselee. Though it possesses definite values, this book has not been written from a conservative, evangelical point of view. 616.89.ST4

Stewart, Charles William. *The Minister as Family Counselor.* Nashville: Abingdon Press, 1979.

Designed for pastors. Through the use of charts and diagrams the author describes the family structure, pinpoints the causes of family breakdown, and shows what pastors may do to prevent predicaments from arising. 253.5.ST4

Stone, Howard W. *Crisis Counseling.* Philadelphia: Fortress Press, 1976.

Following his theoretical discussion of crisis intervention, Stone outlines how pastors may best be of service to those in need. His use of case studies is effective and enlightening. 253.5.ST6

Stuart, Irving, and Lawrence E. Abt, eds. *Children of Separation and Divorce: Management and Treatment.* New York: Van Nostrand Reinhold Co., 1981.

Carefully examines the legal, social, and emotional consequences of divorce, and then discusses appropriate therapeutic strategies. Most helpful. 306.8′9.C43

Thompson, David A. *A Premarital Guide for Couples and Their Counselors.* Minneapolis: Bethany Fellowship, 1979.

Composed of tear sheets with questions and space for answers, this workbook can be used to good effect by pastors as they lead a couple through the stages of preparing for marriage. 253.5.T37 (Alt. DDC 362.8′2)

Tiemann, William Harold, and John C. Bush. *The Right to Silence: Privileged Clergy Communication and the Law.* Nashville: Abingdon Press, 1983.

First published in 1964, this work has been updated with new chapters by Bush. In light of recent developments in U.S. legal history, all those engaged in the important ministry of counseling need to be familiar with its contents. 347.3.AM3.T44 1983

Van Hoose, William H., and Maureen Rousset Worth. *Counseling Adults: A Developmental Approach.* Monterey, Calif.: Brooks/Cole Publishing Co., 1982.

Focuses on the counseling of healthy people (as opposed to those exhibiting some definite pathology), and points the way to personal growth through an understanding of the dynamics of personality and the developmental stages through which we all pass. 158.3.V26

**Van Leeuwen, Mary Stewart.** *The Sorcerer's Apprentice: A Christian Looks at the Changing Face of Psychology.* Downers Grove, Ill.: InterVarsity Press, 1982.

Comprising the John G. Finch Lectures, Fuller Theological Seminary, these incisive studies draw attention to recent developments within psychology as a discipline and their impact on psychology as a profession. 150.1.V32

**Van Vonderen, Jeffrey.** *Good News for the Chemically Dependent.* Nashville: Thomas Nelson Publishers, 1985.

More than thirty million Americans suffer from drug or alcohol addiction, and one person's addiction means a whole family suffers. This discussion of the problem explains how family members, co-workers, and friends can help. It is a study of chemical dependency, what causes it, and what can be done to correct its awful effects. A capable handling of a difficult subject. 616.86'3.V37

**Vanderpool, James A.** *Person to Person: A Handbook for Pastoral Counseling.* Garden City, N.Y.: Doubleday and Co., 1977.

Follows Evelyn Duvall's extremely helpful development approach to human maturation. Discusses the way in which pastors may effectively counsel their parishioners so as to help them grow toward full maturity. 253.5.V26

**Vredevelt, Pam,** and **Joyce Whitman.** *Walking a Thin Line: Anorexia and Bulimia.* Portland, Oreg.: Multnomah Press, 1985.

This book extends a lifeline to those suffering from the eating disorders of anorexia nervosa and bulimia. It discusses the physiological and psychological conditions that devitalize young men and women. Not a substitute for professional help, the counsel contained within

these pages offers supportive help, exercises, positive biblical counsel, and hope. No quick cures are promised, but rather long-range solutions are sought. Pastors will find the discussion helpful. 616.89.V95

**Wells, Carl F.,** and **Irving R. Stuart, eds.** *Self-Destructive Behavior in Children and Adolescents.* New York: Van Nostrand Reinhold Co., 1981.

Treats the reasons for juvenile alcoholism, pregnancies, abortion, and suicide from the perspective of those who really wish to help. A valuable acquisition for the pastoral counselor. 618.92.W46

**Wessler, Ruth A.,** and **Richard L. Wessler.** *The Principles and Practice of Relational-Emotive Therapy.* San Francisco: Jossey-Bass Publishers, 1980.

Analyzes and explains the principles of RET and describes its effectiveness in the client-therapist relationship. 616.89.W51

**Wetzel, Janice Wood.** *Clinical Handbook of Depression.* New York: Gardner Press, 1984.

A comprehensive, interdisciplinary approach to the major psychological models of therapy. Deals with the rising incidence, causes, and treatment of depression. An excellent overview. Recommended. 616.89.W53

**White, John.** *The Masks of Melancholy: A Christian Physician Looks at Depression and Suicide.* Downers Grove, Ill.: InterVarsity Press, 1982.

Here is a book for pastoral counselors—one that will help them unlock the chains of the mentally ill and lead them into the freedom of wholeness in Christ. 616.85.W58

**Wicks, Robert J., Richard J. Parsons,** and **Donald E. Capps, eds.** *Clinical Handbook of Pastoral Counseling.* New York: Paulist Press, 1985.

Believing that this book represents the coming of age of pastoral counseling,

M. Scott Peck praised it for its integration and integrity. It covers all the essential areas of counseling, but the theological position of most of the contributors is to the left of center, and most of the chapters are heavily tinged with humanism. What is contained between these covers is nonetheless useful to the discerning reader. 253.5.W63

**Wilke, Richard B.** *The Pastor and Marriage Group Counseling.* Nashville: Abingdon Press, 1974.

An important book outlining some new techniques for those who work with married couples. Well presented. 253.5.W65

**Williams, Daniel Day.** *The Minister and the Care of Souls.* New York: Harper & Row, 1977.

A Rogerian approach to pastoral counseling. Provides a cogent explanation of client-centered therapy. First published in 1961. 253.5.W67 1977

**Wilson, G. Terence,** and **Cyril M. Franks, eds.** *Contemporary Behavior Therapy: Conceptual and Empirical Foundations.* New York: Guilford Press, 1982.

Delineates the relationship between theory and practice in contemporary behavior therapy, shows how the science has developed over the decades, describes the theoretical ramifications of the new cognitive theorists, and shows how all of these ramifications aid the therapist. 253.5.W69 (Alt. DDC 616.89)

**Wise, Jonathan Kurland,** and **Susan Kierr Wise.** *The Overeaters: Eating Styles and Personality.* New York: Human Sciences Press, 1979.

The best work to appear on the subject of obesity. Distinguishes between different personality types and shows how these require different approaches if the problem is to be corrected. Though psychoanalytic, the counsel offered is worthy of serious consideration. Pastoral

counselors will find this book well worth the investment of their time and money. 616.3'98.W75

**\*Worthington, Everett L., Jr.** *How to Help the Hurting.* Downers Grove, Ill.: InterVarsity Press, 1985.

Deals forthrightly with the problems of, as well as the necessity for, peer-counseling in the church. Provides an overview of the major problems encountered by young people. Shows how people may be led to rethink their difficulties and tackle them realistically. Suggests a step-by-step approach that is easy to follow. This is a useful book and one which pastors may well adapt in training programs. It is the kind of treatise that is happily becoming more frequent. It is welcomed as a fine addition in the educational ministry of the church. 253.5.W89H

**\*Wright, Harry Norman.** *Crisis Counseling: Helping People in Crisis and Stress.* San Bernardino, Calif.: Here's Life Publishers, 1985.

This book may well be described as indispensable. Wright devotes a chapter to each of the major situations crisis counselors are likely to face. The treatment is adequate. This is a welcomed addition to the books pastors may read and then refer to again as occasion requires. 253.5.W93C

**\*_____.** *Marital Counseling: A Biblical, Behavioral, Cognitive Approach.* Cambridge: Harper & Row, 1983.

"Deal[s] effectively with the myriad complexities of human relationships in the home. . . . [Provides] a comprehensive text for Christian marriage counselors that will, I believe, become the standard against which other books in its field will be measured" (James C. Dobson). 253.5.W93M

**\*_____.** *Premarital Counseling.* Chicago: Moody Press, 1981.

"Wright does his homework well and is a master at providing help for pastors and counselors in selecting appropriate resources. Both current popular and professional literature are sifted through in his writings" (*Journal of Psychology*). 253.5.W93P

**Zaccaria, Joseph S.,** and **Stephen G. Bopp.** *Approaches to Guidance in Contemporary Education.* 2d ed. Cranston, R.I.: Carroll Press, 1980.

Surveys guidance counseling within the context of the school and explores guidance counseling in our contemporary society. Compares policies in the U.S. with the practices of educational institutions in other countries. Of value to the pastor who, of necessity, must frequently counsel young people in the church regarding their career choices. 371.4.Z1 1980.

**Zander, Alvin.** *Making Groups Effective.* San Francisco: Jossey-Bass Publishers, 1982.

Written for people who work with others, this book describes the ways in which all kinds of leaders may accomplish set objectives through those with whom they serve. Though secular in orientation, this study abounds with useful information. 302.3.Z1

## CHURCH LEADERSHIP AND ADMINISTRATION

**Adams, Arthur Merrihew.** *Effective Leadership for Today's Church.* Philadelphia: Westminster Press, 1978.

Sifts through the maze of approaches to leadership, and shows how pastors may increase their effectiveness. Practical. 254.AD1

**Adams, Jay Edward.** *Pastoral Leadership.* Shepherding God's Flock 3. Grand Rapids: Baker Book House, 1975.

Runs the gamut of the administrative tasks pastors are called on to face. Adams exhibits a warmth and genuine concern seldom in evidence in works of this nature. His comments are perceptive and his books are to be recommended. 254.AD1

**Anderson, Philip,** and **Phoebe Anderson.** *The House Church.* Nashville: Abingdon Press, 1975.

Emphasizes the sharing experience that lies behind Christian fellowship and contributes so much to personal growth. A valuable treatise that provides helpful suggestions for starting and maintaining such local assemblies. 254'.6.AN2

**Argyris, Chris.** *Reasoning, Learning, and Action: Individual and Organizational.* San Francisco: Jossey-Bass Publishers, 1982.

In the aftermath of the decline of management techniques and organizational effectiveness, Argyris offers some alternatives to the present stalemate. 658.4'03.AR3R

*****Arnold, John D.** *Shooting the Executive: The First Crucial Year of a New Assignment.* New York: McGraw-Hill Book Co., 1981.

Though secular in its orientation, this work nevertheless is permeated with practical counsel that pastors as well as businessmen will find helpful whenever they take over a new responsibility. 658.4.AR6

**Barber, Cyril John,** and **Gary (Gerhard) Henry Strauss.** *Leadership: The Dynamics of Success.* Greenwood, S.C.: Attic Press, 1982.

Grounds leadership squarely on a biblical understanding of human personality. "The authors are knowledgeable of the findings in other disciplines and fuse them with biblical doctrine, developing a unique perspective on an approach to successful leadership. . . . With helpful objectivity they appraise the strengths and weaknesses of various modalities. Offering a triple typology . . . [they point the way to an] effective style of leadership" (Vernon C. Grounds). 658.4.B23

**Barker, Steve, et al.** *Good Things Come in Small Groups.* Downers Grove, Ill.: InterVarsity Press, 1985.

Realizing that each person is a combination of hurts and hopes, and that the church exists to promote a caring community, Barker and a few friends met regularly to discuss and then put into practice the principles of personal and corporate growth. The result exceeded their fondest dreams, so they decided to share their experience with others. Hence this book. It is a must. 259.7.B24

**\*Batten, Joe D.** *Expectations and Possibilities.* Reading, Mass.: Addison-Wesley Publishing Co., 1981.

The author of the best-seller *Tough-Minded Management* here provides fresh support for his innovative, revitalizing ideas. He explains the failure of MBO (management by objective) as a system, discusses the tasks required of those who wish to be dynamic leaders, analyzes the effects of various philosophies of management, and shows how a vital esprit de corps is essential to any kind of organization. Excellent. 650.1.B32E

**Baumann, J. Daniel.** *All Originality Makes a Dull Church.* Santa Ana, Calif.: Vision House, 1976.

Traces the history of churches over the past quarter century, and analyzes the successful ones. Classifies the progressive ones into four categories: soul-winning, teaching, life-situations, and social action. Recommends the "general practitioner" church that combines all four characteristics. 254'.5.B32

**Belknap, Ralph L.** *Effective Use of Church Space.* Valley Forge, Pa.: Judson Press, 1978.

A carefully presented, well-outlined,

thorough treatment. Of value to all pastors and church leaders faced with the problems of expansion. Recommended. 254.7.B4

**Benge, Eugene Jackson,** and **John V. Hickey.** *Morale and Motivation: How to Measure Morale and Increase Productivity.* New York: Franklin Watts, 1984.

Though designed for those in the secular arena, there is enough material in this book to stimulate the thinking of any creative pastor. Part I provides a straightforward system for surveying the contours in worker morale. Part II introduces the reader to the tools that will help solve problems in morale. Part III describes the experiences of managers on the firing line of corporate motivation and productivity. The authors explain their ideas and offer sound suggestions for success. 658.3.B43

**Bittel, Lester R.** *Leadership: The Key to Management Success.* New York: Franklin Watts, 1984.

Combines time-tested know-how with easy-to-follow illustrations. The result is a work of rare merit that shows how to maximize personal skills in on-the-job situations. Excellent. 658.4.B54

**Borst, Diane,** and **Patrick J. Montana, eds.** *Managing Nonprofit Organizations.* New York: American Management Association, 1977.

Though not written for Christian insitutions, this collection of essays by educators and administrators, industrial relations experts and directors of large corporations, contains a mine of information on the running of schools, daycare centers, and other nonprofit enterprises. 658'.04'8.B64

**Broadwell, Martin M.** *The New Supervisor.* 3d ed. Reading, Mass.: Addison-Wesley Publishing Company, 1984.

A sequel to *The Practice of Supervising.* Designed for new supervisors who face the challenge of motivating others. Helpful. 658.3.B78N 1984

————. *The Practice of Supervising: Mak-*

*ing Experience Pay.* 2d ed. Reading, Mass.: Addison-Wesley Publishing Co., 1984.

Senior ministers often have to supervise a multiple staff. This secular work contains some important features that will facilitate their task. Insightful. 658.3.B78 1984

**Burns, James MacGregor.** *Leadership.* New York: Harper & Row, 1978.

"An important book . . . that combines an analysis of the past and a penetrating observation of the present with implications for the future stability of American democracy" (Kenneth B. Clark). 301.15′53.B93

**Callanan, Joseph A.** *Communicating: How to Organize Meetings and Presentations.* New York: Franklin Watts, 1984.

This book is really two books in one. The first part shows how one may organize meetings from one-on-one discussions to company-wide conferences. The second half uncovers practical ways in which each leader can analyze, prepare, and deliver compelling speeches, whether facing a single individual or a room full of strangers. Excellent. 658.4.C13

**Click, J. W.,** and **Russell N. Baird.** *Magazine Editing and Production.* 3d ed. Dubuque, Iowa: Wm. C. Brown Co., 1983.

"Magazines," the authors believe, "disseminate more specialized information than any other medium of mass communication." They conceive of their mission as providing all of the data needed for people (pastors included) to publish their own magazines and newsletters. Their book covers all of the bases and explains the logistics in clear and simple terms. 254.4.C61

**Clinebell, Howard John, Jr.** *The People Dynamic: Changing Self and Society Through Growth Groups.* New York: Harper & Row, 1972.

Having pioneered a formula for personal growth, and having tested his theory in clinical settings, the author makes available to a wider readership the strategies he has used. Readers, however, should be forewarned that Clinebell is eclectic and does not hesitate to use a variety of modalties, including Eastern mysticism. 301.11′3.C61P

**Corbett, Jan.** *Creative Youth Leadership: For Adults Who Work with Youth.* Valley Forge, Pa.: Judson Press, 1977.

Of importance to all who work with young people and seek to develop them for positions of responsibility in the church. 303.34.C81

**Cornwall-Jones, A. T.** *Education for Leadership: The International Administrative Staff Colleges, 1948-84.* London: Routledge and Kegan Paul, 1985.

In this book the writer outlines the origin and growth of the college at Henley and the overseas colleges that have been established after the Henley model. He discusses the unique approach to the principles and practices of management, and also gives a personal account of his own association with the school. Cornwall-Jones also describes the experiences of the seven international schools and their perspectives on management. On the one hand, this book can serve as a useful resource for those schools with courses in leadership/administration, and on the other it provides information for seminaries offering D.Min. degrees in church management. 658′.007.EN3.C81

**Cunningham, Richard B.** *Creative Stewardship.* Nashville: Abingdon Press, 1979.

An intensely practical book that takes a positive approach to the subject of stewardship. This is the kind of work pastors, elders, and deacons should read. 254.8.C91

**Dale, Robert D.** *To Dream Again.* Nashville: Broadman Press, 1981.

A scientific assessment of the organizational problems of churches and the ways in which they may be revitalized through changed policies, personnel, people, and a new sense of purpose. 254.D15

**Daniels, Madeline Marie.** *Realistic Leadership: How to Lead Others in Achieving Company and Personal Goals.* Englewood Cliffs, N.J.: Prentice-Hall, 1983.

Discusses the distinction between collaboration and therapy, conflict resolution and stress management. In doing so, Daniels shows how personal and corporate goals can be realized by a distinctive kind of leadership. 658.4.D22

**Dayton, Edward Risedorph.** *God's Purpose/Man's Plans.* Monrovia, Calif.: MARC, 1971.

A workbook designed for the manager involved in Christian organizations. 254'.01.D33

————, and **Theodore Wilhelm Engstrom.** *Strategy for Leadership.* Old Tappan, N.J.: Fleming H. Revell Co., 1979.

Treats church management and Christian leadership from the perspective of establishing goals, setting priorities, planning, and then working to accomplish set objectives through people. For the neophyte.
254.D33 (Alt. DDC 658.91'25).

**Dressel, Paul Leroy.** *Administrative Leadership.* San Francisco: Jossey-Bass Publishers, 1981.

Designed for those in higher education. This down-to-earth guide reveals the experience gained by the author during his fifty years as an administrator. The basic issues in the decision-making process are dealt with and applied to a variety of everyday situations. Excellent. 378.73.D81

**Driggers, B. Carlisle.** *Models of Metropolitan Ministry: How Twenty Churches are Ministering Successfully in Areas of Rapid Change.* Nashville: Broadman Press, 1979.

This compilation of case studies from across America pinpoints the ways in which these churches are coping with change. The discussion includes examples of central city, inner city, suburban, and rural-urban churches. Ecumenical. 254.22.M72

**\*Drucker, Peter Ferdinand.** *The Changing World of the Executive.* New York: Truman Talley Books, 1982.

Wide-ranging in its scope, this practical treatise explores changes in today's work force, job functions, relationships, and sense of fulfillment. Challenging. 658.4.D84C

\*————. *Management: Tasks, Responsibilities, Practices.* New York: Harper & Row, 1973.

Pastors who have benefited from Drucker's practical treatises on the development of management and executive skills, will welcome his magnum opus. It ably fulfills the subtitle and abounds with useful insights into management problems as well as opportunities for growth. 658.4.D84M

————. *Managing in Turbulent Times.* New York: Harper & Row, 1980.

Important and timely, these chapters concentrate the reader's attention on trends in business, society, and the economy. Issues like inflation, population, and production are documented and discussed with the author's usual foresight and vigor. Preachers will find this volume both stimulating and enlightening. Recommended. 658.4.D84T

**Dubin, Robert.** *Human Relations in Administration.* 4th ed. Englewood Cliffs, N.J.: Prentice-Hall, 1973.

This is an extremely valuable work. It is designed for those who work for big organizations. Its use, therefore, is particularly in line with the needs of people in denominational or missionary headquarters, or those who have the administrative oversight of large churches. 658.4.D85 1973

**Dudley, Carl S., ed.** *Building Effective*

*Ministry: Theory and Practice in the Local Church.* San Francisco: Harper & Row, 1983.

†This is a book that demands consideration. It integrates various disciplines (e.g., anthropology, ethnology, sociology) with the needs of Christian ministers and the overall work of the church. 254.D86

_____. *Making the Small Church Effective.* Nashville: Abingdon Press, 1978.

Abounds with new and important insights. Falls short of providing a biblical model, but does go a long way toward counteracting the negative ideas often associated with small churches. 254.D86

*Eims, LeRoy. *Be a Motivational Leader.* Wheaton, Ill.: Victor Books, 1981.

A challenging sequel to the author's earlier work on leadership. Deals forthrightly with the issues and responsibilities of a motivational leader. 301.155.EI5M

**Engstrom, Theodore Wilhelm.** *The Making of a Christian Leader.* Grand Rapids: Zondervan Publishing House, 1976.

Working from the premise established by Bernard Montgomery that leaders are made not born, the author details the successive steps in the development of one's potential. 254.EN3

_____. *Your Gift of Administration: How to Discover and Use It.* Nashville: Thomas Nelson Publishers, 1983.

Written for Christians, this work "has mingled [Engstrom's own] experiences, biblical insights, and personal convictions to give us this new perspective on the exercise of administration" (Gordon MacDonald). 254.EN3Y

_____, and **Edward R. Dayton.** *Christian Leader's 60-Second Management Guide.* Waco, Tex.: Word Books, 1984.

This book purports to offer pastors, managers, and Christian leaders of organizations a guide that is both "competent and Christian," but it lacks originality and appears to be a take-off from and adaptation of secular principles that have already become widely known as a result of the writings of others. Disappointing. 254.EN3

_____. *The Act of Management for Christian Leaders.* Waco, Tex.: Word Books, 1976.

A compilation of monthly "Christian Leadership Letters." Practical. 254.EN3A

**Falwell, Jerry,** and **Elmer L. Towns.** *Stepping Out on Faith.* Wheaton, Ill.: Tyndale House Publishers, 1984.

A new look at church growth. Focuses on the importance of faith and its relationship to building a church. Provides an excellent research model for adaptation in other settings. A welcome addition to this genre of literature. 254.5.F19

**Fisher, Roger, William Ury,** and **Bruce Patton, eds.** *Getting to Yes.* Boston: Houghton Mifflin Co., 1981.

In the wake of those books treating self-assertion, we have been faced with issues surrounding successful negotiation. This book offers straightforward, no-nonsense counsel that readers may sift, evaluate, and use as occasion requires. 158.5.F53

**Fordyce, Jack K.,** and **Raymond Weil.** *Managing with People: A Manager's Handbook of Organizational Development Methods.* 2d ed. Reading, Mass.: Addison-Wesley Publishing Co., 1979.

Pastors who would like to learn how to accomplish more through others will welcome this handy, well-outlined, thoroughly researched little volume. It is replete with ideas, procedures, and counsel. Secular. 658.4.F75 1979

**Garrett, Annette.** *Interviewing, its Principles and Methods.* 3d ed. Revised by Margaret M. Mangold and Elinor P.

Zake. New York: Family Service Association of America, 1982.

Designed for social workers and those who, as with those in the ministry, frequently deal with people having problems of one sort or another. First published in 1942. Helpful. 361.3'22.G19 1982

**\*Getz, Gene A.** *Building Up One Another.* Wheaton, Ill.: Victor Books, 1976.

Builds on passages of Scripture mentioning "one another." Stresses the function of Christ's Body in Christian growth. Also shows how these biblical principles may be worked out in the life of a local assembly. Excellent. 254.G33

**Harrington, Arthur.** *What the Bible Says About Leadership.* Joplin, Mo.: College Press Publishing Co., 1985.

Approaches the matter of leadership topically (e.g., evangelistic, missionary, pastoral, eldership, women in leadership, etc.). Relates the teaching of the Bible to each of these areas. Though far-ranging and helpful, this work does not assess what leadership is, but concentrates instead on what leaders do. 253.H23

**Hartley, Loyde H.** *Understanding Church Finances: The Economics of the Local Church.* New York: Pilgrim Press, 1984.

Based on extensive research, this work provides a candid evaluation of churches and their attitude toward finances. Offers sound, though at times secular, counsel for pastors and those in positions of responsibility. 254.8.H25

**Hendrix, Olan.** *Management and the Christian Worker.* Fort Washington, Pa.: Christian Literature Crusade, 1974.

An important work for those in the ministry who wish to know how to make better, more efficient use of their time. 254.H38

————. *Management for the Christian Worker.* Libertyville, Ill.: Quill Publications, 1976.

Concentrates on developing the inner qualities that will contribute to self-improvement and result in greater efficiency. 254.H38

**Hersey, Paul.** *The Situational Leader: The Other 59 Minutes.* San Diego: University Associates, 1984.

A response to *The One Minute Manager.* "Provides a brief, easily understandable introduction to Situational Leadership theory and dramatically illustrates the ease and generality of its application. I believe that this volume represents a significant contribution to our continuing search to improve the quality of American management, especially the management of our most precious resource—our people" (J. William Pfeiffer). 658.4.H45

**Hill, George H.,** and **Lenwood David.** *Religious Broadcasting, 1920-1983: A Selectively Annotated Bibliography.* New York: Garland Publishing, 1984.

An important collection of books, dissertations, theses, and journal articles. Contains a vast amount of information—information that is sure to supply D.Min. students with resource material for numerous dissertations. 016.791.H55

**Hocking, David Lee.** *Be a Leader People Will Follow.* Glendale, Calif.: Regal Books, 1979.

Exhibits the experience of the author. Contains plain, practical pointers on the gifts of the Spirit and how to develop the traits of a leader whom people can relate to, look up to, and follow. 303.34.H65

**Holck, Manfred, Jr.** *Church Finance in a Complex Economy.* Nashville: Abingdon Press, 1983.

Writing to help churches in an inflationary economy, Holck provides some important guidelines for those charged with the responsibility of preparing budgets and making ends meet. A valuable monograph. 254.8.H69

————. *Complete Handbook of Church*

*Accounting*. Englewood Cliffs, N.J.: Prentice-Hall, 1978.

Explains in lay terms how to keep a set of financial records and make simple, easy-to-understand reports to the congregation. 254.8.H69

————. *How to Pay Your Pastor More and Balance Your Budget Too!* King of Prussia, Pa: Religious Publishing Co., 1976.

This book, written by an expert, should be regarded as essential reading by all those who serve on church finance committees. 254.8.H71

**Holcombe, Mary W.,** and **Judith K. Stein.** *Writing for Decision Makers: Reports and Memos with a Competitive Edge.* Belmont, Calif.: Lifetime Learning Publications, 1981.

A comprehensive guide to effective written communication that pastors and church administrators will find helpful. 808.H69

**Hunter, Kent R.** *Your Church Has Personality.* Nashville: Abingdon Press, 1985.

The author, a Lutheran, puts his finger on an important aspect of church history—the respective assembly's history, character, and philosophy of ministry. The information gleaned from this introspective look is then used to assess the church's overall health (or personality), needs, and mission. An eye-opening book. 254.5.H91

**Johnson, Douglas W.** *The Care and Feeding of Volunteers.* Nashville: Abingdon Press, 1978.

Treats the "backbone" of the church, and explains how volunteers can be recruited, helped, encouraged, and given appropriate direction. Of great importance is maintaining them as a viable part of the work force of the local assembly, and this is where Johnson's information is particularly helpful. 254.6.J63

**Kamm, Robert B.** *Leadership for Leadership: Number One Priority for Presidents and Other University Administrators.* Washing-

ton, D.C.: University Press of America, 1982.

For the increasing number of pastors who have established Christian schools as part of their church's ministry. This book attempts to define the somewhat elusive element of leadership as the single most important factor in a college or university's successful achievement of its higher education goals, emphasizing the point that interaction is the key ingredient in effective leadership. Suitable for higher education administrators, persons working in business and industry, and also for graduate level seminars dealing with educational leadership. 371.2.K12

**Kendall, Robert Tillman.** *Tithing: A Call to Serious Biblical Giving.* Grand Rapids: Zondervan Publishing House, 1982.

"I am in hearty agreement with the principle Dr. Kendall expounds, that tithing our income is a minimum Christian obligation, and that the church and its mission are bound to suffer when we disobey. God still loves a cheerful giver" (John R. W. Stott). 254.8.K31

**Kennedy, Roger G.** *American Churches.* Falls Church, Va.: McGrath Publishing House, 1982.

A magnificent volume, as handsome as the subject it addresses. More than 120 American churches and temples, with 200 superb full-color and 60 black-and-white photographs, illustrate the diversity of this country's religious life, the richness of its architectural forms, and the importance of the church in American history and culture. The buildings illustrated are located throughout the United States, representing Catholic, Protestant, and Jewish faiths; they range from the simplicity of a New England Puritan church to the Gothic splendor of St. Patrick's Cathedral in New York City, from a university chapel designed by E. Saarinen to a Spanish adobe mission, from a Russian Orthodox frame church to California's Crystal Cathedral. 254.7.K38

**Kernberg, Otto F.** *Internal World and External Reality: Object Relations Theory Applied.* New York: Jason Aronson, 1980.

An incisive evaluation of organizations with an analysis of those individuals who rise to prominence within them. Inherent in the author's masterful presentation is an assessment of why organizational decline sets in. The analysis differs from the one presented by Barber and Strauss in *Leadership: The Dynamics of Success* (chap. 2), but what Kernberg lays out before the reader is of great value. His neo-Freudianism is evident, but he has much to contribute, and it is hoped that students of ecclesiastical organizations and management will read what he has to say. 616.89.K45

**Knight, George W.** *How to Publish a Church Newsletter.* Nashville: Broadman Press, 1983.

Thoughtful, innovative, this book contains useful ideas as well as sound suggestions for publishing a church newsletter. 254.4.K74

**Knox, Alan B., ed.** *Leadership Strategies for Meeting New Challenges.* New Directions for Continuing Education. San Francisco: Jossey-Bass Publishers, 1982.

The editor, an educator, appears to have contributed each of the chapters that make up this book. They cover the salient points of business leadership with verve and skill. Shows how administrators may employ these concepts to enhance their managerial expertise. 658.4.K77

**Lambert, Norman M.** *Managing Church Groups.* Dayton, Ohio: Pflaum Publishing House, 1975.

A manual based on MBO (management by objective). The aim is to help priests determine the purpose of their parish, set goals, and institute workable plans that will help them systematically achieve their objectives. 254.L17

**Larson, Philip M.** *Vital Church Management.* Atlanta: John Knox Press, 1977.

The emphasis is on practicality in Larson's treatment of the ways in which sound administrative practices can be applied to the management of the church. 254.L32

**Lawson, Leslie Griffin.** *Lead On!* San Luis Obispo, Calif.: Impact Publishers, 1982.

An insightful introduction to working with volunteers, working with groups, and maintaining healthy interpersonal relations. 303.3′4.L44

**\*Levinson, Harry.** *Executive.* Cambridge, Mass.: Harvard University Press, 1981.

First published in 1968 under the title *The Exceptional Executive*, this completely rewritten work provides one of the most authoritative overviews of administrative executive psychology. 658.4′2.L57E 1981

**Lewis, G. Douglass.** *Resolving Church Conflicts: A Case Study Approach for Local Congregations.* San Francisco: Harper & Row, 1981.

By combining theology and the behavioral sciences, Lewis shows how the unavoidable conflicts (which are part of our existence) may be handled with a minimum of harm to individuals and the church. 254.L58

**Lindgren, Alvin J.,** and **Norman L. Shawchuck.** *Management for Your Church.* Nashville: Abingdon Press, 1977.

Goes a long way toward showing pastors who feel called to preach that they can also sustain an effective ministry of management in the church. Also illustrates how practical plans can be established, what pastors can do when problems arise, and how they may function effectively and solvently. 254.L64

**Lundberg, Louis B.** *The Art of Being an Executive.* New York: The Free Press, 1981.

The former chairman of the board of

Bank of America brings to the writing of this book his mastery of managerial theory and practice. He tackles seventy different kinds of problems and probes the central issues before suggesting possible solutions. 658.4.L97

**Maccoby, Michael.** *The Leader: A New Face for American Management.* New York: Simon and Schuster, 1981.

With American management in a state of flux, Maccoby calls for a new breed of manager—one who knows how to keep abreast of changing technology but is still able to motivate people to achieve their goals. Uses the casebook method. Helpful. 658.4.M13

**MacDonald, Charles R.** *Administration of the Work of the Local Church.* Minneapolis: Central Seminary Press, 1973.

A brief, practical treatise designed for those who lack administrative expertise. 254.M14

**MacNair, Donald J.** *The Growing Local Church.* Grand Rapids: Baker Book House, 1975.

A well-defined statement of the organization and function of the local church. Reformed. 254.M23G

**McCormack, Mark H.** *What They Don't Teach You at Harvard Business School.* New York: Bantam Books, 1984.

"Truly gives an insight into many critical issues in the business world which cannot be taught at any school or university and can only be learned through experience" (Christopher Lewinton). 650.1.M13

**McFarland, Dalton E.** *Action Strategies for Managerial Achievement.* New York: American Management Association, 1977.

A well-written, practical treatise from which pastors and church officials may draw important principles that will help them better to lead the congregations they serve. 658.4.M16

*****McGavran, Donald Anderson,** and **Win Arn.** *Back to Basics in Church Growth.* Wheaton, Ill.: Tyndale House Publishers, 1981.

Seeks to provide a workable plan for world evangelism, whether in democratic or totalitarian countries. Shows how the principles of church growth can be applied without sacrificing the essentials of an evangelical theology. 254.5.M17B

————, and **George G. Hunter, III.** *Church Growth: Strategies That Work.* Nashville: Abingdon Press, 1980.

Emphasizes the ways in which the local assembly can realize maximum outreach via the principles of church growth. Practical, informative, stimulating. 254.5.M17C 1980

**Meininger, Jut.** *Success Through Transactional Analysis.* New York: Grosset and Dunlap, 1973.

The application of TA to problem solving, decision making, and other administrative procedures. A good book for those who lack training in these areas. 650'.13.M47

**Milton, Charles R.** *Human Behavior in Organizations: Three Levels of Behavior.* Englewood Cliffs, N.J.: Prentice-Hall, 1981.

Runs the gamut of those influences contributing to individual and corporate behavior. Has excellent chapters on motivation, on-the-job effectiveness, leadership, communication, and change. 302.3'5.M64

**Moss, Leonard.** *Management Stress.* Reading, Mass.: Addison-Wesley Publishing Co., 1981.

Probes the causes of stress and the crises that leaders frequently experience. Explains the strategies managers may use to cope with the tensions of everyday life. 658.4'07.M85

**Mylander, Charles.** *Secrets for Growing Churches.* San Francisco: Harper & Row, 1979.

In five tightly-packed chapters, the author applies the principles of church growth to congregational renewal. The insights provided in this book will undoubtedly prove helpful to pastors. 254.5.M99

**Naisbitt, John,** and **Patricia Aburdene.** *Re-inventing the Corporation: Transforming Your Job and Your Company for the New Information Society.* New York: Warner Books, 1985.

This book is vitally geared to the present (in contrast to many schools of business administration that are often twenty years behind the times), but what the writers have to say prepares effectively for the future. They advocate numerous principles that are surprisingly biblical once the humanistic overcoating of our contemporary corporate climate has been peeled away. The best thing to do is to read this work carefully, and with fitting discernment. The reward in new insights and a clearer perception will come automatically. 658.4.N14R

**Ouchi, William G.** *Theory Z: How American Business Can Meet the Japanese Challenge.* Reading, Mass.: Addison-Wesley Publishing Co., 1981.

Describes the art of Japanese management and demonstrates how the principles may be applied to American corporations. Theory Z warrants comparison with the Scriptures and particularly the dynamics of success contained in the book of Nehemiah. 658.3.OU2

**Parkinson, Cyril Northcote.** *Parkinson: The Law.* Boston: Houghton Mifflin Co., 1980.

Parkinson's Law is as famous as the Peter Principle or Murphy's Law. And here, for the benefit of those who no longer have access to the 1957 edition, is a revised and updated version with several new "laws." These chapters are excellent as satire and devastating in their critique of bureaucrats and their methods. 350.P22 1980

**Perry, Lloyd Merle.** *Getting the Church on Target.* Chicago: Moody Press, 1977.

Continues the thrust of this author's long and influential ministry. Concentrates attention on things that will revitalize the church's life and provides constructive guidelines for those either in or entering the ministry. 254.P42G

**Peters, Tom,** and **Nancy Austin.** *A Passion for Excellence: The Leadership Difference.* New York: Random House, 1985.

Challenges accepted methods of management and shows them to be wanting. Provides clear guidelines toward the establishment of sound principles and viable procedures for achieving excellence. Well executed. 658.4.P44

**Porter, Jack Nusan.** *Conflict and Conflict Resolution: A Historical Bibliography.* New York: Garland Publishing, 1982.

As an introduction to the field of social conflict, this bibliography uses classical and contemporary sources to trace conflict theories from ancient times to the present. Though selective in its inclusion of more recent works, this book is comprehensive in its historical dimension, making it unique among sociological studies. With its categorizing of books, articles, and dissertations, it is a valuable handbook or text for research. It should prove invaluable to D.Min. students doing dissertation research in the area of interpersonal communication. 016.3.P83

**Powell, Paul W.** *The Nuts and Bolts of Church Growth.* Nashville: Broadman Press, 1982.

Concentrates on those issues that will lead to increasing church attendance. Deals realistically with issues such as leadership, preaching, evangelism, and the ministry of the church. 254.5.P92

**Powers, Bruce P., ed.** *Church Administration Handbook.* Nashville: Broadman Press, 1985.

This comprehensive handbook provides readers with basic principles in the area of church administration. As a guidebook, it brings together theology and management as these relate to the work of the church. 254.P87C

**Reed, Harold William.** *The Dynamics of Leadership: Open the Door to Your Leadership Potential.* Danville, Ill.: Interstate Printers and Publishers, 1982.

"Leadership is known by the personalities it enriches, not by those it dominates or captivates. Leadership is not a process of exploitation of others for extraneous ends. It is a process of helping others to discover themselves in the achieving of aims which have become intrinsic to them. The proof of leading is in the qualitative growth of the led as individuals and as group members. Any other test is trivial and unworthy" (Ordway Tead). That is the goal of this book. 658.4.R25

**Richards, Lawrence O.** *Three Churches in Renewal.* Grand Rapids: Zondervan Publishing House, 1975.

A candid discussion of the differences of opinion between those who advocate renewal for the church and the ever-present proponents of the big church. Selects three churches for close investigation and considers their impact on those around them—churched and non-churched. Concludes with an assessment of the leadership style of the pastor. 254.R39

**Robert, Marc.** *Managing Conflict: From the Inside Out.* San Diego: University Associates, Inc., 1982.

Robert analyzes the different kinds of situations that cause conflicts and then shows his readers how they may cope with them. Applies his findings to managerial situations. 658.3′15.R54

**Rudge, Peter F.** *Management in the Church.* London: McGraw-Hill Book Co., 1976.

Written by an Anglican. This work reflects the ideas of one who is a specialist in church administration. Aside from that,

the reader has the feeling that the material is eminently practical and can be applied to a variety of situations. Recommended. 254.R83

**\*Rush, Myron D.** *Management: A Biblical Approach.* Wheaton, Ill.: Victor Books, 1983.

In this work, the author, a management consultant, "focuses . . . on how to lead people and manage organizations and businesses from a biblical viewpoint" (Lorne Sanny). 658.4.R89

**Rust, Brian,** and **Barry McLeish.** *The Support-Raising Handbook: A Guide for Christian Workers.* Downers Grove, Ill.: InterVarsity Press, 1984.

Deals with the principles of support-raising and charts a course to ease out the wrinkles and help those involved in this task make efficient use of their time. 254.8.R89

**Schaller, Lyle E.** *Assimilating New Members.* Nashville: Abingdon Press, 1978.

Practical, down-to-earth counsel on how to make new members feel welcome and become active participants in the church. 254.5.SCH1A

————. *Effective Church Planning.* Nashville: Abingdon Press, 1979.

Zeroes in on the needs of groups, the kind of surroundings that make for congeniality, why some people are never satisfied, and what the pastor can do to establish appropriate esprit de corps. As with other books in this series, this one abounds with practical information. 658.91′25.SCH1E

————. *Growing Pains.* Nashville: Abingdon Press, 1983.

A clear, concise assessment of the place and importance of visitation in the life of a growing church. Shows how laypeople may be trained for that important function. 254.5.SCH1G

\*————. *Looking in the Mirror: Self-Appraisal in the Local Church.* Nashville: Abingdon Press, 1984.

One of the best works of this genre. Deals perceptively and realistically with the goals churches may set for themselves. Though there is a tendency to major on assumptions and goals, readers should remember that beliefs precede the establishment of values, and values affect the goals a church may set for itself. 254.SCH1L

_____. *The Medium-sized Church: Problems and Prescriptions.* Nashville: Abingdon Press, 1985.

This sequel to *The Multiple Staff and the Larger Church* and *The Small Church Is Different,* focuses on the special needs of those with a membership between 100 and 200 people. Schaller stresses the importance of understanding congregational culture, distinctive personality, and internal dynamics. An important monograph. 254.SCH1Me

_____. *Survival Tactics in the Parish.* Nashville: Abingdon Press, 1977.

This work is filled with practical pointers for pastors. Personal as well as church-related matters are dealt with, and those who have read Schaller's other works will appreciate this one too. 254.SCH1S

_____, and **Charles A. Tidwell.** *Creative Church Administration.* Nashville: Abingdon Press, 1975.

Calls attention to crucial administrative issues, but fails to solve the problems satisfactorily. Missing is an emphasis on biblical principles. 254.SCH1

**Schul, William D.** *How to Be an Effective Group Leader.* Chicago: Nelson-Hall, 1975.

Pastors who are looking for an easy-to-read, down-to-earth manual on the techniques of effective group work will find their answer in this handy book. 301.15.SCH8

**Schuller, Robert Harold.** *Your Church Has Real Possibilities!* Glendale, Calif.: Regal Books, 1975.

Contains a presentation of the church growth principles taught by Schuller and his associates in the Institute for Successful Leadership. Presents Schuller's brand of PMA. Lacks authenticity. 254'.008.SCH9

**\*Sell, Charles M.** *Family Ministry: The Enrichment of Family Life Through the Church.* Grand Rapids: Zondervan Publishing House, 1981.

Runs the gamut of the multifaceted ministry of the church to families. Covers everything from the present challenge facing the church to all aspects of family life, education, and counseling. Recommended. 259.2.SE4

**Seraydarian, Patricia McKenna.** *The Church Secretary's Handbook.* Wheaton, Ill.: Tyndale House Publishers, 1982.

An indispensable work. Buy a copy for the secretary of your church. 254'.08.SE6

**Sine, Tom.** *The Mustard Seed Conspiracy.* Waco, Tex.: Word Books, 1981.

"Raises the church's collective vision to see that He wants to use 'insignificant people' to institute His righteousness through the world" (Mark O. Hatfield). 254.5.SI6

**Slaught, Lawrence T.** *A Single Board for Churches: Organizing for Action.* Valley Forge, Pa.: Judson Press, 1979.

This handy manual on church management procedures admirably fulfills the subtitle. It is helpful, clear, and concise. 658.91.SL1

**\*Smith, Harold T.,** and **William H. Baker.** *The Administrative Manager.* Chicago: Science Research Associates, 1978.

Doctor of ministry students in church administration and pastors lacking training in management will find this volume to be made-to-order. It covers the principle areas of administration, shows how effective leaders operate, and provides extensive sections on motivation, communication, and personnel management. Excellent. 651.SM5

**Smith, Robert.** *When All Else Fails . . .*

*Read the Directions.* Waco, Tex.: Word Books, 1974.

Offers biblical counsel on the ways in which new life can be infused into the church. Helpful. 254.S6

**Southard, Samuel.** *Training Church Members for Pastoral Care.* Valley Forge, Pa.: Judson Press, 1982.

A concise, able guide describing how each pastor may train believers in his church for visitation and the work of the ministry. 259'.07.SO8

**Spaan, Howard B.** *Christian Reformed Church Government.* Grand Rapids: Kregel Publications, 1971.

Deals with the government of the Christian Reformed Church. 254'.057.SP1

**\*Stogdill, Ralph M.** *Handbook of Leadership.* New York: The Free Press, 1974.

Based on more than forty years of research into the subject of leadership, these chapters cover virtually every aspect of this thoroughly analyzed field. What Stogdill presents needs to be read repeatedly by all who are interested in making an impact in a world of continual change. Anything he may lack concerning the different types of personality that are evident in styles of leadership can be obtained from *Leadership: The Dynamics of Success.* 158.4.ST6

**Tibbetts, Orlando L.** *The Work of the Church Trustee.* Valley Forge, Pa.: Judson Press, 1979.

Demonstrates the biblical basis for, and extent of, the church trustee's functions. Those who hold office in the church will find this discussion helpful. 254.T43

**Tidwell, Charles A.** *Church Administration: Effective Leadership for Ministry.* Nashville: Broadman Press, 1985.

Books on church administration are numerous. This one incorporates tested principles from the world of business and applies them to the function of the church. Comprehensive in scope and generally reliable. There needs to be a sensitivity to biblical principles if the church is not to become a carbon copy of secular practices. Tidwell's treatment has both strengths and weaknesses in that respect. 254.T43C

**Timm, Paul R.,** and **Brendt D. Peterson.** *People at Work: Human Relations in Organizations.* St. Paul: West Publishing Co., 1982.

Pastors and all who work with people will find this work helpful. Of particular interest is Part III on leadership as well as Part IV on communication. Challenging. 658.4.T48

**Towns, Elmer L.** *Getting the Church Started.* Nashville: John T. Benson Publishing Co., 1975.

A presentation of how ten small congregations came into being. Contains practical guidelines concerning finding the right location, advertising, and establishing credibility in the neighborhood. 254.T66

———. *Have the Public Schools Had It?* Nashville: Thomas Nelson Publishers, 1974.

Packed with startling comments about the violence, lack of discipline, and ineffective teaching that characterizes so many of our public schools. Provides guidelines on what concerned citizens may do about this. This book deserves careful reading. 371.01.AM3.T66

**Wagner, C. Peter.** *Church Growth and the Whole Gospel: A Biblical Mandate.* San Francisco, Calif.: Harper & Row, 1981.

Brings into focus the biblical teaching on social concerns. Examines the dimensions of the church growth movement and develops a strong case for a new social consciousneess. 254'.5.W12

———. *Your Church Can Be Healthy.* Nashville: Abingdon Press, 1979.

Humorous and relevant, these vibrant messages challenge pastors to minister in the power of the Holy Spirit. Latent in these studies is Wagner's commitment to the principles of church growth. 254.W12

**Walrath, Douglas Alan.** *Leading Churches Through Change.* Nashville: Abingdon Press, 1979.

Contains important case studies of churches confronted with the inevitability of change. Ideal for promoting a discussion of the issues. 254.5.W16

**Werning, Waldo J.** *Vision and Strategy for Church Growth.* Chicago: Moody Press, 1977.

This conservative approach to the principles of the church growth movement seeks to apply the strategies in ways that are biblical and practical. Pastors as well as missionaries will find Werning's insights helpful. 254.5.W49

**Westing, Harold J.** *Multiple Church Staff Handbook.* Grand Rapids: Kregel Publications, 1985.

Several words can be used to describe this work. It is at once an in-depth, practical, sagacious handbook. Its goal is to unite the efforts of the church staff members in order to further the ministry of the local assembly through their joint efforts. Westing writes as a result of twenty-five years experience in leadership consultation, and his material can be applied to churches of all sizes. Recommended. 254.W52

**Womack, David A.** *The Pyramid Principle of Church Growth.* Minneapolis: Bethany Fellowship, 1977.

This layman's guide to church growth emphasizes the way in which laypeople within the church may become intelligently involved in the spreading of the gospel. 254.5.W84

**Zaccaria, Joseph S.** *Facing Change: Strategies for Problem Solving in the Congregation.* Minneapolis: Augsburg Publishing House, 1984.

Charts a course for congregations that will help keep them growing, open to new opportunities, and free from the dangers that exist at both ends of the continuum. 254.Z1

## RELIGIOUS GROUPS

**Baird, John E., Jr.,** and **Sanford B. Weinberg.** *Group Communication: The Essence of Synergy.* 2d ed. Dubuque, Iowa: Wm. C. Brown Co. Publishers, 1981.

Shows how groups may function efficiently to the benefit of the work they are doing and their mutual profit. Also discusses the dynamics of leadership and decision making. 302.34.B16

**Bloesch, Donald George.** *Wellsprings of Renewal: Promise in Christian Community Life.* Grand Rapids: Wm. B. Eerdmans Publishing Co., 1973.

†A historical and theological analysis of community life within Protestantism. Bloesch draws particular attention to various movements within the evangelical tradition. This citing of relevant examples is interesting and informative (not to mention mind-stretching to the person who has not thought in terms of these constructs before), but the reader is left with the lasting impression that the author's theology has become broadly ecumenical, even though he still claims to be evangelical. 255.8.B62

**Dausey, Gary, ed.** *The Youth Leader's Sourcebook.* Grand Rapids: Zondervan Publishing House, 1983.

Contains chapters by a variety of authorities. Each chapter is designed to help those who work with youth to enrich and improve their ministry. Replete with ideas that are workable. Recommended. 259.23.D26

**Fritz, Mary.** *Take Nothing for the Journey: Solitude as the Foundation for the Non-Possessive Life.* New York: Paulist Press, 1985.

This book will especially appeal to those who have chosen to live as celibates in the church and have determined to live apart from any earthly or material benefits. Such a simplified life-style still has an appeal, and to those who are thus inclined this book will meet a need. 255.F91

**\*Griffin, Emory.** *Getting Together: A Guide for Good Groups.* Downers Grove, Ill.: InterVarsity Press, 1982.

Groups of people exist for all sorts of reasons, to meet all sorts of needs. In this book Griffin discusses the different kinds of groups, their composition, and purpose. Excellent for use in churches. 302.3′4.G87

**Manees, Bill.** *Recreation Ministry: A Guide for All Congregations.* Atlanta: John Knox Press, 1983.

Discusses the rise of recreation as a part of the church's outreach. Provides ideas for the implementation of a vigorous program. 259.8.M31

**Olson, Richard P.,** and **Carole Della Pia-Terry.** *Ministry with Remarried Persons.* Valley Forge, Pa.: Judson Press, 1984.

As an in-depth discussion of the church's ministry to the widowed and divorced who desire to remarry. Lays a biblical foundation before discussing the process of remarriage counseling, the wedding, and integrating the new couple into the life of the church. 259.OL8M

**\*Richards, Lawrence O.** *Youth Ministry: Its Renewal in the Local Church.* Rev. ed. Grand Rapids: Zondervan Publishing House, Ministry Resources Library, 1985.

This is a practical guide to working with youth. It is designed for the pastor and DCE and explains the principles of church renewal that Richards has developed and applied to work with young people. In its earlier format this book explored the characteristics of the youth culture. In this newer volume Richards has changed his emphasis and views in-stead the needs of young people on a continuum. His goal is to help Christian workers relate to the needs of those to whom they minister. In the decade and a half since the appearance of the first edition, Richards has also shifted from an analysis of a particular generation to the use of a paradigm by which the full spectrum of their needs may be met. Those who acquired the earlier edition will welcome this one too. 259.2.R39 1985

**\*Stevens, Douglas.** *Called to Care: Youth Ministry for the Church.* Grand Rapids: Zondervan Publishing House, 1985.

An important book on an important subject, for the youth of today form the backbone of the church tomorrow. To ensure that young people are built up in the faith, Stevens grounds his approach in the Scriptures and relates the functioning of the church to the meeting of their needs. 259.2.ST4

**Warren, Michael.** *Youth and the Future of the Church: Ministry with Youth and Young Adults.* Minneapolis: Seabury Press, 1985.

†Speaks to the concerns of young people and treats their friendships, sexual identities, and relationships with teachers, parents, and pastors. Warren is not afraid to criticize what he sees as inadequacies and points out the blatant sexism of their songs, their contempt for tradition, their inability to communicate outside their small circle of friends, and their apparent comfort with isolationism. Provocative. 259.2.W25

**\*Wiersbe, Warren Wendell,** and **David W. Wiersbe.** *Comforting the Bereaved.* Chicago: Moody Press, 1985.

This book is both timely and relevant. Its importance lies in the biblical advice it offers on counseling those who mourn. It also treats specifics like the funeral and issues such as suicide and the death of a child. Most helpful. 259.6.W64

# 7

# Social and Ecclesiastical Theology

In his book *Involvement,* Dr. John Stott writes of the evidence he sees for an awakened social conscience.

> One of the most notable features of the worldwide evangelical movement during the last ten to fifteen years has been the recovery of our temporarily mislaid social conscience. For approximately fifty years (c. 1920-70) evangelicals were preoccupied with the task of defending the historic biblical faith against the attacks of liberalism and reacting against its "social gospel." But now we are convinced that God has given us social as well as evangelical responsibilities in his world. Yet the half century of neglect has put us far behind in this area.[1]

Evidence of this awakening may be seen in the writings of Chuck Colson, the monographs issued by the Christian Legal Society, and the pioneer efforts of the late Francis Schaeffer and his son, Franky Schaeffer V. Other competent writers have sought to apply the principles of Scripture to the nitty-gritty issues of life. In England there is Sir Norman Anderson, Harry Blamires, John Gladwin, Edward Norman, and many others. And in the United States there is Earl E. Cairns with his *Saints in Society,* Donald Dayton and his book *Discovering Our Evangelical Heritage,* and of course, the ever-popular works of Francis Schaeffer.

Though books on ethics were treated in chapter 5, the books included in this chapter focus specific attention on the controversial issues of our day. They deal with the areas in which theology and sociology meet. Books in this chapter, therefore, will treat matters of church and state, economics and politics, racial prejudice and segregation, the true nature of the church and its function(s), unity and ecumenism, public worship and the ordinances of the local assembly, and related topics.

1. John R. W. Stott, *Involvement,* 2 vols. (Old Tappan, N.J.: Revell, 1985), 1:13.

Discernment is needed in the formulation of one's belief in this area. Now more than ever, those who are committed to the inerrancy of Scripture need to be in the vanguard so that change may be in accordance with God's Word.

## SOCIAL THEOLOGY

**Adams, Q. M.** *Neither Male nor Female: A Study of the Scripture.* Ilfracombe, Devon, England: Arthur H. Stockwell, 1973.

Attempting to answer questions such as, What functions does God envisage for women? What responsibilties do they have? And what limitations (if any) does He impose upon them? Adams provides one of the best assessments of the biblical material available to date. 261.8'34.AD1

**Anderson, James Norman Dalrymple.** *Christianity and World Religions: The Challenge of Pluralism.* Downers Grove, Ill.: InterVarsity Press, 1984.

This book is a companion volume to the author's famous *Christianity and Comparative Religion.* It shows how the old-fashioned syncretism has given way to a full-fledged pluralism. This change is vitally related to the study of comparative religions, making this modern assessment essential reading for all who are engaged in campus work, inner-city evangelism, or missions. 261.2.AN2

**Bainton, Roland Herbert.** *The Travail of Religious Liberty.* Hamden, Conn.: Shoestring Press, 1971.

Biographical studies of Thomas R. Torquemada, John Calvin, Miquel Servetus, Sebastian Castellio, David Joris, Bernardino Ochino, John Milton, Roger Williams, and John Locke. First published in 1951. 261.7'2.B16T 1971

**Baker, William H.** *On Capital Punishment.* Chicago: Moody Press, 1985.

First published in 1973 under the title *Worthy of Death,* this volume tackles a difficult and emotionally laden topic that has our contemporary society at odds

with the courts, law enforcement, and one another. Baker skillfully relates the teaching of Scripture to our modern milieu. He presents his material in a humane, honest manner, and inasmuch as there are no comparable biblical works, it is hoped that the book will enjoy the success it deserves. 261.8'3366.B17C 1985

**Bancroft, John,** and **Philip Myerscough.** *Human Sexuality and Its Problems.* New York: Churchill Livingstone, 1983.

A scientifically verified study conducted in the U.K. in which Bancroft assessed problems in human sexuality from gender identity through homosexuality to problems relating to impotence, frigidity, and forms of deviant behavior. This is a work that pastoral counselors will find helpful. 612.6.B22

**Barrs, Jerram.** *Who Are the Peacemakers? The Christian Case for Nuclear Deterrence.* Westchester, Ill.: Crossway Books, 1983.

Though slender in scope, this work exposes the fallacies that lie latent in the "Pied Piper" mentality found in many modern, popular works. In assessing the need for watchfulness in order to preserve peace, Barrs advocates a hierarchical chain of command. His purpose is laudable, but his political theory is not based on the Bible, and he makes several dangerous assertions that the unwary are not likely to pick up. 261.873.B27

**Bartlett, David L.** *Paul's Vision for the Teaching Church.* Valley Forge, Pa.: Judson Press, 1977.

Based on lectures given at the American Baptist Seminary in 1976, these chapters contain some stimulating ideas for seasoned ministers but fail to come to grips with the dynamics of Paul's life and ministry. 261.1.B28

**Beals, Art,** and **Larry Libby.** *Beyond Hunger: A Biblical Mandate for Social Responsibility.* Portland, Oreg.: Multnomah Press, 1985.

"World hunger is on the rise. Poverty and starvation are critical problems facing much of the world. The spectre of famine has cast its shadow over us all. But the average American's existence is too far removed from the poor and starving of Africa and Asia to allow them to fully comprehend the extent of these problems. In this book [the authors] attempt to present the realities of poverty and starvation, painting vivid pictures of the suffering and despair that characterizes the lives of so many of the world's peoples" (Mark Hatfield). 261.8'325.B36

**Bloesch, Donald George.** *The Invaded Church.* Waco, Tex.: Word Books, 1975.

An exposition of the writer's belief that the real division in the church is not between evangelism and social action, but between the secular humanism of our technological society and the transcendent claims of Christianity. 261.1.B62

**Boesak, Allan.** *Black and Reformed: Apartheid, Liberation, and the Calvinistic Tradition.* Edited by L. Sweetman. Maryknoll, N.Y.: Orbis Books, 1984.

†Though *not* written in the vein of evangelical Calvinism, this work by a South African pastor does provide readers with a devastating critique of apartheid. The writer denounces the supposedly Calvinistic premise of the Dutch Reformed Church and then points the way to revitalizing that movement. 261.8'348.B63

**Bonar, John,** et al. *The Revival of Religion.* Carlisle, Pa.: Banner of Truth Trust, 1984.

Wrongly titled "revival," these messages focus on spiritual *renewal* and furnish penetrating insights into the nature of the "rise and progress of religion in the soul" of man. 269.24.B64

**Bontrager, G. Edwin.** *Divorce and the Faithful Church.* Scottdale, Pa.: Herald Press, 1978.

Divorcing church members constitute one of the most difficult questions facing churches today. The problems for all concerned are many and varied. This study seeks to assess the biblical evidence and then outlines the guidelines laid down by eleven major denominations relating to those in their fellowship who are divorced. Bontrager concludes with a statement about legal and religious implications of excluding certain people from the fellowship. 261.8'34'284.B64

**Braaten, Carl E.** *The Apostolic Imperative: Nature and Aim of the Church's Mission and Ministry.* Minneapolis: Augsburg Publishing House, 1985.

Missions confront two major crises: the existential crisis of meaning and the global crisis of misery. The existential crisis of meaning has become epidemic in the midst of Western affluence. The corresponding crisis of misery places the needy at enmity with those who may wish to bring them the gospel. Resolving these issues is difficult, but Braaten has undertaken to do so. He challenges the church with biblical data to engage in the kind of NT witness that "turned the world upside down." 260.B72

————. *The Flaming Center: A Theology of the Christian Mission.* Philadelphia: Fortress Press, 1977.

†A brief liberal Lutheran statement treating the whole issue of modern missiology in light of the kingdom of God concept in liberation theology. 260.B72

**Bridston, Keith R., ed.** *Casebook on Church and Society.* Nashville: Abingdon Press, 1974.

†Produced by members of the Case-Study Institute of the Episcopal Theological Seminary, these papers direct the reader's attention to ethical, theological, and social problems found in all levels of society. This study is of value for its case studies, but beyond that, it offers little or no help to counselors or anyone else, for that matter, because the contributors have an unscriptural view of the nature of man. 261.1.C26

**Bromiley, Geoffrey William.** *God and Marriage.* Grand Rapids: Wm. B. Eerdmans Publishing Co., 1980.

Brief and to the point, these chapters deal with the Trinity and note how each member of the Godhead affects the marriage of the Christian couple and contributes toward its stability. 261.8′358.B78

**Brown, Raymond Kay.** *Reach Out to Singles: A Challenge to Ministry.* Philadelphia: Westminster Press, 1979.

Examines the hard questions single people are asking, and attempts to provide candid and helpful answers. An important resource for pastors and those who work with single people in the church. 261.8′34.B81

**Browning, Don S.** *Religious Ethics and Pastoral Care.* Philadelphia: Fortress Press, 1983.

†Without grounding his theory of ethics in Scripture, Browning advocates five levels of moral thinking that provide a distinct advance on Lawrence Kohlberg's theory of moral development. His material is backed up with impressive evidence of its viability and is worthy of serious consideration. 261.1.B81

**Bryant, Marcus David,** and **Charles F. Kemp.** *The Church and Community Resources.* St. Louis: Bethany Press, 1977.

A new, expanded version of the author's earlier work. Discusses the tradition of compassion that has charac-terized the Christian church throughout the ages. 361.8.B84

**Buzzard, Lynn Robert, ed.** *Freedom and Faith: The Impact of Law on Religious Liberty.* Westchester, Ill.: Crossway Books, 1982.

The U.S. was founded on the principles of religious freedom and the separation of church and state, but these freedoms have been increasingly impinged on by civil authorities. This book was conceived of and compiled by those who have seen the erosion of these liberties. It should be in every church library, and all Christians should be encouraged to read it. 322.1.B98

_____, ed. *Schools: They Haven't Got a Prayer.* Elgin, Ill.: David C. Cook Publish ing Co., 1982.

Explains the issues surrounding th "prayer in public schools" debate. Deline ates the issues supporting democrac and the rights of parents, teachers, an those who run private schools. 322.1.AM3.B98

\*_____, and **Samuel Ericson.** *The Bc tle for Religious Liberty.* Elgin, Ill.: David Cook Publishing Co., 1982.

A much needed work that, it is hope will awaken Christians to their civil re-sponsibilities and the importance of maintaining a separation between church and state. 261.7′2.B98

_____, and **Paula Campbell.** *Holy Dis-obedience: When Christians Must Resist the State.* Ann Arbor, Mich.: Servant Books, 1984.

Calls attention to the drift of the past several decades and shows how our tradi-tional, Constitutional liberties have been undermined. Provides sage legal coun-sel, and at the same time illustrates the principles set forth by citing case histo-ries that have been the focal point of recent court battles. A provocative and very necessary treatise. Recommended. 261.7.B98

**Carter, John Daniel,** and **Stanley Bruce Narramore.** *The Integration of Psychology and Theology: An Introduction.* Grand Rapids: Zondervan Publishing House, 1979.

The first in the Rosemead Psychology series, this work consists of articles that initially appeared in the *Journal of Psychology and Theology.* 261.5.C24

**Chambers, Carol, ed.** *Our Aging Population: The Social Security Crisis.* New York: Facts on File, 1983.

This highly informative source of information cannot easily be dismissed. Chambers makes available a vast amount of information on the problems of the aged and the growing inability of governmental agencies to care for them. The information challenges those in the church with the need to care for those of their number. 305.6.AM3.C35

***Chilton, David.** *Productive Christians in an Age of Guilt Manipulators: A Biblical Response to Ronald Sider.* 3d ed. Tyler, Tex.: Institute for Christian Economics, 1985.

We have long needed a *biblical* answer to Sider's much publicized, extensively advertized books. This work meets the need. It is biblically respectable, economically reliable, sociologically viable, and it truly champions the cause of the poor and the underprivileged. 261.8'5.C43

**Christenson, Laurence.** *A Charismatic Approach to Social Action.* Minneapolis: Bethany Fellowship, 1974.

The basic thesis of the author is that involvement in social concerns should be based on the leading of the Holy Spirit rather than the clamors of society. Christenson provides a valuable corrective to prevailing trends in many denominations. All of his conclusions cannot be endorsed, but he has placed the emphasis in the right place: on seeking direction from the Spirit of God. 261.8'3.C46

**Clement, Marcel.** *Christ and Revolution.* New Rochelle, N.Y.: Arlington House, 1974.

A well-reasoned rebuttal to the popular idea that Christ was a revolutionary and that Christianity and radical politics go hand-in-hand. 261.7.C59

**Clouse, Robert G., ed.** *Wealth and Poverty: Four Christian Views of Economics.* Downers Grove, Ill.: InterVarsity Press, 1984.

Building on the premise that the Bible portrays God as concerned with the plight of the poor, historian Clouse and four economists evaluate various theories that are claimed by advocates as "biblical." The results may appear contradictory, but the fact remains that there is much to learn from this seminal work. It should not be looked on as an end in itself, but rather as a catalyst to prod other experienced individuals to share their insights as well. 261.8'5.C62

**Colangelo, Nicholas, Dick Dustin** and **Cecelia H. Foxley.** *The Human Relations Experience: Exercises in Multicultural Nonsexist Education.* Monterey, Calif. Brooks/Cole Publishing Co., 1982.

Not designed for those in churches. This work may nevertheless be adapted to the needs of assemblies in culturally mixed communities. 302.C67

**Collins, Gary R.** *Psychology and Theology: Prospects for Integration.* Nashville: Abingdon Press, 1981.

Edited with a contribution by H. Newton Malony, the chapters of this book constitute the ninth Finch Symposium in Psychology and Religion, Fuller Theological Seminary. Well researched, up-to-date. 261.5'15.C69

**Connery, John R.** *Abortion: The Development of the Roman Catholic Perspective.* Chicago: Loyola University Press, 1977.

This scholarly study of the historic development of opinion within various branches of the Roman Church focuses on the present interregnum and seeks to develop a modus operandi that will unite the people on the issue of abortion. 261.83.C76

**Cosgrove, Mark P.** *Psychology Gone Awry: Analysis of Psychological World Views.* Grand Rapids: Zondervan Publishing House, 1979.

This sorely needed treatise examines the presuppositions of naturalistic, humanistic, and transpersonal psychologies, and finds them wanting. In their place Cosgrove suggests a different approach based on an understanding of the *imago Dei*. 150′.1.C82P

**\*Culver, Robert Duncan.** *The Peace-Mongers.* Wheaton, Ill.: Tyndale House Publishers, 1985.

This is a valuable, timely book. Subtitled "A Biblical Answer to Pacifism and Nuclear Disarmament." Recent writers (e.g, Ronald Sider) have advocated views that have been widely disseminated as biblical. Culver has performed a valuable service by exposing these fallacious theories. He has given us in their place a definitive and reliable work. It is hoped that this carefully prepared monograph will enjoy widespread acceptance. 261.873.B89

**David, James Hill,** and **Woodie W. White.** *Racial Transition in the Church.* Nashville: Abingdon Press, 1980.

Produced by two leaders of the United Methodist Church, this work documents six years of extensive research in most of the major metropolitan areas in the U.S. Records changes within society and the problems attending integration. Well done. 261.8.D29

**Davis, John Jefferson.** *Your Wealth in God's World: Does the Bible Support the Free Market?* Phillipsburg, N.J.: Presbyterian and Reformed Publishing Co., 1984.

Tackles the issues of wealth, poverty, and the role of government in economics. Provides clear, biblical guidelines on

Christian stewardship. A thought-provoking book. 261.8′5.D29

**Dayton, Donald W.** *Discovering an Evangelical Heritage.* New York: Harper & Row, 1976.

Based on articles published in the *Post-American* (now *Sojourners*), a left-wing political-theological paper. Dayton urges evangelicals to engage in social action and reclaim society. Good case histories. 260′.001.D33

**DeGruchy, John,** and **Charles Villa-Vicencio.** *Apartheid Is a Heresy.* Grand Rapids: Wm. B. Eerdmans Publishing Co., 1983.

The writers are Christian leaders in South Africa who grasped the urgency of what needed to be done before the riots that made headlines in the news broke out. They make a strong polemic against racial injustice and have written to clarify the issues so that outside pressure can be brought to bear on the Pretoria government. 305.8.SO8.D36

**\*DeMar, Gary.** *God and Government.* 2 vols. Atlanta: American Vision Press, 1982-1984.

Never has there been a greater need for Americans to understand the biblical and social foundations on which our democracy was built. These timely volumes emphasize the historic basis of the Constitution and the purpose behind the governmental policies enacted. The contents furnish a forthright, readable account of our history. This work should be required reading in Christian schools and colleges throughout the land. Recommended. 350.D39

**Diggins, John P.,** and **Mark E. Kann, eds.** *The Problem of Authority in America.* Philadelphia: Temple University Press, 1981.

Examines the issues of political legitimacy, literary tradition, and the use of manipulative psychological devices as areas in which authority may be abused. A revealing discussion. 303.3'6.D56

**Douglas, Jane Dempsey.** *Women, Freedom, and Calvin.* Philadelphia: Westminster Press, 1985.

†This volume composes the Annie Kinkead Warfield Lectures, Princeton Theological Seminary, 1983. The chapters fulfill the scope of the title and relate Reformed doctrine to the issues of freedom and the role of women in Calvinism past and present. 261.8'344.D74

**Dow, Robert Arthur.** *Ministry with Single Adults.* Valley Forge, Pa.: Judson Press, 1977.

Deals with the challenge of ministry to singles. Discusses their unique needs. Overflows with practical suggestions. 261.8'34.D75

**Drakeford, John W.** *A Christian View of Homosexuality.* Nashville: Broadman Press, 1977.

A candid and, in many respects, compassionate approach to the growing problem of homosexuality. Of particular interest is the author's chronicling of the growing homosexual lobby. 261.834.D78

**Drescher, John M.** *What Should Parents Expect?* Nashville: Abingdon Press, 1980.

Covers the stages of child development and offers pointers on how parents may instill moral values in their sons and daughters. 261.8'342.D81

**Edge, Findley B.** *The Greening of the Church.* Waco, Tex.: Word Books, 1971.

Beginning with personal renewal, the writer enlarges on his theme and ultimately includes every aspect of church life. Lacking in dynamic. 269.2.ED3

**Eidsmoe, John.** *God and Caesar: Biblical Faith and Political Action.* Westchester, Ill.: Crossway Books, 1984.

Challenges Christians to rethink their civic responsibilities and become involved in political issues. Demonstrates how conservatives can impact society through social reform, social welfare, and the judicial system. Recommended. 261.7.EI2

**Ellisen, Stanley A.** *Divorce and Remarriage in the Church.* Grand Rapids: Zondervan Publishing House, 1977.

A valuable corrective to Small's *The Right to Remarry.* Sets out in plain language the teaching of Scripture. Brief, pointed, helpful. 261.8'34.EL5

**Ellul, Jacques.** *Money and Power.* Translated by L. Neff. Downers Grove, Ill.: InterVarsity Press, 1984.

Discusses the ethics of wealth and incidentally elucidates the biblical teaching on money and its use. An excellent discussion. 261.8'5.EL5M

————. *Perspectives on Our Age: Jacques Ellul Speaks on His Life and Work.* Edited by W. H. Vanderburg. Translated by J. Neugroschel. New York: Seabury Press, 1981.

Born in Bordeaux, and now a professor in the university in that city, Ellul narrates his intellectual and spiritual odyssey. Explains the inner tensions between Marx and Barth, the effects of the technological system, and his life as an author. 261.8.EL5

**Evans, Mary J.** *Woman in the Bible.* Downers Grove, Ill.: InterVarsity Press, 1984.

"The modern debate about the role of women in the church has been approached from many points of view. . . . Although there are several treatments of the subject that appeal to the biblical evidence, not many of them concentrate on an exegetical approach. . . . Not all will agree with [Prof. Evans'] exegetical conclusions, but they will discover that she marshals her evidence in a fair manner and carefully weighs up the issues involved" (Donald Guthrie). 261.8'344.EV1

**Faber, Heje.** *Striking Sails: A Pastoral-*

*Psychological View of Growing Older in Our Society.* Translated by K. R. Mitchell. Nashville: Abingdon Press, 1984.

A compassionate treatment of the plight of the aged in our society. Explains what the church can do to make their declining years meaningful and fulfilling. 261.8.F11

**Fife, Robert O.** *Teeth on Edge.* Grand Rapids: Baker Book House, 1971.

An honest attempt toward finding an adequate solution to the contemporary problem of racial conflict. The writer feels that racism is fundamentally a spiritual problem and must be answered within its theological dimension. 261.83.F46

**Fishwick, Marshall William.** *Seven Pillars of Popular Culture.* Westport, Conn.: Greenwood Press, 1985.

The "pillar" metaphor is a popular literary device. Fishwick uses it to good effect. He avoids stereotypes and comments instead on *demos, ethos, heros, theos, logos, eikons,* and *mythos* as the basic structures of society. He also makes available an excellent model for evaluating modern American culture. Provocative. 306.4.AM3.F53 1985

**Fleck, John Roland,** and **John Daniel Carter, eds.** *Psychology and Christianity: Integrative Readings.* Nashville: Abingdon Press, 1981.

Essays reprinted from the *Journal of Psychology and Theology.* Valuable for their effort to integrate theology and psychology. 261.5'15.F62

**Fowler, Richard A.,** and **H. Wayne House.** *The Christian Confronts His Culture.* Chicago: Moody Press, 1983.

Assesses the impact of the feminist movement, the controversy surrounding abortion, and homosexuality on our contemporary society. Presents viable ethical alternatives that should enable Christians to confront those whose life-styles and attitudes are having a negative effect on others. 261.8'35.F82

**Franz, Raymond.** *Crisis of Conscience.* Atlanta: Commentary Press, 1983.

Joseph F. Zygmunt of the department of sociology, University of Cincinnati, said of this work: "[It] is a poignant document, reaffirming the value of 'freedom of conscience,' and inviting renewed attention to the classic problem of how this value is to be kept alive in the face of the perennial resurgence of bureaucratic and authoritarian structures." Recommended. 261.1.F85

**Friedman, Edwin H.** *Generation to Generation: Family Process in Church and Synagogue.* New York: Guildford Press, 1985.

Applies the principles of family therapy to the emotional life of the congregation. Challenges his readers as well as fellow-pastors to cultivate those processes that will result in better mental and emotional health. 261.8.F88

**Friedman, Milton,** and **Rose Friedman.** *Free to Choose: A Personal Statement.* New York: Harcourt, Brace and Jovanovich, 1980.

This sequel to *Capitalism and Freedom* examines specific issues and provides a theoretical framework with practical application to the economic structure of our society. Making no pretense at adhering to a Judeo-Christian theory of economics, this work nonetheless serves a valid and valuable purpose. Hopefully, in time, there will be those who will develop a sound biblical approach to economics. Until then, *Free to Choose* remains an important treatise on this neglected subject. 330.12'2.F91F

**\*Gaebelein, Frank Ely.** *The Christian, The Arts, and Truth: Regaining the Vision of Greatness.* Edited by D. B. Lockerbie. Portland, Oreg.: Multnomah Press, 1985.

Gaebelein's writings on truth and beauty—collected and introduced by his protégé—motivate believers to pursue the highest standards in their appreciation of the arts. Such a pursuit will mean the rejection of mediocrity that has permeated our society. Gaebelein gives his readers a clear presentation of excellence, from integrity in art to the highest principles in education, and from painstaking care in research to the joy of holiness that a believer begins to experience within his soul after many years of walking with the Lord. This is a dynamic book. Read it carefully. 261.5'7.G11

**Gaede, S. D.** *Where Gods May Dwell: Understanding the Human Condition.* Grand Rapids: Zondervan Publishing Company, 1985.

Explains the need for Christian thinking where sociology is concerned, but without the usual fears that often accompany a constructive in-depth analysis and critique. In these pages Gaede reasons his way through problematical areas that impinge on everyday life, and what he presents challenges as well as informs. 261.5.G11

**Galbraith, John Kenneth.** *The Anatomy of Power.* Boston: Houghton Mifflin Co., 1983.

Based on a lifetime of study and observation, this work provides a comprehensive assessment of power—its use and abuse—by politicians, corporate executives, TV personalities, and religious leaders. 303.3.G13

**\*Gallup, George, Jr.,** and **David Poling.** *The Search for America's Faith.* Nashville: Abingdon Press, 1980.

An epochal work that probes the attitudes and desires of youth, the family, different religious groups, the church; assesses the validity of religious experience; and explores prospects for the future. Points to the needs of the hour, and provides an analysis of the questions people are asking. Should be read by all in the ministry. 261.G13

**Gardella Peter.** *Innocent Ecstasy: How Christianity Gave America an Ethic of Sexual Pleasure.* New York: Oxford University Press, 1985.

Claims that sexual experience should be both innocent and ecstatic. Gardella points out, however, that in Western countries this has not been the case, for fear and guilt have complicated the issue and deprived couples of pleasure. Some of the complicating factors are religious, psychological, and sociological. By tracing opinion through the writings of different people, Gardella exposes the sources of the problem. 261.8'357.GG16

**\*Getz, Gene A.** *Loving One Another.* Wheaton, Ill.: Victor Books, 1979.

Lays a secure foundation for an evangelistic life-style. Discusses the concept of discipleship within the context of a willingness to serve one another. Corrects many of our earlier false impressions about evangelism. Timely. 260.G33L

**Gilder, George.** *Wealth and Poverty.* New York: Basic Books, Inc., 1981.

A comprehensive assessment of contemporary economic and political trends, coupled with a clear analysis of our modern middle-class American milieu. Will give preachers much to think about. 261.8'5.G38

**Gilmore, J. Herbert.** *When Love Prevails.* Grand Rapids: Wm. B. Eerdmans Publishing Co., 1971.

A selection of sermons in which the writer addresses himself to the racial issues that ultimately brought about his resignation from his pastorate. 261.834.G42

**Gordon, Burgess L.** *Understanding and Promoting the Resources of Aging People: A Guide to Care, Proper Environment, and Well-Being.* Smithtown, N.Y.: Exposition Press, 1981.

Describes the conditions that affect the health of the aged. Written more for those who work extensively with senior citizens, this work nevertheless brings into sharper focus the unique needs of the elderly. 362.61.G65

**Goudzwaard, Robert.** *Idols of Our Time.*

Translated by M. Vander Venner. Downers Grove, Ill.: InterVarsity Press, 1984.

First published in Holland in 1981. This work causes us to take a careful look at ourselves and our contemporary society with a view to assessing those impediments that hinder the spread of the gospel. 261'.09.G72

**Graham, William Franklin.** *The Jesus Generation.* Grand Rapids: Zondervan Publishing House, 1971.

A provocative analysis of those who repudiated the cold intellectualism of their forebears in favor of emotionalism and a religion of the senses. 155.5.G76

**Grant, Robert McBride.** *Early Christianity and Society.* New York: Barnes and Noble, 1977.

An astute analysis of the relationship of the early church with the surrounding Roman society. Sheds considerable light on the cultural milieu of the early Christians. 261.1.G76

**Griffiths, Brian.** *The Creation of Wealth: A Christian's Case for Capitalism.* Downers Grove, Ill.: InterVarsity Press, 1984.

Few people have attempted a biblical approach to economics. Griffiths considers the theological implications after divesting contemporay theories of their humanistic values. The result is a major step forward and the proposal of a solution to the abuses that presently prevail. 330.12'2.G87

**\*Griffiths, Michael C.** *God's Forgetful Pilgrims: Recalling the Church to Its Reason for Being.* Grand Rapids: Wm. B. Eerdmans Publishing Co., 1975.

A contemporary restatement of the biblical doctrine of the church. Contains a powerful presentation of the church as the Body of Christ and the relationship of believers to one another. 261.G87

**Grounds, Vernon Carl.** *Revolution and Christian Faith.* Philadelphia: J. B. Lippincott Co., 1971.

An important book that interacts with the arguments of those who advocate revolutionary strategies to achieve social change. Grounds calls for a Christian radicalism based on NT principles. 261.8.G91

**\*Guinness, Os.** *The Dust of Death.* Downers Grove, Ill.: InterVarsity Press, 1973.

After exposing man's vain search for meaning in the "counter culture" movement, the author proposes what he refers to as a "Third Way," namely, Christianity. He shows how the believer can avoid the extremes of humanism and existentialism by submitting to the authority of Christ. Guinness describes the promises as well as the unfulfilled dreams of Eastern mysticism and the pre-Christian West, and deals with psychedelic drugs and the occult as counterfeits of a true experience with the living God. 261.83.G94 (Alt. DDC 901.24)

**Gundry, Patricia.** *The Complete Woman.* Garden City, N.Y.: Doubleday and Co., 1981.

Having suffered much for her beliefs in the equality of men and women—though refusing all identification with "Women's Lib" and the ERA—Gundry here expounds her understanding of Proverbs 31 and, with material relevant to the needs of her sex, establishes a biblical basis for womanhood in our contemporary society. Excellent. 261.835.G95C

**Hamilton, Kenneth,** and **Alice Hamilton.** *To Be a Man—To Be a Woman.* Nashville: Abingdon Press, 1975.

An examination of the traditional roles of male and female in contemporary society with an evaluation of the causes that have led up to the present state of affairs. A well-reasoned discussion. 261.8'34.H17

**Hamilton, Michael Pollock,** and **Helen F. Reid.** *A Hospice Handbook: A New Way to Care for the Dying.* Grand

Rapids: Wm. B. Eerdmans Publishing Co., 1980.

Each chapter in this book was contributed by a specialist. It surveys the distinctive needs of patients and discusses such areas as relief from pain, handling fear, and the skills required by doctors and nurses. 362.1.H79

**Harkness, Georgia Elma.** *Women in Church and Society: A Historical and Theological Inquiry.* Nashville: Abingdon Press, 1974.

†Although there are some excellent features in this book, the author's obvious rejection of biblical revelation leads her first to challenge and then to reinterpret the teachings of the apostle Paul. 261.8'34'2.H22

**Harrison, Bob,** and **James Montgomery.** *When God Was Black.* Grand Rapids: Zondervan Publishing House, 1971.

Deals with the feelings and frustrations, emotions and desires, prejudices and hatred that are frequently experienced by blacks. Explains the transformation that takes place when God enters that life. A very important treatise. 261.83.H24

**Hatch, Nathan Orr.** *The Sacred Cause of Liberty: Republican Thought and the Millennium in Revolutionary New England.* New Haven, Conn.: Yale University Press, 1977.

Explores the tensions between Christianity and patriotism in eighteenth-century New England. Provides an interesting commentary on one facet of the theological thought of that era. 261.7.AM3.H28

**Henry, Carl Ferdinand Howard.** *A Plea for Evangelical Demonstration.* Grand Rapids: Baker Book House, 1971.

Designed to stir evangelical Christians from their lethargy and make them aware of the social and ethical commitments that demand their attention. 261.8.H39

**Herbert, Jerry S., ed.** *America, Christian or Secular? Readings in American Christian History and Civil Religion.* Portland, Oreg.: Multnomah Press, 1984.

With essays contributed by competent authorities who critique America socially, historically, and politically, the thrust of this book is to awaken people to a realization of what the Bible teaches and what has been lost. This work constitutes a clear, convincing call to the kind of social involvement that should have characterized the evangelical wing of the church for the past six or seven decades. Recommended. 261.7.H41

**Hick, John,** and **Brian Habblewaithe.** *Christianity and Other Religions.* Philadelphia: Fortress Press, 1980.

†Excerpts material from the writings of men such as Ernst Troeltsch, Karl Barth, Karl Rahner, and Paul Tillich to demonstrate the wide range of attitudes toward other faiths. Does so with the intention of providing a basis for interfaith dialog, though lamely affirming the uniqueness of Christianity. 261.2.C46

**Hiltner, Seward.** *Theological Dynamics.* Nashville: Abingdon Press, 1980.

†One of the pioneer works in the correlation of psychology and theology. Insightful. 261.5.H56 1980

**Hopler, Thom.** *A World of Difference: Following Christ Beyond Your Cultural Walls.* Downers Grove, Ill.: InterVarsity Press, 1981.

A concise discussion of Christianity and culture and the ways in which believers may share their faith. The material is varied and stimulating. 261.H77

**Hudnut, Robert K.** *Church Growth Is Not the Point.* New York: Harper & Row, 1975.

A forthright attack on the principles of the Church Growth movement. Exposes the fallacy inherent in the idea that bigger is better and demonstrates that greater effectiveness is achieved by smaller congregations of committed Christians. 260.H86

**Johnston, Olaf Raymond.** *Christianity in a Collapsing Culture.* Exeter, England. Paternoster Press, 1976.

Faces squarely the disintegration of Western civilization, and advocates a cultural renewal based on a clear differentiation between good and evil and a strong infusion of the Spirit's power into the life of every believer. Persuasive and biblical. 261.J64

**Johnston, Robert K.** *Evangelicals at an Impasse.* Atlanta: John Knox Press, 1979.

Assesses the major issues facing the church today: inerrancy, the role of women, homosexuality, social ethics. Critical of evangelicals, but has only words of praise for those who have redefined inerrancy, such as David A. Hubbard, Clark H. Pinnock. Though interesting, this work will be welcomed only by those advocating theological compromise. 261.8.J64

**Kasper, Walter.** *Theology and Christian Marriage.* New York: Seabury Press, 1980.

†Having set the Scriptures aside as normative, Kasper attempts to reconstruct from historical research what different groups throughout history have thought about marriage and how social mores have brought us to the present state of evolution (a better word would have been "deterioration"). 261.8′34.K15

**\*Kilpatrick, William Kirk.** *Psychological Seduction.* Nashville: Thomas Nelson Publishers, 1983.

"Kilpatrick writes with the lucidity of C. S. Lewis, whom he often and aptly quotes. [His] greatest strength is his ability to describe in detail the many common assumptions and ideas of psychology that have replaced the faith of numerous Christians who have bitten the apple of psychology over the last few decades. . . . His book is an easily readable major contribution to the recently emerging Christian critique of psychology" (Paul C. Vitz). 261.5.K55

**\*Knight, George William, III.** *The Role Relationship of Men and Women: New Testament Teaching.* Rev. ed. Chicago: Moody Press, 1985.

One of the best works of its kind. Treats all the NT passages that perplex modern minds. Because so much confusion has arisen over whether or not *kephale* means "source" or "authority," an appendix by Wayne Grudem has been added in which that issue is discussed at length. This work is both reliable and accurate. It is too much to hope that it will put an end to controversy, but at least thoughtful people—both men and women—can and will be instructed by it. 261.8.K74 1985

**Kosnik, Anthony.** *Human Sexuality: New Directions in American Catholic Thought.* New York: Paulist Press, 1977.

A historical survey by the Catholic Theological Society of America, chronicling the changes in attitude toward sexuality from OT times, through the period of the apostolic Fathers, to the present. Tackles problem areas realistically, and shows how much the Catholic church has changed in recent decades. 261.8′34.C28

**Kotesky, Ronald L.** *Psychology from a Christian Perspective.* Nashville: Abingdon Press, 1980.

Discusses the role of psychology in the world today, warns against its abuse, explains the rise of different systems of thought, and then handles issues within the discipline from an integrative point of view. 150.19.K84

**Kraft, Charles H.** *Christianity in Culture: A Study in Dynamic Biblical Theologiz-*

*ing in Cross-cultural Perspective.* Maryknoll, N.Y.: Orbis Books, 1979.

A valiant effort to pioneer a new approach to cross-cultural communication —one that is distinctively Christian and does not foist Western social mores upon other cultures. 261.K85

**Lee, Robert.** *Faith and the Prospects of Economic Collapse.* Atlanta: John Knox Press, 1981.

Written during the last year of Jimmy Carter's presidential administration, this candid assessment of Christianity and economics paints a gloomy picture of the effects of socialism. Attempts to show how a person's faith can carry him through the hard times ahead. Provocative. 261.8′5.L51

**Leslie, Robert C.** *Sharing Groups in the Church: An Invitation to Involvement.* Nashville: Abingdon Press, 1979.

First published a decade ago, this practical work introduces pastors and counselors to the needs of people in the church and the way in which these needs may be met through small care groups. 254.6.L56 1979

**Lieberman, Morton A., et al.** *Self-Help Groups for Coping with Crisis.* San Francisco: Jossey-Bass Publishers, 1979.

Of interest to pastors, for it focuses on two kinds of care groups—those designed to modify their members' behavior or attitudes (including, for example, groups for alcoholics and their families, for child abusers, or for former mental patients), and those formed to aid in coping with particular life crises (ranging from major illness to aging to the loss of one's spouse or child)—both of which can and should function as a part of the *koinonia* of the local church. 361.7.L62

**Lightner, Robert Paul.** *Church Union: A Layman's Guide.* Des Plaines, Ill.: Regular Baptist Press, 1971.

A conservative examination of ecumenical trends. Ideal for laypeople. Provides a convincing exposé. Recommended. 261′.001

**Lockerbie, D. Bruce.** *The Cosmic Center.* Grand Rapids: Wm. B. Eerdmans Publishing Co., 1977.

Draws information from the common elements of life, and shows how man today has cut himself off from the past, is unsure of the future, and can make no sense or meaning out of life. As an apologetic, this book has value, for it continually draws the readers thoughts back to the deepset needs of the human heart, which can only be met through a vital relationship with the risen Lord. 261.8.L79

**\*Lowell, C. Stanley.** *The Great Church-State Fraud.* Washington: Robert B. Luce, 1973.

A sorely needed exposé of the persistent efforts of politicians to alter the First Amendment and bring about an ecclesiastical system that is dependent on and regulated by government. Deserves careful reading and widespread circulation. 261.7.AM3.L95

**Lyon, David.** *Sociology and the Human Image.* Downers Grove, Ill.: InterVarsity Press, 1983.

This scholarly, clearly reasoned apologetic is designed for those who have some familiarity with sociology. Lyon evidences a thorough mastery of history, economic theory, and philosophy and relates that knowledge to such divergent (yet often related) areas of investigation as Communism and the emerging Third-World countries. Insightful. 261.L99

**\*MacKay, Donald MacCrimmon.** *Science and the Quest for Meaning.* Grand Rapids: Wm. B. Eerdmans Publishing House, 1982.

Constituting the Pascal Lectures, delivered at the University of Waterloo, Canada, in 1979, these studies probe the real issue of life, examine the findings of science, and point the way for a greater emphasis on human dignity, personal accountability, and recognition of man's spiritual nature, which demands a Godward relationship. Recommended. 261.5'5.M19

**Malik, Charles Habib.** *A Christian Critique of the University.* Downers Grove, Ill.: InterVarsity Press, 1982.

A challenging assessment of the role of the university in Western civilization and its responsibility to investigate and declare the truth impartially. 377.1.M29

**Mayers, Marvin Keene.** *Christianity Confronts Culture: A Strategy for Cross-Culture Evangelism.* Grand Rapids: Zondervan Publishing House, 1974.

Does not deal with evangelism per se, but does provide handy models for cross-cultural communications. 261'.001.M45

**McCarthy, Rockne M., James W. Skillen,** and **William A. Harper.** *Disestablishment a Second Time: Genuine Pluralism For American Schools.* Grand Rapids: Wm. B. Eerdmans Publishing Co., 1982.

The framers of the U.S. Constitution took pains not to establish any particular religion in a privileged position in the new republic. The authors of *Disestablishment a Second Time* argue that the time is ripe for a second "disestablishment"— the disestablishment of a single, monopolistic system of schools. More than other studies on the subject, this work explores the philosophical and historical roots of the distinction between public, secular schools and private, religious schools in America. After examining the move toward a consensus, civil religion in the colonial period, the authors focus on the Enlightenment rationalism of Thomas Jefferson, which shaped both the Constitution and the common school movement. 370.AM3.M12

**McFadden, Charles Joseph.** *The Dignity of Life: Moral Values in a Changing Society.* Huntington, Ind.: Our Sunday Visitor, 1976.

Aims at acquainting the reader with the scientific nature of many factors that tear society apart. Offers a wholesome corrective. Roman Catholic. 261.8'3.M16

**McGavran, Donald Anderson.** *The Clash Between Christianity and Culture.* Grand Rapids: Baker Book House, 1974.

Attempts to explain how Christians may adjust to another culture and remain true to biblical Christianity. McGavran is an authority in these matters, but he leaves many questions unresolved. 261.1.M17

**McKenzie, Richard B.** *Bound to Be Free.* Stanford, Calif.: Hoover Institution Press, 1984.

Why is it that in the land of the free, special interests control what we eat, wear, and drive, whereas government tells us how our children will be educated and how much we will pay for life's essentials? In this book McKenzie identifies the forces destroying us bit by bit, and shows what can be done now to stop the erosion of individual and marketplace freedom before it's too late. In a daring departure, he argues that the key to each person's freedom is a business community free of government favor and interference. Only a reassertion of the principles of constitutional democracy will really speak to the people's deeply felt need to "get the government off our backs." This book goes beyond a tough, objective delineation of our economic malaise. It provides a hard-hitting, multifaceted program that includes a free market consitutional amendment, an enforceable way to limit the government's ability to levy taxes and print money, and a novel procedure to eliminate the control of Congress by special interests. The result is a message of hope and freedom for all Americans. 261.87.M13

**Middleton, Robert G.** *Charting a Course for the Church: Snug Harbor or Open Sea?* Valley Forge, Pa.: Judson Press, 1979.

A book for the times. Needs to be read with an open mind. 261.8.M58

**Miles, Herbert Jackson,** and **Fern Harrington Miles.** *Husband-Wife Equality.* Old Tappan, N.J.: Fleming H. Revell Co., 1978.

Attempts to dispel the myth propagated by some recent writers, both Christian and non-Christian, that a wife's submission to her husband is tantamount to admitting her inferiority. This husband-wife team stresses equality in all areas of life. 261.8′34.M59

**\*Mitchell, Arnold.** *The Nine American Lifestyles: Who We Are and Where We're Going.* New York: Macmillan Publishing Co., 1983.

A penetrating and, in many respects, disturbing account of the values, beliefs, needs, and trends of our contemporary society. May prove to be as significant a work as Riesmann's *The Lonely Crowd,* Toffler's *Future Shock,* and Nasibitt's *Megatrends.* Should be high on the reading list of every pastor.

**Monsma, Stephen V.** *The Unraveling of America.* Downers Grove, Ill.: InterVarsity Press, 1974.

This critical analysis of government traces the origins of the unraveling of the American dream, and after showing the weaknesses of the various political ideologies, proposes an alternative—a progressive realism. Most helpful when read in conjunction with R. D. Culver's *Towards a Biblical View of Civil Government* and A. J. McClain's *The Greatness of the Kingdom.* 261.7.M75

**Morey, Robert A.** *When Is It Right to Fight?* Minneapolis: Bethany House Publishers, 1985.

Provides a biblical approach to the tension that exists between the "doves" and the "hawks," the so-called peace-mongers and warmongers. Deals with the different issues involving freedom and responsibility. All things considered, this is a sober, realistic book, and it deserves widespread reading. 261.8′73.M81

**Mouw, Richard.** *Political Evangelism.* Grand Rapids: Wm. B. Eerdmans Publishing Co., 1973.

This clear, concise, pointed study argues that political action is part of the church's evangelistic task. Working from the perspective of a covenantal theologian, Mouw does not make a distinction between the OT and the NT, or between Israel and the church. He overestimates the benefit of community and plays down the possibility that on account of man's depravity a sense of *koinonia* may eventually be dominated by people with a lust for power and degenerate into tyranny. 261.7.M86

**Naisbitt, John.** *Megatrends.* New York: Warner Books, 1982.

Describes ten major trends taking place in our contemporary society. Is must reading for all who wish to become more effective in their ministry. 306.AM3.N14

**Niebuhr, Helmut Richard.** *The Purpose of the Church and Its Ministry: Reflections on the Aims of Theological Education.* New York: Harper & Row, 1978.

First published in 1956, this sociological treatise stresses the need for community involvement and emphasizes the importance of ministerial preparation equipping men and women for this task. The essence of the gospel and the need for redemption is either overlooked or subsumed under the author's universalism. 261.8.N55 1978

**Norman, Edward R.** *Church and Society in England, 1770-1970.* Oxford: At the Clarendon Press, 1976.

Devoted almost entirely to a discussion of Anglican (Episcopal) social theology. Disappointing. 261.N78

**North, Gary.** *Backward, Christian Soldiers? An Action Manual for Christian Reconstruction.* Tyler, Tex.: Institute for Christian Economics, 1984.

Part of a growing corpus of literature on Christianity and our contemporary society. Provides a valid and valuable challenge to modern manifestations of humanism. Also makes a strong case for reconstruction and the launching of an evangelical offensive so as to recover what Christians have lost through passivity and biblical illiteracy. Postmillennial. 261.2.N81

_____. *Moses and Pharaoh: Dominion Religion Versus Power Religion.* Tyler, Tex.: Institute for Christian Economics, 1985.

Based on selected passages from the book of Exodus, this work deals realistically with the rival sources of power and authority. The analysis of human power ("Gentileism") and the delegated authority given by God is excellent. The outworking of these rival systems is illustrated in the confrontation between Moses and Pharaoh. This is an important discussion and deserves careful reading. The author advocates a militancy (based on God's instructions to Israel on entering Canaan) that is disturbing. Reformed. Postmillennial. 261.1.N81

**Oates, Kim, ed.** *Child Abuse: A Community Concern.* New York: Brunner/Mazel Publishers, 1982.

Based on an Australian study, this work combines the disciplines of psychology, anthropology, law, medicine, nursing, and sociology in assessing the reasons for child abuse as well as the effect of such abuse on the victims. An excellent discussion. 362.7.AU7.OA8

**Ogden, Schubert Miles.** *Faith and Freedom: Toward a Theology of Liberation.* Nashville: Abingdon Press, 1979.

†Traces the background and development of modern liberation theologies, analyzes their strengths and weaknesses,

and points out their failures. The writer's presuppositions rob his work of unction. 261.8.OG2

**Ohsberg, H. Oliver.** *The Church and Persons with Handicaps.* Scottdale, Pa.: Herald Press, 1982.

A warm and compassionate account of the ways in which those in churches may alleviate the sufferings of the handicapped. Thoughtful and of vital importance to those who work with "special people." 261.8'324.OH6

**Pape, Dorothy R.** *In Search of God's Ideal Woman: A Personal Examination of the New Testament.* Downers Grove, Ill.: InterVarsity Press, 1976.

This book is based on the author's diligent study of the NT coupled with her own observations on the attitudes of others toward women. Her material is clearly presented. This book, however, serves to illustrate that an understanding of womanhood must be built on all that God has chosen to reveal. By limiting a discussion of God's ideal woman solely to the NT, we ignore all that He chose to reveal in the OT and end up distorting the biblical data. 261.8'34.P19

**Parker, William.** *Homosexual Bibliography: Supplement, 1970-1975.* Metuchen, N.J.: Scarecrow Press, 1977.

_____. *Homosexual Bibliography: Second Supplement, 1976-1982.* Metuchen, N.J.: Scarecrow Press, 1985.

Containing more than 3,000 and 3,500 entries respectively, these bibliographies arrange the material in twelve categories according to the kind of publication in which they appear. In addition, books, pamphlets, and dissertations are included, together with religious, legal, and medical information. This is a most comprehensive work and should serve well the needs of the person doing research in this area. 016.301.P22

**Pemberton, Prentiss L.,** and **Daniel Rush Finn.** *Toward a Christian Economic*

*Ethic: Stewardship and Social Power.* Minneapolis: Winston Press, 1985.

†Presents an overview of the history of economic ethics in the Judeo-Christian tradition. Provides a theory of economics, social justice, and sociology that is designed to correct inequalities, poverty, and the supposed deficiencies of democracy. As much as we would like to recommend this work, the theological shortcomings are of such a nature as to render the material presented unreliable. Only those well trained in economics will be able to profit from this work. 261.8′5.P36

**Perkins, John.** *With Justice for All.* Ventura, Calif.: Regal Books, 1982.

This passionate plea for justice in America is a sequel to *Let Justice Roll Down.* It advocates principles and ideals that if acted on, would enable Americans to shoulder their responsibilities and reverse the social and economic conditions of blacks. 261.8.P41W

**Poggi, Gianfranco.** *Calvinism and the Capitalist Spirit: Max Weber's Protestant Ethic.* Amherst, Mass.: University of Massachusetts Press, 1983.

Facilitates the reader's understanding of Weber's work, and then evaluates the viability of his thesis from economic, political, and religious points of view. 261.8′5.P75

**Rahner, Karl.** *The Shape of the Church.* Translated by E. Quinn. London: S. P. C. K., 1974.

†First published in Germany in 1972, this analysis of the situation facing Christendom today is of value because it presents the latest attempts of Romanism to make an impact on society. It describes the way teaching should be conducted and the best means for the church to regain its lost authority. 260.R12

**\*Richards, Lawrence O.,** and **Paul Johnson.** *Death and the Caring Community: Ministering to the Terminally Ill.* Portland, Oreg.: Multnomah Press, 1980.

An excellent statement of the needs of the community and the response of those who can make up the caring nucleus of the church. Should be mandatory reading in all practical theology courses. 259.4.R39

**Richardson, William J.** *Social Action vs. Evangelism: An Essay on the Contemporary Crisis.* South Pasadena, Calif.: William Carey Library, 1977.

An examination of (1) the impact of liberal theology on the church's understanding of her mission, and (2) the question of whether evangelism is compatible with a humanistic understanding of man in society. Well presented. Recommended. 261.8.R39

**Rickerson, Wayne E.** *How to Help the Christian Home.* Glendale, Calif.: Regal Books, 1978.

Should be required reading for all engaged in the pastoral ministry. Outlines eight specific steps for the planning and implementing of a program of ministry to families. 261.8′34.R42H

**Sawin, Margaret M.** *Family Enrichment with Family Clusters.* Valley Forge, Pa.: Judson Press, 1979.

One of the most important books to be published in recent years. Shows how small groups operating in the church can strengthen family ties. 306.8.SA8

**Scanzoni, Letha,** and **Nancy Hardesty.** *All We're Meant to Be.* Waco, Tex.: Word Books, 1975.

†Though this book became the "Number 1 Best Seller,' according to polls taken by *Eternity* magazine and certain other Christian organizations, the fact remains that it is an extremely detrimental work. The authors set out to provide an approach to women's liberation within an evangelical framework. They affirm the equality of women in leadership in church and home but fail to deal with issues involving different roles. They write off Scriptures that do not support

their thesis as culturally conditioned, make a great display of using the original languages (but do so incorrectly), and provide nothing of lasting significance. 261.8′34′12.SC6

————, and **Virginia Ramey Mollenkott**. *Is the Homosexual My Neighbor? Another Christian View.* New York: Harper & Row, 1978.

†Advocates the acceptance of homosexuals, claiming that the Bible does not teach that homosexual acts in and of themselves are wrong. The reasoning of the authors is fallacious, their distortion of the plain intent of Scripture is harmful, and their portrayal of the plight of the homosexual is lopsided. Instead of helpful counsel, they offer implied consent for such practices, and those who wish to excuse their homosexuality have been quick to pick up on the oblique statements, misrepresentations, and misconstructions that abound in this book. 261.8′34′157.SC1

**\*Schaeffer, Francis August.** *A Christian Manifesto.* Westchester, Ill.: Crossway Books, 1981.

Continues the writer's treatment of the lordship of Christ over all of life. In this work he extends his discussion to a Christian's relationship to government, law, and civil disobedience. 261.7.SCH1C

————. *The Church Before the Watching World.* Downers Grove, Ill.: InterVarsity Press, 1971.

Emphasizes that the church is constantly on trial before God and the world. Stresses that the deeds and words of the church reveal to men something of the character and nature of God. 261.8.SCH1C

**\*Schaeffer, Francis August, V.** *A Time for Anger: The Myth of Neutrality.* Westchester, Ill.: Crossway Books, 1982.

This long overdue critique of our contemporary social and political milieu challenges Christians with the erosion of

their civil rights and calls them to let their voices be heard. A vital work. 342.08.SCH1T

**Schneider, Louis, et al.** *Human Responses to Social Problems.* Homewood, Ill.: Dorsey Press, 1981.

An analysis of the issues surrounding sexism, racism, poverty, suicide, drug addiction, bureaucracy, and other problems of our era. Illustrative of current social mores providing food for thought for a score of messages. 362′.042.SCH5

**Sichel, Betty A.** *Value Education for an Age of Crisis.* Washington, D.C.: University Press of America, 1982.

A valiant attempt to return to the values embodied in the Declaration of Independence—values that made America great but that have been almost entirely lost in our contemporary society. 371.SI1

**Sider, Ronald J.,** and **Richard K. Taylor.** *Nuclear Holocaust and Christian Hope: A Book for Christian Peacemakers.* Downers Grove, Ill.: InterVarsity Press, 1982.

†This apologetic for a Christian pacifism makes some ludicrous recommendations and then applies them to sociology and international relations. It is weak eschatologically—an area in which we need to be found cooperating with God's plan, not working at cross-purposes with it. Nevertheless, the work has been well written. Knowledgeable Christians need to be aware of Sider's views, if only to refute them. 261′873.SI1

**Simons, Joseph.** *Living Together: Communication in the Unmarried Relationship.* Chicago: Nelson-Hall, 1978.

Probes the reasons young people and others choose to live together. Includes a discussion of the repression of feelings, fear, insecurity, jealousy, and anger that such a relationship generates. Provides insights that pastors and counselors will find helpful. Secular. 306.7.SI5

**Smedes, Lewis B.** *Sex for Christians: The*

*Limits and Liberties of Sexual Living.* Grand Rapids: Wm. B. Eerdmans Publishing Co., 1976.

A detailed, informative, and very necessary discussion of sexuality and sexual morality. Recommended. 261.8'34'1.SM3

**Snyder, Howard.** *The Problem of Wineskins: Church Structure in a Technological Age.* Downers Grove, Ill.: InterVarsity Press, 1975.

An agenda for future discussion on the interplay between the message of the gospel (the "new wine") and church traditions, structures, and formalities (the "old wineskins"). A refreshing treatise. 260.S9

**Sweet, William Warren.** *The Story of Religion in America.* Grand Rapids: Baker Book House, 1973.

First published in 1930, this old standby takes readers on an excursus through the many and varied aspects of American religious life. Now very much out of date and in need of revision. 261.7.AM3.SW3 1973

**Tavard, George Henri.** *Woman in Christian Tradition.* South Bend, Ind.: University of Notre Dame Press, 1973.

Part of the growing corpus of literature on the place of women in church and society. Concentrates on the teachings of the church Fathers and sees in the unmarried state a solution to the problems of the age. Roman Catholic. 261.8'34.T19

**Toynbee, Arnold.** *Surviving the Future.* New York: Oxford University Press, 1971.

Toynbee gives his views on the world's most pressing problems and tells how history may help contemporary man solve them. 301.6.T66

**Turner, Nathan W.** *Effective Leadership in Small Groups.* Valley Forge, Pa.: Judson Press, 1977.

A helpful summary of group dynam-ics. Explains the way in which these principles may be used in the larger context of the church. 303.34.T85

**Welter, Paul.** *Family Problems and Predicaments: How to Respond.* Wheaton, Ill.: Tyndale House Publishers, 1977.

Practical and insightful, this psychological assessment of the origin and manifestation of anxiety, hurt and anger, depression, and other forms of tension can be read with profit by all who want better marriages and improved mental health. Recommended. 261.8'34'27.W46

**Wheeler, Richard.** *Pagans in the Pulpit.* New Rochelle, N.Y.: Arlington House, 1974.

With moderate evangelicals producing a massive amount of literature on the need for Christians to become involved in social action, and with these evangelicals using the pulpit to propagate their ideas as well as their ideals, it is refreshing to find someone who states unequivocally that the need of the church is for priorities with individual salvation high on the list. 261.8.W57

**Wilke, Harold H.** *Creating a Caring Congregation.* Nashville: Abingdon Press, 1980.

The subtitle captures the theme of this book: "Guidelines for Ministering with [not to] the Handicapped." The author, an M.D., treats the special needs of the handicapped and the ways in which unconditional love and acceptance may be shown them. Recommended. 261.8'324.W65

**Wilkerson, David,** and **Don Wilkerson.** *The Untapped Generation.* Grand Rapids: Zondervan Publishing House, 1971.

An examination of the hidden problems and potentials of the "now" generation. The conclusions are sobering and so is the analysis of the failure of the "other" generation. Dated. 261.83.W681

**Wilkes, Peter, ed.** *Christianity Challenges the University.* Downers Grove, Ill.: InterVarsity Press, 1981.

Exposes the fallacy of an anthropocentric education, and demonstrates the superiority and viability of a Christocentric approach. Recommended. 261.5.C46

**\*Wilson, Carl W.** *Our Dance Has Turned to Death: But We Can Renew the Family and Nation!* Atlanta: Renewal Publishing Co., 1981.

A substantive account of the major causes of America's national decline and what each family can do about it. Highly recommended. 261.8.W69

**Wilson, Howard A.** *Invasion from the East.* Minneapolis: Augsburg Publishing House, 1979.

Evaluates the impact of Eastern religions on Western society and culture. Voices justifiable concern over the spiritual barrenness that has made America vulnerable to such inroads. Sobering. 261.2.W69

**Wright, Harry Norman.** *The Family That Listens.* Wheaton, Ill.: Victor Books, 1978.

A well-written, perceptive approach to communication. Ideal for use in adult discussion groups. 261.8′34.W93F

## ECCLESIOLOGY

**Avis, Paul D. L.** *The Church in the Theology of the Reformers.* New Foundations Theological Library. Atlanta: John Knox Press, 1981.

Examines Luther's concept of the church and then provides guidelines for the development of an ecclesiology based on Luther's views. Scholarly, but of little value to those who wish to base their beliefs squarely on the Scriptures. 262′.009.AV5

**Banks, Robert.** *Paul's Idea of Community: The Early House Church in Their Historical Setting.* Grand Rapids: Wm. B. Eerdmans Publishing Co., 1980.

Correlates Paul's method of establishing churches and the teaching of the NT with the needs of people for close, intimate fellowship. Ably delineates between different kinds of churches and avoids the extremes between legalistic churches and those that are more permissive. 262.B22

**Barnett, James Monroe.** *The Diaconate: A Full and Equal Order.* New York: Seabury Press, 1981.

An elaborate treatment of the biblical and historical data with great emphasis placed on the development of doctrine throughout the history of the church. Sacramental. 262.14.B26 1981

**Barrett, Charles Kingsley.** *Church, Ministry, and Sacraments in the New Testament.* Grand Rapids: Wm. B. Eerdmans Publishing Co., 1985.

Writing for a general audience, Barrett examines the NT texts as well as some writings from the early church Fathers to see to what extent the early Christians were motivated by the local assembly, its ministry, and the sacraments. Barrett, an Anglican, favors a sacramental theology. This book, however, is designed to serve a second purpose. The principles he draws from history are used to further interchurch cooperation and reunion. 262.B27

**Berkouwer, Gerrit Cornelis.** *The Church.* Studies in Dogmatics. Translated by James E. Davison. Grand Rapids: Wm. B. Eerdmans Publishing Co., 1976.

Emphasizes the unity, catholicity, apostolicity, and holiness of the church with a view to expounding its true ministry— something that denominational polity has not always been able to clarify. 262.B45

**Brand, Paul,** and **Philip Yancey.** *In His*

*Image.* Grand Rapids: Zondervan Publishing House, 1984.

In a certain sense this work may be regarded as a sequel to *Fearfully and Wonderfully Made.* The treatment, however, is more substantive and opens up the reader's thoughts about God, His relationship to the world, and how He works. Exciting reading. 262'.77.B73

**Bridges, Jerry.** *True Fellowship: The Biblical Practice of Koinonia.* Colorado Springs, Colo.: NavPress, 1985.

What we call fellowship is often just a time of talking sports, kids, or mortgage rates over coffee and doughnuts. We need more than that. This book cuts through our misconceptions and helps us rediscover the wonder of true fellowship about the Person and work of Christ and the things God has chosen to reveal to us in and through His Word. 262.7.B76

**Buzzard, Lynn Robert,** and **Laurence Eck.** *Tell It to the Church.* Elgin, Ill.: David C. Cook Publishing Co., 1982.

This "legal" monograph instructs Christians in the ways in which Christ's command in Matthew 18 may be used to settle disputes in the church. Such instruction is sorely needed, but the authors' presentation manifests a lack of understanding of the divine origin of civil government. It is also limited to select biblical passages of Scripture, with the result that the advice given is biased, inadequate, and unreliable. 262.8.B98T

**Campbell, Thomas Charles,** and **Gary B. Reierson.** *The Gift of Administration.* Philadelphia: Westminster Press, 1981.

Makes a plea for management as a special form of ministry. This book then blends secular and biblical principles into a practical treatise for pastors and seminarians. 262'.1.C15

**Carroll Press.** *Career Guide to Professional Associations: A Directory of Organizations by Occupational Field.* Cranston, R.I.: Carroll Press, 1980.

Compiled and edited by the staff of Carroll Press, this detailed alphabetical directory of organizations provides, in addition to the name, address, and telephone number of each organization, a note on its purpose, date of founding, membership (numbers as well as requirements), frequency of meetings, titles of publications, career fields represented, and career aids offered. Includes a brief description of the major occupational classifications as they are defined in the *Dictionary of Occupational Titles.* The classification of all organizations by occupational field follows this introduction to the D.O.T. system. Organizations are listed under each classification in which they are active. 262.2.C18

**\*Clark, Stephen B., ed.** *Patterns of Christian Community Order.* Ann Arbor, Mich.: Servant Books, 1984.

Contains essays by those who have lived "in community" in response to Christ's words to love one another. Seeks to relate Scripture to life in ways that illustrate the essence of *koinonia.* 262.C54

**Coote, Robert T.,** and **John R. W. Stott, eds.** *Down to Earth: Studies in Christianity and Culture.* Grand Rapids: Wm. B. Eerdmans Publishing Co., 1980.

These papers, delivered at the Lausanne Consultation on Gospel and Culture, contain some excellent chapters by well-known authors, but most of the essays that make up this book are deficient in their biblical content and quite unable to relate the teaching of what God has chosen to reveal to the needs of people. Disappointing. 262'.001.D75 1980

**Dulles, Avery Robert.** *Models of the Church.* Garden City, N.Y.: Doubleday and Co., 1974.

One of the most prolific of Roman Catholic writers challenges his readers with the church's mission. He is not as avant garde as some outspoken clergymen because his theology remains firmly embedded in the Scripture/Tradition teaching of his church. 262.7.D88

**Fries, Heinrich,** and **Karl Rahner.** *Unity of the Churches: An Actual Possibility.* Translated by R. C. L. Gritsch and E. W. Gritsch. Philadelphia: Fortress Press/ Paulist Press, 1985.

The authors discuss eight theses they believe are essential to union. Because the thrust of this work is ecumenical, conservative and some evangelical churches are excluded from the discussion. Of limited value. 262'.001.F91

**\*Getz, Gene A.** *Sharpening the Focus of the Church.* Extensively rev. ed. Wheaton, Ill.: Victor Books, 1984.

As valuable as the earlier edition was, this revision is even more so. It reveals Getz's growing expertise in church renewal. This book will be worth its weight in gold to the pastor who puts these principles into practice. In the course of time, as people's minds are renewed and they come to value the good and acceptable and perfect will of God, the focus of the church will be sharpened by the Word. 262.7.G33 1984

**Gibbs, Eddie.** *I Believe in Church Growth.* Grand Rapids: Wm. B. Eerdmans Publishing Co., 1981.

Of this work, Michael Green says, "For a long time the churches in the West have been accustomed to think in terms of survival, not of growth. . . . Yet in the rest of the world it is not so. There are far more Christians in the world than there have ever been. Church growth is taking place in most parts of the world. The deadest areas are those traditionally associated with Christian culture, namely Western Europe." In this book Gibbs gives a fascinating diagnosis of the disease in the Western church and offers some prescriptions. The book explains some of the principles that seem to underlie the church's growth and makes apparent that in other parts of the world such growth can happen anywhere if we are prepared to pay the price. 254.G35

**Girard, Robert C.** *Brethren, Hang Together: Restructuring the Church for Relationships.* Grand Rapids: Zondervan Publishing House, 1979.

This sequel to *Brethren, Hang Loose,* advocates and applies the principles of the relational revolution to the church. In contrast to other books of this genre, Girard does attempt to maintain a solid theological foundation as he provides pointers that show how loving concern can be developed with the community. 262'.001.G44T

**Guder, Darrell L.** *Be My Witnesses: The Church's Mission, Message, and Messengers.* Grand Rapids: Wm. B. Eerdmans Publishing Co., 1985.

Written out of Guder's wide-ranging experience as a minister and professor, this book challenges students of ecclesiology as well as educated laypeople with the need to advance the cause of Christ. Guder grapples seriously with the teaching and traditions of the church as these relate to the work of evangelism. 262.G93

**Hale, James Russell.** *The Unchurched: Who They Are and Why They Stay That Way.* San Francisco: Harper & Row, 1980.

Following extensive interviews, the author analyzes in a tenfold way the causes that keep many people away from church. Illuminating. 306.6.H13

**Hoekstra, Harvey Thomas.** *The World Council of Churches and the Demise of Evangelism.* Wheaton, Ill.: Tyndale House Publishers, 1979.

Well-documented and insightful, this historico-theological analysis of the missionary activity of the WCC traces the movement from 1910 to 1975. Of value is the author's exposé of the subtle ways in which, over the years, the WCC has turned attention away from world evangelism to social involvement, which in some instances borders on Marxism. Highly readable. Recommended. 262'.001.H67

**Howe, E. Margaret.** *Women and Church Leadership.* Grand Rapids: Zondervan Publishing House, 1982.

A scholarly attempt to interact with the biblical data and formulate a definitive statement on the place of women in the church. Of course, a most controversial section treats the ordination of women to the ministry. 262.14.H83

**Inrig, Gary.** *Life in His Body.* Wheaton, Ill.: Harold Shaw Publishers, 1975.

A capable, overall presentation of the biblical data on the leadership and organization of the local church. Commendable. 262′.001.IN7

**Jenson, Ronald Allen, and Jim Stevens.** *Dynamics of Church Growth.* Grand Rapids: Baker Book House, 1981.

Demonstrates a witting or unwitting adherence to behavioral psychology. This pervades each chapter. Coverage of the techniques of church expansion is adequate but lacks a sound biblical base. Uninspiring. 262′.01.J45

**Kirk, J. Andrew.** *Liberation Theology: An Evangelical View of the Third World.* Atlanta: John Knox Press, 1979.

Surveys the roots of liberation theology and assesses the contribution of five of the most influential "liberation" thinkers. Looks at the application of this form of theology to the Latin American scene, and concludes with a view of the way these theologians approach the Scriptures and the fundamentals of the faith. 262.8.K63

***Kuen, Alfred F.** *I Will Build My Church.* Chicago: Moody Press, 1971.

A frank discussion of God's plan for the church. Tackles the problems facing the established church and seeks to find answers to them in the pages of biblical revelation. Highly recommended. 262.K95

***Laney, J. Carl.** *A Guide to Church Discipline.* Minneapolis: Bethany House Publishers, 1985.

"[Laney's] message is one which pas-

tors, church leaders, and church members can no longer brush aside. The contemporary church is faltering, threatened more by impurity from within than by persecution from without. Its health, testimony, and usefulness for the Lord are at stake" (John F. MacArthur, Jr.). Laney deals with these issues in this book. 262.9.L24

**Lawrence, Edgar D.** *Ministering to the Silent Minority.* Springfield, Mo.: Gospel Publishing House, 1978.

Treats the ministry the church may have to the deaf, and discourses on the difficulties faced by the hard-of-hearing. 362.42.L43

***MacArthur, John F., Jr.** *Body Dynamics.* Wheaton, Ill.: Victor Books, 1982.

Formerly issued under the title *The Church, the Body of Christ* (1973), this discussion of the place of the church in the plan and purpose of God is ideal for laypeople's discussion groups. 262.7.M11B 1982

*————. *The Church, the Body of Christ.* Grand Rapids: Zondervan Publishing House, 1973.

Presents important truths relating to the believer's place in the Body. Also provides a discerning elucidation of the gifts of the Spirit. Maintains a careful balance between God's sovereignty and man's responsibility. Recommended. 262.7.M11

**Macquarrie, John.** *Christian Unity and Christian Diversity.* Philadelphia: Westminster Press, 1975.

†Holds that diversity is essential to unity and that through the principles of ecumenism the church can achieve its greatest potential. The chapter "Rome, the Centre of Unity" is typical of his trend of thought. 262′.001.M24

**Martin, Ralph Philip.** *The Family and the Fellowship: New Testament Images of the Church.* Grand Rapids: Wm. B. Eerdmans Publishing Co., 1979.

Purports to be an explanation of

*koinonia* for church members. Unfortunately, the reader may get lost in a maze of questionable textual and higher critical theories. Disappointing. Of value only to the discerning reader. 262.7.M36

**McGavran, Donald Anderson,** and **Win Arn.** *Back to Basics in Church Growth.* Wheaton, Ill.: Tyndale House Publishers, 1981.

Believing that practitioners of church growth principles have departed from the essence of the movement, the founder and the executive director issue a plea for a return to basics. 262′.001.M17 1981

**Moltmann, Jurgen.** *The Church in the Power of the Spirit: A Contribution to Messianic Ecclesiology.* Translated by M. Kohl. New York: Harper & Row, 1977.

Designed to help the church meet the challenge of the present as it prepares for the future, these studies reflect more of Moltmann's pastoral experience and association with ecumenical leaders around the world than they do the teaching of the NT. 262′.001.M73

**\*Moore, John,** and **Ken Neff.** *A New Testament Blueprint for the Church.* Chicago: Moody Press, 1985.

"The authors are not armchair strategists throwing rocks at the church; for years they have been deeply involved in the struggle to build a bridge between the revealed Scriptures and the daily life of a local body of believers. . . . This book is . . . an honest attempt to conform the church's life to the patterns of the New Testament" (Howard G. Hendricks). 262.M78

**Ortlund, Raymond C.** *Let The Chu ch Be the Church.* Waco, Tex.: Word Books, 1983.

Brief yet perceptive messages that help readers evaluate the kind of church to which they wish to belong, and also explain to pastors how the church may meet the needs of the entire person—mental, emotional, relational, spiritual—and the needs of the community at large. 262.7.OR8

**Pickering, Ernest.** *Biblical Separation: The Struggle for a Pure Church.* Schaumburg, Ill.: Regular Baptist Press, 1979.

Well outlined and well documented, this biblically based study demonstrates conclusively the imperative necessity of doctrinal purity and holiness of life if the church is to have an effective ministry to the world. Recommended. 262.P58

**Richards, Lawrence O.,** and **Clyde Hoeldtke.** *A Theology of Church Leadership.* Grand Rapids: Zondervan Publishing House, 1980.

This seminal assessment of the needs of the church denounces authoritarian and secular methods of managerial leadership and stresses, instead, the authority of the Word, submission to Christ as the true Head, and servant leadership, which is dynamically different from the usual methodologies practiced by many "shepherds" today. 262.1.R39T

**\*Saucy, Robert Lloyd.** *The Church in God's Program.* Chicago: Moody Press, 1972.

Deals with the church in both its universal and local aspects, emphasizing the biblical principles for its organization, ministry, and worship. Eminently readable; one of the best treatments available. It is deserving of an honored place in the library of every evangelical minister. Recommended. 262.SA8

**Schillebeeckx, Edward.** *The Mission of the Church.* New York: Seabury Press, 1973.

†In this provocative work, the author, a Dutch theologian, shows his disenchantment with many of the practices of the Roman Catholic Church. 262.SCH3

**Schultz, John Howard.** *Paul and the Anatomy of Apostolic Authority.* New York: Cambridge University Press, 1975.

Investigates the nature of authority as

applied to the apostles, particularly to Paul, and discusses the ramifications of that in terms of man's need for structures and his tendency to abuse power. 262'.8.SCH8

**Singer, Charles Gregg.** *The Unholy Alliance.* New Rochelle, Va.: Arlington House, 1975.

This book is not calculated to win friends among adherents to the National Council of Churches. It provides convincing evidence of the tremendous gap that has developed between the NCC and its critics and demonstrates the NCC's inability to achieve its objectives. 262'.001.S6

**Spencer, Aida Besancon.** *Beyond the Curse: Women Called to Ministry.* Nashville: Thomas Nelson Publishers, 1985.

†Mrs. Spencer, an ordained minister of the Presbyterian Church, U.S.A., with a Ph.D. from Southern Baptist Seminary, is also an assistant professor of NT, Gordon-Conwell Seminary, Massachusetts. She believes the "curse" of Genesis 3:15 was done away in Christ and that Paul claimed men and women had become one in Christ. Dr. Spencer believes in a woman's sharing a ministry with her husband or with men who are in positions of responsibility. 262.1.SP3

**Torrance, Thomas Forsyth.** *Theology in Reconciliation.* Grand Rapids: Wm. B. Eerdmans Publishing Co., 1976.

Essays that, in the name of Christian unity, attempt to blur the distinction between evangelicalism and Catholicism. Misleading and unreliable. 262'.001.T63

**Tucker, Michael Ray.** *The Church: Change or Decay.* Wheaton, Ill.: Tyndale House Publishers, 1978.

An authority on the subject of *change* discusses how pastors may keep pace with all that is taking place about them and still keep their churches geared to the task of winning the lost to Christ. 262'.008.T79

**Wagner, C. Peter.** *Our Kind of People: The Ethical Dimensions of Church Growth in America.* Atlanta: John Knox Press, 1979.

Contains a sociological explanation of what is taking place in the U.S. Challenges Christians to reach out to different ethnic groups. 262'.22.W12

**Watson, David.** *I Believe in the Church.* Grand Rapids: Wm. B. Eerdmans Publishing Co., 1979.

Written by an Episcopalian, this popular yet substantive work covers all the major facets of the church, including its purpose and ministry. Challenging. 262.W33

**Wirt, Sherwood Eliot, ed.** *Evangelism: The Next Ten Years.* Waco, Tex.: Word Books, 1978.

A festschrift honoring Billy Graham. Chapters have been contributed by a variety of leading thinkers, some conservative and some neo-evangelical. The value of this work is that students of evangelism and missions will be able to look back on these essays, interact with their content, and from the perspective of hindsight, evaluate which theories worked and which did not and why. 262.G76.W74

ELDERS, DEACONS

**Armerding, Hudson T.** *Leadership.* Wheaton, Ill.: Tyndale House Publishers, 1978.

Based squarely on the Scriptures, these chapters discuss thirteen aspects of Christian leadership that must be mastered and applied if success in any area of service is to be assured. 262.1.AR5

**Deweese, Charles W.** *The Emerging Role of Deacons.* Nashville: Broadman Press, 1979.

Explains the effect of changing times on the role and function of the deacon in Southern Baptist Churches. 262.2.D51

**Warkentin, Marjorie.** *Ordination: A*

*Biblical-Historical View.* Grand Rapids: Wm. B. Eerdmans Publishing Co., 1982.

Examines the historical, exegetical, and theological sources of the rite of ordination. Presents the thesis that the priesthood of all believers loses its meaning unless true ministry can be practiced by each Christian according to his or her spiritual gifts, regardless of ordination. "The vocabulary of the New Testament," says Warkentin, "permits no pyramidal forms. . . . Ordination can have no function in such a system, for it sets up barriers where none should exist, that is, between one Christian and another, and hinders the mutual service by which the church is edified." 262.14.W23

NATURE OF THE CHURCH

**Lang, George Henry.** *The Local Assembly.* Miami Springs, Fla.: Conley and Schoettle Publishing Co., 1985.

Describes some essential differences between Open and Exclusive Brethren. Assesses the scriptural and historical data. Provides a clear explanation of the beliefs and practices of each group. 262.7.L25 1985

**\*Pember, George Hawkins.** *The Church, the Churches, and the Mysteries, or Revelation and Corruption.* Miami Springs, Fla.: Conley and Schoettle Publishing Co., 1984.

First published in 1901, this volume has met with widespread acceptance. It is a definitive, biblical statement of ecclesiology, and throughout is characterized by the author's usual thoroughness. It includes a discussion of baptism, the Lord's Supper, and gifts of ministry. Recommended. 262.7.P36 1984

DAYS, TIMES, CALENDARS

**\*Beckwith, Roger T.,** and **Wilfred Stott.** *This Is the Day: The Biblical Doctrine*

*of the Christian Sunday in Its Jewish and Early Christian Setting.* Greenwood, S.C.: Attic Press, 1978.

A scholarly treatment ably refuting some recent, left-wing works that cast aspersion on the usual "Lord's day" teaching of the NT. This work blends biblical and historical data together and provides a valuable apologetic for Sunday as the day of worship for believing Christians. 263'.2.B38

**\*Carson, Donald A., ed.** *From Sabbath to Lord's Day: A Biblical, Historical, and Theological Investigation.* Grand Rapids: Zondervan Publishing House, 1982.

These essays fall into the three categories of the subtitle. They evaluate the teaching of the gospels, book of Acts and the epistles as these relate to the Sabbath and the Christian's worship on Sunday. 263.C23

**Jewett, Paul King.** *The Lord's Day: A Theological Guide to the Christian Day of Worship.* Grand Rapids: Wm. B. Eerdmans Publishing Co., 1971.

A responsible and valuable discussion of the Lord's day. Builds on a thorough biblical and historical foundation and provides a survey of redemptive history and the change that took place between the Jewish Sabbath and Sunday as the day of worship. 263.3.J55

PUBLIC WORSHIP

**Berglund, Robert D.** *A Philosophy of Church Music.* Chicago: Moody Press, 1985.

Tries to update pastors and seminarians so that they may have a better understanding of the changes that have taken place in church music in recent decades. 783'.02.B45

**\*Colquhoun, Frank.** *Hymns That Live: Their Meaning and Message.* Downers Grove, Ill.: InterVarsity Press, 1981

Proves the origin of forty famous

hymns and shows how a knowledge of their history may enhance our worship. 264'.2.C71

**Cullmann, Oscar.** *Early Christian Worship.* Translated by A. S. Todd and J. B. Torrance. Philadelphia: Westminster Press, 1978.

Contains a series of essays on the general topic of worship, worship services, and the place and importance of the sacraments. Includes studies on John's gospel that further highlight the sacramental aspects of the author's thesis. 264'.009.C89

**Davidson, James Robert.** *A Dictionary of Protestant Church Music.* Metuchen, N.J.: Scarecrow Press, 1975.

Designed to give users information about music, and in particular, to provide clear definitions and a historical perspective of the development of Protestant musicology. Indices of names, persons, titles of books, and various musical works complete this valuable work. 783'.026.D28

**Davies, Horton.** *Worship and Theology in England from Andrews to Baxter and Fox, 1603-1690.* Princeton, N.J.: Princeton University Press, 1977.

Evidences all the qualities of mature scholarship. Indispensable to those doing research in this era of British history. 264'.009.D28

**Davies, J. G., ed.** *The Westminster Dictionary of Worship.* Philadelphia: Westminster Press, 1979.

Formerly published in England under the title *A Dictionary of Liturgy and Worship,* this handy reference volume covers everything from Ablutions to Witsunday, and Architecture to Watch-night services. Heavy emphasis is placed on sacerdotalism. 264'.003.W52 1979

**Espina, Noni.** *Vocal Solos for Christian Churches.* 3d ed. Metuchen, N.J.: Scarecrow Press, 1984.

First published in 1965, this work soon became the main source of information on sacred solo literature for churches, schools, singers, and teachers of singing. Now in an enlarged edition it fully describes 785 songs and arias by 224 composers. 016.7836.ES6 1984

**Hiller, Carl E.** *Caves to Cathedrals: Architecture of the World's Great Religions.* Boston: Little, Brown and Co., 1974.

An assessment of the way man's beliefs have influenced the kind of buildings he has erected for worship. Well illustrated, with a glossary of architectural terms. 726.H55

**\*Hustad, Donald P.** *Jubilate! Church Music in the Evangelical Tradition.* Carol Stream, Ill.: Hope Publishing Co., 1981.

A definitive description of the history and philosophy of music and its place as an integral part of worship. A most helpful discussion. 783'.02'6.H96

**\*Julian, John, ed.** *Dictionary of Hymnology.* 2 vols. Grand Rapids: Kregel Publications, 1984.

This is a monumental work. It also exhibits outstanding scholarship. It covers the origin and history of Christian hymns from all ages and nations up to and including the early part of the twentieth century. A 200-page cross-referenced index listing more than 30,000 English, American, and German hymns is a valuable resource that all pastors and choir directors will use again and again. The publisher is to be commended for undertaking the reprinting of this indispensable work. Recommended. 264.2.J94 1984

**Laster, James H.** *Catalogue of Choral Music Arranged in Biblical Order.* Metuchen, N.J.: Scarecrow Press, 1983.

"A most useful book to have by one's side when choosing anthems which reflect the words of any of the readings at a service" *(Church Music).* 016.7836.L33C

———. *Catalogue of Vocal Solos and*

*Duets Arranged in Biblical Order.* Metuchen, N.J.: Scarecrow Press, 1984.

This new *Catalogue* is designed to assist churches who use soloists to find appropriate worship materials. This volume serves as a companion volume to the author's *Catalogue of Choral Music Arranged in Biblical Order* (1983), and ministers as well as choir directors will find it invaluable. 016.7836.L33V

**Maxwell, William D.** *A History of Christian Worship: An Outline of Its Developments and Forms.* Grand Rapids: Baker Book House, 1982.

This work by a specialist was first published in 1936 under the title *An Outline of Christian Worship.* It provides a concise outline of worship from the earliest times to the present. 264.M45 1982

**Osbeck, Kenneth W.** *Singing with Understanding.* Grand Rapids: Kregel Publications, 1979.

This is a handy guide that can enrich one's worship experience. It contains the words, tunes, and a brief history of the circumstances surrounding the composition of the hymn/poem. Pastors will find that this book abounds with sermonic material drawn from 101 different hymns. It is difficult to think of anyone reading this book without being blessed by what the author presents. 783.9'09.OS1

**\*Rayburn, Robert O.** *O Come, Let Us Worship: Corporate Worship in the Evangelical Church.* Grand Rapids: Baker Book House, 1980.

Forcefully confronts Christians with the importance of and need for true worship. Supplies guidelines showing how the neglect of this important activity may be remedied. 264.R21

**Robertson, James Douglas.** *The Minister's Worship Handbook.* Grand Rapids: Baker Book House, 1974.

An innovative manual replete with programs and prayers. 264'.002.R54

**Sallee, James E.** *A History of Evangelistic Hymnody.* Grand Rapids: Baker Book House, 1978.

A valuable work covering the rise of modern hymnody. Ideal for use as a college text. Preachers will also find its contents valuable as they seek for ways to enrich the worship service. 783.9.AM3.SA3

**\*Stedman, Ray C.** *Body Life.* Glendale, Calif.: Regal Books, 1979.

The reissue of this famous work in an enlarged format. 264.ST3 1979

**Thayer, Lynn W.** *The Church Music Handbook.* Grand Rapids: Zondervan Publishing House, 1971.

A complete and exhaustive treatment that includes a discussion of the duties of the music director, the music committee and its responsibilities, and an examination of the various problems and situations that must be faced if the church is to have a well-balanced musical program. 783.026.T33

**Tucciarone, Angel,** and **Nicholas P. Cafardi.** *Copyright and the Church Musician.* Pittsburgh: Folk Liturgies Unlimited, 1977.

The combined efforts of a church musician and an attorney, both Roman Catholics, in which they survey the history of the copyright law, evaluate the new ruling governing copyrighted material, and offer valuable legal counsel on what may and may not be done. The authors are to be commended for having undertaken, and then carried through to a conclusion, this important task. 341.758.T79

**Welles, Amos Russel.** *A Treasury of Hymns.* Freeport, N.Y.: Books for Libraries Press, 1971.

Contains brief biographies of 120 leading hymn writers and their best-known hymns. Excellent for its homiletic illustrations. 264.2.W45

**White, James F.** *Introduction to Christian*

*Worship.* Nashville: Abingdon Press, 1980.

This treatment of liturgics deals with historical and theological dimensions of sacramentalism and then describes how a pastor may encourage real worship in the church. Ecumenical. 264.W58

ORDINANCES AND CEREMONIES

**Alexander, James W.** *God Is Love.* Carlisle, Pa.: Banner of Truth Trust, 1985.

First published in 1860 under the title *Sacramental Discourses,* these communion meditations have been published from Alexander's handwritten MSS without further editing. They are clear, evangelical, and reveal the New York divine's deep piety. 265.AL2 1985

**Bromiley, Geoffrey William.** *Children of Promise: The Case for Baptizing Infants.* Grand Rapids: Wm. B. Eerdmans Publishing Co., 1979.

An articulate defense of infant baptism in which the author combines history with theology in order to establish a basis in covenant theology for pedobaptism. 265.12.B78

**Bruce, Michael,** and **G. E. Duffield.** *Why Not? Priesthood and Ministry of Women.* Appleford, Berkshire, England: Marcham Manor Press, 1972.

Anglican and Episcopal clergymen discuss the problems associated with the ordination of women to the priesthood. They show an awareness of the history of women's movements in the church from the earliest times to the present, and conclude that women should not be ordained because such action is theologically, exegetically, and historically untenable. 265.4.B83

**\*Carson, Alexander.** *Baptism, Its Mode and Subjects.* Grand Rapids: Kregel Publications, 1981.

The author makes a welcome and important contribution by providing a comprehensive and scholarly examination of the biblical doctrine of baptism. In this treatise he makes available to his readers the fruits of his wide reading and careful reflection. His views are presented clearly and cogently, and within these pages both Baptist and Pedobaptists will find much for reflection. 265.1.C23 1981

**Chemnitz, Martin.** *The Lord's Supper.* Translated by J. A. O. Preus, St. Louis: Concordia Publishing House, 1979.

A refreshing volume, ably combining scholarship with devotion. Supplements the author's *Two Natures of Christ.* 264.3.C42 1979

**Christensen, James L.** *Difficult Funeral Services.* Old Tappan, N.J.: Fleming H. Revell Co., 1985.

A comprehensive guide containing samples of twenty-nine different, difficult funeral services. Well presented and most usable. 265.85.C46

———. *The Minister's Marriage Handbook.* Old Tappan, N.J.: Fleming H. Revell Co., 1985.

Many ministers are indebted to Christensen for his helpful books on different ceremonies associated with the work of the church. This one begins by describing the changes that have taken place in recent years and the effect these have had on premarital counseling and the wedding ceremony. Recommended. 265.5.C46

**Cochrane, Arthur.** *Eating and Drinking With Jesus.* Philadelphia: Westminster Press, 1974.

†An ethical and quasi-biblical study of the Lord's Supper. 265.3.C64

**Cullmann, Oscar.** *Baptism in the New Testament.* Translated by J. K. S. Reid. Philadelphia: Westminster Press, 1978.

A scholarly work that tends to confuse the meaning of *baptizein* with the mode and strangely supports pedobaptism. 265.12.C89

**Eller, Vernard.** *In Place of Sacraments: A*

*Study of Baptism and the Lord's Supper.* Grand Rapids: Wm. B. Eerdmans Publishing Co., 1972.

A vigorous critique of what the author considers the unbiblical method of observing church ordinances, coupled with suggestions for old and new ways to enhance them. 265.EL5

*Howard, James Keir.* New Testament Baptism. London: Pickering and Inglis, 1971.

A careful review of the NT teaching on baptism that concludes that it is not an effecting agent *ex opere operato* but an effective sign requiring a responsible act by a mature person who "gets himself baptized." The writer also stresses the fact that immersion was the "normal mode." 265.13.H83

**Jewett, Paul King.** *Infant Baptism and the Covenant of Grace: An Appraisal of the Argument That As Infants Were Once Circumcised, So They Should Now Be Baptized.* Grand Rapids: Wm. B. Eerdmans Publishing Co., 1978.

Building on the tenets of Reformed theology, Jewett seeks to demonstrate the logical inconsistency of infant baptism and the practical necessity of believer's baptism. Well reasoned, judicious. 265.12.J54

**Muzzy, Ruth,** and **R. Kent Hughes.** *The Christian Wedding Planner.* Edited by C. S. Hastings. Wheaton, Ill.: Tyndale House Publishers, 1984.

One of the best and most comprehensive works of its kind. Should be in every church library. 265.5.M98

*Warns, Johannes.* Baptism: Studies in the Original Christian Baptism, Its History and Conflicts. Minneapolis: Klock & Klock Christian Publishers, 1980.

Reprinted from the 1957 edition published in England. This thorough apologetic for believer's baptism evidences a remarkable mastery of philosophy and history, diverse ecclesiastical practices and theology. It is practical and relevant, and has been written with conviction. Recommended. 265.13.W24 1980

ASSOCIATIONS FOR RELIGIOUS WORK

**McKinley, Edward H.** *Marching to Glory: The History of the Salvation Army in the United States of America, 1880-1980.* San Francisco: Harper & Row, 1980.

From its insignificant beginnings a century ago, McKinley traces the rise of the Salvation Army, its "dough-nut" ministries, involvement in prohibition, work during the Depression, and social commitments. 267.15.M21

# 8

# Missions and Evangelism

It took at least a score of centuries for the population of the world to reach the 1 billion mark in 1850; to that another billion had been added within eighty years; a billion more had inflated that tally to 3 billion by 1960; today, twenty-five years later, population figures are moving rapidly beyond the 5 billion mark.

The juggernaut of population growth is no mere statistical abstraction for Christ's disciples. The world's peoples constitute the fields that, to use Christ's words, are white unto harvest. In spite of the chronic shortage of harvesters, prodigious results have been achieved. The Christian population of our globe is increasing by an estimated 21.6 million annually. But this is only a fraction of the total number of persons swelling population statistics each year. An estimated 1.3 billion persons—fully 27 percent of the inhabitants of our planet—are not yet evangelized in *any* sense of the word.

What has been the response of the church in North America to this need? Many have given their lives in the cause of Christ, but many others have ignored the challenge. They are like those referred to in Ezekiel 16:49 and are arrogant, over-fed and unconcerned; they do not help the poor and needy. Statistics again prove the accuracy of that statement. Church-goers in North America contribute about $4.07 per capita per week to the work of the Lord. Of that an estimated $.20 per week goes to missions.

That is not merely sad; it reveals a sickness that could well be unto death, for the Lord of the churches holds out little hope for either ancient or modern Laodicean churches. Material poverty and numerical weakness He can and does not abide, for He opens up a door of opportunity for struggling Philadelphians. And what of Laodicea? He can only spew the lukewarm out of His mouth.

But there is hope. And an important element of that hope lies in the fact that ministers within our churches have, as never before, the means for informing themselves and their people of the state of the harvest. As the books listed on the following pages reveal, there is an unprecedented plethora of challenging books to relate to the cause of Christ and the challenging of the complacent to action. To further the analogy of the harvest, the various activities constituting life on a farm lose interest and become irrelevant without a harvest. That is the goal of all endeavor. Harvesting is what farming is all about. And the same is true for the church.

The select books in this bibliography, together with their annotations, are prayerfully dedicated to helping busy pastors and earnest laypeople be and do all that God requires of us. We have been sent into the world—to be and to do—unto the uttermost parts of the earth.

JONATHAN J. BONK

## MISSIONS

**Alexander, John W., ed.** *Confessing Christ as Lord: The Urbana 81 Compendium.* Downers Grove, Ill.: InterVarsity Press, 1982.

Contains messages given at the thirteenth InterVarsity Student Missions Convention, 1981. The theme centers in Philippians 2:11 and the relevance of the message of the gospel for all who will heed it. 266.C76

**Allen, Roland.** *The Compulsion of the Spirit: A Roland Allen Reader.* Edited by David MacDonald Paton and Charles H. Long. Grand Rapids: Wm. B. Eerdmans Publishing Co., 1983.

Roland Allen (1868-1947) was an Anglican missionary and pioneer missiologist. His views on the missionary effort of the church were not widely appreciated in his day, but subsequent generations have found his ideas stimulating and relevant. In fact, Allen is now regarded as a visionary and a man of prophetic gifts. This collection of his writings will be welcomed by all who wish to sense something of the immediacy of the challenge facing the church today. 266.33.AL5C

**\*Beals, Paul A.** *A People for His Name: A Church-Based Missions Strategy.* Pasadena,

Calif.: William Carey Library, 1985.

"The most easy-to-read, all-encompassing source book on [this] subject that I have encountered" (Don Richardson). 266′.02.B36

**Beyerhaus, Peter.** *Missions: Which Way? Humanization or Redemption.* Translated by Margaret Clarkson. Grand Rapids: Zondervan Publishing House, 1971.

A valuable reappraisal of the theological issues in Christian missions by one of the chief architects of the Frankfurt Declaration. Strikes a crippling blow at the World Council of Churches concept of missions and the universalistic tendencies in theology today. 266′.01.B46

―――. *Shaken Foundations.* Grand Rapids: Zondervan Publishing House, 1973.

Designed for students of missions, this book may be read with profit by all evangelicals. It documents the rise of theological liberalism in Germany and describes its tragic consequences, first in relation to the Bible and second in its outworking in missions and evangelism. Recommended. 266′.001.B46

**Bonk, Jonathan James.** *An Annotated and Classified Bibliography of English Liter-*

*ature Pertaining to the Ethiopian Orthodox Church.* Metuchen, N.J.: Scarecrow Press, 1984.

Designed to provide readers with access to widely scattered sources of information pertaining to the ancient but little known Ethiopian Orthodox church since its founding in the fourth century. Includes approximately 750 annotated and indexed items arranged alphabetically by author under five general classifications. Of great help to missiologists in tracing the development, teachings, practice, literature, scriptures, organization, and government of that group. 016.281.B64

**Bosch, David J.** *Witness to the World: The Christian Mission in Theological Perspective.* Atlanta: John Knox Press, 1980.

Published simultaneously in the U.S. and the U.K., this insightful study contributes immeasurably toward an understanding of missionary impact around the world, particularly as shaped by political and theological opinion—both from the left wing and the right—and modified by Third World churches. 266′.001.B65

**Chaney, Charles L.** *The Birth of Missions in America.* South Pasadena, Calif.: William Carey Library, 1976.

A study of the theological foundations of early missionary societies together with a clear statement of the origin of the missionary character of American churches. 266′.009.AM3.C36

**Clark, Dennis E.** *The Third World and Mission.* Waco, Tex.: Word Books, 1971.

A hardhitting, provocative work by a leading evangelical missionary statesman. Contains a potent plea for an honest reappraisal of missionary methods in the light of new conditions existing in the Third World. 266′.001.C54

**Coggins, Wade T.** *So That's What Missions Is All About.* Chicago: Moody Press, 1975.

A veteran missionary discusses the sine qua non of missions and mission support. Intended for a lay audience. Recommended. 226′.001.C65

**Collins, Marjorie A.** *Manual for Accepted Missionary Candidates.* South Pasadena, Calif.: William Carey Library, 1978.

A valuable introduction to the period of time that transpires between choosing a mission and leaving for the field. Intensely practical, this book is a *must* for missionary candidates. Pastors and those on church boards should read it as well, so as to be better able to assist those who feel called to service in some foreign country. 266.C69

————. *A Manual for Missionaries on Furlough.* Pasadena, Calif.: William Carey Library, 1972.

An intensely practical guide for all missionaries home on furlough but especially valuable to those facing their first return from the field. 266′.008.C69F

**\*Conn, Harvie M.** *Eternal Word and Changing Worlds: Theology, Anthropology, and Mission in Trialogue.* Grand Rapids: Zondervan Publishing House, Academie Books, 1984.

Makes a strong plea for a radical re-evaluation of current Western approaches to missions. Exposes common inadequacies and points to a viable alternative. Recommended. 266′.001.C76E

————, ed. *Reaching the Unreached: The Old-New Challenge.* Phillipsburg, N.J.: Presbyterian and Reformed Publishing Company, 1984.

These essays call on Christians to fulfill the mandate of Christ and engage in the work of missions, but without compromising the truth of Scripture. Readers will be challenged and given a new vision as they interact with these relevant, perceptive chapters. This is a work that can be warmly recommended. 266.5.C76R

————, and **Samuel F. Rowen, eds.** *Missions and Theological Education in World*

*Perspective.* Farmington, Mich.: Associates of Urbanus, 1984.

This collection of essays focuses on Third World countries. The contributors seek to promote and deepen the responsibility of different churches to the task of worldwide missions. This is a provocative work, and pastors will do well to become acquainted with it. Recommended. 266′.001.C76M

**\*Cook, Harold R.** *Introduction to Christian Missions.* Rev. ed. Chicago: Moody Press, 1971.

A classic study of missions from an evangelical viewpoint. 266′.009.C77

**Cowan, George M.** *The Word That Kindles.* Chappaqua, N.Y.: Christian Herald Books, 1979.

More than just another book on modern missions, this work emphasizes the dedication and skills that are required of Wycliffe Bible Translators. It is also replete with encouraging accounts of those who have preceded contemporary translators in the work of reducing formerly unknown languages to writing. 266′.023.C83W

**\*Culver, Robert Duncan.** *A Greater Commission: A Theology of World Missions.* Chicago: Moody Press, 1984.

The writer, a biblical and systematic theologian of the finest order, focuses attention on missions and world evangelism. His approach is to carefully expound certain key passages. He formulates his credo based on the explicit teaching of God's Word. Recommended. 266′.001.C89

**Danker, William J.,** and **Wi Jo Kang, eds.** *The Future of the Christian World Mission.* Grand Rapids: Wm. B. Eerdmans Publishing Co., 1971.

The title is somewhat misleading. The contents consists of ten essays by various authors—some ecumenical and some evangelical. Some essays have real merit. 266′.001.D23

**Davies, John D.** *The Faith Abroad.* Faith and the Future. Oxford: Basil Blackwell, 1983.

This work by a Roman Catholic in Wales provides a vivid and controversial account of Christian missions. He dispenses with stereotypes, and his work has value for his ability to assess what needs to be done and how to set about doing it. 266.D28

**Dayton, Edward R.,** and **David Allen Fraser.** *Planning Strategies for World Evangelization.* Grand Rapids: Wm. B. Eerdmans Publishing Co., 1980.

A comprehensive consideration of the issues and alternatives facing evangelicals in missions today. Recommended 266.D33P

**\*Duncan, Homer.** *Divine Intent.* 3d rev. ed. Lubbock, Tex.: World-wide Missionary Crusader, 1982.

Brief and to the point, this study guide deals factually and from a biblical perspective with issues of importance to church members, pastors, and missionaries. Excellent for use as a text in elective adult study-groups in churches. 266.D91 1982

**\*Elliot, James.** *The Journal of Jim Elliot.* Edited by Elisabeth Elliot. Old Tappan, N.J.: Fleming H. Revell Co., 1978.

This work may well become a devotional classic. It treats Jim Elliot's life from his junior year at Wheaton College (1948) to his martyrdom in Ecuador (1955). It reveals the heart of the man and his dedication to doing the will of God no matter what the cost. Young people especially should be encouraged to read this fine work. It is a glowing testimony to the grace of God in the life of one committed to the service of the King of kings. Recommended. 266′.023.EL5E 1978

*The Encyclopedia of Missions.* 2d ed. Detroit: Gale Research Library, 1975.

The entries included cover two general topics: (1) the organized work—the societies, their origin and growth at home, and their work abroad; (2) the countries in which mission work is carried on and the religious beliefs that are encountered. Appendixes include a directory of foreign mission societies, Bible translations into non-Western languages, and statistical tables. Covers mission work of both Protestants and Catholics. 266'.003.EN1

**Gill, Sam D.** *Beyond "The Primitive": The Religions of Nonliterate Peoples.* Englewood Cliffs, N.J.: Prentice-Hall, 1981.

One of the best works of its kind. No missiologist should be without this handy treatise. 306'.6.G41

**Greenway, Roger S.** *Apostles to the City: Biblical Strategies for Urban Missions.* Grand Rapids: Baker Book House, 1978.

This vigorous apologetic by a Reformed theologian lays stress on the need to engage in urban evangelism. Greenway uses a combination of Bible character studies coupled with renewal strategies to get his point across. 266.1.G85A

————, ed. *Discipling the City: Theological Reflections on Urban Mission.* Grand Rapids: Baker Book House, 1979.

The recent Council on Biblical Exposition, Los Angeles, highlighted the importance of spiritual renewal in urban areas if the suburbs are to be spared from the same kind of fate that has overtaken the inner cities. In this book, Reformed theologians come to grips with the problems of urban outreach and present an agenda that those who work in the inner city would do well to consider. 266.1.D63G

**Griffiths, Michael.** *The Church and World Mission.* Grand Rapids: Zondervan Publishing House, 1982.

Subtitled "Arousing the People of God to Witness." This work treats missions and church growth in an effective, stimulating, and enlightening manner. 266.G87

**Grunlan, Stephan A., and Marvin K. Mayers.** *Cultural Anthropology: A Christian*

*Perspective.* Grand Rapids: Zondervan Publishing House, 1979.

Directed to Bible school students, this sociological treatise seeks to explain the basis of cultural diversities in an endeavor to help evangelical students minister cross-culturally. Recommended. 301.2.G92

**Hesselgrave, David John, ed.** *New Horizons in World Mission.* Grand Rapids: Baker Book House, 1979.

Contains messages delivered at the Second Consultation on Theology and Mission, Trinity Evangelical Divinity School (Ill.), 1979. Lays a solid foundation for missions in the 1980s. 266'.008.H46 1979

*————.* *Planting Churches Cross-Culturally: A Guide for Home and Foreign Missions.* Grand Rapids: Baker Book House, 1980.

A wide-ranging book on the theory, theology, methodology, and history of missions. Explains each facet of cross-cultural communication in the missionary enterprise. Recommended. 266'.001.H46

**Hinson, E. Glenn.** *The Evangelization of the Roman Empire: Identity and Adaptability.* Macon, Ga.: Mercer University Press, 1981.

Traces the history of Christianity through A.D. 451. Deals concisely with the crises or persecutions of the period, traces the rise of sacramentalism and the establishment of Christianity as the state religion. 266.11.R66.H61

**Hodges, Melvin L.** *A Guide to Church Planting.* Chicago: Moody Press, 1974.

A contemporary discussion of principles that have engaged the attention of missiologists for many years. 266'.08.H66

*————.* *The Indigenous Church and the Missionary.* South Pasadena, Calif.: William Carey Library, 1978.

This is a sequel to Hodges's other book on indigenous church polity. It is addressed directly to the missionary and spells out the kind of attitude he/she should have toward the work being done. Provides valuable counsel on the training of workers. Recommended. 266.1.H66C

**Howard, David M., ed.** *Declare His Glory Among the Nations.* Downers Grove, Ill.: InterVarsity Press, 1977.

Contains the major messages delivered at the eleventh Missionary Conference, Urbana, Illinois, 1976. Will provide grist for missionary conferences held in or sponsored by the local church. 266'.001.H83

**\*Kane, J. Herbert.** *Christian Missions in Biblical Perspective.* Grand Rapids: Baker Book House, 1976.

Beginning with the OT, the author expounds the biblical principles concerning missions. He explains their place and purpose in the plan of the Trinity and shows missions to be the imperative task of the church. Kane's writing is clear, his burden unmistakable, and his task executed with consummate skill. 266.K13C 1976

\*_____. *The Christian World Mission: Today and Tomorrow.* Grand Rapids: Baker Book House, 1981.

A vigorous challenge to Christians to engage in the kind of missionary activity that will be effective today and lay a foundation for the future evangelization of peoples around the world. 266'.01.K13C

\*_____. *A Concise History of Christian World Mission: A Panoramic View of Missions from Pentecost to the Present.* Grand Rapids: Baker Book House, 1978.

Kane is one of the leading missiologists of our time. In his writings he shows his phenomenal grasp of both history and missionary strategy. In this introductory survey he opens up to his readers the whole scope of missions—Catholic as well as Protestant—and traces the rise

and fall of movements, the inception of ideas, and the lack of flexibility and reluctance to respond to change. This is an ideal work for all who wish to be better informed on this important subject. 266'.09.K13C

\*_____. *A Global View of Christian Missions: From Pentecost to the Present.* Grand Rapids: Baker Book House, 1971.

A comprehensive survey of the progress of Christian missions with a record of advances made and problems encountered. A must! 266.09.K13

_____. *Life and Work on the Mission Field.* Grand Rapids: Baker Book House, 1980.

Charts a course through the shoals of missionary work and gives prospective missionaries numerous valuable ideas based on the author's many years of service abroad. Treats adequately aspects of missionary preparation, life on the field, and the work to be done. Recommended. 266.K13L 1980

\*_____. *Understanding Christian Missions.* Grand Rapids: Baker Book House, 1974.

Describes the contemporary problems facing Christian missions and explains the present-day opportunities. Well deserves the status of a college or seminary text and should be required reading for all missionary candidates. 266'.001.K13U

_____. *Winds of Change in the Christian Mission.* Chicago: Moody Press, 1973.

These exciting chapters by a veteran missionary provide honest answers to young people's questions and also present the challenge of today's missionary opportunities in a clear, positive light. 266'.008.K13W

**Kenney, Betty Jo.** *The Missionary Family.* Pasadena, Calif.: William Carey Library, 1983.

"I hope [this book] will be read by many and mastered by those whose callings demand they go through with the logistics necessary to reach the lost. . . . [A] warm manual for missionary living" (J. Philip Hogan). 266'.023.K39

**Keyes, Lawrence E.** *The Last Age of Missions: A Study of Third World Missionary Societies.* Pasadena, Calif.: William Carey Library, 1983.

"This book presents a milestone in the history of missions for the Christian church. With the face of the world changing, strategy must adapt to the new countenance of the 1980s" (John F. MacArthur, Jr.). 266'.063.K52

**Kyle, John E., comp.** *Perspectives on the Unfinished Task.* Ventura, Calif.: Regal Books, 1984.

Harkening back to 1806 when five Williams College students, caught in a thunderstorm and sheltered under a haystack, spent time praying about the missionary task facing the church. This work assesses what remains to be done. A challenging monograph. 266'.001.K98

**Livingstone, William Pringle.** *Mary Slessor of Calabar.* Grand Rapids: Zondervan Publishing House, 1984.

A beautifully written, factual, and captivating account of Mary Slessor's life and ministry. Quite apart from its stimulus on behalf of missions, this work reminds us of the courage, dedication, and selflessness of a single woman who pioneered work in this part of Africa. 266.52.SL2.L76

**\*Lockerbie, D. Bruce.** *Education of Missionaries' Children: The Neglected Dimension of World Mission.* South Pasadena, Calif.: William Carey Library, 1975.

A sobering assessment based on the author's visits to fifteen mission schools in Asia, India, and Africa. Needs to be read by missionary candidates. 377'.6.L79

**McGavran, Donald Anderson, ed.** *The Conciliar-Evangelical Debate: The Crucial Documents, 1964-1976.* South Pasadena,

Calif.: William Carey Library, 1977.

An expanded edition of *Eye of the Storm* (1972), containing ten additional essays and important documents dealing with the issues currently under discussion. Though the earlier work still is of importance to laypeople (and may be preferred to the material in this book), missiologists will be interested in the materials dealing with the policies and decisions of the fifth Assembly of the World Council of Churches, Nairobi, 1975. 266'.01.M17C

———, ed. *Eye of the Storm.* Waco, Tex.: Word Books, 1971.

Twenty eminent leaders collaborate in providing thought-provoking essays on the need for the nature of effective communication in the world today. 266'.01.M17

———. *Understanding Church Growth.* Rev. ed. Grand Rapids: Wm. B. Eerdmans Publishing Co., 1980.

First published in 1970, this revision updates and refines McGavran's seminal work. In contrast to the earlier edition, this study relates the principles of the church growth movement to churches in the U.S. today. Recommended. 266.M17U 1980

**McQuilken, J. Robertson.** *Measuring the Church Growth Movement.* Rev. ed. Chicago: Moody Press, 1974.

A cautious examination of the five presuppositions underlying the church growth movement. Concludes that the movement is biblical, but he fails to provide a solid theological critique of its position. 266'.001.M24

**Neill, Stephen, Gerald H. Anderson,** and **John Goodwin, eds.** *Concise Dictionary of the Christian World Mission.* Nashville: Abingdon Press, 1971.

Here for the first time is a wealth of comprehensive information on the whole scope of world missions. It has been made available to students of missionary history and strategy by acknowledged leaders (few of whom, however, are evangelical). The contents covers every facet of missions from the earliest times to the present. Bibliographies are appended to the major articles. 266'.003.N31

**Nevius, John Livingstone.** *Planting and Development of Missionary Churches.* Nutley, N.J.: Presbyterian and Reformed Publishing Co., 1974.

Although first published in 1885, this book contains an abundance of practical counsel that is still relevant today. 266'.01.N41 1974

**Nicholls, Bruce J., ed.** *In Word and Deed: Evangelism and Social Responsibility.* Grand Rapids: Wm. B. Eerdmans Publishing Co., 1986.

Contains eight papers presented at the Reformed Bible College in Grand Rapids, Michigan, and the responses given. Deals with missiological issues and relates evangelism to social responsibility. 266'.001.N51

**\*Pentecost, Edward C.** *Issues in Missiology: An Introduction.* Grand Rapids: Baker Book House, 1982.

In this clear, candid presentation of contemporary missiology the author deals adequately with the theology of missions and the relationship of the teaching of Scripture to cultural anthropology. A valuable introduction. 266'.01.P38

**\*Peters, George William.** *A Biblical Theology of Missions.* Chicago: Moody Press, 1973.

Directs attention to the fundamental issues of missions today and draws from the Scriptures God's blueprint for missionary principles and strategy. 266'.01.P44

————. *A Theology of Church Growth.* Grand Rapids: Zondervan Publishing House, 1981.

J. Herbert Kane writes of this book, "This is the first definitive work devoted entirely to the theology of church growth. As such, it will make a significant contribution to the growing body of literature on this important topic. I heartily recommend it." 266'.001.P44

**\*Piggin, Stuart, and John Roxborough.** *The St. Andrews Seven: The Finest Flowering of Missionary Zeal in Scottish History.* Carlisle, Pa.: Banner of Truth Trust, 1985.

Fittingly dedicated to Andrew F. Walls, this remarkable volume recounts the story of a university professor, Thomas Chalmers, and his influence on six of his students. Their story is in certain respects the story of missions in the early nineteenth century. The model Chalmers established is one this generation should strive to recover. This book is warmly recommended. 266'.099.P59

**Reed, Lyman E.** *Preparing Missionaries for Intercultural Communication: A Bi-Cultural Approach.* Pasadena, Calif.: William Carey Library, 1985.

"This book was born out of years of faithful and fruitful service in a most demanding Third World missionary situation . . . it reflects the breadth of the author's personal training in schools noted for their efforts to take the full measure of today's world order to responsibly train missionary and national church leaders" (Arthur F. Glasser). 266'.007.R25

**\*Richardson, Donald.** *Eternity in Their Hearts.* Ventura, Calif.: Regal Books, 1981.

Recounts in a series of documented stories examples of how a monotheistic belief existed for centuries in hundreds of cultures throughout the world. 266'.092.R39

\*————. *Lords of the Earth.* Glendale, Calif.: Regal Books, 1977.

This sequel to *Peace Child* describes the experiences of the author and his wife as they worked among the proud Yali tribe, who rule the Snow Mountains of Dutch New Guinea. It is an absorbing account of missionary daring, persistence, and eventual success. Recommended. 266.9′9.R39L

*_____. *Peace Child.* Glendale, Calif.: Regal Books, 1977.

Describes the call the author and his wife felt and their ministry to Stone Age head-hunters in the disease-ridden swamps of Dutch New Guinea. Also relates how they found there, among the Sawi people, a legend of a specially chosen child who would bring peace to the tribes. A compelling book. 266.9′9.R39

**Ridder, Richard R. de.** *The Dispersion of the People of God.* Grand Rapids: Baker Book House, 1971.

An important, technical study of the theology of missions based on Matthew 28:18-20 and interpreted against the background of Jewish, pre-Christian proselyting and the Diaspora. 266′.01.R43

**Seamands, John Thompson.** *Tell It Well: Communicating the Gospel Across Cultures.* Kansas City, Mo.: Beacon Hill Press of Kansas City, 1981.

A valuable treatise on cross-cultural communication. Illustrates his principles from the Scriptures. Ideal for those with no previous training in this area. 266′.001.SE1

**Shenk, Wilbert R.** *Henry Venn—Missionary Statesman.* Maryknoll, N.Y.: Orbis Books, 1983.

"Henry Venn is perennially up-to-date. Anyone reading him who is concerned with today's Church in today's world will find echoes ringing all the time. It is good to have a comprehensive presentation of him; doubly valuable when it is from one who, like Dr. Shenk, is both a scholar and a missionary administrator himself" (Andrew F. Walls). 266.3.V56.SH4

**Steele, Francis Rue.** *Not in Vain: The Story of the North Africa Mission.* Pasadena, Calif.: William Carey Library, 1981.

Traces a century of evangelistic work to Muslims. Shows how the sacrifices endured by NAM's faithful missionaries and their families has not been in vain. 266′.00961.ST3

**Steven, Hugh.** *Never Touch a Tiger.* Nashville: Thomas Nelson Publishers, 1980.

Though it reads like a novel, this account of missionary work by Wycliffe Bible translators in Central and South America conveys some of the humor and challenge of missions. 266′.023.J63.ST4

***Stott, John Robert Walmsey.** *Christian Mission in the Modern World.* Downers Grove, Ill.: InterVarsity Press, 1975.

Crammed with on target observations relating to the most keenly debated facets of contemporary missiology. A must. 266.S6

***Tatford, Frederick Albert.** *That the World May Know.* In process. Bath, Avon, England: Echoes of Service, 1980-.

Scheduled for ten volumes, this assessment of the far-ranging ministry of the Brethren seeks to show how extensive and diverse their missionary work has been. Tatford's material covers the history and religious beliefs of each area, as well as the way in which the gospel has been established. 266′.09.T18

**Townsend, William Cameron.** *They Found a Common Language.* New York: Harper & Row, 1971.

Communicates the author's passion for universal literacy, and, at the same time, proposes guidelines for bilingual education. Excellent. 266′.023.T66

**Troutman, Charles.** *Every Thing You Want to Know About the Mission Field but Are Afraid You Won't Learn Until You Get There.* Downers Grove, Ill.: InterVarsity Press, 1976.

Purporting to be correspondence between a mission leader and a prospective missionary couple, this lively exchange touches on virtually every aspect of missionary life and work. 266'.023.T74

**Trueblood, David Elton.** *The Validity of the Christian Mission.* New York: Harper & Row, 1971.

A forthright presentation of what the writer believes to be the central mission of the church. Provocative. 266'.01.T76

**Warren, Max.** *I Believe in the Great Commission.* Grand Rapids: Wm. B. Eerdmans Publishing Co., 1979.

A brilliant assessment of the nature and scope of Christ's last words to His disciples. Also describes in clear, cogent terms the impact His commission should have on the church. 266'.001.W25

**Weiss, G. Christian.** *God's Plan, Man's Need, Our Mission.* Lincoln, Nebr.: Back to the Bible, 1971.

A timely book designed to stir up interest in missions. 266'.01.W83

**Wells, Tom.** *A Vision for Missions.* Carlisle, Pa.: Banner of Truth Trust, 1985.

A clear, concise apologetic for missions. Contains illustrative vignettes drawn from the lives of great men and women of the past. 266'.001.W46

**Winter, Ralph D.,** and **Steven C. Hawthorne, eds.** *Perspectives on the World Christian Movement: A Reader.* Pasadena, Calif.: William Carey Library, 1981.

An extensive compilation of essays constituting a text of readings by leading missiologists. Should be required reading in evangelical seminaries. 266.W73

## EVANGELISM

*****Aldrich, Joseph Coffin.** *Life-Style Evangelism: Crossing Traditional Boundaries to Reach the Unbelieving World.* Portland, Oreg.: Multnomah Press, 1981.

Sets forth the basic principles of personal evangelism, describes how the local church can become involved in an evangelistic outreach that works, and concludes with a discussion of the most rewarding ways of communicating one's faith. 253.7.AL2

**Bloesch, Donald George.** *The Evangelical Renaissance.* Grand Rapids: Wm. B. Eerdmans Publishing Co., 1973.

†The author attempts to capitalize on the evident signs of evangelical renewal and also to itemize some of the dangers. His stated purpose is to bring evangelicals and liberals closer together. The concessions he makes to those who do not hold conservative theological beliefs should be sufficient to warn off evangelicals. 269.2.B62

**Bright, William Rohl.** *Come Help Change the World.* San Bernardino, Calif.: Campus Crusade for Christ, 1979.

Updates the story of Campus Crusade for Christ and presents the writer's vision to fulfill the Great Commission. Manifests an emphasis on externalism in religious matters and a lack of insight into the plan and purpose of God. Work appears naive when it comes to an understanding of NT evangelism and the development of a biblical view of mission. 269.2.B76C 1979

**Brow, Robert.** *"Go Make Learners:" A New Model for Discipleship in the Church.* Wheaton, Ill.: Harold Shaw Publishers, 1981.

A valuable discussion of the means of grace used by the evangelical wing of the Anglican church. Questions for study and discussion conclude each chapter. Good bibliographies. 253.7.B81

*****Cocoris, G. Michael.** *Evangelism: A Biblical Approach.* Chicago: Moody Press, 1984.

A different approach to evangelism in that the author, both a pastor and an evangelist, is also a biblicist. He seeks, therefore, to ground his rationale for evangelism squarely in the Scriptures and bypasses many discussions and/or techniques used by others because they have little or no foundation in God's Word. Recommended. 269.2.C64

**Conley, Thomas Herbert.** *Pastoral Care for Personal Growth.* Valley Forge, Pa.: Judson Press, 1977.

Shows how the church may facilitate growth, and suggests ways in which personal and spiritual development may be accomplished through small group interaction. 253.7.C76

**Dayton, Edward R.** *That Everyone May Hear: Reaching the Unreached.* Monrovia, Calif.: MARC, 1979.

This special edition of a well-received. work produced by World Vision illustrates how Christians may reach out and evangelize others. Recommended. 269.2.D33T

**Douglas, J. D., ed.** *Let the Earth Hear His Voice.* Minneapolis: World Wide Publications, 1975.

This official reference volume contains the papers (and responses) delivered at the International Congress on World Evangelism, Switzerland, 1974. Some of the contributors are well known and others make their debut in this volume. The work as a whole is of uneven value, but its message is sorely needed. 269.2.IN8D

**Eichhorn, David Max.** *Evangelizing the American Jew.* Middle Village, N.J.: Jonathan David, 1978.

Deals with the history of Christian attempts to convert Jews to Hebrew Christianity and messianic Judaism. 253.7.EI2

**Ellens, Harold J.** *Models of Religious Broadcasting.* Grand Rapids: Wm. B. Eerdmans Publishing Co., 1974.

In an era of mass media communication, this book takes its place as one of the

most helpful and informative works available. 253.7'8.EL5

**Fletcher, William M.** *The Second Greatest Commandment: A Call to a Personal and Corporate Life of Caring.* Colorado Springs, Colo.: NavPress, 1983.

The author's quest for an effective outreach for himself and his church led him to a profound discovery: the power of love to reach the lost. This book is the result of a life-changing experience, and it deserves careful reading. 253.7.F63

***Gillies, John.** *Historical Collections of Accounts of Revival.* Carlisle, Pa.: Banner of Truth Trust, 1982.

Originally published in 1754, this work contains a fuller, more complete account of the work of the Holy Spirit in revivals than published heretofore. 269.2'09.G41 1982

**Hanks, Billie, Jr.,** and **William A. Shell, eds.** *Discipleship.* Grand Rapids: Zondervan Publishing House, 1981.

A compilation based on the writings of R. E. Coleman, LeRoy Eims, G. W. Kuhne, Dawson Trotman, and others. Unfolds the whys and hows of discipleship. 253.7.H19

**Johnston, Arthur P.** *The Battle for World Evangelism.* Wheaton, Ill.: Tyndale House Publishers, 1978.

Continues the discussion begun in *World Evangelism and the Word of God.* Discourses on the history of different conferences for world evangelism, and shows how modern evangelical movements are contributing toward the renewal of the church. Valuable for its historical survey and its insights into the contemporary scene. 253.7.J64B

**Kantzer, Kenneth S., ed.** *Evangelical Roots: A Tribute to Wilbur Smith.* Nashville: Thomas Nelson Publishers, 1978.

Designed as a festschrift, this work became a "Tribute" when Wilbur M. Smith was asked to contribute a concluding essay. The writers are all men of distinction, noted for their evangelical stand and thoroughly abreast of recent trends in Christian theology. Their studies center in the cause of the gospel and the Christian's responsibility. 269.2.SM6.K13

**Kendall, Robert Tillman.** *Stand Up and Be Counted.* Grand Rapids: Zondervan Publishing House, 1985.

"An incisive and biblical analysis of the importance of calling people to take a public stand for Christ" (Billy Graham). 269.2.K33

**Kennedy, D. James.** *Evangelism Explosion.* 3d ed. Revised by D. J. Kennedy and T. M. Moore. Wheaton, Ill.: Tyndale House Publishers, 1983.

Contains the essence of the evangelism program used by Kennedy in Florida for two decades. The results can only be described by the word *growth.* This book explains the how, why, and what of Kennedy's outreach into the community. 253.7.K38 1983

**Korthals, Richard G.** *Agape Evangelism: Roots That Reach Out.* Wheaton, Ill.: Tyndale House Publishers, 1980.

Korthals explores the motives for, as well as the means of, evangelism. His thesis is rooted firmly in the NT. What he presents is in fact a valuable supplement to Chafer's *True Evangelism: Winning Souls by Prayer.* He emphasizes the relational aspect of ministering out of a heart overflowing with God's love. 269.2.K84

***Kraft, Charles H.** *Communication Theory for Christian Witness.* Nashville: Abingdon Press, 183.

This able discussion of the principles and techniques of communication introduces the reader to the methods that result in success via examples illustrating the theory. Excellent. 001.51.K85

**Kuhne, Gary W.** *The Dynamics of Personal Follow-up.* Grand Rapids: Zondervan Publishing House, 1976.

Designed for the training of lay evangelists, the practical insights contained in this book can and, indeed, should be used by churches of different persuasions. 253.7.K95

**Owens, Virginia Stem.** *The Total Image: Or, Selling Jesus in the Modern Age.* Grand Rapids: Wm. B. Eerdmans Publishing Co., 1980.

A social critique of the use of mass media in the U.S. for the purpose, ostensibly, of propagating the gospel. Worthy of serious discussion. 269.2.OW2

**Peace, Richard.** *Small Group Evangelism: A Training Program for Reaching Out with the Gospel.* Downers Grove, Ill.: InterVarsity Press, 1985.

Seizes on a NT principle and expands on it to develop a most effective means of evangelism. This is an excellent book. Its major weakness is its lack of emphasis on the dynamic power of the Word of God. 269.2.P31

**Pentecost, Edward C.** *Reaching the Unreached: An Introductory Study on Developing an Overall Strategy for World Evangelization.* South Pasadena, Calif.: William Carey Library, 1974.

Makes use of research technology and modern scanning methods in order to locate and identify the unevangelized people of the world and facilitate their evangelization. 269'.2.P38

**Pippert, Rebecca Manley.** *Out of the Saltshaker and into the World: Evangelism as a Way of Life.* Downers Grove, Ill.: InterVarsity Prss, 1979.

Twelve well-written chapters in true IVCF style. Designed to defuse the reader's anxiety over witnessing. 269.2.P66

**Reisinger, Ernest C.** *Today's Evangelism: Its Message and Methods.* Phillipsburg, N.J.: Craig Press, 1982.

A carefully reasoned, Reformed exposition of the church's responsibility for evangelism. Rich in biblical emphasis. Excellent. 269.2.R27

***Richards, Lawrence O.** *Sixty-Nine*

*Ways to Start a Study Group and Keep It Growing.* Grand Rapids: Zondervan Publishing House, 1980.

First published in 1973, this important how-to manual focuses on the people as well as the purpose of Bible study groups. Highly recommended. 269.2.R39

**Smith, Glenn C., ed.** *Evangelizing Adults.* Washington, D.C.: Paulist National Catholic Evangelistic Association/Wheaton, Ill.: Tyndale House Publishers, 1985.

This work by Catholic and Protestant authors is designed to promote cooperate evangelistic efforts aimed at bringing men and women from both segments of Christendom to a saving knowledge of Christ. 253.7.SM5

**Sogaard, Viggo B.** *Everything You Need to Know for a Cassette Ministry.* Minneapolis: Bethany Fellowship, 1974.

An important handbook dealing with the place and importance of cassette tapes in the total program of the local church. Recommended. 269.2.SO2

**\*Southard, Samuel.** *Pastoral Evangelism.* Rev. ed. Atlanta: John Knox Press, 1981.

Applies the principles of interpersonal relations to the work of evangelism and shows how these principles may be used by different groups of people. 269.2.SO8 1981

**Stafford, Tim.** *The Friendship Gap: Reaching Out Across Cultures.* Downers Grove, Ill.: InterVarsity Press, 1984.

Reflecting back on missionary experience in Central Africa, Stafford discusses ways to transcend cultural differences and overcome the barriers that hinder the spread of the gospel. 303.4'82.ST1

**Trites, Allison A.** *The New Testament Concept of Witness.* New York: Cambridge University Press, 1977.

A careful examination of the NT terms for "witness" and "testimony." A valuable contribution. 269.2.T73

**Watson, David.** *I Believe in Evangelism.* Grand Rapids: Wm. B. Eerdmans Publishing Co., 1977.

A British pastor and author lays bare his heart as he pleads with people in the church to engage in a style of evangelism that is biblically based and yet meets people where they live. His thesis is cogently stated, and his material is eloquently presented. This is a welcome addition to the usual genre on this subject. 269.2.W33

**Webber, Robert Eugene.** *Common Roots: A Call to Evangelical Maturity.* Grand Rapids: Zondervan Publishing House, 1978.

Well outlined, this college-type text lends itself more to the classroom than the church. It is designed to challenge and direct the efforts of concerned students so that they will be able to cooperate with other religious groups—hopefully, without compromise. 269.2.W38

**\*Woodbridge, John D., Mark A. Noll,** and **Nathan O. Hatch.** *The Gospel in America: Themes in the Story of America's Evangelicals.* Grand Rapids: Zondervan Publishing House, 1979.

Retraces American religious history, showing how, through the ministry of great men of God as well as through a variety of political figures, the movements and events that have transpired have been related to religious experience. Describes the numerous turning points that have either instilled a greater God-consciousness in people or caused them to depart from Him. Recommended. 269.2.AM3.W85

# 9

## Christian Education

Christ's last command to His followers was "Go . . . and make disciples [*mathetes*, "learners, pupils, apprentices"; NASB]." To the extent that the educational program of the church has that as its goal, it is participating in Christ's commission.

In many parts of the country the Christian education program of the church has taken on new challenges. In addition to the traditional Sunday school, many churches now have grade schools, and some have even sponsored the establishment of colleges and seminaries.

During the last few years the Sunday school has celebrated its two-hundredth anniversary. By contrast, grade schools, colleges, and seminaries that have been started by local congregations are of recent origin.

The Sunday school's anniversary was an occasion for celebration. Few man-made institutions have done as much to help, encourage, mold, and instruct people as has the Sunday school. The lingering questions that must constantly be addressed, however, are, "Are we adequately meeting people's needs?" and, "How can we make the Sunday school more effective?"

In spite of considerable effort to convince all concerned that the Sunday school is continuing to meet people's needs, there have been rumblings of discontent across the land. Complaints related to curriculum include failure to keep abreast of the times and the tendency to focus on improving teacher skills rather than providing teaching substance. In some quarters, time spent in Sunday school has been regarded as the most wasted hour of the week. Teenagers as well as their parents have begun looking elsewhere for something more challenging. They work with quantum physics, advanced logic, PASCAL and COBOL, and read *Time* or *Newsweek* or *U.S. News and World Report,* but when it comes to Sunday, the challenge is gone. That is unfortunate, for a recent survey conducted by radio Bible preachers found that the primary desire of people from Boston to Brownsville, and from New York to

417

Los Angeles, was for information that would help them to *mature* in the faith.

Happily, a change is discernible. Books that are popular yet substantive are beginning to make their appearance. These are being slated for elective use in many churches. The trend is commendable, but people's appetites will need to be whetted for this new kind of material. And even when their appreciation is aroused, it will take many, many years to offset the deplorable lack of the past two decades.

Many of the books included in the following enumeration are suggestive of the kind of materials that can be used in Sunday schools and in home Bible study groups. (The available works can easily be augmented by referring to the chapter on "Devotional Literature" and the sections on Christian living and the Christian home.) Furthermore, included in this section are certain select titles that will be found useful in church grade school programs. These are of necessity limited, but additional source material can easily be obtained by consulting the bibliographies listed in my *Introduction to Theological Research*.

The mushrooming of private schools now constitutes one of the greatest challenges of the present day. Secular humanism and poor education permeates most state systems. Only as Christians catch the vision of a qualitative education, involving biblically based beliefs, sound practices, a commitment to excellence in each discipline, and viable attitudes that facilitate the teaching-learning process, can we begin to offer the kind of training that will effectively prepare our young people for life.

To grapple realistically with these problems, we need to face openly and honestly any weaknesses and/or problems that exist at present, then chart a course for improving and strengthening the *beliefs, values*, and *goals* modeled for our students, developing the kind of personnel who will help to achieve these objectives through a policy of continuous evaluation of one's basic philosophy of education and the implementation of needed changes.

**Allen, Charles Livingstone,** and **Mildred Parker.** *How to Increase Your Sunday School Attendance.* Old Tappan, N.J.: Fleming H. Revell Co., 1979.

Two veterans in the field of Christian education team up to show how a vigorous Sunday school ministry can build a church. 268.AL3

**Alpert, Judith L., et al.** *Psychological Consultation in Educational Settings.* San Francisco: Jossey-Bass Publishers, 1982.

Wide ranging. This work focuses the reader's attention on areas of contemporary methods of instruction that are of importance to Christian educators within the church as well as in Christian institutions. 371.2′07.AL7

**Astolfi, Douglas M., ed.** *Teaching in the Ancient World.* Chico, Calif.: Scholars Press, 1983.

This volume should prove indispensable to biblical scholars, classicists, historians, philosophers, and educators. It combines theoretical and practical data into a vivid presentation of educational systems from earliest times to the Roman civilization. A valuable contribution. 930′.07.AS8

**Barber, Lucie W.** *Teaching Christian Values.* Birmingham, Ala.: Religious Education Press, 1984.

†Here is a well-researched, scholarly treatment of the best ways of inculcating Christian values in our topsy-turvey world. A weakness in the author's approach lies in the failure to establish biblically based beliefs before seeking to understand what values are important. By failing to realize that beliefs precede values in the same way that values precede the establishment of goals, Barber's approach becomes behavioristic instead of life-changing. In spite of this fundamental weakness, the contents of this book will provide educators and parents with a thorough analysis of what needs to be done with some plausible ideas on the process. 370.11.B23

**Bossant, Donald E.** *Creative Conflict in Religious Education and Church Administration.* Birmingham, Ala.: Religious Education Press, 1980.

Describes conflict—theological, psychological, and sociological—and shows how an understanding of its dynamics may help educators and administrators turn conflict into an asset that will work for them instead of a liability that works against them. 268.B65

**Boys, Mary C.** *Biblical Interpretation in Religious Education: A Study of the Kerygmatic Era.* Birmingham, Ala.: Religious Education Press, 1980.

Written with Roman Catholics in mind, this informative and perceptive recounting of the history of biblical interpretation and its impact on parochial education stresses the role of *Heilsgeschichte* and the importance of ecumenical dialog if meaningful progress is to be made. Needs to be read with discernment. 268'.001.B71

**Brubacher, John Seiler.** *On the Philosophy of Higher Education.* Rev. ed. San Francisco: Jossey-Bass Publishers, 1982.

Re-examines, refines, and extends earlier arguments in light of significant new social, economic, legal, and educational developments. Makes stimulating reading. 378'.001.B83 1982

**Byrne, Herbert W.** *Improving Church Education.* Birmingham, Ala.: Religious Education Press, 1979.

A valuable addition to the author's other works that have stood the test of time. This treatise meets a need for pastors, DCEs, and those who teach CE courses in colleges and seminaries. Byrne shows how the church's educational program can be enhanced and made relevant to the times. 268'.01.B99I 1979

**Clark, R. E., et al, comps.** *Books for Christian Education Ministry.* Wheaton, Ill.: Evangelical Teacher Training Association, 1982.

Contains a list of 500 books of importance to all who work in CE departments of our churches. 016.268.EV1

**Cochrane, Donald B., Cornell M. Hamm,** and **Anastasios C. Kazepides, eds.** *The Domain of Moral Education.* New York: Paulist Press, 1979.

This symposium introduces the reader to various ways in which people have tended to think erroneously about moral problems and thus escape the demands of moral thinking. Following that, the contributors explore the heart of moral education with a view to providing moral principles for both conduct and education. 370'.114.D71

**Cove, Mary K.,** and **Mary Louise Mueller.** *Regarding Religious Education.* Mishawaka, Ind.: Religious Education Press, 1977.

Directed to those responsible for parish educational programs, this study treats all aspects of the church's teaching-learning function. 268'.01.C83

**Deighton, Lee C. ed.** *The Encyclopedia of Education.* 10 vols. New York: Macmillan Co., 1971.

An extensive, modern treatment of every facet of education with informative sections on colleges and universities, learning centers, and an assessment of modern trends in education. Also contains a mine of information on how people learn, what leadership styles are in vogue, trends within secular education, and the effects of humanism on educational theory. 370.3.EN1

**Dykstra, Craig R.** *Vision and Character: A Christian Educator's Alternative to Kohlberg.* New York: Paulist Press, 1981.

Kohlberg's theory of values has been widely accepted by evangelicals, so much so that many seminarians have used his theories as the basis of their integrative research. Now Dykstra uses biblical revelation as a basis of the development of a new educational theory. 301.21.D99

**Flagel, Claric.** *The DRE Ministry: Issues and Answers.* Dubuque, Iowa: Wm. C. Brown Company Publishers, 1983.

This book is divided into two sections. The first deals with the person of the DRE—his/her training, goals, and duties. The second discusses professional aspects: recruitment and training of volunteers, handling turnover, ethics, accountability, and so on. In all, about eighteen specific topics are treated, making this a practical handbook. 268'.01.F59

**\*Gangel, Kenneth Otto,** and **Warren S. Benson.** *Christian Education: Its History and Philosophy.* Chicago: Moody Press, 1983.

Emphasizing the fact that people make history, the writers deal with those who have influenced educational concepts of teaching and then show how a distinctively Christian education can have a formative effect on the leaders of tomorrow. Recommended. 268.G15H 1983

**Garlett, Marti Watson.** *Who Will Be My Teacher? The Christian Way to Stronger Schools.* Waco, Tex.: Word Books, 1985.

The chapters of this book deal with those components that Garlett feels are desperately needed in schools: teachers who model, who love, and who heal deep hurts; teachers who not only facilitate learning but even prod and push as occasion requires; and teachers who will interpret for students what is important to know about life, as well as demonstrate a commitment to learning themselves. This book is to be heartily recommended. 370.9.AM3.G18

**Graendorf, Werner C., ed.** *Introduction to Biblical Christian Education.* Chicago: Moody Press, 1981.

This symposium treats contemporary Christian education from the perspective of its dynamic process, impact on people, the family, and the church. Includes a discussion of Christian schools as well as an analysis of the current state of the art. Well-done. 268.G75

**Groome, Thomas H.** *Christian Religious Education: Sharing Our Story and Vision.* San Francisco: Harper & Row, 1980.

Giving evidence of sophistication, yet readable and nonparochial, this work makes a unique contribution to the nature, purpose, context, and approach of religious education. 268'.01.G89

**\*Harper, Norman E.** *Making Disciples: The Challenge of Christian Education at the End of the 20th Century.* Memphis: Christian Studies Center, 1981.

An important monograph calling believers back to the primary role of Christian education in the local church. Well presented. 268'.01.H23

**Holmes, Arthur F.** *The Idea of a Christian College.* Grand Rapids: Wm. B.

Eerdmans Publishing Co., 1975.

With tuition increasing and private colleges closing, what rationale is there for maintaining a Christian liberal arts college? In this timely treatise Holmes sets forth the sine qua non of Christian higher education: The integration of faith and learning. 377.8.H73

**Laqueur, Thomas Walter.** *Religion and Respectability: Sunday Schools and English Working Class Culture, 1780-1850.* New Haven, Conn.: Yale University Press, 1976.

Focusing attention on the origin and growth of Sunday schools, this wide-ranging investigation unravels the history of the movement in England and the way in which it reflected the values of the working-class men and women who taught in them. 268'.09'42.L31

**Lee, James Michael.** *The Content of Religious Instruction: A Social Science Approach.* Birmingham, Ala.: Religious Education Press, 1985.

This is a *big* book that took more than ten years to write. It deals with the content communicated verbally and nonverbally, received cognitively and emotionally, and its effect on the life of the receiver. No one in the ministry can afford to neglect what Lee has set forth in this timely and important work. 268'.01.L51

**Leming, James S., comp.** *Foundations of Moral Education: An Annotated Bibliography.* Westport, Conn.: Greenwood Press, 1983.

This bibliography is designed to be used in two ways. The first, through the author and subject indexes, should enable the user to identify items and subjects of interest. The second approach may be more efficient. The arrangement of the bibliography allows the user to peruse related items of interest and determine the amount of information available on a given subject. Whichever

method is chosen, the information contained within these covers should help to facilitate research on the all-important issue of moral education. 016.17'07.L54

**Lynn, Robert W.,** and **H. Elliott Wright.** *The Big Little School: Two Hundred Years of the Sunday School.* 2d ed. revised. Birmingham, Ala.: Religious Education Press, 1980.

Commemorates the two hundred years of the Sunday school in the U.S. Analyzes the reasons for its success and explains the origins of the problems presently being experienced in Sunday schools across the country. 268'.09.L99

**Miller, Randolph Crump.** *The Theory of Christian Education Practice: How Theology Affects Christian Education.* Birmingham, Ala.: Religious Education Press, 1980.

A lucid application of theological truths to educational principles. Ably blends theory and practice. Recommended for serious discussion. Will be appreciated by CE majors. 268'.01.M61

**Moore, Mary Elizabeth.** *Education for Continuity and Change: A New Model for Christian Religious Education.* Nashville: Abingdon Press, 1983.

Faces squarely the issues and needs of modern religious education and provides a carefully reasoned basis for the reformulation of the church's educational program. 268.M78

**\*Morris, Henry Madison.** *Education for the Real World.* 2d ed. San Diego: Master Books, 1983.

Designed for use in Christian colleges, this work sets forth a clear, concise, and convincing philosophy of education. Recommended to all who teach in Christian schools. 370.1'14.M83 1983

**Murray, Lawrence L.** *The Celluloid Persuasion: Movies and the Liberal Arts.* Grand Rapids: Wm. B. Eerdmans Publishing Co., 1979.

Described as a nuts-and-bolts approach to the use of film materials, this work shows how the use of audio-visual equipment can enhance classroom education. A must for DCEs. 378.1′7.M96

**\*Richards, Lawrence O.** *A Theology of Christian Education.* Grand Rapids: Zondervan Publishing House, 1975.

Divided into three parts, this fine treatment evaluates the church theologically and practically. The teaching mission of the church is assessed against the research of Piaget and Kohlberg. Richards then applies the implications of this correlation to the role of leadership in the teaching program. He concludes with a challenge to pastors and Christian educators. Excellent. 268′.08.R39

**Ringenberg, William C.** *The Christian College: A History of Protestant Higher Education in America.* Grand Rapids: Wm. B. Eerdmans Publishing Co., 1984.

"[This is a] well-researched and informative guide to the institutional history of Protestant liberal arts education in America. . . . It should become a widely read resource on the campuses of the Christian colleges themselves, and it should serve as a valuable fount of information for the general study of American higher education" (Mark A. Noll). 377′.8.R47

**Sowell, Evelyn J.,** and **Rita J. Casey.** *Research Methods in Education.* Belmont, Calif.: Wadsworth Publishing Company, 1982.

This introductory work seeks to apprise readers of the skills they need to develop if they are to analyze the research of others or engage in research of their own. Ideal for CE majors. 3370.′78.SO9

**Taylor, Marvin J., ed.** *Changing Patterns of Religious Education.* Nashville: Abingdon Press, 1984.

Essays by theological liberals as well as some conservatives. This work makes a bold attempt to keep pace with change and relate advances in education to Protestant-Catholic-Jewish communities. No reader is expected to agree with everything presented in this volume, but Christian educators have much to learn from the contents of this volume. 268′.01.T21C 1984

────. *Foundations for Christian Education in an Era of Change.* Nashville: Abingdon Press, 1976.

These uneven but thoroughly professional essays explore areas of concern such as theology, curriculum, pedagogy, and administration. 268′.01

**Thompson, C. E., ed.** *The Resource Guide for Adult Religious Education.* Revised ed. Kansas City, Mo.: National Catholic Reporter, 1975.

This annotated guide to books, films, cassettes, and other media is designed for the instruction of Catholics ranging in age from high school students to senior citizens. It is complete with indexes and addresses of suppliers. If nothing else, it shows Protestants what needs to be done and how the task may be brought to completion. 268.R31

**Willis, Wesley R.** *Two Hundred Years— and Still Counting.* Wheaton, Ill.: Victor Books, 1979.

An intriguing story of the history and accomplishments of the Sunday school, together with an assessment of what remains to be done. 268′.09.W67

ADMINISTRATION

**\*Gangel, Kenneth Otto.** *Church Education Handbook.* Wheaton, Ill.: Victor Books, 1985.

These well-outlined and clearly presented chapters tackle a whole range of issues facing the church in its recruitment of workers and the setting up of its educational program. Recommended. 268.1.G15C

**Westing, Harold J.** *Make Your Sunday*

*School Grow Through Evaluation.* Wheaton, Ill.: Victor Books, 1976.

A combination of sound theory and practical suggestions on how to measure the performance of a program—both qualitatively and numerically. 268'.1.W52

BUILDINGS AND EQUIPMENT

**Darkes, Anne Sue.** *How to Make and Use Overhead Transparencies.* Chicago: Moody Press, 1977.

An important, inexpensive manual that all engaged in communicating the Word of God will find helpful. Few works of this genre have mastered as much material and presented it as simply. Recommended. 741.2.D24

**Greenberg, Alan M.,** and **Carole R. McIver.** *LC and AACR2: An Album of Cataloging Examples Arranged by Rule Number.* Metuchen, N.J.: Scarecrow Press, 1984.

Indispensable. The kind of work every church librarian should have at his/her fingertips. Since the Library of Congress officially implemented the 2d ed. of the *Anglo-American Cataloguing Rules* in 1981, Greenberg and McIver have combed through tens of thousands of LC cards for examples that illustrate the rules themselves. In this volume there are 1,100 examples, and they are arranged by rule number. Now, for the first time, librarians have access to an official body of catalog entries to help them apply the rules in an orderly manner. 025.3'2.G82

**\*Towns, Elmer L.,** and **Cyril J. Barber.** *Successful Church Libraries.* Grand Rapids: Baker Book House, 1971.

A Christian educator and a theological librarian team up and provide a basic reference tool for use in the development of new church libraries and the strengthening of the 50,000 already in existence. This work deals with the matter of cataloging, classification, and the processing of materials in a nontechnical way. 027.78.T747

LEADERSHIP AND PERSONNEL

**Hawley, Gloria Hope.** *True Confessions of a Sunday School Teacher.* Wheaton, Ill.: Victor Books, 1983.

A timely book illustrating the ways in which laypeople can be trained to teach with conviction and creativity. Helpful. 268.3.H31

**Murray, Dick.** *Strengthening the Adult Sunday School Class.* Nashville: Abingdon Press, 1981.

Part of the Creative Leadership Series. This work lacks a solid biblical basis but does offer a plethora of practical suggestions. 268.3'4.M96

**\*Zuck, Roy B.** *The Holy Spirit in Your Teaching: The Relationship That Makes All the Difference.* Revised and expanded ed. Wheaton, Ill.: Victor Books, 1985.

Corrects the emphasis on externalism that places stress on methods and materials, gadgets and gimmicks, instead of reliance on the Holy Spirit and His use of the Word. Recommended. 268.2.Z8H 1985

TEACHING DEPARTMENTS

**Barber, Lucie W.** *The Religious Education of Preschool Children.* Birmingham, Ala.: Religious Education Press, 1981.

Opens up new areas of understanding and avenues for ministry with this age group. 268.432.B23

**Benson, Dennis C.,** and **Bill Wolfe.** *The Basic Encyclopedia of Youth Ministry.* Loveland, Colo.: Group Books, 1981.

Arranged alphabetically by topic, this work covers everything from Aaugh to Zits. Well illustrated. It provides concise ideas that youth workers will find valuable. Cross-references are frequent, and some entries conclude with information on resources from which users of this encyclopedia may draw added information. 268.4.B44

**Caldwell, Irene Catherine (Smith), Richard Hatch,** and **Beverly Welton.** *Basics for Communication in the Church.* Anderson, Ind.: Warner Press, 1971.

A practical study guide on teaching groups or individuals. 001.54.C11

**Chadwick, Ronald Paul.** *Teaching and Learning: An Integrated Approach to Christian Education.* Old Tappan, N.J.: Fleming H. Revell Company, 1982.

A practical introduction to the theory and practice of effective teaching. Should be required reading on the part of all CE majors. 268.4.C34

**\*Clark, Robert E., Joanne Brubaker,** and **Roy B. Zuck, eds.** *Childhood Education in the Church.* Revised and expanded ed. Chicago: Moody Press, 1975, 1986.

This volume is designed to educate, challenge, and direct the activities of those responsible for children in the church. Recommended. 268.432.Z8

**Evans, C. Stephen.** *Preserving the Person: A Look at the Human Sciences.* Downers Grove, Ill.: InterVarsity Press, 1977.

An educator takes a hard look at the presuppositions that permeate academia. He exposes their weaknesses and demonstrates how only a Christocentric approach can adequately meet the cognitive and affective needs of mankind. 128.3.EV1P

**Freese, Doris.** *Children's Church: A Comprehensive How-To.* Chicago: Moody Press, 1982.

Basing her philosophy on the thesis that "children's church is a program geared to the child's level so he truly worships the Lord with understanding and has opportunity to actively participate," Freese leads her readers through the steps that can make this time meaningful in the experience of each child. 264.F87

**Fulbright, Robert G.** *New Dimensions in Teaching Children.* Nashville: Broadman Press, 1971.

A book designed to assist teachers guide their pupils to a real-life involvement with Jesus Christ. 268.43.F95

**Gangel, Elizabeth,** and **Elsiebeth McDaniel.** *The Creative Cradle Roll.* Wheaton, Ill.: Victor Books. 1976.

Focusing on a home-centered ministry, this book presents the twofold aim of this department of the church. 268.43211.G15

**McDaniel, Elsiebeth.** *There Is More to Teaching Primaries.* Wheaton, Ill.: Victor Books, 1976.

Drawing on years of experience, the author lays down helpful principles for teaching primaries and provides practical examples of the how, why, when, and what to teach. 268.4323.M14

**Paul, James L., ed.** *The Exceptional Child: A Guidebook for Churches and Community Agencies.* New York: Syracuse University Press, 1983.

A valuable guide for all who work with children who are handicapped mentally or physically. Recommended. 362.4.P28

**Richards, Lawrence O.** *The Theology of Children's Ministry.* Grand Rapids: Zondervan Publishing House, 1983.

This book provides a clear theological framework for those whose ministry is with children. It gives an overview of children as persons, provides significant insights into their growth process, and suggests many practical approaches to a ministry of love and nurture. Excellent. 268.4.R39C

**Rogers, Sharee,** and **Jack Rogers.** *The Family Together: Inter-Generation Education in the Church School.* London: Action House, 1976.

An innovative and, in some respects, revolutionary approach to the educational program of the church. Advocates a plan to bridge the generation gap through the removal of artificial age barriers. 306.8.R63

**Vogel, Linda Jane.** *The Religious Education of Older Adults.* Birmingham, Ala.: Religious Education Press, 1984.

Integrates psychology, sociology, education, and theology with the task facing the church. Challenges those in positions of authority to find meaningful ways to use the talents of those who still have much to contribute. The breadth of this work, coupled with the counsel offered, makes this book a valuable resource. 268.434.V86

**Willey, Ray, comp.** *Working with Youth: A Handbook for the 80's.* Wheaton, Ill.: Victor Books, 1982.

Containing contributions by some of the leading Christian educators of the day, this work meets a long-felt need for a definitive, practical manual to place in the hands of those who work with youth. 268.433.W67

METHODS OF INSTRUCTION

**\*Barlow, Daniel Lenox.** *Educational Psychology: The Teaching-Learning Process.* Chicago: Moody Press, 1985.

Designed as a college text, this work may nonetheless be read by all engaged in the incomparable art of communicating the truth to others. Although the author covers developmental, learning, and teaching theory, he stresses the teacher's actual task and the dynamics of the teaching-learning situation. 370.15.B24

**Beechick, Ruth.** *A Biblical Psychology of Learning: How Your Mind Works.* Denver: Accent Books, 1982.

"May be the finest book on the contemporary scene that explains the learning process, while allowing the Scriptures to judge the vast array of learning theories. The model of learning the author presents and her discussion of creativity, higher thinking, and the spiritual developmental tasks are provocative. But her use of the Biblical concept of the heart marks the book with its uniqueness. It pries open a variety of areas with a new touch" (Warren S. Benson). 370.152.B39

**Breneman, Lucille N., and Bren Breneman.** *Once upon a Time: A Storytelling Handbook.* Chicago: Nelson-Hall, 1983.

This far-ranging book is excellent and deserves to be read by those in the ministry who wish to master the art of making the narrative portions of Scripture live in the minds of their auditors. The principles of good storytelling technique are explained and illustrated in a most capable manner. 372.6'4.B75

**Brown, Velma Darbo, and Henry Clifton Brown, Jr.** *Preparing for Effective Bible Teaching.* Nashville: Broadman Press, 1971.

A modern approach that takes full advantage of the latest research in education and psychology. Presents pertinent and helpful information for teachers and instructors. 268.6.B81

**\*Cooper, Joseph, and William Hovey.** *The Laws of Teaching.* Chicago: Moody Press, 1976.

This set of sixteen colored transparencies gives valuable help in the field of teaching and emphasizes the ministry of the Holy Spirit. Teacher-training will benefit both from the message presented and from demonstration of the use of the overhead projector. 268.635.C77

**Cully, Iris V.** *Planning and Selecting Curriculum for Christian Education.* Valley Forge, Pa.: Judson Press, 1983.

†Explores the issues facing churches

today and charts a course for the reconstruction of the educational program. Provides valuable guidelines that can be implemented by different churches to meet their specific needs. 268.6.C89

**Fulbright, Robert G.** *New Dimensions in Teaching Children.* Nashville: Broadman Press, 1971.

Filled with information that will be of value to both the layperson and the professional in the field of Christian education. The principles and practical suggestions are designed to assist teachers teach elementary school children in the church today. 268.6.F95

**\*Gregory, John Milton.** *The Seven Laws of Teaching.* Owatonna, Minn.: Pillsbury Press, 1976.

An unabridged reprint of the 1886 edition. Each principle of education is supported by Scripture, a factor alone that makes this edition an invaluable reference tool. 268.635.G86 1976

**\*Hall, Terry.** *Getting More from Your Bible.* Wheaton, Ill.: Victor Books, 1983.

Growing out of the author's extensive seminar ministry, this work succeeds in making Bible study both relevant and exciting. Warmly recommended. 268.6.H14

**\*Lee, Rachel Gillespie.** *Learning Centers for Better Christian Education.* Valley Forge, Pa.: Judson Press, 1982.

An able treatise in which the author advocates a new method of education in the church. Describes how to set up and administer a learning resource center. Deserves careful reading. Recommended. 268.6.L51

**Lowman, Joseph.** *Mastering the Techniques of Teaching.* San Francisco: Jossey-Bass Publishers, 1984.

Outlines the basic principles of good teaching, and shows how teachers may improve their skills and communicate effectively. Well researched and ably presented, this is a valuable book for all engaged in the educational ministry of the church. 378'.125.L95

**May, Philip.** *Which Way to Educate.* Chicago: Moody Press, 1975.

This leading British educator speaks out on the dilemma of values relating to modern educational theories. He argues convincingly that basic Christian beliefs about the nature of man and society radically affect educational theory and practice. 370.1.M45

**Perkinson, Henry J.** *Learning from Our Mistakes: A Reinterpretation of Twentieth-Century Educational Theory.* Westport, Conn.: Greenwood Press, 1984.

†How may one determine if the diverse educational theories of Piaget, Skinner, Montessori, Neill, or Rogers really work? Ironically, their very success forces educators to face the fact that not one of these theories can explain why they are successful. This book deals with the seemingly incompatible educational views and concludes that a radical reinterpretation is necessary. Perkinson claims that education is Darwinian-based. This concept of how knowledge is acquired provides him with a supposedly unifying denominator for all five models of learning. Though well researched and containing impressive documentation, Perkinson's theory fails to account for intellectual, social, moral, and emotional growth. In spite of this, he has forced readers and users of those other theories to answer some very hard questions. 370.1.P41

**Reissman, Frank, Mary Kohler,** and **Alan Gartner.** *Children Teach Children: Learning by Teaching.* New York: Harper & Row, 1971.

A modern approach to education. Contains principles Christian teachers can use to good effect. 370.1.R27

**Smith, Ruth S.** *Getting the Books Off the*

*Shelves: Making the Most of Your Congregation's Library.* New York: Hawthorn Books, 1975.

A most important publication that stresses the ways in which church libraries can extend their influence. 659.2'0.S6

**Sudman, Seymour,** and **Norman M. Bradburn.** *Asking Questions.* San Francisco: Jossey-Bass Publishers, 1982.

Subtitled "A Practical Guide to Questionnaire Design," this comprehensive work details the ways in which experimental research may be conducted. An excellent work for D. Min. students. 300'.723.SU2

SERVICES, CAMPING, ETC.

**Mackay, Joy.** *Creative Camping.* Wheaton, Ill.: Victor Books, 1984.

An important contribution to the literature on camping. Includes sections on innovative ideas, the development of skills, and how to plan different activities. Replete with a comprehensive bibliography. 796'.5422.M19

# 10

# Church History

The "relational revolution" has done great disservice to church history. With its emphasis on relevancy and the present, a new generation has arisen to whom the events of the past are of little worth. Theirs is a system of beliefs based on the senses, and to them history holds little significance.

The Christian church has always battled the tension between orthodoxy and heterodoxy, dry formalism and the need for a faith that meets one's emotional needs. In the second century, Montanism placed emphasis on the senses. That was countered by Gnosticism with its insistence on the intellect. Monasticism in the third through the tenth centuries gave prominence to one's feelings and the quest for inner peace. With scholasticism, however, in the eleventh through the fourteenth centuries, the pendulum swung back again. The intellect was to be used in the search for truth. By the fourteenth and fifteenth centuries, mysticism had replaced the stifling discussions that engaged the mind of the intelligentsia. The emphasis was again on what could be experienced in religion. With the Reformation there was a swing back to an intelligent faith. In the centuries that followed, Pietism and Methodism stressed the need for an experiential faith. Liberalism, which began in the nineteenth century, reverted to a pedanticism that even modern liberals have indicted for its sterility. But all was not well in evangelical circles. A dry orthodoxy had begun to characterize the teaching and preaching of the church. Out of this came Pentecostalism and the charismatic movement. The subjectivity of a religion based on ever-fluctuating human experience, however, led some to attempt a synthesis so that the mental and emotional needs of each believer might be met. And so the "evangelical renaissance" came into being. But within a decade, however, with the publication of Keith Miller's *Taste of New Wine*, there was born the relational revolution.

The decision of modern, younger believers to focus on the present was easy to reach. Rapid change, advances in technology that have made discoveries of

**429**

ten and fifteen years ago obsolete, all appeared to herald the dawning of a new age. What was anticipated in the future, they theorized, would bear little resemblance to anything that has taken place in the past. It was easy to conclude, therefore, that history cannot teach us anything about the world of tomorrow.

The tendency to discard history as a viable means of understanding the past or the present has been aided because various philosophies of history have failed to measure up to expectations. Though initially greeted with enthusiasm, internal inconsistencies soon became apparent, and this resulted in an eventual loss of credibility of history per se. As we review the past, we find that linear and cyclical theories have had to be jettisoned. So has the "great man" theory, in which notable individuals were thought to have influenced the destiny of nations. The geographical view of Frederick Jackson Turner and the economic theory of Karl Marx have failed to gain long-standing support. Frederich Hegel's theory of progress was matched with Darwin's "survival of the fittest," but these have not lived up to expectations. The pessimism of Oswald Spengler is now contrasted with the optimism of H. G. Wells. But two world wars, continuous strife among nations, and the ever present threat of an atomic holocaust demand a more comprehensive, internally consistent approach.

With the discarding of history on the part of a new generation, the door has been opened for all sorts of modern cults (really, old heresies in modern garb) to replace traditionally held Christian beliefs. The time has come, therefore, for a return to Scripture and a clear understanding of what the Bible teaches about the past, the present, and the future. Such a study necessitates a thorough knowledge of what God has chosen to reveal about Himself. We cannot separate Him from either creation or history. These must be properly understood before an accurate philosophy of history can be reached.

A careful analysis of Christology also becomes important. Various heretical groups have attacked Christ's Person, as well as His work. (A glance at the next chapter will show how crucial an understanding of this facet of doctrine really is.) History is replete with these controversies. The clearer our understanding of the past, the more readily will we discern the errors inherent in certain deviant forms of belief that are with us now. The importance of a Christocentric approach to history cannot be underestimated.

Neither can we afford to be ignorant of the *imago Dei*. In the past, various religious groups have had an improper understanding of the biblical doctrine of man. This has led to all sorts of abuses. By having a clear picture of mankind as God's representatives on the earth, we see more clearly the responsibilities He has laid on each one of us in terms of His theocratic administration.

And whatever may be the view of certain historians concerning the future, the Bible very clearly shows that we are moving toward the consummation of the age. In this respect, theology in the form of eschatology again comes to our aid. Instead of being overly optimistic or unduly pessimistic, Scripture invests the future with realism. By understanding the progress of events, we can cooperate with God's program rather than seek to mold the future in terms of our own ideas and dissipate our energies on a variety of lost causes. The strength of having a clear view of eschatology is that it grounds our confidence in the eventual triumph of righteousness and culminates in God's rule over the nations through His Son, Jesus Christ.

The following books need to be considered in light of those contained in Volume 1 of *The Minister's Library*. Only by reading widely and integrating what we read with the whole spectrum of theological belief can we begin to develop a clear, biblical philosophy of history.

**Bainton, Roland Herbert.** *Yesterday, Today, and What Next? Reflections on History and Hope.* Minneapolis: Augsburg Publishing House, 1978.

Important reflections on history, the discernible patterns that may be used to guide our decisions today, and what we may expect in the future. 901.B16

**Bebbington, David W.** *Patterns in History: A Christian View.* Downers Grove, Ill.: InterVarsity Press, 1979.

Develops a philosophy of historiography but omits the theocracy (or *kingdom* concept) that is an integral part of biblical revelation. The author's critiques of the cyclical theory, the idea of progress, historicism, and Marxism are of great value. 901.B38

**Bowden, Henry Werner.** *Dictionary of American Religious Biography.* Westport, Conn.: Greenwood Press, 1977.

Provides page-length biographies of 425 American religious leaders who died before July 1, 1977. Transcends denominational and ethnic boundaries. Includes clergy as well as laity. 277.B67 1977

**Brauer, Gerald C.** ed. *The Westminster Dictionary of Church History.* Philadelphia: Westminster Press, 1971.

†Affords immediate, accurate definition and explanation of the major men, events, facts, and movements in the history of Christianity. Emphasis is on the western spread of Christianity from the eighteenth century onwards. The section dealing with developments within the U.S. is particularly full. Includes data on art, politics, and philosophical movements within church history. Major doctrines are dealt with, biographies of Christian theologians are given, and crises in history receive adequate coverage. The bibliographies are excellent. 270'.03.B73

**Cairns, Earle Edwin.** *God and Man in Time: A Christian Approach to Historiography.* Grand Rapids: Baker Book House, 1979.

A well-written, balanced discussion of the nature, materials, methodology, schools of thought, and philosophies of history. Though comprehensive in scope, what is presented in these pages can be read with relative ease. Cairns has given evangelicals a valuable apologetic that will be appreciated the more it is used. 907.2.C12

**Church, F. F.,** and **T. George,** eds. *Continuity and Discontinuity in Church History: Essays Presented to George Hunston Williams.* Leiden, The Netherlands: E. J. Brill, 1979.

Contains twenty-six essays by leading

church historians. Reflects (1) "Communion and Atonement," (2) "The Radical Reformation," and (3) "Wilderness and Paradise" in the experience of different religious movements. Makes stimulating reading. 270'.08.C74

**Cross, F. L.,** and **E. A. Livingstone.** *The Oxford Dictionary of the Christian Church.* 2d ed. London: Oxford University Press, 1974.

†This predominantly Anglican work was first published in 1958. The articles are arranged alphabetically by topic and include biographical, theological, and ecclesiastical themes. Many have valuable bibliographies appended to them. The new edition includes data from Vatican II, a chronological listing of popes, recent trends within different denominations, and more. Though scholarly, there is an absence of articles on evangelical events, beliefs, and the people associated with them. 270.03.OX2.C88 1974 (Alt. DDC 203)

**\*Douglas, James Dixon, ed.** *The New International Dictionary of the Christian Church.* Grand Rapids: Zondervan Publishing House, 1974.

Representative of the latest international scholarship, and far more evangelical than Cross's *Oxford Dictionary of the Christian Church.* This volume nevertheless lacks the decisive quality of a consistently conservative work. The articles make available to busy pastor's a wealth of practical and illustrative material, and in spite of the weaknesses alluded to, *NIDCC* is deserving of a place on every pastors desk. 270.03.N42 1974 (Alt. DDC 203).

**Dowley, T., ed.** *Eerdmans' Handbook to the History of Christianity.* Grand Rapids: Wm. B. Eerdmans Publishing Co., 1977.

Designed as a companion to *Eerdmans' Handbook to the Bible,* this work seeks to present briefly, yet succinctly, the salient facts of the progress of the church from apostolic times to the present. Well illustrated. 270.EE7D

**Hammack, Mary L.** *A Dictionary of Women in Church History.* Chicago: Moody Press, 1984.

A useful compendium containing biographical sketches of women in fifty denominations, thirty missionary societies, and numerous other organizations. 270'.092.H17

**\*Littell, Franklin Hamlin.** *The Macmillan Atlas History of Christianity.* New York: Macmillan Co., 1976.

Embellished with the work of expert cartographers, this fine atlas provides indispensable data on the history of Christianity and ably treats such matters as church discipline, relations with secular structures, missions, ecumenism, and others. 912'.1'2.L71

**Manschreck, Clyde Leonard.** *A History of Christianity in the World: From Persecution to Uncertainty.* Englewood Cliffs, N.J.: Prentice-Hall, 1974.

Surveys the history of Christianity, emphasizes the main trends, and treats fairly and objectively the elements that have shaped its course in the world. 270.M31

**\*Moyer, Elgin Sylvester.** *Wycliffe Biographical Dictionary of the Church.* Revised and edited by Earle E. Cairns. Chicago: Moody Press, 1982.

Thoroughly revised with some information deleted or corrected from the previous revised edition, and with some new material added, this work will continue to serve the needs of seminarians for years to come. Researchers will appreciate the chronological index. Pastors will also find the brief biographical sketches valuable as they illustrate their messages with material taken from the lives of well-known and lesser-known personalities. 270'.092'2.M87C 1982

**Petry, Ray C.,** and **Clyde L. Man-schreck, eds.** *A History of Christianity.* 2 vols. Grand Rapids: Baker Book House, 1981.

Originally published as separate volumes in 1962 and 1964, these works, covering the early and medieval church and the church from the Reformation to the present, have here been published as a set. Scholarly. Well worth reading. 270.P44 1981

**\*Renwick, A.M.,** and **A. M. Harman.** *The Story of the Church.* 2d enlarged ed. Grand Rapids: Wm. B. Eerdmans Publishing Co., 1985.

First published in 1958, this concise summary of the history of the church is one of the very best for laypeople. Since its first appearance, this work has attained the status of a classic. Its reappearance is welcomed. Unfortunately it is not well-produced. A work of this nature was deserving of something better. 270.R29 1985

**Vos, Howard Frederick.** *An Introduction to Church History.* Rev. ed. Chicago: Moody Press, 1984.

Formerly published under the titles *Highlights of Church History* (1960) and *Beginnings in Church History* (1977), this lay-level text should be read by all lay leaders in the church. 270.V92 1984

**Walton, Robert C.** *Chronological and Background Charts of Church History.* Grand Rapids: Zondervan Publishing House, Acadamie Books, 1985.

"Presents significant facts of the past in useful charts and diagrams so that the student can see what facts are important and what their relationship is to the story of the church" (Earle E. Cairns). 270'.02.W17

## CREEDS AND CONFESSIONS

**Baumann, J. Daniel.** *Dare to Believe.* Glendale, Calif.: Regal Books, 1977.

Popular messages on the Apostles' Creed. Provides a clear presentation of Christian doctrine. 238.11.B32

**\*Kelly, John Norman Davidson.** *Early Christian Creeds.* 3d ed. New York: David McKay Co., 1972.

Ably surveys the rise, development, and use of creedal formulas. Perhaps the best work of its kind in print today. The author's Anglican background leads him to be more sacramental than the evidence really permits. Nevertheless, this is a scholarly resource, and it deserves repeated consultation. 238.1.K28

**Lockerbie, D. Bruce.** *The Apostles' Creed: Do You Really Believe It?* Wheaton, Ill.: Victor Books, 1977.

Brief studies by a layman. Ably expounds this early doctrinal statement. 238.11.L79

**Pink, Arthur Walkington.** *The Divine Covenants.* Grand Rapids: Baker Book House, 1973.

Omitting the New Covenant, Pink discusses the other covenants from a strongly Reformed point of view. 238.P65

**Redding, David A.** *Faith of Our Fathers.* Grand Rapids: Wm. B. Eerdmans Publishing Co., 1971.

A popular commentary on the Apostles' Creed. 238.11.R24

**\*Reid, James.** *Memoirs of the Westminster Divines.* Edinburgh: Banner of Truth Trust, 1983.

"As far as I am able to judge," wrote Richard Baxter about the Westminster Assembly, "the Christian world, since the days of the apostles, had never a synod of more excellent divines than this." The Assembly was called into being by the English Parliament, and convened on

July 1, 1643. The result of their deliberations was a *Confession of Faith* and the famous *Shorter Catechism*. The synod met over a period of several years and comprised the finest church historians, Hebraists, Greek scholars, theologians, and pastors of their time. This book records their activities. It is a fine work and should be read for its intrinsic worth. 238.41.R27

**Sproul, Robert Charles.** *The Symbol: An Exposition of the Apostles' Creed.* Nutley, N.J.: Presbyterian and Reformed Publishing Co., 1973.

An evangelical exposition. Recommended. 238.11.S7

## GENERAL WORKS

**Bavinck, J. H.** *The Church Between Temple and Mosque: A Study of the Relationship Between the Christian Faith and Other Religions.* Grand Rapids: Wm. B. Eerdmans Publishing Co., 1981.

Presents the kind of information that may be used when engaged in dialog with people of other religious persuasions. A valuable apologetic. 270'.09.B32

**\*Latourette, Kenneth Scott.** *A History of the Expansion of Christianity.* 7 vols. Grand Rapids: Zondervan Publishing House, 1971.

Surveys the whole scope of church history, including the Eastern Orthodox church, from the first century to 1914. No one can afford to ignore this monumental work. 270.L35H

**Quasten, J., W. J. Burghart,** and **T. C. Lawson, eds.** *Ancient Christian Writers.* 40 vols. Ramsey, N.J.: Paulist Press, 1979.

This mammoth work has now been concluded. These volumes bring to the English-speaking world the writings of the church Fathers. Few ministers will be able to own this set of books. They can always consult them in a public, college, or seminary library. 270'.01.AN2

**Ridley, Jasper.** *The History of England.* London: Routledge and Kegan Paul, 1985.

Ridley, a barrister turned historian, has already favored the world with masterful biographies of several notable men and women of the past, including John Knox, Mary Tudor, and Thomas Cranmer. This brilliant unfolding of the history of England highlights her religious history and comments on the notable people of the times. 942'.01.R43

**Smith, John Holland.** *Constantine the Great.* New York: Charles Scribner's Sons, 1971.

By sifting through the idealized images of legends and early historical accounts, the author reconstructs the life and work of Constantine and the power he exercised in Europe and Asia Minor. 270.1.C76S

## APOSTOLIC CHURCH

**Arnold, Eberhard.** *The Early Christians.* Grand Rapids: Baker Book House, 1979.

Originally published in German. This work makes available to English readers source material from the first centuries of the Christian era and tacitly allows users to glimpse the worship, witness, and, in some cases, martyrdom of those who were followers of Christ. 270.1.AR6 1979

**Bainton, Roland Herbert.** *Early Christianity.* New York: D. Van Nostrand Co., 1984.

First published in 1960. This important work ably correlates secular history with the rise and expansion of the early

Christian church. A valuable excursus. 270.1.B16 1984

**Benko, Stephen.** *Pagan Rome and the Early Christians.* Bloomington, Ind.: Indiana University Press, 1984.

Goes beyond the traditional approach and treats the social, cultural, and intellectual atmosphere in which pagans and Christians coexisted. As such, this book makes available to all readers a candid, critical description of what the pagans said about Christians and the life situations that, though seemingly counterproductive to Christianity, actually contributed to the dynamic growth of the believers' faith and the spread of the gospel. This is an important work, largely because of its approach. The reading of it should inspire courage in the hearts of many who fear that the pressures of our contemporary milieu are more than they can bear. 270.1.B43

**Brown, Raymond Edward.** *The Churches the Apostles Left Behind.* New York: Paulist Press, 1984.

†Studies seven different NT churches after the death of the apostles — churches with diverse emphases, social settings, and doctrinal problems. Enlightening. 270.1.B81

**Bruce, Frederick Fyvie.** *The "Secret" Gospel of Mark.* London: Athlone Press, 1974.

Working in the library of the monastery of Mar Saba in 1958, Morton Smith came across a copy of Voss's 1646 edition of Ignatius. In the end papers was a MS purporting to be from Clement of Alexandria, containing an expanded text of part of Mark 10. In this lecture Bruce assesses the significance of that discovery. 273.1.B83

**Frend, W. H. C.** *Martyrdom and Persecution in the Early Church: A Study of a Conflict from the Maccabees to Donatus.* Grand Rapids: Baker Book House, 1981.

First published in 1965, this work remains the standard treatment of the interplay between church and state in the early centuries of the Christian era. Excellent. 272.1.F88 1981

**Goppelt, Leonhard.** *Apostolic and Post-Apostolic Times.* Translated by R. A. Guelich. Grand Rapids: Baker Book House, 1977.

These studies deal with the origin and growth of the church and her witness to the Person and work of Jesus Christ. 270.1.G64

**Greenslade, Stanley Lawrence, ed.** *Early Latin Theology.* Library of Christian Classics. Philadelphia: Westminster Press, 1978.

The reissue of the 1956 edition of this work makes available again an important selection of primary resource material from the second century to the fifth century A.D. 281.3.G85L 1978

**Grossu, Serginn, comp.** *The Church in Today's Catacombs.* Translated by Janet L. Johnson. New Rochelle, N.Y.: Arlington House, 1975.

A collection of essays, stories, letters, poetry, and appeals testifying to the religious persecution presently going on behind the bamboo and iron curtains. 272.G89

**Harrison, Everett Falconer.** *The Apostolic Church.* Grand Rapids: Wm. B. Eerdmans Publishing Co., 1985.

The author, who earlier gave us a commentary on the book of Acts, here makes available a brief yet definitive work on the development of the early church. He begins with a description of the essential political and religious characteristics of the culture in which the early church began and then moves on to sketch some of the major points of apostolic church history from the birth of the church at Pentecost to the era of persecution and beyond. In an expanded chapter he deals with various aspects of the internal development of the church, including its organization, theology, creeds, ordinances, ministry, and discipline. Comprehensive in its coverage. 270.1.H24

**Ide, Arthur Frederick.** *Woman as Priest, Bishop and Laity in the Early Catholic Church to 440 A.D.* Mesquite, Tex.: Ide House, 1984.

Basing his thesis primarily on Romans 16, Ide surveys the teaching of the church Fathers and demonstrates thereby the Roman Catholic church's approach to the ordination of women. 270.1.W84.ID2

*The Lives of the Desert Fathers: The "Historia Monachorum in Aegypto."* Translated by Norman Russell. Kalamazoo, Mich.: Cistercian Publications, 1981.

Contains biographical sketches of the most influential leaders of monasticism in the early church. 270.M75.L75

**Maier, Paul L.** *The Flames of Rome: A Documentary Novel.* Garden City, N.Y.: Doubleday and Co., 1981.

Covers the history of imperial Rome during the administration of Flavius, Claudius, and Nero. Describes the fluctuating fortunes of Christians during these years of debauchery, excess, and oppression. Recommended. 813'.54.M28F

**Malherbe, Abraham J.** *Social Aspects of Early Christianity.* 2d ed. enlarged. Philadelphia: Fortress Press, 1983.

†First published in 1977, this monograph deals specifically with the social and literary level of the culture of the early church, the problems of house churches, and the need for hospitality. 270.1.M29 1983

**Meeks, Wayne A.** *The First Urban Christians: The Social World of the Apostle Paul.* New Haven, Conn.: Yale University Press, 1983.

Assesses the organization of early Christian groups and shows how they perceived their world and coped with reality. A sociological study. 270.1.M47

**Quasten, Johannes.** *Patrology.* 3 vols. Westminster, Md.: Christian Classics, 1984.

First published in 1950. This is a work "for the student of early Church history as well as the development of Christian doctrine. Quasten's work is an outstanding contribution. Indeed one may confidently predict that it will be a standard work in the field for many years to come" *(Princeton Seminary Bulletin).* 270.1.Q2 1984

**Salway, Peter.** *Roman Britain.* Oxford: Clarendon Press, 1981.

A mammoth work that deals adequately with all features of Rome's conquest of Britain, together with the rise and fall of their influence there. Careful attention is paid to the various campaigns and the administration of the parts brought under Roman rule. A lengthy section is devoted to religion and society, and here Salway has some pertinent observations on the failure of Catholicism to establish a Romano-British church. 936.1'04.SA3

**Schmithals, Walter.** *The Apocalyptic Movement.* Nashville: Abingdon Press, 1975.

†Seeks to understand both the background and the message of biblical apocalyptic literature. Speculative. 273.1.SCH4

————. *Gnosticism in Corinth: An Investigation of the Letters to the Corinthians.* Translated by J. E. Seely. Nashville: Abingdon Press, 1971.

†A critical treatment of the influence of the gnostics on the beliefs of those in Corinth. 273.1.SCH6

**Sherwin-White, Adrian Nicholas.** *Roman Foreign Policy in the East, 168 B.C. to A.D. 1.* Norman, Okla.: University of Oklahoma Press, 1983.

Utilizing the ample documentation available for this period, Sherwin-White gives attention to physical factors, logistics, the nature of warfare, and the effects on relations between the victor and the vanquished. He also explores the course of Roman wars, the strategies of the commanders, the fortunes of the contending peoples, and the size of military forces available to Rome when its commitments in Europe were outstripping its resources. 327.3.SH5

**Smith, Michael A.** *From Christ to Constantine.* London: InterVarsity Press, 1971.

A well-written, illustrated, captivating volume dealing with the history of the early church as seen against the background of the times. 281.3.SM6

**Stevenson, James.** *The Catacombs: Life and Death in Early Christianity.* Nashville: Thomas Nelson Publishers, 1978.

In this well-written and informative book, Stevenson brings to the fore little known facts that are often overlooked by historians of the period, or where known that are misinterpreted or shrouded in myth. He looks at the reason for the catacombs, explores their use as burial sites, and portrays the builders' motives and beliefs. His work is replete with copies of the artwork, and through his skillful handling of the data, this era is made to come alive for the reader. 270.1.ST4

**Wilken, Robert Louis.** *The Christians as the Romans Saw Them.* New Haven, Conn.: Yale University Press, 1984.

Covering the second through the fourth centuries, Wilken provides a fascinating portrayal of Christianity as seen through the eyes of contemporary historians. 270.1.W65

**Workman, Herbert B.** *Persecution in the Early Church.* New York: Oxford University Press, 1980.

This important assessment of persecution in the early centuries of the Christian era analyzes the clash between church and state, probes the causes of hatred, chronicles the great persecutions, and recounts the experiences of those who were persecuted for their faith. 272.1.W89

## PERIOD OF THE ECUMENICAL COUNCILS

**Benko, Stephen,** and **John J. O'Rourke.** *The Catacombs and the Colosseum.* Valley Forge: Judson Press, 1971.

A scholarly analysis of the social and political forces that resulted in the persecution of the early Christian church. 272.1.B43

**Donaldson, Christopher.** *Martin of Tours: Parish Priest, Mystic and Exorcist.* London: Routledge and Kegan Paul, 1980.

Contains excerpts from the writings of Martin that illustrate the epochs through which he passed in his quest for spiritual wholeness. 270.2.M36.D71

**Gray, Patrick T. R.** *The Defense of Chalcedon in the East (451-553).* Studies in the History of Christian Thought. Leiden, The Netherlands: E. J. Brill, 1979.

A perceptive record of the internal struggle over Christological traditions. Ably presents the teaching of the various schools of thought and the defense of the truth against the errors of Eutychianism, and the like. 270.2.C35.G79

**Hodges, Richard,** and **David Whitehouse.** *Mohammed, Charlemagne and the Origins of Europe: Archaeology and the Pirenne Thesis.* Ithaca, N.Y.: Cornell University Press, 1983.

Views the leaders of this period in relation to their influence and accomplishments. Interacts with Henri Pirenne's thesis and finds it still viable. 940.1.H66

**Hunt, E. D.** *Holy Land Pilgrimage in the Later Roman Empire.* A.D. 312-460. Oxford: Clarendon Press, 1982.

Beginning with Constantine's defeat of Maxentius, Hunt deals with the rise to popularity of pilgrimages to the Holy Land and the prominence given sacred sites, the importance of relics, and so forth. A consummate historian and a skilled storyteller, Hunt has succeeded in blending history and early devotion into a captivating book. 273.2.H91

**Kamer, Henry.** *Inquisition and Society in Spain in the Sixteenth and Seventeenth Centuries.* Bloomington, Ind.: Indiana University Press, 1985.

This complete revision of the author's *The Spanish Inquisition* (1965) makes use of the most recent research and seeks to ground the events in the socio-historical outlook of the time. Kamer appears to tone down the suffering inflicted on those who dared to question the right of the Roman Catholic church. This is a decided weakness and does a great disservice to the truth. 272.2.SP1K12 1985

**Magnusson, Magnus.** *Lindisfarne: The Cradle Island.* Illustrated by Sheila Mackie. Boston: Oriel Press, 1984.

Beautifully illustrated. This fine volume traces the history of Lindisfarne, including the remarkable evangelical work of Aidan and the church extension and administration of Cuthbert. Too much is made of the influence of Romanism in connection with Aidan, and too little has been said of the work he did in "kindling the flame of Christianity in the north." 942'.01.M27

**Smith, Michael A.** *The Church Under Siege.* Downers Grove, Ill.: InterVarsity Press, 1976.

A companion volume to the author's *From Christ to Constantine,* this book deals with the history of the church from Constantine to Charlemagne. 270.2.S6

**Young, Frances Margaret.** *From Nicea to Chalcedon: A Guide to the Literature and Its Background.* Philadelphia: Fortress Press, 1983.

Believing that the period from Nicea to Chalcedon is one of the most significant in the formation of the doctrine of the church, Young deals thoroughly with the events surrounding the apologists of the day and the controversies they engaged in. 270.2.Y8

## PERIOD OF PAPAL SUPREMACY

**Augustinus, Aurelius.** *Augustine of Hippo: Selected Writings.* Translated by M. T. Clark. New York: Paulist Press, 1984.

This volume offers translations of some of Augustine's writings that specifically reveal the character and depth of his spirituality. Includes portions of his *Confessions,* homilies on the Psalms, and the gospel of John. Valuable only as it stimulates an interest in all of Augustine's writings. 282.496.AU4C

**Bury, John Bagnell.** *The Life of St. Patrick and His Place in History.* Freeport, N.Y.: Books for Libraries Press, 1971.

Has long been regarded as a standard treatment of the life and labors of this early Celtic missionary to Ireland. Reprinted from the 1905 edition. 282.415.P27B 1971

**Geisler, Norman Leo, ed.** *What Augustine Says.* Grand Rapids: Baker Book House, 1982.

A well-outlined presentation of the

essence of Augustine's thought. Useful as a text or for ready reference. 282.61.AU4.G27

**Howarth, David.** *One Thousand Sixty-Six: The Year of the Conquest.* Homewood, Ill.: Dorsey Press, 1977.

Covers the Norman conquest of England with a dramatic clarity seldom encountered in works of this nature, and succeeds in making this epochal year come alive in the mind of the reader. The pen-portraits of the leading figures are minutely and brilliantly drawn, and this amazingly lucid volume will delight students of the period as well as those who merely wish to read for pleasure. 942'.02.H83

**McNeill, John Thomas.** *The Celtic Churches: A History, A.D. 200 to 1200.* Chicago: University of Chicago Press, 1974.

An important study of a long-neglected, missionary-minded movement. There is much to learn from their zeal, doctrine, and the way in which they made an impact on the paganism and superstition of their times. 274.M23

**Payne, Robert.** *The Dream and the Tomb: A History of the Crusades.* New York: Stein and Day, 1984.

Covers the Holy Land from Petra and its Crusader Church to Beirut, with its abundance of reminders of the drama of the times. With the author, the reader will walk along the shores of the Sea of Galilee; view the Horns of Hattin, where the most devastating of all Crusader battles was fought and lost; and see recreated before his/her mind's eye the colorful battalions assembled to rid the Holy Land of the infidel. Well researched and graphically presented. 909.07.P29

**Smalley, Beryl.** *Historians in the Middle Ages.* New York: Charles Scribner's Sons, 1974.

This distinguished medieval historian examines the basic ideas that shaped historical inquiry and systematically describes the different kinds of treatment. 909.07'07'2.S1

**Southern, Richard William.** *Western Society and the Church in the Middle Ages.* Grand Rapids: Wm. B. Eerdmans Publishing Co., 1972.

This important survey of eight hundred years of history concentrates attention on the connection between the religious organizations and the social environment of the medieval church. 270.4.SO4

**Thomas, Charles.** *Christianity in Roman Britain to A.D. 500.* Berkeley, Calif.: University of California Press, 1981.

The first work of its kind in seventy years. Traces the history of Christianity by highlighting biographical, archaeological, and literary information. Blends the material into an informative account. 274.1.T36

## LATE MIDDLE AGES, RENAISSANCE

**Coe, Benjamin.** *Christian Churches at the Crossroads!* Pasadena, Calif.: William Carey Library, 1981.

Writing with conviction, Rear Admiral Coe discusses the present condition of the church and the cure of the shallowness and spiritual apathy so prevalent today. 280'.4.C65

**Hudson, Anne, ed.** *Selections from English Wycliffite Writings.* New York: Cambridge University Press, 1978.

Contains new translations of writings that illustrate the main views of the Lollards, their eucharistic theology, and their criticism of contemporary church life. 270.5.SE4H

## REFORMATION

**Atkinson, James.** *The Trial of Luther.* London: B. T. Batsford, 1971.

A definitive study of Luther's defense at the Diet of Worms, 1521. 270.6.AT5

***Bainton, Roland Herbert.** Women of the Reformation in Germany and Italy.* Minneapolis: Augsburg Publishing House, 1971.

These frequently neglected women were faithful to their commitments and often displayed courage equal to that of the Reformers themselves. 270.6′092.B16W

**Crossley, Robert.** *Luther and the Peasant's War.* Jericho, N.Y.: Exposition Press, 1974.

A careful presentation of Luther's actions and reactions and of the effects of this war on the people and his work. 943′.031.C88

**Donaldson, George.** *The Scottish Reformation.* Cambridge: At the University Press, 1972.

A brilliantly written treatment of the way in which Protestantism was established in Scotland. 285.2′41.D71

**Hambrick-Stowe, Charles E.** *The Practice of Piety: Puritan Devotional Disciplines in Seventeenth-Century New England.* Chapel Hill, N.C.: University of North Carolina Press, 1982.

A valuable historical résumé in which the author attempts to probe the Godward relationship of our founding fathers in an endeavor to recapture something of their lost piety. 273.7.H17

**Hillerbrand, Hans Joachim.** *Christendom Divided.* Philadelphia: Westminster Press, 1971.

A different approach to the beginnings of Protestantism. Stresses the role of Luther in the midst of the religious, theological, and political ferment of his times. Attributes the division among Christians to the Reformation movement. The writer's desire for unity appears to overpower his loyalty to the teaching of Scripture. 270.6.H55

**Olivier, Daniel** *The Trial of Luther.* Translated by J. Tonkin. St. Louis: Concordia Publishing House, 1978.

A well-documented account of this famous trial. Traces Luther's steps from the obscurity of an Augustinian monastery to his prominence as a leader of the people and a champion of the Reformation. Well written. 270.6.L97.OL4

**Reardon, Bernard Morris Garvin.** *Religious Thought in the Reformation.* New York: Longman Inc., 1981.

Directs the attention of his readers to the central dynamic of the Reformation, and shows how the leaders were activated by life and death issues. 270.6.R23

**Sainsbury, R. M.** *Russell.* London: Routledge and Kegan Paul, 1979.

Describes the growth of Bertrand Russell's ideas, but fails to account for or defend his rejection of Christianity. Of value to those interested in Russell's philosophical ideas. 192.R91.SA2

**Spitz, Lewis William.** *The Protestant Reformation, 1517-1559.* New York: Harper & Row, 1985.

Written to commemorate the five-hundredth anniversary of Zwingli's birth, this scholarly assessment of the social and religious ferment of the times contributes substantially to our understanding of that important period of history. 270.6.SP4

**Wilkie, William E.** *The Cardinal Protectors of England: Rome and the Tudors Before the Reformation.* New York: Cambridge University Press, 1974.

A painstaking discussion of the period from 1485 to 1539, focusing special attention on the protectors in office until Henry's divorce and remarriage in 1533. 282.42.W65

## PEACE OF WESTPHALIA TO THE FRENCH REVOLUTION

**Goodwin, Thomas.** *The Object and Acts of Justifying Faith.* Vol. 8: *The Works of Thomas Goodwin.* Carlisle, Pa.: Banner of Truth Trust, 1985.

Reprinted from the Nichol's edition of Goodwin's *Works*, this is one of the greatest collections of sermons ever put together. As an exegete and an expositor, Goodwin had no equal. What is contained between these covers, therefore, is of unsurpassed merit. 270.7.G63 v.8

**Klaits, Joseph.** *Servants of Satan: the Age of the Witch Hunts.* Bloomington, Ind.: Indiana University Press, 1985.

Throughout his investigation of the rise, spread, and decline of witch-hunting, the author reveals his masterful grasp of the sociology and psychology of the times (sixteenth and seventeenth centuries). The result is a work of distinction that all Christians would do well to read. 909.K66

**Parker, Geoffrey, ed.** *The Thirty Years' War.* London: Routledge and Kegan Paul, 1984.

Regarded by many historians as the beginning of modern history, this work treats the respective contributions of Wallenstein and Richelieu, Gustavus Adolphus and Tilly, the Winter King and the Hapsburg emperors. Though partial to Catholicism, the coverage is excellent, and it makes a valuable contribution to our understanding of the period. 940.2'4.P22

## MODERN CHURCH

**Backman, Milton V., Jr.** *Christian Churches of America: Origins and Beliefs.* Rev. ed. New York: Charles Scribner's Sons, 1983.

Focuses attention on the basic issues of Catholicism and Protestantism, including orthodox and liberal groups, before assessing the contribution of the mainline denominations. Concludes with an account of the rise of the leading cults. 280.AM3.B38 1983

**Baer, Hans A.** *The Black Spiritual Movement: A Religious Response to Racism.* Knoxville, Tenn.: University of Tennessee Press, 1984.

Attempts to shed light on the nature of specific religious movements within the black community. In addition to presenting a history and general description of these spiritual phenomena, Baer also draws attention to people and teachings that have been largely overlooked by other historians. 277.3.N31.B14

**Baker, Frank.** *From Wesley to Asbury: Studies in Early American Methodism.* Durham, N.C.: Duke University Press, 1976.

Based on years of research into the origin and development of British and American Methodism, this study brings to light some of the aspects of early history not found in other works. 287.'0973.B17

**Baker, Robert Andrew.** *The Southern Baptist Convention and Its People, 1607-1972.* Nashville: Broadman Press, 1974.

A comprehensive history of the S.B.C. by one who taught Baptist history for nearly four decades. 286'.132'09.B17

**Barlow, Frank.** *The English Church, 1000-1066: A History of the Later Anglo-Saxon Church.* 2d ed. London: Longmans Group Ltd., 1979.

This comprehensive and authoritative account of the Anglo-Saxon church has been neglected by historians. Barlow corrects this in the present work that will be welcomed by all historians of the period. 274.2.B24

—————. *The English Church, 1066-1154.* London: Longmans Group, Ltd., 1979.

The author's aim is to provide a definitive account of this period. He treats with consummate skill the lives of men such as Anselm, Abelard, and John of Salisbury, together with the rise of Monasticism. An excellent treatise. 274.2.B24E

**Bauer, Jerald C., ed.** *Religion and the American Revolution.* Philadelphia: Fortress Press, 1976.

Shows how Puritanism and revivalism were prime forces in the development of the heart and mind that characterized the American Revolution. Controversial. 209'.73.R27

**Beale, David O.** *S.B.C. House on Sand?* Greenville, S.C.: Unusual Publications, 1985.

This critique of the Southern Baptist Convention uses quotations from its leaders to show how modernism has permeated the structure. Interesting case histories add credibility to the author's presentation. The emphasis is placed on theological liberalism, which all agree is present in the S.B.C. Little stress is placed on the fundamentals of the faith: Christ's virgin conception, sinless life, vicarious atonement, bodily resurrection, and the like. The primary fundamental—and, of course, the foundational one—commented on is the inspiration and inerrancy of the Word of God. 286.132.B36

**Benne, Robert,** and **Philip Hefner.** *Defining America.* Philadelphia: Fortress Press, 1974.

Building on the three basic American values of freedom, initiative, and opportunity, the writers reappraise Christianity in the United States and attempt to chart a course for the future. In spite of their pessimistic outlook and lack of eschatological awareness, theirs is still a work worth consulting. 917.3.B43

**Bloesch, Donald George.** *The Future of Evangelical Christianity: A Call to Unity Amid Diversity.* Garden City, N.Y.: Doubleday and Co., 1983.

Though aiming at unity amid diversity, Bloesch attempts to construct a basis of evangelism acceptable to conservative theologians. It is doubtful that this work will appeal to either conservatives or liberals, however, for too much is included necessitating compromise, and it is unlikely that conservatives—who have been in the forefront of evangelical effort for decades—will see any advantage in following Bloesch's recommendations. 270.8'2. B62F

**Brandenburg, Hans.** *The Meek and the Mighty: The Emergence of the Evangelical Movement in Russia.* New York: Oxford University Press, 1977.

Following a brief survey of Russian church history, the author traces the progress of three different groups of "Baptists" that today make up the evangelical movement in the U.S.S.R. What is presented is a truly absorbing saga. 280.4.R92.B73

**Bready, John Wesley.** *England: Before and After Wesley.* New York: Russell and Russell, 1971.

Traces the evangelical revival and the social reform that saved England from revolution. A reprint of the 1938 edition. 274.2.B74 1971

**Brill, Earl H.** *The Future of the American Past.* New York: Seabury Press, 1974.

An attempt on the part of an Episcopalian to find out what has gone wrong with the American dream and to provide guidelines whereby Christians may become better citizens. Sociological. 277.B76

**Brown, Harold O. J.** *The Reconstruction of the Republic.* New Rochelle, N.Y.: Arlington House, 1977.

Brown notes that the American republic was founded on biblical principles and that only on account of the apathy of believers to secular concerns was humanism able to gain a foothold and finally gain the upper hand. In a persuasive apologetic Brown calls on evangelicals to return to the fundamentals on which this nation was founded. The course he charts for the future is viable, and he needs to be given a hearing. 277.B81

**Brown, Stewart Jay.** *Thomas Chalmers and the Godly Commonwealth in Scotland.* New York: Oxford University Press, 1982.

Though many honor Chalmers as a champion of independency, Brown believes that more is involved. This book reevaluates the Disruption of 1843 and seeks to present the antecedents of Chalmers's belief in a godly commonwealth. Well reasoned. 285.2.C35.B81

**Christenson, Lawrence.** *The Charismatic Renewal Among Lutherans: A Pastoral and Theological Perspective.* Minneapolis: Lutheran Charismatic Renewal Services, 1976.

Contains pertinent information on the introduction of glossolalia into the Lutheran church. Treats the specific problems, and concludes with an annotated bibliography. 282.C46

**Clabaugh, Gary K.** *Thunder on the Right: The Protestant Fundamentalists.* Nashville: Thomas Nelson Publishers, 1974.

†This study of fundamentalism focuses attention on political reactionaries such as Carl McIntire and Billy James Hargis. Although based on extensive research, it identifies theological fundamentalism with these men. Misleading. 280′.4.C51

**Clebsch, William A.** *American Religious Thought: A History.* Chicago: University of Chicago Press, 1973.

This history of the philosophy of religion in America concentrates on three

principal figures: Jonathan Edwards, Ralph Waldo Emerson, and William James. The author claims that these men abandoned a "moralistic spirituality" for an "aesthetic spirituality," and that only as this concept is adequately understood can their contribution be properly appraised. The analysis given is helpful, but the writer's theological position ill prepares him to understand the doctrinal commitments of a man such as Edwards. 277.C58

**Cracraft, James.** *The Church Reform of Peter the Great.* London: Macmillan Co., 1971.

A definitive study of the Russian emperor together with an evaluation of the reforms that he instituted. 281.9′47.C84

**Cragg, Gerald Robertson.** *Puritanism in the Period of the Great Persecution, 1660-68.* New York: Russell and Russell, 1971.

This worthy study focuses on Puritanism in England and is of interest to all students of church history. First published in 1957. 285.9.C84 1971

**Cunningham, Lawrence S.** *The Catholic Experience.* New York: Crossroad Publishing Company, 1985.

Cunningham writes not as a professor of religion but as a concerned layman in a small, middle-class, middle-of-the-road American church. He is trying to make sense of his faith and to see how it evolved historically and relates to him personally. In that sense, this book is an experiential approach to Roman Catholicism. He asks the right questions but does not always receive the right answers. 282.C91

**Dabney, Robert L.** *Discussions.* Vol. 4: *Secular.* Edited by C. R. Vaughan. Vallecito, Calif.: Ross House Books, 1979.

These chapters give evidence of Dabney's involvement in political and civic functions and events. They demonstrate the extent to which a theologian and pastor can play a role in influencing those in positions of responsibility. In a day such as our own, they serve as a model for similar involvement on the part of knowledgeable people. 285.1.D11 v.4

**Dawson, Jan C.** *The Unusable Past: America's Puritan Tradition, 1830 to 1930.* Chico, Calif.: Scholars Press, 1984.

An examination of how American thinkers and writers reinterpreted the Puritan tradition from the Romantic period to the Great Depression. Drawing from major literary, historical, religious, and journalistic sources, this study traces the reasons for the decline of Puritan influence from the time when New Englanders still wrestled with the inscrutability of divine providence to the indifference and even hostility toward Puritanism of the late 1920s. 285.9.AM3.D32

**Dayton, Edward R.** *What Ever Happened to Commitment?* Grand Rapids: Zondervan Publishing House, 1984.

Laments the fact that although Christian numbers in this country are multiplying, the depth of belief and commitment is shallow. Assesses the reasons for this superficiality and traces it to the grip of narcissism on our lives and culture. Also evaluates the value system held by American evangelicals and sees a greater need for a new commitment to God, church, and each other. This book is good as far as it goes. It overlooks the one essential ingredient in slowly reversing the trend—the Word of God. 280.4.D33

**Demos, John Putnam.** *Entertaining Satan: Witchcraft and the Culture of Early New England.* New York: Oxford University Press, 1982.

Deals with the history and psychology surrounding the Salem trials. Provides fresh evidence from a variety of sources about the attitudes and social mores of those times. Deals respectively with the careers of the witches and the motives of their accusers. 277.4.D39

**\*Dobson, Edward.** *In Search of Unity: An Appeal to Fundamentalists and Evangelicals.* Nashville: Thomas Nelson Publishers, 1985.

Desiring to put a stop to the differences between fundamentalists and evangelicals, Dobson examines many of the crucial issues facing these two groups. He is cognizant of extremism on both sides as well as the problems generated by egocentric leaders. He does not minimize the difficulties created by those who manifest a subtle drift away from Scripture, nor does he turn a blind eye to the need for a consistent life-style, a Christian response to social issues, or the importance of sound doctrine. His appeal is based on love, and though he pleads for unity, in the final analysis some may be compelled to follow Mark Twain's advice, "Let those who cannot agree, agree to disagree, agreeably." 380.4.D65

**Dorough, C. Dwight.** *The Bible Belt Mystique.* Philadelphia: Westminster Press, 1974.

A candid (but not always impartial) discussion of revivalism in the South during the eighteenth and nineteenth centuries, with comments on twentieth-century revivalism and the perpetuation of a special "Bible Belt" mystique. 277.8.D73

**Drummond, Lewis A.** *A Fresh Look at the Life and Ministry of Charles G. Finney.* Minneapolis: Bethany House Publishers, 1985.

As an evangelist, Finney reached uncounted thousands of people for Christ. He was also a self-made theologian and exercised a profound influence through his writings. This stimulating biography is readable as well as precise in its recounting of Finney's life and ministry. 285.8.F49.D84

**Edwards, David Lawrence.** *Christian England.* Vol. 2: *From the Reformation to the Eighteenth Century.* Grand Rapids: Wm. B. Eerdmans Publishing Co., 1983.

In this, the second of three volumes, Edwards begins with the Reformation in the 1540s and recounts the story of English Christianity through the Protestant revolution, the Catholic reaction, the Protestant and Catholic objections to the settlement under Elizabeth I, and the Puritan explosion of the seventeenth century. Concludes his recounting of this stormy period with the relative security and tolerance of the eighteenth century. 274.2.ED9 v.2

——. *Christian England: From the Eighteenth Century to the First World War.* Grand Rapids: Wm. B. Eerdmans Publishing Co., 1984.

In this third and final volume of the series, Edwards takes up the story in the eighteenth century and tells of the evangelical and Catholic revivals that helped to make the Victorian Age as religious as it was. His portrait of this era demonstrates that, for all its faults, it was an age full of courage and creativity, one of the peaks of Christian civilization. The book concludes with a discussion of the controversies between English Christians in the early years of the twentieth century and the decline of conventional Christianity. That decline was in part occasioned by the War, and the War in part revealed the dry rot within liberalism, which until that time had been apparent only to conservatives. 274.2.ED9 v.3

*****Edwards, Jonathan.** *The Great Awakening.* Vol. 4, *The Works of Jonathan Edwards.* Edited by C. C. Goen. New Haven, Conn.: Yale University Press, 1972.

This book focuses attention on a movement begun in New England between 1735 and 1751. In presenting Edwards's material, the editor has endeavored to delineate a series of historical developments in and through which the great preacher's thought was formulated. This volume, therefore, becomes a narrative construction of the history of the times and enables the reader to sense the process of reflection that Edwards followed. 285.873.ED9G 1972

**Egan, Eileen.** *Such a Vision of the Street: Mother Teresa—The Spirit and the Work.* Garden City, N.Y.: Doubleday and Co., 1985.

Through her profound spiritual commitment and her tireless devotion to the poor, the unwanted, and the dying, Mother Teresa has touched hearts and minds beyond all barriers of creed and nation. This is a biography worthy of widespread acceptance. 271.97.T34.EG1

**Elliott, Emory.** *Power and the Pulpit in Puritan New England.* Princeton, N.J.: Princeton University Press, 1975.

The author holds that the religious literature, especially the sermons of the Puritans, changed during the course of the seventeenth century. He traces the cause to the psychological needs that arose from a conflict between generations and the methods used in rearing their children. The most notable change he believes, occurred in the content of theology. Their emphasis on the angry, wrathful God the Father was replaced by emphasis on the gentle, loving Christ. 285'.9'0974.EL5

**Falk, Peter.** *The Growth of the Church in Africa.* Grand Rapids: Zondervan Publishing House, 1979.

A careful history by a pastor and missionary to Zaire, in which he discusses the conditions affecting the spread of Christianity, surveys modern missionary methods, and provides a critique of the Africa Independent Church movement. 276.F18

**Falwell, Jerry, Edward Dobson,** and **Edward Hindson.** *The Fundamentalist*

*Phenomenon: The Resurgence of Conservative Christianity.* Garden City, N.Y.: Doubleday and Co., 1981.

This apology for fundamentalism, coupled with a historical resumé of that facet of America's heritage, brings readers up to date on the growth of the movement since the 1930s. Concludes with Falwell's "Agenda for the Eighties." 280.4.F18

**Fletcher, John.** *The Works of John Fletcher.* 4 vols. Hobe Sound, Fla.: Hobe Sound Bible College Press, 1974.

Long out of print, this material by one of the foremost apologists of early Methodism will be welcomed by evangelicals of all denominations. Though all will not agree with Fletcher's teaching on perfectionism, all will be influenced by his piety and zeal for the Lord. 287.1'41.F63

**Fraser, Gordon H.** *Rain on the Desert.* Chicago: Moody Press, 1976.

Describes the effects of the gospel on Navajo, Kickapoo, Apache, and other Indian tribes. 277.91.F86

**Friedman, Jean E.** *The Enclosed Garden: Women and Community in the Evangelical South, 1830-1900.* Chapel Hill, N.C.: University of North Carolina Press, 1985.

A fascinating piece of Americana. Portrays nineteenth-century society accurately and chronicles women's struggle for equality. Well researched and well written. 305.4'2.AM3.F91

**Gaustad, Edwin Scott.** *Dissent in American Religion.* Chicago: University of Chicago Press, 1973.

This analysis of dissent in a highly pluralistic society claims that religion today is passé and that a conservative reaction to prevalent trends is the only way to recover a lost dynamism. 277.G23

———, ed. *A Documentary History of Religion in America Since 1865.* Grand Rapids: Wm. B. Eerdmans Publishing Co., 1983.

"I am amazed by Professor Gaustad's diligence in seeking out these selections, and most admiring of his learned and well-written introductions. The 'coverage' is far more ample than that of previous anthologies, and entirely in tune with our current concern to look beyond the 'mainstream,' or to enlarge its definition. The guides to further reading are also carefully drawn up, and will be useful to students. Teachers [and we might add, pastors as well] who wish to select short, pungent primary documents to enrich the survey [or sermon] will enjoy very good hunting in this volume. So far as I know, we have nothing even approaching it in range and quality" (William R. Hutchinson). 291.AM3.G23

*———. Historical Atlas of Religion in America.* New and revised edition. New York: Harper & Row, 1977.

A revision of a standard work that has been much used and greatly appreciated ever since its first appearance. Gaustad successfully demonstrates the development of the major religious bodies in America. Even those who do not lay claim to being church historians should be familiar with this work. 277.3.G23A 1976

**Gray, Janet Glenn.** *The French Huguenots: Anatomy of Courage:* Grand Rapids: Baker Book House, 1981.

A popularly written, well-researched history of French Calvinism. Makes enlightening reading. 284.5.G79

**Gritsch, Eric Walter.** *Born Againism.* Philadelphia: Fortress Press, 1982.

†Presents an analysis of the histories of evangelism, millennialism, fundamentalism, and Pentecostalism in the United States. The origin of the "born-again" movement and its principle leaders come in for particularly severe criticism. 270.8.G88

**Halevy, Elie.** *The Birth of Methodism in*

*England.* Translated and edited by B. Semmuel. Chicago: University of Chicago Press, 1971.

Based on two French journal articles, these studies show how Methodism was perceived from abroad. As such, they provide a unique perspective and are worthy of consideration. 287.1'42.H13

**Hamilton, Neill Q.** *Recovery of the Protestant Adventure.* New York: Seabury Press, 1981.

Uses Mark's gospel as a basis for recovering the "Protestant Adventure." Challenges Americans to reappropriate their former religious zeal. Omits the foundational fact that the tradition he wishes to see recovered was an evangelical one. Does provide readers with an interesting use of Mark's gospel. 280.4.AM3

**Handy, Robert Theodore.** *A Christian America: Protestant Hopes and Historical Realities.* 2d ed. New York: Oxford University Press, 1984.

First published in 1971. This volume traces the attitudes of Christians in America from the optimism of our founding fathers to the pessimism (resulting from disorientation over the decline of denominationalism) to the disillusionment of the present day. Handy provides an excellent summary of the history of the period but fails to come to grips with the real reason for spiritual decline, the failure of religious externalism and the desperate need for the development of a strong internal Godward orientation. Furthermore, Handy betrays his own theological position when he fails to show that the nadir may be traceable to a lack of real Bible teaching in our churches. 277.3.H19 1984

————. *A History of the Churches in the United States and Canada.* New York: Oxford University Press, 1977.

Part of the new twenty-one volume *Oxford History of the Christian Church.* Pro-

vides an extensive survey of the major Christian movements in North America. Coverage extends from Colonial times to the present. 277.H19

**Hardman, Keith J.** *The Spiritual Awakeners: American Revivalists from Solomon Stoddard to D. L. Moody.* Chicago: Moody Press, 1983.

Argues for the credibility as well as the positive impact of religious revivals that have made a significant impact on American life. Though sociological rather than spiritual, this work nevertheless provides a good survey of the course of American revivals but with a disappointing interpretation of the history of events. 277.H22

**Harmon, Nolan B., ed.** *The Encyclopedia of World Methodism.* 2 vols. Nashville: Abingdon Press, 1974.

Replete with information on all boards and agencies. Also contains extensive appendixes that readily lead researchers to a variety of social, missionary, and statistical information. Provides data on the prominent people and places, doctrines and practices of Methodism. 287.EN1H

**Hastings, C. Brownlow.** *Introducing Southern Baptists: Their Faith and Their Life.* New York: Paulist Press, 1981.

A work published by Roman Catholics to promote greater understanding between themselves and Southern Baptists. A series is contemplated. 286.132.H27

**Hatch, Nathan,** and **Mark A. Noll, eds.** *The Bible in America: Essays in Cultural History.* New York: Oxford University Press, 1982.

Comprises papers delivered at the conference "The Bible in American Culture," Wheaton College, Illinois, 1979. Provocative. Worthy of careful reading. 277.H28

**Henry, Carl Ferdinand Howard.** *Evangelicals in Search of Identity.* Waco, Tex.: Word Books, 1976.

Writing in the wake of the evangelical renaissance, Henry issues a prophetic call to evangelicals to capitalize on the opportunities now facing them. 277.3.H39

**Hesselink, I. John.** *On Being Reformed: Distinctive Characteristics and Common Misunderstandings.* Ann Arbor, Mich.: Servant Publications, 1983.

Emphasizes the latter aspect of the subtitle more than the former. Contains an extensive annotated bibliography. 285.H46

**\*Hoffecker, W. Andrew.** *Piety and the Princeton Theologians: Archibald Alexander, Charles Hodge, and Benjamin Warfield.* Grand Rapids: Baker Book House, 1981.

Demonstrates from the lives of these men that devotional experience can be vitally united to, and an outgrowth of, a solid evangelical theology. 285.1.P93.H67

**Holbrook, Clyde A.** *The Ethics of Jonathan Edwards: Morality and Aesthetics.* Ann Arbor, Mich.: University of Michigan Press, 1973.

The author blends Edwards's theological objectivism and practical subjectivism into a work that reveals not only the New England minister's Puritan theology, but his Lockean psychology as well. The truths thus gleaned are then applied to the areas of morality and aesthetics. 285.8.ED9.H69

**\*Hudson, Winthrop Still.** *Religion in America.* 2d ed. New York: Charles Scribner's Sons, 1973.

†Updates the author's 1965 survey of American religious history by including a study of the occult, the charismatic movement, the impact of Vatican II on contemporary Roman Catholicism, and other topics. 277.H86 1973

**Hutcheson, Richard G., Jr.** *Mainline Churches and the Evangelicals: A Challenging Crisis?* Atlanta: John Knox Press, 1981.

With mainline denominations declining in membership and influence, Hutcheson probes for the cause. His insights are provocative and should be discussed by clergy, laypeople, and seminarians. 280.4.AM3.H97

**Hutchinson, William R.** *The Modernist Impulse in American Protestantism.* Cambridge, Mass.: Harvard University Press, 1976.

Traces the history of liberal thought from 1870 to the 1930s and shows the close connection between philosophical liberalism and Protestant modernism. Should be read in the light of Dollar's *History of Fundamentalism in America.* 273'.9.H97

**Inch, Morris Alton.** *The Evangelical Challenge.* Philadelphia: Westminster Press, 1978.

Describes the distinctive features of evangelicalism. Includes a careful consideration of the place of evangelism in missions, ecumenism, social action, politics, and culture. Opens up to readers the possibilities of effecting change in these areas. Stimulating. 270.82.IN2

**Ironside, Henry Allan.** *A Historical Sketch of the Brethren Movement.* Neptune, N.J.: Loizeaux Brothers, 1985.

First published in 1942, this book covers an often overlooked and much misunderstood aspect of Christian history. Ironside interacts with the writings of others—pro and con—and succeeds in providing a balanced treatment of the movement that clarifies the distinctives of the Plymouth Brethren. Recommended. 289.9.IR6 1985

**Jones, Charles Edwin.** *A Guide to the Study of the Pentecostal Movement.* 2 vols. ATLA bibliography series. Metuchen, N.J.: Scarecrow Press, 1983.

Both religious and social researchers will find this comprehensive bibliographic guide indispensable. The four-part work includes historical information concerning churches, associations, evangelistic and missionary organizations, schools, and also evaluations of the movement both pro and con. More than 6,000 entries are included. 016.2708.J71

**\*Jones, James William.** *The Shattered Synthesis: New England Puritanism Before the Great Awakening.* New Haven, Conn.: Yale University Press, 1973.

An important assessment of the issues the Puritans faced and the manner in which these issues were handled. 974.4'02.J71

**Katsh, Abraham Isaac.** *The Biblical Heritage of American Democracy.* New York: Ktav Publishing House, 1977.

This important treatise traces the roots of democracy to the impact of the Hebrew Bible on Western civilization and culture. Katsh's discussion of the issues is excellent. We applaud his efforts and are grateful for his insights. 973.2.K15

**Kauffman, J. Howard,** and **Leland Harder.** *Anabaptists Four Centuries Later: A Profile of Five Mennonite and Brethren in Christ Denominations.* Scottdale, Pa.: Herald Press, 1975.

Based on the findings of the "Church Member Profile" representing 70 percent of the total Anabaptist membership, these studies present a discerning analysis of their present beliefs, spiritual awareness, and Christian commitment. 289.7'73.K16

**Keeley, Robin, ed.** *Christianity in Today's World.* Grand Rapids: Wm. B. Eerdmans Publishing Co., 1985.

Written by sixty-three specialists drawn from six continents, this reference work gives the insider's view of what it means to be a Christian. More than 200 photographs illumine the places, people, and differing aspects of Christianity in diverse parts of the world. Twenty-five diagrams and maps assist readers to understand the key ideas and movements that are part and parcel of the growth of the church. Fully indexed. 270.8'29.K24

**Kelley, Dean M.** *Why Conservative Churches Are Growing.* New York: Harper & Row, 1972.

A sociological study of the attitudes (rather than the doctrines and practices) of conservative churches, including Mormons and other sects. Lacks an understanding of theological distinctives and fails to discriminate where cultic groups are concerned. Needs to be read in light of Murch's *The Protestant Revolt.* 280.7.K28

**Kirk, J. Andrew.** *The Good News of the Kingdom Coming: The Marriage of Evangelism and Social Responsibility.* Downers Grove, Ill.: InterVarsity Press, 1985.

First published in England under the title *A New World Coming,* this historical, sociological, and theological approach to cross-cultural evangelism lays a foundation for the assumption of human responsibility in the propagation of the gospel. Kirk provides his readers with a well-reasoned, wide-ranging discussion that, for all its merit, lacks a solid biblical foundation. 270.8'2.K63

**Kraybill, P., ed.** *Mennonite World Handbook.* Lombard, Ill.: Mennonite World Conference, 1978.

A compact guide to the many and varied aspects of ministry carried on by Mennonites throughout the world. 289.7.M52K 1978

**Lawrence, Carl.** *The Church in China.* Minneapolis: Bethany House Publishers, 1985.

"This moving story . . . marks the end of one age and the beginning of another. It tells of a dramatic new power available for world evangelization. Until [recently] the spread of the Christian faith was done primarily by the spoken word. . . . This process has been speeded up by a second means, the written/printed word.

. . . During the past twenty years, however, in China these two means of spreading the gospel have been greatly assisted by radio broadcasts" (Donald A. McGavran). And that is the story of this book. 275.1'082.L41

**Loetscher, Lefferts A.,** and **George Laird Hunt.** *A Brief History of the Presbyterians.* 4th ed. Philadelphia: Westminster Press, 1983.

A useful introductory work to this aspect of Christian history. Well documented. 285.L82 1983

**London, Herbert Ira,** and **Albert L. Weeks.** *Myths That Rule America.* Washington, D.C.: University Press of America, 1981.

A candid look at American life and culture based on an astute assessment of our contemporary milieu. 303.3'72.L84

**\*Marquart, Kurt E.** *Anatomy of an Explosion: A Theological Analysis of the Missouri Synod Conflict.* Grand Rapids: Baker Book House, 1978.

A clear, concise explanation of the gradual and almost imperceptible encroachment of theological liberalism within this denomination with an account of the radical purge that sent shock waves throughout the nation. History shows that such institutions tend to erode from within. The action taken by the Lutheran Church Missouri Synod is the first such reversal of such a trend in modern history. What Marquart has presented provides outsiders with an objective account of an often misunderstood and sometimes maligned saga. 284.1322.M34

**Mather, Cotton.** *The Great Works of Christ in America: "Magnalia Christi Americana."* 2 vols. Edinburgh: Banner of Truth Trust, 1979.

First published in 1702, this work provides an ecclesiastical history of New England from the founding of the first colony to 1698. A memoir of Cotton Mather is included. A valuable piece of Americana. 277.4.M42G 1979

**Mathews, Donald G.** *Religion in the Old South.* Chicago: University of Chicago Press, 1977.

Traces the rise of white Protestantism in the Old South between 1750 and 1860. Emphasizes the sociology of that era more than the theology. Contains some good information on the growth and development of black Christianity during that period. 277.5.M42

**Miller, Glenn T.** *Religious Liberty in America: History and Prospects.* Philadelphia: Westminster Press, 1976.

Recounts the saga of religious liberty from colonial times to the present. Pays special attention to the changing social climate in which freedom has had to be maintained. 323.44'2.M61

**Miller, Perry.** *The New England Mind: From Colony to Province.* Cambridge, Mass.: Harvard University Press, 1983.

First appeared in 1953. This work is noted for its "depth and thoroughness [which is] matched only by the clarity and wit of [Miller's] presentation. Few scholars would have had the patience for such an investigation; even fewer could have made their results delightful and absorbing reading" *(New York Times Book Review).* 974.M61F 1983

―――. *The New England Mind: The Seventeenth Century.* Cambridge, Mass.: Harvard University Press, 1982.

First published in 1939, this work has received plaudits from many sources. Henry Nash Smith described it as "an authoritative description of Puritanism, the most subtle and most fully coherent intellectual system which has ever functioned as the official code of an American regional society. . . . the book is the best single illustration of what is meant by 'the history of ideas' as a method of dealing with American materials." 974'.02.M61N 1982

**\*Montgomery, John Warwick.** *The Shaping of America.* Minneapolis: Bethany Fellowship, 1976.

Issued specifically for the bicentennial, this timely treatise describes the American character—both good and bad—and issues a prophetic call to the nation to return to the principles of righteousness and godliness that made America great. 200'.AM3.M76

**Murray, John.** *Collected Writings of John Murray.* In process. Edinburgh: Banner of Truth Trust, 1976-.

Long overdue. These writings from the pen of John Murray cover bibliology, Christology, the history of Westminster Seminary, the Christian life, moral law, the church, and his lectures on systematic theology. Volume 3 contains a biographical sketch together with letters and other papers of theological significance. Readers of these volumes will find that they are filled with interest (e.g., a critique of William Barclay's views of the virgin birth, the possibility of a Christian world order, Christian education, etc.). The appearance of these volumes is welcomed. It is hoped that the others will be forthcoming soon. 285.1.M96

**\*Neal, Daniel.** *The History of the Puritans.* 3 vols. Minneapolis: Klock & Klock Christian Publishers, 1979.

Reprinted from the latest edition and containing critical notes, this outstanding presentation of Protestant nonconformity (from 1517 to 1688) delineates the course of action taken by those dubbed Puritan, describes the seeds of liberty and democracy that they spread and that lie latent in their history and teachings, and presents a vivid picture of the effect of their stand for the truth. This is an excellent work and is welldeserving of careful study. The benefits of reading these volumes is too great to be tabulated here. We can only hope that a new generation of men and women who are loyal to the Lord and His Word will peruse these pages to their own great profit. 285.3.N25 1979

**Neill, Stephen Charles.** *Anglicanism.* 4th ed. New York: Oxford University Press, 1978.

Surveys the history, organization, and spirit of Anglicanism. This edition differs little from its predecessors except for a twenty-one-page epilogue. 283.N31 1978

**Nelson, E. Clifford, ed.** *The Lutherans in North America.* Philadelphia: Fortress Press, 1975.

This history of Lutheranism in North America covers the period from 1650 to the present. It is the most modern treatment available. 284'.173.N33

**Noll, Mark A., ed.** *Eerdmans Handbook to Christianity in America.* Grand Rapids: Wm. B. Eerdmans Publishing Co., 1983.

The book tells the story of individual Christian leaders, the organized church, and the popular movements. It is about Christians as believers and Christians as behavers. It describes their faith, culture, and the nation to which they belong. The editor's narrative is supplemented by essays on people and movements. It also contains numerous references to documents. The sixty-five contributors are all men of distinction and represent a broad spectrum academically, geographically, and theologically. 277.3.EE7N

**Noll, Mark A., Nathan O. Hatch,** and **George M. Marsden.** *The Search for Christian America.* Westchester, Ill.: Crossway Books, 1983.

Believing, and rightly so, that the key to understanding the present lies in the past, the authors provide their readers with a realistic approach to the true nature of America's spiritual heritage. Recommended. 277.N72

**O'Conner, Edward Dennis.** *The Pentecostal Movement in the Catholic Church.* Notre Dame, Ind.: Ava Maria Press, 1971.

A modern assessment of the impact of the tongues movement on the Roman Catholic church. 282.OC5

**Pierson, Arthur Tappan.** *Forward Movements of the Last Half Century.* New York: Garland Publishing, 1984.

First published in 1900, this handy

historic volume reviews the philanthropic, missionary, and deeper life movements that were at the height of their power and influence during the latter part of the nineteenth century. 270.8'1.P61 1984

**Prince, Harold B., comp.** *A Presbyterian Bibliography*. ATLA Bibliography series, no. 8. Metuchen, N.J.: Scarecrow Press, 1983.

Librarians, historians, researchers, theologs, and others interested in studying the literary work of Southern Presbyterian ministers will find this bibliography invaluable. It contains 4,187 entries covering 1861-1961. Users will find in this volume a wealth of information for theses or dissertations. 016.285.P93

**Quebedeaux, Richard.** *The Worldly Evangelicals*. San Francisco: Harper & Row, 1978.

A contemporary evaluation of changes within evangelical circles. Quebedeaux, who identifies himself as a neo-evangelical, has directed his special talents to an evaluation of the evangelical movement. He uses Niebuhr's fivefold model for his analysis of where certain leaders stand in their relation to Christ and culture. What he presents makes stimulating reading, even though Quebedeaux's theology is not in accord with the men he is critiquing. 270.82.Q3W

**Ramsden, William E.** *The Church in a Changing Society*. Nashville: Abingdon Press, 1980.

Another work sponsored by the United Methodist Church, assessing change within society and charting a course for the church in the coming decades. Serves as a model for other organizations. 287.673.R14

**Rifkin, Jeremy,** and **Ted Howard.** *The Emerging Order: God in the Age of Scarcity*. New York: G. P. Putnam's Sons, 1979.

"An exciting, fascinating book. . . . provides a blue print for the economic

and spiritual challenges facing the Christian community in the remainder of this century. Rifkin dramatically illuminates the wayward self-destructive course of modern society's values and points to the potential saving role that can be played by people of faith. . . . I trust that Evangelicals in particular will put it at the top of their reading lists" (Senator Mark Hatfield). 277.3.R44

**Robinson, David, ed.** *William Ellery Channing: Selected Writings*. New York: Paulist Press, 1985.

Robinson provides an excellent historical and interpretative essay on Channing's life, intellectual development, and influence. In his view, Channing's works are still fresh, and an understanding of them can help readers appreciate Channing's place in America's cultural development. He neglects Channing's influence on the rise of Unitarianism, opposition to Jonathan Edwards, and the effects his beliefs had on the obscuring of the gospel. It is hoped that this book will stimulate interest in the writings of the conservatives of the period. If this happens then Robinson's book will have fulfilled a beneficial purpose. 277.C36.R56

**Rowe, H. Edward.** *Save America!* Old Tappan, N.J.: Fleming H. Revell Co., 1976.

Outlines the specific ways Christians can exert a positive influence on those around them and challenges believers to stay abreast of, and become involved in, political, social, and cultural concerns. 209'.73.R79

**Rowe, Kenneth E.** *Methodist Union Catalog: Pre-1976 Imprints*. 20 vols. In process. Metuchen, N.J.: Scarecrow Press, 1975-.

A repertory of catalogued holdings on Methodism in more than two hundred libraries in the U.S., Canada, the United Kingdom, and the Continent. 016.287.R79

**Schaeffer, Francis August.** *The Great Evangelical Disaster.* Westchester, Ill.: Crossway Books, 1984.

Continuing the theme found in all of Schaeffer's books, namely, the lordship of Christ in the totality of life, this work restates and reapplies some of the ideas and themes from earlier works. Designed for use with the film of the same title. 277.3.SCH1

**Shaw, Bynum.** *Divided We Stand; The Baptists in American Life: A History.* Durham, N.C.: Moore Publishing Co., 1974.

An account of the origins of the Baptist church in America and its impact on American life and institutions. 286'.0973.SH2

**Simonson, Harold P.** *Jonathan Edwards: Theologian of the Heart.* Grand Rapids: Wm. B. Eerdmans Publishing Co., 1974.

A brilliant literary and theological analysis of one of America's leading figures. Draws principles from Edwards's messages and applies them to the needs of the present hour. 285.8'73.ED9.SI5

**Springer, Nelson P.,** and **A. J. Klassen,** comps. *Mennonite Bibliography, 1631-1961.* 2 vols. Scottdale, Pa.: Herald Press, 1977.

Contains 28,155 entries. Continues the *Bibliography of Anabaptism, 1520-1630,* by H. J. Hillerbrand. Includes journal articles, books, pamphlets, dissertations, and the like. Of value to researchers and students of church history who are looking for a suitable dissertation topic. 016.289'7.SP8

**Stoeffer, F. Ernest.** *German Pietism During the Eighteenth Century.* Studies in the History of Religions. Leiden: E. J. Brill, 1973.

An indispensable introduction to the influence of A. H. Francke, P. J. Spener, Count Zinzendorf, and many others who infused new life into a dull and seemingly lifeless orthodoxy. 274.3.ST6

————. *The Rise of Evangelical Piety.* Studies in the History of Religions. Leiden: E. J. Brill, 1971.

Traces American Protestantism's indebtedness to the Pietistic movement and culls an abundance of information in support of his thesis from the writings by and about the Founding Fathers as well as the books they brought with them. Insightful. 277.ST6

**Strayer, Joseph Reese.** *The Albigensian Crusades.* New York: Dial Press, Inc. 1971.

A well-written, informative account of this cruel and yet significant persecution of the medieval dissenters. 284.4.ST8

**Sullivan, Francis A.** *Charisms and Charismatic Renewal: A Biblical and Theological Study.* Ann Arbor, Mich.: Servant Books, 1982.

Treats a phenomenon that has made deep inroads into the Roman Catholic church. Includes a discussion of tongues, renewal, and healing. Unconvincing. 282.SU5

**Thompson, James.** *Tried As By Fire: Southern Baptists and the Religious Controversies of the 1920's.* Macon, Ga.: Mercer University Press, 1982.

A clear, carefully researched work showing how decisive the 1920s were in shaping the trends and theology of the SBC. A helpful critique to which all students of American religious history will be indebted. 286.132.T37

**Toon, Peter.** *Evangelical Theology, 1833-1856: A Response to Tractarianism.* Atlanta: John Knox Press, 1979.

A brilliant study of the Oxford Movement and the influence of Newman, Pusey, and Keble on early Tractarianism. 283.41.T6

**Towns, Elmer L.** *Is the Day of the Denomination Dead?* Nashville: Thomas Nelson Publishers, 1973.

Towns contends that although denominationalism may have made a contribution to the past, now urbanization, advancing technology, and a rapidly changing society make it more of a hindrance than a help to the advance of the gospel. He points, therefore, to sociological forces as the cause of denominational decline. It might have been more accurate to have advanced the theory that denominations have gone the way of their seminaries, and with theological liberalism increasing across the country, denominations have been weakened by internal feuding over cardinal doctrinal issues. People slowly began to lose confidence in their denominations and first one family and then another would leave to go to a place where they would receive food for their souls. What Towns has said is valid, but his book should be read along with Murch's *The Protestant Revolt* and Brown's *Protest of a Troubled Protestant.* 280.07′73.T66

**Tucker, William Edward,** and **Lester F. G. McAllister.** *Journey in Faith: A History of the Christian Church.* St. Louis: Bethany Press, 1975.

Traces the history of the Disciples of Christ from 1876 to the present. 286′.6.T79

**Turner, Harold W., ed.** *Bibliography of New Religious Movements in Primal Societies.* Vol. 1, Black Africa. Boston: G. K. Hall, 1977.

The first of a scheduled four-volume series, this work covers black Africa south of the Sahara. Other volumes will cover North America, Latin America and the Caribbean, and Asia and Oceania. Of importance to historians and missiologists. 016.2.T79 v.1

**Watson, Philip S., comp.** *The Message of the Wesleys: A Reader of Instruction and Devotion.* Grand Rapids: Francis Asbury Press, 1984.

Treats the specifics surrounding the Wesleyan doctrine of conversion, the process of growth in grace, and the way in which a person may prepare for eter-

nity. Samples the devotional literature of the Wesleys, and exhorts his readers to emulate their example. 287.W51.W29

**Watts, Michael R.** *The Dissenters.* Vol. 1, *From the Reformation to the French Revolution.* New York: Oxford University Press, 1978.

A full and complete treatment of this formative period of English and Welsh history. Covers the English Anabaptists, the emergence of the sixteenth-century Separatists, and later, in the seventeenth century, the rise of the Baptists, Quakers, and Presbyterians. A valuable addition to our knowledge of the free church movement. 274.1.W34

**Webber, Robert Eugene.** *Evangelicals on the Canterbury Trail.* Waco, Tex.: Word Books, 1985.

Deals with the phenomenon of evangelicals joining the Episcopal church. Chronicles the experiences of several who have made the switch and explains the attraction of the Anglical/ Episcopal church. 270.8′2.W38

**Wells, David F.,** and **John D. Woodbridge, eds.** *The Evangelicals.* Nashville: Abingdon Press, 1975.

†Apart from a few chapters by evangelicals, the majority of these essays are by men who have long been identified with the theological left. The emphasis is sociological and historical. 280′.4.AM3.W46

**Wells, William W.** *Welcome to the Family: An Introduction to Evangelical Christianity.* Downers Grove, Ill.: InterVarsity Press, 1979.

Beginning with the Bible, its origin, and principles of interpretation, Wells shows how in NT times believers became a part of a new community and were thus able to withstand adversity. In the history of the church, whenever persecution broke out, the same sense of belonging sustained believers. Wells continues to trace this familial theme through the Reformation to the present. He uses the sense of community to strengthen believers so that they will be able to reach out and help others. 280.4.W46

**Wesley, John.** *The Appeals to Men of Reason and Religion and Certain Related Open Letters.* Edited by Gerald R. Cragg. In process. New York: Oxford University Press, 1975-.

This new, critical edition of volume 2 of Wesley's Works forms part of a projected 34-volume series. When completed, the set will contain all of Wesley's original prose works (e.g., letters, sermons, journals, diaries) as well as his doctrinal writings. 287.442.W51 v.2

**Whitehead, John W.** *The Stealing of America.* Westchester, Ill.: Crossway Books, 1983.

Believing that the state and federal governments are encroaching on the freedom of American people, Whitehead, an attorney, demonstrates how secularism and bureaucracy have abrogated the foundation of the Constitution. Recommended. 277.W58

**Wood, J. E., Jr., ed.** *Baptists and the American Experience.* Valley Forge, Pa.: Judson Press, 1976.

Contains papers read at the National Bicentennial Convocation, January 12-15, 1976. Ties history to the needs of individuals. 286'.0973.B22

# BIOGRAPHY

**Almond, Philip C.** *Rudolf Otto: An Introduction to His Philosophical Theology.* Chapel Hill, N.C.: University of North Carolina Press, 1984.

Best known for his *Idea of the Holy*, Otto has been "discovered" belatedly by evangelicals. This biographical sketch helps readers interpret Otto's works in light of his philosophical presuppositions and personal growth. 200'.1.OT8.AL6

**Angoff, Charles, ed.** *Jonathan Edwards: His Life and Influence.* Cranbury, N.J.: Fairleigh Dickinson University Press, 1975.

The two papers that make up this brief book concentrate on the relationship of imagery (emotion) to analysis (reason) and evaluate Edwards's sermons as literature. Thought provoking. 285.8.ED9.AN4

**Ash, James L., Jr.** *Protestantism and the American University: An Intellectual Biography of William Warren Sweet.* Dallas: Southern Methodist University Press, 1982.

An appreciative review of the life, literary contribution, and impact on religion in America of W. W. Sweet. 277.3.SW3.AS3

**Ayling, Stanley.** *John Wesley.* Nashville: Abingdon Press, 1979.

A full-length portrait of the father of Methodism by an authority on eighteenth-century church history. Stimulating. 287.W51.AY4

**Bangs, Carl.** *Arminius: A Study in the Dutch Reformation.* Grand Rapids: Zondervan Publishing House, 1985.

A vivid portrait of the man and his background. Combines scholarship with lively writing style, and ably depicts the emergence of Arminius's theology. 284.92.AR5.B22 1985

**Barclay, William.** *A Spiritual Autobiography.* Grand Rapids: Wm. B. Eerdmans Publishing Co., 1975.

In this book, which is illustrated with quotations from a wide variety of literary sources, Barclay explains his belief in a universal salvation, theistic evolution, sin and suffering, work (on which he is particularly good), and the family and the home. His reminiscences make delightful reading and clarify for conservatives why this renowned Scot's theology has been viewed with a jaundiced eye. 285.241.B23

**Barker, Esther T.** *Lady Huntington,*

*Whitefield and the Wesleys.* Maryville, Tenn.: Esther T. Barker, 1984.

A fascinating volume about one of the remarkable women in the Wesleyan Reformation. This slender book does more than dramatize the phenomenal contributions of this laywoman; it also brings a fresh understanding of the ministry of John and Charles Wesley and George Whitefield. 287.H92.B24

**Beetz, Kirk H.** *Algernon Charles Swinburne: A Bibliography of Secondary Works, 1861-1980.* Metuchen, N.J.: Scarecrow Press, 1982.

Lists approximately 2,300 numbered works about Swinburne and his writings. The entries are arranged in chronological order, then by category—book, dissertation, periodical—and then alphabetically by author. Important events in Swinburne's life and significant primary publications are mentioned at the beginning of each year. Important secondary works are accompanied by annotations and/or commentary. Swinburne was no lover of Christianity and this bibliography will provide researchers with valuable information about his opinions as well as his genius as a man of letters. 016.821′8.SW6.B39

———. *Tennyson: A Bibliography, 1827-1982.* Metuchen, N.J.: Scarecrow Press, 1984.

Few authors have been studied in greater detail than Tennyson, a committed Christian. His writings have brought inspiration to people in all parts of the English-speaking world. Even the most careful reader, however, can become lost in the confusion of publications about this man and his writings. Hence this work. It catalogs more than 5,100 entries by year, then by category—book, dissertation, periodical—and then alphabetically by author. Book reviews of primary and secondary materials are included. 016.821′8.T25.B39

**Beidelman, T. O.** *W. Robertson Smith and the Sociological Study of Religion.* Chi-cago: University of Chicago Press, 1974.

Evidence of Smith's abiding influence may be found in this volume. Though his development of social anthropology has been superseded (and, in many respects, refined), he did chart a course for the study of the sociology of religion, and this biography provides the perspective of history on his labors. 200.SM6.B39

**Bergin, Joseph.** *Cardinal Richelieu: Power and the Pursuit of Wealth.* New Haven, Conn.: Yale University Press, 1985.

Drawing on a large body of previously unknown sources, Bergin reconstructs Richelieu's avarice for wealth, prestige, benefices, and all the other accoutrements of power. He also portrays him against the backdrop of his times, and this proves helpful as we try to ascertain the struggle for religious liberty that was waged at such cost. 944′.032.R39.B45

**Bockelman, Wilfred.** *Gothard: The Man and His Ministry.* London: Quill Publications, 1976.

An evaluative critique of the man behind the Basic Youth Conflicts seminars. 267.61.G71.B63

**Booth, Frank Carlton.** *On the Mountain Top.* Wheaton, Ill.: Tyndale House Publishers, 1984.

This humorous biographical sketch recalls eighty years of history, tells of the "greats" whom the author has known, and recounts the ministry Carlton Booth has had—a ministry, as he describes it, of "service and song." 270.8.B64

**Bornkamm, Heinrich.** *Luther in Mid-Career, 1521-1530.* Edited by K. Bornkamm. Translated by E. T. Bachmann. Philadelphia: Fortress Press, 1983.

Covering the years between Luther's thirty-seventh and forty-sixth birthdays, this work reflects the Reformer grappling with the consequences of his determination to preach the gospel—which he had championed at the Diet of Worms —and the events that elapsed between his translation of the NT (1521) and the publication of his two catechisms. 284.1.L97.B64 1983

**Brabazon, James.** *Albert Schweitzer: A Biography.* New York: G. P. Putnam and Sons, 1975.

A comprehensive, well-illustrated, interpretative biography based on extensive interviews and original research. 266'.025.SCH9.B72

**Brodie, Fawn (McKay).** *No Man Knows My History.* 2d rev. ed. New York: Alfred P. Knopf, 1971.

†The life story of Joseph Smith, the self-styled Mormon prophet. 289.3'09.B78 1971

**Bruce, Frederick Fyvie.** *In Retrospect: Remembrance of Things Past.* Grand Rapids: Wm. B. Eerdmans Publishing Co., 1980.

Brief chapters, partly historical and partly topical, in which Bruce recalls significant events throughout his long, scholarly career. Includes discourses on his friends, a discussion of his love of books, and a description of his literary activities. 286.542.B83

**Bryant, Arthur.** *Macaulay.* London: Weidenfeld and Nicholson, 1979.

A captivating biography of one of the great Victorian politicians who was also a man of letters, and a historian. There is much to learn from a consideration of Macaulay's life. He lived at a time in history when affairs of state called for greatness and the educational institutions of the day were capable of producing them. Bryant describes with verve and skill the process by which Macaulay achieved his well-deserved renown. 824.M11.B84

**Cairns, Earle E.** *V. Raymond Edman: In the Presence of the King.* Chicago: Moody Press, 1972.

The authorized biography of one of America's great Christian statesmen who served as a missionary in South America before becoming president of Wheaton College. 268.573.ED5.C12

**Chadwick, Henry.** *Priscillian of Avila:*

*The Occult and the Charismatic in the Early Church.* New York: Oxford University Press, 1976.

Focuses on the contribution of this misguided ascetic and the charismatic movement that sprang up about him. Carefully documented. 273.4.P93.C34

**Clements, Kendrick A.** *William Jennings Bryan: Missionary Isolationist.* Knoxville, Tenn.: University of Tennessee Press, 1982.

A severe critique of Bryan's views on international relations with an assessment of his desires for neutrality. Points out that Bryan conceived of keeping America out of World War I as his Christian duty so that America might set an example to the world. 973.91.B84.C59

**Colp, Ralph, Jr.** *To Be an Invalid: The Illness of Charles Darwin.* Chicago: University of Chicago Press, 1977.

By gleaning information from the state of medical research in Darwin's time and combining this with the psychology of stress, Colp, a psychiatrist, exposes the anxiety Darwin experienced as he contemplated the impact of his theory of natural selection on the scientific and religious world of his day. 575.016.D25.C71

**Conforti, Joseph A.** *Samuel Hopkins and the New Divinity Movement: Calvinism, the Congregational Ministry, and Reform in New England Between the Great Awakenings.* Grand Rapids: Wm. B. Eerdmans Publishing Co., 1981.

Marks a new and important advance in the interpretation of the impact of Jonathan Edwards's successors in New England. Shows how popular was the character and social impact of the movement, and describes the place and influence of Hopkins in the shaping of the cultural, social, and religious ideas of the day. 230.58.C76

**\*Coray, Henry W. J.** *Gresham Machen: A Silhouette.* Grand Rapids: Kregel Publications, 1981.

A brief, factual account of the life of

this remarkable evangelical scholar. 285.1'73.M18.C81

**\*Dallimore, Arnold A.** *George White-field: The Life and Times of the Great Evangelist of the Eighteenth Century Revival.* Vol. 2. Westchester, Ill.: Cornerstone Books, 1979.

At last, after several years of delay, the author has provided us with the concluding volume to his excellent treatment of Whitefield's life and labors. He picks up from where he left off in volume one and gives his readers numerous insights into Whitefield's friendship with the Wesleys. Dallimore also treats fairly the controversies that plagued Whitefield's later years, describes his evangelistic work on two continents, and succeeds in indelibly impressing his readers with Whitefield's love for the Lord and commitment to His service. An extensive bibliography is appended. Recommended. 285.873.W58D v.2

**\*_____.** *Spurgeon.* Chicago: Moody Press, 1984.

Although Spurgeon is often lauded by evangelicals today, few who hold him in such high honor fully understand his personality and the forces that made him great. That is Dallimore's goal—and he has executed his task with remarkable skill. 286.13.SP9.D16

**Darwin, Charles.** *The Collected Papers of Charles Darwin.* Edited by Paul H. Barrett. 2 vols. Chicago: University of Chicago Press, 1977.

Exposing the breadth of Darwin's interests, these papers provide insight into the way in which he analyzed problems. They demonstrate not only the logic of some of his theories, but the fallacies as well. 575.016.D25 1977

**Dobbins, Austin C.** *Gaines S. Dobbins: Pioneer in Religious Education.* Nashville: Broadman Press, 1981.

A brief biography chronicling the pioneer efforts of this great Southern Baptist educator. 286.132.D65

**Dodds, Elizabeth D.** *Marriage to a Diffi-*

*cult Man.* Philadelphia: Westminster Press, 1971.

An account of the "uncommon union" between Jonathan Edwards, the theologian, and Sarah Pierrepont, his saintly wife. 285.873.ED9D

**Doig, Desmond.** *Mother Teresa: Her People and Her Work.* San Francisco: Harper & Row, 1980.

First published in 1976, this touching book chronicles in pictures as well as words the life, labors, and accomplishments of Mother Teresa, a remarkable humanitarian and deserved winner of the Nobel Peace Prize. 266.2.T27.D68

**Drewery, Mary.** *William Carey: A Biography.* Grand Rapids: Zondervan Publishing House, 1979.

Discusses the crises, both spiritual and personal, of Carey's life and shares with readers a captivating account of his missionary vision and venture of faith. 266.6.C18.D82

**Dunker, Marilee Pierce.** *Man of Vision; Woman of Prayer.* Nashville: Thomas Nelson Publishers, 1980.

This is a candid, inside look at the lives of the author's parents, their ministry to underprivileged children around the world, and the pain of separation. Bob Pierce is best remembered for his involvement with World Vision and later The Samaritan's Purse. 269.2.P61.D92

**Edwards, Brian H.** *God's Outlaw.* Wheaton, Ill.: Tyndale House Publishers, 1981.

Published in England in 1976, this study of William Tyndale traces the vicissitudes of his life, and the ever-present opposition of those who sought opportunity to betray him. Also reflects on his indefatigable efforts to translate God's Word into English. Readers will find this a captivating work. It is to be warmly recommended. 283.42.T97.ED9

**\*Edwards, Jonathan.** *The Life of David Brainerd.* Vol. 7, *The Works of Jonathan Edwards.* Edited by N. Pettit. New Haven, Conn.: Yale University Press, 1985.

This is a rare, almost forgotten document depicting life in prerevolutionary America during the period when religious enthusiasm swept the frontier. From 1743 to 1747 Brainerd had been a missionary to the Indians. Riding thousands of miles alone on horseback, he kept a journal of his spiritual pilgrimage as well as a record of events as they transpired. He continued this practice until a week before his death at age twenty-nine. This edition of *Brainerd's Life* is complete, annotated, and well-deserving of repeated consultation. Highly recommended. 285.873.B73.ED9 1985

**Ehrlich, Leonard H.** *Karl Jaspers: Philosophy as Faith.* Amherst, Mass.: University of Massachusetts Press, 1975.

A definitive interpretation of Jaspers's thought that attempts to tone down his pessimism and emphasize instead the quality of his faith. 193.EH8

**Emery, Noemie.** *Alexander Hamilton: An Intimate Portrait.* New York: G. P. Putnam's Sons, 1982.

Recounts the colorful life of one of the most influential men of his time, and deals candidly with his tragedies as well as his triumphs. Breathes a spirit of such realism that readers cannot fail to be moved by the greatness of the man. 973.4.H18.EM3

**Endy, Melvin B.** *William Penn and Early Quakerism.* Princeton, N.J.: Princeton University Press, 1973.

A detailed examination of Penn's relationship with the Quakers and the development of his own religious convictions. Contains some surprising statements about the origin and development of the movement. 289.6.P37.EN2

**English, Eugene Schuyler.** *Ordained of the Lord: H. A. Ironside, a Biography.* Neptune, N.J.: Loizeaux Brothers, 1976.

This revision of the author's 1946 biography has been condensed and completely rewritten. It also includes new material from the latter years of Iron-

side's long and illustrious life. 269.2.IR6.EN3 1976

**Ericson, Edward E., Jr.** *Solzhenitsyn: The Moral Vision.* Grand Rapids: Wm. B. Eerdmans Publishing Co., 1980.

Written before the publication of *The Oak and the Calf,* this work traces Aleksandr Solzhenitsyn's life through his writings. The result is a valuable interpretative approach to the thinking of a man who understands the issues of the twentieth century from a unique perspective. Recommended. 891.73'44.ER4

**Ferguson, John.** *Clement of Alexandria.* New York: Twayne, 1974.

A brief survey of the life and times of this early church Father with an analysis of each of his major works. 270.1.C59.F38

**Finlay, Ian.** *Columba.* London: Victor Gollancz, 1979.

A scholarly recounting of the life and labors of Columba and of the missionary work that he began on the Island of Iona, by means of which he sought to evangelize England. 274.42.C72.F49

**Flood, Charles Bracelin.** *Lee: The Last Years.* Boston: Houghton, Mifflin Co., 1981.

Traces Robert E. Lee's emergence from defeat to his acceptance of the presidency of Washington College, and the development of a model of education that set the standard for other institutions for many years. Also shows how he spent his time trying to heal the national wounds left as a result of the Civil War. 973.8'1.L51.F65

**Fuller, Reginald C.** *Alexander Geddes, 1737-1802: Pioneer of Biblical Criticism.* Sheffield, England: Almond Press, 1984.

Based on the author's doctoral dissertation at Cambridge University, this biography assesses the importance and influence of Alexander Geddes on biblical scholarship. 220.6.G26.F95

**Gilbert, Martin.** *Winston Churchill: The Wilderness Years.* Boston: Houghton, Mifflin Co., 1982.

Reminds readers that even great men have had to endure opposition and defeat, slander and rejection. This recounting of Churchill's life from 1929 to 1939 is vital to an understanding of Churchill's character, but more important still, to a knowledge of how he coped with adversity without giving way to despair. 941'.082.C47.G37

**Goddard, Donald.** *The Last Days of Dietrich Bonhoeffer.* New York: Harper & Row, 1976.

A reconstruction of the last two years of this social reformer and theologian's life. 230.41.B64.G54

***Gordon, Ernest B.** *Adoniram Judson Gordon, a Biography.* New York: Garland Publishing, 1984.

A candid biography of one of the great evangelical leaders of the nineteenth century. As a pastor, conference speaker, missionary statesman, author, and advocate of biblical Christianity, Gordon had few peers. This work is based largely on his letters and sermons. 286.1.G65G

**Green, Roger Lancelyn,** and **Walter Hooper.** *C. S. Lewis: A Biography.* New York: Harcourt, Brace and Jovanovich, 1974.

The credentials of the authors provide an unbeatable merger for an accurate biography of the enigmatic Lewis coupled with an assessment of his writings. Green is an English scholar and author of children's books, and Hooper was Lewis's secretary. They combine their skills to provide an enlightening evaluation of the Oxford don's life, world, and work. 828'.9'1209.L58.G82

**Gundry, Stanley N.** *Love Them In: The Life and Theology of D. L. Moody.* Grand Rapids: Baker Book House, 1982.

First published in 1976, this dissertation reads well and reveals a great deal about the evangelist as well as the development of his beliefs. Excellent. 285.8.M77.G93 1982

**Hardesty, Nancy A.** *Great Women of the Faith: The Strength and Influence of Christian Women.* Grand Rapids: Baker Book House, 1980.

No one will dispute the adage that "the hand that rocks the cradle rules the world." In these brief, informative chapters readers are not only reminded of this fact but are given the impression that this book is really a vehicle for feminist propaganda. Disappointing. 922.H21

**Hefley, James C.,** and **Marti Hefley.** *Uncle Cam.* Waco, Tex.: Word Books, 1974.

A sympathetic presentation of William Cameron Townsend, founder of the Wycliffe Bible Translators/Summer Institute of Linguistics/Jungle Aviation Radio Service. Includes his many trials as well as the triumphs that he saw after long years of patient and persistent effort. Includes his reasons for working with Pentecostals as well as the many internal and external controversies that have plagued the mission. Makes an important contribution to our knowledge of the man and the work he started. 266'.023.T66.H36

**Heitzenrater, Richard P.** *The Elusive Mr. Wesley.* 2 vols. Nashville: Abingdon Press, 1984-1985.

This work deciphers Wesley's journals and discusses the role he played in the founding of Methodism. Included is a candid and revealing discussion of Wesley as seen by his contemporaries. 287.W51.H36

**Henry, Stuart C.** *Unvanquished Puritan.* Grand Rapids: Wm. B. Eerdmans Publishing Co., 1973.

A discerning discussion of Lyman Beecher and his famous family (including the authoress of *Uncle Tom's Cabin* and Isabelle Beecher—an early crusader for female liberation). 285.9.B39.H39

**Hindley, Geoffrey.** *Saladin.* New York: Barnes and Noble, 1976.

Church historians, and particularly those interested in the Crusades, will enjoy this fascinating study of the enigmatic Muslim leader of the Saracens whose wits and military daring was pitted against the best that Europe could muster. 956'.01.SA3.H58

**Hopkins, C. Howard.** *John R. Mott, 1865-1955: A Biography.* Grand Rapids: Wm. B. Eerdmans Publishing Co., 1979.

Stressing the ecumenical influence of Mott, his biographer also describes how the provincial Midwestern youth became one of the most influential men of his generation. Includes accounts of Mott's struggles, failures, and successes. Omits Mott's contribution to evangelical Christianity—and in that we have the book's greatest weakness. 267'.392.M85.H77

**Hunter, Archibald Macbride.** *P. T. Forsyth.* Philadelphia: Westminster Press, 1974.

A brief but important monograph on the theological contribution of one of the great leaders in the Congregational church in England. 285.8.F77.H91

**Hunter, Ian.** *Malcolm Muggeridge: A Life.* Nashville: Thomas Nelson Publishers, 1980.

Published before Muggeridge embraced Romanism, this biographical sketch traces the fascinating saga of his varied and colorful life. Describes his conversion from agnosticism to Christianity, and the events and books that followed. Well researched; provocative. 070.92'4.M89.H92

**Hutton, Richard Holt.** *Cardinal Newman.* 2d ed. New York: AMS Press, 1977.

This warmly appreciative study of Newman concentrates on recounting the events of his life before leaving the Anglican church. 262.135.N46.H97 1977.

**Iacocca, Lee,** and **William Novak.** *Iacocca: An Autobiography.* New York: Bantam Books, 1984.

A fascinating self-portrait of a uniquely gifted entrepreneur. Offers a compelling and thought-provoking assessment of American business, ably illustrated with contemporary examples of good and bad managerial practices. Pastors will find many sermon illustrations between these covers, and Christian leaders have much to learn from the principles that Iacocca presents. 658.IA1

**Jenkins, Peter,** and **Barbara Jenkins.** *The Road Unseen.* Nashville: Thomas Nelson Publishers, 1985.

The authors of the national bestsellers, *A Walk Across America* and *The Walk West*, discuss their Christian faith—and what it meant to them on their journeys. In doing so, they describe what it was like to struggle with nature and themselves; know weariness and fatigue, hunger and the need for rest; and look to God for guidance and to the American people whom they met for encouragement and hope. Included in this volume are previously untold stories of their adventures, plus how the Lord continues to work in their lives. 248.2.J41U

————. *The Walk West: A Walk Across America 2.* New York: William Morrow and Co., 1981.

This sequel to the national bestseller, *A Walk Across America,* describes Peter Jenkins's conversion and marriage. It chronicles the journey he and his wife took as they went on foot from New Orleans to Florence, Oregon, with only one book (the Bible) and the belongings they could carry on their backs. A stimulating work. 917.3.J41 v.2

**Kaplan, Fred.** *Thomas Carlyle: A Biography.* Ithaca, N.Y.: Cornell University Press, 1983.

This major new biography provides a modern interpretation of Carlyle's life and scholarship. Kaplan deals with a vast body of materials, published and unpublished, and out of them shapes a comprehensive and credible study of the man and his contribution to Scottish society and world literature. 824.8.C19.K14

**Kelly, Henry Ansgar.** *The Matrimonial Trials of Henry VIII.* Stanford, Calif.: Stanford University Press, 1976.

Based on much hitherto unknown or unexplored documentary evidence, this volume treats the canonical and procedural questions involved in the trials. Demonstrates how Henry sought to justify himself in public and in private, and records his wrestlings with his conscience. 262.9'35.K29

**\*Kelly, John Norman.** *Jerome: His Life, Writings, and Controversies.* New York: Harper & Row, 1975.

A work of unsurpassed excellence. Historically, theologically, and psychologically accurate. Contains a mine of valuable information. 270.2.J48.K29

**Koob, Kathryn.** *Guest of the Revolution.* Nashville: Thomas Nelson Publishers, 1982.

Recounts the saga of one of the hostages in Tehran during the Carter administration. The story is complete with little known facts about the circumstances of the Americans imprisoned in Iran for 444 days. 955'.054.K83

**LeJoly, Edward.** *Mother Teresa of Calcutta: A Biography.* San Francisco: Harper & Row, 1983.

A richly detailed, full biography based on private conversations. Reveals her remarkable courage and dedication. Makes inspiring reading. 271.97.T27.L53

**Lockerbie, D. Bruce.** *A Man Under Orders: Lieutenant General William K. Harrison, Jr.* San Francisco: Harper & Row, 1979.

The inspiring story of a Christian who knew and worked with the great men of his era, served his country in the best tradition of an American gentleman,

and whose goal as a believer was to continually exemplify the grace of God. 355.3'31.H24.L79

**Longford, Elizabeth.** *The Life of Byron.* Boston: Little, Brown and Co., 1976.

Graphically portrays Byron's political and romantic misfortunes, as she also describes his unexcelled literary ability. Shares with readers the results of his misguided genius and strange complex emotions. 821.7.B99.L86

**Ludwig, Charles.** *Francis Asbury: God's Circuit Rider.* Milford, Mich.: Mott Media, 1984.

"This is more than a fascinating historical narrative; it is the moving experience of a man determined 'to live for God, and to bring others so to do.' Reading the account can not help but inspire one to higher vision and nobler action" (Robert E. Coleman). 287.173.AS1L

**Marshall, George M.,** and **David Poling.** *Schweitzer: A Biography.* Garden City, N.Y.: Doubleday and Co., 1971.

A sympathetic study of the doctor of Lambarene. 276.72.SCH9

**Martin, Brian.** *John Henry Newman: His Life and Work.* New York: Oxford University Press, 1982.

Newman contributed greatly to education, theology, hymnology, and the growth of the Roman Catholic Church in England. This book reflects on his accomplishments and seeks to preserve for posterity something of the vigor that characterized his life. Well illustrated. 282.42.N46.M36

**Martin, Linette.** *Hans Rookmaker: A Biography.* Downers Grove, Ill.: InterVarsity Press, 1979.

A fascinating portrayal of a Dutch art critic, theologian, and sociologist, whose many fine publications have enriched our Western heritage. 739.R67.M36

**McFeely, William S.** *Grant: A Biography.* New York: W. W. Norton and Co., 1981.

A remarkable story of a country boy who became an outstanding general and, later, this nation's president. Shows how the Civil War developed his unique leadership skills so that he was respected by all who knew him and admired even by those who had only heard of his daring exploits. This book, more so than any other, unfolds Grant's personality. 973.8'2.G76.M16

**Middlekauff, Robert.** *The Mathers: Three Generations of Puritan Intellectuals, 1596-1728.* New York: Oxford University Press, 1971.

A comprehensive treatment based on a careful consideration of primary source material. 285.973.M58

**Miller, Perry.** *Jonathan Edwards.* Amherst, Mass.: University of Massachusetts Press, 1981.

First published in 1949. This definitive study of the life and thought of Jonathan Edwards (1703-1758) remains one of the best ever written. Miller, however, is not of the same theological conviction as Edwards, and as a result he lacks sympathy with his subject in this area. 285.8.ED9.M61 1981

**Milmine, Georgine.** *The Life of Mary Baker G. Eddy and the History of Christian Science.* Grand Rapids: Baker Book House, 1971.

A thorough exposé of the origin and teachings of Christian Science. Reprinted from the 1909 edition. 289.573.ED2M 1971

**Mitchell, Curtis.** *Billy Graham: Saint or Sinner?* Old Tappan, N.J.: Fleming H. Revell Co., 1979.

Probes the allegations leveled against the evangelist and his association; vindicates him on all counts. 269.2.G76.M69

**Monod, James L.** *Prophet and Peacemaker: The Life of Adolphe Monod.* Lanham, Md.: University Press of America, 1984.

This scholarly study of a leading figure in the French Reformed church chronicles Monod's quest for truth. This led to his abandonment of the Enlightenment and conversion as a result of Robert Haldane's teaching on the epistle to the Romans. The rest is a history of his remarkable life and service. 274.4.M75.OS2

**Montgomery, Elizabeth Ryder.** *Albert Schweitzer, Great Humanitarian.* Champaign, Ill.: Garrard Publishing Co., 1971.

A biography of a musician, theologian, and educator who relinquished a comfortable teaching career in order to become a missionary doctor in the jungles of Africa. 276.72.SCH9M

**Moore, John Allen.** *Anabaptist Portraits.* Scottdale, Pa.: Herald Press, 1984.

A valuable excursus into the past, providing readers with a pleasing portrait of some Anabaptist Reformers. 284.3.M78

**Morrow, Honore Willsie.** *Splendor of God: The Life of Adoniram Judson.* Grand Rapids: Baker Book House, 1982.

First published in 1929, this missionary biography recounts the struggles of Adoniram Judson and his talented and dedicated wife, Ann. Also catalogs the accomplishments of this couple as together they worked to establish the gospel in Burma. This record of their unremitting sacrifice serves to encourage others to persevere even as they did. 275.91.J92.M83

**Muir, Edwin.** *John Knox: Portrait of a Calvinist.* Freeport, N.Y.: Books for Libraries Press, 1971.

A revealing book. Well written. Reprinted from the 1929 edition. 284.241.K77.M89 1971

**Murray, Iain Hamish.** *Arthur W. Pink: His Life and Thought.* Edinburgh: Banner of Truth Trust, 1981.

A laudacious work that still meets the need for a suitable biography of this great man of God. 230'.09.P65.M96

**Murray, William J.** *My Life Without God.*

Nashville: Thomas Nelson Publishers, 1982.

The son of atheist Madalyn Murray O'Hair speaks out about his home life, relationship with his mother, and conversion to Christianity. On his conversion, he gave up drugs, smuggling, and left-wing causes for the emotional stability of a relationship with Christ. 248.24.M96

**Neely, Lois.** *Fire in His Bones: The Official Biography of Oswald J. Smith.* Wheaton, Ill.: Tyndale House Publishers, 1982.

An intimate glimpse into the life of a man of God whose ministry has spanned seven decades and who has been a prime mover in the cause of Christian missions. 285.2'71.SM6.N29

**Olsen, Viggo,** and **Jeanette Lockerbie.** *Daktar: Diplomat of Bangladesh.* Chicago: Moody Press, 1973.

An exciting study of the life of a dedicated medical missionary among the poor of Pakistan before Bangladesh became the world's 147th nation. 954.9'205.OL8

**\*Owen, George Frederick.** *Abraham Lincoln: The Man and His Faith.* Wheaton, Ill.: Tyndale House Publishers, 1981.

Originally published under the title *The Heart That Yearned for God,* this clear, concise biographical sketch is permeated with new insights into Lincoln's character and convictions. 973.7.OW2 1981

**\*Parker, Thomas Henry Louis.** *John Calvin: A Biography.* Philadelphia: Westminster Press, 1975.

A definitive account of Calvin's life and labors with special attention being paid to Calvin's doctrine, writings, and influence. 230'.42.C13.P22

**Petillo, Carol Morris.** *Douglas MacArthur: The Philippine Years.* Bloomington, Ind.: Indiana University Press, 1981.

Points out that for more than a quarter century MacArthur's professional career

was spent in the Philippine Islands. Describes his growing influence as well as the complex relationships he formed. A revealing biography of a great, though enigmatic, man. 959.9'03.M11.P44

**\*Phillips, John Bertram.** *The Price of Success: An Autobiography.* Wheaton, Ill.: Harold Shaw Publishers, 1984.

An amazingly candid, factual account of the life of the man who gave to the world *Letters to Young Churches* and then continued to popularize the need for a paraphrase of the Bible. Warm, at times witty, and always honest, this is the kind of work that both inspires and edifies. 283.3.P54

**Phillips, Vera,** and **Edwin H. Robertson.** *J. B. Phillips: The Wounded Healer.* Grand Rapids: Wm. B. Eerdmans Publishing Co., 1984.

In this book Phillips's widow and his close friend Edwin Robertson have drawn on their biographee's vast correspondence to produce a sensitive and revealing account of a well-loved pastor and author. The book reveals the private turmoil Phillips endured, even while continuing to minister to others. 283.3.P54P

**Poling, David.** *Why Billy Graham?* Grand Rapids: Zondervan Publishing House, 1977.

Analyzes Graham's impact on people, foreign policy, and the media. Concludes that his success can be attributed to his love for people. 269.2.G76.P75

**Pollock, John Charles.** *A Foreign Devil in China.* Grand Rapids: Zondervan Publishing House, 1971.

The biography of Dr. Nelson Bell, Southern Presbyterian missionary to China from 1916 to 1941. 275.1.P76

———. *Amazing Grace: John Newton's Story.* San Francisco: Harper & Row, 1981.

A delightful and compelling biography of the prodigal who became a dedicated servant of Christ and one of Christianity's finest hymnwriters. 283.3.N48.P76

**\*Potter, George Richard.** *Zwingli.* New York: Cambridge University Press, 1977.

Based on primary and secondary resource material, this scholarly study of the life and beliefs of the Swiss Reformer sheds light on his writings, the controversies of his times, and the way in which he affected subsequent history. 270.6.Z9.P85

**Rawlins, Clive L.** *William Barclay: The Authorized Biography.* Grand Rapids: Wm. B. Eerdmans Publishing Co., 1984.

"Now we can learn what kind of man William Barclay was, and what the influences were which directed his life and thought. Mr. Rawlins has given us an authoritative account of a great man" (F. F. Bruce). 285.2.B23.R19

**Rayburn, James, III.** *Dance, Children, Dance.* Wheaton, Ill.: Tyndale House Publishers, 1984.

This is the story of the founder of Young Life. "From our first meeting to the last [Rayburn] was for me the prototype of what a servant of Christ should be. He relished life. His gutsy courage was legendary. His ability to communicate the love of God in Christ was simply incomparable" (Richard C. Halverson). 259.8.R21

**Read, David H. C.** *This Grace Given.* Grand Rapids: Wm. B. Eerdmans Publishing Co., 1984.

In tracing the hand of God as it shaped his life, Read looks back over the first period of his life—from his birth in 1910 to the end of World War II—and reminisces over his ancestry, childhood, religious impressions, passion for travel, education in the U.K. as well as on the Continent, and wartime experiences as a chaplain held prisoner by the Germans. This is a very humane account and makes stimulating reading. It is hoped the narrative will be furthered by a later volume. 285.1.R22

**Reid, William Sanford.** *John Calvin: His Influence in the Western World.* Grand Rapids: Zondervan Publishing House, 1982.

A festschrift in honor of Paul Wooley. The essays cover the impact of the Genevan Reformer on the theology and culture of the West. 284.2.C13.R27

**Ridley, Jasper.** *Henry VIII.* New York: Viking Press, 1985.

The dust cover carries the subtitle *The Politics of Tyranny.* Ridley chronicles the changes in English political and social life during Henry's thirty-seven year reign. His is a detailed and revealing account. 942.05'2.H39.R43

**\*Roberts, W. Dayton.** *Strachan of Costa Rica: Missionary Insights and Strategies.* Grand Rapids: Wm. B. Eerdmans Publishing Co., 1971.

Traces the mental and spiritual development of Kenneth Strachen's ideas and the origin of Evangelism-in-Depth. 277.286.ST8R

**Ruffin, Bernard.** *Fanny Crosby.* Philadelphia: United Church Press, 1976.

An important and needed book that, in addition to treating the life of one of America's beloved songwriters, also provides sidelights on the status of religious life in the late nineteenth and early twentieth centuries. 811'.4.R83

**Running, Leona Glidden,** and **David Noel Freedman.** *William Foxwell Albright: A Twentieth-Century Genius.* New York: Two Continents Publishing Group, 1975.

A sympathetic and discerning tribute to a man who spent his life opening up the OT and NT to a new generation of Bible students. 220.93.AL1.R87

**Rupp, Gordon.** *Thomas More: The King's Good Servant.* London: William Collins, 1978.

Describes Sir Thomas's place in the England of Henry VIII. Reveals his devotion to the Catholic Church, influence on learning, and loyalty to the crown. 283.3.M81.R87

**Ryun, James,** and **Michael Phillips.** *In Quest of Gold: The Jim Ryun Story.* San Francisco: Harper & Row, 1984.

His life is replete with triumph and tragedy, days of sunshine as well as periods of gloom, fame as well as obscurity. Here is his story, and it is worth reading. 796.4.R99.P54

**Sage, Michael M.** *Cyprian.* Cambridge, Mass.: Philadelphia Patristic Foundation, 1975.

This careful examination of the ecclesiastical milieu of the third century A.D. clarifies the context of Cyprian's writings and uses what he wrote to illumine this obscure period of Roman history. 270.1.C99.SA1

**Sandmel, Samuel.** *Philo of Alexandria.* New York: Oxford University Press, 1978.

Assesses the place of Philo in Alexandrian Jewry, scholarship, and influence on early Christian theology. A valuable contribution. 932.P54.SA5

**Schaeffer, Edith.** *The Tapestry: The Life and Times of Francis and Edith Schaeffer.* Waco, Tex.: Word Books, 1981.

A warm, intimate look at a couple who have endeared themselves to thousands of people in every country of the world. Records the good times as well as the bad, the seasons of blessing as well as the trials they endured, and shows how they triumphed through faith and perseverance in doing what they believed to be right. 285.1.SCH1S

**Schurmann, Reiner.** *Meister Eckhart, Mystic and Philosopher: Translations and Commentary.* Bloomington, Ind.: Indiana University Press, 1978.

Uses quotations from Eckhart's writings to clarify his thought and explain the development of his views. 193.EC5.SCH8

**Shackleton, Ernest.** *Shackleton.* His Arctic Writings Selected and Introduced by Christopher Ralling. London: British Broadcasting Corporation, 1983.

Exemplifies the daring of great men of the past. Abounds with anecdotes and homiletic illustrations. Enhanced with maps, black-and-white and color photographs. Is the record of one of the most daring ventures of all time. 914.2.SH1R

**Skinner, John.** *Journal of a Somerset Rector, 1803-1834.* Edited by H. and P. Coombs. New York: Oxford University Press, 1984.

Skinner is known to students of the OT for his commentaries. Few, however, are aware of his years spent as a pastor. This work concentrates attention on his family and his work. It is a revealing portrait. 914.23′8.SK3 1984

**Smith, Warren Thomas.** *Augustine: His Life and Thought.* Atlanta: John Knox Press, 1980.

Ably combines biographical facts relating to Augustine's life with the history of the times and the development of his beliefs. Scholarly, readable, stimulating. 281.4.AU4.SM6

**Smith, Wilbur Moorehead.** *Before I Forget.* Chicago: Moody Press, 1971.

One of America's great bibliophiles reminisces about his life as a writer, teacher, and biblical scholar. Selective, nostalgic, chatty. 285.173.SM76B

**Snyder, Howard A.** *The Radical Wesley and Patterns for Church Renewal.* Downers Grove, Ill.: InterVarsity Press, 1980.

Writing out of a heart of concern for the church, Snyder uses Wesley as a model of spiritual-sociological renewal. He then applies principles from Wesley's work to the task facing Christians today. Missing, however, is a biblical foundation. Absent, too, is a discussion of the weaknesses attending any human movement. 287.W51.SN9

**\*Spurgeon, Charles Haddon.** *C. H. Spurgeon Autobiography.* Vol. 2, *The Full Harvest, 1860-1892.* Edinburgh: Banner of Truth Trust, 1973.

This long-awaited companion volume to *The Early Years* (1962) will stimulate, encourage, and edify those presently engaged in a pastoral ministry and challenge those who are preparing for it. Recommended. 286.142.SP9 v.2

**Stauffer, Richard.** *The Humanness of John Calvin.* Translated by George Shriver. Nashville: Abingdon Press, 1971.

A Swiss pastor's approach to and an assessment of, the great Reformer. Thematic. 284.294.C13.ST2

**Steer, Roger.** *George Müller: Delighted in God!* Wheaton, Ill.: Harold Shaw Publishers, 1975.

A definitive work on an outstanding man of God. Deserves a place in the forefront of Christian biographies. 286.542.M91.S4

**Stohlman, Martha Lou Lemmon.** *John Witherspoon: Parson, Politician, Patriot.* Philadelphia: Westminster Press, 1976.

A popular treatment of this Scottish Presbyterian who became the sixth president of Princeton College and was active in both ecclesiastical and political spheres of New Jersey life. 973.3.W77.S6

**Strong, Augustus Hopkins.** *Autobiography of Augustus Hopkins Strong.* Edited by C. Douglas. Valley Forge, Pa.: Judson Press, 1981.

Strong is widely known for his systematic theology. This important personal sketch describes the life and labors of one who knew he would one day stand before the *bema* of Christ, and therefore disciplined himself accordingly. 230.61.ST8D 1981

**Toon, Peter.** *God's Statesman: The Life and Work of John Owen.* Grand Rapids: Zondervan Publishing House, 1973.

A brilliant biography of one of the important political and ecclesiastical figures of the Puritan era. 285.342.OW2.T61

**\*Tucker, Ruth A.** *From Jerusalem to Irian Jaya: A Biographical History of Christian Missions.* Grand Rapids: Zondervan Publishing House, Academie Books, 1983.

A well-written, informative résumé of missions with material covering every facet: ancient, medieval, and modern, specialized as well as nationalistic. It is at once interesting and informative. A must for informed laypeople. 266'.0092.T79

**Turner, Charles, ed.** *Chosen Vessels: Portraits of Ten Outstanding Christian Men.* Ann Arbor, Mich.: Servant Publications, 1985.

Ten outstanding contemporary writer/theologians provide excellent biographical essays on C. S. Lewis, Paul Brand, William Wilberforce, Thomas Aquinas, Otto Keller, D. M. Lloyd-Jones, and others. Provocative. 209'.2.T84

**Vanauken, Sheldon.** *Under the Mercy.* Nashville: Thomas Nelson Publishers, 1985.

*A Severe Mercy* was the story of Vanauken's love for Davy; *Under the Mercy* is his autobiography since Davy's death. It chronicles his mistaken crusades and misguided idealism. It also shows his eventual emergence into the light of God's love and the realization that he had always been under God's mercy. 283.3.V26

**\*Walker, Williston.** *Ten New England Leaders.* New York: Arno Press, 1976.

Reprinted from the 1901 edition. These brief yet perceptive biographies do justice both to the history of the times in which each person lived and to the impact they made on the educational, social, and religious life of their day. A valuable work. 285.8.W15 1976.

**Wallace-Hadrill, Andrew.** *Suetonius: The Scholar and His Caesars.* New Haven,

Conn.: Yale University Press, 1983.

After dealing with the difference between history and biography, and the factual data in Suetonius's *Annals*, Wallace-Hadrill of Magdalene College, Cambridge, assesses the reliability of this ancient biographer as well as the lives of those about whom he wrote. 937.SU2.W15

**Walter, Altina L.** *Reverend Beecher and Mrs. Tilton: Sex and Class in Victorian America*. Amherst, Mass.: University of Massachusetts Press, 1982.

Uses the temporary moral lapse of Henry Ward Beecher to illustrate the Victorian attitude of many Americans toward sex and also chronicles the reaction of middle-class America with its corresponding rejection of Beecher and his message. 285.8'32.B39.W17

**Weatherhead, Andrew Kingsley.** *Leslie Weatherhead: A Personal Portrait*. Nashville: Abingdon Press, 1975.

Although it is not easy for a son to write a biography of his father, Andrew K. Weatherhead manifests a marked degree of objectivity in this lengthy work. Methodists and those interested in religious psychology will welcome it. 287'.1.W37.W37

**Wesley, Charles.** *The Journal of Charles Wesley*. 2 vols. Grand Rapids: Baker Book House, 1980.

Photographically reproduced from the 1849 edition, this reprint makes available to modern readers the journal, poetry, and correspondence of this great leader of the Christian church. 287'.142.W51C 1980

**White, William, Jr.** *Van Til: Defender of the Faith*. Nashville: Thomas Nelson Publishers, 1979.

Views the theology and apologetics of Cornelius Van Til in the context of his times. Provides interesting and informative sidelights on his contemporaries. A worthy acquisition. 285.731.V36.W58

**Wiersbe, Warren Wendell.** *Walking with the Giants: A Minister's Guide to Good Reading and Great Preaching*. Grand Rapids: Baker Book House, 1976.

Reprinted from articles that appeared in *Moody Monthly*, 1971-1975. Makes stimulating reading. 922.W63

————. *William Culbertson: A Man of God*. Chicago: Moody Press, 1974.

This biography captures the deeply devotional spirit that motivated William Culbertson, and at the same time carefully describes the path that God chose in preparing him for the work He wanted to accomplish through him. Those who knew Dr. Culbertson were moved by the relevance of his piety and quiet godliness, and Wiersbe reveals this saintly man's influence on old and young alike. 285.3.C91.W61

**Wilkinson, John Thomas.** *Arthur Samuel Peake: A Biography*. London: Epworth Press, 1971.

An appreciative presentation of Peake's contribution to biblical scholarship. 287.142.P31

**Williams, E. T., and C. S. Nicholls, eds.** *Dictionary of National Biography, 1961-1970*. Oxford: Oxford University Press, 1981.

Contains biographical sketches of 745 British men and women who died between 1961 and 1970. Included are Winston Churchill and Evelyn Waugh, C. S. Lewis and J. E. Masefield, T. S. Eliot and E. M. Forester. Also contains a cumulative index covering those entries from 1901 to 1970. A very useful volume. 920'.041.D56

**Williams, John Bickerton.** *The Lives of Philip and Matthew Henry*. Carlisle, Pa.: Banner of Truth Trust, 1974.

Contains two volumes in one. These accounts of a notable father and his illustrious son provide an important study of the effect of godliness in the home and the way in which a parent's spiritual commitment and practical wisdom influenced his children. This is a remarkable volume that deserves to be read, and reread. 285.2'42.H39.W67

**Winebrenner, Jan.** *Steel in His Soul.* Chicago: Moody Press, 1985.

A graphic study of Dick Hillis, a human, vulnerable, and weak person who nonetheless was mightily used of the Lord as a missionary in China, and whose influence extended beyond the bounds of his own mission. 266.H55.W68

**Winslow, Ola Elizabeth.** *Jonathan Edwards, 1703-1758: A Biography.* New York: Octagon Books, 1973.

Reprinted from the 1940 edition, this indispensable work accurately portrays the life and labors of Edwards. 285.873.ED9.W73 1973

**Wolfe, Tom.** *The Right Stuff.* New York: Farrar, Straus, Giroux, 1979.

Looks behind the scenes and favors his readers with the perceptions and goals of the astronauts who not only made headlines in the newspapers but also achieved certain personal ambitions. Replete with information illustrating the courage and resourcefulness of these people. 629.1.AM3.W83

**Wooden, John,** and **Jack Tobin.** *They Call Me Coach.* Waco, Tex.: Word Books, 1985.

Wooden became the legendary coach of the UCLA basketball team. His leadership skills were remarkable. In addition to the obvious human interest that attaches to a work such as this, pastors will find that it abounds with homiletic illustrations. 796.32'3.W85T

**Wright, Wendy M.** *Bond of Perfection: Jeanne de Chantal and Francois de Sales.* New York: Paulist Press, 1985.

Can men and women be just friends? There are many who say no. One thing all will agree on is that we lack contemporary models of such friendships. In this book the author takes her readers back to the seventeenth century and, after describing the social, political, and religious context of the times, describes the rich and many-faceted nature of the friendship of these two unlikely people. In the process she introduces her readers to the powerful dynamics of interaction between male and female and also explains the overpowering love of God that both felt. Their nineteen-year friendship brought each to a better understanding of himself/herself as together they sought to develop a "bond of perfection." This is a truly remarkable book, and one that will serve to illustrate the possibility of rich, rewarding relationships quite apart from any sexual overtones. 270.8.W93

## OTHER RELIGIOUS GROUPS

**\*Ahmanson, John.** *Secret History: A Translation of "Vor Tids Muhamed."* Translated by G. L. Archer, Jr. Chicago: Moody Press, 1984.

This eye-witness account of the rise of Mormonism in the United States was published in Danish in 1876. Only three copies of the original are extant. This translation, with copious marginal notes, is essential to a proper understanding of the history of the period. It should be read by Mormons as well as those who work with them. Recommended. 289.3.AH5

**Anderson, Robert Maples.** *Vision of the Disinherited: The Making of American Pentecostalism.* New York: Oxford University Press, 1979.

A study of the formative phase of the Pentecostal movement from the latter part of the nineteenth century to the 1930s. Treats the three major divisions, and provides numerous interesting sidelights on the movement's history and development. 289.9.AN2

**Arrington, Leonard J.**, and **Davis Bitton.** *The Mormon Experience: A History of the Latter-Day Saints.* New York: Alfred A. Knopf, 1979.

A pro-Mormon history of the origin and growth of the movement. Contains information from Mormon archives previously not available to researchers. 289.3'09.AR6

**Baxter, James Sidlow.** *Divine Healing of the Body.* Grand Rapids: Zondervan Publishing House, 1979.

Considers the evidence for divine healing through the centuries, and then takes a sober look at divine healing as it is taught today. 289.9.B33

**Baxter, Ronald E.** *The Charismatic Gift of Tongues.* Grand Rapids: Kregel Publications, 1981.

A careful study of *glossolalia.* Treats the phenomenon biblically as well as theologically. Of particular interest is the chapter on counterfeit unity. 289.9.B33

**Bowden, James.** *The History of the Society of Friends in America.* 2 vols. in 1. New York: Arno Press, 1972.

First published in 1850, this carefully prepared treatise traces the history of the Quakers from the founding of the Colonies to 1820. An important piece of Americana. 289.6.AM3.B67 1972

**Brumback, Carl.** *A Sound from Heaven* and *Like A River.* Springfield, Mo.: Gospel Publishing House, 1977.

A reprint of two primary resource works dealing with the history and doctrine of the Assemblies of God. 289.9.B83

**Cassara, Ernest.** *Universalism in America.* Boston: Beacon Press, 1971.

A documentary history of the rise of universalism in the U.S. 289.1'73.C26

**Chantry, Walter J.** *Signs of the Apostles: An Examination of New Pentecostalism.*

London: Banner of Truth Trust, 1973.

This concise critique of the charismatic movement claims that adherence to and involvement with neo-Pentecostalism necessitates an implicit denial of the doctrine of the authority of the Scriptures and the all-sufficiency of the Word of God. Though not well reasoned, the author's basic thesis is sound, and he deserves a hearing. 289.9.C36

**Culpepper, Robert H.** *Evaluating the Charismatic Movement: A Theological and Biblical Appraisal.* Valley Forge, Pa.: Judson Press, 1977.

Comes to grips with the historical evidence relating to the emergence of the charismatics and interacts with their doctrinal beliefs. Finds them wanting in every area. 289.9.C89

**Davis, Deborah Linda Berg**, and **Bill Davis.** *The Children of God: The Inside Story.* Grand Rapids: Zondervan Publishing House, 1984.

A thorough exposé of this cult by the daughter of the founder. 289.9.D29

**Davis, Howard A.**, et al. *Who Really Wrote the Book of Mormon?* Santa Ana, Calif.: Vision House Publishers, 1977.

This is an excellent treatise. It exposes the fallacies inherent in the Mormons' belief that the book they hold on a par with the Bible is inspired. The contributors show that this work was really a novel written by a retired minister. It was registered with the Library of Congress, but never published. Photostatic copies of all documents are included. This is a devastating critique that leaves Mormons with no alternative but to admit that they have been duped and to seek the truth as presented in the NT. 289.322.D29

**\*Davis, John James.** *Contemporary Counterfeits.* Grand Rapids: Baker Book House, 1973.

An important analysis of the various manifestations of occultism in the lesser-known cults. 133.D29

**Decker, Ed,** and **Dave Hunt.** *The God Makers.* Eugene, Oreg.: Harvest House Publishers, 1984.

"This book is dynamite! The most powerful thing I've read. Get your Mormon friends to read it" (John F. MacArthur, Jr.). 289.3.D35

**Dillow, Joseph C.** *Speaking in Tongues.* Grand Rapids: Zondervan Publishing House, 1975.

A searching inquiry into *glossolalia.* Concludes that the phenomenon was a temporary gift to the early church. Thorough and revealing. 289.9.D58

**Ebon, Martin.** *The Devil's Bride—Exorcism: Past and Present.* New York: Harper & Row, 1974.

Contains case histories of exorcism as well as an abundance of material documenting man's obsession with Satanism and the occult. Provides little biblical support for any of his theories. 133.3.EB7

**Hamilton, Michael P., ed.** *The Charismatic Movement.* Grand Rapids: Wm. B. Eerdmans Publishing Co., 1975.

Of help as a review of the movement, but deficient in that it contains little data not found in other works. Lacks cohesion and fails to provide a thorough analysis of the social and spiritual aspects of the charismatic experience. 289.9.H18

**Hollenweger, Walter J.** *The Pentecostals: The Charismatic Movement in the Churches.* Translated by R. A. Wilson. Minneapolis: Augsburg Publishing House, 1972.

A comprehensive and scholarly book that begins with historical sketches of the movement in the U.S. and then analyzes the beliefs of those who are the adherents of Pentecostalism. The author, an ardent supporter of the movement, is sympathetic to the cause, and though there is merit to a work written by an insider, there is also the danger that such a study may lack objectivity. This one does. Its chief value lies in the informa-

tion that can be gleaned on the attitudes of the adherents. 289.9.H72

**Hopkins, Joseph Martin.** *The Armstrong Empire.* Grand Rapids: Wm. B. Eerdmans Publishing Co., 1974.

A capable handling of the *history* of H. W. Armstrong and his Worldwide Church of God. Does little to delineate Armstrong's *doctrine.* 289.9.H77

**Jorstad, Erling, ed.** *The Holy Spirit in Today's Church.* Nashville: Abingdon Press, 1973.

A handbook of neo-Pentecostalism that attempts to answer the basic questions raised about the movement. 289.9.J76

**Kaufman, Robert.** *Inside Scientology: How I Joined Scientology and Became Superhuman.* New York: Olympia Press, 1972.

A candid exposé that deserves to be read by all who have been approached by adherents of this movement. 289.9.K16

**Kemperman, Steve.** *Lord of the Second Advent.* Ventura, Calif.: Regal Books, 1981.

A sorely needed critique of the "Moonies" and the impact of that mind-controlling cult on America's youth. An essential work. 289.9.K32

**Kildahl, John P.** *The Psychology of Speaking in Tongues.* New York: Harper & Row, 1972.

Based on reports of *glossolalia,* personal interviews, tapes, and other research, this approach to neo-Pentecostalism seeks to provide a factual answer to questions such as: Who is involved? Why do they speak in tongues? What does this all mean? The research is highly commendable; the approach sound; the conclusions, however, are not related to a clear understanding of the teaching of God's Word and as a result will need some modification. 289.9.K55

**Lang, George Henry.** *The Earlier Years of the Modern Tongues Movement: A Historical Survey and Its Lessons.* Miami Springs,

Fla.: Conley and Schoettle Publishing Co., 1985.

Written before the emergence of neo-Pentecostalism, this study makes available some excellent, little-known facts pertaining to the beginning of the movement. Lang is always perceptive. His work can be recommended as supplying important sidelights that now explain later trends. 289.9.L25 1985

**Larson, Bob.** *Bob Larson's Book of Cults.* Wheaton, Ill.: Tyndale House Publishers, 1982.

An encyclopedic work that surveys the major as well as the newer cults with a brevity and clarity that makes this an ideal resource. 289.L32

————. *The Guru.* Denver: The Author, 1974.

A candid polemic against the claims and teachings of the teenage Maharaj Ji. 133.42.L32

**\*MacArthur, John F., Jr.** *The Charismatics: A Doctrinal Perspective.* Grand Rapids: Zondervan Publishing House, 1978.

Counselors know that many of their clients are deeply disturbed, disillusioned charismatics. Because the Bible equates "healthy mindedness" with the practice of sound doctrine, MacArthur has provided a clear, direct evaluation of the charismatic movement. He is thoroughly biblical. Drawing on his years of pastoral experience, he examines the doctrinal distinctives and ecclesiastical practices of the movement and finds them to be woefully deficient. This book will not win MacArthur many friends among charismatics, but its message is sorely needed, and he is to be commended for having undertaken such a difficult task. We cannot recommend this book too highly. 289.9.M11

**Magnani, Duane,** and **Arthur Barrett.** *The Watchtower Files: Dialogue with a Jehovah's Witness.* Minneapolis: Bethany House Publishers, 1985.

This book goes beyond the usual works on this subject. It describes the fallacies inherent in Jehovah's Witness doctrine and also exposes the crises facing the Church of Jesus Christ of the Latter Day Saints. 289.9′2.M27

**\*Martin, Walter Ralston.** *The Kingdom of the Occult.* Santa Ana, Calif.: Vision House, 1974.

A comprehensive examination of the history and theology of occultism. Recommended. 133.M36

**Mayhue, Richard L.** *Divine Healing Today.* Chicago: Moody Press, 1983.

This book is for those who are confused over divine healing. The scope is thoroughly biblical. Mayhue examines the biblical teaching and draws valid conclusions that will bring peace to troubled hearts. The presentation is simple, and what is presented can be read through in less than half an hour. This is a *must* for those in doubt. 289.9.M45

**Mills, Watson E.** *Understanding Speaking in Tongues.* Grand Rapids: Wm. B. Eerdmans Publishing Co., 1971.

Insists that a distinction must be drawn between the form and the meaning of *glossolalia.* Claims that those who reject the form of *glossolalia* as no longer relevant should at least be prepared to concede that tongue-speaking may attest to genuine experience. A weak defense. 289.9.M62

————. *Charismatic Religion in Modern Research: A Bibliography.* Macon, Ga.: Mercer University Press, 1985.

In this first volume of a new series sponsored by the National Association of Baptist Professors of Religion and designed to sponsor new scholarship, Mills, an acknowledged authority on *glossolalia,* has compiled an invaluable guide to the literature in this complex and expanding field. The 2,105 entries are listed by author. There are two indexes—editors/joint authors, and title. 016.289.M62

**\*Montgomery, John Warwick.** *Prin-*

*cipalities and Powers: The World of the Occult.* Minneapolis: Bethany Fellowship, 1974.

Few men possess the personal resources Montgomery has at his disposal. Having studied in Europe, he has amassed a vast library on all aspects of the history and doctrines of demonism and the occult. Here is an able synthesis that makes available to contemporary students an analysis of the many forms of Satanism. Every well-informed person should read this book. 133.M76

**Neal, Julia.** *The Kentucky Shakers.* Lexington, Ky.: University of Kentucky Press, 1982.

Describes the events of 1805 when three Shakers from New York visited the frontier and established centers of ecstatic worship and communal life. An interesting piece of Americana. 289.8.K41.N25

**Pardington, G. P.** *Twenty-five Wonderful Years, 1889-1914: A Popular Sketch of the Christian and Missionary Alliance.* New York: Garland Publishing, 1984.

First published in 1914. This historic volume recounts the work of A. B. Simpson in founding the Christian and Missionary Alliance and also deals with the outreach of its members into various parts of the world. 289.9.P21 1984

**Parham, Sarah E.** *The Life of Charles F. Parham: Founder of the Apostolic Faith Movement.* New York: Garland Publishing, 1985.

First published in 1930, this intimate study lays bare the vision behind the founding of Parham's movement. The story is well told. 289.9.P15P 1985

**Paxton, Geoffrey J.** *The Shaking of Adventism.* Grand Rapids: Baker Book House, 1978.

Shockwaves have gone through the Seventh-Day Adventist Church. This study by an Australian assesses the real heart of the movement, describes the main trends, and shows how divergent ideas have affected the message of justification and shaken the faith of the adherents. 286.73.P28S

**Penton, M. James.** *Apocalypse Delayed: The Story of Jehovah's Witnesses:* Toronto: University of Toronto Press, 1985.

A fourth-generation Jehovah's Witness (he was disfellowshiped in 1981), Penton tells the story of the movement and provides interesting information on the numerous predictions made by the sect about the coming of Christ and the end of the world. Weak ecclesiologically and eschatologically, but interesting for its data about the movement. 289.9'2.P38

**Pritchett, W. Douglas.** *The Children of God/Family of Love: An Annotated Bibliography.* New York: Garland Publishing, 1985.

This book is about the largest, best organized, and most controversial of the "Jesus People" groups. Although starting with a thoroughly fundamentalist orientation, the Children of God evolved into a highly unorthodox cult that is both mobile and secretive. This timely reference volume presents a broad selection of material from 1968 to the present. The topically arranged citations include articles, reviews, books, papers, and dissertations. This is an invaluable resource for scholars as well as students of modern cults. 016.2899.P93

**Quebedeaux, Richard.** *By What Authority: The Rise of Personality Cults in American Christianity.* San Francisco: Harper & Row, 1981.

Provides a probing, insightful analysis of the relationship between celebritydom and religious authority. Traces the formation of charismatic Christianity as well as the growing popularity of TV evangelists and media-oriented spiritual leaders who claim an insider's right to speak out on a variety of social/ethical issues. The position these "instant successes" now hold was once reserved for those whose formal training and experience equipped them to speak with authority. But all of that has changed. Central in Quebedeaux's discussion is the increasingly important role of electronic media. Advances in technology over the past three decades now allow these celebrity figures to beam themselves into homes all across America with their brand of popular religion—defined by Quebedeaux as "popular because it is fashioned for everyday people with the aim of solving everyday problems." Scant attention is paid by these individuals to a full-orbed theology that has the power to build a strong, dynamic faith. Though readers cannot be expected to agree with all that is contained in this book, the author has nevertheless placed his finger on an important issue. 289.Q3B

————. *The New Charismatics: The Origins, Development, and Significance of Neo-Pentecostalism.* Garden City, N.Y.: Doubleday and Co., 1976.

A revision of the author's doctoral thesis at Oxford, this work fulfills the intent of the sub-title. The biographical sketches are of particular importance. Considerable space is devoted to the doctrine of charismatic renewal, but little is done to systematize the beliefs of the widely divergent groups presently participating in this phenomenon. 289.9.Q3

**Robinson, David.** *The Unitarians and the Universalists.* Westport, Conn.: Greenwood Press, 1985.

†An important discussion of the origin and rise of unitarianism, universalism, and theological liberalism. Provides a helpful résumé of the different views. 288.73.R56

**Ropp, Harry L.** *The Mormon Papers: Are the Mormon Scriptures Reliable?* Downers Grove, Ill.: InterVarsity Press, 1977.

Why is Mormonism one of the fastest spreading religions in the world today? What are the beliefs of Mormons? How do they differ from evangelical Christianity? These questions receive a full exposé in this enlightening book. Ropp demonstrates from Mormon writings the logical inconsistencies of the movement and the fallacy of believing in the "revelations" given Joseph Smith. His work is well reasoned and is well deserving of wide circulation. 289.32.R68

**Samarin, William J.** *Tongues of Men and Angels.* New York: Macmillan Co., 1972.

A thorough assessment of the modern *glossolalia* movement. Among the conclusions reached by the author is that the phenomenon of Acts 2 was an example of *xenoglossolalia*, and that the modern counterpart of that has a beneficial effect because it makes the individual feel good. The linguistic analysis of *glossolalia* is excellent, but the writer's exegetical and theological expertise leaves much to be desired. 289.9.SA4

***Smith, Charles R.** *Tongues in Biblical Perspective: A Summary of Biblical Conclusions Concerning Tongues.* Winona Lake, Ind.: BMH Books, 1976.

This is an important discussion of *glossolalia*, surveying it biblically, historically, and theologically. In only one small area does Smith err, and that is in his treatment of tongues as a sign to the Jews. In all other respects he has given his readers a fine, balanced, accurate treatment. Recommended. 289.9.SM5

**Synan, Vinson.** *The Holiness Pentecostal Movement in the United States.* Grand Rapids: Wm. B. Eerdmans Publishing Co., 1971.

A sympathetic study of the origin and growth of the Pentecostal and Holiness movements. Of particular interest is Synan's recounting of recent developments and the growth of the charismatic movement in non-Pentecostal denominations. 289.9′09.SY7

**\*Unger, Merrill Frederick.** *Beyond the Crystal Ball.* Chicago: Moody Press, 1973.

Provides a balanced treatment of the limitations of occultism in determining the future, links biblical prediction with world events, and exposes the origin, power, and delusion of Satanism. A must in every pastor's library. 133.3.UN3

**Warner, James A.,** and **Styne M. Slade.** *The Mormon Way.* Englewood Cliffs, N.J.: Prentice-Hall, 1976.

A beautifully illustrated portrayal of Mormon life and history. 289.3′3.W24

**Zaretsky, Irving I.,** and **Mark P. Leone, eds.** *Religious Movements in Contemporary America.* Princeton, N.J.: Princeton University Press, 1975.

Isms appear to be mushrooming in the American milieu. These collected papers analyze a single facet of a specific religious movement and, though in no way complete, they do provide a careful appraisal of the different sects a pastor is likely to encounter. 289.9.Z1

# 11

---

# Comparative Religions

"Counterfeits to Christianity" is perhaps the best descriptive term for the plethora of false religions and cults that seem to be taking over the Western world. In November 1978, when the world was shocked into wakefulness by the unforgettable tragedy that took place in the remote jungle village of Guyana in South America, we were forcefully reminded of the power of deviant beliefs. Jim Jones and his followers participated in a gruesome act of annihilation. It was a tragedy of unspeakable proportions that still reminds us that only in Judaism and Christianity do we find beliefs based on the self-disclosure of God to man.

The events in Guyana confirm that religious evil is the worst form of evil. It masquerades under the guise of social concern, but in its outworking, its adherents are deprived of all that is decent and ennobling.

Even in Old Testament times there were charlatans who "prophesied falsely." They were intent on lining their own pockets and found in the gullibility of people and their religious sensibilities a ready market for their avarice and greed. In our day we have evidence of that continued trait.

But who can properly account for the popularity of Bahaism or Zen Buddhism, the supposed "Church of the Living Word" or Eckankar, Hare Krishna or the Jehovah's Witnesses? Books by cultists sell in the hundreds of thousands. That has certainly been true of *Dianetics—The Modern Science of Mental Health,* the *Kama Sutra of Vatsyayana,* the so-called *Secret Doctrines of Jesus,* and the revival of interest in the *Tibetan Book of the Dead.*

To the astute student of church history and historical theology, all of the new movements are seen to be old heresies in modern dress. Never before, however, has a need existed for Christians in all walks of life to be well read in both Bible and theology. That will enable them to discern error when they see it. They can then help those who are young in the faith to maintain their beliefs in the midst of plausible contradictions from false religionists.

The following is a very brief summary of some of the more popular works that have appeared in recent years. Works on the major religions have also been included. However, because large numbers of Americans, particularly young teenagers and those in their early twenties, have been attracted to unconventional religious movements, it is important for pastor-teachers to be aware of the issues so they can declare truth and establish people firmly in the faith.

**Faruqi, Ishra'il Ragi al.** *Historical Atlas of the Religions of the World.* New York: Macmillan Co., 1974.

†Interspersed throughout this handsome volume are essays on the history of various religions—their growth and interesting phenomena relating to their practices. Beautiful black and white pictures and helpful chronological charts, bibliographies, appendixes, and indexes further enhance the usefulness of this important work. 912.H62

**Ferguson, John.** *Encyclopedia of Mysticism and Mystery Religions.* New York: Crossroad Publishing Co., 1982.

First published in England in 1976, this work is crammed with information from "Abhidharma" to "Zoroastrianism" and includes meaningful discussions of all facets of spiritual endeavor and spiritist phenomena. 291'.03.F38

_____. *An Illustrated Encyclopedia of Mysticism and the Mystery Religions.* New York: Seabury Press, 1976.

Ferguson is an acknowledged authority on the subject of the mystery religions. The steady rise of Satanism, the preoccupation with the occult, and the ever-present recurrence of ancient religions in modern dress is forcing many pastors to take a fresh look at the history of these groups as well as their rites and practices. This handy encyclopedia contains a veritable smorgasbord of information. It explains terms currently in vogue, concepts that underlie certain beliefs, and doctrines that were not a part of one's seminary training. This is a book compiled by a specialist, and it will be of inestimable help to the busy pastor who must be aware of these teachings. 291'.42.F38

**Parrinder, Edward Geoffrey.** *A Dictionary of Non-Christian Religions.* Philadelphia: Westminster Press, 1973.

Helps the researcher find valuable and reliable data on a wide range of religious themes. 290.3.P24

## GENERAL STUDIES

**\*Beyerlin, Walter, ed.** *Near Eastern Religious Texts Relating to the Old Testament.* Old Testament Library. Translated by J. Bowden. Philadelphia: Westminster Press, 1979.

Similar in scope to Pritchard's indispensable *Ancient Near Eastern Texts,* this work likewise highlights many features of OT interpretation encountered in commentaries. Now preachers may have this scholarly translation of important

documents within easy reach. The result is that they can use the information to sharpen the focus of their exposition through a fresh understanding of the passage under consideration. 291.8'0956.N27.B46 1979

**Boa, Kenneth.** *Cults, World Religions, and You.* Wheaton, Ill.: Victor Books, 1977.

A handbook that treats concisely the history and doctrinal beliefs of twenty-seven deviant religious groups. Designed for small group discussion and, if used in this manner, will ensure that laypeople in the church are informed of the dangers of heterodoxy. 291.B63

**Bowker, John Westerdale.** *The Religious Imagination and the Sense of God.* New York: Oxford University Press, 1978.

A sequel to *The Sense of God* (1973), this work surveys the major emphases of Judaism, Islam, Christianity, and Buddhism. It provides a good overview, but is lacking when it comes to explaining adequately the dynamic of revealed religion. 291.2'11.B67

**Brandon, Samuel George Frederick.** *Men and God in Art and Ritual.* New York: Charles Scribner's Sons, 1975.

A pioneer work that adequately surveys the iconography, architecture, and ritual of religious groups throughout the world. Establishes a method of procedure and reviews religious beliefs and practices. 291.1.B73

**Bregman, Lucy.** *The Rediscovery of Inner Experience.* Chicago: Nelson-Hall, 1982.

A candid study of a new trend in American society. Bregman probes the usual sources of inner experience from a psychological point of view, and then interprets these findings in their relation to mankind's predisposition to develop religious beliefs. Provides a rationale for hedonism, narcissism, sadism, and the like. 291.4'2.B74

**Carmen, John Braisted.** *The Theology of Ramanuja: An Essay in Irreligious Understandings.* New Haven, Conn.: Yale University Press, 1974.

An attempt on the part of an Occidental to understand the concepts of supremacy *(paratva)* and accessibility *(saulabhya)* as experiencing two sides of Ramanuja's concept of God. 181.483.C21

**Carmody, Denise Larder,** and **John Tully Carmody.** *Shamans, Prophets, and Sages: An Introduction to World Religions.*

Belmont, Calif.: Wadsworth Publishing Co., 1985.

Focusing on the typologies that world religions have in common, the Carmodys elicit three standards (identified in the title) and explain common denominators in light of these similarities. Though antisupernaturalistic in regard to Christianity, this is nonetheless a fine introduction that readily reveals the authors' expertise in the area of comparative religions. 291.C21

**Cassuto, Umberto.** *The Goddess 'Anat: Canaanite Epics of the Patriarchal Age.* Translated by Israel Abrahams. Jerusalem: Magnes Press, 1971.

Based on the original texts with Hebrew translation and commentary. This standard work on the Semitic goddess Anat and the Phoenician deity Baal illuminates the biblical record and supplements the OT narrative with material from the Ugaritic texts. 291.211.C27

**Catoir, John T.** *The Way People Pray.* New York: Paulist Press, 1974.

A brief introduction to the history of religious belief. 291.C29

**Cinnamon, Kenneth,** and **David Farson.** *Cults and Cons: The Exploitation of the Emotional Growth Consumer.* Chicago: Nelson-Hall, 1979.

Two psychologists team up to provide a vigorous exposé of the false premises and false promises of modern cultic groups. This book deserves careful reading, for though it does not purport to be evangelical, it does expose the beliefs and practices of some quasi-evangelical groups. 158.C49

**Coward, Harold.** *Pluralism: Challenge to World Religions.* Maryknoll, N.Y.: Orbis Books, 1985.

†A comprehensive treatment of how each major world religion has understood its particular claim to absolute truth. As a compendium, this work may well be regarded as a valuable resource.

It also meets a felt need. 291.1'72.C83

**Davies, Douglas James.** *Meaning and Salvation in Religious Studies.* Studies in the History of Religions. Leiden: E. J. Brill, 1984.

Two different kinds of data have been used in this book: historical and theoretical. The one deals with the development of ideas; the other tends toward a unified approach to man's innate need for meaning. 291.2.D28

**Dixon, Jeane.** *Yesterday, Today, and Forever.* New York: William Morrow and Co., 1976.

†The widely acclaimed "seer" writes on how astrology can help a person find his or her place in God's program. Dixon concentrates on the twelve apostles, gives each an astrological sign, and proceeds to draw lessons for daily living. Sin (as in the case of Peter) is explained on the grounds of an Arien trait. Heretical. 133.5.D64

**Doria, C.,** and **H. Lenowitz, eds. and trans.** *Origins: Creation Texts from the Ancient Mediterranean.* New York: AMS Press, 1976.

A rich collection of cosmogonies—Grecian, Mycenaean, Egyptian, Babylonian—including chants and invocations, and suggesting an Ur-text of the world's beginning. 291.2'2.OR4

**Duddy, Neil T.** *The Godmen: An Inquiry into Witness Lee and the Local Church.* Downers Grove, Ill.: InterVarsity Press, 1981.

This book by the staff of the Spiritual Counterfeits Project in Berkeley, California, provides a critique of the theology of the Local Church movement and its teaching on authentic religious experience. 291.63.D86

**Eliade, Mircea.** *Death, Afterlife and Eschatology.* New York: Harper & Row, 1974.

A secular approach to the historical development of these doctrines in pagan religions. Insightful. 291'.09.EL5D

———. *Gods, Goddesses, and Myths of Creation.* New York: Harper & Row, 1974.

Containing part of the author's *From Primitives to Zen,* this study focuses on the cosmological beliefs of pagan societies. A valuable compendium of thought. 291.2.EL5G

———. *A History of Religious Ideas.* In Process. Translated by W. R. Trask. Chicago: University of Chicago Press, 1978-.

The first volume in this new series probes the mysteries of death in Stone Age and early Grecian thought. It provides a valuable resource tool to the phenomena encountered and also helps the researcher understand these ancient cultures and their beliefs. 291'.09.EL4 v.1

———. *Occultism, Witchcraft, and Cultural Fashions: Essays on Comparative Religions.* Chicago: University of Chicago Press, 1976.

These chapters do not have a uniform theme. They deal with widely divergent aspects of paganism. They explain such beliefs as the cosmic symbolism of sacred space, mythologies of death, European witchcraft, and the rise of occultism in the West. This is a sobering book, and one that should not be ignored. 291'.08.EL4E

**Enroth, Ronald.** *Youth, Brainwashing, and Extremist Cults.* Grand Rapids: Zondervan Publishing House, 1977.

Written to prepare parents and those who work with young people of the psychological, sociological, and pseudospiritual onslaughts of cultists who yearly ensnare into their totalitarian systems large numbers of America's youth. Provides timely warning. 301.5'8.EN3

**Frankfort, Henri.** *Kingship and the Gods: A Study of Ancient Near Eastern Religion as the Integration of Society and Nature.* Chicago: University of Chicago Press, 1978.

The reissue of a standard work first published in 1948. Beautifully and lucidly written, and imaginatively illustrated, this classic treatment establishes the fundamental differences between the peoples of ancient Egypt and Mesopotamia. 291.2.F85 1978

**Gratus, Jack.** *The False Messiahs.* New York: Taplinger, 1976.

Attorney Jack Gratus extensively treats the numerous false messiahs from biblical times to Charles Manson. In his book he unwittingly does evangelicals a great service. He shows the motives as well as the schemes of the self-seekers, and that information is easy to contrast with the teaching of the NT. 291.6'3.G77

**Hardy, Alister.** *The Spiritual Nature of Man: A Study of Contemporary Religious Experience.* Oxford: Clarendon Press, 1979.

An historical record of the work done by the Religious Experience Research Unit, Oxford. Darwinian in approach; believes man's spiritual nature is intimately linked with the evolutionary process. 291.4'2.H22

**Hawkins, Gerald S.** *Beyond Stonehenge.* New York: Harper & Row, 1973.

Dealing with the same data as *Chariots of the Gods,* Hawkins explores the many fascinating aspects of the wisdom of early man. His sane, sensible approach highlights the prowess of ancient civilizations. In his concluding chapters he presents modern man with startling facts concerning ecology and survival. A worthy sequel to *Stonehenge Decoded* and *Splendor in the Sky.* 523.H31

**Hinnells, John R.** *The Facts on File Dictionary of Religions.* New York: Facts on File, 1984.

Intended to provide users with a precise understanding of religious phenomena and the vocabulary of the major world religions. Articles have been contributed by twenty-nine international scholars. The contents include historical, classical, archaeological, sociological, anthropological, and linguistic data. Well presented and highly usable, this work will delight students who need clear and concise information. 291'.03.H59

**Hudson, Winthrop Still.** *Religion in America.* 3d ed. New York: Charles Scribner's Sons, 1981.

A thorough résumé of the development of American religious history. Includes a statement on the turn to conservatism in the 1970s and 1980s. 291.AM3.H86 1981

**Huxley, Francis.** *The Way of the Sacred.* Garden City, N.Y.: Doubleday and Co., 1974.

An assessment of the place of symbols, rites, and ceremonies in religious worship. Sacramental. 291.H98

**Jacobsen, Thorkild.** *The Treasures of Darkness: A History of Mesopotamian Religion.* New Haven, Conn.: Yale University Press, 1976.

A work of exemplary scholarship that brings to light a long dead civilization and traces the rise, progress, and eventual demise of their religious beliefs. 291.17.J15

**James, Edwin Oliver.** *Origins of Sacrifice: A Study in Comparative Religion.* Port Washington, N.Y.: Kennikat Press, 1971.

First published in 1933. This work deals with the origin of blood sacrifices, fertility rites, human sacrifices, cannibalism, and the mystery cults. 291.3.J23 1971

**Johnson, David L.** *A Reasoned Look at Asian Religions.* Minneapolis: Bethany House Publishers, 1985.

The mixing of philosophy and religion and the introduction of Marxism to Islam, Hinduism, Buddhism, and Confucianism has perplexed the Occidental mind. Johnson sets out to clear up the problem, and succeeds in providing a clear, reliable assessment of the history and development of changes within these Oriental religions. 291'.095.J63

**Jung, Leo.** *Fallen Angels in Jewish, Christian, and Mohammedan Literature.* New

York: Ktav Publishing House, 1974.

Reprinted from the 1926 edition, this treatise provides an informative and comparative study of demonology. 291.2'16.J95 1974

**Katz, Steven T., ed.** *Mysticism and Religious Traditions.* New York: Oxford University Press, 1983.

†Ably bridges the seeming void between mysticism and the development of religious traditions. Shows how a regnant orthodoxy can correlate these separate areas—the one, high and lofty, and the other, the result of the implementation of ideals by less insightful devotees. 291.42.K15

**Lewis, Gordon R.** *Confronting the Cults.* Grand Rapids: Baker Book House, 1975.

This work contains more than an evaluation of different sects and an analysis of their beliefs. It exhibits several important distinctives. In attitude, it is fair and devoid of hostility; in purpose, it is evangelical and seeks to present the truth in an appealing manner; and in style, it is easy-to-read and ideal for use with young people in discussion groups. 291.L58

**Long, Charles H.** *Alpha: The Myths of Creation.* Chico, Calif.: Scholars Press, 1983.

First published in 1963, this work provides researchers with a handy resumé of cosmological beliefs covering everything from Navaho myths to Babylonian creation epics. 291.2'4.L85 1983

**\*Martin, Walter Ralston.** *The Kingdom of the Cults.* Revised and expanded edition. Minneapolis: Bethany House Publishers, 1985.

The product of a lifetime of research, this work is essential to every pastor. In its earlier edition it was widely recognized as an outstanding book tabulating and chronicling the history and doctrinal aberrations of a variety of cultic groups. This revised edition is no less valuable. 291.9.M36 1985

**Marty, Martin Emil.** *Pilgrims in Their Own Land: 500 Years of Religion in America.* Boston: Little, Brown and Co., 1984.

The story of American religious institutions has been told often and well, but it has reached only a small portion of the public. This work focuses on the men and women of vision who were pathfinders and who attracted followers in search of a home. Well-researched and well-presented. 291.AM3.M35

**McDonald, Henry.** *The Ethics of Comparative Religion.* Lanham, Md.: University Press of America, 1984.

This far-ranging work includes a study of Emile Durkheim and the ethics of comparative religions. Social, cultural, scientific, mythological, moral, philosophical, and individual matters are brought under the author's scrutiny. The result is a work of rare scholarship that will delight as well as challenge those in the field. 291.5.M14

**Melton, J. Gordon.** *The Encyclopedia of American Religions: First edition, Supplement.* Detroit: Gale Research Co., 1985.

The edition of *The Encyclopedia of American Religions* (1979) provided the first comprehensive study of religious and spiritual groups in the U.S. since 1936 when the *Census of Religious Bodies* was published. Now, supplementing the first edition of the *Encyclopedia* is this supplement containing information to more than 100 groups that have undergone changes in name or status since they were first mentioned. Following the entry number and name of the organization is a detailed paragraph of the origin and history, beliefs and organizational structure of the group. Separate headings are given for mailing address, membership statistics, and periodicals. Each entry is also accompanied by a bibliography of source materials. 200.2.AM3.M49 Supp. 1

**Miller, Calvin.** *Transcendental Hesitation: A Biblical Appraisal of TM and Eastern*

*Mysticism.* Grand Rapids: Zondervan Publishing House, 1977.

A brilliant analysis and exposé of this Eastern religious movement that appears to have taken America by storm. 158.1.M61

**Montgomery, John Warwick, ed.** *Demon Possession: A Medical, Historical, Theological, and Anthropological Symposium.* Minneapolis: Bethany Fellowship, 1976.

Establishes a biblically based analysis for the investigation of demonism today. 133.42.M76

**Moulton, James Hope.** *The Treasure of the Magi: A Study of Modern Zoroastrianism.* New York: AMS Press, 1975.

Ably fulfills the subtitle. Reprinted from the 1917 edition. 925.M86 1975

**Neusner, Jacob.** *The Idea of Purity in Ancient Judaism.* Leiden: E. J. Brill, 1974.

This brilliant treatise by a noted Jewish historian draws attention to the biblical basis for purity in the OT and its postbiblical practice in Judaism. A careful perusal of Neusner's work will enhance one's understanding of much that is taught in the OT. 291.22.N39

**Ochshorn, Judith.** *The Female Experience and the Nature of the Divine.* Bloomington, Ind.: Indiana University Press, 1981.

A capable contribution to the study of androgeny. Draws together different strands of thought into a coherent presentation of the conflicting ideas. 291.1.OC3

**Parrinder, Edward Geoffrey.** *Avatar and Incarnation.* New York: Oxford University Press, 1982.

Based on the Wilde Lectures in Natural and Comparative Religion, Oxford, 1966-1969, this work discusses the principal sources underlying these primarily Indian beliefs before comparing Avatar teachings with Christian doctrines. 291.2.AV1.P24

———, ed. *Mysticism in the World's Religions.* New York: Oxford University Press, 1977.

Ably covers pagan religions and clearly distinguishes between monastic and theistic mysticism. Provides an indispensable guide to all who are interested in comparative studies. 291.42.P24M

———. *Something After Death?* Niles, Ill.: Argus Communications, 1975.

Of value to those engaged in a study of thanatology. Includes the views of psychologists as well as the beliefs and practices of the major religions. 291.2'3.P24S

———, ed. *World Religions, From Ancient History to the Present.* New York: Facts on File Publications, 1984.

An incredibly perceptive study, well illustrated and accurate, this work provides readers with an overview of the major religions of the world. It lends itself for use in introductory courses in college and seminary. 291.P24W 1984

**Perowne, Stewart.** *Holy Places of Christendom.* New York: Oxford University Press, 1976.

Similar in scope to the National Geographic Society's *Great Religions of the World,* this work concentrates on the spread of Christianity (both East and West) and, by means of narration and color photographs, provides a most lucid and moving portrayal of our Christian heritage. 291.P42 1976

**Perry, W. J.** *The Origin of Magic and Religion.* Port Washington, N.Y.: Kennikat Press, 1971.

First published in 1923, this study recounts in a clear, unobtrusive way the story of the development of the magical element in religious thought and practice. 291.3.P42 1971

**Preston, James J., ed.** *Mother Worship: Theme and Variations.* Chapel Hill, N.C.: University of North Carolina Press, 1982.

This important study of comparative religious beliefs takes the mother-goddess concept as the central tenet to be explored. Also considers the role of women as priestesses in pagan religions and the elevation of the Virgin Mary to sainthood and a position of veneration. 291.P92

**Saborin, Leopold.** *Priesthood: A Comparative Study.* Leiden: E. J. Brill, 1973.

In this important study a Jesuit priest investigates the nature and function of the priesthood in ancient religions. When dealing with the OT he focuses primarily on the Aaronic order, although there is brief mention of Melchizedek. A final chapter is devoted to Jesus the High Priest. As a comparative study, this work has a great deal to commend it. It is pertinent and revealing. 291.61.SA1

**Saggs, H. W. F.** *The Encounter with the Divine in Mesopotamia and Israel.* London: Athlone Press, 1978.

Surveys the way in which different branches of Semites viewed their deities. Includes in his treatment a discussion of their beliefs about creation, history, theodicy, and revelation. 291.4.SA1E

**Sharpe, Eric J.** *Comparative Religion: A History.* New York: Charles Scribner's Sons, 1975.

After a brief introduction surveying the antecedents of comparative religion, Sharpe describes the events of the mid-nineteenth century that gave rise to the objective and scientific approach to religion. During the rest of the book he maintains a careful balance between history and methodology. An important contribution. 291.SH2

**Smart, Ninian.** *The Religious Experience of Mankind.* 2d ed. New York: Charles Scribner's Sons, 1976.

†Contains some revisions and corrections and a completely new chapter on African religions. 291.SM2 1976

**Stone, Merlin.** *Ancient Mirrors of Womanhood: A Treasury of Goddess and Heroine Lore from Around the World.* Boston: Beacon Press, 1984.

Includes virtually every country of the world and assesses the place of woman in mythology and history. Reveals the strength women have often contributed to different cultures in times of crisis as well as in the normal affairs of their race. 291.2'11.ST6

**Streicker, Lowell D.** *Mind-bending: Brainwashing, Cults, and Deprogramming in the '80s.* Garden City, N.Y.: Doubleday and Co., 1984.

Deals forthrightly with the process by which those who are entrapped in certain cultic practices have their perceptions of reality, values, and self-image bent or distorted by specific techniques. This is a very sobering book and explains how the process may be reversed. Helpful. 291.ST8

**Thompson, Reginald Campbell.** *The Devils and Evil Spirits of Babylonia.* 2 vols. New York: AMS Press, 1976.

Details Assyrian and Babylonian incantations against evil spirits. Provides informative background material on the religious and cultural milieu of the ancient Near East. 133.4'27.T37 1976.

**Toynbee, Arnold Joseph, ed.** *Life After Death.* New York: McGraw-Hill Book Co., 1976.

Of importance because it shows how philosophers, theologians, social scientists, psychics, and historians view death and the possibility of life beyond the grave. 291.2'3.T66

**Van Bensberger, Wim,** and **Matthew Schoffeleers, eds.** *Theoretical Explorations in African Religion.* London: Routledge and Kegan Paul, 1985.

Takes a fresh look at African religions and presents some surprising new facts concerning the origin of certain beliefs. This is a good book for missiologists. 291.AF8.V27

**Wilson, John Frederick,** and **Thomas P. Slavens.** *Research Guide to Religious Studies.* Chicago: American Library Association, 1982.

Concentrates the reader's attention on

areas of importance to the student of comparative religions. Of value to all D.Miss. students. Well indexed. A *must* for every academic library. 291'.072.W69

**Witt, R. E.** *Isis in the Graeco-Roman World.* Ithaca, N.Y.: Cornell University Press, 1971.

A detailed study that evaluates the place, worship, and doctrine of Isis in the Graeco-Roman world. Includes both a theological and an archaeological investigation. Aids in understanding the religious beliefs of the world into which Christ was born and in which the apostolic church was established. 291.211.W78

## GREEK AND ROMAN RELIGION

**Apollodorus of Athens.** *Gods and Heroes of the Greeks: The Library of Apollodorus.* Translated by Michael Simpson. Amherst, Mass.: University of Massachusetts Press, 1976.

More than a recounting of the religious beliefs of the ancient Greeks. The notes at the end of each chapter provide insights into the origin and growth of these seminal ideas that exerted such influence upon the Western world. 292.2'11.AP4.S15 1976

**Banier, Antoine.** *The Mythology and Fables of the Ancients Explained from History.* 4 vols. New York: Garland Publishers, 1976.

This set includes an introduction to the whole phenomenon of mythology, coupled with a detailed explanation of the theogony of ancient civilizations, an account of the rise of idolatry, an analysis of the evils of witchcraft and occultism, and the emergence of various gods. These volumes, more so than in any other work, describe the local situation(s) in which certain myths developed and how man created deities fashioned after his own likeness or according to the likeness of animals whose skills he held in esteem. The treatment is comprehensive and informative. It sheds light on mankind's insatiable religiosity. 292.1'3.B22

**Barthell, Edward E., Jr.** *Gods and Goddesses of Ancient Egypt.* Coral Gables, Fla.: University of Miami Press, 1971.

A modern treatment of the role of the gods in worship of the ancient Egyptians. 292.211.B31

**Campbell, Lewis.** *Religion in Greek Literature.* Freeport, N.Y.: Books for Libraries Press, 1971.

Long recognized as a work of considerable merit. It sketches briefly and concisely the main tenets of Greek religion, traces their origin and development, and shows the incipient reasons for their decay. First published in 1898. 292'.08.C15

**Downing, Christine.** *The Goddess: Mythological Images of the Feminine.* New York: Crossroad Publishing Co., 1981.

Relates the female deities of antiquity to the present and future of women and the perpetuation of ancient matriarchal traditions. Sees in each of the goddesses an archtype of some facet of the modern feminist situation. 292.211.D75

**Grant, Michael.** *Roman Myths.* New York: Charles Scribner's Sons, 1971.

A survey of the myths that underlay Roman culture. Provides important sidelights of Paul's ministries in Ephesus and Corinth, and highlights the study of his epistles. 292'.07.G76

**Kimpel, Ben.** *Philosophies of Life of the Ancient Greeks and Israelites.* New York: Philosophical Library, 1981.

This is an analysis of the parallels between these widely divergent cultures on the nature of man and the essence of human life. Provides insights into the philosophy, religion, and literature of each group. 109.G81.K57

**MacDonald, William L.** *The Pantheon: Design, Meaning, and Progeny.* Cambridge, Mass.: Harvard University Press, 1976.

The Pantheon in Rome was built by Hadrian. It is one of the grand architectural feats of all time. In this richly illustrated book the reader is introduced to the gods of the ancient Romans and shown how they controlled every aspect of civil, religious, and personal life. 292.13.M14

**MacMullen, Ramsay.** *Paganism in the Roman Empire.* New Haven, Conn.: Yale University Press, 1981.

Describes the whole range of pagan religious belief of the ancient Romans that arose as a result of the uniting of the world under Roman rule. A valuable summary that casts light on the first century as well. 292.M22

**Palmer, Robert E. A.** *Roman Religion and Roman Empire: Five Essays.* Philadelphia: University of Pennsylvania Press, 1974.

An extensive volume detailing the progress of Roman beliefs at the time of the Republic. 292'.07.P18

**Spetnak, Charlene.** *Lost Goddesses of Early Greece: A Collection of Pre-Hellenistic Myths.* Boston: Beacon Press, 1984.

Useful for the light it sheds on the early origins of religious belief, but is also replete with the kind of illustrative material preachers will find helpful. 292.2'11.SP7

## INDIC RELIGIONS

**Beyer, Stephan.** *The Cult of Tara.* Berkeley, Calif.: University of California Press, 1974.

This scholarly appraisal of Buddhist origins and ritual concentrates on the goddess Tara and her influence on Tibetan life and thought. 294.3'4'38.B46

**Buhler, G., trans.** *The Laws of Manu.* New York: AMS Press, 1971.

A translation with extracts from seven commentaries. 294.5'92.M31

**Fernando, Antony,** and **Leonard Swidler.** *Buddhism Made Plain: An Introduction for Christians and Jews.* Rev. ed. Maryknoll, N.Y.: Orbis Books, 1985.

†Designed to foster dialog, this book presents the practical wisdom of personal liberation in its Theravada form. 294.3.F39 1985

**Humphreys, Christmas.** *A Popular Dictionary of Buddhism.* Totowa, N.J.: Rowman and Littlefield, 1976.

Buddhist terms from seven languages are explained, including theological concepts, persons, places, and objects. 294.3'03.H88

**Jaini, Padmanabh S.** *The Jaina Path of Purification.* Berkeley, Calif.: University of California Press, 1979.

This description of the traditions of the followers of the Jina, records the religious beliefs and practices of those of the Indian subcontinent who have followed these teachings for more than two and a half millennia. The treatment provided here explains Janian cosmology, philosophy, and the attainment of eternal salvation. Of value to the student of comparative religions.294.4'38.J19

**Kinsley, David R.** *Hinduism: A Cultural Perspective.* Englewood Cliffs, N.J.: Prentice-Hall, 1981.

A brief, yet compact introduction to Hinduism. Describes the cardinal beliefs as well as the dissension within the Hindu community. 294.5.K62

**Levine, Faye.** *The Strange World of Hare Krishnas.* Greenwich, Conn.: Fawcett Books, 1974.

A secular evaluation of the history, structure, beliefs, and practices of this mystic group. Written by a journalist who spent a month with group members in their New York temple. 294.L57

**MacDonell, Arthur Anthony.** *Vedic Mythology.* New York: Gordon Press, 1974.

Based on an earlier German work by George Buhler, this analysis of Hindu beliefs will prove to be of value to those whose ministry brings them into contact with these primitive practices. 294.1.M14

**Parrinder, Edward Geoffrey, comp.** *The Wisdom of Early Buddhists.* New York: New Directions Press, 1977.

A brief selection of traditional instructions culled from the sayings of the Buddha. 294.34.P24W

**Shaku, Soyen.** *Zen for Americans.* Translated by Daisetz Teitars Suzuki. LaSalle, Ill.: Open Court, 1974.

This reprint of the 1906 publication is designed to take advantage of the resurgence of interest in Oriental mysticism and make Buddhism more appealing to Occidentals. 294.3'08.SH1 1974

**Smith, Bardell L., ed.** *Hinduism: New Essays in the History of Religions.* Leiden: E. J. Brill, 1976.

These essays deal with various aspects of the Bhakti movement. They provide sidelights on their reinterpretation of epic mythology. 294.52.SM5

**Stutley, Margaret, and James Stutley.** *Harper's Dictionary of Hinduism: Its Mythology, Folklore, Philosophy, Literature, and History.* New York: Harper & Row, 1977.

Admirably fulfills the promise of the subtitle. Includes numerous cross-references that will aid the student in locating information in related areas of investigation. Also contains an extensive bibliography together with an index of English subjects and their Sanskrit equivalents. 294.95.ST8

**Yamamoto, J. Isamu.** *Beyond Buddhism: A Basic Introduction to the Buddhist Tradition.* Downers Grove, Ill.: InterVarsity Press, 1982.

A candid reflection on Japanese Buddhism, with a discussion of Zen and its impact on American life and culture. Shows how the demands of a faith that fully satisfies the human heart leads one to embrace the teachings of Christ and Christianity. 294.3.Y1

## ZOROASTRIANISM

**Boyce, Mary.** *Zoroastrians: Their Religious Beliefs and Practices.* London: Routledge and Kegan Paul, 1979.

A detailed examination of the historical development of the Zoroastrian beliefs over 3,500 years. Recommended to those interested in the history of religious ideas. 295'.09'27.B69

## JUDAISM

**Bildstein, Gerald J.** *Honor Thy Father and Mother: Filial Responsibility in Jewish Law and Ethics.* New York: Ktav Publishing House, 1975.

An insightful description and interpretation that adequately outlines the nature and scope of a Jewish child's responsibility. Surveys the history of tradition, and shows how this ethos is to be maintained. 296.3'85.B49

**Bloch, Abraham P.** *The Biblical and Historical Background of the Jewish Holy Days.* New York: Ktav Publishing House, 1978.

A detailed discussion providing valuable historical material heightening one's understanding of the OT teaching and giving readers a new appreciation of Jewish traditions perpetuated from ancient times to the present. 296.43.B63

**Boer, P. A. H. de.** *Fatherhood and Motherhood in Israelite and Judean Piety.* Leiden: E. J. Brill, 1975.

Examines the nature of God and concludes that God is more an "Eternal Parent" than the Father. The author mars his treatment by introducing mother-goddess mythology in unlikely and unwarranted places. 296.1.C99.B63

**Buchanan, George Wesley.** *Revelation and Redemption: Jewish Documents of Deliverance from the Fall of Jerusalem to the Death of Nahmanides.* Dillsboro, N.C.: Western North Carolina Press, 1978.

Treats a variety of themes, including history, doctrine, prophetic movements, poetry, prayer, messianic expectations, the Holy City, the day of vindication, and various eschatological ideas, all of which aid our understanding of the exilic and postexilic periods of Israel's history. Insightful. 909'.04.B85

**Coggins, R. J.** *Samaritans and Jews: The Origins of Samaritanism Reconsidered.* Atlanta: John Knox Press, 1975.

Basing his views on diligent research, Coggins concludes that the hostility between Samaritans and Jews took time to develop. His supportive data are most enlightening. 296.8.C65

**Collins, John J.** *The Sibylline Oracles of Egyptian Judaism.* Missoula, Mont.: Scholars Press, 1974.

A unique volume that draws attention to a long-neglected aspect of Jewish religious life in Egypt. 296.1.C69 (Alt. DDC 133.2)

**Croner, Helga, ed.** *More Stepping Stones to Jewish-Christian Relations: An Unabridged Collection of Christian Documents 1975-1983.* Studies in Judaism and Christianity. New York: Paulist Press, 1985.

The goal behind the founding of the Stimulus Foundation (which sponsors colloquia between Jews and Christians) is truly praiseworthy. These papers, however, deal only with the issues of the ecumenical branch of the church, leaving out evangelicals. As a consequence, the consensus aimed at will be more divisive than unifying. Disappointing. 296.C88

**Davies, William David.** *The Territorial Dimension of Judaism.* Berkeley, Calif.: University of California Press, 1982.

As with all the books of this author, this work is marked by a diligent scholarship and a clear explanation of his chosen theme. He provides his readers with a fine companion volume to *The Gospel and the Land.* 296.3'877.D28

**\*Dolman, Dirk Hermanus,** and **Marcus Rainsford.** *The Tabernacle.* 2 vols. in 1. Minneapolis: Klock & Klock Christian Publishers, 1982.

Two exemplary works that explain the significance of the Tabernacle in Israel's worship and reveal the mysteries of Christ's Person and work in the Old Testament. 296.4.D69 1982

**Eckstein, Yechiel.** *What Christians Should Know About Jews and Judaism.* Waco, Tex.: Word Books, 1984.

The author "is uniquely qualified to explain Judaism to Christians in general and to those of Evangelical persuasion in particular. . . . His [work] is informative, reflects the pious commitment of his Jewish faith, and is sensitively tuned to his Christian readers" (Morris Inch). 296.3'87.EC5

**Eidelberg, Shlomo, trans. and ed.** *The Jews and the Crusaders: The Hebrew Chronicles of the First and Second Crusades.* Madison, Wis.: University of Wisconsin Press, 1977.

Contains translations of and comments on four Hebrew chronicles dealing with what happened to the Jewish communities of Europe that lay along the route taken by the Crusaders. 943'.004.EI2

**\*Fairweather, William.** *The Background*

*of the Gospels, or Judaism in the Period Between the Old and New Testaments.* 3d ed. Minneapolis: Klock & Klock Christian Publishers, 1977.

An important older work that is neither too technical nor too superficial in its handling of the history of the times. Ably sets the stage for our understanding of the "fulness of times" when God sent forth His Son, born of a woman and born under the law to redeem those under the law. Provides all that the busy pastor could desire. The only weakness inherent in Fairweather's treatment is his late dating of certain books (e.g. Daniel). Otherwise his work is to be highly recommended. 296.F16 1977

**Finkel, Asher.** *The Pharisees and the Teacher of Nazareth.* Leiden: E. J. Brill, 1974.

Describes the progress of tradition from the Great Synagogue to the time of Christ, deals with the controversial Halachic teaching of the Pharisees, explores the written and oral traditions during the Hasmonaean and Herodian periods, and then discusses the message of Jesus and His conflict with the religious leaders. 296.81.F49

**Fitzmyer, Joseph A.** *Essays on the Semitic Background of the New Testament.* London: Jeffrey Chapman, 1971.

†A collection of essays by a leading Aramaic scholar. Revealing. Fills in the gaps in our thinking. 296.1.F57

**Foakes-Jackson, Frederick John.** *Josephus and the Jews: The Religion and History of the Jews as Explained by Flavius Josephus.* Grand Rapids: Baker Book House, 1977.

First published in 1939, this work serves to introduce the reader to the strengths and weaknesses of Josephus's writings. A valuable reprint. 933'.072.F68 1977

**Gordis, Robert.** *Love and Sex: A Modern Jewish Perspective.* New York: Farrar, Strauss and Giroux, 1978.

In the wake of the modern sexual malaise, Gordis expounds the historic roots of Jewish belief and passes on to his readers an appreciation of the rich heritage of the OT. 296.3'87.G65

**Greenstein, Howard R.** *Judaism—An Eternal Covenant.* Philadelphia: Fortress Press, 1983.

Part of a series to cover the faiths of Jews, Catholics, and Protestants. This work was written for both Jews and Gentiles and was designed as an apologetic to promote an understanding of Judaism. An admirable explanation. 296.G85

**Gutmann, Joseph.** *The Jewish Sanctuary.* Iconography of Religions, 23. Leiden: E. J. Brill, 1983.

A beautifully illustrated, authoritative account of the rise of the synagogue and its establishment over the last two millennia. 296.4.G98

**Halpern, Baruch.** *The Constitution of the Monarchy in Israel.* Harvard Semitic Monographs. Chico, Calif.: Scholars Press, 1981.

A comprehensive examination of *nagid* in the OT and the establishment of the monarchy in Israel. Provides sidelights on the qualities of leadership inherent in the monarchy. 296.3'877.H16

**Haut, Irwin H.** *Divorce in Jewish Law and Life.* Studies in Jewish Jurisprudence, 5. New York: Sepher-Hermon Press, 1983.

This work by an attorney/rabbi evaluates the teaching of the Talmud and other Jewish religious traditions before applying the evidence of Judaistic legislation to the rising tide of divorce within the Jewish community. Haut makes available to his readers a wealth of information, and inasmuch as much of it comes from the Talmud (which fairly represents beliefs in vogue in biblical times), there is much useful information to be gleaned from this volume concerning marriage as well as divorce. 296.1'8.H29

**Hengel, Martin.** *Judaism and Hellenism: Studies in Their Encounter in Palestine During the Early Hellenistic Period.* Translated by John Bowden. 2 vols. Philadelphia: Fortress Press, 1975.

†This monumental study deals specifically with the political, economic, intellectual, and religious climate. Sets the stage for the NT era. 296'.09'014.H38

**Higgens, Elford.** *Hebrew Idolatry and Superstition.* Port Washington, N.Y.: Kennikat Press, 1971.

Reprinted from the 1893 edition. Surveys the critical works to that time, deals with the interchange of religious thought in the ancient Near East, and enlarges on the pagan religious worship inherent in divination, witchcraft, and enchantment. 296.3.H53 1971

**Levine, Baruch A.** *In the Presence of the Lord.* Leiden: E. J. Brill, 1974.

An exacting study of sacrificial systems in Ugaritic and Israelite religions. 296.L57

**Mann, Thomas W.** *Divine Presence and Guidance in Israelite Traditions: The Typology of Exaltation.* Baltimore: Johns Hopkins University Press, 1977.

Probes the form and function of the divine presence in the OT and assesses the guidance motifs that form an integral part of Hebrew tradition. 296.311.M31

**Neusner, Jacob.** *The Pharisees: Rabbinic Perspectives.* Studies in Ancient Judaism. Hoboken, N.J.: Ktav Publishing House, 1985.

This major work was first published in Holland in 1973. This edition represents a condensation of the author's earlier three volumes. Neusner deals with the fundamental issues of the history of the rabbinate and how this movement is viewed in the Mishnah and the Talmuds. Though it does not verify the gospel records, the material in this volume provides new and interesting sidelights on the movement. 296.812.N39 1985

————, ed. *Understanding Rabbinic Judaism from Talmudic to Modern Times.* New York: Ktav Publishing House, 1974.

Contains chapters contributed by modern Jewish historians and theologians. This work illustrates the way in which rabbinic Judaism laid the foundations of Jewish history. Casts light on many OT concepts and practices. 296.N39U

**Newman, Louis E.** *The Sanctity of the Seventh Year: A Study of Mishnah "Tractate Shebit."* Brown Judaic Studies, no. 44. Chico, Calif.: Scholars Press, 1983.

This is an interpretation of Mishnah rules concerning the Sabbatical year as it was understood by those who redacted the document in the second century. A translation and commentary of the Tosefta Shebit is also provided. Readers have available in this handy volume a work of immense erudition. It readily opens up the tradition of the Jewish people on this important OT concept. 296.1.N46

**Newsome, James D., Jr.** *By the Waters of Babylon: An Introduction to the History and Theology of the Exile.* Atlanta: John Knox Press, 1979.

A well-written account of Jewish history from the Babylonian Captivity to the restoration after the Exile. Informative and helpful in understanding the attitude of the people. 933.N47

**Nickelsburg, George W. E.** *Resurrection, Immortality, and Eternal Life in Intertestamental Judaism.* Harvard Theological Studies. Cambridge, Mass.: Harvard University Press, 1972.

An important contribution that adds considerably to our understanding of how different ideas were formed that appear as well-developed doctrines in the gospels. A valuable supplement to Charles's *Eschatology.* 296.3'3.N53

**Novak, David.** *Law and Theology in Judaism.* New York: Ktav Publishing House, 1974.

The first and last chapters of this work are of great importance to non-Jewish readers. The first emphasizes the fact that it is possible to understand Judaism only as one understands the relationship between the *halakhah* ("law") and *aggadah* ("theology"). The last discusses the relationship of faith and knowledge. The chapters in between elaborate on chapter 1 and are more distinctively Jewish in orientation. Makes rewarding reading. 296.1′79.N85

**Olford, Stephen F.** *The Tabernacle: Camping with God.* Neptune, N.J.: Loizeaux Brothers, 1971.

A stimulating and challenging devotional exposition of the typology of the Tabernacle. 296.4.OL2

**Priesand, Sally.** *Judaism and the New Woman.* New York: Behrman House, 1975.

The first woman to be ordained into the privileges of the rabbinate exposes what she believes to be the obvious discrimination of Jewish law against women, acknowledging that although they have always been held in honor in Jewish tradition, they have never been equals with men. 296.3′87′83412.P93

**Rajak, Tessa.** *Josephus: The Historian and His Society.* Philadelphia: Fortress Press, 1983.

Investigates the various aspects of Josephus's life and thought and, by interpreting his writings in light of his times, reveals his real contribution to posterity. 933′.05.J77.R13

**Rowland, Christopher.** *Christian Origins: From Messianic Movement to Christian Religion.* Minneapolis: Augsburg Publishing House, 1985.

†Assesses the teaching of the NT against the broader background of first-century Judaism, Hellenistic culture, and Roman domination. Provides a fine synthesis of Jewish thought, and presents the beliefs of the various religious and political groups that emerged in the intertestamental period. In seeking to explore Christian origins, Rowland deals with the messianic sects that arose, attempts to explain the ministry of Jesus and Paul against the ferment of the zealous but misguided movements of the times, and completely ignores revealed religion. Although this is an overview, the author has presented a scholarly review of the material. 296.R79

**Safrai, S., et al.** *The Jewish People in the First Century.* In progress. Philadelphia: Fortress Press, 1974-.

The work of a team of Jewish and Christian scholars, this projected ten-volume set will survey Jewish historical geography; political history; and social, cultural, and religious life and institutions. Special attention is given to Jewish oral and literary traditions. 296.J55

**Sanders, E. P.** *Paul and Palestinian Judaism: A Comparison of Patterns of Religion.* Philadelphia: Fortress Press, 1977.

By building his thesis on Talmudic literature, the DDS, the Apocrypha, and pseudepigrapha, Sanders is able to advance the claim that the majority of NT scholars have totally misunderstood the nature of Judaism in the time of Christ. And, according to Sanders, they have also misunderstood Paul's attitude toward Judaism. 296.4.SA5P

**Sandmel, Samuel.** *Judaism and Christian Beginnings.* New York: Oxford University Press, 1978.

Traces the history, institutions, and religious beliefs of the Jews from 200 B.C. to A.D. 175. Provides good insights into the era of the Maccabees, the development of apocalyptic literature, and the growth of the Apocrypha and pseudepigrapha. Includes an assessment of Jewish attitudes toward Josephus and of the value of the Qumran materials. 291′.09.SA5J

**Smallwood, E. Mary.** *The Jews Under Roman Rule from Pompey to Diocletian.* Leiden: E. J. Brill, 1978.

Beginning with Pompey's control over Palestine and the arrival in Rome of thousands of prisoners of war, this discussion of Jewish history covers three hundred years of Roman rule, during which time the Jews enjoyed the unique position of a protected cult. Smallwood traces the history of the period with consummate skill and then closes her narrative with the transition of the empire from pagan to Christian, with a corresponding decline in the fortunes of the Jews. 933.SM1

**Strassfeld, Michael.** *The Jewish Holidays: A Guide and Commentary.* New York: Harper & Row, 1985.

Dealing with the "festival cycle," this book chronicles Israel's religious calendar. Based on the Torah, it deals with the history and purpose of the feasts and also Yom Kippur. 296.4'3.ST8

**Surburg, Raymond F.** *Introduction of the Intertestamental Period.* St. Louis: Concordia Publishing House, 1975.

After surveying the history of the Jews from Persian times to the fall of Jerusalem in A.D. 70, Surburg assesses the origin and importance of the major religious sects and the development of their beliefs. He concludes with a survey of Jewish literature during this period. 296'.09'014.SU7

**Trever, John C.** *The Dead Sea Scrolls: A Personal Account.* Rev. ed. Grand Rapids: Wm. B. Eerdmans Publishing Co., 1977.

Formerly published under the title *The Untold Story of Qumran*, this work details the history of the finds, their value to biblical scholarship, and the author's involvement with the MSS. 296.81.T72D 1977

**Vaughan, Patrick H.** *The Meaning of "Bama" in the Old Testament: A Study of the Etymology.* Textual and Archaeological Evidence. New York: Cambridge University Press, 1974.

*Bama* is used frequently in the OT to describe cultic sites, and this in-depth study reveals the threefold meaning of the word—topographical, anatomical, and cultic. An important technical treatment. 296.4.V46

**Vermes, Geza,** and **Pamela Vermes.** *The Dead Sea Scrolls: Qumran in Perspective.* Cleveland: Collins World Publishing Co., 1978.

A reexamination of the DDS and their translation. Treats the discovery of the scrolls, the date of their composition, and their authenticity. Contains an extensive bibliography. 296.81.V58 1978

**Wigoder, Geoffrey, ed.** *Encyclopedic Dictionary of Judaica.* New York: Leon Amiel Publications, 1974.

Compiled by the editors of and condensed from the sixteen-volume *Encyclopedia Judaica*. Covers all aspects of Jewish life and culture. A handy reference volume for the pastor. 296.03.EN1D

**Yadin, Yigael.** *The Temple Scroll: The Hidden Law of the Dead Sea Sect.* New York: Random House, 1985.

The account of Yadin's strange acquisition and careful decoding of this scroll has now shown the find to be one of the most important of the DDS discovered thus far. This is a welcome volume that sheds new light on the Qumran community. 296.1'55.Y1

## ISLAM

**Abu-Izzeddin, Nejla M.** *The Druzes: A New Study of Their History, Faith and Society.* Leiden: E. J. Brill, 1984.

Places the beliefs of the Druzes in the context of the development of Shi'ism in its Isma'ili-Fatimid form; describes the role of the Druze community in Lebanon and Syria. 956.92.AY9

**Bakhtiar, Laleh.** *Sufi: Expressions of the Mystic Quest.* New York: Avon Books, 1976.

Describes the inner dimension of Islam and explains the hidden archetypes of Islamic belief in terms of concrete symbols. 297.4.B17

**Bjorling, Joel.** *The Baha'i Faith: A Historical Bibliography.* New York: Garland Publishing, 1985.

Disenchanted with the confusion of tongues so evident among many groups today, Bjorling seriously investigated the Baha'i faith. His bibliography will be of immense help to apologists and missiologists. The entries are grouped under the main divisions of this organization. Chapter 11 contains an informative essay on the history of the movement. 016.297'89.B55

**Burton, John.** *The Collection of the Qur'an.* New York: Cambridge University Press, 1977.

Examines the various aspects of Islam. Sheds light on the origins of Muslim scripture and deals with their dating, manner of collection, and promulgation. 297.B95

**Chittick, William C.** *The Sufi Path of Love: The Spiritual Teachings of Rumi.* Albany, N.Y.: State University of New York Press, 1983.

Traces the spiritual lineage of Baha' Walad and the exotic sciences related to the "divine law" and the "spiritual path" of devotees. As a work for comparative religionists, this one is worthy of serious consideration. 297.4.C49

**Edmonds, I. G.** *Islam.* New York: Franklin Watts, 1977.

A brief introduction to the history, principles, and customs of Islam. Should prove valuable to the missionary who desires to have a comprehensive overview of the beliefs of those to whom he ministers. 297.ED5

**Esposito, John L.** *Voices of Resurgent Islam.* New York: Oxford University Press, 1983.

Provides, through biographical sketches and Muslim statements, a fresh and challenging new perspective on the rise of Islam in politics and world affairs. A helpful and in some respects alarming treatise. 297'.09.ES6

**Hatcher, William,** and **J. Douglas Martin.** *The Baha'i Faith: The Emerging Global Religion.* San Francisco: Harper & Row, 1984.

Written by an academician and a business administrator, this book boldly defends the Bahai faith. It examines the current persecution of Bahais in Iran and purports to show how this false religion meets the need of the human heart (see *The Minister's Library*, 1984, pp. 439-40 for an explanation). 297'.89.H28

**Ingrams, Doreon.** *Mosques and Minarets.* St. Paul, Mich.: EMC Corporation, 1974.

A revealing discussion of the basic teachings of Islam, illustrating through photographs and narration the unifying effect of their beliefs on the Arab nations of the Middle East. 297.IN4

**Kahn, Muhammed Zafrulla, trans.** *The Koran: The Eternal Revelation Vouchsafed to Muhammad.* New York: Frederick A. Praeger, 1971.

An accurate, modern translation. 297.1224.K84

**Martin, Richard C.** *Islam: A Cultural Perspective.* Englewood Cliffs, N.J.: Prentice-Hall, 1982.

With Islam having gained more than a foothold in the U.S. and increasing in adherents in many quarters of the world, it behooves Christians to be aware of the cultural background and religious beliefs of those who call themselves Muslim. This brief introduction serves that purpose. 297.M36

**Miller, William McElwee.** *What Is the Baha'i Faith?* Grand Rapids: Wm. B.

Eerdmans Publishing Co., 1977.

Written by a veteran missionary to Iran, this thorough evaluation traces the rise, progress, and beliefs of this cult from its origin in the mid-1800s to modern times. An excellent discussion. 297.89.M61

————. *The Baha'i Faith: Its History and Teaching.* South Pasadena, Calif.: William Carey Library, 1974.

An excellent exposé of this fast-growing sect. Of special value to collegians who have been invited to join syncretistic groups. Recommended. 297.89.M61

**Momen, Moojan.** *An Introduction to Shi'i Islam: The History and Doctrines of Twelver Shi'ism.* New Haven, Conn.: Yale University Press, 1985.

This major work in the area of Middle Eastern religion shows how Shi'i doctrine differs from other aspects of Islam. The explanation of the beliefs and rituals, social practices, and jurisprudence is of particular value to missiologists and students of comparative religions. 297.82.M73

**Parrinder, Edward Geoffrey.** *Jesus in the Qur'an.* New York: Oxford University Press, 1977.

A scholarly study of the ties between Islam and Christianity. Opens up numerous veins of thought that missionaries working with Muslims can use to good effect. 297'.1228.P24J

**Schimmel, Annemarie.** *And Muhammad Is His Messenger: The Veneration of the Prophet in Islamic Piety.* Chapel Hill, N.C.: University of North Carolina Press, 1985.

Based on the author's own experience

in Turkey, this work contains information from poetry and folk tradition not found in other sources. An important contribution. 809.1.M72.SCH3

**Smith, Margaret.** *The Way of the Mystics: The Early Christian Mystics and the Rise of the Sufis.* New York: Oxford University Press, 1978.

Draws parallels between the writings of Anthony, Simeon the Stylite, and Augustine, on the one hand, and such Sufi mystics as Rabi'a of Basra and Harith al-Muhasibi, on the other. The commonality of certain ideals in no way discounts the need to explain the divergencies of belief that are also evident to the student of comparative religions. 297.4.SM6

**Smith, Wilfred Cantwell.** *Islam in Modern History.* Princeton, N.J.: Princeton University Press, 1977.

Written with profound insight, this remarkable work may be regarded as must reading for all who deal with Muslims or wish to understand modern Islamic thought. 297.SM6

**Trimingham, J. Spencer.** *The Sufi Orders in Islam.* Oxford: At the Clarendon Press, 1971.

Directs the attention of readers to the organizational aspects and mystical practices of this branch of Islamic belief. 297.T73

**Watt, William Montgomery.** *Muhammad: Prophet and Statesman.* New York: Oxford University Press, 1974.

A full treatment, even though it gives evidence of being an abridgement of the author's earlier work. 297.63.W34

# Index of Authors

# Index of Titles

# Index of Subjects

Moody Press, a ministry of the Moody Bible Institute, is designed for education, evangelization, and edification. If we may assist you in knowing more about Christ and the Christian life, please write us without obligation: Moody Press, c/o MLM, Chicago, Illinois 60610.